Philosophy

Philosophy

A Guide to the Reference Literature
Third Edition

Hans E. Bynagle

Reference Sources in the Humanities

LIBRARIES
UNLIMITED
A Member of the Greenwood Publishing Group

Westport, Connecticut • London

Library of Congress Cataloging-in-Publication Data

Bynagle, Hans E. (Hans Edward), 1946–
    Philosophy : a guide to the reference literature / Hans E. Bynagle.— 3rd ed.
        p.   cm. — (Reference sources in the humanities)
    Includes indexes.
    ISBN 1–56308–954–8
    1. Philosophy—Bibliography.   I. Title.   II. Series: Reference sources in the
humanities series.
Z7125.B97 2006
[B72]
016.1—dc22   2006004702

British Library Cataloguing in Publication Data is available.

Library of Congress Catalog Card Number: 2006004702
ISBN: 1–56308–954–8

First published in 2006

Libraries Unlimited, 88 Post Road West, Westport, CT 06881
A Member of the Greenwood Publishing Group, Inc.
www.lu.com

Printed in the United States of America

The paper used in this book complies with the
Permanent Paper Standard issued by the National
Information Standards Organization (Z39.48–1984).

10   9   8   7   6   5   4   3   2   1

Contents

Preface

This guide to reference sources in philosophy has been compiled and written with a diversity of users in mind. It is intended for professional philosophers and teachers of philosophy; for students of philosophy at both undergraduate and graduate levels; for librarians, as an aid in reference service and collection development; and, to a lesser extent, for the general reader or inquirer who may come to philosophy with little or no background. Not everyone, needless to say, will be equally well served by every part of this guide, and that is undoubtedly true also of the work as a whole. Nonetheless, I have tried to keep all of these potential audiences in mind throughout, and have tried in particular to gear the level of information provided in the annotations to the audience(s) most likely to take an interest in them and to use and benefit from the work in question. That same principle applies to the introduction (ch. 1), which is addressed primarily to those without a close acquaintance with the field of philosophy, though readers who are not in that position may find parts of it helpful as well.

The present guide succeeds two previous editions of *Philosophy: A Guide to the Reference Literature,* also published by Libraries Unlimited (1st ed., 1986; 2nd ed., 1997). The most radical departure from its predecessors is represented by its organization. It employs what is predominantly a subject arrangement, classifying sources first of all in relation to the various divisions of philosophy and its history, in contrast to the primary arrangement by types of reference sources (bibliographies, indexes, dictionaries and encyclopedias, etc.) employed previously. Each approach has its pros and cons. I am persuaded, however, that a striking increase in the number and variety of philosophical reference sources over the last decade or so has tipped the balance in favor of the subject-dominated approach. As the sheer number of sources in each type-of-source category grows, it becomes increasingly imperative to split them into subcategories, usually based on subject matter. At some point it seems better to invert the structure and adopt primary categories based on subject matter, subdivided as necessary or desirable by type-of-source. This also has the virtue of grouping together, or at least in close proximity, different types of sources within the same general subject area. There is a drawback to this, however. Any subject arrangement, particularly in philosophy, is imperiled by the overlapping of subjects and the resistance of many sources to easy categorization. This poses, I can testify, many challenges for the author: first in devising an effective scheme of subject categories, and secondly in adjudicating the best fit for many sources that overlap the defined categories or reside on their boundaries. For users of this guide, on the other hand, it may pose the temptation to rely too much on the subject classification to identify sources of potential interest or utility. Cross-referencing provides a partial remedy, but I found that can quickly get out of hand. As a more comprehensive antidote, consultation of the subject index is strongly recommended; I have sought not to skimp on that despite adopting a subject-dominated arrangement.

Four broad categories provide the overarching structure of this guide: general sources, history of philosophy, branches of philosophy, and miscellanea. Part I, "General Sources," covers publications and Web sites whose purview takes in all or most of the field and is not confined to one or a few branches or aspects. It is subdivided into several chapters by type of source. Part II, "History of Philosophy," includes a chapter for comprehensive history sources, a chapter for non-Western philosophy, one for Western philosophy in general, and four for sources specific to the major historical periods into which Western philosophy is conventionally divided. Each chapter in this section includes subsections on individual philosophers. Part III, "Branches of Philosophy," has eight chapters on the major subdisciplines of the field: aesthetics, epistemology, ethics, logic, metaphysics, philosophy of religion, philosophy of science, and so forth. In several cases branches with close affinities due to the nature of their subject matter or their historical development, or both, have been grouped together in one chapter. The final chapter in this section encompasses several minor branches—minor if only in terms of numbers of reference sources specific to them—and some special topics that cut across several branches. Finally, part IV, the "Miscellanea" section has a chapter on some philosophical currents, schools, and movements that do not fit readily into either the history or the branch rubrics of parts II and III, and ends with a chapter covering directories and miscellaneous reference sources that again do not fit readily into other chapter categories.

Most chapters in parts II and III include explicit type-of-source divisions in the following sequence: (i) bibliographies and indexes; (ii) dictionaries, encyclopedias, and handbooks; (iii) other types of sources. The same order is observed, though usually not explicitly identified, whenever applicable in chapter subsections, including those on individual philosophers.

The present guide expands on the second edition by the addition of some 290 new entries, an increase of more than 50 percent. Nearly all of these represent new sources; five correct previous oversights. Over the past decade or so, the proliferation of philosophy reference publications that occurred between the completion dates of this guide's two predecessors (1985 and 1996, respectively) seems only to have accelerated, and this is coupled, of course, with considerable growth in online reference sources. The quality of these new sources, both print and online, is generally quite high, so the opportunity to incorporate them in this revision is all the more gratifying. At the same time, the growth in quantity seems to make the kind of guidance this work seeks to offer all the more valuable. In addition to new sources, this revision also records changes affecting around 50 previous entries. These include new editions of monographic publications, additional volumes published in monographic series or multivolume sets, and changes to serial publications and Web resources. Some sources previously listed and described, rendered increasingly out-of-date or reduced in significance by the passage of time or the appearance of newer competitors, have been de-emphasized; a few very marginal ones have been dropped altogether. I have also decided to omit in this revision the former chapters on core journals and on principal research centers, associations, and other organizations, in part to make room for so many new reference sources in the narrower sense, and in part because information about journals and organizations, besides being always changeable, is nowadays readily available online and can be located via several of the directories and gateways listed in chapter 6.

A few general comments about online sources. Representation of these has increased by some 600 percent over the second edition of *Philosophy: A Guide to the Reference Literature*. Even so, they still constitute a minority—about 7 percent—of the entries in this guide; a few more are mentioned in annotations. In part this reflects the fact that, in philosophy at least, online reference sources—especially sources of creditable quality—are still far from equaling, let alone displacing, print reference publications. But it also reflects the fact that I have been more selective with respect to online sources than is the case for print sources. The Web remains—indeed, is essentially—a volatile medium in which resources regularly appear, disappear, move, and change—and also (what is sometimes worse) fail to change as they could and should, with projects often incomplete or suffering from lack of updating. This fact was brought home to me repeatedly in the course of preparing this guide, as I would discover that even some excellent Web sites (including several listed previously) that seemed to carry high promise of stability had disappeared, while others were no longer being updated, resulting in rapid erosion of value due to obsolescence. For these reasons, I have kept a focus on Web sites that are substantial, reasonably well developed, and at respectable levels of quality and authority, as well as holding out a good likelihood (though rarely any guarantee) of enduring and, if applicable, being kept up to date, even if they change their content, their design, or their host locations. The latter criterion favors, as a rule of thumb, Web sites maintained by institutions and organizations over those maintained by individuals as personal projects, even if the latter are sometimes comparable in quality and authority. But a number of Web resources selected for inclusion represent well-justified exceptions to this rule of thumb; and any or all of the foregoing criteria are apt to have been relaxed for sites that seem particularly valuable, especially if they are unduplicated by alternate print or online sources. Readers are urged to bear in mind that any information this guide provides on online sources can be rendered obsolete in an instant.

I should emphasize also that inclusion of digital sources is restricted to sources that perform reference functions similar or analogous to those performed by the printed reference works listed in this guide. There is no attempt here to provide guidance to Web sites or other digital media whose functions are like those of published nonreference philosophy texts and serials, or that serve as vehicles for informal communication and exchange of information, such as mailing lists ("listservs") and newsgroups. For guidance to these, as well as to many additional online reference sources that are narrowly specialized, marginal, ephemeral, or more apt to be transitory than those selected for inclusion here, readers should consult one or more of the general directories or gateways to philosophy-related internet resources listed in chapter 6. Also, when appropriate, consult the more specialized sites, to be found in several other chapters, that provide links to related Web sites in their specific subject areas. Finally, I should clarify that availability of online or other electronic versions of printed books or serials listed in this guide, insofar as these simply reproduce the content of the printed versions, is generally *not* noted. That includes, for example, titles offered by netLibrary, Xrefer, and individual publisher services such as Oxford Reference Online, or included in so-called "aggregator" databases. (Access to all of these is generally limited to subscribing libraries or individuals.) Because this is a constantly changing scene, any attempt to reflect it here would be quickly out of date and misleading. This general disclaimer does not apply to online counterparts of print publications that incorporate significant value-added content or features beyond those in the print versions—for example, the online *Routledge Encyclopedia of Philosophy* (entry 152). It also does not apply to online versions of indexes and serial bibliographies, though these typically do have value-added features such as additional indexing points and search engines that support sophisticated search strategies.

The cutoff date for this guide is October 2005, though attentive readers will note that some Web sites are listed as accessed after that date as I had occasion to revisit them while polishing the manuscript. It is entirely possible that some sources, particularly foreign publications, issued close to this temporal limit did not come to my attention in time to be included. I apologize in advance for any omissions that may come to light. As to its scope, this guide is intended to encompass the entire realm of philosophy: sources dealing with any movement, school, period, branch, major figure, or geographical-cultural subdivision, non-Western as well as Western, have been candidates for inclusion. This inclusiveness may falter, admittedly, with regard to certain borderline areas. However, important interdisciplinary or multidisciplinary sources (concerned, for instance, with the history of ideas, or with ethics from the perspectives of several disciplines) have also been included, provided they give substantial attention to distinctly philosophical subject matter and do so in a way that does not have ready parallels in more exclusively philosophical sources.

This broad definition of scope is qualified by certain emphases. Because it is aimed primarily at English-speaking users, this guide emphasizes English-language sources. It does include important sources in other European languages, however, particularly if they offer significant content or distinct perspectives not available or well represented in English-language sources. There is further emphasis, in the case of non-English items, on sources likely to be useful even at a low to medium level of specialization (but not necessarily a low to medium level of requisite language ability); foreign-language sources reserved for very advanced or specialized scholarship are generally omitted. Possibly this does not account for the exclusion of works that are not accessible without substantial facility in one or more non-Western languages. My own lack of any such facility, in any case, plays the major part in that exclusion.

A second emphasis, applicable mainly to print sources, is recency. In general, the older a work, the more stringently it has been judged as to its importance and usefulness. Availability has also been a positive consideration, to the extent that any English-language publication in print at the time of compilation was almost automatically included. Wide availability in U.S. libraries was also a strong factor. Two points need to be mentioned in this connection. One is that for any work first published before 1950, the chances for inclusion are substantially improved when there has been a subsequent reprinting, because that provides some evidence (admittedly weak) of importance and usually implies wider availability. The second point is that quality has not been a significant criterion for inclusion with works published within the last half century or so. The annotations in many cases are critical and evaluative as well as descriptive, and I have taken the approach that it is more useful to include a work of dubious quality and signal its shortcomings than to omit it. The judgments expressed in the annotations, incidentally, unless explicitly attributed to others, are ultimately mine, whatever help I may have gotten from other sources, and I take responsibility for them.

It has been my goal to examine firsthand as many sources as possible, and I was able to realize that goal for better than 98 percent of the sources eventually selected for inclusion. For the remainder, I have endeavored to corroborate bibliographic and descriptive information by using at least two independent sources, and to draw critical comments, if any, from authoritative sources.

No precise definition of "reference source" is assumed here or, to my knowledge, available. I take it that, as employed for over a century by librarians who built and used "reference collections," the term "reference work" generally refers to a publication intended for brief consultation to obtain information in relatively small quantities or discrete segments, rather than to be read from cover to cover. But this description does not quite amount to what philosophers call a "sufficient condition," and at any rate allows for a good many borderline cases. Such borderline cases tend to occur especially in the category "handbook," commonly lumped together with "dictionaries and encyclopedias." Quite possibly I have not achieved perfect consistency in decisions about borderline cases. For example, several individual works or series with the words *handbook* or *companion* in their title are not represented here because I judge them to be more like conventional collections of essays on their topic (some clearly intended as textbooks) than reference works. On the other hand, I list and describe all extant volumes in the important Blackwell Companions to Philosophy series. Many of these belong here without argument—for example, those organized in a standard alphabetical dictionary or encyclopedia format. Others definitely fall on the "reference work" borderline but have been included because they offer specific reference features (e.g., a glossary or exceptionally extensive bibliography), feature largely self-standing articles, or provide exceptionally authoritative and comprehensive coverage of their subject, frequently not readily available otherwise. And in a few instances I included them because it seemed odd, or might elicit puzzlement, to exclude them while including the rest of the series; but this may raise the question why other works or series closely similar to these particular volumes did not make it in, too. Again, I will not claim perfect consistency when it comes to such borderline cases. I also recognize that the characterization for "reference work" given previously, when broadened to "reference source," likely applies to many more Web sites with philosophy content than are in fact included in this guide. But I have already addressed the rationale for being more selective when it comes to online sources.

In the introductory chapter, I discuss the factor of perspective as an important and sometimes problematic dimension of many reference sources in philosophy. I also provide an overview of major philosophical traditions that it is helpful to be aware of in this connection. Some comment on the question of perspective as it relates to this guide seems apropos here. A certain element of perspective is no doubt entailed by the emphasis on English-language sources: these more often embody or emphasize the perspective of the Anglo-American tradition than they do any other. However, the perspectives of the Continental and other philosophical traditions are increasingly well represented by sources in English, as well as many in other languages represented in this guide. In any case, I have not knowingly imposed any particular perspective beyond what I've just indicated. But because one is often blind, if not to one's biases, then to their full effect, it is best to identify my own orientation. My philosophical training and, it seems, my intellectual propensities fall largely within the Anglo-American tradition, more specifically within Analytic philosophy though only in the widest sense distinguished in the introduction. Never completely satisfied with this tradition, and in any case curious and hopefully open-minded, I am apt to make modest excursions into other traditions, intrigued often by the questions they raise, their motivations, or even their mood; but I confess I often find them ultimately disappointing or fundamentally misguided (by my lights), not to mention in some cases bewildering. As a Christian, I have a special interest in the intersection between philosophy and religious faith, though I do not identify myself with any particular school of Christian philosophy. If any of these commitments and predilections have affected either my selectivity (i.e., decisions on what to include and exclude) or my descriptive efforts, I am not aware of it. It is more likely, I suppose, that they do color my critical and evaluative judgments here or there. I have tried, however, to be fair to all perspectives, judging all sources so far as possible on their own terms, and I hope I have avoided any heavy-handedness.

As I complete this substantial revision of my previous efforts, I am mindful once again of many debts of gratitude and more: to Whitworth College, for continued support and encouragement, and for a congenial environment in which my professional responsibilities as library director are enriched by teaching and other opportunities to use my academic training and interest in philosophy; to the college's Information Systems staff for assistance with computer challenges; to the library staff, for all the ways they help and support me, and particularly to our able program coordinator, Deb Fry, and to Gail

Fielding for interlibrary loan assistance; to Forrest Baird, my colleague in philosophy at Whitworth, for helpful comments on earlier versions of the introduction; to my sister Ida for translation-assistance once again with Russian-language entries; and to James Rettig, the series editor, and the publisher's staff for patience with missed deadlines and for good counsel. My thanks also to various libraries beyond my own in which I had opportunity (often incidental to other travel) to pursue my research or examine an elusive item, including especially Gonzaga University, Eastern Washington and Washington State Universities, Northwestern University, Cambridge and Oxford Universities, and the Universities of Washington, Arizona, and Chicago—and, not to forget, the public libraries of Chicago and of Spokane and Issaquah, Wash. No library I know of has all the resources listed in this guide, and I appreciate increasingly that the welcome most libraries extend to visitors (sometimes with understandable minor hurdles) represents a benefit of our intellectual and civic cultures not to be taken lightly or for granted. Finally, my wife, Jan, has once again endured substantial deprivations of my time and attention as I worked on this project. I am indebted and grateful to her most of all.

1
Introduction

Anyone familiar with reference sources in general will not be struck immediately by anything exceptional about those in philosophy. The types of reference sources, both print and online, that are listed in this guide are, for the most part, also common in other disciplines: encyclopedias, dictionaries, bibliographies, indexes to periodical literature either with or without abstracts, directories, and, of late, guides or gateways to internet resources. One will also meet up with some types of reference tools that may not exist in every field: concordances, lexicons, or directories, for example. Yet these are certainly not unique to philosophy. And on the whole, there is little that distinguishes the field in terms of the sorts of reference tools one will need or encounter. So if there is any special difficulty in using its reference resources—apart from the inevitable idiosyncrasies of individual works or Web sites—the source of such difficulty will probably lie elsewhere.

THE PROBLEMS OF SCOPE AND PERSPECTIVE

The most likely sources of difficulty in using philosophical reference sources, in my estimation, are two closely related problems, which I'll call the problems of *scope* and *perspective.* For many sources, effective and judicious use requires some understanding of their scope or perspective, or both. On the one hand, one may need to know how much of the philosophical universe, so to speak, a work or online source takes into its purview (i.e., what its scope is). On the other hand, one may need to know from what position or point of view it regards whatever parts of the philosophical universe it takes in (its perspective). Yet scope and perspective are often not immediately obvious on coming to a philosophical reference source. For example, chapter 7 of this guide lists more than a dozen different English-language dictionaries titled simply *Dictionary of Philosophy* or *Philosophical Dictionary* (in a few instances adding other terms that are not essentially descriptive of their content, for example, *Cambridge Dictionary of Philosophy*), and almost as many works similarly titled in other languages. All of these differ significantly with respect to either scope or perspective, or both, yet most do not bear any obvious signs of such differences. True, there are clues, which professionals and advanced students can usually pick up rather quickly. But the beginner may well feel confused or bewildered, or may be led unwittingly into situations somewhat akin to exploring a country without knowing what country it is, or seeing part of a country and taking it as representative of the whole, or getting a description of a country from someone who doesn't live there and wouldn't care to.

The problems of scope I am thinking of are not primarily those having to do with the scope of one or another branch of philosophy, though there are indeed problems in that regard. What one philosopher includes in the branch of philosophy called "ethics" may not coincide with what another subsumes under that label, and the same is true for other branches, say metaphysics or social philosophy or philosophy of history. A set of questions which one thinker considers an important part of a field, another will exclude for any of a variety of reasons: as not properly philosophical, as meaningless, as trivial, or perhaps simply as outside his or her own predilections or expertise. Such divergences may be more pronounced in the nonreference literature of philosophy—of actual philosophical argumentation, especially—but they can assert themselves even in such seemingly nonpolemical works as bibliographies, not to mention philosophical dictionaries and encyclopedias.

Still, to reiterate, the problems of scope to which I wish to call attention are not primarily those just noted, but another sort, which are sometimes at the root of the former. I refer to problems occasioned by the diversity of philosophical traditions, schools, and movements that characterizes the world of philosophy. These traditions, schools, and movements are differentiated not simply by their answers to philosophical questions, but by particular conceptions of what philosophical problems are, or which are the more important problems, and of how such problems may be resolved or, if not resolved, fruitfully debated and clarified. It is in relation to such differences that problems both of scope and perspective tend to become acute. A work which presents itself as concerned with philosophy or some branch of philosophy, without any explicit qualification, may limit its scope to the concerns, doctrines, thinkers, or writings of only one movement, or perhaps a few. On the other hand, even if it encompasses several or many different traditions, schools, or movements, it may and almost inevitably will treat them from the perspective of one in particular. (A case in point would be the *Oxford Companion to Philosophy* [entry 131], which includes in its scope the whole history of philosophy worldwide, yet clearly does so from the perspective of Anglo-American philosophy, described later in this introduction.) Such a perspective may be deliberate or not; it may be overt or subtle; and it may assert itself in a variety of ways: in explicit critiques of opposing positions, in matters of selection or emphasis, in failures of accuracy or fairness in presentation of competing viewpoints, even in the kind of background knowledge that is presupposed.

It would be pointless to decry in general either restrictions of scope or the manifestations of perspectives. Any author must be granted the right to limit the range of his or her concerns. The effects of perspective are to some extent inevitable, and even where they are not, they may have a legitimate function and positive value. (It is not a fault of an astronomy text to describe the configuration of the heavens from the perspective of earth, that usually being the perspective of interest to its readers). What one might decry is a tendency of philosophical works and resources, including reference sources, not to "wear on their sleeves" any clear indications of either perspective or scope. This leaves the reader or the user to figure it out, or suffer the consequences. There is certainly a case to be made for better disclosure, more "truth in labeling." Even if philosophical reference sources were to become uniformly explicit in this regard, however, problems would not vanish. To be aware of scope or perspective is one thing, to attach some meaningful content to that awareness is another, and it is still another, no doubt, to act appropriately and effectively on that awareness.

SURVEYING THE PHILOSOPHICAL LANDSCAPE

To appreciate adequately the dynamics of scope and perspective in philosophy and its reference literature, and to be somewhat equipped against their hazards, it is helpful, even essential, to have at least a basic orientation to the philosophical landscape. For the uninitiated, this can pose some difficulty. Even to get a sense of the major philosophical traditions, to say nothing of countless lesser schools and movements both within and outside the major traditions, is not altogether easy. Familiarizing oneself with the labels that are conventionally attached to them is not difficult, but this is only minimally useful. One needs to be able to place these labels, metaphorically speaking, on at least a rough philosophical map, a map that represents something of the general character of the major philosophical "regions" and how they relate to one another. It is hard, however, to provide much help in this regard within a brief compass—the compass, for instance, of this introduction. The major philosophical traditions are notoriously difficult to characterize in a nutshell, at least in a way that is meaningful apart from a more detailed antecedent acquaintance with them. Generalizations, especially, are perilous and apt to be misleading.

Fortunately, one can begin to sketch a philosophical map, albeit a *very* rough one, in terms that are largely geographical (a circumstance which makes the metaphor of a "map" somewhat more than just a metaphor). The major divisions of philosophy, while they do not by any means fall neatly along geographical boundaries, do accord to a significant extent with geographical regions, at least in terms of their dominance. So an elementary geographical schema can make a somewhat useful starting point, provided one keeps in mind from the outset that as a philosophical map it is very rudimentary indeed.

THE MAJOR DOMAINS

The most basic division to begin with is that between Western and non-Western philosophy. With regard to non-Western, one may think particularly of eastern and southern Asia, highlighting perhaps China and India, which have the most substantial philosophical traditions. Non-Western also takes in parts of western Asia (the Middle East), and certainly includes other parts of the world not usually considered part of "the West" (a term I take to refer chiefly to Europe and areas in which transplanted European cultures are dominant, such as Australia and most of the Americas). A case in point would be Africa, insofar as we are thinking of philosophies that are indigenous or built on indigenous traditions. Despite its broader connotation, "non-Western philosophy" was long used interchangeably with "Eastern philosophy," both having in view Asian philosophies. But that equation has been undermined by growing recognition of non-Western philosophical traditions, albeit generally informal ones, outside Asia in the native cultures of Africa, the Pacific, and the Americas, and even contemporary development of such traditions in academic philosophy. (Incidentally, the term "Oriental," now largely out favor, was often used in older literature, sometimes to designate philosophies of far eastern Asia only—that is, China and Japan and their near neighbors—and sometimes to encompass also philosophies of southern Asia, mainly India, and even the Middle East.)

The line between Western and non-Western philosophy is one that runs through most of the history of philosophy. The next line we need to draw, demarcating major areas within Western philosophy, represents a modern development with roots going back several centuries but dating primarily from the twentieth century. This line serves to divide the philosophical tradition which dominates most of the European continent, known accordingly as Continental philosophy, from the dominant philosophical tradition of England, the United Sates, and some other countries subject to strong British or American influence, such as Canada and Australia, known as Anglo-American philosophy. This line is perhaps less "clean" even than the previous one, but it does mark a real and well-recognized division.

So far, then, we have demarcated in rough fashion the following philosophical regions: non-Western and Western, and within Western, Continental and Anglo-American. Just two decades ago, when I wrote an earlier version of this introduction for a predecessor volume, I could readily add to this philosophical geography, with similarly rough precision, two other major realms. The first was Marxist philosophy, which at that time dominated the Soviet Union and the countries of Eastern Europe. This constituted a large and quite active domain, identifiably Western but relatively isolated from both the Continental and Anglo-American domains; extensive contacts between philosophers on either side of the divide, at least, were uncommon. Today, as a result of convulsive political and social changes in the region it once dominated, Marxist philosophy can hardly be said to exist as a distinct domain, at least not in geographical terms.

A second domain that 10 years ago seemed important enough to recognize along with the others named so far was labeled Neo-Scholasticism. This disrupted the tidiness of our mapping scheme, because it overlapped geographically the two regions already labeled Continental and Anglo-American. Neo-Scholasticism—the name derives from Scholasticism, referring to the various philosophical "schools" of the medieval period, from which this tradition takes its primary inspiration—had been for almost a century the reigning, though by no means exclusive, orientation among Catholic philosophers. It had a sufficiently large following both in Europe and in the Americas (North as well as South) to be ranked among the major extant traditions of Western philosophy. Though Neo-Scholastic philosophy certainly has not suffered the traumatic dislocations experienced by Marxism since 1985, erosions of its status and stature that were already well under way two decades ago have continued to the point where, arguably, it no longer merits recognition at the level of major philosophical domains.

But if the respective fortunes of Marxism and Neo-Scholasticism imply that we need to take erasers to the old map, it might be well if our erasures were incomplete, leaving something of the old patterns discernible. Neither domain has vanished entirely by any means—and who knows what their future may yet be? More to the point for present purposes, many reference works listed in this guide antedate the developments of the last few decades and still reflect the older realities. It remains important, accordingly, to know what those realities were. We'll keep Marxism and Neo-Scholasticism, therefore, on our "short list" of the major traditions it's most useful to be aware of, and will say something more about them in the following paragraphs.

To sum up, then, we have distinguished five very broad domains that either dominate the philosophical landscape presently or did so until recently: Non-Western, Marxist, Continental, Anglo-American, and Neo-Scholastic. It must be emphasized again that the map we have sketched to identify these domains is a very crude one. We shall need at least to introduce some of the more important refinements, as well as to characterize these philosophical domains in more substantive terms. We can begin by saying a bit more about non-Western philosophies.

NON-WESTERN PHILOSOPHIES

This is a very large area, and one of tremendous diversity. Just a few of the major movements can be listed here: Buddhism; Jainism; Hindu philosophies (at least six distinct systems more or less loosely allied to Hindu religion, including Vedānta, Mīmāmsā, Yoga, and Vaiśesika); Confucianism and Neo-Confucianism; Taoism; the Chinese Yin-

Yang School; and Islamic philosophy. These are some of the historically important traditions. Not all of them are active today, and those that are may be caught up in considerable interaction with Western philosophy. We should also mention the largely oral philosophical traditions of, for instance, Africa and Oceania, about which a great deal more is known in the West now than even 20 years ago. Up until the modern period, all of these non-Western philosophies developed in total or near-total isolation from Western philosophy, with one major exception. The exception is Islamic philosophy, which developed under strong influence from Western, particularly Greek, philosophy, and in fact played a crucial role in the transmission of Greek thought and Greek philosophical texts to medieval European culture. Thus it straddled from its earliest beginning what was otherwise a fairly clear line between Western and non-Western philosophy, and in some contexts is actually included within Western philosophy.

The line between Western and non-Western philosophy is less clear now than it once was. Western philosophies have penetrated deeply into the non-Western world, not merely as subjects of study but as adopted positions and modes of philosophizing. Marxism, if not the example likely to come to mind first, may have been for a time the most significant. But Continental, Anglo-American, and even Neo-Scholastic philosophies have also drawn much interest and considerable followings in parts of the non-Western world. There is a significant current as well in the opposite direction, that is, from the non-Western to the Western world. Whether this is as yet equally significant may be doubted. But certainly there is in the West a widespread interest, scholarly as well as popular, in non-Western thought (often in association with religious interests or motives), and by some accounts the number of philosophers in the West who "do philosophy" in a non-Western mode or at least draw significantly on non-Western traditions is far from negligible.

The close association between philosophy and religion in much of non-Western thought requires some comment. Most of the philosophical traditions mentioned previously are also religious traditions, and probably better known as such. This association of philosophy with religion is so prevalent and in many instances so close that it is often assumed to be universal in the non-Western world. To combat this notion, some scholars have been at pains to emphasize philosophical elements that are largely independent of direct religious concern, notably in the areas of epistemology (or theory of knowledge), logic, philosophy of language, and social philosophy, and to bring to the fore historical movements that were non- or anti-religious, for example the materialistic Cārvāka school which sprang up in India about the seventh century A.D. When all is said and done, however, there remains a vast area where religion and philosophy are not only closely intertwined but where it is virtually impossible to disentangle them. In addition to the many theoretical questions this raises—what constitutes religion and what constitutes philosophy?—it poses, for a guide such as this, the practical problem of what works to include as pertaining to non-Western philosophy, and which to exclude as being chiefly concerned with religion. The solution I have adopted is a pragmatic one, and forced in part by my relatively impoverished knowledge of non-Western thought. If a work presents or describes itself as dealing with non-Western philosophy, it has been considered for inclusion; if it presents or describes itself as concerned with religion, or chiefly with religion, it has generally been left out of consideration. The user of this guide is urged to keep in mind, however, that reference sources that cover non-Western religion, or some aspect thereof, may contain a great deal that is relevant for philosophy. The problem discussed here, by the way, is not unique to non-Western philosophy. In a broad sense, it is ubiquitous, while it arises in a more focused way in connection with, for instance, avowedly Christian philosophies such as Neo-Scholasticism. Nevertheless, the problem tends to be less acute in these cases, partly because a distinction between philosophy and theology has been explicitly addressed, debated, and often embodied in practice as a vocational division of labor, whereas in traditional non-Western thought such a distinction is seldom even contemplated.

WESTERN PHILOSOPHY

Let's turn now to Western philosophy. The terms "Continental" and Anglo-American" have been in currency for many years to distinguish the main twentieth-century philosophical traditions of the non-Communist West, yet they are something less than official names for well-defined movements. Philosophical dictionaries seldom included entries for them until quite recently. Neither the illustrious *Routledge Encyclopedia of Philosophy* (entry 150) nor its eminent predecessor from the 1960s, the *Encyclopedia of Philosophy* (entry 125), has an article on either term or even so much as an index entry (apart from one minor, secondary index reference in the *Routledge* for "Anglo-American philosophy"). Yet the terms are used in both works. As noted previously, the traditions these somewhat indeterminate terms designate are comparatively recent developments— that is, twentieth-century developments—though they do have roots in an older bifurcation between Continental Rationalism and British Empiricism dating back to the seventeenth century.

Continental Philosophy

Until the late 1980s, "Continental philosophy" was frequently used as practically synonymous with two related movements, Phenomenology and Existentialism. This is no longer feasible. It was always true that the term could be used in a wider sense to encompass other movements that have flourished on the European continent, including for instance an older strain somewhat inadequately labeled Idealism, with roots especially in the eighteenth- and nineteenth-century philosophies of Kant and Hegel, and a more recent movement which goes by the name of Structuralism. An important development in the last quarter century, however, has been the meteoric rise to prominence of several newer philosophical positions or orientations originating primarily in Europe, especially in France. Among the labels most commonly associated with them are Post-Structuralism, Deconstruction, and Postmodernism. All of these currents have a strongly interdisciplinary character and all tend toward left-of-center political and social positions. They have generated so much interest and discussion not only on their home ground but in the United States, Britain, and other strongholds of Anglo-American philosophy that it becomes necessary to speak of a significant blurring and bridging of the boundary between the Continental and Anglo-American domains during the past two decades. It's probably true, as some have observed, that Anglo-American interest in (and certainly enthusiasm for) these newer Continental currents runs much stronger in departments of literature, communication, women's studies, multicultural studies, and others than it does in philosophy departments. If only because of the presence of this wider interest in the academy, however, it's harder now than formerly for Anglo-American philosophers (and the reference works they use!) simply to ignore Continental philosophy. By way of illustration, I'll mention here a couple of events that are symptomatic of this blurring and bridging of the Continental/Anglo-American boundary and at the same time demonstrate its continuing reality. First is the start-up in the late 1980s and early 1990s of least three journals by American or British publishers explicitly devoted to philosophical exchanges across this boundary. Second is the awarding in 1992 of an honorary doctorate to French philosopher Jacques Derrida, the leading exponent of Deconstruction, by Cambridge University, long an epicenter for Anglo-American philosophy—a gesture preceded by a heated dispute at Cambridge that drew in outside participants as well.

I can offer here only the most rudimentary characterizations of a few of the main strands of Continental philosophy already mentioned, beginning with *Phenomenology.* Founded around the beginning of the last century by Edmund Husserl, Phenomenology is essentially a philosophical method, one which focuses on careful inspection and description of phenomena or appearances, defined as any object of conscious experience, that is, that which we are conscious *of.* The inspection and description are supposed to be effected without any presuppositions, and that includes any presuppositions as to whether such objects of consciousness are "real" or correspond to something "external," or as to what their causes or consequences may be. It is believed that by this method the essential structures of experience and its objects can be uncovered. The sorts of experiences and phenomena which Phenomenologists have sought to describe are highly varied, including, for instance, time consciousness, mathematics and logic, perception, experience of the social world, our experience of our own bodies, and moral, aesthetic, and religious experience.

Existentialism, unlike Phenomenology, is not primarily a philosophical method. Neither is it exactly a set of doctrines (at least not any *one* set) but more an outlook or attitude supported by diverse doctrines centered about certain common themes. These themes include the human condition, or the relation of the individual to the world; the human response to that condition (described often in strongly affective and preponderantly negative terms such as "despair," "dread," "anxiety," "guilt," "bad faith," "nausea"); being, especially the difference between the being of persons (which is "existence") and the being of other kinds of things; human freedom; the significance (and unavoidability) of choice and decision in the absence of certainty; and the concreteness and subjectivity of life as lived, over against abstractions and false objectifications.

Existentialism is often thought to be antireligious (and is, in some of its versions), but there has in fact been a strong current of Christian Existentialism, beginning with the figure often credited with originating Existentialism, the nineteenth-century Danish philosopher Kierkegaard. Existentialism's relationship to Phenomenology is a matter of some controversy, but one can safely say that many of the later Existentialist thinkers, Sartre among them, have employed Phenomenological methods to arrive at or support their specific variations on Existential themes. While Existentialism has been on the wane since the 1960s, it has enjoyed exceptional prominence, even popularity, for a philosophical movement, in part because of its literary expressions by writers such as Sartre, Camus, De Beauvoir, and Marcel.

Structuralism is an interdisciplinary movement united by the principle that social and cultural phenomena, including belief systems and every kind of discourse (literary, political, scientific, etc.), are best understood by analogy with language, itself best understood as a structure of relations among its component parts. Just as in language the crucial determinant of meaning (according to the early structural linguist Ferdinand de Saussure) is neither individual words nor their reference to things outside language but their interrelationships within the linguistic structure, so the crucial element in all social and cultural phenomena is the underlying structure that determines the functions of the various parts. A good deal of Structuralist analysis has been concerned with a kind of unmasking, that is, with revealing political, social, or psychological phenomena as (allegedly) not what they seem or what participants believe them to be but as determined by structures often concealed from view.

This unmasking impulse persists with the group of thinkers sometimes designated *Post-Structuralists,* who both rejected certain presuppositions of Structuralism and added their own more radical ideas about the fundamental role of language in constructing all human perceptions and conceptions of reality. A particular form of this unmasking tendency is *Deconstruction,* introduced in the work of Jacques Derrida, who is generally counted among Post-Structuralists. Any attempt to define Deconstruction must labor in the shadow of Derrida's apparent rejection in advance of all such attempts. Nonetheless, it has seemed fair to many interpreters to characterize it as a form of textual criticism or interpretation whose aim is to unmask and overcome hidden "privileging" that occurs in texts of all kinds. This privileging, for example the privileging of reason, the masculine, the sacred, the literal, the objective, and so on, entails the exclusion, suppression, or marginalization of their opposites—passion, the feminine, the profane, the metaphorical, the subjective, etc.—while at the same time it must presuppose these opposites even to make sense of the privileged concept. As a reading technique uncovering alleged hidden agendas behind the ostensible meaning of a text, Deconstruction takes the further step of denying that the text has a definite meaning. This has become a key thesis for the currents of literary theorizing and criticism that followed in Derrida's wake.

Postmodernism, finally, has come into vogue as the name for a rather diffuse family of ideas and trends that in significant respects reject, challenge, or aim to supersede "modernity": the convictions, aspirations, and pretensions (as they are now alleged to be) of modern Western thought and culture since the Enlightenment. In architecture, where the term first gained currency, it signified the rejection of the highly rationalized, sterile functionalism of modern architecture in favor of an eclecticism that is often playful and, by mixing seemingly incongruous styles, mocks its own seriousness. In philosophy and adjacent disciplines, Postmodernism has come to mean, somewhat analogously, a rejection of the modern mind's confidence in rationality, including, for instance, its pretensions to the attainment of universally valid and objective truth and its confidence in the achievability of progress. As expounded by the French thinker Jean-François Lyotard, it also entailed a profound suspicion and abandonment of what he called "metanarratives," grand narratives or theories purporting to disclose the overall meaning of history and to assign particular events and phenomena, and to deny to others, a place in the grand scheme of things. For Lyotard, such "totalizing" metanarratives, whether offered by religion, Marxism, Darwinism, psychoanalysis, or whatever, need to be deconstructed as coercive and oppressive in their purpose or effect. Certain Anglo-American philosophical strains also meet under the banner of Postmodernism. The American philosopher Richard Rorty, notably, developing themes from Pragmatism and certain quarters of Analytic philosophy and bringing these together with Continental themes, challenged the modern rationalist presumption that philosophy or any branch of knowledge can find secure foundations or achieve genuine representation of reality.

Anglo-American Philosophy

This provides a handy segue to our closer characterization of Anglo-American philosophy. It is not uncommon to equate Anglo-American philosophy with what is called *Analytic* or *Analytical philosophy,* but the term is also used in a broader sense to encompass other movements that have flourished chiefly on British and American soil, for instance Pragmatism, Naturalism, and Process philosophy. There is much to be said for the wider meaning, which avoids the suggestion that philosophy in England and America is more monolithic than it really is. The equation of Anglo-American with Analytic is also unfortunate from another point of view, in that Analytic philosophy has become the dominant mode of philosophizing in some other areas as well, notably the Scandinavian countries, to say nothing of the inroads it has made in areas where other approaches still dominate the field (the other side of the blurring and bridging of the Continental/Anglo-American boundary), for example, in Germany. Granting all those qualifications and others, however, there is no question that Analytic philosophy has been the most important philosophical current within the Anglo-American sphere. It is also the one most often contrasted with (and actively opposed to) the Continental movements described previously.

What constitutes Analytic philosophy is not so easy to say. I believe it is possible to distinguish at least three variants, though they probably represent points on a spectrum rather than discrete alternatives. In the widest and loosest sense, Analytic philosophy is hardly more than a philosophical style, one that takes extreme care with the meanings of words (sometimes with precise definitions of terms and consistency in their use, sometimes with the nuances of ordinary language), that tends to present arguments in meticulous step-by-step fashion (often endeavoring to leave nothing implicit), and that pays close, sometimes minute attention to logical relations (often using logical symbolism or specialized logical terminology to render such relations transparent). In a narrower sense, "Analytic philosophy" designates a philosophical outlook that holds the primary task or even (in its more extreme version) the only proper task of philosophy—the primary or proper method for attacking philosophical problems—to be analysis of one sort or another: of meanings, of concepts, of logical relations, or all of these. We can call this the methodological version. Finally, one may occasionally encounter the term "Analytic philosophy" in contexts where it is reserved for one or more specific doctrines regarding the outcome of correct philosophical analysis. While the Analytic tradition (in either of the two wider senses) owes a great deal to certain specific doctrinal versions—and to major figures who propounded them, such as Bertrand Russell, G. E. Moore, and Ludwig Wittgenstein—it would be incorrect to say that Analytic philosophy is the dominant orientation among British and American philosophers if one has in mind this narrower meaning. In fact, it is not clear that this is or ever has been true under any but the widest meaning distinguished previously.

Common to those who subscribe to the Analytic approach, whether in the broadest sense or a narrower one, is the conviction that to some significant degree, philosophical problems, puzzles, and errors are rooted in language, and can be solved or avoided, as the case may be, by a sound understanding of language and careful attention to its workings. This has tended to focus much attention on language and on its close relative, logic, as objects of study for their own sake. (The relationship between language and logic is itself a question subjected to considerable inquiry and debate.) Detractors are apt to point to this concern—they might say an obsession—with language and logic as one aspect of the trivialization of philosophy with which they charge the Analytic movement. Many who are generally loyal or sympathetic to Analytic philosophy may agree that, especially in its heyday during the middle third of the twentieth century, it tended to draw philosophy away from "deep" questions. In any case, the last several decades have seen, on the one hand, increased self-searching as to the limitations of the Analytic approach, and on the other, more efforts to apply it to such deeper questions—about the meaning of life, for instance, or the nature of the moral life—in a way that takes them seriously. There has also been more extensive application to "real-life" moral and social issues, so that Analytic approaches and perspectives are well represented in the burgeoning literature of professional ethics, bioethics, and political and social thought.

Marxist Philosophy

We turn now to Marxist philosophy, whose recent precipitous decline was previously noted. Like other aspects of Marxism, such as economics, this derives its impetus and its fundamental ideas from the writings of Karl Marx and his associate, Friedrich Engels, despite the fact (ironically) that Marx himself considered philosophy an activity proper only to the pre-Communist order. (While this is one notion of Marx that clearly was *not* taken up in Marxist philosophy, there is some continuity between it and the prevalent hostility in Marxist philosophy toward other philosophical positions, which are regarded as not simply mistaken but as manifestations of class interests and instruments of political struggle.) Marxist philosophy is not easily summarized, but its two central tenets can be readily identified by their conventional labels: dialectical materialism and historical materialism. The former asserts the primacy of matter as the fundamental reality and attempts to state general principles concerning the organization and development of matter. The latter is a theory about history and attempts to state general principles concerning the development of human thought and society in the historical process. Marx's well-known thesis concerning the primacy of economic factors in history is one ingredient of historical materialism. In most Communist countries, Marx's thought was wedded to that of Lenin and known accordingly as Marxism-Leninism.

The crude map with which we began indicated the dominance until recently of Marxist philosophy in the Iron Curtain countries, but it has really been far more widely dispersed than that. We have already noted its presence in the non-Western world, and we need only think of China to recognize the rather formidable "refinement" this requires in our philosophical map. Nor has Marxist philosophy been confined to the Communist world. Marxist philosophers were found in many countries, and still are, though dramatically fewer in number now. Some qualify their Marxism rather considerably, or combine it with other philosophical orientations, giving rise to the label "Neo-Marxism." A well-known instance of this is Jean-Paul Sartre's attempt to wed, rather incongruously on the face of it, a somewhat unorthodox Marxism to French Existentialism. An important German movement, the Frankfurt School, associated with the names of Adorno and Habermas (among others) and represented in the United States for a while by Marcuse, likewise developed ideas and themes from Marx without accepting, unless severely qualified, key Marxist dogmas such as historical materialism. Acquaintance with Marxism in the non-Communist West has tended to be more by way of such exponents working outside than those working inside the Communist sphere.

With the fall of Communism and the break-up of the Soviet Union and its East-European alliance in the early 1990s, Marxism lost not only its status as the official philosophy of the countries concerned but much of its cultural and ideological influence. Is it dead in this region? It would be premature to say. Defenders of orthodox Marxism still remain in Russia and elsewhere, and may be regaining strength as these countries struggle with their transitions to capitalism. Others are striving to develop compromise positions, combining various strands of Marxist thought with other ideas and orientations, including Eastern-Orthodox Christianity and pre-Communist Russian philosophies as well as Continental and Anglo-American philosophical positions. Still others reject Marxism in toto. In any case, the era when one could simply label this region "Marxist" on one's philosophical map is over and does not seem about to return, though the future is unknown.

Neo-Scholasticism

We turn, finally, to Neo-Scholasticism. Like the labels connected with other philosophical traditions we have discussed, "Neo-Scholasticism" has a somewhat variable denotation. Not uncommonly, it is used interchangeably with "Neo-Thomism," a term derived from St. Thomas Aquinas, a medieval philosopher whose thought was revived in spirit and to a considerable extent in substance by Catholic thinkers in the mid-nineteenth century, and given quasi-official status in Catholicism by a papal encyclical in 1879. Insofar as Neo-Thomism is the major force within Neo-Scholasticism, the equation is not too far wrong. But in a stricter sense, Neo-Scholastic philosophy harkens back to medieval Christian philosophy more generally, and may draw on and seek to develop the views of other philosophers besides St. Thomas, such as Bonaventure, Duns Scotus, and William of Ockham. Like its medieval ancestor, Neo-Scholasticism owes a great deal to Aristotle (St. Thomas is often credited with achieving a great synthesis of Aristotelian philosophy and Christian theology) and to other classical philosophers. However, it has also interacted with contemporary currents in both the Anglo-American and Continental spheres, depending to some extent, as one might expect, on the setting in which it is pursued. Neo-Scholasticism largely lost its quasi-official status with the Second Vatican Council of the early 1960s, and its institutional support within Catholicism gradually weakened in the years following. Catholic philosophers now tend to represent a wide range of philosophical positions and orientations. Symptomatic of the trend is the change of title in 1989 of the American Catholic Philosophical Association's journal from *New Scholasticism* to *American Catholic Philosophical Quarterly.*

This concludes our brief overview of the main philosophical traditions that characterize the present and recent philosophical landscape. Dozens, even hundreds of lesser movements within, without, and overlapping the boundaries of these traditions have not been mentioned, let alone described. Nor have I said anything, beyond a bare mention here or there, about historical schools and movements that may have been among the major philosophical alternatives in their time, but have since died out, been absorbed, or reduced to minor outposts on the philosophical landscape. However, most problems of scope and perspective that crop up in connection with modern reference sources (and many other types of philosophical literature, such as histories, introductory texts, journals, etc.) can be characterized and clarified with reference to the five traditions discussed. Even how (or whether) a given work deals with philosophies of the past often depends on its perspective in relation to one of these extant traditions.

FEMINIST PHILOSOPHY

Our overview is incomplete, nonetheless, without some discussion of feminist philosophy. It would be inaccurate, or at least premature at this point, to place this as a major philosophical tradition alongside the five previously described. On the other hand, it is too important a part of the contemporary philosophical scene to go unmentioned here. As a movement or perspective within philosophy, feminist philosophy is broadly concerned with philosophical issues surrounding sexual differences. There is considerable diversity and sometimes disagreement within it, however, regarding the levels at which these issues are important. Some feminist philosophers are centrally concerned with political and social inequalities between men and women and with the philosophical groundwork necessary or helpful for combating those inequalities. Others undertake a more "radical" (i.e., fundamental) critique of traditional philosophy (and other domains of knowledge, such as science) as allegedly dominated by masculine concerns and categories, and are concerned to assert the value and legitimacy, and perhaps the superiority, of women's ways of being, knowing, and doing that are claimed to be different from those of men. These feminist philosophers have proposed distinctively feminist epistemologies, ethics, and metaphysics. Such ground-level concerns overlap with concerns about equality, of course, and often complement them; but the two can also collide—for example, when some who insist on the radical nature of gender differences interpret "equity feminists" as purchasing equality at the price of suppressing those differences (thus maintaining the essential subordination of feminine to masculine).

Feminist philosophy is not independent of the traditions previously described; many who claim the feminist label identify strongly with one or another of the Anglo-American, Continental, Marxist, and even Neo-Scholastic traditions. (Whether there are specifically non-Western forms of feminist philosophy I am not sure; certainly there are explorations of the relations between feminism and non-Western philosophical traditions.) Even when identification with a major tradition is not strong, or is explicitly rejected, the various groupings and viewpoints identifiable within feminist philosophy—liberal, Marxist, radical, psychoanalytic, existentialist, socialist, postmodern, Christian—clearly differ in the extent to which they draw significant support, inspiration, terminology, and so forth, from one or several of these traditions.

From a pragmatic point of view, it is relevant for our purpose here to observe that feminist philosophy is included within the *scope* of many reference sources, particularly recent ones, representing various perspectives, especially Anglo-American or Continental; and particular parts of those works may represent or express specifically feminist *perspectives*. On the other hand, only a few sources listed in this guide can be said either to represent a feminist perspective when taken as a whole or to take feminist philosophy as their exclusive scope. Several early sources that came close were chiefly concerned with recovering and making accessible the contributions of women to philosophy throughout its history (see entries 35, 36, and 203). Such efforts do represent an important feminist concern, and the sources in question may evidence, in varying degrees, additional feminist motivations and convictions. None, however, confined their attention to women whose philosophical ideas are specifically feminist, nor did they presume or assert feminist implications in women's philosophical thought that is not itself (overtly) feminist. The last decade, however, began to yield several reference publications, listed in chapter 23, that can be said to represent feminist philosophy in a much stronger sense. The trend seems likely to continue.

Part I
GENERAL SOURCES

2
General Bibliographic and Research Guides

1.　　　De George, Richard T. **The Philosopher's Guide: To Sources, Research Tools, Professional Life, and Related Fields**. Lawrence: Regents Press of Kansas, 1980. 261p.

　　　This work succeeds De George's earlier *Guide to Philosophical Bibliography and Research* (1971). Aimed particularly at the professional philosopher and the advanced student, it has served as a solid, reputable, and broadly useful resource, but has now lost a great deal of ground to obsolescence. Roughly half the volume is a comprehensive bibliography of research resources in philosophy, including bibliographies, indexes, dictionaries and encyclopedias, standard histories and biographies, collected editions of major philosophers, and major series and journals. This half is divided into three sections: (1) "General"; (2) "History of Philosophy," with period chapters that include subsections for individual philosophers; and (3) "Systematic Philosophy," with chapters (amply subdivided) for branches, selected schools and movements, and nations and regions. Liberal use is made of cross-references. There follows a section which groups a bibliography of philosophical serials with a chapter covering aids to writing and publishing and a directory of philosophical organizations, institutions, and other facilitators of professional life. The final third of the volume is devoted to research tools outside philosophy proper but potentially useful for philosophical studies, either general in scope or in related fields. The latter include most of the standard academic disciplines, with religion distinguished by a chapter of its own.

　　　The Philosopher's Guide is annotated only selectively, with minimal and exclusively descriptive annotations.

2.　　　Ellwood, Robert S., ed. **The Best in Philosophy and Religion.** New Providence, N.J.: R. R. Bowker, 1994. 1054p. (The Reader's Adviser: A Layman's Guide to Literature, 14th ed., vol. 4).

　　　This volume is one of six under the common title *The Reader's Adviser,* which bills itself as a comprehensive guide to literature that "booksellers, reference and acquisitions librarians, lay readers, teachers, academics, and students alike can readily use to identify the best of nearly everything available in English in the United States today" (series preface). It lists books only. The proportion of the volume devoted to philosophy is a little less than half—or possibly a little more, once one counts in philosophical materials from several chapters in the Religion section where religion and philosophy are actually treated together: ancient religions and philosophies (apart from Greek and Roman), Islam, and Judaism. Following a short opening chapter on key reference works in both fields, the Philosophy section (pp. 11–415) comprises a chapter on "general philosophy," five chapters on Western philosophy by historical periods, and a chapter each (new since the thirteenth edition) on Asian and African philosophy since 1850 and on contemporary issues in philosophy. The Religion section has chapters, besides those aforementioned, on Eastern religions, Christianity (three, including one on the Bible and related literature), minority religions and contemporary religious movements, and contemporary issues in religious thought. All are apt to include some material of potential interest to philosophers and philosophy students.

This work has substantial virtues, as one might predict from an impressive pedigree (13 previous editions of *The Reader's Adviser* since 1921) and several distinguished names among its contributors. Coverage of philosophy includes citations of several thousand books, each with a succinct one- or two-sentence description, together with excellent thumbnail sketches of the field's major geographic and historical divisions and key figures. But alongside these strengths are some weaknesses as well. These result mainly from an organization scheme and selection criteria that are focused too intently on individual thinkers, each treated in some depth, while attention to specific branches of philosophy (ethics, epistemology, philosophy of religion, etc.) is neglected or slighted. This leads to under-representation of important topics (e.g., aesthetics, free will) and a lack of balance, in the sense that less important books are "in" while more important ones are "out." For example, 10 titles are listed by or about philosophical system-builder James Feibleman, not well known even to most professional philosophers, compared with just one each by John Searle and Arthur Danto, none by Julia Kristeva, though each has several books sure to be more widely read and discussed than most of Feibleman's—but they were not ranked as major philosophers meriting a section of their own (itself a debatable judgment at least in Kristeva's case). However, credit must be given for a considerable mitigation of this problem compared to what it was in the corresponding volume in the previous edition of the *Reader's Adviser* (William L. Reese, ed., *The Best in the Literature of Philosophy and World Religions*, New York: R. R. Bowker, 1988, 801p.), thanks in part to an expanded and more judicious selection of recent and contemporary philosophers but also to the addition of the more topically oriented "Current Issues in Philosophy" chapter.

3.   Erratic Impact's Philosophy Research Base. Maintained by Danne Polk. http://www.erraticimpact.com (accessed October 13, 2005).

This Web site has some claim to inclusion in this chapter, as it describes itself as a "study guide [that] attempts to aid both academic and general interest in all philosophical genres and their related fields," and seeks to accomplish this by "integrating text resources with the best online resources" (home page). But it can be commended for this function only with substantial reservations. As a directory to Web-based resources, it stands alongside *EpistemeLinks* (entry 104) as among the best of such sites that is still undergoing continuous updating at this writing in October 2005 (see entry 105 for more on this aspect). And it does, in a sense, "integrate" information about thousands of print resources. Select any topic or philosopher from those offered, and you're likely to be presented with information about an introductory text or other recent study, often with an extended quotation or a brief summary. Besides these one typically finds links for "Texts" on the selected topic and related topics—links that turn out to invoke searches of the catalogs of online bookseller Amazon.com, or Powell's Books for used texts. This is by no means useless even if one is not interested in buying, but it does both too much and too little. Too much in that such searches are often imprecise, tending to capture many marginal or downright irrelevant titles, and in any case quite nondiscriminating among the important, less important, and worthless. At the same time, it does too little in that it is limited to what is in the catalogs of the affiliated booksellers at the time, which may easily leave one unaware of key publications that are out of print and not necessarily in the second-hand catalogs at the moment. And, of course, there is no guidance to periodical literature. In sum, it is not wise to rely on this site for general guidance to print resources, though it's a useful supplement to other sources.

4.   Follon, J. **Guide bibliographique des études de philosophie.** Louvain-la-Neuve: Editions de l'Institut Supérieur de Philosophie; Paris: J. Vrin; Louvain-la-Neuve: Librairie Peeters, 1993. 220p. (Bibliothéque philosophique de Louvain, 37).

Though now more than a decade away from being current, this guide retains some usefulness for French or French-speaking students and "apprentice philosophers" (preface). By its own account, it is also intended for English-speaking readers (ibid.). And indeed, it lists many English as well as French-language sources in all chapters, including the first two dealing respectively with introductions and with textbooks for philosophy in general or its significant subfields, as well as later chapters listing historical studies and collected editions of major philosophers. Chapters on reference works—dictionaries, encyclopedias, bibliographies, and so forth—also list important works in German, Italian, Latin, Spanish, and occasionally other languages. But except for a preface in both French and English, narrative material such as chapter introductions and (selective) annotations are in French only. An appendix explains the *International Philosophical Bibliography* (entry 43) and its use. A second appendix provides concise guides to philosophical schools and major philosophers. Index of names only.

5.   Graybosch, Anthony, Gregory M. Scott and Stephen M. Garrison. **The Philosophy Student Writer's Manual.** 2nd ed. Upper Saddle River, N.J.: Prentice Hall, 2003. 259p.

Offers a smorgasbord of advice and guidance for undergraduate students facing writing assignments in philosophy. Topics covered include an introduction to the discipline intended to give "a feel for philosophical argumentation" (p. 2); generic advice on the process and the mechanics of writing, even including basic grammar; principles of argument; logical fallacies, both formal and informal; documentation of sources; the research process; and finding information "in your library and similar places" and on the World Wide Web. Parts of the last-named section are sadly disappointing. While coverage of Web resources is spotty, more so than a reasonable concern about rapid obsolescence might justify, the impoverished and often ill-chosen selection of print reference works seems particularly inexcusable. Of just 41 titles listed, fewer than half are specific to philosophy, and several of those are far from core titles. The 1967 *Encyclopedia of Philosophy* (entry 125) is listed, the much newer *Routledge Encyclopedia of Philosophy* (1998, entry 150) is not. That a slight majority are general works or sources in related disciplines (e.g., religion, political studies) might be defensible, except that most of the choices seem arbitrary and do not represent titles most likely to aid undergraduate philosophy research. The book's final section makes suggestions for some specific kinds of writing assignments, focusing on the areas of ethics and history of philosophy, and presents several sample papers. An eight-page glossary of philosophic terms is appended.

6.   Jordak, Francis Elliott. **A Bibliographical Survey for a Foundation in Philosophy.** Washington, D.C.: University Press of America, 1978. 435p.

Intended to serve the particular needs of the philosophy program in the two-year colleges of the Wisconsin Center System (some of its subject divisions are actually course titles), this guide also claimed a broader usefulness "for small and medium sized libraries . . . both public and private" and "for the people who use these libraries in order to obtain a firm foundation in philosophy." Such usefulness was undermined, however, by uneven selection, lack of consistent focus as to the intended audience, and poor categorization of some items. Even when new it could not be commended as a reliable guide, and obsolescence has substantially eroded what merits it may have had. One unique feature that may still serve occasional uses, however, is its provision of lengthy quotations from standard sources such as *Choice,* Sheehy's *Guide to Reference Works,* and Katz's *Magazines for Libraries,* which generally constitute the sole content of its annotations.

7.　　　List, Charles J. and Stephen H. Plum. **Library Research Guide to Philosophy.** Ann Arbor, Mich.: Pierian Press, 1990. 102p.

Aimed primarily at the undergraduate student facing a "research paper" assignment, but also useful for graduate students or for scholars venturing outside their specialty, this guide takes the user through the typical steps of the research process. Successive chapters cover the construction of a preliminary bibliography with the help of such basic resources as the *Encyclopedia of Philosophy* (entry 125); surveying the frontiers of one's topic via more specialized bibliographical resources; finding one's way through the library using tools such as the catalog, the *L.C. Guide to Subject Headings,* and the *Book Review Index;* "what to do if it's not in the library"; and identifying recent literature through, for example, the *Philosopher's Index* in either its print or online versions (entries 47 and 48), as well as (in a separate chapter) more general sources such as the *Arts and Humanities Citation Index.* Appendices offer a "library knowledge test," advice on the actual writing of a philosophy paper, and a 20-page classified bibliography of basic reference sources. Finally, there is a title index of the sources treated in depth in the body of the work. List and Plum's guide now requires considerable supplementing to reflect recent changes in the field, but it retains some measure of its original utility even 15 years after publication.

8.　　　Matczak, Sebastian A. **Philosophy: Its Nature, Methods and Basic Sources.** New York: Learned Publications; Louvain: Editions Nauwelaerts; Paris: Beatrice-Nauwelaerts, 1975. 280p. (Philosophical Questions Series, 4).

The goal set by Matczak for this work was "to meet the need of a concise and yet all-embracing work of the essential questions and sources in philosophy" (preface). Part 1, "The Nature of Philosophy," is a short treatise, liberally augmented with bibliographic references, on "the notion of philosophy and its methods . . . as distinguished from the methods of other sciences" (introduction). Some attempt is made to represent diverse perspectives, though Matczak's own Christian and Catholic orientation can be discerned. Part 2, "Basic Bibliographical Sources," has chapters ranging in generality from multidisciplinary bibliographies to those on individual philosophers. Part 3, "Basic Descriptive Sources," covers encyclopedias, dictionaries, and biographical sources. Part 4 is devoted to periodicals, part 5 to philosophical institutions, including a chapter on libraries.

Among the older research guides, Matczak's competed with DeGeorge's (entry 1) in terms of generality and comprehensiveness. It lists an even larger and more varied selection of philosophical and general resources, but was somewhat less reliable and arguably more partisan in orientation. Being five years older, it has of course lost even more ground to obsolescence.

Several other philosophy research guides that are now more than a quarter of a century old and obsolete for most purposes still retain, each of them, some utility for a variety of special and sometimes unique features. Martin A Bertman's *Research Guide in Philosophy* (Morristown, N.J.: General Learning Press, 1974, 252p.) offers practical guidance for research and writing that is largely timeless, with sections titled "On Giving One's Opinion," "What is a Philosophical Problem?" "Taking Notes," and "Marking Up Books: A Shorthand System." Still worthwhile also are a sketch of the history of philosophy and a glossary of philosophical terms. An earlier work by Sebastian Matzcak, *Research and Composition in Philosophy* (2nd ed., Louvain: Editions Nauwelaerts, 1971, 88p.), could serve to a large extent as a generic introduction to the processes and techniques of scholarly research and writing, with the advantage for the philosophy student of employing philosophical examples. On the other hand, it is outdated even with regard to such matters as footnote and bibliography forms, not to mention its basic list of philosophical bibliographies, encyclopedias, dictionaries, biographical sources, histories, and periodicals in the major European languages as well as English. Dietrich Hans Borchardt's *How to Find Out in Philosophy and Psychology* (Oxford: Pergamon Press, 1968, 97p.) remains of some value for its chatty but informative historical surveys of the major types of comprehensive reference sources: dictionaries, encyclopedias, general retrospective bibliographies and handbooks, current bibliographies and reviewing journals, and national bibliographies. Its unusual pairing of philosophy with psychology is supported with the observation that "many standard reference works have done so" and that "it is impossible to disentangle their common history until the second half of the nineteenth century" (introduction). In actuality, though, Borchardt usually segregates the two fields within each chapter or section. Finally, Henry J. Koren's *Research in Philosophy: A Bibliographical Introduction to Philosophy and a Few Suggestions for Dissertations* (Pittsburgh: Duquesne University Press, 1966, 203p.) may still be worth an occasional consultation for its coverage of some older and more out-of-the way bibliographies; a five-page explanation of the *Répertoire bibliographique de la philosophie* (see entry 43), including its history, arrangement, and scope; general information about books and their classification; and "a few suggestions about dissertations." More generally, it affords rather more emphasis on Thomistic and Continental philosophy than most other guides.

9.   Retlich, Norbert. **Literatur für das Philosophiestudium.** Stuttgart: J. B. Metzler, 1998. 179p. (Sammlung Metzler, Band 308).

An excellent guide principally for German philosophy students and researchers, from beginning through graduate level to professional. Others with even a modicum of German-language ability may find it useful for some purposes as well. Retlich lists and describes not only German-language sources but many *fremdsprachige* (foreign language) works, particularly English-language, though giving preference to German translations when available. He covers not just philosophical reference literature but also several other categories such as recommended introductions to the field and its subregions, historical overviews, print and online collections of primary texts, standard editions of major philosophers, and philosophical journals and other serial publications. Among reference sources, he includes besides those specific to philosophy a variety of multidisciplinary works—general biographical sources, for example—deemed particularly useful for philosophical research. And he offers general chapters on research and information-seeking methods and even general helps for students such as guides to financial aid or foreign study opportunities. A regrettable omission in this work is an index of any kind.

The nearest English-language counterpart to Retlich's guide, *The Philosopher's Guide* by De George (entry 1), is seriously outdated.

10.   Tice, Terrence N. and Thomas P. Slavens. **Research Guide to Philosophy.** Chicago: American Library Association, 1983. 608p. (Sources of Information in the Humanities, no. 3).

While the title may suggest similarity to works by De George (entry 1) or List and Plum (entry 7), this guide is primarily a systematic-*cum*-bibliographical survey of the field, more akin to the work by Ellwood (entry 2) but restricted in this instance to philosophy and possessed of a more encompassing organizational scheme. It does include a well-annotated list of reference works, compiled by Slavens, but this is highly selective, listing just under 50 works, and was less up-to-date even in 1983 (the copyright date) than one might justly expect.

The 500-page survey portion, the work of Tice, a member of the University of Michigan philosophy faculty, comprises 13 chapters on the history of philosophy, including leading modern schools and movements (Marxism, Existentialism, Analysis, etc.), and 17 on areas of philosophy. The latter include boundary areas such as philosophy of psychology and psychoanalysis, as well as traditional core areas such as metaphysics. The important area of practical ethics, however, including the burgeoning fields of bioethics and professional ethics, is given surprisingly short shrift. Throughout, there is a focus on "the principal changes since the late 19th century," and treatment of earlier periods concerns itself primarily with later (especially recent) secondary literature, not primary sources. Attention is largely confined to monographic literature; some key journal articles are mentioned, but neither cited in full nor indexed. Coverage is through 1982. Well over 4,000 works—an estimated 3,400 cited in full and included in the author/title index—are identified, succinctly characterized, and not infrequently accorded critical or evaluative comment, all in the course of systematic profiles of the major periods and divisions of the field. Some inadequacies may be inevitable in such an ambitious undertaking, but on the whole the feat is carried off with remarkable success. One would like to see the effort updated.

3
General Bibliographies

This chapter lists bibliographies and bibliographic series that are "general" in that the scope of their subject coverage ranges comprehensively, or at least very widely, over the history of philosophy and all or many of its branches. Many cover publications from a particular period of time. Those listed in the first part cover books, often in combination with other types of materials, such as journal articles, and do so without any special discrimination as to authorship or other factors. Those listed in the second part are confined to special classes of material defined either by type of publication (such as bibliographies, dissertations, Festschriften, and periodicals), by source (conference proceedings), or by a special authorship criterion, such as women philosophers. Not included in this chapter are serial bibliographies that are or were ongoing. These are covered in chapter 4.

11.   Bochenski, Innocentius M., ed. **Bibliographische Einführungen in das Studium der Philosophie.** Berne: Francke, 1948–1953. Nos. 1–23.

This series of brief, selective bibliographies featuring mainly twentieth-century materials is decidedly out-of-date, but the annotations (in German) provided in most issues may still be of some interest or utility. In addition, some issues may have continuing value because updated or similarly convenient coverage is not widely available, or because they include references to German materials not readily identifiable otherwise. Following is a list of the individual numbers.

1. I. M. Bochenski and F. Montelone, **Allgemeine philosophische Bibliographie.** 1948. 42p.
2. Ralph B. Winn, **Amerikanische Philosophie.** 1948. 32p.
3. E. W. Beth, **Symbolische Logik und Grundlegung der exakten Wissenschaften.** 1948. 28p.
4. Régis Jolivet, **Kierkegaard.** 1948. 33p.
5. Olaf Gigon, **Antike Philosophie.** 1948. 52p.
6. P. J. de Menasce, **Arabische Philosophie.** 1948. 49p.
7. Michele F. Sciacca, **Italienische Philosophie der Gegenwart.** 1948. 36p.
8. M.-D. Phillippe, **Aristoteles.** 1948. 48p.
9. Regis Jolivet, **Französische Existenzphilosophie.** 1948. 36p.
10. Michele F. Sciacca, **Augustinus.** 1948. 32p.
11. Karl Dürr, **Der logische Positivismus.** 1948. 24p.
12. Olaf Gignon, **Platon.** 1950. 30p.
13/14. Paul Wyser. **Thomas von Aquin.** 1950. 78p.
15/16. Paul Wyser. **Der Thomismus.** 1951. 120p.

16. Paul Wyser. **Der Thomismus.** 1951. 120p.

17. Fernand van Steenberghen, **Philosophie des Mittelalters.** 1950. 52p.

18. Othmar Perler, **Patristische Philosophie.** 1950. 44p.

19. Georges Vajda, **Jüdische Philosophie.** 1950. 40p.

20/21. C. Régamey, **Buddhistische Philosophie.** 1950. 86p.

22. Odulf Schäfer, **Johannes Duns Scotus.** 1953. 34p.

23. Otto Friedrich Bollnow, **Deutsche Existenzphilosophie.** 1953. 40p.

12. Brie, G. A. de. **Bibliographia Philosophica, 1934–1945.** Vol. 1: **Bibliographia Historiae Philosophiae.** Brussels: Ed. Spectrum, 1950. 644p. Vol. 2: **Bibliographia Philosophiae.** Antwerp: Ed. Spectrum, 1954. 798p.

De Brie's outstanding accomplishment was to fill the gap left by the discontinuation or debilitation of the major serial bibliographies during the war years 1939–45, when "European scholars were unable to get in touch with the bibliographical literature of Great Britain and the American continent, whereas overseas [i.e., British and American] students lost contact with continental philosophers" (introduction). In particular, his work supplements, as well as cumulates and revises, the *Répertoire bibliographique de la philosophie* (entry 43), which during that period was being published as a supplement to two Neo-Thomist journals.

De Brie's first volume deals with the history of philosophy and is arranged generally in chronological order. Volume 2 covers philosophy systematically; its arrangement, by branches, virtually duplicates that of the *Répertoire bibliographique.* Between the two volumes, there are over 48,000 entries representing books and articles in a dozen languages: Danish, Dutch, English, French, German, Italian, Latin, Norwegian, Portuguese, Spanish and Catalan, and Swedish. Entries for books, marked with an asterisk, also have citations to reviews appended to them. An unusual feature is the use of Latin for headings and subheadings: *theoria cognitionis, cosmologia,* and so forth. This can present difficulties for the user who does not know Latin, but most of the terms are readily decipherable. The introduction is in English as well as five other European languages.

The editor's intention to continue this work with five-year supplements, announced in the introduction and repeated by others for many years afterward, was never carried out.

13. Burr, John R., and Charlotte A. Burr. **World Philosophy: A Contemporary Bibliography.** Westport, Conn.: Greenwood, 1993. 380p. (Bibliographies and Indexes in Philosophy, no. 3).

This work essentially supplements the bibliographies of John Burr's 1980 *Handbook of World Philosophy* (entry 198), without replicating or updating the latter's narrative material. The Burrs' selective list includes 3,919 representative books and monographs (no articles) published between 1976 and 1992, with significantly more emphasis on the first decade of this period than its later years. Following a list of 32 general items under the heading "World Philosophy" are sections for each of the following regions: Africa; the Middle East; Asia; Eastern Europe; Western Europe, Australia and New Zealand; Latin America; and North America. Each region is further subdivided by country. Books listed usually represent a mix of local-language and English-language titles. Some entries have annotations; most do not. An author index and fairly detailed subject index are provided.

14. **Catalog of the Hoose Library of Philosophy, University of Southern California**. Boston: G. K. Hall, 1968. 6 vols.

Reproduced in these volumes, by means of photolithography, are catalog cards representing some 37,000 volumes in the Hoose Library at the time of publication. Author, title, and subject entries are presented in a single alphabetical sequence. According to the introduction, the library's scope encompasses "all titles of significance for the study of Western philosophy," but it also offers several areas of special strength. These include the classical philosophers, German philosophy, Personalism, Phenomenology, and Latin American philosophy. For at least two historical periods, the Enlightenment and Romanticism, it offered (at the time) something approaching "the bibliographical ideal of comprehensiveness." Numerous first editions of philosophical texts as well as incunabula and manuscript holdings are all reflected here.

The utility of this and similar works (cf. entry 15) as access tools for particular libraries has been largely supplanted by the widespread online accessibility of library catalogs via the Word Wide Web. (Hoose Library collections can be accessed via the USC Libraries online catalog at http://www.usc.edu/isd/locations/libraries.html.) This set retains some value, however, as a philosophical bibliography of extremely broad scope for the period before 1968.

15. Harvard University Library. **Philosophy and Psychology.** Cambridge, Mass.: Harvard University Library, distributed by Harvard University Press, 1973. 2 vols. (Widener Library Shelflist, 42–43).

Some 59,000 books, periodicals, and pamphlets are reflected in these two volumes, part of a massive series, begun in 1965, documenting the rich resources of Harvard's Widener Library. Subjects covered, according to the preface, include "metaphysics in general, cosmology, ontology, epistemology, logic, aesthetics, and psychology." Philosophy of religion is encompassed, but not the philosophies of other disciplines (science, history, law, etc.).

The series title, "Widener Library Shelflist," may be misleading, because only a portion of volume 1 corresponds to what librarians understand by a shelflist, that is, a listing in classification (or call number) order. Also in volume 1 is a chronological listing by date of publication—an unusual and occasionally valuable aid to historical research. Volume 2 contains a listing by author and title (interfiled). Thus, not only is this in effect a very comprehensive bibliography of philosophy to around 1973, but one that affords a unique variety of access points. Its utility as a library access tool is largely rendered moot by the online access currently provided to the Harvard Libraries catalog (via the libraries' Web site at http://lib.harvard.edu/).

16. May, Thomas, ed. **Philosophy Books 1982–1986.** Bowling Green, Ohio: Philosophy Documentation Center, Bowling Green State University, 1991. 211p.

Although this was intended as the first volume of a triennial series, it was apparently not successful enough to warrant successors. May's aim was "to help philosophers increase their awareness of important recent work in philosophy outside their own areas of specialization" by identifying "the English-language books receiving the most attention from the philosophical community" (introduction). His primary strategy for identifying such books was to select, from all titles listed in the book review section of the *Philosopher's Index* (entry 47) for the years indicated, those that received multiple reviews in the philosophical literature, then narrowing that group to those most frequently cited in other publications as reflected in the *Arts and Humanities Citation Index.* The roughly 600 books selected by this method, plus another 50 identified otherwise, are arranged into 16 major thematic and historical categories, further divided by subcategories, within each of which they are listed in order of "importance" defined by citation frequency. Entries have descriptive, nonevaluative annotations of typically five to eight lines.

Conceivably, the reason May's project didn't catch on is that "most important," "receiving the most attention," and "most reviewed and cited" are not obviously equivalent; nor do they necessarily coincide with either "the best" or "the most useful," which may be what the audience for this sort of bibliography is more likely to look for.

17.   Oxford University. Oxford Sub-Faculty of Philosophy. **Study Aid Series.** Vols. 1–9. 1975–1987.

This series of selective bibliographies, issued mostly in mimeographed form (or, in a late instance, via "desk-top publishing") but more widely distributed than this might suggest, was intended mainly to meet the needs of graduate students. It was conceived, one may guess, to plug some gaps (some filled by now with more conventional publications) in convenient bibliographic coverage of specific fields and topics, particularly those emphasized in recent Anglo-American philosophy. The individual issues (latest editions) are as follows:

1. C.A.B. Peacocke, et. al. **A Selective Bibliography of Philosophical Logic.** 3rd ed. 1978. 125p.

2. R. Harré and J. Hawthorn. **A Selective Bibliography of Philosophy of Science.** 2nd ed. 1977. 69p.

3. P.A.M. Seuren. **A Selective Bibliography of Philosophy of Language.** 1975. 30p.

4. M. Moss and D. Scott, **A Bibliography of Logic Books.** 1975. 106p.

5. R.C.S. Walker. **A Selective Bibliography on Kant.** 2nd ed. 1978. 68p.

6. Swinburne, Richard. **A Selective Bibliography of the Philosophy of Mind.** New ed. 1987. 36p.

7. J. Barnes, et. al. **Aristotle: A Bibliography.** Rev. ed. 1981. 88p.

8. W. Newton-Smith. **A Study Guide to the Philosophy of Physics.** Rev. ed. 1979. 49p.

9. J. Baker. **A Select Bibliography of Moral Philosophy.** 1977. 144p.

10. Susan L. Hurley, Jeff McMahan, and Madison Powers. **A Select Bibliography of Moral and Political Philosophy.** 1987. 95p.

Swinburne's compilation on the philosophy of mind (vol. 6) supplements rather than fully supersedes the previous edition by R. C. Lindley and J. M. Shorter (*Philosophy of Mind: A Bibliography,* part 1: *The Self,* 1977; part 2: *Philosophy of Action,* 1978, 62p.), because it omits all writings before 1960.

18.   **Philosophische Bücherei: Kommentierte Internet-Ressourcen zur Philosophie.** Claus Osausky, ed. Philosophie-Institut der Universität Wien. http://buecherei.philo.at/index.htm (accessed October 13, 2005).

See entry 108. Includes bibliographies of printed books.

19.   Rand, Benjamin, comp. **Bibliography of Philosophy, Psychology and Cognate Subjects.** New York: Macmillan, 1905. 1 vol. in 2. Reprinted: New York: Peter Smith, 1949.

Rand's bibliography constitutes volume 3 (in two parts) of J. M Baldwin's *Dictionary of Philosophy and Psychology* (entry 117). It is often, as here, cited separately. Among the most ambitious bibliographical efforts in philosophy by a single individual, it aimed to be "though not exhaustive, . . . comprehensive in its scope" (preface). Some 60,000 titles are listed, journal articles and reviews as well as books. One limitation on its scope was set by Rand's decision to concentrate mainly on philosophical literature available at the time. There are no annotations.

Rand's work divides into two major sections. The first, labeled "Bibliography A, History of Philosophy," occupies most of part 1. Though it begins with the main historical and geographical divisions, the bulk of it is devoted to individual philosophers, in alphabetical, *not* chronological sequence. Bibliographies B through G, occupying part 2, deal systematically with the major branches of philosophy and with psychology.

Rand has been criticized, in his own time and since, for omitting certain topics (e.g., philosophy of history and philosophy of language) and for other shortcomings. However, the magnitude of his effort is generally acknowledged and acclaimed, and its product remains even now of some value, particularly for its nearly exhaustive coverage of nineteenth-century authors. Furthermore, its conjunction with Baldwin's encyclopedia gave it an unusually wide distribution, so that it is available, even now, in many libraries that do not have in-depth philosophy collections.

20.   Varet, Gilbert. **Manuel de bibliographie philosophique.** Paris: Presses Universitaires de France, 1956. 2 vols. (Logos: Introduction aux etudes philosophiques).

Varet's is a selective bibliography ranging over the entire field of philosophy, and often beyond. Tobey (entry 267) characterizes it, in fact, as "close to being the only bibliographical survey of the entire history of ideas"—alluding, presumably, to the pervasive inclusion of literature on theology, the history of science, and the history and criticism of the arts. Its overall arrangement falls into two parts. Volume 1, *Les philosophies classiques,* covers the history of philosophy more or less chronologically through Kant and neo-Kantian schools. Volume 2, *Les sciences philosophiques,* treats systematically the major areas of philosophical thought, grouped under three headings: "Philosophy of history and culture" (including the philosophies of religion and art), "Philosophies of sciences" (including logic and general epistemology), and "Philosophies of man" (comprising moral, social, political, and educational philosophy, and also philosophy of being, existence, and value). This grouping, and likewise the arrangement within groups, reflects specific conceptions held by Varet regarding the nature and structure of philosophy, and the bibliographer's task of exhibiting and elucidating the same. The working out of these sometimes idiosyncratic conceptions in their finer details may pose obstacles for the unwary user (who will probably not expect, for example, to find sensation and perception covered in a chapter on the philosophy of physics). Varet's peculiarities are more fully described by Jasenas (entry 22), pages 107–11.

Despite the idiosyncrasies, this is, with some 20,000 to 25,000 entries, a rich and very comprehensive resource. Coverage is especially strong for the period 1914–1934. Headings, occasional notes, and prefatory matter are all in French.

BIBLIOGRAPHIES OF BIBLIOGRAPHIES

21. Guerry, Herbert, ed. **A Bibliography of Philosophical Bibliographies.** Westport, Conn.: Greenwood Press, 1977. 332p.

Covering philosophical bibliographies in all countries from 1450 to 1974, this comprehensive work is divided into two lists. The first, labeled "Bibliographies of Individual Philosophers," is arranged alphabetically by names (it includes some coverage of schools designated by individuals' names: Thomism, Hegelianism, etc.). The second list, labeled "Subject Bibliographies," is arranged alphabetically by topic. Coverage is confined, with few exceptions, to bibliographies published separately, either as monographs or in journals. Annotations are few and usually limited to indicating the number of items cited. Cross-referencing is not always thorough. An index of editors/compilers is at the back of the volume.

22. Jasenas, Michael. **A History of the Bibliography of Philosophy.** Hildesheim: Georg Olms, 1973. 188p.

An extended bibliographic essay which describes and discusses philosophical bibliographies, from a pioneering work by Frisius in 1592 through the major serial bibliographies being published as of 1960, this book focuses on works that aimed at comprehensive coverage of the field of philosophy. In addition to describing content and arrangement, Jasenas dwells extensively on historical details concerning the compilation and publication of such bibliographies, and the influences at work upon the bibliographers.

Jasenas divides the history of philosophical bibliography into five major phases: Renaissance, modern, German *Aufklärung,* post-Kantian, and twentieth century. Appendices contain lists of bibliographies included, arranged chronologically and alphabetically; a list of other bibliographies, *not* discussed by Jasenas; and, somewhat anomalously, a "short-title list of major philosophical works discussed in standard histories of philosophy."

23. Totok, Wilhelm. **Bibliographischer Wegweiser der philosophischen Literatur.** 2nd ed., rev. by Horst-Dieter Finke. Frankfurt am Main: Vittorio Klostermann, 1985. 53p.

This German "bibliographical guide to philosophical literature" covers serial bibliographies, bibliographies of bibliographies, reviewing journals, bibliographies on countries and regions, bibliographies for specific subject areas and topics, and so forth. Notably absent are bibliographies on individual philosophers. Annotations are limited to a line or two here and there; many entries have none. The advantage of Totok's compilation over the bibliography listings in this guide—beside the obvious one for German-speakers or others more comfortable with German than English—is its wider inclusion of older and more specialized European bibliographies, particularly from before 1940. Though its primary coverage begins at the start of the twentieth century, an appendix lists philosophical bibliographies from the sixteenth through nineteenth centuries. There are author and title indexes for the 200 items listed, but no subject index. In lieu of the latter, a subject subarrangement is used within some of the chapters.

CONFERENCE PROCEEDINGS

24. Geldsetzer, Lutz. **Bibliography of the International Congresses of Philosophy: Proceedings, 1900–1978 / Bibliographie der internationalen Philosophie Kongresse: Beiträge, 1900–1978**. Munich: K. G. Saur, 1981. 208p.

A handy index to the proceedings of 16 World Philosophical Congresses, from Paris 1900–1903 to Düsseldorf 1978, many of them published in multiple volumes (e.g., 12 volumes for the 1958 Venice Congress). Gives tables of contents and provides collective indexes of authors and subjects.

DISSERTATIONS

25.   Bechtle, Thomas C., and Mary F. Riley. **Dissertations in Philosophy Accepted at American Universities, 1861–1975.** New York: Garland, 1978. 537p.

Listed are 7,503 dissertations from 120 universities. As a rule, these include only dissertations for degrees earned in departments of philosophy (thus not, for instance, philosophical dissertations done in seminaries). The compilers made an unusual effort, described in the preface, to identify dissertations not reflected in standard sources such as *Dissertation Abstracts* and *Comprehensive Dissertation Index,* notably those completed prior to 1912. Information provided includes, besides author and title, the university, year submitted, and when applicable the *Dissertation Abstracts* number, handy for locating the abstract or for ordering a copy of the dissertation itself from University Microfilms.

Arrangement is by author, not a particularly useful approach unless accompanied with a good subject index. There *is* a subject index, but not a good one. Too many subject terms, being too broad, have long, undiscriminating strings of references (numbers only). Worse, some dissertations cannot be found where they would reasonably be expected (e.g., one titled "Eros and Philosophy" is absent under the word "eros"; another, on historical objectivity, could not be located under "history," "objectivity," or any other likely term).

26.   **Bibliographien zur Philosophie.** Cologne: Gemini, 1980–1989. Hürth-Efferen: Gemini, 1992–.

All bibliographies in this series to date are edited by Gernot U. Gabel. Its generic title notwithstanding, the series to this point is devoted, with one exception and one borderline case, to dissertations and theses on German philosophy and philosophers. The exception is an issue on Sartre; the borderline case is one on Wittgenstein, an Austrian who wrote his major works in German but taught at Cambridge and is generally claimed by Anglo-American philosophy. Each issue focuses either on an individual philosopher or on one or more countries of origin, or on a combination of the two. Issues are slim, ranging from 34 to 89 pages in length, and list from around 300 to around 700 dissertations and theses each. Entries normally provide the author, title, university, and year of completion, and are arranged chronologically. All issues include a subject index, and most an author index as well. There are no annotations.

A few volumes have already seen multiple editions. Whether the series remains open (as of late 2003) is unclear. Available issues are as follows (latest editions only):

1. **Friedrich Nietzsche: Ein Verzeichnis westeuropäischer und nordamerikanischer Hochschulschriften, 1900–1980.** 3rd ed. 1985. 68p.

2. **Hegel: Ein Verzeichnis der Dissertationen aus sieben westeuropäischer Ländern, 1885–1980.** 1986. 68p.

3. **Immanuel Kant: Ein Verzeichnis der Dissertationen aus den deutschschprachigen Ländern, 1900–1980.** 2nd ed. 1987. 70p.

4. **Die deutsche Philosophie im Spiegel französischer Hochschulschriften, 1885–1985: Eine Bibliographie.** 2nd ed. 1993. 64p.

5. **Bibliographie österreichischer und schweizerischer Dissertationen zur deutschen Philosophie, 1885–1975.** 1982. 89p.

6. **Canadian Theses on German Philosophy, 1925–1980: A Bibliography.** 3rd ed. 1985. 60p.

7. **Leibniz: Eine Bibliographie europäischer und nordamerikanischer Hochschulschriften, 1875–1980.** 2nd ed. 1986. 49p.

8. **Index to Theses on German Philosophy Accepted by the Universities of Great Britain and Ireland, 1900–1980.** 1984. 50p.

9. **Fichte: Ein Verzeichnis westeuropäischer und nordamerikanischer Hochschulschriften, 1885–1980.** 1985. 44p.

10. **Schleiermacher: Ein Verzeichnis westeuropäischer und nordamerikanischer Hochschulschriften, 1880–1980.** 1986. 45p.

11.**Schelling: Ein Verzeichnis westeuropäischer und nordamerikanischer Hochschulschriften, 1885–1980.** 1986. 34p.

12. **Ludwig Wittgenstein: A Comprehensive Bibliography of International Theses and Dissertations, 1933–1985.** 1988. 60p.

13. **Schopenhauer: Ein Verzeichnis westeuropäischer und nordamerikanischer Hochschulschriften, 1885–1985.** 1988. 45p.

14. **Kant: An Index to Theses and Dissertations Accepted by Universities in Canada and the United States, 1879–1985.** 1989. 67p.

15. **Sartre: A Comprehensive Bibliography of International Theses and Dissertations, 1950–1985.** 1992. 79p.

16. **Heidegger: Ein internationales Verzeichnis der Hochschulschriften, 1930–1990.** 1993. 83p.

17. **Husserl: Ein Verzeichnis der Hochschulschriften aus westeuropäischen und nordamerikanischen Ländern, 1912–1990.** 1995. 60p.

FESTSCHRIFTEN AND SIMILAR COLLECTIONS

27. Geldsetzer, Lutz. **In Honorem: Eine Bibliographie philosophischer Festschriften und ihrer Beiträge.** Düsseldorf: Philosophia, 1975. 226p.

Despite the title, not all of the essay-collections listed and indexed in this volume are strictly *Festschriften* (intended to honor a particular individual, typically presented on retirement). Notable exceptions include the Library of Living Philosophers series and some volumes in the Boston Studies in the Philosophy of Science (e.g., one on Ernst Mach). It covers, as these examples indicate, English-language as well as German collections, and also some French. It reproduces tables of contents and provides collective author and subject indexes (the latter in German).

PERIODICALS

28. Hogrebe, Wolfram, Rudolf Kamp, and Gert König. **Periodica philosophica: eine internationale Bibliografie philosophischer Zeitschriften von den Anfängen bis zur Gegenwart.** Düsseldorf: Philosophia, 1972. 728 columns.

This is an international listing of some 5,000 journals, both extant and defunct, in the field of philosophy broadly defined (broadly enough to include borderline journals in religion, psychology, general humanistic studies, etc.). Data provided typically include country and dates of publication, first and (if applicable) last issue numbers, sponsoring organization(s), and previous and subsequent titles. A special section, labeled *Kettenregister* ("chain index"), diagrams complex series of title changes, splits, mergers, and so forth. There is also a classified subject index *(Bereichsregister)* and a country index *(Länderregister).*

29. Maison des Sciences de l'Homme, Paris. Service d'Echange d'Informations Scientifiques. **Liste mondiale des périodìques spéciales en philosophie / World List of Specialized Periodicals in Philosophy.** Paris: Mouton, 1967. 124p. (Publications série C: Catalogues et inventaires).

This fully bilingual (English and French) work lists and describes philosophical periodicals by country and indexes them by subject, by publishing bodies, and by titles.

30. **Online Information about Journals in Philosophy and Related Disciplines.** Peter Milne, comp. http://homepages.ed.ac.uk/pmilne/links_html/journals.html.

See entry 106.

31. Ruben, Douglas H. **Philosophy Journals and Serials: An Analytical Guide.** Westport, Conn.: Greenwood Press, 1985. 147p. (Annotated Bibliographies of Serials: A Subject Approach, no. 2).

Unlike the other periodicals bibliographies listed in this section (entries 28, 29, and 32), Ruben's is limited to English-language serials. It lists, however, over 300 titles. The extensive annotations for each entry include much that is now seriously obsolete or unreliable—price, circulation, manuscript selection, acceptance rates, and, to some extent, coverage in indexes and abstracts—but characterizations of target audience and evaluative comments on strengths and weaknesses remain of some value. Arrangement is alphabetical by title, with subject and geographical indexes.

32. U.S. Library of Congress. General Reference and Bibliography Division. **Philosophical Periodicals: An Annotated World List.** Comp. by David Baumgardt. Washington, D.C.: Government Printing Office, 1952. 89p.

This list of 489 titles was "designed to give some basic information on the variegated philosophical interests of periodicals being issued currently [i.e., ca. 1952] in some 71 political areas" (introduction). For countries with extensive periodical publishing, inclusion is limited to professional publications, but for those "whose literary production is more limited, the nonformal philosophical press has been liberally taken into account." The latter feature, together with some of the brief notes characterizing scope or emphasis, give this dated work some residual value.

PERIODICAL ARTICLES

33.   Philosophische Dokumentation aus dem Philosophischen Institut der Universität Düsseldorf. 1. Zeitschriften-Bibliographien. Vols. 1–8. Various publishers, 1968–80.

This series of "bibliographies"—more accurately, indexes—covers exhaustively, for specified periods of time, the contents of a number of the most historically significant journals in nineteenth- and twentieth-century Western philosophy—journals which regularly provided venues for the most important philosophers of their time, including figures of the stature of, for example, Heidegger and Russell. The extremely—maybe excessively—thorough indexing afforded by these volumes goes well beyond the titles of articles, beyond even abstracts or descriptors, to include indexing by significant words of the actual contents, that is, the full text, of the articles. Other indexing varies by journal, but typically includes titles with abstracts, authors, and subject descriptors. The following volumes have been issued:

1.1 **Gesamtregister zur Zeitschrift für philosophische Forschung 1–21 (1946–1967)**. Meisenheim/Glan: Anton Hain, 1968. 618p.

1.2 **Gesamtregister der Kant-Studien, Teil I, 1–30 (1897–1925)**. Meisenheim/ Glan: Anton Hain, 1969. 192p.

1.3 **Gesamtregister der Kant-Studien, Teil II, 31–60 (1926–1969)**. Meisenheim/ Glan: Anton Hain, 1970. 381p.

1.4 **Register der Revue philosophique de Louvain 44–68 (1946–1970)**. Ed. Monique Jucquois. Nendeln/Liechtenstein: Kraus Reprint, 1973. 428p.

1.5 **Gesamtregister der Annalen der Philosophie (u. philos. Kritik) 1–8 (1919–1929); Erkenntnis 1–7 (1930/31–1937/38); The Journal of Unified Science (Erkenntnis) 8 (1939/40); Forum philosophicum 1 (1930/31)**. Ed. Felicitas Belke. Nendeln/Liechtenstein: Kraus Reprint, 1973. 754p.

1.6 **Mind (Old Series) 1–16 (1876–1891)**. Ed. Ariane Iljon. Munich: Kraus International , 1980. 209p.

1.7 **Zeitschrift für Sozialforschung 1–7 (1932–1938); Studies in Philosophy and Social Science 8–9 (1939–1941)**. Munich: Kraus International , 1980. 287p.

1.8 **Revue de msetaphysique et de morale 51–78 (1946–1973)**. Ed. Monique Jucquois. Munich: Kraus International, 1980. 720p.

[handwritten margin note: is this all part of Erkenntnis?]

REFERENCE BOOKS

34.   ARBA In-depth: Philosophy and Religion. Martin Dillon and Sharon Graff Hysell, eds. Westport, Conn.: Libraries Unlimited, 2004. 230p.

This volume gathers 436 reviews chosen from *American Reference Books Annual* (*ARBA*) for the years 1997–2003. Just 60 come under the heading of philosophy, drawn from a total of 65 in that category in the annual volumes for those years. Being somewhat selective, the volume constitutes what the introduction terms "an abridged version of *ARBA*," but each selected review is reprinted in full. Philosophy reference works are divided into subsections for bibliography, biography, dictionaries and encyclopedias, directories, handbooks and yearbooks, and indexes. The much larger religion section has many topical divisions including the major world religions and Biblical studies. *ARBA* reviews reference sources published in the United States and Canada, along with some English language titles form other countries.

WOMEN PHILOSOPHERS

35. Barth, Else M. **Women Philosophers: A Bibliography of Books through 1990.** Bowling Green, Ohio: Philosophy Documentation Center, Bowling Green State University, 1992. 236p.

On the principle that "women's work, and women's voices, are not to be tucked away into separate corners of the academic world" but belong "right in the heart of each academic field and (sub)discipline" (preface), Barth has organized her bibliography of books both *by* and *about* women philosophers according to a largely traditional classification of philosophical domains and subdomains. The main division is between what she labels "systematical philosophy" and history of philosophy, the former subdivided by the major branches and approaches (e.g., analytic philosophy, epistemology, logic, metaphysics, philosophy of culture, ethics and morality, etc.), the latter including both general history of philosophy and the histories of specific subdisciplines, studies of individual philosophers, and finally a section on broad philosophical traditions (e.g., American, Asian, psychoanalytical), including the feminist tradition. This last is one of only two places in the scheme where feminism is an explicit rubric; the other is a subheading under political philosophy. A few other section titles reflect characteristic concerns of feminist philosophy (e.g., "Sexual/gender Oppression and Politics," "Images of 'Man'"), and certainly many books listed throughout have a feminist perspective or deal with "women's issues." Yet feminism is not (contrary, perhaps, to stereotypes of women philosophers) the dominant focus. Philosophical books written or edited by women are included whatever their subject matter or point of view. Judgments of quality, too, do not come into play, and the only bounds are certain limitations of language and geography dictated by practical considerations: Eastern Europe and non–English-speaking countries outside Europe are not covered. Doctoral dissertations, even those not published, are included "wherever possible" (p. 3), that is, if the information was somewhat readily available. More than 2,800 items are listed, and more than 1,900 names appear in the author index. Entries are not annotated.

36. **Collaborative Bibliography of Women in Philosophy.** Ed. Noël Hutchings and William D. Rumsey. Bowling Green, Ohio: Philosophy Documentation Center, Bowling Green State University, 1997. 375p.

Lists and often annotates more than 11,000 philosophical works produced by more than 3,500 women, from the pre-Socratics to near the close of the twentieth century. It is not restricted to "philosophers" in a narrow sense, including for instance such figures as Theosophist Helena Blavatzky and writer Virginia Woolf. The "collaborative" description incorporated in the title reflects the fact that this print volume derived from an online bibliography that invited contributions, corrections, and suggestions from anyone—and provided a mechanism for submitting them—while maintaining editorial control to assure acceptable levels of authenticity and scholarly quality. Lamentably, this online project, known as *Noema: Collaborative Bibliography of Women in Philosophy,* despite holding up an intriguing model for the future of Web-based bibliography, went off-line in July 2003. With it have vanished, at least for now, additions entered subsequent to this print version, which even by mid-2001 (my latest figures) had expanded the bibliography to more than 16,000 records representing over 5,000 women.

Entries are arranged alphabetically by authors' last names. Books and (occasionally) works in nonprint media are listed first, then articles, as applicable, by date of publication within each category. There is an index of named persons and subjects. Topical entries in this index tend to be overly broad: an article on adultery, for instance, can't be found under that subject entry (there isn't one) or even under "sex, philosophy of," but only under "ethics, applied." As for indexed names, their most distinctly valuable aspect would seem to be the references to women philosophers writing about *other* women philosophers. These render this in some measure a secondary bibliography on women philosophers, though *not* in a full-fledged sense: a work about a woman philosopher written by a male would find no place here.

4

General Indexes, Abstract and Review Sources, and Serial Bibliographies

37. **Bibliographie de la philosophie,** 1937–53. Vols. 1–10. Paris: Librairie Philosophique J. Vrin, 1937–1958. Semiannual.

Compiled by the staff of the Institut International de Philosophie, this serial bibliography and index attempted to cover exhaustively philosophical publications, books as well as journal literature, in most Western languages. It did not appear for several years during World War II (1940–1945); the gap is filled by De Brie's *Bibliografia philosophica* (entry 12). The two major sections of each issue are (1) an integrated, alphabetical author listing of books and journal articles and (2) a systematic subject index subdivided into a chronological/geographical section, an index of philosophers, and an index of concepts and terms. In addition, there is a directory of publishers by country and a directory of periodicals.

Volume 10 of this series, not published until 1958, is a "hybrid" bridging the transition of the *Bibliographie* to a radically revised scope and format (see entry 38).

38. **Bibliographie de la philosophie/Bibliography of Philosophy,** 1954–. Paris: Librairie Philosophique J. Vrin, 1954–. Vol. 1–. 3 issues per year.

The adoption of joint English and French titles marked the transition of this publication from a bibliography listing both books and periodical articles to one covering books only. A new volume numbering also began with this change. However, a transitional volume, covering the years 1952–1953, was published belatedly (1958) as the final volume (number 10) of the original series (entry 37); this covered only books and carried the dual-language title, but followed the old format and lacked the abstracts which are a major virtue of the new series.

The present publication is not only international in scope but also polylingual, providing abstracts in the language of origin for books in English, French, German, Italian, and Spanish, and in either English or French for books in other languages. In a typical year, well over a thousand books are covered in the *Bibliographie*. The signed abstracts are intended to be factual and not critical. They vary in length from a few to sometimes more than 30 lines. Entries and abstracts are contributed via "centers of philosophical bibliography" in over 50 countries represented in the Institut International de Philosophie, the Paris-based organization responsible for the *Bibliographie* and one of several international bodies (UNESCO is another) associated with its publication.

The *Bibliographie* employs a systematic arrangement with 10 broad and rather standard divisions (philosophy in general; logic and philosophy of science; ethics and values; etc.). Indexes are not provided in each quarterly issue—only cumulated annual indexes in the final issue of each volume. One index formerly combined authors, titles, and title catchwords, but has been reduced since volume 34 (1987) to just an author index, except for anonymous works or others listed by title only. A second, labeled "Index of Names," combines publishers, translators, authors of prefaces, and individuals mentioned in titles or in abstracts. Volume 41 (1994) brought the addition of a subject index, divided into three distinct parts: (1) periods; (2) doctrines, disciplines, and trends of thought; and (3) concepts and categories.

A *Glossaire / Glossary*, published as a supplement in 1995, lists translation equivalents for frequently occurring terms and expressions across the five languages used in the *Bibliographie.*

39.   Bibliographie de la philosophie/Bibliography of Philosophy, 1998–. CD-ROM. Paris: Librairie Philosophique J. Vrin, 2000–.

A CD-ROM version of entry 38. At this writing in November 2005, three installments, each of the last two superseding its predecessor(s), are listed on the Web site of the sponsoring Institut International de Philosophie (http://www.umr8547.ens.fr/Productions/iip-Publications.html). The first disk, issued in 2000, covered 1998 only; the second, issued in 2001, provided cumulated coverage for 1998–2000; and the latest installment, issued in 2004, covers 1998–2002. (That the latest disk listed actually exists is consistent with plans described in a May 2004 communication from the Institut to the author of this guide, but could not be independently confirmed.) Issuance of files for years prior to 1998 was also foreseen but has not occurred to date. Similarly, reported negotiations toward the goal of making the database available online, with implementation originally anticipated sometime in 2005, have not yet come to fruition. Efforts to obtain updated information on these plans have been unsuccessful as of late 2005.

40.   Dietrich's Index philosophicus, 1983–. Munich: K. G. Saur, 1997–. CD-ROM.

As of late 2005, this CD-ROM resource comprised a retrospective disc *(Basisdatenbank)* covering the years1983–1996 and a cumulated file for the period *(Berichtszeitraum)* 1997–2004, supplemented by twice-annual updates. The 1983–1996 compilation, originally issued at Osnabrück by Felix Dietrich Verlag, 1998, was marketed in North America for a time by the Philosophy Documentation Center as *Index Philosophicus.* Both it and subsequent issues are scarce in U.S. libraries at this writing.

DIP is a multilingual index to journal articles, book reviews, and essays from *Festschriften* on philosophy, theology, and religious studies. It is compiled by drawing material in these areas from three interdisciplinary indexes: *the Internationale Bibliographie der Zeitschriftenliteratur (IBZ),* the *Internationale Bibliographie der Rezensionen (IBR),* and the *Internationale Jahresbibliographie der Festschriften (IJBF).* Searchable subject headings are assigned in both German and English, and the retrieval program supports a standard variety of additional access points and search strategies. The publisher's Web site (September 2005) advertises that a combined total of 696,852 items are represented on the two cumulative discs.

Although *DIP*'s coverage overlaps significantly with that of the *Philosopher's Index* (entry 47) as well as the *International Philosophical Bibliography* (entry 43), wider inclusion of European philosophical publications provides an advantage over the former, while advantages over both lie in the comprehensive indexing of the *Festschriften* literature and (for some users) the subject coverage combining philosophy with theology and religious studies.

41.   Francis bulletin signalétique 519: Philosophie/Philosophy, 1991–1994. Vols. 45–48. Nancy, France: Institut de l'information scientifique et technique, 1991–1994.

This publication was part of the immense indexing and abstracting program carried on by the French Centre National de la Recherche Scientifique (C.N.R.S.) under the umbrella title *Francis bulletin signalétique.* This particular part, which covered the serial literature of Western philosophy on a worldwide scale and with something approaching exhaustiveness, has a complex bibliographic history. It first appeared under the title *Bulletin analytique: Philosophie* (1947–55, vols. 1–9), and subsequently, through 1990, as the *Bulletin signalétique,* in varying combinations of subject coverage, with varying subtitles and section numberings:

1956–1960, volumes 10–14: *Philosophie, Sciences humaines.*

1961–1968, volumes 15–21: *Sciences humaines (Section 19: Philosophie, Sciences religieuses).*

1969, volume 22: *Philosophie, sciences religieuses.*

1970–90, volumes 23–44: *519. Philosophie.*

The final title change (including addition of the subtitle in English) occurred in 1991. Surprisingly, a single continuous sequence of volume numbers was maintained throughout all these changes. Print publication ceased with the 1994 volume. Since then this publication's coverage has been effectively carried forward, and retrospectively duplicated, by the online and CD-ROM datebase *FRANCIS,* which provides interdisciplinary coverage of the humanities and social sciences but no longer affords the distinct identity for philosophy that existed in the print era. *FRANCIS* remains under the provenance of the Institut de l'information scientifique et technique. Its retrospective coverage, as of early 2004, reached back to 1972 in the online database, to 1984 in the CD-ROM version (distributed by Ovid Technologies). English-language searching of the Web version is available via the Eureka search interface of the U.S. Research Libraries Group (RLG).

Francis bulletin signalétique 519 employs a classified arrangement, with the *plan de classement* or classification scheme (both French and English-language versions) printed in the front of each issue. Abstracts, usually brief, are in French, regardless of the language of the article or the origin of the journal in which it is published. Book reviews, but *not* books themselves, are included, and are often summarized in a short abstract as well. An index of journals covered in each issue is provided, as well as separate author and subject indexes. All three indexes are cumulated in annual indexes, or *tables annuelles,* which appeared as a fifth issue supplementing the regular quarterly issues.

42.   Index Philosophicus. CD-ROM.

See entry 40.

43.   International Philosophical Bibliography/Répertoire bibliographique de la philosophie/Bibliografisch repertorium van de wijsbegeerte, 1991–. Vol. 43–. Louvain: Institut superieur de Philosophie, Université Catholique de Louvain/Hoger Instituut voor Wijsbegeerte, Katholieke Universiteit te Leuven, 1991–. Frequency varies.

From 1949 through 1990 (volumes 1–42), this trilingually titled publication carried only the French title *Répertoire bibliographique de la philosophie.* For convenience, it will be referred to here as the *IPB/Répertoire.*

Writing before the advent of the *Philosopher's Index* (entry 47), H. J. Koren (see note under entry 8) called this "perhaps the *most important* tool for assembling a bibliography on a particular subject." While the importance of the *IPB/Répertoire* has unquestionably diminished since then, at least for the typical English-speaking scholar or student, it remains for some an alternative and for others a significant supplement to the *Philosopher's Index.* It covers a number of non-English journals not included in the *Phil Index,* and also many non-English books, which the *Phil Index* excludes as a matter of policy. Unlike the *Phil Index,* however, the *IPB/Répertoire* does not provide abstracts.

The scope and arrangement of the *IPB/Répertoire* are thoroughly explained—in French, English, Dutch, German, Spanish, and Italian—in the introduction to the first issue of each annual volume. As it has since 1949, it focuses its attention on materials in these languages: Catalan, Dutch, English, French, German, Italian, Latin, Portuguese, and Spanish. Works in other languages *may* be included, but the exhaustiveness claimed for the languages mentioned is specifically disclaimed for any others. Entries for books and journal articles are intermingled in the classified arrangement, but those for books and collections (such as conference proceedings) are distinguished by an asterisk. The classification scheme divides broadly into a historical section, with both chronological and geographical subdivisions, and a systematic section, subdivided for major branches of philosophic thought. Prior to 1997, annual volumes consisted of three regular issues listing articles and books, but lacking indexes, plus a fourth (the November issue) reserved for book reviews and a cumulated annual index. Since 1997, though the *IPB/Répertoire* remains formally a quarterly, issues have regularly been combined: into a single issue for 1997 (vol. 49) and into double issues (numbered "1–2" and "3–4") for subsequent years. Each combined issue now incorporates book review listings and has its own index. The latter remains limited to a general name index for authors, translators, and reviewers, and also, in a feeble gesture toward subject indexing, philosophers mentioned in the titles of works cited.

As an independent publication under its former French-only and present trilingual titles, the *IPB/Répertoire* succeeds a previous incarnation, from 1934 to 1948, as a supplement to the *Revue néo-scholastique de philosophie,* later the *Revue philosophique de Louvain,* and also, for part of the same period, as a supplement to the Dutch *Tijdschrift voor philosophie* under the title *Biliographisch repertorium.* (Most of this period has since been more thoroughly covered by De Brie's *Bibliografia philosophica,* entry 12). Both the *IPB/Répertoire*'s origins and its present sponsorship suggest, and explain, a Neo-Scholastic orientation. However, any bias is noticeable in the inclusion of material others might consider marginal rather than in the exclusion of anything generally considered central to philosophy.

44.   International Philosophical Bibliography/Répertoire bibliographique de la philosophie/Bibliografisch repertorium van de wijsbegeerte, 1997–. CD-ROM. Louvain: Peeters Press, n.d.

The CD-ROM version of the *IPB/Répertoire* (entry 43) is limited at this writing in November 2005 to a single disc covering 1997–2000. Plans for a cumulative CD-ROM file for 1997–2003, reported by the publication's staff in mid-2004, have not materialized at this time; updated information on this was not available. An online version of the database (entry 45) debuted in late 2004.

The 1997–2000 CD-ROM, corresponding to volumes 49 to 52 of the printed publication, was advertised as containing records for some 24,000 books, 20,000 articles, and 13,000 book reviews. Search software included on the disc permits "simple searches" via no less than 18 different indexes. Advanced searching using Boolean operators, wildcards, and so forth, is also supported.

45.   International Philosophical Bibliography/Répertoire bibliographique de la philosophie/Bibliografisch repertorium van de wijsbegeerte. Online.

The online version of the *IPB/Répertoire* (cf. entries 43 and 44) became available in 2004. It shares the classified structure as well as the content of the print index, but it affords additional access points including article or book titles, journal titles, subject keywords (limited to specifically philosophical expressions in English only), and ISBNs for books; and it also provides Boolean search capabilities and the ability to limit searches by language, type of document, year of publication, or specific personal name categories such as authors, editors, collaborators, or translators. The database is divided into a retrospective file (1990 through 1996) and a current file (1997 forward). Access is by institutional subscription. Provisions originally made for limited "daypass" access by individuals had been suspended by late 2005. Information about the database as well as access to it from authorized locations are available at http://pob.peeters-leuven.be/.

46.   Novaia literatura po sotsialnym i gumanitarnym naukam: filosofiia i sotsiologiia, 1993–. Moscow: INION RAN, 1993–. Monthly.

The principal Russian-language index to periodical literature in philosophy, covered in combination with sociology. It is part of the larger indexing project designated by its main title. Russian and other Slavic-language journals are particularly well represented, but the scope is international. It is not uncommon that half or more of the entries in a given subject section represent articles or reviews in English and other non-Slavic European languages, printed in roman alphabet. Brief abstracts, where present, are always in Russian. Main entries are organized by a detailed subject classification encompassing branches and subbranches of philosophy and historical periods. The sociology section is distinct from that for philosophy but follows it without interruption in the classification scheme.

The index under its present title was formed by the merger of *Novaia inostrannaia literature po obschestvennyym naukam: filosofiia i sotsiologiia* (Moscow: Akademiia nauk SSSR, 1976–1992) and *Novaia otechestvennaia literatura po obshchestvennym naukam: filosofiia i sotsiologiia,* the latter issued for only a single year (Moscow: INION RAN, 1992) and preceded by *Noviaia sovetskaia literatura po obshchestvennym naukam: filosofskie nauki* (Moscow: Akademiia nauk SSSR, 1976–1991).

47.   The Philosopher's Index, 1967–. Vol. 1–. Bowling Green, Ohio: Philosophy Documentation Center, Bowling Green State University, 1967–1998; Bowling Green, Ohio: Philosopher's Information Center, 1998–. Quarterly with annual cumulation.

Launched in 1967, *The Philosopher's Index* quickly established itself as the preeminent indexing and abstracting service for philosophers and students in the Anglo-American orbit, and for many beyond it as well. All major philosophy journals in English, French, German, Spanish and Italian are indexed, along with selected journals in other languages and related interdisciplinary publications. By 2005, more than 550 journals from 40 countries and in 30 languages were being indexed in full or in part. Coverage was extended to books in 1980, but only to books in English. The subtitle, *An International Index to Philosophical Periodicals,* had the words *"and Books"* added in 1982 to reflect this widened scope.

After some initial variation, the *Index* settled into its present pattern of organization, a highly satisfactory one that deserves wider emulation. The basic division is into subject and author listings, with full bibliographic information and abstract (always in English) furnished in the author section. The subject index refers to the full entries in the author section, but because it provides the title and author of the cited article or book (not, e.g., just an entry number), the user can often assess an item's likely relevance from the information in the subject index alone. This reduces laborious flipping between indexes. Subject descriptors, while mostly narrow and specific, sometimes cast so wide that they net unmanageably large numbers of entries (especially in the annual cumulation). In compensation, however, items are usually listed under several, even many, descriptors. A thesaurus of descriptors has been published separately (*The Philosopher's Index Thesaurus,* rev. 2nd ed., revisions by Kelly M. Broughton, Philosophy Documentation Center, 1998, 105p.)

Book reviews are covered in a separate section of the *Index.* From 1975 to 1988, every issue also had a section explaining the *Philosophy Research Archives,* initially a microfilm-only journal, after 1982 an annual print journal with a microfiche supplement, sponsored by the Philosophy Documentation Center and geared as much to on-demand publication as subscriptions. Articles in the *Archives* were covered in the main sections of the *Index.* Regularization as a journal in 1989 was followed by a title change in 1990 to *Journal of Philosophical Research.*

For retrospective coverage of materials published prior to 1967, see entries 49 and 50. For electronic versions of the *Philosopher's Index,* see entry 48.

48. **The Philosopher's Index.** Online and CD-ROM. Bowling Green, Ohio: Philosopher's Information Center.

The electronic version of the *Philosopher's Index,* available both online and on CD-ROM, embraces the content of the current print index from its commencement in 1967 (entry 47) as well as two retrospective print indexes that extended coverage back to 1940 (entries 49 and 50). At this writing in October 2005, both electronic formats are available through Ovid Technologies (formerly SilverPlatter), the online version also through the database services of OCLC FirstSearch and Cambridge Scientific Abstracts (CSA). When multiple databases are licensed from these same vendors, it is often possible to search *Philosopher's Index* and other indexes simultaneously. Each vendor applies its own search interface to the content of the index, but all afford most of the standard access points and search techniques, such as Boolean searching and use of truncated terms. Of course, search software is highly subject to change—as are database vendors. A vivid reminder of this comes if one consults the "Hints for Effective Searches" in the 1998 printed *Philosopher's Index Thesaurus,* rev. 2nd ed., which is geared to the now defunct Dialog Corporation version of the database. Incidentally, the actual thesaurus of subject descriptors in that publication can certainly be used to abet online searching, but the various vendor platforms provide handier and more up-to-date equivalents for identifying appropriate descriptors, such as the "Index" and "Suggest" functions of the Ovid interface or CSA's browsable indexes.

The database is reported to contain some 328,000 records as of 2005 and to add some 14,000 each year. Until recently, the electronic version of the *Philosopher's Index* notoriously omitted book reviews, which command a separate section in the printed index. Citations to book reviews began appearing in late 2004, however, and are now included back to 1994 (vol. 28 of the print version).

Readers are advised to consult the Philosopher's Information Center Web site, http://www.philinfo.org, for current information on the electronic *Philosopher's Index.*

49.   The Philosopher's Index: A Retrospective Index to U.S. Publications from 1940. Bowling Green, Ohio: Philosophy Documentation Center, Bowling Green State University, 1978. 3 vols.

This retrospective index includes articles published in American philosophy journals between 1940 and 1966, and original philosophy books (i.e., not including new editions, reprintings, etc.) published in the United States between 1940 and 1976. The difference between dates of coverage for journal literature and those for books is presumably due to the fact that books began to be included in the regular *Philosopher's Index* series only in 1980 (though this seems still to leave a small gap: some, though certainly not all, books published in 1976 and 1977 appear to have fallen through the "crack").

Arrangement is identical to that used in the current series, with volumes 1 and 2 containing the subject index and volume 3 the author index with abstracts. Many of the abstracts are reprinted from other sources, including the *Bibliographie de la philosophie, Philosophic Abstracts,* and journals such as the *Review of Metaphysics.*

50.   The Philosopher's Index: A Retrospective Index to Non-U.S. English Language Publications from 1940. Bowling Green, Ohio: Philosophy Documentation Center, Bowling Green State University, 1980. 3 vols.

This work is similar to entry 49 but covers books and journal literature published outside the United States. While international in scope and encompassing material published in countries which are not English-speaking, it does include only material written in English, differing in that respect from the current *Philosopher's Index.*

51.   Philosophiae Ianua Bibliographica. Compiled by Joachim Aul. Cuxhaven and Dartford: Traude Junghans, 1999–.

Its title ("Annual Bibliography of Philosophy") indicates that although this bibliography commenced by periodically issuing subject volumes covering successive parts of the alphabet—an apparently finite project—it was intended to be an ongoing endeavor. A loose-leaf format evidently was meant to accommodate annual supplements, though the first several volumes failed to explain this. It is not clear that this plan was ever implemented or even whether progress continues on the base set. The author of this guide personally examined three base volumes covering the letters A (1999), B (2000), and C/D (2000); additional volumes through P/Q (2004) and a separate one for Kant (2002) are attested by various library catalogs. Ongoing effort or future plans could not be confirmed. In any event, the project seems to have met a chilly reception. A reviewer on the *Reference Reviews Europe Online* Web site (October 27, 2001, no longer accessible) made the following assessment: "A statement in a brochure obtained separately from the publisher, in which the author describes himself as a 'collector, with a side interest in philosophy,' explains the lack of discrimination in the inclusion and organization of the articles. One would be best off utilizing existing retrospective and current printed and electronic bibliographies. There is certainly no need for this one." In that light, it's not surprising that only a few exemplars of early volumes are to be found in North American and British libraries.

52.   Philosophic Abstracts, 1939–54. Vols. 1–16. New York: Philosophical Library, 1939–1946 (vols. 1–6). New York: Russell F. Moore, 1947–1954 (vols. 7–16).

Evidently conceived more as a current awareness and reviewing publication than as a comprehensive bibliographic tool, *Philosophic Abstracts* typically covered 50 to 100 books in each of its quarterly issues. While selective, it did provide international coverage, including non-English- as well as English-language books, and employed a geographical arrangement by country of publication. Until 1950, it also carried lists of periodical literature, that is, journal articles; but these, too, were highly selective, and they did *not* include abstracts.

Many of the abstracts for books were quite lengthy and would more accurately be called reviews—especially those that contained critical and evaluative comment as well as factual information. No doubt this explains why, especially in its early years, so many of its abstracts, which were signed, could be contributed by distinguished figures such as George Boas, Rudolf Carnap, Paul O. Kristeller, Richard McKeon, Ernest Nagel, I. M. Bochenski, and Vernon J. Bourke.

For its first half decade, *Philosophic Abstracts* was edited by Dagobert Runes. Later editors were Ralph Winn and the publisher, Russell F. Moore. Moore also brought out a cumulated index under the title *Decennial Index to Philosophical Literature, 1939–1950* (n.d., 115p.).

53.   Philosophical Books, 1960–. Vol. 1–. Leicester, England: Leicester University Press, 1960–1978. Oxford: Basil Blackwell, 1979–. Quarterly.

Philosophical Books is a quarterly journal that "aims to provide prompt, scholarly reviews of new professional books and journals in philosophy and the history of philosophy" (from a statement printed at the back of each issue). Founded in 1960 by the editorial committee of the journal *Analysis,* it is highly selective. Emphasized predominantly, though not exclusively, are books reflecting the concerns of Anglo-American analytic philosophy. A typical issue contains 20 or so substantial review articles that normally are critical as well as descriptive. A regular discussion feature allows authors of selected titles an opportunity to respond to reviewers. Special issues may be devoted to a single theme.

A *Cumulative Index to Philosophical Books: Volumes 1–15 (1960–1974),* compiled by Julius F. Ariail, has been published separately (Statesboro, Ga.: Sweet Bay Press, 1980, 40p.).

54.   Philosophischer Literaturanzeiger: Ein Referateorgan für die Neuerscheinungen der Philosophie und ihrer gesamten Grenzgebiete, 1949–. Publisher varies, 1949–1989, vols. 1–42 (no. 2). Frankfurt am Main: Vittorio Klostermann, 1989–. Vol. 42 (no. 3)–. Quarterly.

This review journal is published in conjunction with the *Zeitschrift für philosophische Forschung.* Currently published quarterly (frequency has varied in the past), it carries reviews of 25 to 30 new books in each issue. Although the majority of these are German, or at least German translations, some significant non-German titles are also reviewed in most issues. The board of editors includes philosophers from several countries.

There exists a cumulative index for 1948–1977*, Gesamtregister der Jahrgänge 1–30 (1948–1977): Philosophischer Literaturanzeiger,* compiled by Georgi Schischkoff (Meisenheim/Glan: A. Hain, 1977, 90p.), but it is not widely available. Tables of contents for recent years were available (as of October 2005) on the publisher's Web site: http://www.klostermann.de/zeitsch/phli_hmp.htm.

55.   Philosophy in Review/Comptes rendus philosophiques, 1997–. Edmonton, Alta.: Academic Printing & Publishing, 1997–. Vol. 17–.

Formerly titled *Canadian Philosophical Reviews/Revue canadienne de comptes rendus en philosophie* (1981–1996, vols. 1–16), this bimonthly review journal publishes up to 200 reviews annually of books encompassing any area of philosophy. It is not restricted to Canadian books or authors. Reviews, which may be in English or French, are generally timely, within a year of publication.

56.   POIESIS: Philosophy Online Serials. Intelex and the Philosophy Documentation Center. http://www.nlx.com/posp/index.htm (accessed October 15, 2005).

POIESIS is in the first instance a full-text database of philosophy journals that contract with its two sponsoring organizations, Intelex and the Philosophy Documentation Center, to make their content available online to subscribing institutions only. Its search software, however, makes it an effective index to the journals included in the database—43 at this writing (October 2005), ranging from core comprehensive journals such as *The Journal of Philosophy* and *The Philosophical Quarterly* to highly specialized titles like the *Leibniz Review* or the *Journal of Consciousness Studies.* More than 20 others are slated to be added. Search options include table of contents browsing, author/title searches, and full-text searching by keyword or phrase. In general, searching, like full-text access, is restricted to subscribers, but visitors who register at the site are permitted to search tables of contents.

5
National and Regional Bibliographies and Indexes

National and regional bibliographies vary widely in their aims and scope. Some intend to record all or a representative selection of philosophical publications within a country or other geographically, politically, or linguistically defined region, either for a specified period or on a continuing basis. Such bibliographies are typically "general" in the sense that the publications they include may deal with any area of philosophy as their subject matter, including philosophies of other places and times. They may even incorporate publications by foreign authors, particularly translations. Others, drawing a narrower circle of inclusion, aim to provide bibliographic guidance to philosophical thought that is native to, or characteristic of, the subject country or region. Some of these include secondary studies by "outsiders," others do not. And there are yet other variations. This chapter is largely indifferent to such distinctions, apart from endeavoring to reflect them in the annotations for the works comprehended under its broad umbrella. National or regional bibliographies that pertain narrowly to a specific historical period or to some alternate chapter rubric in this guide are cross-referenced in those chapters. A few bibliographies that encompass chiefly secondary or "outsider" studies of philosophy in a particular country or region, particularly Western studies of non-Western philosophy, have their primary entries elsewhere but are cross-referenced here.

WESTERN EUROPE

AUSTRIA

57.   **International Bibliography of Austrian Philosophy/Internationale Bibliographie zur österreichischen Philosophie**, 1974/75–. Amsterdam: Rodopi, 1986–. (Studien zur österreichischen Philosophie, Supplement, vol. 1–).

This bibliographic series set out to provide comprehensive, if somewhat tardy, coverage of Austrian philosophy in the form both of works *by* and writings *about* Austrian philosophers. Certain limitation apply in the case of major figures whose work falls into Austrian and non-Austrian periods (e.g., Wittgenstein, Carnap) or is philosophically relevant only in part (e.g., Freud). Articles, essays in collections, books, and book reviews are all included. The chronologically defined volumes, offering two- to four-year overviews, have not appeared sequentially. The inaugural 1974/75 volume, issued in 1986, was followed by a volume for 1980/81, issued in 1988; a volume filling the gap, 1976/79, was not published until 1993. At this writing in October 2005, chronological coverage stretches without interruption from 1974 through 1994, with the latest volume published (2005) filling a previously existing gap for 1991/92.

FRANCE

58.   Bibliography of Philosophy. Sainte Ruffine, Moselle, France: Imprimerie Maisonneuve, n.d. 2 vols.

Hiding behind the nondescript title is a bibliography of French philosophical books from 1945 to 1965. It is divided into studies of the history of philosophy (volume 1, 102p.) and original and systematic works of philosophy (volume 2, 80p.). The former are arranged by major periods, from antiquity to the twentieth century; the latter, by individual philosophers, with works about an individual (e.g., Sartre) following those by him or her. Substantial descriptive and occasionally critical annotations, in English, are particularly valuable. A 10-page introduction by Paul Ricœur gives a concise overview of French philosophical currents during the period covered.

GERMANY AND GERMANIC COUNTRIES

59.   Bibliographie Philosophie, 1967–1987. Berlin: Akademie für Gesellschafts-wissenschaften beim Z.K. der S.E.D., Institut für Marxistisch-leninistische Philosophie, Zentralstelle für philosophische Information und Dokumentation, 1967–1987. Vols. 1–21.

See entry 78.

60.   Bibliographien zur Philosophie. Cologne: Gemini, 1980–1989. Hürth-Efferen: Gemini, 1992–.

See entry 26.

61.   Ersch, Johann Samuel, and Christian Anton Geissler. **Handbuch der philoso-phischen Literatur der Deutschen, von der Mitte des 18. Jahrhunderts bis zum Jahre 1850.** Düsseldorf: Stern-Verlag Janssen, 1965. 218p. (Instrumenta Philosophica. Series Indices librorum, 1).

Apart from the addition of an introduction by Lutz Geldsetzer and an updated index of author names with birth and death dates, this is an unaltered reprinting of the third edition of the *Bibliographisches Handbuch der philosophischen Literatur der Deutschen von der Mitte des achtzehnten Jahrhunderts bis auf die neuste Zeit* (Leipzig: Brockhaus, 1850). The bibliography is a classified listing of monographs encompassing both the history of philosophy and the various philosophical subdisciplines. It includes German editions of non-German authors. There are no annotations, but as a historical curiosity the 1800s purchase prices are preserved in the photomechanical reproduction. Besides the aforementioned name index there is an original subject index.

62.   Gumposch, Victor Philipp. **Die philosophische Literatur der Deutschen von 1400 bis um 1850.** Regensburg: G. Joseph Manz, 1851. Reprinted, with a foreword by Lutz Geldsetzer, Düsseldorf: Stern-Verlag Janssen, 1967. 640p. (Instrumental Philosophica; Series Indices Librorum, 2).

Gumposch used the format of the bibliographic essay to present a comprehensive, if not exhaustive, record of Germanic philosophical literature from late-Scholasticism to his own time, the period just after Hegel. Bibliographic references are imbedded in a text that surveys major and minor philosophical currents and often identifies briefly the intellectual and institutional affiliations of authors. Within three broad historical divisions (pre-Leibniz, Leibniz to Kant, and post-Kant), a fluid organizational scheme yields chapters and subchapters devoted variously to particular schools or movements, branches (e.g., political philosophy), geographical locations (often individual university towns), and types of literature (e.g., periodicals, acts of academies), or combinations of these categories. A fourth division offers brief characterizations of and general sources on each philosophical subdiscipline (logic, metaphysics, ethics, etc.). Geographical coverage is not confined to Germany, either modern or historical, but extends at least in selective fashion to Austria, Switzerland, the low countries, Scandinavia, and even Russia. A subject index lists names and locations as well as subject terms. The text is set in *fraktur.*

63.   Koehler & Volckmar. **Philosophie und Grenzgebiete, 1945–1964.** Stuttgart: Koehler & Volckmar, 1965. 434p. (Koehler & Volckmar Fachbibliographien).

A bibliography of books and periodicals in philosophy and bordering areas published in Germany or German-speaking countries, especially Switzerland, and some German-language works published elsewhere. Arrangement is by subject classification, with general works (including dictionaries, bibliographies, yearbooks, etc.) gathered in chapter 1 and periodicals in chapter 9.

64.   Marti, Hanspeter, with Karin Marti. **Philosophische Dissertationen deutscher Universitäten, 1660–1750: eine Auswahlbibliographie.** Munich: K. G. Saur, 1982.

An introduction by the compiler begins by noting the inadequacy of the modern concept of "dissertation" to convey the particular character of the texts represented in this selective bibliography, and places them in the context of the traditions and conventions of disputation that prevailed in German education during the period in question. This clarifies the otherwise puzzling fact that the nearly 10,000 dissertations in the main section, the *Titelnachweise,* are arranged hierarchically under *two* names: first, that of the *Präsens* or senior faculty member under whose direction (and at times coauthorship) the text was composed and who often presided over its public defense, then the *Respondent,* typically a junior scholar seeking an academic degree but sometimes representing other circumstances, including ones in which *Präsens* and *Respondent* are the same (e.g., inaugural disputations or dissertations). Because the primary arrangement is by *Präsens'* names, there is an index to *Respondents.* There are also indexes by place of origin (university towns) and by subject using almost exclusively Latin keywords.

65.   **Philosophy and History: A Review of German-Language Research Contributions on Philosophy, History, and Cultural Developments.** Vols. 1–24. Tübingen: Institute for Scientific Co-operation, 1968–1991 (German Studies, Section 1).

This semiannual publication, now discontinued, featured substantial reviews (typically a page or more), in English, of selected German books, plus a selective bibliography of new books and articles. Philosophy took up a third to half of each issue. The practice of listing works under English translations of their titles, followed by the original German title in brackets, should not be construed to mean that the works themselves are available in English translation.

66. Sass, Hans-Martin. **Inedita Philosophica: Ein Verzeichnis von Nachlässen deutschsprachinger Philosophen des 19. und 20. Jahrhunderts.** Düsseldorf: Philosophia, 1974. 86 numbered columns. 43p.

This catalog of unpublished papers of nineteenth- and twentieth-century German-speaking philosophers lists primarily manuscripts but also diaries, letters, personal papers, lecture notes, extracts and drafts. Papers of Hannah Arendt, Buber, Hegel, Herder, Jaspers, Mach, Nietzsche, and Schopenhauer are among those included. Gives locations, mainly German libraries and archives, but also some elsewhere, including the Library of Congress (e.g., for Arendt, Friedrich Kapp) and a few other U.S. locations.

GREECE

67. Voumvlinopoulos, Georges E. **Bibliographie critique de la philosophie grecque depuis la chute de Constantinople a nos jours, 1453–1953.** Athens: [Impr. de l'Institut Français d'Athènes], 1966. 236p.

Philosophers of "modern" Greece—spanning a 500-year period beginning with the fall of Constantinople in 1453—are arranged in chronological sequence. Perhaps five or six hundred in number, they are obscure for the most part. Their names are given in both Roman and modern Greek alphabets. Literature cited includes "works by" and "works about." Annotations, headings, and other nonbibliographic information are in French. A historical introduction and overview is provided on pages 5–22.

ITALY

68. **Bibliografia filosofica italiana,** 1949–. Publisher varies. 1951–.

This annual bibliography, sponsored by the Centro di Studi Filosofici di Gallarate (formerly Centro di Studi Filosofici Cristiani di Gallarate), continues a four-volume work covering 1900 through 1950 (entry 71). It differs in its arrangement, however, using a classification scheme that includes both historical periods and branches of philosophy. Initially published at Milan by C. Marzorati, the bibliography has been published since 1978 at Florence by Leo S. Olschki.

69. **Catalogo di manoscritti filosofici nelle biblioteche italiane.** 11 vols. Vols. 1–8: Florence: Leo S. Olschki, 1980–1996. Vols. 9–11: Florence: Sismel—Edizioni del Galluzo, 1999–2003 (Subsidia al Corpus philosophorum Medii Aevi, Unione Accademica Nazionale).

See entry 338.

70. Istituto di Studi Filosofici. **Bibliografia filosofica italiana dal 1850 al 1900.** Rome: ABETE, 1969. 644p.

Similar in coverage and basic arrangement to the previously issued bibliography for 1900–1950 (see entry 71).

71. Istituto di Studi Filosofici. **Bibliografia filosofica italiana dal 1900 al 1950.** Rome: Edizioni Delfino, 1950–56. 4 vols.

This comprehensive bibliography of Italian philosophical literature of the first half of the last century encompasses primary works by philosophers of the period, secondary studies, editions and reprints of older works, and translations of non-Italian authors. Journal articles are included as well as books. Arrangement is alphabetical by names of individuals, integrating both "works by" and "works about." Volume 4 (U–Z) also includes an extensive section of additions and corrections to volumes 1–3 (A–T), a section for anonymous and pseudonymous works, and an annotated bibliography of Italian journals in philosophy and related fields.

Italian org ✦

This work was compiled and published under the auspices of the Istituto di Studi Filosofici of the Centro Nazionale di Informazioni Bibliografiche, with collaboration from the Centro di Studi Filosofici Cristiani di Gallarate. See also entries 68 and 70 for coverage of earlier and later periods.

NETHERLANDS

72. Poortman, Johannes Jacobus, et. al. **Repertorium der nederlandse wijsbegeerte.** Amsterdam: Wereldbibliotheek, 1948. 403p. **Supplements 1–3,** Amsterdam: Wereldbibliotheek (suppl. 1 and 3), 1958, 1983; Amsterdam: Buijten en Schipperheijen (suppl. 2), 1968.

This Dutch bibliography and its supplements record two general categories of publication: (1) philosophical works printed in Dutch in the Netherlands or in the Flemish part of Belgium, regardless of the nationality of the author, and thus including translations from other languages; (2) works by Netherlanders in any language and wherever published. The first three volumes have subject and author listings (the latter restricted to books until Supplement 2), replaced in the fourth volume with a classed arrangement by periods and topics, augmented by personal name and subject indexes. The base volume covers the period from the Middle Ages to 1947, the supplements, respectively, 1947–1957, 1958–1967, and 1968–1982.

PORTUGAL

73. Ganho, Maria de Lourdes Sirgado and Mendo Castro Henriques. **Bibliografia filosófica Potuguesa, 1931–1987.** Lisbon: Editorial Verbo, 1988. 402p.

Lists Portuguese philosophical publications from the period indicated in its title, both books and articles, by author within four broad subject divisions. Items are not necessarily by Portuguese authors but include many translations/editions of non-Portuguese works. The bibliography was compiled and issued under the auspices of the Sociedade Científica da Universidade Católica Portuguesa. *Portuguese organization*

SPAIN / IBERIA

74. **Anuario bibliográfico de historia del pensamiento ibero e iberoamericano.** 1986–1990. Athens, Ga.: University of Georgia, Moore College, Department of Romance Languages, 1989–1993.

This annual bibliography, published for just five years, provided a comprehensive listing of books, articles, and periodicals published throughout the world on all aspects of Hispanic philosophy both on the Iberian peninsula and in Hispanic America, arranged by country of publication.

75. Díaz Díaz, Gonzalo. **Hombres y documentos de la filosofía española.** Madrid: Consejo Superior de Investigaciones Científicas, Instituto de Filosofía "Luis Vives," Departmento de Filosofía Española, 1980–. Vol. 1–.

See entry 293.

76. Díaz Díaz, Gonzalo, and Ceferino Santos Escudero. **Bibliografia filosofica Hispanica (1901–1970).** Madrid: Consejo Superior de Investigaciones Científicas, Instituto de Filosofía "Luis Vives," Departmento de Filosofía Española, 1982. 1371p.

This comprehensive listing of philosophical books published in Spain and Hispanic America during the first seven decades of the last century, together with selected articles from the same period, is arranged thematically by the major areas of philosophy—metaphysics, cosmology, philosophical systems (i.e., schools), philosophical psychology, ethics, history of philosophy, philosophical theology, and so forth—each with an abundance of subdivisions. An alphabetical subject index refers to these sections and subsections, not individual entries. There is an author index as well. Book and article entries are intermingled, and entries are not annotated.

77. Martínez Gómez, L. **Bibliografía filosófica española e hispanoamericana (1940–1958).** Barcelona: Juan Flors, 1961. 500p. (Libros "Pensamiento"; Serie: Difusion, no. 1).

This 10,166-item bibliography of Spanish and Hispanoamerican philosophy covers not only writings by and about Hispanic philosophers, but also Spanish translations of non-Hispanic authors and writings. It is based chiefly on bibliographies from the quarterly journal _Pensamiento._ The two basic divisions comprise historical materials (chronological arrangement) and systematic materials (with chapters on logic, metaphysics, ethics, etc.). There is an author index.

EASTERN EUROPE

EAST GERMANY

78. **Bibliographie Philosophie,** 1967–1987. Berlin: Akademie für Gesellschafts-wissenschaften beim Z.K. der S.E.D., Institut für Marxistisch-leninistische Philosophie, Zentralstelle für philosophische Information und Dokumentation, 1967–1987. Vols. 1–21.

This East German serial bibliography, now defunct, is sometimes cited with the words *"mit Autoren und Sach Register"* appended to its title; these did not appear on the title pages of later volumes, however. It emphasized books articles, dissertations, and other literature published in the former East Germany but also gave selective attention to Soviet, other East-European, and some West German publications. The orientation is overtly Marxist; non-Marxist writings considered important to Marxist thinkers are included, but are segregated from Marxist works within each section of the classified arrangement. Entries are not annotated, but frequently do include descriptors. Each also includes a location (holding library) code. Name and title indexes are provided.

POLAND

79. **Bibliografia filozofii polskiej.** Vols. 1–3, Warsaw: Panstwowe Wydawnictwo Naukowe, 1955–1971. Vol. 4, Warsaw: Wydawnictwo IFiS PAN, 1994.

The four volumes of this bibliography of Polish philosophical writings, which include writings about non-Polish philosophers, cover respectively the years 1750–1830, 1831–1864, 1865–1895, and 1896–1918. Their arrangement uses a single alphabetical sequence for both authors and individuals who are the subjects of "works about." All volumes are issued under the auspices of the Polska Akademia Nauk, the first three through its Komitet Filozoficzny, the fourth through the Instytut Filozofii i Socjologii.

Polish org

RUSSIA / SOVIET UNION

80. **Bibliographie der sowjetischen Philosophie / Bibliography of Soviet Philoso-phy.** Ed. J. M. Bochenski, et. al. Dordrecht, Netherlands: D. Reidel, 1959–1968. Vols. 1–7. (Sovietica: Veröffentlichen des Osteuropa-Instituts, Universität Freiburg/ Schweiz).

The seven volumes of this bibliography vary considerably in content. Volume 1 is an index to the major Soviet philosophical journal, *Voprosy filosofii,* for 1947–56. Volume 2 lists books from 1947–56 plus books and articles (from a variety of journals) for 1957–58. Volumes 3, 6, and 7 cover books and articles for, respectively, 1959–60, 1961–63, and 1964–65. Volumes 4 and 5 contain, respectively, a supplement and cumulative index for 1947–60. Subject indexes are in English.

Soviet journal

From 1967 through 1989, bibliographic coverage of Soviet philosophy was continued in the journal *Studies in Soviet Thought.*

THE AMERICAS

ARGENTINA

81. Lértora Mendoza, Celina Ana and Matilda Isabel García Losada. **Bibliografía filosófica argentina (1900–1975).** Buenos Aires: Fundación para la Educación, la Ciencia y la Cultura, 1983. 359p.

This unannotated bibliography of Argentine philosophy for the first three quarters of the twentieth century presents 5,182 publications, including monographs, articles, and collected works, arranged thematically in roughly the order of the philosophy division of the Universal Decimal Classification. Entries are numbered consecutively, but a second column of numbers is used, not altogether perspicuously, to distinguish types of publications and to cross-reference publications contained in larger works to the parent entry. Author and subject indexes are provided.

CANADA

82. Mathien, Thomas, Louise Girard, and Lori Morris. **Bibliographie de la philosophie au Canada: une guide à recherche / Bibliography of Philosophy in**

Canada: A Research Guide. Kingston, Ont.: Frye, 1989. 157p. (Frye Library of Canadian Philosophy, suppl. vol. 1).

The core of this work, part 3, lists and annotates 670 works by English-Canadian philosophers active before 1950, arranged by surname. Parts 1 and 2 provide, respectively, background information for philosophical research in Canada and a list of 440 bibliographies and secondary sources (historical studies, etc.). The introduction, provided in both English and French, contains a lengthy discussion of the criteria for inclusion. A projected companion volume for French-Canadian philosophers seems not to have appeared.

LATIN AMERICA

83.   **Anuario bibliográfico de historia del pensamiento ibero e iberoamericano.** 1986–1990. Athens, Ga.: University of Georgia, Moore College, Department of Romance Languages, 1989–1993.

See entry 74.

84.   Díaz Díaz, Gonzalo, and Ceferino Santos Escudero. **Bibliografia filosofica Hispanica (1901–1970).** Madrid: Consejo Superior de Investigaciones Científicas, Instituto de Filosofía "Luis Vives," Departmento de Filosofía Española, 1982. 1371p.

See entry 76.

85.   **Fuentes de la filosofía latinoamericana.** Washington, D.C.: Union Panamericana, 1967. 100p. (Union Panamericana. Bibliografías básicas, 4).

Some 800 *fuentes* (sources) on Latin American philosophy are listed in this bibliography, all of them secondary sources; primary sources are outside its scope. "Philosophy is interpreted broadly to include the history of ideas and social and political thought" (introduction). Chapters cover (1) general works, (2) works by country, (3) articles, also subdivided by country, (4) bibliographic sources, and (5) journals. Items listed are mainly in Spanish or Portuguese, but some are in English or other languages. Many entries include descriptive annotations, in Spanish.

86.   **Los "fundadores" en la filosofía de América Latina.** Washington, D.C.: Secretaría General, Organización de los Estados Americanos, 1970. 199p. (Union Panamericana. Bibliografías básicas, 7).

Complementing the earlier *Fuentes de la filosofía latinoamericana,* this bibliography covers 20 founders of Latin American philosophy. Born between 1839 to 1893 and active in some cases up to the mid-twentieth century, they constitute a diverse group, united only, the introduction suggests, by "an identity of motivations (the dedication to philosophy) and a community of objectives (the effort to diffuse philosophy and normalize its study)." The more eminent figures among them include Caso and Vasconcelos (Mexico), Deustua (Peru), Farias Brito (Brazil), Ingenieros and Korn (Argentina), Molina (Chile), Varona (Cuba), and Vaz Ferreira (Uruguay). Each thinker is treated with a brief chronology and a bibliography divided into "works by" and "works about." Most items are in Spanish or Portuguese. Annotations are few and brief.

87. Martínez Gómez, L. **Bibliografía filosófica española e hispanoamericana (1940–1958).** Barcelona: Juan Flors, 1961. 500p. (Libros "Pensamiento"; Serie: Difusion, no. 1).

See entry 77.

88. Redmond, Walter Bernard. **Bibliography of the Philosophy in the Iberian Colonies of America.** The Hague: Martinus Nijhoff, 1972. 174p. (International Archives of the History of Ideas, 51).

See entry 827.

MEXICO

89. **Bibliografía filosófica mexicana,** 1968–1996. Mexico City: Instituto de Investigaciones Filosóficas, Universidad Nacional Autónoma de México, 1970–98.

This annual bibliography of Mexican philosophy used a classed arrangement with a name index. Publication was suspended following the issue for 1996. Coverage of Mexican philosophy has subsequently been assumed by the online index *FILOS* (entry 90).

90. **FILOS: Base de datos sobre filosofía en México.** Mexico City: Instituto de Investigaciones Filosóficas, Universidad Nacional Autónoma de México. http://www.filosoficas.unam.mx/basefilos/index.html (accessed October 18, 2005).

This online bibliography and index of philosophical publications in Mexico is freely accessible on the Web at this writing. It has taken over the role formerly filled by the printed *Bibliografía filosófica mexicana* (entry 89). Retrospective coverage has been extended to 1950. *FILOS* aims to provide a comprehensive record of books, theses, journal articles, reviews, bibliographies, and reference works concerned principally with philosophy and issued in Mexico. The database comprised nearly 28,000 records by late 2005. Its search engine supports a wide variety of search options, including keyword or browse searches by author, title, series title, or subject as well as Boolean combinations, and allows truncated terms under most search options.

UNITED STATES

91. Sandeen, Ernest R., and Frederick Hale. **American Religion and Philosophy: A Guide to Information Sources.** Detroit: Gale, 1978. 377p. (American Studies Information Guide Series, vol. 5; Gale Information Guide Library).

This bibliography "appears in a series of guides to American Studies because religion and philosophy are treated with special attention to their relationship with the rest of American culture," and it combines religion with philosophy because "they grew up as Siamese twins until separated in the late nineteenth century" (preface). Religion, however, gets far more attention than philosophy; there is undeniably more to attend to. The bulk of philosophically oriented material is in chapter 19, "From Pragmatism to Contemporary Philosophy," material on earlier periods and figures (e.g., Edwards, nineteenth-century moral philosophy) being scattered though earlier chapters. General works are in chapter 1. Philosophy since about 1920 is scantily covered, on the rationale that it has become increasingly specialized and has ceased to be distinctively American. Despite its limited aim, this is a useful selective guide to books (and a few journal articles).

ASIA

CHINA

92. Chan, Wing-tsit. **Chinese Philosophy, 1949–1963: An Annotated Bibliography of Mainland China Publications**. Honolulu: East-West Center Press, 1967. 290p.

This bibliography of Chinese-language works is concerned with studies of traditional Chinese philosophy and modern developments thereof; it does not deal with Chinese Marxist philosophy. Books and articles are in separate sections, each identically arranged by periods, schools, and major philosophers, in roughly chronological order. References are given both in transliteration and in Chinese characters, the former being primary. English translations are provided for titles. Most entries include library locations in the United States, Hong Kong, or Tokyo.

93. Chan, Wing-tsit. **An Outline and Annotated Bibliography of Chinese Philosophy.** Rev. ed. New Haven: Yale Far Eastern Publications, 1969. 220p. (Sinological Series, no. 4).

See entry 227.

94. Fu, Charles Wei-hsun, and Wing-tsit Chan. **Guide to Chinese Philosophy.** Boston: G. K. Hall, 1978. 262p. (Asian Philosophies and Religions Resource Guides).

See entry 228.

INDIA

95. **A Bibliography of Indian Philosophy.** Madras: Published by the C. P. Ramaswani Aiyar Research Endowment Committee, 1963/68. 2 vols.

The two parts of this bibliography that have been issued list source-books in Sanskrit and, where available, translations in English, relating to: (part 1) the *Upanishads,* the *Bhagavad Gita,* the Nyāya, Vaiśeshika, Sāmkhya, Yoga, and Mīmāmsā systems, and the Vedānta systems comprising Advaita, Viśishtādvaita, and Dvaita; (part 2) Navya Naya, Jainism, Buddhism, Śaiva Siddhānta, the Vedas, the Dharma Sutras, Śākta Tantra, and works on Bhakti. Projected volumes for recent studies of Indian systems have not materialized, possibly because of the appearance of the bibliography volume of the *Encyclopedia of Indian Philosophies* (entry 97).

96. Centre of Advanced Study in Sanskrit, University of Poona. **CASS Bibliography Series. Class H.** V. N. Jha, gen. ed. 1993–.

See entry 225.

97. Potter, Karl H., et. al. **Encyclopedia of Indian Philosophies.** Vol. 1, **Bibliography.** 3rd rev. ed. Delhi: Motilal Banarsidass, 1995. 2 vols.

The first edition of this ambitious work, published in 1970 with the title *Bibliography of Indian Philosophies,* inaugurated the *Encyclopedia of Indian Philosophies* (see entry 239). Even as other volumes of the encyclopedia slowly made their appearance, the bibliography attained a second edition (Delhi: Motilal Banarsidas, 1983; Princeton: Princeton University Press, 1984, 1023p.) in which the number of authors and works cited was greatly expanded. Among the additions were references to summaries of works in English where such exist. On the other hand, citations of secondary literature written in non-Western languages were dropped. The third edition maintains a similar scope, but the addition of newer works entailed an expansion into two physical volumes, labeled "sections."

Part 1 (in section 1) lists Sanskrit and Tamil primary texts in chronological order; parts 2 and 3 (also in section 1) cover authors and texts of unknown date. All known editions and translations into European languages are cited. If no published versions are known, locations of manuscripts are indicated. Part 4 (in section 2) is devoted to secondary literature in European languages, arranged according to the various philosophic movements and systems. Indexes are by names, titles, and topics.

As of late 2005, an electronic version of this bibliography incorporating updates was available on the World Wide Web. See entry 98.

98. Potter, Karl H., et. al. **Encyclopedia of Indian Philosophies: Bibliography.** http://faculty.washington.edu/kpotter (accessed October 20, 2005).

This Web site provides the content of the third edition of the bibliography volume (vol. 1; see entry 97) of the *Encyclopedia of Indian Philosophies* (entry 239) augmented with continuous updating to reflect materials published or discovered since completion of the print version. It offers the option of viewing either with or without diacritics for romanized Sanskrit terms and names. Users are asked to accept restrictions on copying, printing, or distribution of the content.

99. Potter, Karl H., with Austin B. Creel and Edwin Gerow. **Guide to Indian Philosophy.** Boston: G. K. Hall, 1988. 159p. (Asian Philosophies and Religions Resource Guides).

See entry 235.

JAPAN

100. Holzman, Donald, with Motoyama Yukihiko, et. al. **Japanese Religion and Philosophy: A Guide to Japanese Reference and Research Materials.** Ann Arbor, Mich.: University of Michigan Press, 1959. Reprinted, Westport, Conn.: Greenwood Press, 1975. 102p.

This guide is limited to Japanese books (no periodical articles) published since the Meiji era (ca. 1868–). It lists books on all significant religions and philosophical schools, including Shinto, Buddhism, Confucianism, and Christianity (restricted in all cases to Japanese aspects). There is no separation of philosophical materials from religious until the Meiji and post-Meiji periods (entries 826–914), when a distinction between religion and philosophy emerged in Japanese thought under Western influence. Of the earlier schools, the most philosophical is Confucianism (entries 545–695).

AFRICA

101.   Ofori, Patrick E. **Black African Traditional Religions and Philosophy: A Select Bibliographic Survey of the Sources from the Earliest Times to 1974**. Nendeln, Liechtenstein: Kraus-Thomson, 1975. 421p.

See entry 263.

102.   Smet, A. J. **Bibliographie de la pensée Africaine: Répertoire et suppléments I–IV.** Kinshasa-Limete: Faculté de Theologie Catholique, 1972–1975. 285p.

See entry 264.

6

General Internet Resource Directories and Gateways

Most of the internet directories and gateways covered in this chapter are fully general in scope, providing guidance and links to Web sites of all types and across the entire spectrum of philosophical thought and activity. A few are restricted to sites that perform a particular function, for example sites that host online papers, but they are still "general" with respect to the philosophical subject areas and topics to which they give access.

103.   **APA Online.** American Philosophical Association. http://www.apa.udel.edu/apa/index.html (accessed October 20, 2005).

The primary function of this Web site is to provide information about the American Philosophical Association, particularly for its members. However, under the rubric "Web resources" it offers several pages of links that comprise a good selective guide to some of the best or most broadly useful online resources in philosophy. Categories include associations and societies, centers and institutes, bibliographies, directories, electronic texts, guides to philosophy. A separate area provides a directory of Web pages for U.S. college and university philosophy departments. See also entry 860.

104.   **EpistemeLinks.com: Philosophy Resources on the Internet.** Thomas Ryan Stone, comp. http://www.epistemelinks.com (accessed October 20, 2005).

This is arguably the most widely useful guide at present to philosophy-related Web resources. Among its several virtues is that it is often not content to simply list and link to significant sites in their totality, but will burrow in to a site to link to specific information on individual pages. For example, its online encyclopedia section does not simply offer a directory of titles, but provides a consolidated index to several key online encyclopedias both philosophical (e.g., the *Stanford Encyclopedia of Philosophy*) and general (e.g., *Wikipedia, Columbia Encyclopedia*), linking directly from a specific topic to the relevant articles in one or more encyclopedias. Similarly, its e-text section does not simply list sites where one can find a directory or collection of e-texts, but permits searching by author across many such sites to locate online books or other texts.

Labeled "main sections" on the *EpistemeLinks* site are the twin categories "Philosophers" and "Topics." The former offers pages on individual philosopher, some 450 at this writing, searchable alphabetically, by historical periods, or by subject categories such as ethics or Eastern philosophy. The "Topics" section classifies Web sites by historical periods, by philosophical subdisciplines (applied ethics, metaphysics, political philosophy, etc.), by schools and traditions (e.g., analytic philosophy, postmodernism), and by aspects of the practice of philosophy. Other substantial categories on this site include a journal directory, which accommodates searching by title, topic, or publisher for either online journals or print-journal home pages or both; a comprehensive directory of college/ university philosophy department pages; a directory of organizations searchable by name or topic; a calendar of events searchable by date, topic, and even location; and a directory of classroom teaching resources, with both general and subject-specific resources.

As a commercial site, this has unobtrusive advertisements sprinkled throughout, and there is a list of "affiliate links" including, for example, Amazon, eBay, Alibris, and HotJobs. The Webmaster seems committed to keeping this aspect low-key.

105.   Erratic Impact's Philosophy Research Base. Danne Polk, comp. http://www. erraticimpact.com (accessed October 20, 2005).

As a directory to philosophy Web sites, this ranks (in my judgment) somewhere behind *EpistemeLinks* (entry 104) but in any case stands with it as one of the two most comprehensive directory sites that are actively maintained and updated at this writing (October 2005). Interestingly, these two sites frequently cross-reference each other. The Erratic Impact site stakes a claim to serving a broader function by "integrating text resources with the best online resources," implying that its role as a "research base" is more general than just a directory of online sources. For comments on this aspect, see entry 3 in chapter 2.

The principal organizational categories of the site are three: history of philosophy (i.e., major periods and some general categories such as American philosophy and women in philosophy), philosophical topics (mainly branches of philosophy and schools of thought, but also a few general topics such as philosophy for children and teaching philosophy, and some major "issues" such as freedom and consciousness), and philosophers by name. Other significant rubrics include directories of academic philosophy departments worldwide, of philosopher home pages (not limited to important philosophers), of organizations, and of journals, as well as a calendar of events. Links sometimes go to specific subsections of larger sites.

Philosophy Research Base has particular strengths in cross-disciplinary areas associated with radical or left-of-center social-political views, for example, critical theory, queer theory, ecofeminism, environmental philosophy, but it is certainly not confined to these. As a commercial site, its advertising is somewhat more obtrusive than that of *EpistemeLinks* and its linkages with affiliated booksellers and other shopping sites are more prominent and pervasive.

106.   Online Information about Journals in Philosophy and Related Disciplines. Peter Milne, comp. http://homepages.cd.ac.uk/pmilne/links_html/journals.html (accessed October 21, 2005).

Housed at the University of Edinburgh, this site "aims to be complete" in listing and linking both e-journal sites and the home pages of print journals in philosophy and closely related areas. It provides listings by subject as well as alphabetical lists.

107.   Online Papers in Philosophy. Brian Weatherson, comp. http://opp.weatherson. net (accessed October 21, 2005).

A specialized but extremely valuable directory to Web sites, nearly a thousand at this writing, that host online papers in all areas of philosophy. A majority of the sites are personal Web pages of philosophers, including a number of prominent figures, mainly though not exclusively Anglo-American. Others are, for example, university department sites that house some faculty papers, or subject-oriented Web sites that either house online papers in their area of interest or provide links to them. Around 30 are philosophy journals that are available online; their content, however, is typically restricted to subscribers, save for some sample articles or issues. Surprisingly, Weatherson's directory does not track papers published in open-access e-journals.

Facility for basic word/phrase searching is incorporated in this site. A complementary site that formerly served a similar function, *The International Directory of Online Philosophy Papers* (http://philosophy.hku.hk/paper, accessed October 21, 2005), now describes itself as a search engine for the papers tracked by Weatherson's site. However, for reasons unclear, identical searches on the two sites rarely yield precisely identical results.

108.   Philosophische Bücherei: Kommentierte Internet-Ressourcen zur Philosophie.
Claus Osausky, ed. Philosophie-Institut der Universität Wien. http://buecherei.philo.at/index.htm (accessed October 21, 2005).

A very good German-language comprehensive internet directory, based in Austria, that also incorporates bibliographies of philosophical books that for the most part are not available online. German-language sites are emphasized and identified with a "D," but numerous English-language and other sites are listed and linked as well. Principal categories are history of philosophy (subdivided by periods and major schools), philosophers (listed A to Z), philosophical subdisciplines, and philosophy periodicals. Minor categories include, for example, internet philosophy projects, publisher sites, online text collections, and philosopher portrait sources. The bibliographies *(Literaturliste)* are largely restricted to German-language books, including translations from other languages, with the notable exception of reference works.

109.   Philosophy in Cyberspace. Dey Alexander, comp. http://www.personal.monash.edu.au/~dey/phil/index.htm (accessed October 21, 2005).

At this writing in October 2005, this veteran among comprehensive directories to philosophy-related online resources is no longer being updated. It remains available, however, at its longtime home on the Web site of Australia's Monash University. Dey Alexander, who launched *Philosophy in Cyberspace* in 1993 as a text-based resource distributed via Gopher and FTP and presided over its subsequent evolution, confirmed the site's currently frozen status in late 2004. He would not confirm any plans for its reactivation, though at the time a notice on the Monash Web site held out that prospect.

Philosophy in Cyberspace still provides many useful links, not always duplicated by other comprehensive philosophy directories (e.g., entries 104 and 105), but clearly it will need to be used in conjunction with those others as a rule. Its usefulness, already much diminished, will inevitably decline rapidly if updating is not resumed in the near future. The existing site's overall organizing scheme employs five major categories: (1) branches of philosophy; (2) text-related sites (online bibliographies, encyclopedias, e-journals, print-journal home pages, etc); (3) organizations, including academic philosophy departments; (4) "forums" (newsgroups and mailing lists); (5) miscellaneous resources.

Another pioneer in the field of comprehensive philosophical internet gateways, the *Guide to Philosophy on the Internet* compiled and maintained for many years (as Web sites go) by Peter Suber (http://www.earlham.edu/~peters/philinks.htm, accessed October 21, 2005) has also ceased being updated as of February 2003. It remains available, though frozen, in late 2005, and retains some residual value as a complement to currently maintained directories (e.g., entries 104 and 105); but this is bound to decline rapidly. It employs a standard set of categories and is comparatively uncluttered.

110.　　Philosophy in Cyberspace: A Guide to Philosophy-Related Resources on the Internet. 2nd ed. Dey Alexander, ed. Bowling Green, Ohio: Philosophy Documentation Center, Bowling Green State University, 1998. 404 pp.

This print directory corresponding to an earlier stage of the *Philosophy in Cyberspace* Web site long maintained by Alexander (entry 109) is now so dated as to be virtually obsolete. The publisher's original intention to issue a new edition annually was evidently abandoned after the second edition—understandably, given the pace of change on the Web and its wide availability, the hypertext linking advantages of the Web version, and the vanishing need to cover non-Web online resources for individuals with computers but no Web access.

111.　　PHILTAR: Philosophy, Theology, and Religion. Lancaster, U.K.: Division of Religion and Philosophy, St. Martin's College. http://philtar.ucsm.ac.uk (accessed October 21, 2005).

A very uneven site, even allowing for its somewhat circumscribed interest in philosophy alongside religion and theology. Its chief selling points are its useful links in the areas of Chinese, Indian, and Islamic philosophy, including many individual thinkers. Other categories singled out for special attention are, somewhat surprisingly, philosophy of mathematics and Russian philosophy.

112.　　Sito Web Italiano per la Filofia (SWIF). www.swif.uniba.it/lei/index.html (accessed October 22, 2005).

In 2004 this well-regarded Italian Web site bowed out of its role as a comprehensive Web portal for philosophy to focus on an expanding role as a content provider with an online journal, e-book survey of philosophy, and other full-text resources. It still serves something of its former function in several limited areas: philosophy of mind, medieval philosophy, history of science, and philosophy and schools (precollege philosophy). It also maintains a guide to Web sites for individual philosophers (some accompanied by biographical-intellectual sketches) and classic texts; and it hosts the online dictionary *FOLDOP* (entry 126). Some sections of *SWIF,* such as that on philosophy of mind, are entirely in English; a few others are to some degree bilingual. Discontinued portal pages produced from 1995 to 2004 are archived on the site as downloadable PDF files.

113.　　www.PhilSearch.de: Philosophische Suchmaschine. Administered by Uwe Wiedemann. http://www.philsearch.de/ (accessed November 8, 2005).

As its subtitle suggests, this Web site offers virtually no content of its own—only a handful of links to other sites, including several likewise administered by Wiedemann— but serves as a Google-style search engine for German philosophy-related Web content. "German" here encompasses Austrian and Swiss sites that carry the country identifiers ".at" and ".ch" in their URL's, as well as ".de" sites based in Germany. Most are German-language sites, predictably, but some are in, or include content in, other languages, most often English. The search engine gives access to a wide variety of Web-based material, including online papers and bibliographies, dictionary entries, digital texts, philosophical humor, and information about philosophy departments, institutes, and associations. It does not just search home pages but frequently drills down to lower-level pages. Topical content accessible via this useful tool is not limited to Germanic philosophy but spans the entire philosophical spectrum.

7
General Encyclopedias, Dictionaries, and Handbooks

For purposes of this chapter, an encyclopedia, dictionary, or handbook is considered "general" if it treats terms and concepts that are generically philosophical or drawn from all or most of philosophy's commonly recognized branches. Many works listed here have a particular perspective—Western, Anglo-American, Marxist, Thomistic, and so forth—and some restrict their historical coverage of philosophers and philosophical schools to those embraced by their perspective or congenial to it.

ENGLISH-LANGUAGE

This section includes English translations of foreign-language works.

114.   Adler, Mortimer. **Adler's Philosophical Dictionary.** New York: Scribner, 1995. 223p. New York: Simon & Schuster, 1996. 223p. Paperbound ed.: New York: Touchstone, 1996. 223p.

Throughout a career that included associations with the University of Chicago, the *Encyclopedia Britannica,* and the *Great Books of the Western World* collection (cf. entries 278 and 279), Adler strove to reach a general public concerned about philosophical issues, not just professional philosophers. Continuing that aspiration, this dictionary aims not to explicate philosophical jargon but "to give words of common, everyday speech . . . the precision they should have when they are used for philosophical purposes" (p. 11). This characterization fits comfortably the majority of the 125 entries—such as absolute and relative, anarchy, angels, duty, ends and means, idea, leisure, matter, punishment—which are common in everyday discourse and other nonphilosophical contexts. A very few entries—for example, analytic and synthetic judgments, nominalism—arguably constitute exceptions. Articles tend to be suffused with Adler's personal convictions and reflections, and even autobiographical elements; good examples are those on being, democracy, liberal arts, progress, and theology. Very much a personal statement in the spirit of Voltaire's *Philosophical Dictionary* (entry 159), though more strictly philosophical, this dictionary cites only Adler's other books and is even described by him as "a summation of my philosophical views" (p. 7). However interesting or meritorious on that account, it would be a poor choice to fill the role of a basic philosophical dictionary, even for a general audience.

115.   Angeles, Peter A. **HarperCollins Dictionary of Philosophy.** 2nd ed. New York: HarperCollins, 1992. 343p.

Among the handful of compact single-volume dictionaries of philosophy in English, Angeles's is unusual in sticking rather closely to the narrower meaning of "dictionary"—concentrating, that is, on the lexical function and eschewing any tendency to become encyclopedic. Short definitions predominate, formulated as much as possible in single sentences. (Several such definitions, often numbered, may be needed to indicate variant meanings, competing explanations or views on a topic, or major aspects of the idea, school, theory, etc., being defined.) Etymologies are often furnished as well. But there are few systematic treatments of any topics, and no bibliographic references. The second edition, unlike the first (titled simply *Dictionary of Philosophy;* Barnes & Noble, 1981), does have biographical entries—for about 100 philosophers—and there is also an index of philosophers mentioned in other entries. Certain terms and expressions peculiar to specific thinkers are identified and explained as such: "bad faith (Sartre)," "bundle theory of the mind (Hume)," "slave morality (Nietzsche)." Further, some terms are given multiple entries to reflect the distinctive conceptions of different thinkers, for instance, "knowledge (Aristotle)," "knowledge (Descartes)," "knowledge (Hume)," and so forth. As the latter strategy shows, a strictly lexical approach is not always either possible or desirable, but Angeles succeeds in staying about as close as one can or should.

This dictionary is aimed at the nonspecialist, with emphasis on "terms most commonly covered in beginning philosophy courses" (preface). That does not preclude usefulness to others, but advanced students will find many definitions quite elementary and sometimes simplistic or superficial. Only terms in Western philosophy are covered, but there is no special emphasis on either Anglo-American or Continental philosophy.

116.   Audi, Robert, ed. **Cambridge Dictionary of Philosophy.** 2nd ed. Cambridge: Cambridge University Press, 1999. 1001p.

This excellent dictionary, whose first edition appeared just a few months after Honderich's *Oxford Companion to Philosophy* (entry 131), contends with the latter work for the designation "best all-round single-volume English-language encyclopedic dictionary of philosophy." In the original comparison, the *Oxford Companion* came out slightly ahead in my estimation. But with its second edition the *Cambridge Dictionary* has pulled more nearly even, at least, though each continues to have its particular merits. The *Cambridge* may well be a bit more accessible to beginners than the *Oxford Companion,* though this is difficult to assess and definitely does not apply to every entry-by-entry comparison. It ranges across all areas of philosophy and claims more than 4,400 entries and cross-references, having more of the latter than any comparable work. The *Oxford Companion* can boast a somewhat larger number of unique entries, while the *Cambridge Dictionary* tends to be a bit more expansive. *Cambridge* draws on the expertise of over 440 highly-qualified contributors, some of whom also contributed to the *Oxford Companion* (generally not the same entries). The majority are American scholars, comparing with a fairly even split between British and American contributors for the *Oxford Companion.* However, nearly half of the 60 new contributors for the second edition are from outside North America. Coverage of Continental philosophy is roughly comparable—the *Cambridge Dictionary* is somewhat better with the second edition— as both works follow the lead of Blackburn's *Oxford Dictionary of Philosophy* (entry 118) in giving more than perfunctory attention to this domain while remaining clearly and strongly representative of the Anglo-American tradition. When it comes to non-Western philosophy, Audi's coverage is more detailed, including more entries than does the *Oxford Companion* on narrower terms and concepts (e.g., Atman, Carvaka, ch'eng, yin and yang) as well as specific thinkers and texts (e.g., Buddhagosa, Fung Yu-lan, Shankara, *Vedas*) alongside the survey articles on Chinese philosophy, Hinduism, Jainism, Japanese philosophy, and so forth, and such major highlights as the *Bagahvad Gita,* Confucius, or the *Upanishads.* Audi's original policy of excluding living philosophers—on the respectable rationale that adequate portraits cannot be done while they are still producing philosophical work—has been relaxed somewhat with this edition, but only to admit thinkers in their mid-sixties or older. Some compensation for this restrictive policy is provided by an index of several hundred selected names that do not have their own entries but are mentioned in other articles. Finally, the *Cambridge Dictionary* does not have bibliographies or bibliographic references.

117. Baldwin, James Mark. **Dictionary of Philosophy and Psychology.** New York: Macmillan, 1901–05. Reprinted, Gloucester, Mass.: Peter Smith, 1960. 3 vols. in 4.

In addition to the editions cited here, there have been several reprintings of this long-standard work by Macmillan (e.g., in 1910, 1918, 1928), sometimes labeled "new edition" but merely containing minor corrections; several previous reprintings by Peter Smith (the earliest: New York, 1940); and a more recent reprinting by Gordon Press (1977). Volume 3 of this work, which has two parts (i.e., two physical volumes) is a major bibliography compiled by Benjamin Rand and is often cited separately (see entry 19).

As its title announces, this encyclopedic dictionary covers psychology as well as philosophy. Baldwin himself was a psychologist, and psychological topics constitute a sizeable share of the work's content. One can see this in the first few pages, with entries for "aberration," "abnormal psychology," "aboulia," and "absent-mindedness." There is also selective attention to concepts, terms, and individuals in the fields of anthropology, biology, economics, education, philology, physiology, and physical science, primarily as they relate to philosophy and psychology. Articles are generally short, and many are devoted to definitions or explanations of fairly narrow concepts and to biographical data on minor figures.

A strong recommendation for Baldwin's work at the time of its original publication, and an important factor in its continuing historical significance, was the collaboration of a number of illustrious figures as contributors or editorial advisors. Among the best-known: Bernard Bosanquet, John Dewey, William James, G.E. Moore, Charles Sanders Peirce, Josiah Royce, and Henry Sidgwick. Articles, even very short ones, are signed. Some, such as those by Peirce and Dewey, have been duly recorded in standard bibliographies on their respective authors.

It is conventional to ascribe any enduring value for Baldwin's work exclusively to its historical interest; for other purposes, it has presumably been superseded by more current works. Perhaps, though, this fails to do justice to a great deal of material (biographical entries being only the most obvious example) that is as valid now as it was in 1901, some of it not readily found elsewhere, or not in the convenient combination represented here. It is true, of course, that its usefulness in this regard is contingent on the user's caution and some ability to judge what has or has not been vitiated by time.

118. Blackburn, Simon. **Oxford Dictionary of Philosophy.** Oxford and New York: Oxford University Press, 1994. 408p.

When first published, Blackburn's dictionary, when judged in terms of overall usefulness, readily outdistanced its nearest competitors among single-volume philosophical dictionaries already in the field, those of Flew (entry 124) and Lacey (entry 138). It was in turn soon eclipsed, however—judged by the same criterion—by its younger but bigger Oxford sibling, Honderich's *Oxford Companion to Philosophy* (entry 131), and by Audi's *Cambridge Dictionary of Philosophy* (entry 116). While roughly on a par with Flew and Lacey in quality and authoritativeness—though with considerable variation in this regard among specific corresponding articles—Blackburn offered around 75 percent more total entries than Flew and more than three times as many as Lacey. His dictionary encompasses non-Western as well as Western, Continental as well as Anglo-American philosophical traditions. And while the Anglo-American strain is dealt with in more detail, as might be expected from a work with "Oxford" in its title, Blackburn's treatment of the other traditions is substantial, judicious, and helpful. His coverage of recently prominent strains of Continental thought—represented, for example, by entries on such figures as Althusser, Derrida, Kristeva, Lacan, and Saussure, and on concepts such as deconstruction, Post-Structuralism, *différance,* and *langue/parole,* as well as some attention under more general entries, for example, the reference to Michel Foucault's views in the article on power—was previously unmatched by any similar English-language dictionary. Likewise noteworthy is Blackburn's inclusion of many more women philosophers than included heretofore in other general dictionaries—from Hypathia (fourth century B.C.) through Queen Kristina Wasa of Sweden and Anne Finch Conway (both seventeenth century) and Mary Wollstonecraft (eighteenth century) to contemporary feminists Luce Irigaray, Hélène Cixous, and Julia Kristeva. This breadth of coverage has since been matched generally, if not entry-for-entry, by Honderich and Audi, and to a lesser extent by Mautner (entry 141).

Apart from mention of primary sources within articles, Blackburn provides no bibliographical references.

119.   Brugger, Walter and Kenneth Baker. **Philosophical Dictionary.** Spokane, Wash.: Gonzaga University Press, 1972. 460p.

This is in part a translation, in part an adaptation, conceived and edited by Baker, of the 13th edition of Brugger's *Philosophisches Wörterbuch* (Freiburg im Breisgau, 1967; cf. entry 170 for 17th ed.). The bibliographies of the German work have been omitted in this American edition, along with an outline of the history of philosophy and a number of articles "not suitable for an American readership" (preface). On the other hand, new articles "dealing with contemporary Anglo-American concerns," written by American contributors, have been added. These include, for example, articles on Behaviorism, Lonerganism, and Process Philosophy. Baker has also added an introduction titled "The Future of Christian Philosophy," in which the work's already transparent Catholic and Neo-Scholastic viewpoint is made even more explicit.

Entries are provided in this dictionary for concepts only (which *do* include schools and movements, such as Platonism and Neo-Platonism, Thomism, and Existential Philosophy), not for individuals. It eschews an "atomizing" approach which "devotes a separate article to every expression," opting for medium-length articles on relatively broad topics. Partly for this reason, and partly because of a greater selectivity engendered by its editors' conception of what is most vital in past and present philosophy, it features fewer entries than most other English-language dictionaries of recent vintage. Even so, it offers some 400 articles on topics from Absolute to yoga.

120.   Bunge, Mario. **Philosophical Dictionary.** Enlarged ed. Amherst, N.Y.: Prometheus Books, 2003. 315p.

This idiosyncratic work, titled *Dictionary of Philosophy* in its original edition (Prometheus, 1999), arguably should not be categorized among "general" philosophical dictionaries. But no alternate category fits better. Described by its author as "limited to modern Western philosophy" (foreword), it turns out to be concerned mainly with concepts, problems, principles, and theories—there are no biographical entries—prominent in recent and contemporary philosophy, though many have long-reaching historical antecedents. Yet it does not attempt any balanced representation either of Western philosophy since its "modern" period (in the usual meaning) or its more recent developments. Rather, Bunge has selected terms he considers favored by "usage, usefulness, and enduring value rather than trendiness" (foreword), which in his (highly personal) judgment eliminates, for example, abduction, anomalous monism, logical atomism, and strict implication—though these are terms students of twentieth-century philosophy may readily encounter and want some help understanding. But Bunge seems less interested in assisting general understanding than advancing his own convictions. The latter he often does with considerable aplomb and an entertaining lack of solemnity. Nowhere, probably, is this more evident than in his characterization of Existentialism as "a hodge-podge of enigmatic utterances," "a pseudophilosophy, and one of the greatest swindles of any kind and of all times." Take this for what it's worth—the opinions of an accomplished and respected philosopher—but don't take this work as a candidate for a broadly useful, balanced dictionary of philosophy, even "modern" Western philosophy.

121.   Bunnin, Nicholas and E. P. Tsui-James, eds. **The Blackwell Companion to Philosophy.** 2nd ed. Oxford: Blackwell, 2003. 951p.

"This Companion complements the *Blackwell Companions to Philosophy* series by presenting a new overview of philosophy prepared by thirty-five leading British and American philosophers" (preface to first edition). In the second edition the number of contributors has swelled to 51, the number of essays (some coauthored) to 44, counting 2 reflective introductions on contemporary philosophy by John Searle and Bernard Williams. The first edition's acknowledged Anglo-American emphasis, particularly in the chapters on branches of philosophy in Part 1, is still there, but has been reduced proportionately by the addition, in Part 2 on the history of philosophy, of new chapters on Husserl and Heidegger and on Sartre, Foucault, and Derrida. Non-Western philosophy is not covered. More a survey text—potentially even a textbook, as discussion questions at the end of most chapters would suggest—than a conventional reference work, this volume can nonetheless serve several reference functions with its compact yet authoritative discussions of many of the field's major topics, substantial bibliographies, and 18-page glossary of key terms.

122.   Bunnin, Nicholas and Jiyuan Yu. **The Blackwell Dictionary of Western Philosophy.** Malden, Mass.: Blackwell, 2004. 766p.

Bunnin and Yu in their preface describe this dictionary as "a revised and augmented version" of a work they prepared for Chinese students of Western philosophy, *Dictionary of Western Philosophy: English-Chinese—Xi fang zhe xue Ying Han dui zhao ci dian* (Beijing: Ren min chu ban she, 2001). Its origin in this cross-cultural effort, however, is not readily apparent. It features a fairly standard mix of topical and biographical entries ranging widely over Western philosophy, its history and branches, though with an avowed emphasis on "terms and individuals at the center of current philosophical discussion" (p. vii). The number of entries is comparable to that of the *Oxford Companion to Philosophy* (entry 131) but articles are somewhat shorter on average. Few—mainly those on major philosophers—exceed half a page in length. Articles on difficult topics sometimes are too brief to be helpful to readers not already initiated (those on "idea (Hegel)" and "modality *de dicto*" are cases in point), but on the whole this dictionary achieves a reasonable balance between clarity and conciseness. All topical entries, but not the biographical ones, conclude with an illustrative quote (set of by a shaded background) that often illuminates or reinforces the explanation provided but at times seems merely decorative. Apart from mentions of primary works in the biographical articles, there are no bibliographical references within or accompanying the articles. A 22-page bibliography at the end of the volume is of limited value for lack of either topical or chronological subdivisions in its straight listing, by author, of nearly a thousand books.

Though a useful supplement to other recent dictionaries, Bunnin and Yu's work does not achieve the stature of the front-running *Oxford Companion* and *Cambridge Dictionary of Philosophy* (entry 116).

123.   Concise Routledge Encyclopedia of Philosophy. London: Routledge, 2000. 1,030p.

Describing itself as "a condensed version of the ten-volume *Routledge Encyclopedia of Philosophy*" (introduction; see entry 150), this single-volume offspring has nearly the same number of entries (around 2,000) as found in its parent. Its articles consist, in the vast majority of cases, of the article-summaries that are standard in the larger work, where they precede the full articles. A small class of exceptions is formed by entries representing the major subdisciplines of philosophy (ethics, metaphysics, etc.) and major time periods and regions (ancient philosophy, Indian and Tibetan philosophy, etc.), whose articles are reproduced in full. Suggestions for further reading at the end of each article are usually reduced to an impoverished one or two items, though these do have the benefit of annotation.

While the *Concise REP* inherits the authoritative character bestowed on its parent by some 1,200 expert contributors, it suffers from the rather arbitrary conditions imposed by its derivative nature. For instance, articles on giants such as Aristotle or Kant are similar in brevity to those on relatively obscure philosophers. Consequently, this should not be the first choice for a single-volume philosophical dictionary, though it can usefully supplement such front-runners as the *Oxford Companion to Philosophy* (entry 131) and the *Cambridge Dictionary of Philosophy* (entry 116). Recognizing the *Concise REP*'s shortcomings, Routledge undertook to remedy them with a substantially different *REP* condensation bearing a confusingly similar title, the *Shorter Routledge Encyclopedia of Philosophy,* issued in 2005 (entry 154).

124.   Dictionary of Philosophy. 3rd ed. Antony Flew and Stephen Priest, eds. London: Pan, 2002. 433p.

This concise, easy-to-use dictionary provides explanations of terms, including common abbreviations and shorthand names for arguments and theories, as well as brief articles on key individuals, movements, and ideas, and on branches of philosophy. Short entries predominate and few articles exceed half a page in length. No bibliographies are provided. While some articles are more technical or presuppose more background than others, the work can generally serve both students and professionals. Emphasis is on Anglo-American philosophy, but some attention is given both to Continental and to non-Western philosophy. Coverage of Continental philosophy in particular has been expanded from that in the second edition (New York: St. Martin's, 1984), with new entries on, for example, Derrida, Kristeva, postmodernism, and post-structuralism.

The first and second editions of this work were strongly identified with Flew, whose name, a well-known one in British philosophy, appeared alone on the cover. The extent of his actual responsibility for it, however, was never entirely clear. Front matter in those editions identified him as "consulting editor" and listed 32 other contributors. Updating and expansion for this third edition appears to have been Priest's responsibility entirely.

125. **Encyclopedia of Philosophy.** Paul Edwards, ed. New York: Macmillan and Free Press; London: Collier Macmillan, 1967. 8 vols. Reprinted, 1972. 8 vols. in 4. **Supplement.** Ed. Donald M. Borchert. New York: Macmillan, 1996. 775p.

The aim of this monumental reference work was succinctly stated in Edwards's introduction: "to cover the whole of philosophy as well as many of the points of contact between philosophy and other disciplines." Accordingly, it "treats Eastern and Western philosophy; it deals with ancient, medieval, and modern philosophy; and it discusses the theories of mathematicians, physicists, biologists, sociologists, psychologists, moral reformers, and religious thinkers where these have had an impact on philosophy." The realization of this ambitious undertaking involved the efforts of an international editorial board of 153 distinguished scholars, and an equally international cast of more than 500 contributors.

Notwithstanding its comprehensiveness and its aim of universality, the *Encyclopedia of Philosophy (EP)* has some degree of bias toward Anglo-American philosophy as practiced in the third quarter of the twentieth century, particularly its concerns with logic, language, and analysis. This manifests itself most readily in the choice of topics and the allocation of space. Users are advised to read the introduction, which acknowledges the bias but also describes measures taken to counteract it, for example, the use as much as possible of authors with some sympathy for their topics.

The *EP* is organized on the supposition that most users benefit more "from a smaller number of long and integrated articles than from a multitude of shorter entries." Few if any of its 1,500 articles occupy less than half a page, and some, as the editor suggests, "are in effect small books." (The article "Logic, History of" occupies 58 pages; the twin articles on "Ethics, History of" and "Ethics, Problems of" together take up 53 pages).

Among the *EP*'s more unusual offerings are articles on philosophy in specific countries; a glossary of logical terms; and excellent though now dated survey articles on the history and state of philosophical bibliographies, dictionaries and encyclopedias, and journals.

Useful to both the specialist and the nonspecialist (though not uniformly for each), the *EP* achieved, on the whole, a remarkable combination of informativeness, incisiveness, balance, and readability. These qualities were abetted by editorial policies that encouraged authors to deal freely with controversial material, to take stands if they wished, to break new ground if they could, and, not least, to feel no compulsion to be "serious and solemn at all costs."

The one-volume 1996 *Supplement* to the *EP* by Borchert contains 357 articles reflecting developments since the *EP*'s publication in 1967, divided into four broad types: overview articles of developments in 13 major areas of philosophy (e.g., applied ethics, Continental philosophy), entries on topics newly emerged or not previously treated (e.g., African philosophy, feminist philosophy, fuzzy logic), biographies of newly prominent philosophers (e.g., Derrida, Rawls), and updates to many original articles. While the

Supplement extended the usefulness of the parent set, the *EP*'s standing as the leading philosophical encyclopedia in English was soon taken over by the entirely new *Routledge Encyclopedia of Philosophy* (entry 150). Nonetheless, the *EP* retains a great deal of value for historical purposes and as a source of supplementary information or alternative perspectives to those provided in the *Routledge Encyclopedia*. Libraries and individuals who own the former should keep it even if they have acquired the latter, at minimum until a projected second edition of the *EP,* edited by Borchert and scheduled for release in December 2005, is available. Advance publicity indicates that this will incorporate "the core scholarship of the original set and its . . . 1996 *Supplement* while adding hundreds of new articles" (http://www.gale.com, October 6, 2005).

Borchert has also published *Philosophy and Ethics: Selections from the Encyclopedia of Philosophy and Supplement* (New York: Macmillan Library Reference USA, 1999, 1158p.)

126.   The Free On-Line Dictionary of Philosophy (FOLDOP). Version 3.0. Gian Paolo Terravecchia, chief editor. Sito Web Italiana per la Filosofia (SWIF). http://www.swif.it/foldop (accessed October 21, 2005).

This substantial online dictionary is edited and made available under the aegis of the Italian philosophy Web site *SWIF* (entry 112), but is entirely in English. As of October 2005 it boasts 2,418 entries, ranging widely over the philosophical landscape and including some 339 biographical entries. Explanations are usually brief but in some cases, particularly biographical articles, they run well over the equivalent of a full printed page. Many but not all include bibliographic references and suggested readings. Cross-references, duly hot-linked, are common.

A large share of the entries in *FOLDOP* derive from other online philosophy dictionaries such as *A Dictionary of Philosophical Terms and Names* (entry 136) and are acknowledged as such. *FOLDOP* is particularly rich in terms from cognitive science and logic, where it borrows heavily from its sibling and model, the *Free Online Dictionary of Computing (FOLDOC).* The considerable variation in the substantiality, clarity, and authority of articles in *FOLDOP* is attributable in part to differences among the various sources from which it draws.

The entire dictionary can be viewed as a PDF document and, by its own suggestion, printed from this format (more than 600 pages!) for off-line consultation.

127.   Frolov, Ivan Timofeevich, ed. Dictionary of Philosophy. Trans. from the Russian; ed. Murad Saifulin and Richard P. Dixon. Moscow: Progress Publishers; New York: International Publishing Co., 1985. 464p.

A translation of the fourth edition of a standard Soviet work, *Filosofskii slovar',* this encyclopedic dictionary is universal in scope, covering both Western and (much more spottily) Eastern philosophy; but it wears its Marxist character like the red insignia that adorned Soviet-era military uniforms. Thus, an article on "Criterion of Truth," striking a typically Marxist note, declares dogmatically that "Social practice is the Criterion of Truth." The article on agnosticism announces that it was Lenin who "laid bare the epistemological roots of Agnosticism." And the article on Utilitarianism begins: "a bourgeois ethical theory. . . ." There are also numerous articles on specifically Marxist topics, for example, "Criticism and Self-Criticism," "Internationalism," "Marxism-Leninism," "State of the Whole People," and biographical entries for Soviet philosophical figures.

An earlier version of this dictionary (Moscow: Progress Publishers, 1967) was based on the second edition of *Filosofskii slovar'*, edited by Mark M. Rozental' and Pavel F. IUdin (their names appear on the title page, and in many citations, transliterated as "M. Rosenthal" and "P. Yudin"). *Filosofskii slovar'* is the successor to an earlier work by Rozental' and IUdin, *Kratkii filosofskii slovar'*, an English version of which, adapted and edited by Howard Selsam, was published in 1949. The various editions and printings, since 1939, of these successive dictionaries provide an interesting reflection of the ups and downs of Soviet politics before the fall of communism. Whereas early editions cast Stalin in the role of a major philosophical authority, neither the work cited here nor its immediate predecessor has even an article on him. The editor of the present work, Ivan T. Frolov, was a key figure in officially sanctioned Soviet philosophy.

128.　　Goring, Rosemary, ed.; Frank Whaling, consulting ed. **Larousse Dictionary of Beliefs and Religions.** Edinburgh: Larousse, 1994. 605p.

Originally published as *Chambers Dictionary of Beliefs and Religions* (Edinburgh: W. R. Chambers, 1992, 587 pp.). Religion overshadows philosophy in this dictionary, but it does have significant philosophical content. Particularly useful is its coverage of topics in non-Western thought where religion and philosophy often overlap. Appropriate for students and general readers, it features some illustrations, mostly relating to religious subjects. A list of entries by broad subject categories, at the back of the volume, does not include philosophy as a category, but many philosophical topics are found under "secular alternatives to religion." The 15 contributors are all associated with British institutions.

129.　　Grooten, J. and G. Jo Steenbergen. **New Encyclopedia of Philosophy.** Translated from the Dutch, edited, and rev. by Edmond van den Bossche. New York: Philosophical Library, 1972. 468p.

This one-volume encyclopedic dictionary is a translation, with some adaptation, of a Dutch work, *Filosofisch Lexicon,* originally published in 1958. Over two dozen contributors are listed on its title page. The work can be recommended chiefly for its Continental perspective and emphasis, particularly with regard to somewhat older Continental currents, in contrast to the Anglo-American emphasis of most English-language dictionaries. Illustrative of this are substantial entries (half a column or more) on such Continental figures as Rudolf Stammler, Désiré-Joseph Mercier, and Alphonse Gratry, who typically have no entries or very brief ones elsewhere. (A startling omission, on the other hand, is Maurice Merleau-Ponty.)

For general purposes, this work can usefully supplement but certainly not substitute for more recent and more standard single-volume dictionaries or encyclopedias such as that by Audi (entry 116) or Honderich's *Oxford Companion* (entry 131). Some important terms are absent (e.g., Emotivism, cosmological argument) and a number of its articles are either too obscure or barely informative (cf. those on ethics, goods, ontology, and Nicholas of Cusa). Translation and editorial matters, also, are less than expertly handled. The cross-referencing system, which employs asterisks to signal terms that have their own entries, occasionally fails, and there are instances of cross-references to nonexistent entries (dropped, one conjectures, from the English edition).

130.　　Gutmann, James, et. al*.,* eds. **Philosophy A to Z.** Based on the work of Alwin Diemer, Ivo Frenzel, and others. Trans. by Salvatore Attanasio. New York: Grosset & Dunlap, 1963. 343p. (Universal Reference Library).

The material in this volume is in large part a translation, with some revision and amplification, of the *Philosophie* volume (by Diemer, Frenzel, and others) in a popular German series, the *Fischer Lexikon* (Frankfurt-Main: Fischer Bücherei, K.G., 1958). Entirely new articles were added on Idealism (by Abraham Edel), Christian philosophy (Arthur Holmes), Jewish philosophy (Alexander Altmann), Islamic philosophy (Richard Walzer), and Pragmatism (H. Standish Thayer). Though its articles are in alphabetical sequence, this is more like an introductory overview than a typical dictionary or encyclopedia and features a relatively small number of articles on broad topics—chapters, more or less, on the main areas and branches of philosophy, Eastern included. A brief, very selective bibliography is provided at the end.

131.   Honderich, Ted, ed. **The Oxford Companion to Philosophy.** 2nd ed. Oxford: Oxford University Press, 2005. 1056p.

This entry in the distinguished Oxford Companion series, now in its second edition, can make fair claim to being the premier single-volume encyclopedic dictionary of philosophy in English. Stiff competition for that claim is offered by the second edition of Audi's *Cambridge Dictionary of Philosophy* (entry 116), the *Oxford Companion*'s virtual contemporary in their respective first editions, both published in 1995. Honderich's was and remains in my judgment—no doubt disputable—the most broadly useful dictionary on balance, with Audi's running a very close second. Naturally, other dictionaries—notably those by Mautner (entries 141 and 142), Blackburn (entry 118), Flew (entry 124) and Lacey (entry 138)—may offer advantages in particular situations by virtue of greater brevity, simpler explanations for beginners, or the particularities of individual entries. Suffice it to say, however, that this *Companion* is a superb reference source. To begin, no similar work since Urmson's (entry 157) has elicited the involvement of quite so many eminent figures in contemporary philosophy, including Isaiah Berlin, Sissela Bok, Ronald Dworkin, Paul Feyerabend, Alasdair MacIntyre, W. V. Quine, Anthony Quinton, Nicholas Rescher, John Searle, and Peter Singer, to name just 10 of many prominent names among the nearly 300 contributors. It is true that in their totality these contributors represent an overwhelmingly Anglo-American orientation, which can also be gleaned from the relatively generous representation of entries on living English-speaking philosophers and, on closer readings, from the tone or substance of some of the articles on non–Anglo-American topics. Nonetheless, the *Companion* ranges at some level over all of the world's major philosophical systems and traditions, Eastern and Western, historical and contemporary. It includes, for example, a three-column survey article on Continental philosophy, and entries on such Continental figures, schools, and concepts as Derrida, *différance,* Frankfurt School, Habermas, hermeneutic circle, Irigaray, Lyotard, and Post-Structuralism, along with the more established Existentialism and Phenomenology. As for Eastern thought, the combined index and list of entries at the back (excellent for cross-referencing) reveals a combined total of 64 entries relating to Chinese, Indian, Japanese, and Islamic philosophies. Among these, and new to this edition, is an entry for Islamic philosophy today. There are also, of course, all the usual entries for major branches, figures, concepts, terms, and controversies of Western philosophy, and a few unusual (sometimes entertaining) ones as well. Among the latter are entries for "brain in a vat," "deaths of philosophers," and "nothing so absurd" (from a remark of Cicero's). Entries in this edition total to 2,230, expanded from 1,932 in the first edition. The number of entries for contemporary philosophers, however, was held steady at 150 by deleting some in favor of others—for example, R. Brandt is out, R. Brandom in.

Other noteworthy *Companion* features include brief bibliographies accompanying most entries; portraits of major philosophers; a chronological table; 14 "maps" (diagrams) of philosophical domains, positions, or theories (e.g., philosophy of mind, rationalism); and a table of logical symbols.

132.   Hutchinson Dictionary of Ideas. Oxford: Helicon, 1994; Santa Barbara, Calif.: ABC-CLIO, 1994. 583p.

The more than 4,000 entries in this dictionary range over many disciplines, including religious studies, psychology, mathematics, computing science, political theory, education, and women's studies as well as philosophy. Many of those outside philosophy proper, however, have significant connections to philosophical thought. The work is aimed not at specialists but the general reader. The entries are brief (average length about 50 words, according to the introduction) and concentrate on providing basic definitions and the most important facts on historically significant ideas, theories, and concepts, the people most responsible for or closely associated with them, and their manifestations in movements ("-ologies and -isms") or, less frequently, social and cultural institutions and practices. Non-Western thought gets some attention, but considerably less than Western. Special features include: 21 full-page "feature articles" on major issues or controversies, for example, abortion, animal rights, "mind-body dualism and the riddle of human consciousness," Postmodernism, progress; 27 "useful listings of information" as varied as the books of the Bible, computing chronology, great economists, the Islamic calendar, main language groups, and the seven virtues; 350 selected quotes appended to relevant entries; and separate indexes of topical entries and biographical entries categorized by broad subject areas.

133.   Iannone, A. Pablo. Dictionary of World Philosophy. London: Routledge, 2001. 554p.

An ambitiously comprehensive work that proposes to address "fragmentation" in philosophy, and in contemporary intellectual, social, and cultural life generally, by treating all philosophical traditions as "on a par with each other" (preface). As such it covers both Western and non-Western philosophies, and among the latter not only the long-recognized traditions of Asia, particularly India and China, but also those of the pre-Hispanic Americas, sub-Saharan Africa, and Pacific cultures such as the Māori, provided they have been subjected to scholarly study. Also touted as part of the volume's antifragmentation strategy is its solo authorship, which, it's suggested, secures a degree of cohesiveness and consistency that tends to elude dictionaries with numerous contributors. Author Iannone did, however, supplement his obviously broad knowledge by drawing on the advice of an international group of 14 consulting editors. The result is indeed exceptionally broad coverage of the world's varied philosophical traditions. But it is marred, regrettably, by occasional superficiality, shortcomings in clarity or balance, and injudicious suggestions for "further reading." And at times the volume simply fails to deliver on its promise. A nine-page article on sociopolitical philosophy, for example, mentions only Western thinkers; those on epistemology (4 pp.) and philosophy of mind (7 pp.) take only very brief and perfunctory notice of non-Western, mainly Indian, views.

Entries in this dictionary represent terms and concepts only; there are no biographical articles. Names of philosophers are prominent, however, among the work's many "see" references, which partly substitute for an index. All in all, this is a useful complement to other philosophical dictionaries, but not a first choice.

134.   The Internet Encyclopedia of Philosophy. James Fieser and Bradley Dowden, general editors. http://www.iep.utm.edu (accessed October 22, 2005).

The *IEP* is the product of "a non-profit organization run by the editors" that "receives no funding, and operates through the volunteer work of the editors, authors, and technical advisors." Around two dozen subject area editors are listed, affiliated mainly with universities in the United States but also a few abroad. Articles are divided at this point between signed "original contributions by specialized philosophers around the internet" and "proto-articles," adapted by the editors mainly from public domain sources and intended to be replaced eventually, identified by the initials IEP. While the contributors are indeed specialists on their topics, they are less likely to be top experts than is the case for the *Stanford Encyclopedia of Philosophy* (entry 156). An ongoing project, the *IEP* by now has entries for most of the principal topics and names in Western philosophy, and a modest but growing number in non-Western philosophy; but it still has some significant gaps and maintains an extensive list of desired articles by areas as well as a list of "100 most desired articles." Existing articles (even some of the "proto-articles") are typically quite substantial, running from several pages to several dozen pages if printed. They usually include substantial bibliographies. Avenues of access to entries include alphabetical lists, a keyword list with cross-references to related entries, and a timeline of Western philosophy with links to pertinent entries.

135.   The Ism Book: A Field Guide to the Nomenclature of Philosophy. Peter Saint-Andre. http://www.saint-andre.com/ismbook/ism3.html (accessed October, 2005).

A relatively informal guide to a restricted range of philosophical concepts and terminology, namely, traditions, movements, schools, doctrines, principles, ideas, theories, systems, and approaches designated, quite literally, by terms ending in "-ism," from absolutism to voluntarism. Occasionally the effort to observe this restriction becomes a bit strained as certain significant concepts are forced into the prescribed form though they're rarely if ever encountered that way: immortalism, intrinsicism, Socraticism, for instance. Nonetheless, this is a useful if lightweight guide to many of philosophy's central ideas and movements, suitable particularly for inquisitive laypersons and beginning students. If author Saint-Andre's personal views are at times in evidence, it's usually evident that's just what they are.

136.   Kemmerling, Garth. A Dictionary of Philosophical Terms and Names. http://www.philosophypages.com/dy (accessed October 22, 2005).

Kemmerling describes his online dictionary as "a concise guide to technical terms and personal names often encountered in the study of philosophy. . .meant to be clear, accurate, and fair, a reliable source of information on Western philosophy" (home page). Entries are generally brief, though those on major philosophers (Kant is a good case in point) can run to some length and often have subtopics that are reflected in the alphabetical lists of entries. Most entries include cross-references and recommended readings, and many also have links to other online sites, including notably the *Stanford Encyclopedia of Philosophy* (entry 156), for more expansive treatment. There is some advertising and biographical references often include links to Amazon.com. The dictionary is part of a larger site maintained by Kemmerling, titled *Philosophy Pages,* that also includes a timeline and a brief history of Western philosophy, an introduction to logic, and a guide to the study of philosophy.

137. Klauder, Francis J. **The Wonder of Philosophy: A Review of Philosophers and Philosophic Thought**. New York: Philosophical Library, 1973. 75p.

Thomistic in its perspective and purpose, this brief guide offers thumbnail sketches of selected branches of philosophy and of the main periods and figures of Western philosophy, plus a three-page summary of Oriental philosophy. Even within the legitimate limits set by its perspective and purpose, it is a work of highly idiosyncratic selectivity as well as recurrent superficiality. In addition, it is marked by oddities of organization; the section on the modern period, for instance, consists entirely of brief notes on six philosophers who inexplicably are not included in the alphabetical dictionary of Western philosophers which forms part 3 of the book. Altogether, a work of very limited utility.

138. Lacey, A. R. **Dictionary of Philosophy.** 3rd ed. London: Routledge, 1996. 386p.

When originally published in 1976, Lacey's dictionary was, for general purposes, the first serious competitor to D. D. Runes's long-lived but oft-maligned dictionary of 1942 (entry 153). It was soon joined, however, by roughly similar works by Flew (entry 124) and Reese (entry 148) and a somewhat less similar work by Angeles (entry 115). More recent and considerably more expansive dictionaries such as those by Blackburn (entry 118), Honderich (entry 131), Audi (entry 116), and Mautner (entry 141) leave even this third edition of Lacey's work in the dust when it comes to overall usefulness, yet it remains a worthwhile complement to any or all of them. Lacey's special strength is his bibliographies, sometimes surprisingly extensive for a work of this type. He continues to maintain a decidedly Anglo-American orientation, and emphasizes particularly epistemological and logical topics; but he does cover all periods, branches, and major movements and figures within Western philosophy. There is no coverage of non-Western philosophies. While the second edition (1990) improved on the first with 25 new entries, the third edition adds another 66. It also claims considerable rewriting of older entries, in part to reflect "the change in philosophical outlook that has occurred since the first edition, written still under the influence of the 'linguistic philosophy' era" (preface).

139. MacGregor, Geddes. **Dictionary of Religion and Philosophy.** New York: Paragon House, 1989. 696p. Also published as **The Everyman Dictionary of Religion and Philosophy.** n.l.: Dent, 1990. 696p.

This dictionary joins that by Reese (entry 148) as a second modern English-language dictionary encompassing both religion and philosophy. In MacGregor's case, in contrast to Reese's, coverage of philosophy is largely subservient to a primary focus on religious studies, being premised on the conviction that "any serious study of religion entails some understanding of the philosophical implicates of religious belief and practice" (preface). Despite the subordinate role, philosophy receives substantial and solid treatment that compares respectably with several of the strictly philosophical dictionaries, such as Blackburn's (entry 118) or Flew's (entry 124), except in the areas of logic and the more technical aspects of contemporary philosophy. Like most recent English-language dictionaries, MacGregor provides some coverage of Eastern philosophy as well as Western, enriched in this case by his interest in the intertwined religious aspects of Eastern thought. Entries include philosophers as well as the usual terms and concepts. Some articles (a minority) include bibliographic references. There is also a selective, classified bibliography at the back of the volume, but this slights philosophy, except philosophy of religion.

In his coverage of religion, MacGregor's acknowledged emphasis is on the Judeo-Christian tradition, but other world religions receive significant attention as well.

140. Martin, Robert M. **The Philosopher's Dictionary.** 3rd ed. Peterborough, Ontario: Broadview Press, 2002. 329p.

Dedicated "To Fran, who loves five-dollar words," this dictionary is obviously aimed at the philosophical amateur and beginning student. Definitions aim to be "brief and basic" (prefatory matter), but are sometimes so brief as to be uninformative. There are notes on usage, spelling, and pronunciation of common philosophical terms, and entries on most of the better-known philosophers.

141. Mautner, Thomas. **A Dictionary of Philosophy.** Oxford: Basil Blackwell, 1996. 480p.

The stage of English-language philosophical dictionaries had already begun to seem crowded when Mautner's work joined the cast in 1996. And despite excellent credentials and solid performance, it found itself upstaged on arrival by two other recent entrants, Honderich's *Oxford Companion to Philosophy* (entry 131) and Audi's *Cambridge Dictionary of Philosophy* (entry 116). But if it's not quite in the same league with those two, its particular virtues should not be overlooked. First among these is the sheer number of entries it provides (an estimated 2,300, excluding cross-references), many supplying definitions and brief explanations for technical terms or highly specialized concepts not found in its competitors. These include both specifically philosophical terms (e.g., acosmism, actualism, deduction theorem) or ones that have special meanings in philosophy (abstract, adventitious, definite descriptions) and expressions that, though not distinctively philosophical, occur fairly frequently in philosophical discourse yet may be unfamiliar to many readers: *ad hoc, ceteris paribus, de jure, non sequitur,* and so forth. Another aspect of Mautner's more truly dictionary-like approach is extensive help with pronunciation for foreign or otherwise less familiar terms and names. This is not to suggest that Mautner steers away from all encyclopedic tendencies. He provides substantial and very respectable articles on all of the usual and expected philosophical topics and figures, at lengths generally comparable to Blackburn's *Oxford Dictionary of Philosophy* (entry 118) but less than the *Oxford Companion* or the *Cambridge Dictionary.* Coverage of Continental philosophy is comparable to that provided by all three of the aforementioned works. In contrast to these, on the other hand, Mautner limits his scope to Western philosophy (encompassing, however, some coverage of Islamic thought), submitting that to attempt to cover the rich and varied Eastern traditions "would be a vain presumption" (preface). A dominantly Anglo-American orientation comes in this case with a somewhat Australian cast: Mautner himself is Australian, as are a good share of 80 or so contributors, including such notables as John Passmore, J.J.C. Smart, and Peter Singer. All three of these, incidentally, are among a handful of leading contemporary thinkers who provide self-portraits—a unique feature of this dictionary. Others in that group include, for example, Isaiah Berlin, W.V.O. Quine, Richard Rorty, and John Searle.

A slightly revised paperback version of this dictionary appeared as *The Penguin Dictionary of Philosophy* (entry 142).

142. Mautner, Thomas. **The Penguin Dictionary of Philosophy.** London: Penguin Books, 1997. 641p.

A very modestly revised edition, issued in paperback, of Mautner's 1996 *Dictionary of Philosophy* published by Blackwell (entry 141). A small number of new entries were added, some existing entries rewritten, and some errors corrected. A reprinting in 2000 claims additional minor revisions to a bibliography of "titles in print" at the back of the volume.

143.   McLeish, Kenneth, ed. **Key Ideas in Human Thought.** New York: Facts on File, 1993. 789p.

The 2,500 or so alphabetically arranged "ideas" in this work range widely over intellectual history: economics, the arts, anthropology, science, religion and religious studies, and so forth, as well as philosophy, which is a significant component but not dominant. Many ideas outside philosophy proper, however, have been important for philosophical thought: axiomatization, bourgeoisie, character, Gandhianism, Gödel's incompleteness theorem, representative government, syntax, vitalism—to pick just a few examples from diverse realms of thought. There is some representation of non-Western thought as well as Western. Numerous cross-references, signaled by bold type, serve what the introduction identifies as the work's special mission, namely, "to show the networks of thought" by identifying vital connections (pp. ix–x), though they are hardly as exceptional as this seems to intimate. Many articles end with one or several suggested sources for further reading.

144.   **Meta-Encyclopedia of Philosophy.** Andrew Chrucky, comp. http://www.ditext. com/encyc/frame.html (accessed October 22, 2005).

Provides a single access point to entries in six online encyclopedias and dictionaries of philosophy, all freely available online: the *Internet Encyclopedia of Philosophy* (entry 134), *Stanford Encyclopedia of Philosophy* (entry 156), *Dictionary of the Philosophy of Mind* (entry 634), *Ism Book* (entry 135), *Dictionary of Philosophical Terms and Names* (entry 136), and an online version of D. Runes's 1942 *Dictionary of Philosophy* (cf. entry 153). Also covered is a very old (1913) edition of the *Catholic Encyclopedia* (cf. entry 826). Though I assess the long-term future of this site as a bit more tenuous than is the case for most Web resources selected for inclusion in this guide, it is a very useful tool and, if maintained, should become increasingly valuable.

145.   **New Catholic Encyclopedia.** 2nd ed. Detroit: Thomson/Gale; Washington, D.C.: Catholic University of America, 2003–2004. 15 vols.

See entry 826. Though this is not, obviously, a "general encyclopedia of philosophy," its treatment of philosophy (not limited to Catholic thought) is so wide-ranging that it merits at least a cross-reference in this chapter.

146.   Parkinson, G. H. R., ed. **Encyclopedia of Philosophy.** London: Routledge, 1988. U.S. edition titled **The Handbook of Western Philosophy.** New York: Macmillan, 1989. 935p.

The systematic rather than alphabetical arrangement of this work makes the title of the U.S. edition perhaps a better choice than that of the original British edition. It offers 37 chapters on major philosophical topics or problem areas, each by a different expert, intended to constitute collectively a survey of "contemporary philosophical thought, an account of the current state of philosophical thinking" (p. ix). The editor is careful to qualify this, however, by acknowledging that the Anglo-Saxon tradition (as he prefers to call it) is represented here almost exclusively, sidelining the Continental tradition except where it has had some impact on the Anglo-Saxon, as well as virtually all non-Western philosophy. Historical background is not neglected, but there is "no discussion of issues that belong wholly to the past" (p. ix). Chapters (apart from the introductory "What is Philosophy?") are grouped under six headings: meaning and truth; theory of knowledge; metaphysics; philosophy of mind; moral philosophy; society, art and religion. Examples of individual chapter titles include: "Theories of Meaning: from 'Reference' to 'Use' "; "Truth"; "Science as Conjecture and Refutation"; "Space, Time and Motion"; "Behaviourism"; "Teleological Theories of Morality"; "Defenders of the State"; "The Philosophy of Punishment." Back matter includes a glossary of philosophical terms, a chronology of the history of philosophy from 1600 to 1960, and name and subject indexes.

147. Pence, Gregory E. **A Dictionary of Common Philosophical Terms.** New York: McGraw-Hill, 2000. 57p.

A slight work intended to help students with terms they are likely to encounter in undergraduate philosophy courses. Provides brief definitions, often just a sentence or two, of around 500 common terms.

148. Reese, William L. **Dictionary of Philosophy and Religion: Eastern and Western Thought.** New and enlarged ed. Atlantic Highlands, N.J.: Humanities Press, 1996. 856p.

The combination of philosophy and religion in this single-volume dictionary, whose first edition was published in 1980, offers an advantage wherever there is frequent need for reference to both, or from one area to the other. This advantage might be even greater but for two shortcomings. First, Reese's work is much more adequate as a dictionary of philosophy than as a dictionary of religion. In the former category it compares favorably with, for example, dictionaries by Flew and Lacey (entries 124 and 138), though it's no match for the frontrunning *Oxford Companion to Philosophy* (entry 131) and *Cambridge Dictionary of Philosophy* (entry 116). As a dictionary of religion it does not compare very well with any standard work in that field, for at least three reasons: (1) its understandable focus on the intellectual aspects of religion, rather than, say, its institutional and social aspects; (2) the relative paucity of entries for second-rank religious thinkers, as compared with the generous inclusion of second-rank philosophers; and (3) its relatively perfunctory treatment of religious perspectives on such topics as ethics, immortality, and the soul. This last touches directly on the work's second significant shortcoming: it often fails to make the connections between philosophical and religious thought just where the connections are most important. Still, such coverage of religion as it offers may be taken as a bonus. Another virtue is its fairly extensive coverage of Eastern philosophy, considerably expanded in the second edition. Topical articles in this dictionary tend to emphasize nutshell summaries of the views of individual thinkers, at some expense, frequently, to systematic development. Cross-references are extensive and often refer to a specific numbered point within an article.

While combined treatment of philosophy and religion is also afforded in recent dictionaries by MacGregor (entry 139) and Goring (entry 128), Reese's is unique in giving primacy to philosophy rather than to religion.

149. Rohmann, Chris. **A World of Ideas: A Dictionary of Important Theories, Concepts, Beliefs, and Thinkers**. New York: Ballantine Books, 1999. 477p.

The Library of Congress classifies this work under Philosophy, though as its author explains, the "fields of knowledge gathered here include philosophy, psychology, history, economics, sociology, religion, science, and the arts" (p. x). Still, not only are philosophy and philosophers prominent, but the ideas selected from other fields tend to be those fraught with philosophical implications or evocative of philosophical questions (examples include the Gaia hypothesis, hermeneutics, quantum theory, surrealism, utopianism), consonant with Rohmann's professed predilection for "the theoretical and propositional—debatable, questionable, or unprovable notions" (p. x). There are 444 alphabetically arranged entries, including 111 profiles of major thinkers. Emphasis is on Western thought as well as contemporary thought, though not to the exclusion of either non-Western thought or older ideas and thinkers. Aimed at general readers rather than an academic audience, articles tend to be clear if brief and basic.

150. **Routledge Encyclopedia of Philosophy.** Edward Craig, ed. London: Routledge, 1998. 10 vols.

The *Routledge Encyclopedia of Philosophy* (hereafter *REP*) succeeds the 1967 *Encyclopedia of Philosophy* edited by Paul Edwards as the preeminent multi-volume philosophical encyclopedia in English. It replicates many of the virtues of the Edwards work, including comprehensiveness, readability and good organization, and often improves on them. It broke new ground by being released simultaneously in print format and a CD-ROM electronic format, joined subsequently by an online (Web) version (see entries 151 and 152).

The *REP* covers all areas of philosophy and all of the world's philosophical traditions, drawing on the expertise of over 1,300 contributors from 36 countries. Its team of 33 subject editors headed by Craig (Cambridge University) includes, in addition to an editor for each major branch of the field and for each major period of Western philosophy, specialist editors for African, East Asian, Indian and Tibetan, Islamic, Jewish, Latin American, and Russian philosophy. The publisher's advertising states that a quarter of the entries cover philosophy "from outside the traditional western canon." Perhaps surprisingly, the Continental tradition within Western philosophy is specifically represented on the editorial team only (though importantly) by a subject editor for Postmodern French philosophy. However, other sectors of the Continental tradition (e.g., Existentialism, Frankfurt School, Hermeneutics, Phenomenology, Structuralism, etc.) and their leading thinkers are amply covered by numerous entries and substantial articles. All of that said, the work remains understandably, and appropriately, somewhat weighted toward the concerns and perspectives of Anglo-American philosophy.

Articles in the *REP* fall into three categories: "signpost" articles for each of the major subdisciplines of philosophy (metaphysics, ethics, etc.) as well as several major philosophical traditions (e.g., Analytical philosophy, East Asian philosophy) and major historical periods (e.g., ancient philosophy, medieval philosophy) that provide overviews and direct the reader toward the many related articles; thematic articles on narrower topics, including concepts, terms, schools of thought, and so forth; and biographical articles. A uniform structure is observed for all articles. Each opens with a concise summary overview, followed by a numbered list of section headings for the main article. Following the main article, which often includes cross-references to other articles, is an annotated bibliography of references and suggested sources for further reading. In the case of biographical articles, bibliographies are divided between the subject's own works and secondary sources.

Volume 10 contains a list of contributors and an exhaustive index that includes cross-references.

151.   **Routledge Encyclopedia of Philosophy.** Edward Craig, ed. Luciano Floridi, consultant ed. London: Routledge, 1998. CD-ROM. 1 disc with user's guide.

The CD-ROM version of the *Routledge Encyclopedia* shares the entire text of the print version (see entry 150) and combines it with an electronic index and other search and navigation capabilities afforded by the digital format. It offers both basic and advanced search options that include multiterm searching with Boolean operators *(and, or, not)* as well as free text searching. Cross-references in articles are "hot-linked" for instant access to the referenced article. A thematic index provides "guided paths" to related articles via hierarchical subject relationships. On-screen help features are available, and a user guide is provided both on-screen and in an accompanying printed booklet.

The publisher is no longer marketing the CD-ROM version of the *REP* and confirms it has no plans for any future reissues that might include the updates and revisions being incorporated in the online version (see entry 152). But at this writing in late 2005 OCLC's WorldCat union catalog shows over 100 U.S. and foreign libraries that have the CD-ROM product.

152.   **Routledge Encyclopedia of Philosophy.** Edward Craig, ed. Routledge, 2000–. http://www.rep.routledge.com/index.html (accessed October 22, 2005).

The online *REP* has as its basis the text of the print version (entry 150), but incorporates ongoing revisions and additions that, if its promise and its record to date are maintained, will make this format increasingly advantageous—quite aside from the usual benefits of online resources, such as multiple search capabilities and the ability to offer access to students and faculty in their dorm-rooms and offices. As of late October 2005, the *"REP* Online Updates" page on the Web site listed more than 100 new or revised articles, the great majority new, broken down by a combination of subject categories (e.g., nineteenth-century philosophy, Russian philosophy—two of the largest gainers) and dates of implementation. The articles themselves also include a notice of their new or revised status.

Access options include a basic keyword search that searches not only entry headings but subheadings within articles; advanced search options including full-text searching with a variety of strategies for limiting, Boolean searching, and "concept" and "pattern" (basically wildcard and truncated term) searching; browsing an alphabetical list of entries; and a "subject themes" search via a classification of articles under the broad subject categories represented also by "signpost" articles (cf. description under entry 150). The signpost articles, which can also be accessed quickly via a special tab, themselves serve as a kind of subject guide to related articles. A "Help" function is provided.

It should be emphasized that this is not a free Web site but a subscription resource. However, the site's home page (URL listed previously) and a limited selection of *REP* content, notably 28 "signpost" articles, together with various pages of information about the *REP* Online, are publicly accessible at this time.

153.   Runes, Dagobert D., ed. **Dictionary of Philosophy.** Rev. ed. New York: Philosophical Library, 1982. 360p.

From the time of its original appearance in 1942, this work has been frequently castigated for its sins. Yet it remained in wide use, and in print, for well over 40 years, partly because of the incorrigibility of its several publishers, partly because it long served a need not met by anything better, and partly because of its genuine merits.

The 72 contributors to the original edition included many noted figures in American (and in a few cases European) philosophy: Alonzo Church on logic, William Frankena on ethics, Paul Kristeller on Renaissance philosophy, to name a few. But 13 of them, including Church, Rudolph Carnap, and C. J. Ducasse, felt obliged to publish in several philosophical journals "a public disavowal of any editorial responsibility," prompted, as they explained, by unheeded objections to its publication "in its present form" and Runes's substantial tampering with their articles without their consent (see, e.g., *Mind* 51:296).

As if determined to perpetuate this tarnish on its reputation, various publishers reissued the dictionary in numerous "editions" (at least through a sixteenth) that in fact were merely reprintings with only miniscule corrections and additions. The 1982 "revised and enlarged edition" does go beyond that—but not enough to redeem its reputation. Few articles were updated, not even major ones (e.g., ethics, philosophy of religion, philosophy of science); new articles were confined largely to entries for a few prominent figures (not always a judicious selection); and recent developments indicated in one place went unacknowledged in another (e.g., a biographical entry was added for Karl Popper, but the article on philosophy of science was not revised to mark his substantial influence in that domain).

Still, Runes's work had its uses, and still has a few. It did benefit from the distinction and scholarship of its original contributors. Many of its definitions, explanations, and perspectives can still supplement or complement other sources, and its age can be a virtue when one needs coverage of individuals, ideas, or sources once prominent but now sunk into relative obscurity.

Runes's original 1942 work has recently become available online through the *Meta-Encyclopedia of Philosophy* Web site (entry 144).

154.   Shorter Routledge Encyclopedia of Philosophy. Edward Craig, ed. Abingdon, Oxon, U.K: Routledge, 2005. 1,077p.

The introduction acknowledges that this single-volume encyclopedia, drawn in large measure from the 10-volume 1998 *Routledge Encyclopedia of Philosophy* (entry 150), "emerged out of experience with the *Concise Routledge Encyclopedia of Philosophy*" (entry 123), an earlier condensation effort described as matching the parent set "everywhere for breadth but hardly anywhere for depth" (p. vii). The two should not be confused. While the *Concise REP* has 2,054 entries, the *Shorter REP* is content with just 957, having dropped many considered of lower importance. These include, for instance, entries on Emil Fackenheim, fallacies, John of Paris, and rational beliefs. On the other hand, the *Shorter REP* features 119 articles republished in their full original length from the *REP*, as opposed to a mere two dozen "signpost" articles in the *Concise REP*. The *Shorter REP* has also seized opportunities to update, not only with entirely new entries (examples: corrective justice, globalization, Thomas More, randomness) but by incorporating new and revised material from the online version of the *REP* (entry 152). Major articles with significant revisions include, for example, those on Existentialism, infinity, Kant, Plato, and Socrates. One important article, on Hume, has been completely rewritten.

The *Shorter REP* professes to be "unashamedly 'Western' in its emphasis, being designed to suit the needs of undergraduate philosophy students and the courses they are most likely to encounter" (p. vii). Nonetheless, it has a judicious selection of entries for non-Western philosophy such as Confucius, Confucian philosophy, Hindu philosophy, Japanese philosophy, and Vedanta.

155. Sparkes, A. W. **Talking Philosophy: A Wordbook.** London and New York: Routledge, 1991. 307p.

"*Talking Philosophy* presents an informative and critical look at the basic terminology of twentieth-century Anglophone philosophy. It also examines the more important aspects of the terminology which philosophy shares with common discourse, and the language of argument generally" (prefatory matter). Arranged thematically rather than alphabetically, the book offers short definitions and discussions of terms and expressions, heavily dominated by linguistic and logical concepts but also including a chapter on "-isms, -ists, and -ologies" (e.g., Rationalism, Sophist, ontology) and a chapter titled "Doing" which covers philosophy of action as well as ethics. Numerous text references direct the reader to items in the nearly 30-page bibliography at the back. There is a detailed index.

156. **Stanford Encyclopedia of Philosophy.** Edward N. Zalta., ed. Metaphysics Research Lab, Stanford University. http://plato.stanford.edu (accessed October 22, 2005).

Without question this is the most authoritative and substantial open-access online philosophy encyclopedia, though far from complete at this writing (late 2005). In one sense, it will always be incomplete, by design. From its inception in 1995, it was designed to be a dynamic reference work: authors are expected to maintain and update their entries, even to revise in response to valid criticism (as determined by the editor in consultation with an editorial board). This is no mere intention: many existing entries have indeed been revised at least once. But the encyclopedia is also incomplete in that, of some 1,500 projected entries (itself a moving target), less than a third are finished at this writing, and many are not even assigned yet. But the articles that *are* present, often contributed by leading authorities on their topics, already constitute a resource of astonishing breadth, depth, and scholarly quality. By way of example: recently new entries in October 2005 included articles on other minds equivalent to 14 printed pages; on postmodernism, 22 pages; on collective responsibility, 18 pages; on Continental feminism, 37 pages; and on Socrates, 25 pages. Not all articles run to such lengths, but few are less than 5 or 6 print-equivalent pages. All are accompanied by bibliographies, often extensive; these of course are natural candidates for the work's updating capabilities. At this stage, entries mainly represent or concentrate on Western philosophy, but a few articles on non-Western philosophy have appeared, including a 36-page treatment of Taoism.

In recognition of the problem a dynamic publication poses for citation purposes, a remarkable provision is made to archive "fixed editions" of the encyclopedia every three months. These editions, which remain unmodified once archived, are accessible at the home site. It is of course important in citing them to reference the appropriate edition date.

Though it has enjoyed impressive support from its parent university, foundations, and the philosophical community, the future of the *Stanford Encyclopedia*—at least as an open-access resource—is not entirely secure at this date. In early 2004 it initiated a fundraising drive, including an appeal to libraries, aimed at establishing an endowment that could fund long-term continuation.

157. Urmson, J. O. and Jonathan Rée, eds. **Concise Encyclopedia of Western Philosophy.** 3rd ed. Abingdon, Oxon, U.K.: Routledge, 2005. 398p.

The first edition of this encyclopedia (London: Hutchinson, 1960) boasted a list of 49 contributors that would make a good start on a "Who's Who" of mid-twentieth-century Anglo-American philosophy. Besides the original editor, J. O. Urmson, it included among others A. J. Ayer, Isaiah Berlin, R. M. Hare, H.L.A. Hart, Walter Kaufmann, Alasdair MacIntyre, Ernest Nagel, Gilbert Ryle, Ruth Saw, P. F. Strawson, and B.A.O. Williams. A majority of these contributors were associated with the "linguistic" movement in philosophy centered in Oxford. The encyclopedia's second edition nearly three decades later (London: Unwin Hyman, 1989) brought in 31 additional contributors, not as distinguished on the whole but still including several relatively prominent names, for example, Ian Hacking, Peter Singer, and Charles Taylor. The third edition adds just four more contributors who joined editor Rée in providing new material. Substantial content from the first edition survives, signaled by parentheses enclosing authors' initials at the ends of articles. (In the original 1960 edition articles were unsigned, but a 1967 reprinting introduced the practice of identifying authors by their initials.) Articles that were new with the second edition are marked by square brackets—[ ]—enclosing the author initials, those new to the third by curly brackets—{ }. The "survivors" from Urmson's original work remain virtually intact as originally published, thereby preserving the historical value of the original encyclopedia—which as Rée notes "now has the status of a minor classic" (introduction, p. vi)—but giving the later editions a mildly schizophrenic character, as articles that have not been updated to reflect developments since 1960 mingle with newer articles that do. In the second edition, the majority of new entries dealt with areas such as "psychoanalysis, Marxism, and traditions in European continental philosophy [referring to Hermeneutics, Postmodernism, Structuralism, Post-Structuralism, etc.] which would not have been regarded as intellectually legitimate by English philosophers in the 1950s" (p. vii). A few new articles, however, replaced original articles that had either become seriously obsolete (e.g., philosophy of science, political philosophy) or in some way embarrassing (e.g., Walter Kaufmann's dismissive piece on Heidegger). The small number of entries new to the third edition more often rectify previous omissions—for example, those on aesthetics, categorical imperative, logical atomism, Newton—than they reflect new developments.

Urmson favored longer articles on broad subjects rather than short entries for narrower ones, and explained in his introduction to the first edition that "the total number of articles included has been restricted on the principle that it is better to have a fair number of useful articles than to have a large number of useless ones." Among his principles of selection was a fairly narrow interpretation of what constitutes philosophy, namely, "one conforming to the usage of *professional* philosophers in the *western* tradition" (italics supplied); but at the same time the encyclopedia was aimed primarily at nonspecialists. None of this has changed markedly with the revised editions, but some of the omissions and imbalances for which Urmson has been criticized have been ameliorated. This remains a useful and interesting encyclopedia on the whole, but best used with some sensitivity to its slightly awkward chronological schizophrenia. Its *historical* value is better served by the first edition where available—especially copies that boast the more than 100 handsome plates, chiefly portraits of important philosophers, included in some (not all) printings of the first edition but regrettably not in subsequent editions.

None of the three editions provide bibliographies with the articles, and the suggestions "for further reading" at the back of the first edition have since been dropped.

158.   Vesey, Godfrey and Paul Foulkes. **Collins Dictionary of Philosophy.** London: Collins, 1990. 300p.

This British paperback dictionary, not commonly available in the United States, combines topical and biographical entries to present a concise "Who is Who and What is What in Philosophy" (foreword). Reviewing this work in the journal *Philosophy* (66, no. 255:128–29 (January 1991)), Jenny Teichman critiqued inconsistency in mixing short and long entries (e.g., there's a "shortish" entry on communism with separate entries for exponents such as Marx, Lenin, and Trotsky, but only a long article on psychoanalysis with no separate entry for Freud) as well as a number of inclusions and exclusions. While I demur from her assessment that it's "odd" to treat Einstein and Camus as philosophers, it's easy to agree that it's odd to devote a whole page to the secondary seventeenth-century philosopher Geulincx when there are no references to important thinkers such as De Beauvoir, Foucault, Kuhn, Nozick, or Wollstonecraft, and to concur in regretting that the authors omit entries on functionalism, holism, individualism, just war, liberty, necessity, ontology, and will, among others. Arguably the work is better on balance than these criticisms suggest, but it's clearly not a heavyweight contender among general dictionaries of philosophy of the past two decades.

159.   Voltaire, François-Marie Arrouet de. **Philosophical Dictionary.** Translated and with an introduction and glossary by Peter Gay. New York: Basic Books, 1962. 2 vols. Alternate ed.: Ed. and trans. Theodore Besterman. Harmondsworth, Eng.: Penguin Books, 1971. 400p.

Dictionaries and encyclopedias from past centuries are generally not included in this guide, but Voltaire's (first French edition, 1764) deserves an exception. This is not because it's the only one reprinted in modern times (some others have seen small-run reprintings for specialized scholarly purposes), but rather that, having seen several modern translations and editions (two recent ones cited here), it is more widely available than any other.

De George (see entry 1) observes that Voltaire's work "is now only of historical interest," but one should add "and literary interest," for it is chiefly Voltaire's style, wit, and irreverent opinions that have kept this classic alive. Even in its time, it hardly served as a dictionary of technical philosophy, being concerned mainly with matters of popular philosophy and religious controversy. Among Voltaire's few technical topics are soul, beauty, certainty, chain of events, great chain of being, fate, and necessary.

A few contemporary thinkers have imitated Voltaire's use of the alphabetical dictionary format as a vehicle for informal, often personal, and largely nontechnical commentary and reflection on a miscellany of subjects with a broadly philosophical slant. Examples of the genre include Robert Nisbet's *Prejudices: A Philosophical Dictionary* (1982) , Willard Van Orman Quine's *Quiddities: An Intermittently Philosophical Diction-ary* (1987), and Jaroslav Pelikan's *The Melody of Theology: A Philosophical Dictionary* (1988), all published by Harvard University Press, and Thomas Szasz's *Words to the Wise: A Medical-Philosophical Dictionary* (Transaction, 2004). Dictionaries by Mortimer Adler (entry 114) and Mario Bunge (entry 120) come somewhat closer to being conventional dictionaries of philosophy, but these too share much of the highly personal flavor of Voltaire's prototype. Fittingly mentioned also in this recitation of dictionaries both personal and polemical is the *Anti-Philosophical Dictionary: Thinking, Speech, Science/Scholar-ship* of Danish scientist Peter Naur (Gentofte, Denmark: naur.com, 2001, 102p.). Though this includes many entries common to philosophical dictionaries, its stated purpose is to display "the inanity of the traditional ways of talking of philosophers" including, for example, Descartes, Russell, Ryle, Heidegger, and Wittgenstein, and contrast these with Naur's allegedly more coherent understanding of the matters indicated in his subtitle based upon ideas of William James, Otto Jesperson, and James Watson (cover blurb).

160.   Ward, Keith. **Fifty Key Words in Philosophy.** London: Lutterworth Press, 1968. 85p. (Fifty Key Word Books).

This brief, handy, but now dated reference guide, aimed at general readers, offers a judicious selection of the most significant terms in philosophy, excluding ethics. Articles on schools and movements (e.g., Behaviorism, Pragmatism) and philosophical concepts or issues (determinism, mind, sense-data, truth) average about a page and a half in length. Cross-references are furnished liberally. There is an index of terms not treated in separate articles and also a chronological list of philosophers mentioned in the text.

OTHER LANGUAGES

FRENCH

161.   Auroux, Sylvain and Yvonne Weil. **Dictionnaire des auteurs et des thèmes de la philosophie.** Rev. and enlarged ed. Paris: Hachette, 1991. 526p.

This French dictionary aims to help students and general readers decipher philosophical references and messages encountered in school settings, the mass media, public discourse, personal reading, and other contexts outside of professional philosophy. It features medium-length articles on individual philosophers and on broad topics such as major philosophical schools and theories and core concerns and concepts of philosophical debate (e.g., *alienation, cause, sujet, temps, verité*). Includes brief bibliographies and indexes of concepts, names, and titles of works referenced in the articles.

162.   Blanc, Élie. **Dictionnaire de philosophie ancienne, moderne et contemporaine.** Paris: P. Lethielleux, 1906. Reprinted, New York: Burt Franklin, 1972. 1,248 columns. **Supplément (années 1906, 1907, 1908)** bound with main work. 154 columns (Burt Franklin Bibliography and Reference Series, 461; Philosophy & Religious History, 117).

This early twentieth-century French dictionary, while comprehensive, has a Scholastic emphasis. Its primary continuing value, presumably motivating the 1970s reprinting, lies in its coverage of lesser known figures, especially Catholic and French. It has over 4,000 entries, mostly brief, but some running as long as 2 or 3 pages (e.g., Kant).

163.   Durozoi, Gérard and André Roussel. **Dictionnaire de philosophie.** Paris: Éditions Nathan, 1987. 367p.

This French dictionary is designed to make the specialized vocabulary of philosophy accessible to students and philosophical amateurs. It features brief articles on significant terms and concepts common in philosophical discourse, together with brief entries on the major philosophers, with very selective attention to borderline areas and figures particularly in contemporary thought (e.g., Bataille, Deleuze, Serres). An unusual feature is a series of diagrams showing relationships among major schools and thinkers in various domains of philosophy (e.g., Marxist, English, French, Greek, Classical Arabic, Christian, Medieval, Enlightenment), or among the contributions of significant thinkers on a specific topic such as perception or the person.

164.   Encyclopédie philosophique universelle. André Jacob, general ed. Paris: Presses Universitaires de France, 1989–1998. 4 vols. in 6.

This significant French encyclopedia, published in cooperation with the Centre National des Lettres and involving well over a thousand contributors, features an unusual format comprising four distinctly different sections (designated as *volumes* 1–4), each under separate editorship and each approaching the philosophical universe from a different angle. Volumes 2 and 3 each consist of two physical volumes (designated as *tomes*). Each physical tome comprises from 1,500 to more than 2,700 pages. The approaches and content of this unique set are often as unconventional as its mode of organization.

1. **L'univers philosophique.** André Jacob, ed. 1989. Volume 1 surveys the modern "philosophical universe" by way of a series of essays, some by well-known names such as Paul Ricœur and Jacques Ellul, thematically organized under two major rubrics: "Problématiques contemporaines," which surveys themes and issues in the major branches of the field (metaphysics, ethics, social philosophy, etc.), and "Matériaux pour la réflexion," which explores relationships of philosophy to other disciplines and fields of endeavor (the sciences, mathematics, anthropology, ethnology, etc.) with particular attention to recent developments. Also includes a *bibliographie générale,* compiled by Gilbert Varet, and an index.

2. **Les notions philosophiques: dictionnaire.** Sylvain Auroux, ed. 1990. (2 *tomes,* or physical vols.) Volume 2 is an encyclopedic dictionary of philosophical terms and concepts, generally alphabetical in arrangement but divided first of all into a number of separate sections: *philosophie occidentale* (i.e., Western philosophy, but including in this case Islamic and other Middle Eastern thought) ; *pensées asiatiques,* further subdivided into *Inde, Chine,* and *Japon;* and "Conceptualisation des sociétes traditionnelles," covering African, South American, and other traditional cultures. Signed articles are typically half a page or so in length, but some run to as much as five or six pages. The *"tables analytiques"* list terms from all these areas under broad subjects, such as moral or political philosophy.

3. **Les oeuvres philosophiques: dictionnaire.** Jean-François Mattéi, ed., 1992. (2 *tomes,* or physical vols.). Volume 3 presents individual summaries of, and sometimes critical comment on, some 9,000 significant works over the breadth and depth of philosophical history, divided into the same three major parts as volume 2. The first, *philosophie occidentale* is subdivided into six periods from antiquity to contemporary thought. The second, *pensées asiatiques,* is subdivided into four cultural regions: India, China, Japan, and Korea. Finally, "Conceptualisation des sociétés traditionnelles" treats works from and relating to "oral cultures" by continental subdivisions: Africa, the Americas, Southeast Asia, Europe, Oceania. In this last section, the works analyzed are collections of oral traditions and secondary studies by observers and scholars of the societies considered. Within all subdivisions, arrangement is by author's name or by title for anonymous works. Every entry begins with brief biographical information on the

author or on the historical context for anonymous works, and ends with primary and secondary bibliographies. Tome 2 includes several indexes and tables.

4. **Le discours philosophique.** Jean-François Mattéi, ed., 1998. Volume 4 offers thematic essays on multiple facets, dimensions, and contours of philosophy as a domain of discourse. It includes multichapter sections on the major languages in which philosophical texts have been written; national origins and orientations of philosophical discourse; modes of philosophizing in traditional cultures; avenues *(chemins)* of translation (e.g. Sanskrit to Chinese, Arabic to Latin) and the problems of translation; comparative approaches to philosophy; philosophical genres and styles; texts and their contexts; and philosophy's relation to other fields of thought and endeavor (science, psychology, the arts, etc.). Accompanying each chapter is a selection of texts, in French translation if not originally French, illustrating that chapter's themes or arguments. There is an index of these *textes illustratifs* as well indexes of names, topics, and illustrations.

165. Foulquié, Paul and Raymond Saint-Jean. **Dictionnaire de la langue philosophique.** 6th ed. Paris: Presses Universitaires de France, 1992. 778p.

A work which acknowledges its indebtedness to the long-standard French dictionary by Lalande (entry 169), this is, like Lalande's, a dictionary of terms and concepts. It has no entries for persons, or even for schools or viewpoints such as Aristotelianism or Thomism. Its 1,500 or so terms are generally treated in alphabetical sequence, but in some cases related terms are grouped together. Thus, *essence* and *exister* (to cite an example of some importance in the context of French philosophy) are grouped with other related terms under *être.* Similarly, *indéterminisme* is found under *déterminisme.* Cross-references are of course provided in these instances.

The chief distinguishing feature of Foulquié's work, highlighted by a judicious employment of distinct typefaces, is its use of quotations from significant philosophical writings to illustrate the use or uses of a term, somewhat in the manner of the *Oxford English Dictionary.* Citations identify authors and source-works and even page numbers, but lack further bibliographic data including dates.

166. Godin, Christian. **Dictionnaire de philosophie.** Paris: Fayard / Éditions du temp, 2004. 1,534p.

This recent work claims to be without precedent as a comprehensive French-language philosophy dictionary written by a single author. The sole authorship, its preface argues, provides for exceptional coherence and for consistency in, among other things, the direct and accessible language that is one of its guiding motives. Among the more than 5,000 entries, around 1,000 are biographical; the remainder cover terms, concepts, schools, movements, celebrated philosophical metaphors and images, and principal texts. Godin's single-handed effort takes in the full scope of philosophical history, Eastern as well as Western.

167. **Grande dictionnaire de la philosophie.** Michel Blay, ed. in chief. Paris: Larousse/CNRS, 2003. 1105p.

A significant new French dictionary, issued under sponsorship of the Centre National de la Recherche Scientifique. Lead editor Blay, director of research for the CNRS, marshaled a team of 8 coeditors and around 200 contributors, predominantly French academics. There are some 1,100 standard entries covering terms, concepts, movements, and so forth, but no biographical entries. Interspersed throughout are 70 extended essays on a diverse selection of special topics, for example "Dieu est-il mort?" "L'art contemporain est-il une sociologie?" and "Norme et Nature."

168.   Julia, Didier. **Dictionnaire de la philosophie.** New ed., rev. and corrected. Paris: Larousse, 1995. 301p.

First published in 1964 and previously revised in 1984, Julia's is in some ways a standard sort of encyclopedic dictionary, featuring articles on individuals, concepts, schools of thought, and so forth, and also some on philosophical classics such as Descartes's *Discourse on Method* and Kant's *Critique of Pure Reason.* What is fairly unusual, however, is that it is addressed to the layperson and aims specifically to show the applicability of philosophy to daily life. In the service of this cause it deploys many illustrations, going well beyond routine portraits of philosophers to include paintings, current event photos, and other types of illustrations seemingly calculated to arouse curiosity as to what their connection might be with philosophy. Most of these illustrate topics of popular interest, sometimes borderline or semiphilosophical, which also abound: euthanasia, fanaticism, feminism, hysteria, racism, socialist realism, sublimation, xenism, and others of like nature. Something of the work's outlook is suggested by William Gerber's observation on an earlier edition (*Encyclopedia of Philosophy,* vol. 6, p. 196) that "Marx gets more space than anyone else, and Trotsky gets more than Aristotle." However one assesses its perspective or its success overall, the concept behind Julia's dictionary is appealing; one would like to see it tried more often, and in an English-language work.

169.   Lalande, André, ed. **Vocabulaire technique et critique de la philosophie.** 18th ed. Paris: Presses Universitaires de France, 1996. 1,323p.

Lalande's durable dictionary is published under the *aegis* of the Societé Française de Philosophie, in whose *Bulletin* the first edition appeared in 21 parts (1902–23). Its focus is the clarification of terms and concepts; there are no biographical entries, nor is there historical or systematic treatment of topics *per se.* In addition to definitions, there are examples of use by philosophers (translations for those in Latin and Greek are provided in two appendices at the back), and typically also etymologies and equivalents of the term in German, English, and Italian. A highly unusual feature is the inclusion, in the form of footnotes, of comments on the definitions by members of the Societé Française de Philosophie.

GERMAN

170.   Brugger, Walter. **Philosophisches Wörterbuch.** 17th ed. Freiburg im Breisgau: Herder, 1985. 592p.

A well-regarded dictionary with a Neo-Scholastic orientation. The latter is manifested primarily in emphases and perspective, not in the choice of entries, which range widely over standard topics in Western philosophy with some attention as well to non-Western philosophy. There are no biographical entries. Not only has Brugger's work seen numerous new German editions since its first appearance in 1948, but it has been translated into several other languages, including English (see entry 119), Chinese, and Spanish. The

Spanish version has achieved at least a 13th edition (*Diccionario de filosofía,* Barcelona: Editorial Herder, 1995, 734p.).

171. Eisler, Rudolf. **Wörterbuch der Philosophischen Begriffe.** 4th ed. Berlin: E. S. Mittler, 1927–30. 3 vols.

This three-volume fourth edition evolved from a single-volume work which appeared in 1899, and prevailed for many years as the preeminent encyclopedic dictionary of philosophy in German. It is being superseded, however, by a thoroughgoing revision under the editorship of Joachim Ritter, now nearly complete (entry 172). Though this fourth edition was actually completed after Eisler's death (under the supervision of K. Roretz), it enjoyed the cooperation and consequent imprimatur of the respected Kant-Gesellschaft. It treats terms and concepts only, but tends to follow a historical approach that systematically canvasses the definitions, views, and arguments of major thinkers on a topic.

Eisler also produced a briefer dictionary, the *Handwörterbuch der Philosophie* (2. Aufl., Berlin: E. S. Mittler, 1922, 785p.), aimed more at the nonspecialist and closer to the scope of his original *Wörterbuch.* This has also been very successful, and was reprinted as late as 1949.

172. **Historisches Wörterbuch der Philosophie.** Joachim Ritter, Karlfried Gründer, et al., eds. Basel/Stuttgart: Schwabe, 1971–. 13 vols. projected.

Billed as a thoroughgoing revision of the long-standard *Wörterbuch* of Rudolf Eisler (entry 171), this massive work of mainly German and Swiss scholarship neared completion with the publication of volume 12 (W–Z) in late 2004. An index volume is scheduled to appear late 2006, according to the publisher's Web site. The original editor-in-chief, Joachim Ritter, now deceased, saw this project through the publication of volume 3 (G–H); his name has continued to appear on the title pages of subsequent volumes, joined by those of his successors, Karlfried Gründer and, beginning with volume 11, Gottfried Gabriel. The more than 700 contributing authorities proclaimed on the title page of volume 1 grew to more than 1,500 by volume 12.

What this revision carries over from Eisler's work is more a conception, approach, and set of emphases than its actual content. Ritter's *Vorwort* to volume 1 explains at some length the growth of the project beyond originally modest intentions and the need, soon realized, to rebuild "from the ground up." Articles carried forward with relatively little revision by the editorial staff (a very small minority) are signed "Eisler (red.)."

Volumes of the *Historisches Wörterbuch* run from 526 to 933 pages each, though it numbers columns (two per page) rather than pages. Articles tend to be long, usually at least half a column, with only occasionally a shorter definition. They cover a mixture of concepts, terms, schools, movements, and so forth, but there are no entries for individual philosophers. Extensive bibliographies are provided. There is some coverage of Eastern philosophy, though it is not detailed.

173. Klaus, Georg and Manfred Buhr. **Philosophisches Wörterbuch.** 8th corrected ed. Berlin: Das Europäische Buch, 1972. 2 vols.

The *Ausgangspunkt* (point of departure) for this dictionary issued in the former East Germany is, says its foreword, the works of Marx, Engels, and Lenin as well as the fundamental documents of the German Socialist Party and the international workers movement, in particular the Communist Party of the Soviet Union. Central to its aims, avowedly, is the presentation of Marxist-Leninist philosophy *per se.* However, it is also a general dictionary in the sense that it provides general coverage of philosophical and logical terminology, the history of philosophy, and aspects of other disciplines relevant to philosophy. Even there, of course, the Marxist perspective is operative. An avowed part of its strategy, in fact, is to further understanding of Marxism-Leninism by contrasting it with "bourgeois philosophy and imperialist ideology."

Some 1,800 entries include terms, concepts, schools, movements, and so forth, but not names of individuals.

A West German edition of the previous (7th) edition of this work was issued under the title *Marxistisch-leninistisches Wörterbuch der Philosophie* (Reinbek: Rowolt, 1972, 3 vols.).

174.   Krings, Hermann, Hans Michael Baumgartner, and Christoph Wild, eds. **Handbuch philosophischer Grundbegriffe.** Munich: Kosel-Verlag, 1973–74. 3 vols.

Far from attempting to be a comprehensive encyclopedia, this German reference work takes seriously the focus on *Grundbegriffe,* that is, foundational concepts, signaled in its title. It features no more than about 150 articles on concepts that, in the editors' view, are pivotal for philosophical thought. Examples include such varied concepts as the absolute, consciousness *(Bewusstsein),* evil *(das Böse),* finiteness *(Endlichkeit),* progress *(Fortschritt),* and society *(Gesellschaft).* Each of these is subjected to a substantial conceptual analysis with extensive reference to its history in philosophical thought. Excluded in this approach are concepts which can be explicated with a brief definition; terms which have a purely "designative" character, such as those designating various philosophical disciplines (logic, philosophy of language) or movements (Idealism, Utilitarianism); and biographical entries.

Nearly all the contributors to this work are German. Historically German philosophical tendencies, particularly Idealism, are much in evidence, but do not exclude other perspectives. Extensive bibliographies emphasize German sources but also cite numerous works in other languages, chiefly English and French.

175.   Mittelstrass, Jürgen, et. al. **Enzyklopädie Philosophie und Wissenschaftstheorie.** Vols. 1 and 2: Mannheim: Bibliographisches Institut-Wissenschaftsverlag, 1980, 1984. Vols. 3–4: Stuttgart: J. B. Metzler, 1995–1996.

This German encyclopedia was issued over the course of 16 years by 2 different publishers and with a changing roster of coeditors and contributing editors. As of late 2005, all four volumes were available from Metzler. While this encyclopedia takes into its purview most of the traditional range of philosophy, it concentrates deliberately on developments, concepts, and figures in logic and philosophy of science, and on connections—historical, conceptual, logical, methodological—among philosophy, the natural sciences, the social sciences (to a lesser extent), and mathematics. Some 4,000 articles, mostly of short to medium length, include both brief explanations of concepts and biographical entries. Regrettably, the work lacks a comprehensive index.

176.   **PhilLex: Lexikon der Philosophie.** Uwe Wiedemann, ed. http://www.phillex. de (accessed October 23, 2005).

A useful if not notably authoritative German online dictionary. Covers terms and concepts only, but has linked cross-references to a companion site, *Philosophen und Logiker* (entry 275). Explanations are typically brief, though some on major topics run to several pages when printed.

177.   Sandkühler, Hans Jörg. **Europäische Enzyklopädie zu Philosophie und Wissenschaften.** Hamburg: Felix Meiner, 1990. 4 vols.

As its title indicates, this German encyclopedia is multidisciplinary (the term *Wissenschaften* is translatable variously as "sciences" or, less misleadingly, "scholarly disciplines"), yet heavily philosophical. Its special forte is the dialogue of philosophy with other disciplines: the philosophical questions they raise, and the insights they offer or claims they make that are especially fruitful or challenging for philosophical reflection. This interdisciplinary breadth may be suggested by the following sampling of article titles which mingle with those of a more narrowly philosophical cast: *Armut der Frau; Bürokratie; Entropie; Evolutionsbiologie; Geschichtsphilosophie; Kapital; Kunst, Künste; Metapher; Polizei; Rechtspositivismus; Renaissance; Sozialforschung, empirische; Text; Utopie; Wissenschaftstheorie; Zukunft.* Only lengthy, substantive articles appear—no short entries or definitions—and there are no biographical entries. Some cross-references are provided. The Istituto Italiano per Gli Studi Filosofici cooperated in the publication of this encyclopedia.

178.   Schmidt, Heinrich. **Philosophisches Wörterbuch.** 22nd ed., newly rev. by Georgi Schischkoff. Stuttgart: Alfred Kröner, 1991. 817p.

If one counts all of its 22 editions, stretching from 1912 to 1991, this German dictionary is possibly the most widely used philosophical dictionary ever, in any language. More than half of its editions have been published since Schmidt's death in 1935, under the supervision of a variety of editors. It has survived and overcome a serious smirch on its reputation created by the intrusion of pro-Nazi and anti-Jewish elements in editions published during the Nazi era.

In content, Schmidt is most nearly comparable to the works of Blackburn and Flew in English (entries 118 and 124), though it is somewhat longer and more comprehensive than either. It has articles on individuals, including, predictably, many German and, more generally, European philosophers not commonly found in English-language dictionaries. Coverage of Eastern philosophy is very spotty, but there are articles on, for example, Chinese philosophy, Indian philosophy, Buddhism, and Buddhist logic. Brief bibliographical references are provided.

ITALIAN

179.   Abbagnano, Nicola. **Dizionario di filosofia.** 3rd ed., enlarged and updated. Turin: UTET [Unione Tipografico-Editrice Torinese], 1998. 1173p.

Abbagnano's is the most important and most highly regarded single-volume philosophical dictionary in Italian. It combines short definitions and explanations with lengthy expositions and survey articles. There are entries for terms, concepts, schools, movements, and so forth, but *not* for individuals.

This work has also been translated into Spanish as *Diccionario de filosofía,* 3rd ed. (tr. Alfredo N. Galletti; Mexico: FCE, 1998. 1206p.).

180.   Enciclopedia filosofica. 2nd ed., completely revised. Florence: G. C. Sansoni, 1967–1969. 6 vols.

The six-volume second edition of this Italian encyclopedia succeeds a four-volume edition, published in 1957, which was considered a landmark in its time. This was the largest and most comprehensive encyclopedia of philosophy in any language prior to the *Encyclopedia of Philosophy* edited by Paul Edwards (entry 125). Both editions were produced under the aegis of the Centro di studi filosofici di Gallarate (identified at the head of the title page) and are the work primarily of Italian scholars, with some international collaboration. Reflecting Italian philosophical penchants, the *Enciclopedia* shows some bias toward Idealistic and religious philosophy, and understandably affords more space to Italian thinkers, including obscure ones, than those of other countries. Nonetheless, it is justly admired for the sweep of its coverage and its truly international scope. Eastern thought receives some attention, though much less than Western; there are, for example, articles on Buddhism and Hinduism, and survey articles on India and China. The first edition reputedly contained some 12,000 articles; an estimate for the second is not available, but the number is undoubtedly even larger. Articles range from very short—mainly definitional and biographical—to very lengthy. Longer articles are signed, and usually include bibliographies. Most items cited in the latter are in the major European languages, that is, French, Spanish, and German as well as Italian, but English-language works are cited as well. (A possible use of this encyclopedia for the student with no facility in Italian might be to trace important sources in other languages, including perhaps non-English works on English-speaking philosophers.)

A handsome set physically, the *Enciclopedia filosofica* features a modest number of high-quality plates, mostly portraits but also some other types of illustrations. Columns, rather than pages, are numbered, and each volume has about 1,600 columns. Volume 6 has a classified list of articles as well as an index of terms and names not used as entries.

181.   Mondin, Battista. Dizionario Enciclopedicao di Filosofia, Teologia e Morale. Milano: Masimo, 1989. 855p.

This Italian dictionary of philosophy, theology, and ethics has clearly Catholic loyalties and orientation. It is, as one would anticipate, especially strong on thinkers Italian (e.g., among philosophers, Abbagnano, Banfi, Gentile, Gramsci), Catholic (e.g., Gilson, Lonergan, Maritain), or both (e.g., Bontadini, Gemelli, Guzzo), and on Catholic perspectives on topics such as *bioetica, male* (evil), and *pace* (peace). It ranges, however, over most of the standard topics in Western and to some extent Eastern philosophy, in its topical as well as its biographical articles.

182.   Rossi, Paolo, et. al. Dizionario di filosofia. Scandicci (Florence): La Nuova Italia, 1996. 453p.

This recent Italian dictionary offers a standard array of topical entries—terms and concepts, branches of philosophy, philosophical schools and movements, institutions—but no biographical entries. Numerous individuals are referenced, however, in the detailed index. Many but not all articles include brief bibliographies, usually citing works in Italian only with an occasional exception for works in other languages including English. A total of 18 contributors are listed in the front, but the majority of articles are by the 5-member editorial team.

RUSSIAN

183. **Filosofskaia entsiklopediia.** F. V. Konstantinov, general ed. Moscow: "Sovets-kaia entsiklopediia," 1960–70. 5 vols.

This comprehensive Russian encyclopedia from the Soviet era exhibits a predictable Marxist-Leninist emphasis and viewpoint. Published under the auspices of the Institute of Philosophy of the Academy of Science (Akademii Nauk) of the USSR, it was part of a more comprehensive publishing project, the *Entisiklopedii slovari spravochniki.* The major articles include substantial bibliographies. "Especially valuable for its detailed coverage of the theoretical bases of Communist doctrine" (R. Neiswender, "Guide to Russian Reference and Language Aids," quoted in A. J. Walford, *Guide to Reference Material,* 4th ed., 1982).

184. **Filosofskii entsiklopedicheskii slovar'.** Ed. E. F. Gubskii, G. V. Korableva, and V. A. Lutchenko. Moscow: INFRA-M, 1997. 574p.

This work is rooted in a Soviet-era encyclopedia of the same title whose second edition appeared in 1989 (see entry 185), but it is not specifically identified as a third or new edition of the earlier work. Possibly this is because of its departure from the Marxist perspective and emphasis of its predecessors. It includes many thinkers, both Russian and foreign, not previously afforded a place. There are some 3,500 short to medium-length entries covering all branches and eras of Western philosophy. A glossary of foreign philosophical terms and expressions follows the main body of entries.

185. **Filosofskii entsiklopedicheskii slovar'.** 2nd ed. Ed. S. S. Averintsev, et. al. Moscow: "Sovetskaia éntsiklopediia," 1989. 814p.

Though replaced in one sense by a namesake work issued in 1997 (see entry 184), this single-volume Russian encyclopedia whose first edition appeared in 1983, followed by the second in 1989, remains of distinct interest and value for its Marxist emphasis and perspective dating from the twilight of the Soviet era. Despite the Marxist slant, its roughly 2,000 topical and biographical articles cover the full range of Western philosophy.

186. Gubskii, E. F., et. al. **Kratkaia filosofskaia entsiklopediia.** Moscow: Progress, 1994. 575p.

A blurb in the front of this post-Soviet-era Russian encyclopedia lays claim to its being the first unbiased and comprehensive philosophical reference work in Russia in 75 years. A preface by the editors expands on this theme by noting that it includes both "foreign" schools of thought and many "forgotten" Russian philosophers. Among the areas they specifically mention as being included, besides standard divisions of the field such as metaphysics, ethics, philosophy of history, and so forth, are religious philosophy, Scholasticism, Logical Positivism, Existentialism, and Skepticism. On the other hand, there are, remarkably, no articles on Lenin and Marx. One might infer that in early post-Soviet Russia assessment of philosophical significance was still turning with the political winds. Altogether, there are over 3,500 entries, including many short definitions and brief biographical articles, which attempt, the editors say, to cover all the major philosophical questions.

SPANISH

187.   Ferrater Mora, José and Terricabras, Josep-Maria. **Diccionario de filosofía.** Barcelona: Editorial Ariel, 1994. 4 vols.

Though labeled "1st edition," this 1994 encyclopedia nonetheless emphasizes its continuity with Ferrater Mora's highly regarded work of the same title, first published in 1941 and subsequently reissued five times in new editions (6th ed., Madrid: Alianza, 1982, 4 vols.), several of them widely republished in Latin America. Thus the present work also describes itself as a "nueva edición revisada, aumentada y actualizada por el professor . . . Terricabras" (title page).

William Gerber, in the 1967 *Encyclopedia of Philosophy* (entry 125), called the ancestor of this work "one of the most useful dictionaries published in the twentieth century" and "a monumental one-man contribution." The latter is an apt characterization of its size and scope, if nothing else. In its present reincarnation as in its previous lives, this encyclopedia features articles that tend to be short, seldom running more than a few pages even on major topics; the typical article is one or two columns (of two per page). Entries cover the usual range of an encyclopedic dictionary, but there is a heavy emphasis on individuals. These include many Iberian and Latin-American thinkers little known outside their own linguistic and cultural domain. Bibliographies cite materials in many languages, though Spanish-language sources are emphasized. There are no illustrations.

TRANSLATION DICTIONARIES

188.   Ballestrem, Karl G. **Russian Philosophical Terminology.** Dordrecht, Netherlands: D. Reidel, 1964. 117p.

Published by the Institute of East European Studies, University of Fribourg (Switzerland), to facilitate the study of Soviet philosophy, this glossary contains about a thousand Russian philosophical terms arranged in cyrillic alphabetical order and followed by English, German, and French equivalents. No attempt is made to expand upon a term's meaning or significance. Any terms that appeared regularly in Russian philosophical texts are included, but those central or specific to Soviet philosophy (e.g., *zakony dialektiky*) are marked with an asterisk, allowing the user to identify first the most basic vocabulary. Indexes for English, German, and French terms refer to the corresponding Russian expressions, which are numbered.

189.   **Vocabulaire européen des philosophies: dictionnaire des intraduisibles**. Barbara Cassin, general ed. Paris: Le Robert / Seuil, 2004. 1,531p.

A dictionary of "untranslatables" may seem to fit awkwardly under the heading "translation dictionaries." It deals, however, with philosophical terms in a variety of European languages that give translators headaches as well as create obstacles or pitfalls for scholars and students trying to understand philosophical discourse in, or translated from, a tongue other than their own. "Untranslatable," as an associated Web site (see following paragraph) explains, "does not imply that translation is impossible, but that its difficulty is a symptom of conceptual discrepancies." The terms are drawn from not only the expected principal European languages but also Norwegian, Swedish, Russian, Ukrainian, Portuguese, Basque, and ancient languages including Latin, classical Greek, Hebrew, and even Arabic. Examples include *Bild* and *Dasein* in German, *svet* and *mir* in Russian, *mimêsis* and *logos* in Greek, *agency* in English, *beauté* in French, *virtù* in Italian, *saudade* in Portuguese, *Torah* in Hebrew. There are about 400 entries, though many more terms are treated in discussions under the entry terms and can be located via a detailed index. Most entries represent individual words, but a handful of "meta-entries" take on broader topics such as general features of a specific language, or still more general linguistic phenomena such as word order, that can pose translation challenges. There are also "directional" entries that lead from French terms to related foreign-language terms. Articles on individual terms generally provide common translations into other languages followed by an extended exploration of meaning nuances, connotations, interlinguistic comparisons, and historical and cultural contexts. The work is set against the background supposition of a deep connection between differences of languages and ways of thinking. This thought may tend to discourage anyone who lacks a native or near-native command of French from endeavoring to use this dictionary. Some level of competence in French is of course required in any case. A similar tool someday in English, perhaps an adaptation of this one, would be a welcome development.

A project to make the content of the *VEP* available online, sponsored by European Cultural Heritage Online (ECHO), had some 40 sample articles made available at this writing (http://robert.bvdep.com/public/vep, accessed November 8, 2005).

190. Waible, Elmar and Philip Herdina. **Dictionary of Philosophical Terms—Wörterbuch philosophischer Fachbegriffe**. Munich: K. G. Saur, 1997. 2 vols. Published simultaneously under alternate title **German Dictionary of Philosophical Terms—Wörterbuch philosophischer Fachbegriffe englisch**. London: Routledge, 1997. 2 vols.

Provides equivalences between German and English philosophical terms and expressions, in as succinct a manner as possible, that is, without elaboration or explication of the concepts involved beyond indicating the subdiscipline to which a term pertains or sometimes a philosopher with whom it is especially or uniquely associated. Terms and expressions from related fields, such as mathematics, economics, and art, are included insofar as they are pertinent to constructing philosophies or conducting philosophical analyses of those fields. Occasionally, ordinary language terms, such as the German *Interesse* and *Ironie,* are entered as cross-references to technical terms such as *Erkenntnisinteresse* or *sokratische Ironie.* Terms from languages other than English or German (e.g., Greek, Latin, or Asian languages) may be listed insofar as they play a significant role in technical philosophical language in either domain. Names are included only if they differ between the two languages. Altogether, each language is represented by some 20,000 entries. The introduction/*Vorwort* in each of the respective languages is identically printed, though with their order reversed, in both volume 1 (German-English) and volume 2 (English-German). This covers, besides the afore-summarized matters of scope, such details as alphabetization rules, grammatical and other abbreviations, and, very importantly, the special symbols used to signal synonyms, antonyms, cognate terms, and references to indexes of philosophical titles. The latter, appended to each volume, provide title translations for some 1,300 important philosophical works and are accompanied by author indexes.

Part II
HISTORY OF PHILOSOPHY

8
Comprehensive History Sources

Sources in this chapter are "comprehensive" in geographic and cultural terms: that is, they encompass philosophy throughout the entire world, or at least those parts of the world with long-recognized philosophical traditions commonly comprised under the categories "Western" and "non-Western." Most of these sources are also chronologically comprehensive: they cover the worldwide history of philosophy from its beginnings to present or recent times. A few take in a much narrower slice of time but are still comprehensive in terms of their geographical coverage and the breadth of traditions within their purview.

HISTORY AND BIBLIOGRAPHY

191.   Grundriss der Geschichte der Philosophie. Founded by Friedrich Ueberweg. Completely rev. ed. Vols. 1–. Basel: Schwabe, 1983–. 30 vols. projected.

This work-in-progress represents a drastic revision and updating of a classic work originally issued by Friedrich Ueberweg in the mid-nineteenth century and republished eventually in 12 editions for most of its 5 constituent volumes, 11 in the case of volume 2 (11. & 12. Aufl., Berlin: E. S. Mittler, 1923–1928; variously reprinted). Essentially a history of philosophy, Ueberweg's work was so rich in bibliography, especially by the eleventh and twelfth editions, that it is often listed among the major philosophical bibliographies. Its lengthy publishing history includes a number of further complications that warrant mention. At least one reprinting of the older version by Schwabe (1951–1957) is dubbed *13. Auflage* yet clearly states it is an "unaltered photomechanical reprinting" of the eleventh and twelfth editions. A two-volume English translation (1871 and subsequent) was based on the fourth German edition and omitted the bibliographies. A new edition by Paul W. Wilpert that was reputed in progress for some years (cf. DeGeorge, entry 1, page 6) never appeared under Wilpert's name, but presumably refers to the work now emerging.

This completely new edition continues the tradition of its predecessors by incorporating remarkably full and carefully thought-out bibliographies, generally appended to individual chapters and, often, subsections of chapters. For instance, the chapter on Epicurus (in volume 4 of *Die Philosophie der Antike*) has separate bibliographies associated with subsections on the state of scholarship on Epicurus, on his writings (including descriptive annotations on the content of his letters and collected sayings), on editions and translations of his work, on his life, on specific aspects of his thought, and on his relations to other thinkers. The bibliographies cite monographic and periodical literature, and even dissertations, in all Western European languages; and they encompass older sources (including nineteenth-century and earlier) as well as the immense amount of material published since the 1920s edition. They can be intimidating for their size and comprehensiveness, but the typographical density and extensive use of abbreviations characteristic of the older Ueberweg editions have been substantially mitigated.

Even more than its predecessors, this edition of the *Grundriss* has a complex hierarchical volume structure, exemplified by the parts that have appeared to date. The advertised publication plan (as found on the publisher's Web site in late 2005) includes 10 fundamental divisions: 7 chronological periods of Western philosophy plus 3 non-Western geographical-cultural domains (the Islamic World, Asia, and Africa). Each division (treated by some libraries as an individual publication) has a distinct title, is under separate editorship, and encompasses multiple component volumes *(Bände)* that in some cases are further divided into subparts and/or spread over multiple physical volumes or *Halbbände.* As of late 2005, only a handful of volumes, representing just 3 of the 10 major period and cultural divisions, have seen the light of day. These are as follows:

Die Philosophie der Antike, edited by Hellmut Flashar

Band 2/1: *Sophistik, Sokrates, Mathematiker und Mediziner,* 1998

Band 3: *Ältere Akademie, Aristoteles, Peripatos,* 1983

Band 4: *Die hellenistische Philosophie,* 1994 (2 Halbbände)

(Still in preparation: Band 1, Band 2/2, Band 5)

Die Philosophie des 17. Jahrhunderts, edited by Jean-Pierre Schobinger

Band 1: *Allegemeine Themen, Iberische Halbinsel, Italien,* 1998 (2 Halbbände)

Band 2: *Frankreich und Niederlande,* 1993 (2 Halbbände)

Band 3: *England,* 1988 (2 Halbbände)

Band 4: *Das Heilige Römische Reich Deutscher Nation, Nord- und Osteuropa,* 2001 (2 Halbbände)

(Complete)

Die Philosophie des 18. Jahrhunderts, edited by Helmut Holzhey and Vilem Mudroch

Band 1: *Grossbritannien und Nordamerika, Niederlande,* 2004 (2 Halbbände)

(Still in preparation: Bände 2, 3)

Volumes in the following additional divisions are in preparation or projected:

Die Philosophie des Mittelalters (4 vols.), edited by Ruedi Imbach and Peter Schulthess

Die Philosophie der Renaissance

Die Philosophie des 19. Jahrhunderts

Die Philosophie des 20. Jahrhunderts

Die Philosophie in der Islamischen Welt (3 vols.), edited by Ulrich Rudolph

Die Philosophie Asiens

Die Philosophie Afrikas

BIBLIOGRAPHIES

192. Plott, John C., and Paul D. Mays. **Sarva-Darsana-Sangraha: A Bibliographical Guide to the Global History of Philosophy.** Leiden: E. J. Brill, 1969. 305p.

The authors aspired to promote the "globalization" of the history of philosophy by integrating coverage of Western and non-Western philosophies. This was a laudable aim, though pursued here with rather too much breastbeating about European ethnocentrism and hyperbolical gestures of obeisance to the goal of "the development of WORLD COMMUNITY" (see especially p. xii of the introduction). All the more ironic, therefore, that Plott and Mays organize much of "global history" on a scheme of periodization appropriate mainly for Western history. Thus, in chapters labeled with period names such as "Classical," "Medieval," "Renaissance," and "Modern," references on Western philosophers alternate, in simple alphabetical sequence, with references on roughly contemporaneous non-Western philosophers. Disclaimers about the bugbear of periodization (p. xvii), quotation marks surrounding such period labels, or even a footnote proclaiming that a label such as "Renaissance" is "only for convenience" and "means nothing in the global context" (page 112), cannot adequately mitigate this ill-advised arrangement. The impression it leaves is that there really is no meaningful way to relate Western and non-Western philosophy.

Despite its faults, this volume does have value as a guide to useful European-language materials, some of them obscure, others easy to overlook. It is the only annotated guide that covers a wide range of non-Western philosophies (Chinese, Japanese, Indian, Arabic, etc.). Though quite dated by now, it can still be a help to those for whom it was primarily designed: undergraduate or early graduate students and philosophy faculty with no specialized knowledge of non-Western thought.

A "synchronological chart" is housed in a pocket inside the back cover.

193. Totok, Wilhelm, et. al. **Handbuch der Geschichte der Philosophie.** Frankfurt am Main: Vittorio Klostermann, 1964–1997. Vol. 1, **Das Altertum: indische, chinesische, griechisch-römische Philosophie,** 2nd ed., completely rev., 1997. 733p. Vol. 2, **Mittelalter,** 1974. 676p. Vol. 3, **Renaissance,** 1980. 658p. Vol. 4, **Frühe Neuzeit: 17. Jahrhundert,** 1981. 612p. Vol. 5, **Bibliographie 18. und 19. Jahrhundert,** 1986. 760p. Vol. 6, **Bibliographie 20. Jahrhundert,** 1990. 853p.

Whatever the connotation of *Handbuch,* this is actually a massive bibliography of the history of philosophy. Tobey (entry 267) cites and extols Totok's work frequently, specifically lauding volume 2 as "the best detailed guide to the literature" of the medieval period and mentioning a number of topics for which Totok is an exceptionally good resource (e.g., Aquinas, mysticism), "the best general guide" (Aristotle), or even "indispensable" (Ockham). It should be borne in mind, however, that Totok's work is conceived as supplementing Ueberweg's *Grundriss der Geschichte der Philosophie* in its original incarnation (see entry 191) and as such concentrates on literature from 1920 to the editorial cut-off dates for Totok's individual volumes. Earlier publications are listed only if they are textual editions or other works that still have unusual scholarly significance. Also, despite its monumental coverage, the *Handbuch* does not pretend to be exhaustive, and in fact gives ample warning to the contrary (see vol. 1, *Vorwort*). Volume 1 alone has been issued in a second edition, much expanded from the first (1964, 400 pp.). According to information supplied by the publisher in late 2003, there are no plans for new editions of other volumes.

Materials in Western languages predominate. Periodical articles and essays in collections are listed as well as books. The overall organization is generally chronological, excepting areas outside the mainstream of Western philosophical development (e.g., Oriental, Islamic, and Jewish philosophy), variously subdivided including by types of sources. Within subsections, arrangement is alphabetical by author. Each volume has an author and a subject index.

Two characteristics make this work or parts of it somewhat forbidding. One is a heavy reliance on abbreviations. The second, applying to volumes 2–4 and to volume 1 in its first edition, is a presentation format which presents bibliographic lists set as if ordinary text in paragraph form, stringing citations (occasionally accompanied by brief annotations in italics) together much like sentences. Volume 5 inaugurated a welcome departure from this format, adopting a more user-friendly conventional list format with numbered entries, which persists through the second edition of volume 1.

DICTIONARIES, ENCYCLOPEDIAS, AND HANDBOOKS

194.   Arrington, Robert, ed. **A Companion to the Philosophers.** Malden, Mass.: Blackwell, 1999. 696p. (Blackwell Companions to Philosophy).

Includes articles describing the lives and ideas of a 193 philosophers throughout world history. They are grouped by major geographical-intellectual traditions: European and American (the largest by far with 122 entries), African (8 entries), Chinese (18), Indian (26), Japanese (11), and Islamic & Jewish (8). Contributors, numbering around 130, are mainly philosophy professors in the United States, the United Kingdom, and Canada, and include at least a few prominent names. The work aims to present material "at a level . . . appropriate for a reader who is approaching these figures for the first time," but acknowledges that, given the difficulty of much philosophy, "some of the essays will stretch the minds of many readers" (preface). Articles conclude with bibliographies, typically listing two to eight but sometimes as many as a dozen or more primary and secondary sources.

This work should not be confused with two others in the Blackwell Companions to Philosophy series, the *Blackwell Companion to Philosophy* by Bunnin and Tsui-James (entry 121) and the *Companion to World Philosophies* by Deutsch and Bontekoe (entry 218). The former provides a thematic survey of the history and branches of Western philosophy that includes biographical chapters on just two dozen or so of the most influential philosophers; the latter deals with non-Western philosophies only and has no biographical entries.

195.   Bales, Eugene F. **Ready Reference Guide to Philosophy East and West.** Lanham, Md.: University Press of America, 1988. 289p.

"Ready reference guide" can mean various things but describes in this instance an outline history of philosophy that mainly strings together brief summaries on individual philosophers and, to some extent, schools of philosophy. The summaries are comparable in length and content to the articles typically found in single-volume philosophical dictionaries, and to that extent Bales's work may serve a similar function—facilitated by two "quick alphabetical indexes" placed at the front, one to philosophers, one to philosophical theories and movement—but with the advantage that each summary is placed within a historical context. About a third of the work is devoted to Indian and Chinese philosophy, and the chapter on twentieth-century Western philosophy includes fairly unusual attention to Russian philosophy. Aimed at undergraduate students and the general reader, the work is competently done, though it lacks the authoritative touch of most compact histories or dictionaries published by more "mainstream" publishers.

196.   Biographical Dictionary of Twentieth Century Philosophers. Ed. Stuart Brown, Diané Collinson, and Robert Wilkinson. London: Routledge, 1996. 947p.

While it focuses on only a fraction of the timespan of philosophical history, this admirable volume justifies its self-description as worldwide in scope. To take its measure in this regard, one need only glance at the nationality index. True, among over a thousand names listed, American and British philosophers are generously represented (a combined total of 302), as are Continental philosophers (e.g. France, 117; Germany, 100; Italy, 57; the Netherlands, 22; Switzerland, 11). But China is represented by 51 philosophers, Russia by 50, and numerous countries by smaller contingents that are collectively very substantial and quite without parallel in other works: Japan and Mexico, for instance, by 10 philosophers each; India, 9; Egypt, 8; Czechoslovakia, 6; Brazil, 5; Cuba, 3; Iran, 3; and 1 or 2 each from, for example, Cameroon, Georgia, Ghana, Guinea, Iraq, Morocco, Pakistan, Tibet, Ukraine, Uruguay. Considered for inclusion were thinkers "regarded as philosophers in the communities and cultures to which they belong" (introduction). Additional criteria are spelled out in the introduction.

The biographical articles, while ranging in length from 250 to 1,250 words, all follow a uniform pattern, beginning with a précis of (as applicable and ascertainable) nationality, birth and death dates, birthplace, general category or categories (e.g., Analytical philosopher, Confucian-Buddhist syncretist, Idealist, Marxist philosopher of science), interests (i.e., field or fields of major contributions, such as ethics, philosophy of religion, semantics), higher education, major influences on this philosopher (often self-reported), and academic or other professional appointments. Following this are bibliographies of main publications and secondary literature, and finally a concise exposition of the philosopher's ideas, with some indication of their reception and influence where appropriate. Under an inspired indexing strategy, multiple indexes reference many of the specific elements in the aforementioned précis: nationalities, categories, fields of interest, and influences. Separate name and subject indexes cover persons and subjects specifically mentioned in the text segment of any entry.

Philosophers are the focus in this volume, but the editors commendably add a 26-page guide to schools and movements (e.g., Critical Realism, Existentialism, Frankfurt School, Postmodernism, Pragmatism, Vienna Circle), with a succinct descriptions and basic bibliographies that can help to place individuals in context and give meaning to categorizations. This is the one area, however, where non-Western philosophy is slighted.

197.   Brown, Stuart, Diané Collinson, and Robert Wilkinson. One Hundred Twentieth-Century Philosophers. London: Routledge, 1998. 241p.

Selects from the *Biographical Dictionary of Twentieth Century Philosophers* (see entry 196) 100 figures who, as a cover blurb states, are deemed "most significant"— presumably by the editors, though this is not specified and selection criteria are not otherwise explained. Half a dozen of the selected subjects are non-Western. Articles are reproduced in full from the parent work, with all component elements intact. The guide to schools and movements is also included in full at the end of the volume. There are no indexes.

198.   Burr, John R., ed. **Handbook of World Philosophy: Contemporary Developments since 1945**. Westport, Conn.: Greenwood Press, 1980. 643p.

Twenty-eight essays survey philosophical thought and activity, from 1945 to roughly 1977, in individual countries or in some cases larger geographical/cultural regions (Africa, Islamic countries, Latin America). Each is written by a specialist, generally a so-called insider, but in a few instances not (e.g., those on France and the Soviet Union). A selective but substantial bibliography is provided with each article. Two appendices, a directory of philosophical associations by region and country and a list of more-or-less regular congresses and meetings, have lost much of their value with time, and of course the work as a whole does not reflect activity since 1977.

The chief fault of Burr's *Handbook* is unevenness of coverage. Compare, for example, the 65 pages on France (twice as much as *any* other country), or Australia's 26, with 9- and 15-page articles on Italy and Britain, respectively. Nonetheless, this *Handbook* performs a useful service not fully matched by any other reference work. Its bibliographies only are supplemented by Burr's 1993 *World Philosophy* (entry 13).

199.   Dehsen, Christian von, ed. **Philosophers and Religious Leaders.** Phoenix, Ariz.: Oryx Press, 1999. 256p. (Lives and Legacies: An Encyclopedia of People Who Changed the World).

This is one of a series of four reference volumes on influential figures throughout world history written at a level that appears appropriate for general readers and for high school and lower-level undergraduate students. Philosophers share billing here with religious leaders—in not a few cases the two categories converge—and account for somewhat over a third of the 200 individuals profiled. The label "philosopher" is not construed narrowly: while there are approximately 60 figures who might show up in any comprehensive history or reference work of philosophy, at least another dozen classed as philosophers here (they're not religious leaders, in any case) are actually more strongly identified with other domains of thought or endeavor, for example, Herodotus, Thomas Jefferson, Booker T. Washington, Émile Durkheim, J. M. Keynes, Jean Piaget. Each subject, in egalitarian fashion, is accorded one full page which includes a sketch of "Life and Work," a synopsis of historical impact titled "Legacy," a timeline placing him or her in historical context, and a brief bibliography. Often there is a small portrait as well. Appendices provide a chronology of key events in philosophy plus geographical, chronological, and alphabetical listings of biographees. There are also a general bibliography and general index.

200.   **Dictionary of the History of Ideas.** Philip P. Wiener, editor-in-chief. Electronic Text Center, University of Virginia. http://etext.lib.virginia.edu/DicHist/dict.html (accessed November 6, 2005).

The full text of the 1973–74 *Dictionary of the History of Ideas* (entry 201), digitized under a grant from the director and editors of the *Journal of the History of Ideas,* is made available at this Web site in part to facilitate consultation by users of the 2004 *New Dictionary of the History of Ideas* (entry 207), which acknowledges the continuing relevance of its predecessor and cites this online version in its preface. As in the print version, articles can be accessed alphabetically by their entry titles or via an analytical subject classi-fication. In addition, the site supports keyword or phrase searching of the full text including a variety of combined-search and limiting options, with results sorted by article according to the number of matches. For copyright reasons, the modest number of illustrations in the print set are not included in this online version.

201.   Dictionary of the History of Ideas: Studies of Selected Pivotal Ideas. Philip P. Wiener, editor-in-chief. New York: Scribner's, 1973–74. 4 vols. plus Index vol.

This outstanding reference work stands squarely within the "history of ideas" tradition associated with Arthur O. Lovejoy *(The Great Chain of Being)* and with the *Journal of the History of Ideas,* edited for many years by Wiener. As such, it is cer-tainly not confined to philosophical subject matter, but is multi- and interdisciplinary in content and orientation. Nonetheless, philosophical ideas proper are prominent among the topics it covers; it has, for example, articles titled "Antinomy of Pure Reason," "Design Argument," "Free Will and Determinism," "Necessity," "Perennial Philoso-phy," "Relativism in Ethics," and "Utilitarianism." Other articles deal with topics which at least straddle the boundaries of philosophy; examples include "Alienation in Hegel and Marx," "Causation," "Determinism in History," "Equality," "God," "Progress," and "Taste in the History of Aesthetics from the Renaissance to 1770." Even when the sub-ject is not primarily or explicitly philosophical, there are apt to be philosophical aspects, implications, and connections. This is true, for instance, for articles titled "Behavior-ism," "Game Theory," "Relativity," "Sense of the Tragic," and "Utility and Value in Economic Thought."

Collectively, the foregoing examples should suggest the rich variety represented in this unique resource. A very helpful "Analytical Table of Contents" at the front of volume 1 lists the individual articles under seven broad headings, such as "the history of ideas about the external order of nature studied by the physical and biological sciences," "the historical development of economic, legal, and political ideas and institutions, ide-ologies, and movements," and "the history of religious and philosophical ideas." The editor's preface also identifies three broad types of studies offered by this "dictionary" (a misleading title in view of the typical length of such studies and the absence of any brief entries): "cross-cultural studies limited to a given century or period, studies that trace an idea from antiquity to later periods, and studies that explicate the meaning of a pervasive idea and its development in the minds of its leading proponents." What it does *not* offer, it should be noted, is articles on the ideas of individual thinkers such as Plato or Kant. However, their contributions or those of others to specific topics can be traced via a very thorough index.

Emphasis in this work falls overwhelmingly on the history of Western thought. It does, however, have a few entries representing non-Western thought (e.g., Buddhism) as well scattered references throughout to non-Western ideas (e.g., the articles on cycles and on death and immortality).

A galaxy of distinguished contributors from many fields, ranging from art history to physics and from economics to literary criticism, includes stellar authorities on the his-tory of philosophical ideas such as Monroe Beardsley, Isaiah Berlin, George Boas, Sidney Hook, John Passmore, and Richard Popkin. All articles are signed.

This work is supplemented and updated by the *New Dictionary of the History of Ideas,* released in early 2005; see entry 207.

202.   Huisman, Denis, ed. **Dictionnaire des philosophes.** Paris: Presses Universita-ires de France, 1984. 2 vols.

Huisman's biographical dictionary, totaling 2,725 pages over its two volumes, is especially comprehensive for French philosophers, including a host of lesser-known figures, historical as well as contemporary. However, it covers all major and many minor non-French philosophers as well, including many non-Western figures. Entries range in length from just a few lines (e.g., two for English theologian Edwin Abbott, 1838–1926) to several pages (nine for Montaigne, seven for Descartes, six for Derrida).

203.   Kersey, Ethel M., with Calvin O. Schrag, consulting ed. **Women Philosophers: A Bio-Critical Source Book.** Westport, Conn.: Greenwood Press, 1989. 230p.

Presents an alphabetical procession of about 150 women philosophers from ancient times to the twentieth century, excluding, with a few exceptions, philosophers born after 1920. The geographic scope is worldwide in principle, but in fact includes just one non-Western figure, the Chinese Confuscianist Pan Chao. Kersey concentrates on women who wrote or taught in traditional philosophical fields such as metaphysics, ethics, logic, aesthetics, and so forth, leaving aside writers on "the philosophy of woman" such as Mary Wollstonecraft unless they also wrote on other philosophical topics, on the grounds that the majority of these have been adequately treated elsewhere (preface). About some of her sub-jects precious little is known: her first entry, for instance, on Abrotelia (a fifth century B.C. Pythagorean philosopher), comprises just four lines of the most basic of biographical facts. At the other end of the spectrum are well-known recent figures such as Hannah Arendt, Simone de Beauvoir, Susanne Langer, Ayn Rand, and Simone Weil. Probably the work's greatest value is its coverage of intermediate figures whose substantial contributions are known but who do not generally show up in other standard reference works: for example, the Neo-Platonist Hypatia, the late Medieval Christine de Pisan, seventeenth-century English philosopher Anne Conway, Italian Enlightenment mathematician/philosopher Maria Agnesi, Russian Marxist Liubo Akselrod, and such recent Anglo-American philosophers as Elizabeth Anscombe, Marjorie Grene, and Ruth Barcan Marcus. Accompanying each article is a bibliography of "works by" (if applicable) and "works about." An introduction surveys the history of women's participation in the philosophical enterprise and highlights some of the principal figures.

204.   Kiernan, Thomas P. **Who's Who in the History of Philosophy.** New York: Phil-osophical Library, 1965; Vision Press, 1966. 185p.

Aiming to serve as a "quick, concise and easily accessible source of reference," this volume goes somewhat beyond the typical "Who's Who" format to present, along with dates and important events in the philosopher's life, "a concise exposition or representa-tion of the principal points" in his or her philosophy (preface). The user may take as fair warning Kiernan's acknowledgment of the difficulty and near-presumptuousness of this aim. Included are the predictable major and secondary figures in the history of philosophy, but also some who are more obscure and not often represented in the standard philosophi-cal dictionaries and encyclopedias. Examples include Mary Whiton Calkins (American Idealist), Callicles (known through Plato's *Gorgias*), and Ptah-Hotep (Egyptian, "often considered the first philosopher in history"). The typical entry is 5 to 20 lines in length, but major figures such as Aristotle and Kant may be allotted 2 pages or more.

205.   King, Peter J. **One Hundred Philosophers: The Life and Work of the World's Greatest Thinkers.** Hauppauge, N.Y.: Barron's Educational Series, 2004. Hove, U.K.: Apple, 2004. 192p.

This exceptionally attractive volume features numerous illustrations, many in full color, along with graphics, sidebars, and other design elements calculated to appeal to beginning students and general readers. There is even color coding of the work's five chronological divisions, ancient through the twentieth century. The selection of 100 philosophers, each treated in either a single page or a 2-page spread, includes 6 women philosophers and 22 non-Western thinkers, some of the latter fit a bit awkwardly into the essentially Western periodization. Some inclusions and exclusions, particularly of recent and contemporary figures, may be viewed as debatable (e.g., why David Wiggins but not Richard Rorty?). Each article includes a basic biography, if known, and summaries of major ideas and writings. Sidebars and insets offer key quotations, lists of major works, and sometimes contextual information. Interspersed among the entries for individuals are 11 single-page "overview" articles on topics such as Chinese, Indian, and African philosophy, women in philosophy, human nature, common sense, philosophy of science, and moral philosophy. There are also a general introduction and introductions for each historical period. Back matter includes a list of suggested readings and a basic glossary, each two pages, plus an index.

206.   Kunzmann, Peter, Franz-Peter Burkard, and Franz Wiedmann. **dtv-Atlas zur Philosophie: Tafeln und Texte.** 9th ed. Munich: Deutscher Taschenbuch Verlag, 2001. 264p.

This unique German reference work surveys the history of philosophy by pairing text on odd-numbered pages with a multitude of colorful charts *(Tafeln)* on even-numbered pages. It covers chiefly Western philosophy, in chronological fashion, but actually begins with a chapter on Eastern thought. The text tends to present material in relatively discrete segments that succinctly characterize significant thinkers, concepts, theories, and so forth. Bold type identifies key terms that are also illustrated in the accompanying charts. The latter, ranging stylistically from austerely abstract to (more often) cartoon-like, undertake to represent graphically such highly diverse matters as the relativity of knowledge in Taoism, Empedocles's theory of the elements, the key ideas about human nature and knowledge in Pascal's *Pensées,* the stages of history according to Marx's historical materialism, or the "totemic operator" of Claude Lévi-Strauss. Not all of these efforts can be judged successful, and some must be judged simplistic, but most do communicate difficult ideas in fresh, often entertaining ways, and frequently with a conciseness or a clarity difficult to achieve with text, or with text alone.

This work was first published in 1991. Succeeding editions are essentially reprintings. Translations have been published in French, Spanish, Italian, Slovenian, and Hungarian.

207.   **New Dictionary of the History of Ideas.** Maryanne Cline Horowitz, ed. New York: Charles Scribner's Sons, 2005. 6 vols.

Important to note is that this work does not entirely supplant but rather supplements and updates its illustrious parent, the *Dictionary of the History of Ideas* (entry 201). A substantial number of the *DHI*'s entries are not repeated in the *NDHI,* for instance appearance and reality, Baconianism, and certainty. In other cases articles assume and build on those in the parent set. For example, several lengthy *DHI* articles on the Western concept of law are supplemented in the *NDHI* with a short article that picks up with developments since the 1970s. In yet other instances, treatment of a topic in the *DHI* has been greatly contracted in the *NDHI* even if it is updated with late twentieth-century developments (e.g., the articles on beauty, happiness, and utilitarianism) or broadened to take in non-Western thought (e.g., property, time, utopia).

Not to be minimized, however, are the wealth of completely new topics in the *NDHI*—topics as diverse as Afrocentricity, critical race theory, dystopia, essentialism, leadership, postmodernism, pre-Columbian civilization, privacy, pseudoscience, queer theory, Shinto, virtue ethics—and the significant expansion of scope from the *DHI,* particularly in three respects. First, the *DHI*'s overwhelmingly Eurocentric emphasis is replaced by a strong accent on the global history of ideas, even if this is far from being accorded to every topic where it might be pertinent. Secondly, whereas the *DHI* focused on history of texts, the *NDHI* broadens its reach to encompass the history of ideas as represented or evidenced in oral traditions, in cultural artifacts ("visual ideas"), and in social, political, and religious practices ("experiential ideas"). Thirdly, attention to the historical-geographical contexts and cultural environments of ideas is greatly increased, including clusters of articles on the means of communicating ideas and the role of diverse forms of education. All of these expansions of scope conspire to make philosophy *per se* even less predominant than it was in the *DHI.* Nonetheless, philosophy maintains a vigorous and pervasive presence, and the *NDHI* complements its ancestor as an invaluable resource for the history of philosophy, especially its intersections with other domains of thought and its wider intellectual and cultural backgrounds.

The *NDHI*'s alphabetical organization affords quick access to many readily identifiable terms and concepts from abolitionism to Zionism. Prominently featured, however, is an 80-page Reader's Guide—repeated in full at the front of each volume—that not only aids in locating less obvious entries such as "philosophies: feminist, twentieth century," but facilitates period or area studies through chronologically and geographically organized lists of entries, as well as studies oriented toward a specific discipline (philosophy, fine arts, ethnic studies, etc.) or toward making interdisciplinary connections. The disciplinary grouping for philosophy includes over 300 entries. There is also a comprehensive index in volume 6.

208.   Ritter, Joachim, and Karlfried Gründer, eds. **Historisches Wörterbuch der Philosophie.**

See entry 172.

209.   Thomas, Henry. **Biographical Encyclopedia of Philosophy.** Garden City, N.Y.: Doubleday, 1965. 273p.

"In this book," states Thomas in his introduction, "I have presented the lives and the thoughts of the outstanding philosophers—some four hundred in all—who have offered the healing of wisdom in the epidemic of man's inhumanity to man." The orientation suggested by those words definitely governed the selection of thinkers included in this encyclopedia. Philosophers known primarily as logicians, or for highly technical contributions, tend to be omitted (e.g., Ayer, Carnap, Frege, Mach, Ryle) or deemphasized (Wittgenstein gets 12 lines). Many borderline figures, on the other hand, are included: Einstein, Havelock Ellis, George Fox, Anatole France, Goethe, Gregory I, Oliver Wendell Holmes, Johan Huizinga, Jeremiah, Walt Whitman, and John Wycliff, among others. Eastern thinkers come in for attention as well as Western. Thomas is fond of biographical details, colorful descriptions, and anecdotes, especially to reveal a thinker's human side (see, e.g., the articles on Abelard, Dewey, Gregory I, or Locke). As might be expected, the expositions of an individual's ideas are at a popular level.

210. Ziegenfuss, Werner. **Philosophen-Lexikon: Handwörterbuch der Philosophie nach Personen.** Berlin: Walter DeGruyter, 1949. 2 vols.

Ziegenfuss's work may best be labeled bio-bibliographical; even very short entries on minor figures include bibliographies of their principal works *("Schriften")* and selected secondary sources *("Literatur")*. Short entries, in fact, predominate; they often include just one to three lines of the most basic biographical data and a brief indication of the individual's significance. Longer articles on more important figures provide greater depth and detail: Hume gets 5 pages, Plato 10, Kant 34. German thinkers get more entries and relatively more space than others. Some have critiqued the inclusion of, or the amount of space devoted to, individuals whose significance was more political than intrinsic (the five pages on race-theorist Houston Stewart Chamberlain being perhaps the most egregious example). This is interesting in light of the work's history, to which Ziegenfuss alludes in his *Vorwort.* A substantial part (A through J) was already published before World War II (1936–1937), but the remainder was suppressed for political reasons. The work was finally published as a whole after the war, largely in its original form: the biographical material received only minor updating, while bibliographies were brought up to 1945 for German publications, 1939 for non-German.

This *Philosophen-Lexikon* was planned to supplant an earlier one by Rudolf Eisler (Berlin: Mittler, 1912). It covers all periods and countries, but deliberately emphasizes philosophy since Hegel, and especially that of the twentieth century.

OTHER REFERENCE SOURCES

211. Magill, Frank N., ed., with Ian P. McGreal, assoc. ed. **Masterpieces of World Philosophy in Summary Form.** New York: Harper, 1961. 1166p. New York: Salem Press, 1961. 2 vols.

Two hundred philosophical classics are summarized in the manner of the *Masterplots* series and many similar works with which Magill's name is associated. There are 20 collaborators listed for this project, among them several prominent and well-respected scholars (e.g., Richard Popkin, Roy Wood Sellars, Frederick Sontag). The selection of works covered, if not beyond debate, is judicious, and the summaries are generally well-done. Arrangement is chronological, from the fragments of Anaximander (sixth century B.C.) to Wittgenstein's *Philosophical Investigations* (1953). Eastern philosophers (e.g., Confucius, Chuang Chou, Han Fei, Suzuki) are represented as well as Western philosophers. An alphabetical list of titles is at the front, author index at the back. A glossary of philosophical terms (pages xix–xxxii) can be helpful, though definitions are brief.

Successors to this work, some much expanded, include entries 212, 213, and 214; but where those are not available, this early version can still serve a useful purpose.

212. Magill, Frank N., with Ian P. McGreal, assoc. ed. **World Philosophy: Essay-Reviews of 225 Major Works.** Englewood Cliffs, N.J.: Salem Press, 1982. 5 vols.

This work incorporates all of the material in *Masterpieces of World Philosophy in Summary Form* (see entry 211). The older material is augmented, however, by new material of three kinds:

1. Twenty-five additional summaries of works not covered in the earlier volume. Some are older works previously excluded (e.g., Hegel's *Phenomenology of*

Spirit, the *I Ching),* others are more recent works of exceptional importance (Quine's *Word and Object,* Rawls's *Theory of Justice).*

2. Summary-reviews of at least two secondary studies (labeled "Pertinent Literature") relating to each of the primary texts summarized. For Plato's *Republic,* for instance, there are summaries, each nearly two pages in length, of a book and an article dealing with important aspects of the *Republic.*

3. Short bibliographies of additional recommended readings. In the case of Plato's *Republic,* for example, four additional secondary works are recommended.

The strictly chronological arrangement employed in this set, as in its predecessor, results in a somewhat awkward juxtaposition of Western and non-Western works. The placement of Confucius between Anaximander and Heraclitus may be chronologically sound, but has little meaning in view of the absolute geographical and cultural gap separating the Chinese philosopher from his Greek contemporaries.

The five volumes cover the following periods: (1) sixth to third centuries B.C.; (2) third century B.C. to A.D. 1713; (3) 1726–1896; (4) 1896–1932; (5) 1932–1971.

A successor work, *World Philosophers and Their Works* (entry 214), partly updates and expands this set, but does not entirely supplant it, as it does not include the summary-reviews of secondary literature.

213.   Magill, Frank N., ed.; selection by John K. Roth. **Masterpieces of World Philosophy.** New York: HarperCollins, 1990. 684p.

Apart from an introduction provided by Roth, this work (labeled "first edition") contains no new content but comprises a selection from the 1982 *World Philosophy: Essay-Reviews of 225 Major Works* (entry 212). It reprints material on just 82 of the 225 philosophical classics included in the larger set—evidently those considered most important or worthwhile by Roth, who does not explain his choices. The majority of its summaries were drawn originally from Magill's 1961 *Masterpieces of World Philosophy in Summary Form* (entry 211). To these are added the following from the 1982 set: (a) summaries for several works that were not in the 1961 version, and (b) for each work included, the summary-reviews of two or more significant secondary studies, together with the brief lists of additional recommended readings. Authorship of the summaries is no longer identified. Arrangement is chronological, and title and author indexes are provided.

214.   Roth, John K., et. al., eds. **World Philosophers and Their Works.** Pasadena, Cal.: Salem Press, 2000. 3 vols.

Extending the tradition of Magill and Roth's *Masterpieces of World Philosophy* (entry 213) and its several ancestors (entries 211 and 212), this work offers summary-reviews of 285 major philosophical texts, including many unquestionable classics as well as a selection of recent important or influential works for which the designation "classic" may be (at least) premature. Like its predecessors, it is written "with the needs of students and general readers in mind" (p. ix). Its scope in terms of the number of philosophers and works covered is comparable to that of the 1982 *World Philosophy: Essay Reviews of 225 Major Works* (entry 212), but it does not replicate the latter's summary-reviews of secondary literature. In their stead are newly added overviews of each author's life, work, and influence. Coverage has been expanded to include a number of recently prominent writers and books, such as Thomas Nagel's *The View from Nowhere,* Derrida's *Of Grammatology,* and Alison Jaggar's *Feminist Politics and Human Nature,* but also to improve representation of non-Western philosophy. China and Japan are now represented by 18 thinkers and their works, India by 8, Islam by 3, Judaism by 7, and Africa by 4. A number of works profiled in the 1982 set have been dropped. For older works still included, summaries are in many cases carried forward from the 1982 set or other predecessor volumes with only nonsubstantive revisions such as updated language or some reorganization.

Arrangement of chapters is alphabetical by philosophers' names or, in the case of a few anonymous works, by title.

Supplementary material includes a chronological list of philosophers, which incorporates many figures not treated to articles in these volumes but included in a separate list of "more world philosophers" that provides their dates and the areas in which they made significant contributions; a glossary of terms and concepts; a categorized list of the works analyzed in this set (primarily by broad subject categories such as aesthetics, ethics, and so forth, but also by philosophical traditions such as African philosophy, Buddhism, etc.); and alphabetical title and subject indexes.

215. Runes, Dagobert D., comp. **Treasury of Philosophy.** New York: Philosophical Library, 1955. Reprinted as **Treasury of World Philosophy.** Paterson, N.J.: Littlefield, Adams, 1959. 1280p.

Runes's *Treasury* is a compendium of representative selections, a few paragraphs to several pages in length, from about 375 alphabetically arranged philosophers and others whose writings resonate with philosophical import. Each figure is represented by a single excerpt exposing (usually) just one aspect of his or her thought. Subject to that limitation as well as the compiler's personal predilections, the selections generally do typify their authors' thought.

Preceding each excerpt is a brief biographical sketch with comments on the individual's contributions and significance. These, too, tend to reflect personal tastes and evaluations, but can be useful for the popular audience for whom this work seems designed.

9
Non-Western Philosophy

GENERAL (WORLDWIDE OR PAN-ASIAN)

216.   Carr, Brian, and Indira Mahalingam, eds. **Companion Encyclopedia of Asian Philosophy.** London: Routledge, 1997. 1136p.

A thematically rather than alphabetically structured reference work, this can also serve as a scholarly survey text on Asian philosophy. It is organized by six major philosophical traditions: Persian, Indian, Buddhist, Chinese, Japanese, and Islamic. Some overlaps among these—Buddhism's presence in India, China and Japan, Islamic thought in India—are duly accounted for. Each section begins with a brief introduction by the editors and an essay on the tradition's origins. These are followed by anywhere from 2 to 10 essays on topics deemed most pertinent to that tradition, including for example specific schools of thought within it, subdomains of philosophical thought (typically, logic and language, knowledge and reality, morals and society), or geographical divisions such as Buddhism in Tibet. Concluding each section is an essay on the tradition's contemporary situation. Essays are contributed by 49 scholars "from the four corners of the world," as the editors aptly put it (p. xix). They include a number of prominent names in the study of Asian thought, for example, Charles Wei-Shun Fu, Karl Potter, Ninian Smart, and Li Xi.

Supplementing the essays are glossaries of selected key terms—a separate one for each tradition—gathered at the back of the volume (pp. 1043–84). There is a detailed index.

217.   Collinson, Diané, Kathryn Plant, and Robert Wilkinson. **Fifty Eastern Thinkers.** London: Routledge, 2000. 425p.

Though it includes short overviews of the major Eastern philosophical traditions and a 10-page glossary of terms, this introductory-level work is strongly focused, as its title implies, on individual thinkers. These are presented not alphabetically but grouped in mainly geographical categories, with two exceptions: Zoroaster (in a category by himself) and Islamic thinkers (a category defined more by religious-philosophical commonality than by geography). The geographical divisions are India, Tibet, China, Korea, and Japan. Within each section, individuals are presented in chronological sequence, resulting sometimes in a mingling of different philosophical traditions. Collectively, the 50 thinkers, all men, span a period of more than three millennia, from Zoroaster (sometime before 1000 B.C.) and the Buddha (sixth century B.C.) through Mao Zedong (d. 1976) and Japanese philosopher Nishitani (d. 1991). No living persons are included. Mao represents the only figure who stands essentially outside (though no doubt influenced by) the major Eastern traditions; others, however, among the more recent figures developed their philosophies with at least an eye on Western thought (e.g., Vivekananda, Gandhi, Radhakrishnan, and D. T. Suzuki).

Each essay begins with a short statement summarizing its subject's thought, then proceeds to biographical matters and finally concise expositions of some of his central ideas—often relating these to the thought of other philosophers, not only Eastern but sometimes also Western. Notes and brief primary and secondary bibliographies follow each essay.

This is an expansion of *Thirty-Five Oriental Philosophers* by Collinson and Wilkinson (London: Routledge, 1994, 216p.). Besides adding 15 new figures, including 8 Chinese and 2 Korean (a new category), it incorporates some updating of bibliographies, expansion of the glossary, and a switch in the primary romanization system for Chinese names and terms, from Wade-Giles to *Pinyin*.

218. Deutsch, Eliot and Ronald Bontekoe, eds. **A Companion to World Philosophies.** Malden, Mass.: Blackwell, 1997. 587p. (Blackwell Companions to Philosophy).

Like a number of other Blackwell Companions to Philosophy, this adopts a thematic approach to its domain, but with an unusual twist. Its organizational scheme incorporates seven major non-Western traditions: Chinese, Japanese, Indian, Polynesian, African, Buddhist, and Islamic. But rather than using these for its primary divisions it applies them repeatedly, though with some variation, to structure its three principal sections, titled "Historical Background" (Part 1), "Philosophical Topics" (Part 2), and "The Contemporary Situation" (Part 3). Japanese philosophy, somewhat surprisingly, does not show up as a distinct category until part 3, where the discussion of its contemporary situation focuses on three Japanese thinkers of the last quarter of the twentieth century. The middle section on philosophical topics is the most substantial, comprising nearly two-thirds of the volume, but does not include chapters on topics within the Polynesian and African traditions. For Chinese, Indian, Buddhist, and Islamic traditions, it offers a variable number of essays on selected topics pertinent for that tradition. These do not follow a uniform scheme, but recurrent themes include ideas of the good, reality and divinity, humankind and nature, sociopolitical thought, rationality, causality, and aesthetics. Signed articles are contributed by 42 scholars, the majority affiliated with American universities but some with Asian and European institutions.

A pronunciation guide for romanized Sanskrit, Pali, Chinese, and Arabic terms is at the front. There is an index for names and subjects, the latter only moderately detailed.

219. Leaman, Oliver, ed. **Encyclopedia of Asian Philosophy.** London: Routledge, 2001. 669p.

Inspiration for this volume came in part, editor Leaman explains, from his work as a contributor to Carr and Mahalingam's *Companion Encyclopedia of Asian Philosophy* (entry 216), just four years older. His encyclopedia differs from the latter in that it uses an alphabetical arrangement of entries, offers a combination of short and long articles (a total of around 650 entries), and is the work of a smaller number of contributing authors (14). It is also pitched at a more introductory level. Entries include a standard mix of names and concepts or terms, the latter predominantly English-language terms except in the case of Indian philosophy where entries for Sanskrit terms are common. There are also geographical-cultural survey articles (e.g., Australian, Chinese, Islamic, Korean, Melanesian, etc., philosophies) and entries for broad philosophical topics or branches, such as aesthetics, causality, free will, logic, time and being, and so forth, though these are typically specified to a particular tradition (e.g., "ethics in Islamic philosophy," "fatalism in Indian philosophy") or divided into separate entries for several traditions. A "Thematic Entry List" at the front categorizes entries under nine rubrics: Australasia, China, India, Islam, Japan, Korea, Melanesia, Tibet, and Zoroastrianism.

An explanation of policies for transliteration of terms in Asian languages (pp. x–xi) indicates they aim to assist the average English-speaking reader with approximate pronunciation and do not necessarily adhere to scholarly conventions, including any use of diacritics. Other front matter includes a general bibliography and a reference chart of Chinese dynasties. Separate name and subject indexes are at the back.

220.   Leaman, Oliver. **Key Concepts in Eastern Philosophy.** London: Routledge, 1999. 319p. (Key Concepts Series).

More concise than Leaman's *Encyclopedia of Asian Philosophy* (entry 219), this dictionary is also quite distinct from it, though it may have laid the groundwork for the later and larger work. True to its title, it focuses specifically on concepts, to the exclusion, notably, of biographical entries. Yet its compass is not quite as narrow as this might suggest: it does offer some survey articles, for instance on Japanese, Korean, and Tibetan philosophy and on broad topics such as education, ethics, logic, and mind. Entries for concepts in the narrower sense comprise a mix of original-language and English-language concepts. Eastern philosophy for purposes of this work embraces Islamic and Zoroastrian philosophies as well as those of East and South Asia. Acknowledging the problem of differentiating between philosophy and religion in this domain, Leaman allows that he has "included some material that is far more relevant to religion than to philosophy" (introduction). Most articles conclude with several suggestions for further reading, keyed to a general list of references at the back of the volume. There is a detailed index.

221.   McGreal, Ian P., ed. **Great Thinkers of the Eastern World: The Major Thinkers and the Philosophical and Religious Classics of China, India, Japan, Korea, and the World of Islam.** New York: HarperCollins, 1995. 505p.

Complementing McGreal's *Great Thinkers of the Western World* (entry 272) and following its general format, this volume presents 109 essays summarizing the ideas of outstanding philosophical and religious thinkers of China, India, Japan, Korea, and the world of Islam. In a few cases, these thinkers are anonymous, as essays treat the central themes of highly influential classic works of unknown authorship such as the *Bhagavad Gita* and the *Yi Jing (I Ching)*. Such famous representatives of Eastern thought as Confucius, Buddha, Gandhi, and Mao are present, of course, but the volume also covers most "second tier" figures familiar to students of the various traditions, for example Mencius, Sun-Yat-sen, Fung Yu-lan, Gaudapada, Tagore, Fujiwara, al-Kindī, and Avicenna. McGreal explains in a preface that "to represent the various lines of thought and faith exhibited in the countries concerned, we have included some thinkers who are little known to the general public," and allows that, inevitably, "some philosophers regarded by some scholars and critics as being of more importance that those included have been left out," whether deliberately or inadvertently. The one really inexplicable omission, however, seems to be Muhammad. Thinkers are grouped by country or, in the exceptional case, by religious tradition under the heading "Islamic World"; within each group, they are presented chronologically. Designed for general readers, this volume, like its companion, may invite charges of over-simplification; its roster of contributing scholars, however, shows evidence of solid credentials in Asian and Islamic studies.

222.   Nauman, St. Elmo, Jr. **Dictionary of Asian Philosophies.** New York: Philosophical Library, 1978. 372p.

The "Asian Philosophies" of the title refers to Middle Eastern as well as Far Eastern philosophies. Entries in this dictionary include major thinkers, schools of thought, philosophical texts, terms, and concepts. It also offers some survey articles, for example, on Indian philosophy and Jewish philosophy—but not, curiously, Islamic philosophy. The latter omission represents but one of several disparities in Nauman's work. Another instance is the absence of Fung Yu-lan from the survey article on Chinese philosophy, despite the fact that he gets a 4-page article of his own which describes him as "one of the most important philosophers in contemporary China." Add to these faults an occasional omission of basic information (the article on the Hare Krishna movement neglects to identify it as a form of Hinduism) and the lack of an index to locate topics covered under other headings (e.g., Krishna under Bhagavad-Gita). In sum, the usefulness of this work is less than might have been, and has diminished steadily as alternative coverage of Asian philosophy has improved (cf. esp. entries 216, 219, and 238).

223. Reyna, Ruth. **Dictionary of Oriental Philosophy.** New Delhi: Munshiram Manoharlal, 1984. 419p.

The work of an American Indologist who herself became an adherent of and spokesperson for Indian philosophy and spirituality, Reyna's dictionary is most nearly similar to the *Encyclopedia of Eastern Philosophy and Religion* (entry 238), which it precedes by several years. Due presumably to its publication in India, it is far less common in American libraries. Short definitions predominate, the majority for terms in the original languages of the traditions covered. There are more entries for English-language terms than in the aforementioned *Encyclopedia,* however, and also a larger number of somewhat longer articles (a short paragraph to a page) on broader topics such as dance in India, the Yoga school, or philosophy of polity in China. The work is divided into two volumes within one physical volume with continuous page numbering, and each volume in turn divides into two parts: volume 1, India and the Middle East; volume 2, China and Japan. India takes up 220 of the work's 419 pages. There are some illustrations.

EASTERN AND SOUTHERN ASIA

BIBLIOGRAPHIES

224. **A Bibliography of Indian Philosophy.** Madras: Published by the C. P. Ramaswani Aiyar Research Endowment Committee, 1963/68. 2 vols.

See entry 95.

225. Centre of Advanced Study in Sanskrit, University of Poona. **CASS Bibliography Series. Class H.** V. N. Jha, general ed. 1993–.

These bibliographies on various schools and branches of Indian philosophy are claimed to be "comprehensive" though well short of exhaustive, concentrating as they do on resources available in the issuing institution's home city of Pune [Poona], described as "very rich in oriental libraries" (General Editor's Note, front of each issue). Each issue lists original Sanskrit texts, secondary studies, and reviews in a single alphabetical sequence by author's, editor's, or translator's name. There are indexes by titles and topics, as well as author indexes for the authors of original Sanskrit texts and commentaries. Extant issues are listed below. Additional issues were projected, but it is not clear (as of late 2005) whether any are forthcoming.

1. Kashinath Hota and Arun Ranjan Mishra. **Bibliography of Nyāya-Vaiśesika.** 1993. 104p.

2. Subhas Chandra Dash. **Bibliography of Pali and Buddhism.** 1994. 141p.

3. Nirmala G. Kamat. **Bibliography of Aupādhika Bhedābheda.** 1994. 9p.

4. Nirmala G. Kamat. **Bibliography of Svabhavika Bhedābheda.** 1994. 20, 30p.

5. Nirmala G. Kamat. **Bibliography of Acintya Bhedābheda.** 1995. 51p.

6. Anuradha M. Pujari. **Bibliography of Sāmkya.** 1994. 65p.

7. Kashinath Hota. **Bibliography of Technical Science.** 1995. 75p.

8. Manik Thakar. **Bibliography of Yoga .** 1995. 81p.

9. B. A. Pataskar. **Bibliography of Vyākarana.** 1997. 46p.

10. Kanchan V. Mande. **Bibliography of Viśistādvaita.** 1997. 75p.

11. Shailaja Bapat. **Bibliography of Advaita Vedanta.** 1999. 180p.

12. Shailaja Bapat. **Bibliography of Śudhādvaita Vedānta.** 2000. n.a.

226. Chan, Wing-tsit. **Chinese Philosophy, 1949–1963: An Annotated Bibliography of Mainland China Publications.** Honolulu: East-West Center Press, 1967. 290p.

See entry 92.

227. Chan, Wing-tsit. **An Outline and Annotated Bibliography of Chinese Philosophy.** Rev. ed. New Haven: Yale Far Eastern Publications, 1969. 220p. (Sinological Series, no. 4).

Largely superseded by Fu and Chan's *Guide to Chinese Philosophy* (entry 228), which adapts some of its material and is aimed at a similar, nonspecialist audience, this work remains of value where the later work is not available, and occasionally for differences in the organization of topics and materials. The arrangement by schools and periods in roughly chronological sequence is supplemented with a subject index.

228. Fu, Charles Wei-hsun, and Wing-tsit Chan. **Guide to Chinese Philosophy.** Boston: G. K. Hall, 1978. 262p. (Asian Philosophies and Religions Resource Guides).

Fu and Chan list and annotate predominantly English-language works for nonspecialists who do not have access to primary texts in the original languages. Their first and longest section, "History of Chinese Philosophy," moves from general overviews to specific schools, movements, and periods in approximate chronological sequence, from pre-Confucian and traditional elements through Chinese Marxism. Sections 2–13 cover specific topics as treated in Chinese philosophies: human nature, ethics, philosophy of religion, epistemology, logic, social and political philosophy, and so forth. Concluding sections deal with materials on presuppositions and methods (14), comparisons of various philosophies (15), and authoritative texts and their philosophical significance (16).

229. Hacker, Edward, Steve Moore, and Lorraine Patsco. **I Ching: An Annotated Bibliography.** New York: Routledge, 2002. 336p.

This bibliography limits itself to English-language writings relating to the *I Ching (Book of Changes),* a Chinese classic whose pervasive influence in Chinese thought and culture was mediated particularly by its role in the Confucian and Neo-Confucian schools as well as in Taoism. It does not restrict itself to the *I Ching's* philosophical significance, which lies chiefly in the domains of cosmology and moral and social thought, but also takes in its concerns with, or influences upon, psychology (including its influence in the West on Jungian psychology), spirituality, divination, "alternative sciences," and magic. These latter elements account for much of the popular interest in the *I Ching,* for example in New Age and fortune-telling circles, and thus the substantial amount of popular literature covered here along with the academic. They also account for most of the bibliography's unusual Part C, which lists "I Ching devices and equipment," a category that includes audio-visual resources, software, *I Ching* cards and kits, and various devices (sticks, dice, etc.) used in fortune-telling. No attempt is made to separate out the various strands of *I Ching* interest in the literature references, which are divided simply into books and dissertations (Part A) and journal and magazine articles and book reviews (Part B) and arranged alphabetically by author within each section. However, annotations, ranging from a single line to a full page or more, often provide guidance to a work's content and to its academic or popular character where not already obvious. For the most part, the annotations are nonjudgmental.

230. Holzman, Donald, with Motoyama Yukihiko, et. al. **Japanese Religion and Philosophy: A Guide to Japanese Reference and Research Materials.** Ann Arbor, Mich.: University of Michigan Press, 1959. Reprinted, Westport, Conn.: Greenwood Press, 1975. 102p.

See entry 100.

231. Inada, Kenneth K., et. al. **Guide to Buddhist Philosophy.** Boston, Mass.: G. K. Hall, 1985. 226p. (Asian Philosophies and Religions Resource Guides).

This guide to Buddhist philosophy lists and annotates predominantly English-language sources, but includes some especially important texts in other languages. It is a sister volume to Frank E. Reynolds's *Guide to Buddhist Religion* in the same series (Boston, Mass.: G. K. Hall, 1981), but no explanation is offered as to how the line between religion and philosophy was drawn. Chapter 4 in particular may leave one to wonder about the distinction: titled "Paths to Liberation," it covers materials dealing with meditation, purification, and the Buddhist understanding of salvation. On the other hand, most chapter headings in this volume will ring familiar to Western philosophical ears: ethics, philosophy of religion, philosophy of psychology, epistemology, metaphysics and ontology, philosophy of language, logic, social and political philosophy, philosophy of history, aesthetics. An opening chapter covers surveys of the history of Buddhist philosophy, both pan-Asian and specific to the major Buddhist countries (India, China, Japan, and Tibet). Chapter 14, the longest, lists English translations of original, "authoritative" Buddhist texts, while chapter 15 covers comparisons of Buddhism with Western as well as other Asian thought.

232. Jarrell, Howard R. **International Yoga Bibliography, 1950 to 1980.** Metuchen, N.J.: Scarecrow Press, 1981. 221p.

The 1,713 items listed in this bibliography on Yoga include 1,364 books, 210 journal articles, 95 magazine articles, and no less than 44 periodicals devoted largely or in their entirety to Yoga. Hardly confined to the philosophical aspects of Yoga, this sizeable body of literature deals with all facets of its thought and practice: popular, intellectual, ethical, spiritual, psychological, physiological, and so forth. The compiler disclaims any judgment on the merit or value of works included. Because entries are listed alphabetically by author or, lacking that, by title, specific subject access is via a subject index, generally adequate except for some excessively broad categories such as Hatha Yoga and meditation. The subject index also indexes non-English books by language under entries such as "Dutch, books in," "French, books in," and so forth.

233. Potter, Karl H., et. al. **Encyclopedia of Indian Philosophies.** Vol. 1, **Bibliography.** 3rd rev. ed. Delhi: Motilal Banarsidass, 1995. 2 vols.

See entry 97.

234. Potter, Karl H., et. al. **Encyclopedia of Indian Philosophies: Bibliography.** http://faculty.washington.edu/kpotter

See entry 98.

235. Potter, Karl H., with Austin B. Creel and Edwin Gerow. **Guide to Indian Philosophy.** Boston: G. K. Hall, 1988. 159p. (Asian Philosophies and Religions Resource Guides).

This selective bibliography of English-language *secondary* sources cites 884 books and articles published mainly up to 1985, with a few later items. All are listed in a single alphabetical sequence by author. This places the burden for subject access entirely on two indexes, one for "names"—referring not just to personal names but the names or titles of works treated as subjects—and another for subject terms, including Sanskrit as well as English-language terms. The subject index, while reasonably well-done, is not altogether reliable. All entries in this work include annotations of one to five lines (rarely more), often refreshingly informal in keeping with the volume's aim of serving primarily the nonspecialist.

The compilers state in a preface that they have attempted to include "only works of philosophical (as opposed to religious, literary, etc.) relevance," after defining the scope of Indian philosophy as encompassing "mainly ... the subject of bondage and liberation and the methods of gaining the latter." While this may well leave the user in the dark about the supposed distinction between (especially) philosophy and religion in Indian thought, it is worth emphasizing that the bibliography embraces all the usual subdivisions of philosophy, from epistemology, metaphysics, and logic to ethics and social, political, and legal philosophy.

236. **Viśistādvaita Works, Bibliography.** Melkote, Karnakata: Academy of Sanskrit Research, 1988. 2 vols.

A specialized bibliography of printed works and manuscripts of the Viśistādvaita ("qualified non-dualism") school of Vedānta Hindu philosophy, compiled by scholars of the Academy of Sanskrit Research led by M. A. Lakshmithathachar. Materials, mostly in Sanskrit, Tamil, or their mixture, are organized into 13 subject-oriented sections. Somewhat complex details of presentation and notation are explained in the introduction to volume 1. Author and title indexes are provided separately for printed works and manuscripts.

DICTIONARIES, ENCYCLOPEDIAS, AND HANDBOOKS

237. Cua, Antonio S., ed. **Encyclopedia of Chinese Philosophy.** New York: Routledge, 2003. 1020p.

A substantial and authoritative work, produced with the participation of a 10-member Board of Editorial Consultants and 77 contributing scholars from institutions in North America, the Far East, and Europe. It features 187 in-depth articles supplemented with a separate, 48-page glossary of terms and names. Entries for the former include individual thinkers from Confucius to the twentieth-century Neo-Confucianist Mou Zongsan; schools of thought such as Buddhism, Confuciansim (divided among no less than 20 entries on its various aspects and manifestations), Daoism, and Marxism; several major texts, for example, *Guanzi* and *Huainanzi;* key Chinese-language concepts such as *De* (virtue or power) and *Xu* (emptiness); and general topics such as aesthetics, cosmology, egoism in ethics, philosophy of mind. Less predictable articles include several concerned with approaches to Chinese philosophy from the outside ("Comparative Philosophy," "Intercultural Hermeneutics," and "Translation and Its Problems"); surveys of recent trends in Chinese philosophy on the mainland, on Taiwan, and overseas; an article on Feng Youlan's works on the history of Chinese philosophy; and one on Taiwan Nationalist leader Chiang Kai-shek. All articles include bibliographies.

Arrangement of entries is alphabetical. For Chinese terms, the newer *Pinyin* system of romanization is used, with the older Wade-Giles version often shown in parentheses, for example, *"Junzi (Chün-tzu)."* There is a detailed subject and name index.

238. **Encyclopedia of Eastern Philosophy and Religion: Buddhism, Taoism, Zen, Hinduism.** Ed. Stephan Schuhmacher and Gert Woerner. Boston: Shambhala, 1989. Published in Britain as **The Rider Encyclopedia of Eastern Philosophy and Religion: Buddhism, Taoism, Zen, Hinduism.** London: Rider, 1989. 468p.

This encyclopedia (identical in its U.S. and British versions except for titles) is a translation of a German work, *Lexikon der östlichen Weisheitslehren* (Bern and Munich: Otto-Wilhelm-Barth, 1986). In effect four encyclopedic dictionaries melded into one, it incorporates, yet keeps distinct, material on the four systems of thought named in its subtitle. (Zen, though often considered a school of Buddhism, is treated separately here because of its independent development and its self-understanding as "outside the orthodox teaching" (p. xi).) A single alphabetical sequence prevails, but a highlighted letter (B, T, Z, or H) beside each entry term identifies the system to which it pertains. In cases where a term is common to several systems, it is coded for each; and if used with different meanings in each, separate explanations are provided and labeled accordingly. This approach entails that there is very little comparative treatment that cuts across the various systems; a notable exception is the article on meditation. This is also among the few entries representing a concept expressed in English. The majority of roughly 4,000 entries represent transliterated terms in the five original languages in which the four systems were primarily formulated: Sanskrit, Pali, Tibetan, Chinese and Japanese. Also heavily represented are important thinkers and major texts. Generally speaking, this work is highly useful for help with matters of detail, less so for overviews of broad topics. An 18-page bibliography at the back lists many primary and secondary sources, chiefly in English and German and occasionally French, but none in the original languages.

239. **Encyclopedia of Indian Philosophies.** Ed. Karl H. Potter. Delhi: Motilal Banarsidass, 1970–. Vols. 1–6 also published at Princeton: Princeton University Press, 1978–1992.

Potter (Professor of Philosophy Emeritus, University of Washington) serves as general editor for this ambitiously conceived reference work, which little resembles an "encyclopedia" in the ordinary sense. Apart from volume 1, the *Bibliography,* each volume covers a particular system or phase in Indian philosophy via a two-pronged approach: first, an extended analytical essay, and secondly, summaries of as many as possible of the extant philosophical texts. Notes are collected at the end of each volume, and are followed by a detailed index. In the volumes issued so far, thus presumably in future volumes as well, the summaries comprise the major share of the text. The summaries are intended "to make available the substance of the thought contained in these works" for philosophers unable to read the original languages (mainly Sanskrit) or any of the available translations, or who for other reasons "find difficulty in understanding and finding their way about" in these translations.

Individual volumes published to date are listed and described briefly in the following entries. Additional volumes in progress, as listed on the general editor's Web site in early 2004, will cover the following schools and systems: Buddhist Philosophy from A.D. 600 to 750 and from A.D. 750 to 1300, Yoga, Nyāya-Vais'esika from 150 to 1650, Advaita Vedānta from 1300 to 1600, Jain Philosophy to 1150, Kashmir Saiva Philosophy, Cārvāka, Dvaitādvaita, Visistādvaita, Pūrvamīmāmsā, Dvaita Vedānta, and Acintyabhedābheda. The entire series is projected to comprise some 25 volumes, including the *Bibliography* volume and a concluding Glossary/Index.

240. Volume 1: Karl H. Potter, ed. **Bibliography.** 3rd rev. ed. Delhi: 1995. 2 vols.

See separate listing and description, entry 97.

241. Volume 2: Karl H. Potter, ed. **Metaphysics and Epistemology: The Tradition of Nyāya-Vaiśesika up to Gangeśa.** Part 1. Delhi: 1977; Princeton: 1977. 752p.

Covers the literature of the classical system of Nyāya-Vaiśesika in its earlier stages, that is, from its inception in the *sutras* (the basic Hindu texts, ca. 400 B.C. to A.D. 600) to the time of Gangesa (about A.D. 1350). Following a "Historical Resume," an analytical essay covers topics such as the theory of value, relations, substance, universals, meanings and truth, logical theory. Works summarized include the *sutras* of Gautama, the *bhasya* of Vatsyayana, and writings of Udayana.

242. Volume 3: Karl H. Potter, ed. **Advaita Vedānta up to Śamkara and His Pupils.** Delhi: 1981; Princeton: 1981. 635p.

Deals with only one, but probably the foremost, of several Vedānta systems, based on the Vedic literature known as the *Upanishads,* "the springs of classical Hinduism." Covers only the earliest segment of the literature of this system, that is, the Advaita Vedānta, up to its most famous figure, śamkara. A "Historical Resume" is followed by surveys of major topics addressed in the Advaita Vedānta literature. Pages 115–346 are devoted to summaries of Śamkara's works, the remainder to works by Gaudapāda and others.

243. Volume 4: Gerald James Larson and Ram Shankar Bhattacharya, eds. **Sāmkhya: A Dualist Tradition in Indian Philosophy.** Delhi, 1987; Princeton, 1987. 674p.

A tradition that has been continuously influential for some 25 centuries, Sāmkhya is a Hindu philosophy that posits a dualistic universe comprising nature on the one hand and innumerable souls on the other. Its name, meaning "enumeration," refers to its method of enumerating categories of reality and experience for the purpose attaining liberation from frustration and rebirth. Larson provides an 80-page overview, while the summaries cover some 65 works, including a 16-page treatment of the fundamental *Sāmkhyakārika* that is longer than the original text. One development of Sāmkhya, Yoga, is not treated here but reserved for a separate, forthcoming volume.

244.   Volume 5: Harold G. Coward and K. Kunjunni Raja, eds. **The Philosophy of the Grammarians.** Delhi, 1990; Princeton, 1990. 609p.

Covers the work of numerous Indian thinkers, from the fifth century B.C. (Yāska and Pānini) through the 1970s, who, though diverse in their wider philosophical commitments, share a concern with *vyākarana*—literally "grammar," but more broadly the analysis and theory of language as a conveyor of meaning and, beyond that, of its relation to consciousness and its roles in mediating knowledge, illuminating reality, and effecting liberation. Coward and Raja's introductory overview includes a historical résumé and chapters on metaphysics, epistemology, word meaning, and sentence meaning. Part 2, "Survey of the Literature of Grammarian Philosophy," describes 85 authors or (in some cases) individual works, though some very briefly. Series editor Potter has added a "Bibliography on Grammar" covering both primary and secondary *vyākarana* literature.

245.   Volume 6: Karl H. Potter and Sibajiban Bhattacharyya, eds. **Indian Philosophical Analysis: Nyāya-Vaiśesika from Gangeśa to Raghunātha Śiromani.** Delhi, 1993; Princeton, 1992. 672p.

Continues where volume 2 leaves off, covering a period of two centuries (roughly 1310 to 1510) bounded by "two of India's most remarkable philosophers, Gangeśa and Raghunātha Śiromani" (preface). Situated between these 2 giants are 48 other authors whose writings, like theirs, are summarized or described in the literature survey. The major movement of this period, Navyanyāya (New Logic), introduced new techniques of philosophical analysis and is described by Potter as "comparable in its implications to the burgeoning of symbolic logic and its concomitant philosophical explanations" in late nineteenth and early twentieth century Western philosophy (preface).

246.   Volume 7. Karl H. Potter, et. al., eds. **Abhidharma Buddhism to 150 A.D.** Delhi: 1996. 636p.

Introduces and summarizes the earliest Buddhist philosophical texts, from the *Dhammasangani,* dated in part from the fourth century B.C., through the mammoth *Mahāvibhāsā,* resulting from a convention held in the first or second century A.D.

247.   Volume 8. Karl H. Potter, ed. **Buddhist Philosophy from 100 to 350 A.D.** Delhi: 1999. 827p.

Summaries in this volume cover 207 texts, beginning with the earliest *Prajnaparamita Sutras* and ending with the works of Vasubandhu and his critic Samghabhadra.

248. Volume 9. Karl H. Potter, ed. **Buddhist Philosophy from 350 to 600 A.D.** Delhi, 2003. 762p.

Covers the period that includes the writings of Buddhaghosa and Buddhadatta, Dignaga, Dharmakirti, and the commentators Bhavya, Dharmapala, and Sthiramati.

249. Feuerstein, Georg. **Shambhala Encyclopedia of Yoga.** Boston: Shambhala, 1997. 357p.

This is a revision and expansion of Feuerstein's *Encyclopedic Dictionary of Yoga* (New York: Paragon House, 1990, 430p.). It provides comprehensive coverage of the physical disciplines with which Yoga (a Hindu tradition tracing back nearly three thousand years to the *Upanishads*) is identified in the popular mind; of its spiritual disciplines and meditation techniques, for which the physical disciplines are meant to be preparation; and of the metaphysical system behind all of these. The work is directed at the student or general reader with no (or little) knowledge of Sanskrit. The typical entry represents a transliterated Sanskrit term (e.g., *bhagavat, dharma*), though there are some entries for English-language terms such as hypnosis and sexuality, and even more cross-references from English-language terms, mostly new to the revised edition. Additional entries include biographical entries and titles of Yoga textual sources. Most definitions and explanations are reasonably clear, but the average user may struggle a bit with the sometimes excessive resort to cross-referencing, especially to other Sanskrit terms. Terms or meanings peculiar to one or another of Yoga's several branches are carefully noted. There are some illustrations, notably of Yoga exercise positions and important Yoga teachers. A bibliography of reference sources and recommended readings is on pages 353–55.

250. Grimes, John. **A Concise Dictionary of Indian Philosophy: Sanskrit Terms Defined in English.** New and rev. ed. Albany, N.Y.: State University of New York Press, 1996. 366 + 24p.

Grimes's dictionary can benefit any English-speaker approaching Indian philosophy, whether through its original language or not, because almost any source on the subject makes some use of Sanskrit terms, too often with insufficient explanation for the uninitiated reader. This revised edition lists around 3,000 terms (500 more than the first edition, 1989), drawn from all major schools of Indian philosophy. Perhaps half of these are defined with simple translations (e.g., *pinda*—part of the whole, individual), but many receive more extended treatment to clarify the term's use, summarize particular doctrines related to it, or distinguish the views of different schools. For instance, the key term *moksa,* defined as liberation or release, has 15 brief paragraphs explaining the teachings of various schools on how liberation is achieved. Terms are entered according to their roman alphabet transliteration, which is followed by their equivalent in Devanagari script (a reversal of the order in the first edition). At the end of the volume are 14 useful charts showing important relationships, categories, and sourcebooks pertaining to individual schools.

251. Huang, Siu-chi. **Essentials of Neo-Confuciansim: Eight Major Philosophers of the Song and Ming Periods.** Westport, Conn.: Greenwood Press, 1999. 261p. (Resources in Asian Philosophy and Religion).

Presents major Neo-Confucian thinkers of the Song and Ming periods, from Zhou Dun-yi, 1017–1073, to Wang Yang-ming, 1472–1529. Though the work is in many ways a conventional survey text, its reference value is enhanced by a 20-page glossary of pertinent Chinese terms, phrases, and names, presented both in Chinese characters and in transliterated form using mainly the *Pinyin* system.

252. Padhi, Bibhu, and Minakshi Padhi. **Indian Philosophy and Religion: A Reader's Guide.** Jefferson, N.C.: McFarland, 1990. 413p.

This guide, a borderline reference work that may also function as an introductory text, offers thematic chapters on the sources and schools of orthodox (Hindu) Indian philosophy/religion, from the Vedas through the Vedānta, as well as on Jainism, Buddhism, and materialist schools including Cārvāka. A final chapter deals with Hindu gods and goddesses. Each chapter ends with a short bibliography of works cited and suggestions for further reading, and the book concludes with a 12-page glossary of major terms.

253. Singh, B. N. **Dictionary of Indian Philosophical Concepts.** Varanasi: Asha Prakashan, 1988. 340p.

Singh explains around 200 concepts of Indian philosophy, approached exclusively through (transliterated) Sanskrit terms. His work is similar in concept to Grimes's *Concise Dictionary of Indian Philosophy* (entry 250), except that it concentrates on a far smaller group of central terms (e.g., 43 under "A" in the alphabetical arrangement, compared with over 600 terms for Grimes) and treats these at greater length. Intended as "a compendium for getting a first-hand knowledge of classical concepts without presupposing a certain degree of grounding in the subject," it strives particularly to reflect "how a concept has acquired varying hues nestled by a particular school and ruffled by the adversary school" (preface)—in a number of cases (e.g., *ātman, īśvara, karma, moksa*) providing multiple entries representing the distinct usages of different schools. Names of some schools or movements (e.g., *Vaiśesika*) and of philosophical texts (e.g., *Upanisads*) are included, but not persons.

254. Wood, Ernest. **Vedanta Dictionary.** New York: Philosophical Library, 1964. 225p.

Like other traditional schools of Indian thought, the Vedānta—a Hindu system based on the *Vedānta Sutras* (or *Brahma Sutras*)—represents an inseparable mixture of religious and philosophical elements. However, not only is it among the most philosophical systems, but one that has continued to undergo considerable modern development, particularly in the form known as Advaita. Entries in this dictionary that have some familiarity for a Western philosophical orientation include the absolute, cause and causation, ethics and morals, materialism, space and time, and freedom of the will. There are also many Sanskrit terms—most with no direct English equivalent—and entries for major Vedānta thinkers.

Wood, an intimate but not notably scholarly student of Eastern religious thought, also produced a *Yoga Dictionary* (1956) and *Zen Dictionary* (1962), issued by the same publisher. Both of these, however, are very thin on philosophical content.

255. Wu, Yi. **Chinese Philosophical Terms.** Lanham, Md.: University Press of America, with California Institute of Integral Studies, 1986. 154p.

Wu presents a highly selective group of just 50 single-character Chinese terms from Confucian, Taoist, and Buddhist philosophy. (According to a prefatory note, he planned a later volume, which apparently has not materialized, to cover multicharacter terms.) For each term entered under its Chinese character he provides a transliteration and translation (e.g., *chen,* "true/truth"), followed by a discussion of its philosophical meaning(s) and historical development that may range from two to six pages and typically includes illustrative selections from Chinese texts where the term can be seen in context. Though the selection is small, and Wu's success in adequately conveying the meaning of a concept with the material he provides somewhat uneven, the work should be useful to students of Chinese philosophy. It is liberally cross-referenced, and indexed by transliterated term and English translation.

256. Yao, Xinzhong, ed. **RoutledgeCurzon Encyclopedia of Confucianism.** London: Routledge, 2003. 2 vols.

The Library of Congress classifies this work in the category of Religion. As editor Yao notes, however, "whether or not Confucianism is a religious tradition has been hotly debated among modern scholars" (pp. 6–7), whereas its standing as a philosophical tradition appears to be less controversial. Accordingly, it seems fitting to include this authoritative encyclopedia in a guide to philosophical reference sources. It is, in fact, an outstanding example of the growing body of substantial English-language reference works with very strong scholarly credentials on specific areas of Asian philosophy. It features over 950 articles, ranging from 200 to 5,000 words, contributed by an international group of scholars. It covers both the origins of Confucianism and its transformations and adaptations into a variety of Confucian or Neo-Confucian schools in China as well as in other East Asian countries, including so-called Modern New Confucianism. Also treated is Confucian Studies as an academic discipline. Entries include numerous terms and concepts along with schools, masters, scholars, texts, places, rituals, and institutions. Chinese terms and names are generally romanized using the *Pinyin* system except in cases where the older Wade-Giles romanization or other versions are familiar to Western readers, "Confucius" being a case in point. Romanized entry terms are followed by the corresponding Chinese characters.

MIDDLE EAST / ISLAM

257. Daiber, Hans. **Bibliography of Islamic Philosophy.** Leiden: Brill, 1999. 2 vol. (Handbuch der Orientalistik—Handbook of Oriental Studies; Erste Abteilung, Der nahe und mittlere Osten—The Near and Middle East, Band 43).

Lists 9,525 numbered items representing "as complete[ly] as possible the primary and secondary sources for the study of Islamic philosophical thought," including "all hitherto known publications in western and non-Western languages in the field of Islamic philosophy from the fifteenth century until the present, including Greek and Syriac sources of Islamic philosophy, its impact on Jewish and medieval Latin scholasticism and its repercussions in modern European and Islamic thought" (preface, v. 1). The goal of completeness is qualified by the exclusion of publications that are addressed to a popular audience, do not offer significant new perspectives, and do not refer to primary or relevant secondary sources.

Volume 1 contains an alphabetical list of sources by author or by title for anonymous works. Entries include full bibliographic data and occasional brief annotations that describe the content, identify special features, or mention related literature such as book reviews. Volume 2 contains an index of names, terms, and topics in a single alphabetical sequence. Index entries for major topics (e.g., Fārābi) are elaborately subdivided.

258.   Dictionary of Islamic Philosophical Terms. Islamic Philosophy Online, Inc. http://www.muslimphilosophy.com/pd/default.htm (accessed October 24, 2005).

An online dictionary based on M. S. Sheikh's *Dictionary of Muslim Philosophy* (entry 259) with additions, updates, and corrections. "It includes most of the terminology that was developed by Muslim philosophers in their works and the terms that they borrowed—and sometimes translated—from Greek (Hellenistic), Syriac, Persian, and Indian philosophical works. Also included are concepts that are Islamic but of a philosophical nature and were used by Muslim philosophers. The dictionary also includes the Arabized names of the philosophers and scientists of Greek, Roman, Byzantine, Persian, and Indian origin . . ." (intro.). Pure Arabic or strictly Fiqhi and Sufi terms are not included, nor are Arabic names. Entries can be accessed via an alphabetized list in English transliteration or in Arabic (the latter requires a browser with Arabic encoding). The entire dictionary can also be viewed in PDF format (158 pages). A new version of the dictionary anticipated, according to a note on the site, in Summer 2005 had not yet materialized by October 2005.

259.   Sheikh, M. Saeed. Dictionary of Muslim Philosophy. Lahore, Pakistan: Institute of Islamic Culture, 1970. 146p.

Narrower in scope than its title may suggest, this dictionary focuses on terms and references prevalent in the writings of *medieval* Muslim philosophers such as al-Ghazālī, al-Fārābi, al-Kindī, and Muhammad Bāqir Dāmād, especially in the fields of logic, metaphysics, and psychology. It bears testimony to the important debt of these philosophers to Greek and Hellenistic philosophy and their vital role in transmitting that heritage to the West. A substantial proportion of entries, perhaps a majority, represent either Greek and Hellenistic thinkers, texts, or schools of thought, or concepts whose explanations refer to Greek or Hellenistic origins. Distinctly Muslim terms—for example, *hāl* (a transtemporal state posited by Sufi mysticism), *ibtihāj* (to enjoy God)—seem to be a minority. There are no biographical articles for the Muslim philosophers themselves, though there are entries for several honorific titles by which the most prominent among them were designated by other writers—for example, *al-mu'allim al-thānī*, "the second teacher" [after Aristotle], given to al-Fārābi. All terms are entered in and alphabetized by Arabic script, followed by their English transliteration. Regrettably, there is neither an index for the transliterated terms nor an index for terms and names in English translation.

260.   Islamic Philosophy Online: Philosophia Islamica. Islamic Philosophy Online, Inc. http://www.muslimphilosophy.com (accessed October 24, 2005).

Describing itself as "the Premier Islamic Philosophy resource on the Web," this site is "dedicated to the study of the philosophical output of the Muslim World" (home page). Featured resources include a *Dictionary of Islamic Philosophical Terms* (entry 258); individual pages on major Islamic philosophers, typically including links to online versions of their works, biographies, and other secondary studies; a calendar of events; links to various utilities (e.g., a date converter) useful in the study of Islamic philosophy; and miscellaneous other links.

SOURCES ON INDIVIDUAL PHILOSOPHERS

Fārābi, Abu-Nasr Muhammad al-

261. Rescher, Nicholas. **Al-Fārābi: An Annotated Bibliography.** Pittsburgh: University of Pittsburgh Press, 1962. 54p.

Al-Fārābi (ca. 870–950) "must be numbered among the five or six greatest philosophers of Islam" (introduction) and is also celebrated as a commentator on Aristotle. He influenced both Jewish and Scholastic philosophy in the Middle Ages. Rescher provides a comprehensive inventory of printed materials, including editions and translations of al-Fārābi's works, arranged by author, editor, or translator, followed by classified listings of al-Fārābi's works and of secondary studies. Though many items are in Arabic, Rescher aptly comments on the striking "indication of the very substantial amount of material available in Western languages" (introduction).

Kindī, Abu-Yusuf Ya'qub Ibn Ishaq al-

262. Rescher, Nicholas. **Al-Kindī: An Annotated Bibliography.** Pittsburgh: University of Pittsburgh Press, 1964. 55p.

This work is similar in content and arrangement to Rescher's earlier work on al-Fārābi (entry 261). The first major Arabic-writing philosopher, al-Kindī (ca. 805–870) "made a great contribution to the establishment of Greek learning in the orbit of Islam" (introduction).

AFRICA

263. Ofori, Patrick E. **Black African Traditional Religions and Philosophy: A Select Bibliographic Survey of the Sources from the Earliest Times to 1974**. Nendeln, Liechtenstein: Kraus-Thomson, 1975. 421p.

The 2,541 items cited in Ofori's bibliography—about half of them annotated—concentrate mainly on African indigenous religions. Philosophy is generally not clearly distinguished, no doubt a reflection of the nature of African thought. Arrangement is primarily geographical, with sections for broad regions subdivided by countries and sometimes by ethnic groups. A few of these geographical divisions have sections specifically designated for philosophy, in combinations with related concepts such as values or cosmology and with proverbs. There are indexes for authors and for ethnic groups, but not subjects.

264. Smet, A. J. **Bibliographie de la pensée Africaine: Répertoire et suppléments I–IV.** Kinshasa-Limete: Faculté de Theologie Catholique, 1972–1975. 285p.

"This bibliography on African thought is in principle limited to studies on the philosophical conceptions of the peoples of Black Africa." Besides publications which are "philosophical in the strict sense of that word," it also lists those "presenting a philosophy in the broad sense of the word, i.e., a more or less elaborated interpretation of African cultural values in a language borrowing from one or the other philosophical system" (introduction). An initial list ("Répertoire") and four supplements are bound together.

An analytical table (index) covers the main list plus supplements 1 through 3; a separate table covers supplement 4. Most materials listed are in European languages, including English. No annotations are provided.

265. Wiredu, Kwasi. **A Companion to African Philosophy.** Malden, Mass.: Blackwell, 2004. 587p. (Blackwell Companions to Philosophy, 28).

"This volume is intended to be a comprehensive anthology of essays on the history of African philosophy, ancient, medieval, modern, and contemporary, and on all the main branches of the discipline, including logic, epistemology, metaphysics, aesthetics, ethics, and politics" (preface). As that description suggests, this is more like a conventional survey text than a conventional reference work. But the wide-ranging treatment presented in 47 essays by 40 international authorities, most accompanied by substantial bibliographies, make this probably as good a single-volume source on African philosophy as is available at this time, and one that can meet a good many reference needs in the absence of any conventional dictionary or encyclopedia devoted to this topic. The chief caveat on this score is that some essays present more their author's individual perspective or argument than a representative overview of African thought. Cases in point include "Quasi-Materialism: A Contemporary African Philosophy of Mind" and "Democracy, Kingship, and Consensus: A South African Perspective." Editor Wiredu provides a helpful introduction on "African Philosophy in Our Time."

10
Western Philosophy: General, National, and Regional

GENERAL WESTERN HISTORY SOURCES

BIBLIOGRAPHIES

266.   Risse, Wilhelm. **Bibliographia Philosophica Vetus: Repertorium Generale Systematicum Operum Philosophicorum usque ad Annum MDCCC Typis Impressorum**. Hildesheim: Georg Olms, 1998. 9 vols. (Studien und Materialen zur Geschichte der Philosophie, Band 45).

In something of a *tour de force,* Risse has compiled a comprehensive short-title bibliography that attempts to include all independently published works of Western philosophy from the invention of printing, ca. 1455, up to 1800, in (he carefully qualifies) all Western languages accessible to him. This includes not only works of philosophers who lived and wrote within the specified timeframe, but also editions of philosophers from the ancient, medieval, and early Renaissance periods. They amount to an estimated 76,400 titles. These are divided over eight volumes of varying length, defined by a combination of subject-field and genre categories, as follows:

Pars 1: *Philosophia generalis*

Pars 2: *Logica*

Pars 3: *Metaphysica*

Pars 4: *Etica et politica*

Pars 5: *De anima*

Pars 6: *Philosophia naturalis*

Pars 7: *Doxoscopia*

Pars 8: *Theses academicae,* in three physical volumes (*Tomes*):

    Tomes 1–2: *Index disputationum*
    Tome 3: *Index respondentium*

Parts 1–7 are uniformly arranged chronologically by year of publication, within each year alphabetically by author. Each part includes an author index, index of titles of anonymous works, index of authors who are the subjects of others' commentaries, and a topical index. Part 8, which lists printed academic theses in volumes 1–2, is arranged alphabetically by author of the original thesis *(disputatio),* regardless of publication year. Under each thesis entry it lists, where applicable, published responses to it by other writers. The latter are also indexed in volume 3 of Part 8 with references back to the relevant entries in volumes 1 and 2.

The ninth volume, titled *Syllabus auctorum,* contains a complete author index, with birth and death dates, places of birth and activity, and profession (as available); a concordance of Latin and vernacular place names; and a short list of abbreviations of monastic orders.

For nearly every entry in this bibliography Risse provides, besides the customary bibliographic data, one or more location codes for holding libraries where exemplars are available. These included numerical codes for major German research libraries, alphabetical codes for some 350 additional libraries in Europe and America. As Risse notes, many of the works listed are rare, and some were found only in "smaller" libraries (preface). Those he has personally inspected are marked by an asterisk.

267.   Tobey, Jeremy L. **The History of Ideas: A Bibliographical Introduction.** Santa Barbara, Calif., and Oxford: American Bibliographical Center/Clio Press, 1975–. Vol. 1, **Classical Antiquity,** 1975, 211p. Vol. 2, **Medieval and Early Modern Europe,** 1977, 320p.

Though on the one hand this work limits itself to the period up to about 1727 (the death of Newton), and on the other hand it ranges beyond philosophy, it merits inclusion in this chapter as a rich and useful resource covering a substantial segment of Western philosophy's history. Over a third of each volume is devoted to specifically philosophical materials. Other areas covered are the history of science, religious thought, and "aesthetics" (a term Tobey employs beyond its narrow meaning in philosophy to embrace a wide range of criticism, historical scholarship, and theorizing about the arts). All three areas encompass much that borders on philosophy or is of interest for philosophical thought. Works in English are stressed, but important non-English works are also cited.

Tobey's mode of presentation is the bibliographic essay. References are embedded in a succinct but very readable narrative that describes the topography of the subject area, including the important issues and controversies, and relates the cited work to this in terms of its scope or thesis, and often its specific strength, weakness, or bias. Tobey's personal judgments inevitably come into play; but where apparent, these represent recognized alternatives, not idiosyncratic opinions, and the product of deep immersion in the intellectual history of the periods covered.

Citations are handled well. References in the essays adequately identify the work in question, but full bibliographic details are reserved for the "index"—more accurately, an alphabetical bibliography by author—at the end of each volume.

DICTIONARIES, ENCYCLOPEDIAS, AND HANDBOOKS

268.   Baggini, Julian and Jeremy Stangroom, eds. **Great Thinkers A–Z.** New York: Continuum, 2004. 275p.

Provides snapshots, aimed at the "intelligent non-specialist" (p. vii), of the lives, thought, and impact of 100 "great thinkers" who have shaped Western philosophical tradition from ancient Greece to the present. The editors stipulate that their selection does not aspire to include everyone with a persuasive claim to be counted among the "*top* one hundred. " Rather, it seeks to include, besides the indisputable giants such as Aristotle, Aquinas, Locke, Kant, Hegel, Mill, and Sartre, "an eclectic mix who represent the many styles and strands of philosophy" (introduction). This likely explains the choice, otherwise debatable, of, say, Daniel

Dennett, Frank Ramsey, John Searle, and Peter Singer, among others. For the majority of these 100 figures their primary identity lies clearly with philosophy. But thinkers known for straddling philosophy and other domains of thought are also represented—for example, Erasmus, Pascal, Marx, Turing, Foucault, Chomsky—as are a few chiefly identified with fields such as science, psychology, economics, and so forth, but who had a significant impact on philosophy, such as Darwin, Einstein, Freud, and Hayek. A surprise inclusion may be Gandhi, not obviously classified as Western but undeniably influential on Western thought. Articles are generally clear and accessible, avoiding unnecessary or unexplained technical vocabulary, and end with brief bibliographies. There is a chronological index, a thematic guide (relating thinkers to the major branches of philosophy), and a general index.

269.   Collinson, Diané. **Fifty Major Philosophers: A Reference Guide.** New York: Croom Helm/Methuen, 1987. London: Routledge, 1988. 170p.

Collinson provides concise, nontechnical introductions to 50 major Western philosophers from Thales to Sartre. Her selection contains few surprises: perhaps the inclusion of Moritz Schlick is one, or the fact that she has almost as many presocratics (seven) as twentieth-century figures (nine). The latter may be partly due, however, to the deliberate exclusion of any living philosophers. Under each entry she provides a short statement describing the main thrust of the individual's philosophy; information about his life; brief expositions of one or two aspects of his thought taken to be "especially important, interesting, and characteristic of his work" (preface); notes to the text; a list of the philosopher's major writings; and a selected bibliography for further reading. The arrangement is chronological. At the end of the volume is a glossary of around 50 basic philosophical concepts, which are cross-referenced from the text by bold print.

270.   **Dictionary of the History of Ideas: Studies of Selected Pivotal Ideas.** Philip P. Wiener, editor-in-chief.

See entry 201.

271.   Lange, Erhard, and Dietrich Alexander, eds. **Philosophenlexikon.** Berlin: Dietz, 1982. West Berlin: Das europäische Buch, 1982. 975p.

This "dictionary of philosophers" published in former East Germany is strongly colored by its Marxist-Leninist perspective. It spans the entire history of Western philosophy, but its special strength is its coverage of Marxist and socialist thinkers, including figures little known outside the orbit of Soviet and East European Marxism. The longest articles are on Marx, Engels, and Lenin, but there are none on Stalin or Mao. Similarly symptomatic of the vicissitudes of Marxist intellectual life is the sarcastic characterization of Ernst Bloch as a "bourgeois philosopher who understood himself as a Marxist."

272.   McGreal, Ian P. **Great Thinkers of the Western World: The Major Ideas and Classic Works of More than 100 Outstanding Western Philosophers, Physical and Social Scientists, Psychologists, Religious Writers, and Theologians**. New York: HarperCollins, 1992. 572p.

In the spirit of the *Masterplots* approach common to several previous works with which McGreal has been associated (see entries 211 and 212), this volume attempts to summarize at an introductory level the key ideas of major Western thinkers, focusing in this case on each one's thought as a whole rather than on individual texts. Not all of the thinkers are philosophers, as the subtitle makes clear, but easily two thirds of them would be mentioned in any comprehensive history or dictionary of Western philosophy. Even the nonphilosophers—or quasi-philosophers, in some instances—tend to be figures who have drawn much attention from philosophers: Copernicus, Calvin, Adam Smith, Darwin, Thoreau, Freud, Weber, Einstein, Heisenberg, and Toynbee, among others. Provided for each thinker is a brief biographical sketch, a short list of succinctly formulated "major ideas," a four-to-eight-page discussion of these ideas, and a short annotated bibliography of works for further reading. Articles are arranged chronologically from Parmenides to Camus. Contributors of the signed articles include several well-reputed scholars, such as Richard Popkin and Frederick Sontag.

273.   Metzler Philosophen Lexikon: Von den Vorsokratikern bis zu den Neuen Philosophen. 3rd rev. & enl. ed. Bernd Lutz, ed. Stuttgart: J. B. Metzler, 2003. 794p.

The third edition of this biographical *Lexikon* provides descriptions of the lives and works of some 360 significant Western philosophers, up from 300 in the first edition (1989). A few medieval Islamic philosophers are counted as Western for this purpose. Accompanying the written "portraits" in most cases are literal portraits, though small ones—a fairly unusual feature. Only basic, highly selective bibliographical references, usually three or four books, are appended to each article.

274.   Meyer, Ursula I., and Heidemarie Bennent-Vahle. Philosophinnen-Lexikon. Aachen: ein-FACH, 1994. 382p. (Philosophinnen, 2).

From Agallis of Kerkyra (Greek Grammarian, third to second centuries B.C.) to Clara Zetkin (twentieth-century Soviet philosopher), nearly 200 women philosophers from Western history are represented in this German biographical dictionary. The concept of "philosopher" is taken broadly to encompass literary figures such as Virginia Woolf, activists such as Susan B. Anthony, mystics such as Teresa of Avila, religious spokeswomen such as Phemonoe (Greek priestess of Apollo), and occultists such as Helena Blavatsky. In part, this is reflective of the theme sounded in the *Vorwort* that women generally had to develop their philosophical thought outside the channels open to men, particularly academic channels, and frequently do not allow for classification within the rigid categories impressed on the discipline of philosophy by males. Mainstream contemporary philosophers such as Elizabeth Anscombe and academic feminists such as Luce Irigaray are also well represented, of course. Articles vary in length from a few sentences to several pages, and include bibliographic references. There is also a general bibliography.

275.   Philosophen und Logiker. Uwe Wiedemann, ed. http://www.philosophenlexikon. de (accessed October 24, 2005).

An exceptionally comprehensive online biographical dictionary, covering several thousand major and minor philosophers and logicians throughout the history of Western philosophy, including at the borderline a few Islamic philosophers. The majority of entries are brief, sometimes no more than a single sentence, but those on major figures often run to the equivalent of two to six printed pages. There are occasional cross-references, with links, to a companion German-language online dictionary, *PhilLex* (entry 176), for explanations of terms or concepts.

276. Weate, Jeremy. **A Young Person's Guide to Philosophy: "I Think, Therefore I Am."** New York: DK Publishing, 1998. 64p.

This unusual effort to communicate philosophy for young readers could be characterized as a beginner's handbook to the history of Western philosophy, even if its title may suggest something broader. It divides into two principal sections: a chronological jaunt through history that looks at 34 great philosophers, followed by thumbnail descriptions of major schools of Western philosophy. Write-ups on individuals often continue in the section on schools. Weate by no means picks out lighter-weight thinkers or ideas: he begins with the pre-Socratics (Thales, et. al.), marches right through the likes of Plato, Aristotle, Aquinas, Descartes, Kant, Nietzsche, Wittgenstein, and De Beauvoir right up to Derrida, then tackles such schools as the Idealists, Materialists, Scholastics, Rationalists, Pragmatists, Existentialists, Feminist Philosophers, and Postmodernists. There's also a short introduction on the nature and use of philosophy, and at the end a very brief glossary.

The age level for which this is appropriate is a bit difficult to judge. The book's look and feel, especially the large colorful illustrations in the first part, suggest elementary school level, but some of the content, particularly in the second part, seems well beyond that (how do you explain phenomenology to a fifth grader?). The reviewer in *American Reference Books Annual* 1999 (entry 1258, pp. 522–23) recommends it "for public, elementary, and high school libraries."

OTHER REFERENCE SOURCES

277. Ayer, A. J. and Jane O'Grady, eds. **A Dictionary of Philosophical Quotations.** Oxford: Blackwell, 1992. 528p.

This dictionary of quotations was conceived and begun by the late A. J. Ayer, then finished after his death by Jane O'Grady. Its forte is trenchant statements, averaging a paragraph or so in length, on significant philosophical topics taken from the writings of around 340 philosophers throughout Western history. There is a fair supply here of memorable aphorisms and pithy sayings, from Heraclitus's "It is not possible to step into the same river twice" to Sartre's "Hell is other people" and Wittgenstein's summary of the aim of his philosophy, "To shew the fly the way out of the fly-bottle." But these are more exceptional than typical: most quotations are more substantial, if less "quotable," and present a fuller picture of a position, argument, or conclusion on the topic at hand. Even famous phrases and sentences—for example, Descartes's "I am thinking, therefore I exist" or Hobbes's description of life in the state of nature as "solitary, poor, nasty, brutish, and short"—are more likely to be quoted with their surrounding context. Occasionally, the length of a quoted passage will approach a full page, but 6 to 10 lines is more typical. Only Western philosophers are included, and among these a substantial number of contemporary philosophers. If most of the latter do not approach the great figures of the past in fame and stature, O'Grady justifies their strong representation with the observation that "philosophy is not just a matter of venerable figures or of charm but of continuous dispute and living issues" (introduction). She also acknowledges that there is wider inclusion from Continental philosophy, for instance, than might have been the case had Ayer (a leading Anglo-American philosopher) lived to finish this book; and one wonders whether the same isn't true for the representation of recent feminist philosophers.

Quotations are grouped by authors, arranged alphabetically. Sources are identified, but too often inadequately or inconsistently. Subject access is via an index that is moderately detailed but that falls well short of a keyword index (as found in the best general quotations dictionaries) that would permit retrieval of quoted phrases by almost any significant term. (There's no getting to Bertrand Russell's oft-cited example for his analysis of definite description, "the author of *Waverley*," by looking under Waverley.) O'Grady also supplies a useful glossary of around 140 key terms in which she aims not merely to define terms but to indicate briefly something of their context in philosophical disputes.

278. **Great Books of the Western World.** 2nd ed. Vols. 1 and 2: **The Great Ideas: A Syntopicon.** Mortimer J. Adler, editor-in-chief. Chicago: Encyclopedia Britannica, 1990. 2 vols. Reprinted, in one volume, as **The Great Ideas: A Lexicon of Western Thought,** by Mortimer J. Adler. New York: Macmillan, 1992. 958p.

The *Syntopicon* serves as a thematic guide and index to the more than 400 classics of Western thought collected in the *Great Books of the Western World* (60 vols.), among which philosophical and philosophically significant works easily make up a majority. As its reprinting in a separate volume implies, its utility need not be limited to its use with the *Great Books* set, which, admirable as it is, has its drawbacks (it often does not offer the best available texts or translations, and it lacks either scholarly apparatus or aids for the general reader struggling with archaic language or arcane concepts). In many cases, it is possible to use the *Syntopicon* with other editions of the works represented in the set, though this may require varying degrees of diligence and ingenuity.

Each of the *Syntopicon*'s 102 chapters is devoted to a fundamental term or concept (beauty, democracy, God, happiness, infinity, progress, science, wisdom, etc.) or set of complementary concepts (one and many, virtue and vice), and consists of five parts: (1) an introduction in the form of a survey essay; (2) an outline of topics; (3) references to relevant texts, arranged according to the outline of topics; (4) cross-references to related concepts and topics; (5) additional readings, referring to works not included in the *Great Books*. An inventory of terms at the end lists narrower subject terms (from "a priori" to "zoology") and directs one to the relevant chapters on broader concepts.

279. **Great Treasury of Western Thought: A Compendium of Important Statements on Man and His Institutions by the Great Thinkers in Western History.** Mortimer J. Adler and Charles Van Doren, eds. New York: R. R. Bowker, 1977. 1771p.

The great thinkers in Western history included in this superb compilation of quotations are not all philosophers, at least in any rigorous sense. Nonetheless, philosophers and philosophic writing are more than generously represented. The quotations are organized into 20 chapters on major themes: love, mind, ethics, politics, liberty and equality, art and aesthetics, nature and the cosmos, religion, and others. These are further divided into a total of 127 sections for more specific topics, including for example "Moral Freedom" (under ethics); "Progress, Regress, and Cycles in History" (under history); "Time" (under nature and the cosmos). The quotations, arranged chronologically within these sections, are typically longer than those in other collections of quotations, "running to more than 100 words on the average" (preface) and often much longer. Indexing is very thorough; besides an author index, there is a subject and proper name index with over fifty thousand entries.

That one of the editors (Adler) is prominently associated with the *Great Books of the Western World* is not incidental. The preface alludes to the foundation of the present work in "that collection of the most worthwhile books to be read" and its innovative index, the *Syntopicon* (see entry 278). But while it stands in the *Great Books* tradition, the

Great Treasury is by no means limited to writers and writings included in the *Great Books:* "almost twice as many writers are included," notes the preface. In any case, it is a work that stands by itself and has a value all its own.

280.   Hunnex, Milton D. **Chronological and Thematic Charts of Philosophies and Philosophers.** Grand Rapids. Mich.: Academie Books/Zondervan, 1986. 56p. + 24 charts.

Hunnex describes this unusual work as "a *ready-reference* aid for the student who needs essential information in a hurry" (p. 1). He provides, first, a text with succinct definitions and descriptions, sometimes illustrated with small diagrams, of significant positions within Western philosophy only on the major questions of philosophy, organized into three chapters titled "The Problem of Knowledge," "The Problem of the World," and "The Problem of Values." (The last of these is broader than its title may suggest, encompassing not only ethics and philosophy of art but also philosophy of religion, philosophy of education, and issues of determinism and freedom.) There is also a section summarizing, in short, bullet-like statements, the ideas of 49 philosophers, arranged alphabetically. Secondly, Hunnex provides 24 charts, each stretching across two pages, designed to yield "*orientation* within a historical context" by exploiting the fact that "philosophical theories tend to recur in the history of thought and tend to cluster within the limitations of several possibilities of explanation." With the use of these charts—flow charts, more or less—he seeks to portray "antecedent influences that lead to a particular philosophy . . . as well as consequent influences and the relation to contemporary philosophy" (p. 1). It is not clear whether his lines and arrows necessarily represent actual historical relationships of direct influence or, in some cases, logical relationships among positions. Text accompanying each chart explains concisely the major positions shown, but is often redundant with the text in the book's first half. Red print in the charts (as distinct from black) identifies philosophers and positions discussed in the text in either section. The distinction between red and black lines and arrows in the chart is not explained, but presumably indicates stronger and weaker relationships of influence.

This is a revised edition of Hunnex's *Philosophies and Philosophers* (Chandler, 1971) but does not include developments after 1970.

NATIONAL OR REGIONAL HISTORY SOURCES

This section lists only dictionaries and encyclopedias whose historical coverage spans two or more of the major eras in the history of Western philosophy treated in succeeding chapters. Works of national or regional history confined to a single period or smaller time span are listed in the pertinent period chapter. National and regional bibliographies are listed in chapter 5.

GERMANY / GERMANIC COUNTRIES

281.   **Biographische Enzyklopädie deutschsprachiger Philosophen.** Ed. Bruno Jahn. Munich: K. G. Saur, 2001. 718p.

The content of this work is drawn substantially from the giant *Deutsche biographische Enzyklopädie* edited by Walther Killy and Rudolph Vierhaus (K. G. Saur, 1995–2000, 12 vols.). Roughly 1,200 of its 1,370 articles derive from the parent work, though often revised and supplied with updated bibliographies. An additional 170 or so articles are supplied for philosophers previously overlooked or slighted or who had died since publication of the *DBE*. Living figures remain excluded, as they were from the *DBE*. Apart from that, the encyclopedia encompasses philosophers from the early Middle Ages to nearly the present time. It includes philosophers in Austria and German-speaking Switzerland as well as in present-day Germany and its antecedents. It also includes foreigners who worked in German-speaking lands. "Philosopher" is interpreted generously and encompasses, for example, individuals identified chiefly with other fields, such as theology, science, psychology, or law, but who contributed significantly to philosophical discussion related (usually) to those fields.

The work includes an index of names, which combines individuals who have their own entries with those only mentioned in articles; an index of places of origin; and a chronology of significant philosophical publications from the eighth century to 2001.

IRELAND

282.   Duddy, Thomas, ed. **Dictionary of Irish Philosophers.** New York: Thoemmes Continuum, 2004. 385p.

This unique resource on Irish philosophers complements the three dictionaries published by Thoemmes on British philosophers of the seventeenth, eighteenth, and nineteenth centuries (entries 397, 393, and 395, respectively). A substantial portion is also redundant with those three works, because their broad definition of "British" encompassed many philosophers who are again included here, for instance George Berkeley, Robert Boyle, William Molyneux, and Jonathan Swift. Among those not in the British works, some were excluded because they "would not have qualified as British" for a variety of reasons (p. viii), but the majority simply fall outside the three centuries collectively covered by those dictionaries. No such restriction of chronological scope applies here: the range is from an anonymous seventh century author known as the "Irish Augustine" well into the twentieth century. However, by editorial policy no living figures were included. Debate concerning the finer points of deciding "who is Irish," discussed in the introduction, was often resolved by compromises among the editorial board. As in the British works, a broad definition of "philosopher" has been used. All told, over 180 thinkers are represented, from the quite well-known, such as John Scottus Eriugena (ninth century) and Iris Murdoch (twentieth century), to figures sufficiently obscure that no other secondary literature could be cited in the bibliographies accompanying their entries. Articles were contributed by dozens of scholars representing universities both in and outside Ireland. The dictionary includes an index of names only.

LATIN AMERICA

283.   Díaz Díaz, Gonzalo. **Hombres y documentos de la filosofía española.** Madrid: Consejo Superior de Investigaciones Científicas, Instituto de Filosofía "Luis Vives," Departmento de Filosofía Española, 1980–. Vols. 1–.

See entry 293.

284.   Los **"fundadores" en la filosofía de América Latina.** Washington, D.C.: Secretaría General, Organización de los Estados Americanos, 1970. 199p. (Union Panamericana. Bibliografías básicas, 7).

See entry 86.

RUSSIA / SOVIET UNION / SLAVIC COUNTRIES

285. Abramov, A. I., ed. **Russkaia filosofiia: malyi entsiklopedicheskii slovar'.** Moscow: Nauka, 1995. 624p.

This "concise encyclopedic dictionary" of Russian philosophy is particularly strong on biographical entries but also offers a substantial selection of entries on philosophical institutions and movements, branches of philosophy and their Russian developments, and significant terms or concepts characteristic of Russian philosophy in both Soviet and pre- or post-Soviet eras. Signed articles, contributed by numerous scholars, usually include brief bibliographies.

286. Alekseev, Petr Vasil'evich. **Filosofy Rossii XIX–XX stoletii: biografii, idei, trudy.** 4th ed. Moscow: Akademicheskii Proekt, 2002.

New and significantly expanded editions of this encyclopedia of nineteenth- and twentieth-century Russian philosophy have been appearing in quick succession since the 1993 first edition (Moscow: Kniga i biznes, 1993, 221p.). Though its scope embraces "biographies, ideas, and writings," as the subtitle states, entries are exclusively biographical (i.e., personal names). Well over two thousand philosophers, major and minor, are represented in this fourth edition along with some other figures connected with Russian philosophy, such as publishers. Articles typically include basic biographical data, areas of specialty, and summaries of principal ideas, and conclude with bibliographies, sometimes quite extensive.

287. Ballestrem, Karl G. **Russian Philosophical Terminology.** Dordrecht, Netherlands: D. Reidel, 1964. 117p.

See entry 188.

288. Emel'ianov, B. V., and V. V. Kulikov. **Russkie mysliteli vtoroi poloviny XIX– nachala XX veka: opyt kratkogo biobibliograficheskogo slovaria.** Ekaterinburg: Izd-vo Ural'skogo Universiteta, 1996. 383p.

See entry 398.

289. Lazari, Andrzeja de, ed. **Idee w Rosji—Ideas in Russia: leksykon rosyjsko-polsko-angielski.** 5 vols. Vol. 1: Warsaw: Semper, 1999. Vols. 2–5: Lodz: Ibidem, 1999–2003. 5 vols.

Label this encyclopedia "unconventional." Trilingual throughout, it presents every article in Russian, Polish, and English in parallel columns across facing pages, with a fourth column devoted to substantial bibliographies including materials in these and other languages. And while it employs an alphabetical arrangement by the Russian entry terms, it was issued in stages such that each successive volume contains articles from A to Z (or *A* to *Я*). Finally, although it was planned and announced as a four-volume work, and volume 4 concludes with a cumulated index to volumes 1–4, a fifth volume was already foreseen at that point and appeared two years later.

This is, broadly, a work of intellectual history, aiming to give "freshly considered information on the broad concepts of Russian theological, philosophical, social and political thought from the Middle Ages to the present day" (front matter). Besides entries for significant ideas and concepts from these fields, there are entries for important thinkers, for intellectual institutions and movements, and even for selected social and cultural phenomena (e.g., nobility, balalaika) seen as influencing or revealing something of the "Russian mind." Articles on individuals concentrate on their ideas and writings while providing only minimal biographical details, on the grounds that the latter are mostly available elsewhere.

Contributors represent a variety of nationalities and include some American and Western European scholars, but most are either Russian or (a majority) Polish. The editor is affiliated with Poland's University of Lodz. Despite the prevalence of a Polish perspective on the history of Russian ideas, there is a considerable diversity of views. In some cases several alternative or complementary explanations of the same idea are offered in successive articles.

290. Ogorodnik, I. V., Guberskii, L. V., et. al. **Filosofskaia mysl' vostochnykh slavian: biobibliograficheskii slovar'.** Kiev: Parlamentskoe izd-vo, 1999. 326p.

This biographical dictionary covers some 375 philosophers from the Slavic region of Eastern Europe from the eleventh through the twentieth centuries. Articles typically provide a biographical overview and summary of major ideas and conclude with a bibliography of primary and selected secondary sources.

291. **Russkaia filosofiia: slovar'.** M. A. Maslin, general ed. Moscow: Nauka, 1995. 655p.

One of several post-Soviet era dictionary/encyclopedias (see also entries 285, 286, and 290) that began to recapture, reframe, and reappraise the breadth and depth of Russian philosophical history throughout both the pre-Soviet and Soviet eras. Features many biographical entries along with entries on movements and schools of thought, institutions, significant concepts or ideas, and influential philosophical books. A number of articles explore specifically Russian manifestations of, or responses to, wider philosophical developments, for example, "Kant and Russia," "Marx and Russia." Editor Maslin (also transliterated "Maslina") has at least eight other works on the history of Russian philosophy to his credit.

292. Sukhov, A. D., ed. **Sto russkikh filosofov: biograficheskii slovar'.** Moscow: "Mirta," 1995. 312p.

The 100 Russian philosophers treated in this biographical dictionary span seven centuries, from the fourteenth century to the twentieth. Excluded, however, are philosophers of Marxist orientation—thus no article on Lenin, for instance—leaving the nineteenth century the most numerously represented. Among those included are figures well-known beyond Russia, for example, Kropotkin, Tolstoi, Leontiev, and many who are not. The presence of several pre–eighteenth-century thinkers suggests that "philosopher" is used in a loose, or at least a broad, sense. The work was published under the auspices of the Institut Filosofii of the Rossiskaia Akademiia Nauk.

SPAIN / HISPANIC COUNTRIES

293. Díaz Díaz, Gonzalo. **Hombres y documentos de la filosofía española.** Madrid: Consejo Superior de Investigaciones Científicas, Instituto de Filosofía "Luis Vives," Departamento de Filosofía Española, 1980–2003. Vols. 1–7.

Having reached the end of the alphabet in 2003 with volume 7, covering S through Z, this work now constitutes a virtually exhaustive encyclopedia of Spanish philosophers, the very minor as well as the major. "Philosophers" is interpreted broadly so as to include many theologically oriented thinkers, cultural critics, and so forth. "Spanish" is interpreted to encompass thinkers who were born or who did their work either in the Iberian peninsula or in Spain's various territories, including those overseas, up to the time of their respective independencies. Philosophers are presented in alphabetical sequence, each with a succinct description of life and thought (or as much as is known, sometimes very little), a primary bibliography *(obras),* and a secondary bibliography *(estudios).* Preceding the whole, in volume 1, is a 538-item general bibliography.

UNITED KINGDOM

294.   Dematteis, Philip Breed, Peter S. Fosl and Leemon B. McHenry, eds. **British Philosophers, 1800–2000.** Detroit: Gale, 2002. 420p. (Dictionary of Literary Biography, vol. 262).

Shares the qualities and features common to the *Dictionary of Literary Biography* series; see entry 347 for a general comment. There are 32 nineteenth- and twentieth-century British philosophers profiled. For the nineteenth century, British philosophy claims few front-rank philosophers: John Stuart Mill is one, Herbert Spencer more debatably a second. But besides those two, this dictionary covers a number of significant second-rank figures at a length not readily found elsewhere, especially at a level accessible even to beginning philosophy students. They include, for example, Bernard Bosanquet, F. H. Bradley, William Godwin, James Mill, Henry Sidgwick, and William Whewell. Twentieth-century figures covered here include such leading figures of the Anglo-American and broadly analytical tradition as J. L. Austin, A. J. Ayer, G. E. Moore, Karl Popper, Bertrand Russell, Gilbert Ryle, and Ludwig Wittgenstein (counted here as British despite his Austrian beginnings). Other participants in that tradition represented here are, among others, Elizabeth Anscombe, Michael Dummett, R. M. Hare, Derek Parfit, J.J.C. Smart, and Timothy Sprigge. Somewhat outside the mainstream, at least in large parts of their work, are Whitehead and R. G. Collingwood.

UNITED STATES

295.   Dematteis, Philip Breed and Leemon B. McHenry, eds. **American Philosophers Before 1950.** Detroit: Gale, 2003. 407p. (Dictionary of Literary Biography, vol. 270).

Shares the qualities and features common to the *Dictionary of Literary Biography* series; see entry 347 for a general comment. There are 26 American philosophers covered in this volume, divided about equally between pre–twentieth-century and twentieth-century figures. The earliest is Cadwallader Colden (1688–1776), more famous as a Colonial historian, scientist, and politician. Among the "big names" here are Jonathan Edwards, Emerson, Thoreau, William James, C. S. Peirce, Dewey, and Santayana. Those less famous from the nineteenth century include two women—Mary Whiton Calkins and Marietta Kies—and several figures familiar to American intellectual historians but little known otherwise, for example, Josiah Royce, William Graham Sumner, and Chauncey Wright. From the twentieth century, significant second-rank figures (or arguably third-rank, in a few cases) include, for example, E. S. Brightman, Rudolf Carnap, W. E. Hocking,

C. I. Lewis, Arthur Lovejoy, G. H. Mead, and F.J.E. Woodbridge. At least two philosophers found here, Charles Hartshorne and Suzanne Langer, remained active well after 1950—the boundary between this and a complementary volume for 1950–2000 (entry 527)—but already had well-established careers and reputations by that date.

296. Nauman, St. Elmo, Jr. **Dictionary of American Philosophy.** New York: Philosophical Library, 1973. Paperback ed., Totowa, N.J.: Littlefield, Adams, 1974. 273p.

A balanced work this is not. Two lists at the front identify, respectively, 19 "major" philosophers and a smaller group of 10 who are "the most outstanding" or "have had the greatest influence." Yet a figure on neither list, William Ames, who "never reached America (he died *en route*)," gets 11 pages, while two in the "top ten," Peirce and Whitehead, get two pages each. There are also imbalances between biographical and topical entries (only 15 of the latter); in the choice of topics (an entry for conscience but none for science or philosophy of science); within the topical articles (the one on social philosophy discusses John Adams exclusively!); in the choice of individuals counted as philosophers (Ambrose Beirce but not Edward Bellamy); and between biographical matters and discussion of an individual's ideas (C. S. Peirce's thought gets a half page of the two pages under his name, another page under Pragamatism). The examples could easily be multiplied. Look to this dictionary for informative bits and pieces, and for interesting anecdotes, but not for balanced treatment or even, with any degree of reliability, the most essential information.

11
Western Philosophy: Ancient

BIBLIOGRAPHIES

297.   Bell, Albert A., Jr. and James B. Allis. **Resources in Ancient Philosophy: An Annotated Bibliography of Scholarship in English, 1965–1989.** Metuchen, N.J.: Scarecrow, 1991. 800p.

Though it covers scholarship from only a 25 year period, this ambitious bibliography of ancient Western philosophy from Thales through Augustine lists some 7,076 items: books, journal articles, and essays in anthologies. It is principally a secondary bibliography: primary texts, either in original languages or in translation, are included only if supplied with considerable notes or commentary in English. Each entry includes a concise annotation, often just a single sentence, generally descriptive and not evaluative, though in rare cases the authors note a glaring deficiency or severe bias in a work. A roughly chronological overall organization scheme includes chapters covering major schools (e.g., the Eleatics, Epicureanism), usually with subchapters on individual figures, while Socrates, Plato, and Aristotle each get a chapter of their own, subdivided by specific writings in Plato's case, by broad topical areas (e.g., ethics) in Aristotle's. Christian thinkers such as Tertullian, Origen, and even Augustine are treated in a single, comparatively short chapter because coverage is limited to items that "concern their roles as continuators of the classical philosophical tradition, not as theologians" (p. 2).

Bell and Allis provide a brief narrative introduction to each school or figure—a very useful feature. The chief deficiency of their work is its subject index, which skimps on indexing terms while compiling unmanageably large blocks of undifferentiated entry numbers under some of its broad index headings (e.g., 81 under analogy, 186 under virtue).

298.   **The Classical World Bibliography of Philosophy, Religion, and Rhetoric.** New York: Garland, 1978. 396p. (The Classical World Bibliographies; Garland Reference Library of the Humanities, vol. 95).

This volume reprints a selection of bibliographic surveys published originally in the journal *Classical World* and "directed towards the particular requirements of research and pedagogy in the United States and Canada" (introduction). Each of 19 separately authored bibliographies is devoted to a special topic and offers "a comprehensive, though not exhaustive, listing, summary, and analysis of major books and articles covering a discrete period of time." Those most centrally concerned with philosophy survey works on the pre-Socratics from 1945–66; on Plato, 1945–55; Aristotle, 1945–55, with separate surveys on Aristotle's psychology and the *Poetics;* Epicurus and Epicureanism, 1937–57; Hellenistic philosophy, 1937–57; and Lucretius, 1945–72. Other surveys are concerned with Cicero, Seneca, ancient rhetoric, and Roman religion. Each bibliography is briefly described in the introduction.

299.   Navia, Luis E. **The Philosophy of Cynicism: An Annotated Bibliography.** Westport, Conn.: Greenwood Press, 1995. 232p. (Bibliographies and Indexes in Philosophy, 4).

The Cynics, or "dog philosophers," represented a sporadic ancient movement of philosophical attitudes and practices aiming at individual happiness through ascetic life-styles and denunciation or ridicule of established convention. Major Cynic figures included Antisthenes, Diogenes of Sinope, Crates of Thebes, and Dio Chrysostom. Navia focuses on the secondary literature on Cynicism, including primary sources only if they contain secondary material. Occasionally, he extends his scope to works (e.g., several by Nietzsche) that use the word *cynic* in its modern sense. His 704 entries, encompassing materials in a variety of languages and published from the sixteenth century to 1994, include a fair number of cross-references and some double entries for a work and its translations, as well as some citations of minor sources such as general encyclopedia articles. The annotations are useful and informative.

300. Navia, Luis E. **The Presocratic Philosophers: An Annotated Bibliography.** Hamden, Conn.: Garland, 1993. 722p. (Garland Reference Library of Social Science, vol. 704).

Navia lists and descriptively annotates 2,683 items dealing with the group of Greek thinkers who, in the two centuries before Socrates and Plato, significantly shaped the development of Western philosophy—and Western science, too—with the questions they raised and often their answers as well. Included are materials in many Western languages and, beyond the usual scholarly literature, some fictional works, poetry, and musical compositions with Presocratic subjects. Individual chapters are devoted to 11 key figures: Anaxagoras, Anaximander, Anaximenes, Democritus, Empedocles, Heraclitus, Parmenides, Pythagoras, Thales, Xenophanes, and Zeno. In the case of Pythagoras, coverage is more limited, serving as an addendum to Navia's previously published bibliography on this important thinker (entry 331). Chapters 1 through 3 list bibliographical works, source collections (for the fragments that are the only remains of the Presocratics' writings), and general studies. Navia provides a list of some 450 international journals and periodicals from which articles on the Presocratics have been drawn, but does not otherwise clarify the boundaries (including the timeframe) of the literature he has reviewed. His work overlaps substantially with the French/Canadian bibliography *Les Présocratiques* by L. Paquet, et. al. (entry 301), published five years earlier, but each work lists some items not found in the other—notably, in Navia's case, items published since 1980 (Paquet's closing date).

301. Paquet, Léonce, M. Roussel, and Y. Lafrance. **Les Présocratiques: Bibliographie analytique (1879–1980).** Montreal: Éditions Bellarmin; Paris: Belles Lettres, 1988–1989. 2 vols. (Collection d'études anciennes; Collection Noêsis).

Paquet and his co-bibliographers cover ground similar to that covered by Luis Navia in *The Presocratic Philosophers* (entry 300), and in somewhat similar fashion with a few significant exceptions. Their coverage, while it stops more than a decade earlier, is generally more comprehensive, especially for late eighteenth- and early nineteenth-century materials, and specifically encompasses several individuals and groups left out by Navia, such as Alcmeon, Philolaus, the Sophists, and the Hippocratic school. Altogether, their two volumes yield about twice the number of citations found in Navia. Like Navia, Paquet et. al. provide chapters or subchapters for bibliographic sources, textual sources, and general studies, as well as chapters devoted to individual major thinkers or schools. Their longest chapter, however, comprising over 600 of the 2,436 total entries, is concerned with studies of specific themes, concepts, and terms, and is subdivided into topical sections that have no parallel in Navia's organizational scheme. Book review listings are appended to many of the entries for books. Doctoral theses are listed in an appendix. Annotations, of course, are in French, as is other editorial material. A systematic index *(index général analytique)* is provided along with alphabetical subject and author indexes.

DICTIONARIES AND ENCYCLOPEDIAS

302.   **Encyclopedia of Classical Philosophy.** Donald J. Zeyl, Daniel T. Devereux, and Phillip T. Mitsis, eds. Westport, Conn.: Greenwood Press, 1997. 614p.

More than 270 alphabetically arranged entries illuminate the philosophical world of Greek and Roman antiquity from the sixty century B.C. to the sixty century A.D. Signed articles are contributed by around 90 scholars, most affiliated with major universities throughout North America and Europe. Articles treat philosophical themes, schools, and the intellectual and cultural contexts of the ancient world, but a majority is devoted to individual philosophers, major and minor. All include basic bibliographies. A concise chronological outline is on pages 384–87, a guide to bibliography on pages 589–91. Name/subject index.

303.   Goulet, Richard. **Dictionnaire des philosophes antiques.** Paris: Éditions du Centre National de la Recherche Scientifique, 1989–. Vols. 1–. **Supplement, 2003.** 808p.

The aim of this impressive French publishing project is to provide comprehensive coverage of ancient philosophers, the obscure and minor as well as the great and famous. At this writing (November 2005), the first three volumes only have appeared, carrying its alphabetical coverage through Juvenal. But already the publisher has seen fit to issue a supplement to bring these initial volumes up to date, in part with some previously missed philosophers but primarily with new materials on Aristotle and Cicero, plus some appendices devoted mainly to treatment of Presocratics in the Arabic tradition.

Content, format, and length of the entries vary widely with the individual's significance and the sorts of information available, but a typical entry may include a survey of biographical sources, bibliographies of primary and secondary works (perhaps also spurious works), listing of fragments, and iconography (portraits, etc.). Most include at their head a reference to the relevant article in the authoritative *Paulys Realencyclopädie der classischen Altertumswisswishenschaft* (new ed. by G. Wissowa, et. al., Stuttgart: Metzler, 1893–1972) or its *Supplementbände* 1–15 (1903–1978). The enormous variations in length of treatment are exemplified in volume 1 by a 176-page article on Aristotle contrasted with two lines given to one Artémidore, evidently known only from a mention somewhere as the author of a work titled *Phainomena.*

Each volume lists dozens of contributors, and articles are signed. Volume 1 has an appendix of nearly a hundred pages describing the topology and archeology of the Athenian Academy.

304.   Peters, Francis Edward. **Greek Philosophical Terms: A Historical Lexicon.** New York: New York University Press; London: University of London Press, 1967. 234p.

Peters's dictionary is aimed at neither the scholarly specialist nor the beginner, but at the intermediate student. A useful, authoritative tool for the study of Greek philosophers "on their own terms" (preface), it seeks to strip away as much as possible of the historical baggage accrued through later developments or carried by the common English translations. As a whole, it documents and clarifies the gradual development of philosophical language from its roots in daily life, in myth, and in epic, to an increasingly specialized and technical vocabulary—the latter stage represented particularly by Aristotle. Plato and Aristotle, predictably, dominate this dictionary, but there is also extensive attention to the terminology of both the presocratics and the "post-Aristotelians" (e.g., Stoics, Epicureans, and Neoplatonists).

Entries are arranged alphabetically according to the English transliteration of the Greek terms. Knowledge of Greek or the Greek alphabet is not required, though it is likely that the most common use of this dictionary begins with an awareness of a particular Greek term: perhaps *arete, dike,* or *eidos* (for a student of Plato), or *pathos, psyche,* or *telos* (for a student of Aristotle). However, there is an English-Greek index which permits reference from an English term to its Greek original. Peters describes this as "complete," but at least one omission should make one wonder: the term *eidos* (possibly the most prominent and even notorious term in Plato) is variously translated as "idea" or "form," but only the latter appears in the index. Yet that oversight, striking as it may be, should not detract unduly from a high estimation of Peters's work.

305. Urmson, J. O. **The Greek Philosophical Vocabulary.** London: Duckworth, 1990. 173p.

"This book is designed to be an aid to students of ancient Greek philosophy who have some, but not necessarily a profound, knowledge of the Greek language" (introduction). It aims to clarify the meanings and usage of some 500 to 600 words commonly used by Greek philosophers, chiefly through the strategy of quoting their own statements, abetted by explanatory comments supplied by Urmson. The quotations, like the entry terms themselves, are provided in transliterated Greek, followed by Urmson's own translations into English, intended, he says, "to be helpful rather than literal" (introduction). Drawn from authors spanning the fifth century B.C. to the sixth century A.D., the quotations are not merely illustrative but generally consist of a philosopher's own, or a close follower's, definition or explanation of the word in question. The work supplements rather than replaces use of a standard Greek lexicon, and can profitably be used alongside *Greek Philosophical Terms: A Historical Lexicon* by F. E. Peters (entry 304).

SOURCES ON INDIVIDUAL PHILOSOPHERS

ARISTOTLE (384–322 B.C.)

306. **Aristotle Bibliography.** Richard Ingardia, ed. New York: St. John's University. http://www.aristotlebibliography.com/ (accessed October 24, 2005).

This is not a free Web resource but a Web-based subscription database. At this writing in October 2005 it is "marketed mainly to libraries, although under some circumstances an individual can be issued a permanent UserID" (F.A.Q. page). At this point the bibliography claims some 45,000 entries from 1900 forward, including 7,000 books, 36,000 articles and reviews, and 2,000 dissertations. Search results (short records) are sorted by the aforementioned document types and display in reverse chronological order. Multiple items can be selected for simultaneous full record display. The Web interface provides clean, pleasing displays. A reviewer in *Choice* (41 no. 7 [March 2004]:1308) noted some shortcomings with the search engine, which affords author and keyword/title searching with optional date restrictions but otherwise limited capabilities to refine searches that yield too many hits. Nonetheless, this online resource, assuming it can be maintained, promises to be a boon to serious Aristotelian study and scholarship, which has been comparatively poor in dedicated bibliographic resources.

307.   Barnes, Jonathan, et. al. **Aristotle: A Bibliography.** Rev. ed. Oxford: Sub-Faculty of Philosophy, 1981. 88p. (Study Aid Series, no. 7).

In the absence of a more comprehensive, current, or widely available bibliography on Aristotle apart from Ingardia's recently introduced online bibliography (entry 306), which is not yet widely accessible, this very selective bibliography in the Oxford Study Aid series (see entry 17) merits mention here. "Designed primarily to suit the interests of English-speaking philosophers" (preface), it includes chapters on Aristotle's logic, metaphysics, philosophy of science, science, psychology, ethics, and politics, and on the *Poetics.*

308.   Radice, Roberto, and Richard Davis. **Aristotle's *Metaphysics:* Annotated Bibliography of the Twentieth-Century Literature.** New York: E. J. Brill, 1997. 904p. (Brill's Annotated Bibliographies, vol. 1).

This is an English-language version of a bibliography published in Italian as *La "Metafisica" di Aristotele nel XX secolo: bibliografia ragionata e sistematica* (2. ed. riveduta, corretta e ampliata, by Roberto Radice and Andolfo Mateo; Milan: Vita e Pensiero, 1997, 825p.). The second Italian edition postdated the first (Milan: Vita e Pensiero, 1996. 734p.) by only a year. Davies translated elements such as headings and annotations and simultaneously regularized some of the bibliography's language. Materials listed cover the time span 1900 to 1996 and include, in separate sections, editions of the *Metaphysics,* modern translations, commentaries, bibliographic works, and secondary works arranged chronologically. Annotations are mostly though not exclusively descriptive. There are four excellent indexes: of concepts, Greek terms, authors, and specific passages of the *Metaphysics.*

309.   Schwab, Moïse. **Bibliographie d'Aristote.** Paris: Librairie H. Welter, 1896. Reprinted, Dubuque, Ia.: Wm. C. Brown, [1965]. 380p.

This century-old work, which reproduces a rather dense handwritten text, remains as of this writing in late 2005 the latest comprehensive printed bibliography devoted to Aristotle; but see entry 306 for a new online bibliography by Ingardia. Covering the entire Aristotelian corpus, Schwab's bibliography has a separate section for each work, listing manuscripts, editions and translations, and commentaries on the text from ancient times to the late 1800s. Some, but not all, sections include a subsection with selected critical studies.

310.   Kiernan, Thomas P. **Aristotle Dictionary.** New York: Philosophical Library; London: Peter Owen, 1962. 524p.

See entry 508 for a general comment on the series of which this work is a part. As is typical of the series, its "definitions" and articles are confined to quotations from the philosopher's works. It departs from the general pattern, however, by also including a 162-page introductory overview of Aristotle's works (by Theodore E. James). It is also better than average in two other respects: its selection of terms and concepts, and also of pertinent quotations, is more judicious than most; and it cites the sources of quotes specifically (by references to the standard Bekker edition of the Greek text of Aristotle's works, published in 1831).

311.   Bonitz, Hermann. **Index Aristotelicus.** Vol. 5 of **Aristotelis Opera,** ed. I. Bekker. Berlin: Reimer, 1870. Reprinted separately, Graz: Akademische Druck- und Verlagsanstalt, 1955. Reprinted separately, Berlin: Walter de Gruyter, 1961. 878p.

This is a complete concordance of the Bekker edition of Aristotle's Greek text. "An invaluable index of Greek words" (*Encyclopedia of Philosophy,* vol. 1, p. 162).

312.   Organ, Troy Wilson. **An Index to Aristotle in English Translation.** Princeton: Princeton University Press, 1949. Reprinted, New York: Gordian Press, 1966. 181p.

This is a detailed topical index to Aristotle's works based on the 11-volume English translation edited by W. D. Ross and J. A. Smith (Oxford University Press, 1908–1931). The page numbers cited are those of the Bekker edition of the Greek text (issued by the Berlin Academy, 1831–1870), which are referenced in the margins of the Oxford translations and also in many other English editions of Aristotle's works.

EPICTETUS (CA. 55–CA. 135)

313.   Oldfather, W. A. **Contributions Toward a Bibliography of Epictetus.** Urbana: University of Illinois Press, 1927. 201p. **Supplement.** Ed. Marian Harman, with a preliminary list of Epictetus manuscripts by W. H. Friedrich and C. U. Faye. Urbana: University of Illinois Press, 1952. 177p.

Oldfather, the foremost translator of Epictetus, painstakingly compiled a detailed bibliography of editions and translations of the Stoic philosopher's works (all consisting of transcriptions by his followers) in all languages, together with a secondary bibliography of criticism, including books, articles, and selected reviews. The 1952 supplement updates and augments the original with new or previously missed materials gathered by Oldfather or, after the latter's death, by Harman, though it includes none published after 1946. It also adds a preliminary list of known manuscripts of Epictetus's *Encheiridion.*

EPICURUS (CA. 341–270 B.C.)

314.   Usener, Hermann. **Glossarium Epicureum.** Edited and enlarged by M. Gigante and W. Schmid. Rome: Edizioni dell'Ateneo & Bizzarri, 1977. 873p. (Lessico intellettuale europeo, 14).

Indexes the Greek text of surviving manuscripts and fragments, including scattered and damaged papyrological texts, of Epicurus's writings. No definitions are provided, but lemmatized words are placed in their context, with sporadic elements of Latin or German paraphrase. Preface and other secondary matter are in Latin. Originally prepared by Usener, a nineteenth-century Epicurus scholar responsible for a standard collection of texts, *Epicurea* (1897), the glossary was enlarged by Gigante and Schmid.

PHILO OF ALEXANDRIA (PHILO JUDAEUS)
(CA. 20 B.C.–CA. A.D. 50)

315. Radice, Roberto, et. al. **Philo of Alexandria: An Annotated Bibliography, 1937–1986.** Leiden: E. J. Brill, 1988. 469p. (Supplements to Vigiliae Christianae, vol. 8).

This work is a translation plus expansion of Radice's Italian bibliography, *Filone di Alessandria: Bibliografia generale 1937–1982* (Naples: Bibliopolis, 1983), with coverage brought up to 1986. It includes a primary bibliography of Philo's works and a secondary bibliography of studies about him in Dutch, English, French, Italian, German, Modern Hebrew, Latin, and Spanish. Each is arranged chronologically. Six indexes provide access by authors of secondary studies, reviews, biblical passages, passages from Philo's own works, subjects, and Greek passages.

316. Borgen, Peder, Kåre Fuglseth, and Roald Skarsten. **The Philo Index: A Complete Greek Word Index to the Writings of Philo of Alexandria.** Grand Rapids. Mich.: William B. Eerdmans; Leiden: Brill, 2000. 371p.

An index to all the Greek words in the written corpus of the Hellenistic Jewish philosopher Philo. It is based on four major text editions: Cohn-Wendland (1896–1915), Colson (1941), Petit (1978), and Paramelle (1984). It improves on the older index by Mayer (entry 317) in several respects, most importantly in being more complete by including words from the principal fragments and indexing *all* words except three most frequent *(dev, kaiv,* and *oJ).* Also, index references use abbreviated names (versus Mayer's numbers) to identify texts, and word frequencies are noted. Lemmatising principles (regarding treatment of variants of the same basic word) are explained in the introduction.

317. Mayer, Günter. **Index Philoneus.** Berlin: Walter de Gruyter, 1974. 312p.

An index to Greek words based on the "Editio minor" of Philo's writings by Cohn and Wendland (1896 1915). Index references use numbers to identify the specific texts in which words occur; a key is provided in Mayer's introduction. Remains useful principally where the newer *Philo Index* (entry 316) is not available.

PLATO (CA. 428–347 B.C.)

318. Brisson, Luc, with Frédéric Plin. **Platon: 1990–1995, bibliographie.** Paris: Librairie Philosophique J. Vrin, 1999. 416p. (Tradition de la pensée classique).

Continues as an independent publication a series of bibliographies published for the period 1975–1990 in the German annual *Lustrum* (1983, 1988, and 1992). Includes a primary bibliography of editions and translations of Plato's works that also incorporates commentaries, and a secondary bibliography of *"travaux d'interprétation"*—books, journal articles, essays in *Festschriften,* and so forth. Most entries are annotated. Nearly 1,800 items are listed in the secondary section, arranged by author name. An "analytical index" provides access in the form of a subject outline.

Though the introduction forecasts publication "probably in 2001" of an additional volume for 1995–2000, as well as availability of a CD-ROM compilation covering 1950–2000 (p. 7), no evidence could be found as of July 2004 for the existence of either.

319.   Deschoux, Marcelle. **Comprendre Platon: Un siecle de bibliographie plato-nicienne de langue française, 1880–1980.** Paris: Belles Lettres, 1981. 206p. (Collection d'études anciennes; Travaux du Centre de Documentation et Bibliographie Philosophiques de l'Université de Franche Comté).

A comprehensive bibliography of French-language Platonic studies published from 1880 to 1980. Following brief chapters listing background studies on Greek antiquity and studies on Socrates, the principal part of the bibliography (pp. 33–127) divides into four sections: text editions and translations; books on Plato; articles in philosophical journals; and articles in historical, literary, or other publications, and in foreign journals. A final chapter lists foreign-language works, mainly English and German, treated in French-language reviews or studies. Within each chapter or section, arrangement is chronological. Includes six indexes.

320.   Martinez, Julio A. **Bibliography of Writings on Plato, 1900–1967.** San Diego, Calif.: San Diego State University Press, 1978. 94p.

Though relatively scarce even in U.S. libraries, compared for instance with McKirnahan's Plato bibliography for 1958–1973 (entry 321) with which it overlaps for a few years, Martinez's bibliography affords useful selective coverage for the first two-thirds of the twentieth century. "I have attempted," explains the compiler, "to select those works published between 1900 and 1967 which meet the scholarly and pedagogical needs of philosophers. However, some items of intrinsic philological value were also included" (introduction). Around 1,200 books, articles, dissertations, and reviews are listed, divided between two sections: general works on Plato and writings dealing with individual Platonic dialogues. English-language materials predominate, but items in French, German, and Spanish are also included.

321.   McKirahan, Richard D., Jr. **Plato and Socrates: A Comprehensive Bibliography, 1958–1973.** New York: Garland, 1978. 592p. (Garland Reference Library of the Humanities, vol. 78).

Continues the coverage provided for 1950–1957 by H. F. Cherniss's bibliographies in the German annual *Lustrum* (1959, 1960). Lists over 4,600 items, not counting book reviews, in more than 30 languages. The subject arrangement is facilitated by numerous cross-references and a number of special indexes imbedded within the subject sections. Sections devoted to individual Platonic dialogues include subdivisions for texts and translations, studies, and textual criticism. There are no annotations. An author index is provided.

322.   Ritter, Constantin. **Bibliographies on Plato, 1912–1930.** New York: Garland, 1980. 909p. (in various pagings) (Ancient Philosophy: Editions, Commentaries, Critical Works).

Reprints bibliographic essays in German originally published in *Jahresberichte über die Fortschritt des klassischen Altertumswissenschaft,* published at Leipzig by O. R. Reisland, 1912–1930. Each bears the title "Berichte über die in den letzten Jahrzehnten über Platon erschienenen Arbeiten."

323.   Saunders, Trevor J., and Luc Brisson. **Bibliography on Plato's *Laws*.** 3rd ed. Sankt Augustin: Academia, 2000. 141p. (International Plato Studies, vol. 12).

Covers literature published from 1922 to 1999 relating to one of Plato's longest and most difficult works. It is divided into three sections comprising (A) texts, translations, and commentaries; (B) books and articles; (C) discussions of individual passages. Brisson, who oversaw completion of this third edition after Saunders's death, has provided in an addendum a bibliography on Plato's *Epinomis*.

324.   Skemp, J. B. **Plato.** Oxford: Clarendon Press, 1976. 63p. (Greece and Rome: New Surveys in the Classics, no. 10).

Features concise bibliographic essays surveying various aspects of Platonic scholarship: recent editions of Plato's works, textual scholarship, Plato's relationship to Socrates and the Sophists, key ideas and dimensions of his thought (the Forms, theory of knowledge, ethics, physics, etc.), and "The Latest Phase: The Unwritten Doctrines" (chapter 10).

325.   Stockhammer, Morris. **Plato Dictionary.** New York: Philosophical Library, 1963. Paperback ed., Totowa, N.J.: Littlefield, Adams, 1965. 287p.

See entry 508 for a general comment. Like others in its series, this "dictionary" consists exclusively of quotations from its subject, in this case Plato. Of Stockhammer's several efforts in this vein (cf. entries 374, 448, and 473), this is probably the best. Given Plato's large and varied body of writings, one can readily find passages that cry out to be included but aren't (e.g., under the heading "opinion," some of the discussion in the *Meno* on opinion versus knowledge). On balance, though, Stockhammer has managed an interesting and representative selection of quotes. No more than that, however: the pretentious declaration in the introduction that "a new look at Plato's ethics of moral ideas has occasioned this book" epitomizes the penchant of works in this series for masquerading as more than what they are.

Sources of quotes are referenced using the standard pagination of the Stephanus edition. The text comes mainly from the archaic translations by Jowett (1871).

326.   Ast, Friedrich. **Lexicon Platonicum sive Vocum Platonicarum Index.** Leipzig: Weidmann, 1835–1838. 3 vols. Reprinted, Bonn: Habelt, 1956. 3 vols. in 2. Reprinted, New York: Burt Franklin, 1969. 3 vols.

A Greek-Latin lexicon to Plato's terminology is combined with a keyword index in this work. "The classical dictionary for Plato's original text" (Koren, *Research in Philosophy*, 98). Brandwood, however, in his newer *Word Index to Plato* (entry 327), avers that the *Lexicon Platonicum* "has long been recognized as an inadequate aid to the study of Plato" (p. ix).

327.   Brandwood, Leonard. **A Word Index to Plato.** Leeds, England: W. S. Maney, 1976. 1003p.

Brandwood's index, a product of early computer technology and 15 years of dogged labor, some of it described as a "depressing drudgery," provides complete references to all Greek words occurring in the Platonic corpus, "except for the definite article and *kai*, . . . the latter included only in certain mechanically identifiable combinations with other conjunctions or particles" (introduction). It is based on the Oxford Classical Text edition edited by John Burnet (Oxford, 1899–1907), but can be used with others because its references use the standard page, section, and line numbers of the Stephanus edition. References are grouped by dialogue, ordered according to a broadly chronological scheme. Footnotes comment on problematic words and sometimes give bibliographic references. An index of quotations is appended at the back.

328.   **The Plato Manuscripts: A New Index.** Prepared by the Plato Microfilm Project of the Yale University Library Under the Direction of Robert L. Brumbaugh and Rulon Wells. New Haven: Yale University Press, 1968. 163p.

A catalog of microfilms of "extant pre-1,500 manuscripts containing Plato's works in whole or in part," this work consists of two indexes, one arranged by holding library, and the other by title of Platonic dialogue. A short bibliography (19 items) of textually oriented works is included on page 163.

PLOTINUS (CA. 204–270)

329.   Dufour, Richard. **Plotinus: A Bibliography, 1950–2000.** Leiden: Brill, 2002. 174p.

This primary and secondary bibliography "aims to be exhaustive" for the period covered, though the compiler warns that exhaustiveness no doubt declines gradually for the last five years due to lag times in coverage by the major indexes and running bibliographies (introduction). Primary sources are divided between sections listing editions of the Greek texts of Plotinus's works and translations in all languages; each of these also incorporates secondary sources in the form of textual criticism, commentaries, and linguistic studies. Other secondary literature is gathered under the rubric "Studies" in a single sequence of 1,542 entries representing books and articles in all languages, arranged alphabetically by author.

This monographic publication is identified as a revised edition of a bibliography published in the series *Phronesis,* vol. 46 no. 3, August 2001.

330.   Sleeman, J. H., and Gilbert Pollet, eds. **Lexicon Plotinianum.** Leiden: E. J. Brill and Louvain: University Press, 1980. 1164 columns (Ancient and Medieval Philosophy, 2).

This comprehensive lexicon to the Greek text of Plotinus's works (known as the *Enneads,* from their arrangement into sections of nine treatises each) is designed to serve scholars of Plotinus, Neoplatonism, and more broadly late classical philosophy and philology. Each entry consists of a term in the Greek alphabet and its equivalent in English, succeeded by one or, more typically, a series of references to the term's occurrence(s) in Plotinus's text. References are followed by a full quotation when the term is considered the keyword for the quoted sentence or clause; those without quotations or with only a short quotation are often followed by a cross-reference to the entry where the fully quoted text may be found. Citations provide the number of the *Ennead* (Roman numeral) and chapter and line numbers (Arabic numerals) based on the *Plotini Opera* edition (Paris, 1951–1973). Plotinus's literal quotations of other writers, notably Plato, are marked by parentheses and followed by a reference to the source.

PYTHAGORAS (CA. 550–CA. 500 B.C.)

331.   Navia, Luis E. **Pythagoras: An Annotated Bibliography.** New York: Garland, 1990. 381p. (Garland Reference Library of the Humanities, vol. 1128).

Noting that "either Pythagoras himself or at least the traditions created in antiquity around him have succeeded in constructing a philosophical and scientific edifice of impressive dimensions" (foreword), Navia offers not a complete but "a selective and representative bibliography" of over a thousand works on Pythagoras. These vary considerably, he acknowledges, in the extent to which they are grounded in solid historical evidence as opposed to imaginative reconstruction, speculation, or sheer fantasy. Despite this, Navia's annotations remain descriptive rather than critical. The materials are divided into 10 sections representing major areas of Pythagorean scholarship—from bibliographies and source collections through general studies, relationships to Socrates and Plato, the testimony of Aristotle, Pythogoras's contributions to mathematics, science, music and art, to Pythagoreanism and literature—with an eleventh section for miscellaneous works. Author and name indexes are provided.

SOCRATES (470–399 B.C.)

332.   McKirahan, Richard D., Jr. **Plato and Socrates: A Comprehensive Bibliography, 1958–1973.** New York: Garland, 1978. 592p. (Garland Reference Library of the Humanities, vol. 78p.

Materials concerned with Socrates as a historical figure, and not simply as a character in Plato's dialogues, are listed in a 45-page section near the end of this book. See also entry 321.

333.   Morrison, Donald R. **Bibliography of Editions, Translations, and Commentary on Xenophon's Socratic Writings: 1600–Present.** Pittsburgh, Pa.: Mathesis, 1988. 103p.

Morrison's aim for this bibliography is to amend a perceived neglect in the twentieth century of Xenophon and his Socratic writings—next to Plato the most important source of information (and perhaps misinformation) about Socrates—in part by facilitating recovery and assimilation of past scholarship, which in this field remains exceptionally important. Separate chapters deal with complete editions of Xenophon's works; selective collections; each of his major Socratic writings; two writings of minor interest for Socratic studies; and special topics such as Xenophon's life, views, and relations to other thinkers, and the problems surrounding the "historical Socrates." Of 1,382 entries, just over half represent secondary studies. Annotations are rare and limited to brief indications of content when the title is particularly unhelpful.

334.   Navia, Luis E. and Ellen L. Katz. **Socrates: An Annotated Bibliography.** New York: Garland, 1988. 536p. (Garland Reference Library of the Humanities, vol. 844).

Navia and Katz organize 1,938 selected and representative works, from Socrates's own time to 1987, into 23 chapters encompassing all aspects of scholarship on and interest in Socrates. Besides more predictable categories such as primary sources (Aristophanes, Xenophon, Plato) and secondary studies thereof, works on Socrates's trial, or studies on Plato's *Apology,* there are chapters on, for example, the Aristotelian testimony; the *Crito* and political theory; Socrates, Jesus, and Christianity; the influence of Socrates; and fiction, poetry, and drama (including opera, film, and television) in which Socrates figures as a subject or character. Annotations, descriptive rather than critical, often provide excellent summaries of a work's major themes, arguments, or conclusions.

335.   Patzer, Andreas. **Bibliographia Socratica: Die wissenschaftliche Literatur über Sokrates von den Anfängen bis auf der neueste Zeit in systematisch-chronologischer Anordnung.** Freiburg: Karl Alber, 1985 365p.

Similar in several respects, including thematic arrangement and timespan covered, to Navia and Katz's 1987 bibliography (entry 334), but there are some differences in their respective organizational schemes, in emphases, and in the selection of representative works. Selection criteria are explained in the *Vorbermerkungen* (pp. 20ff). Lists 2,301 items. Occasional annotations and "see also" references. Index combines author names with subjects.

12

Western Philosophy: Medieval and Renaissance

BIBLIOGRAPHIES AND INDEXES

336. Ashworth, E. J. **The Tradition of Medieval Logic and Speculative Grammar from Anselm to the End of the Seventeenth Century: A Bibliography from 1836 Onwards.** Toronto: Pontifical Institute of Medieval Studies, 1978. 111p.

See entry 721.

337. **Bibliographia Patristica: Internationale patristische Bibliographie.** Berlin: Walter DeGruyter, 1959–1997. Vol. 1 (1956)—vol. 33/35 (1998–1990).

This serial bibliography, which lists books and periodical literature relating to the early Church Fathers, was suspended following publication of the volume covering 1998–1990 but provided comprehensive coverage for a period totaling 35 years. Theological subject matter predominates. The *philosophica* section is generally brief, but additional philosophical material appears in sections on individual authors, notably Augustine, Origen, Tertullian. The *auctores* sections include both works by (i.e., new editions and translations) and works about Patristic authors. Entries are not annotated. A separate section lists book reviews *(recensiones)*. Prefatory material is in German; subject headings are in Latin.

Publication frequency and format vary. Annual volumes 1 through 11 covered the years 1956–1966. Subsequent volumes mostly consolidate two years and carry double volume numbers, beginning with volume 12/13, published in 1975 and covering 1967–1968. After reverting back to individual volumes (28 and 29) for 1983 and 1984, the final two issues, published in 1994 and 1997, consolidate three volumes each, 30/32, and 33/35, covering 1985–1987 and 1998–1990, respectively.

A special supplement *(Supplementum 1)*, titled *Voces: Eine Bibliographie zu Wörtern und Begriffen aus der Patristik (1918–1978)* (Berlin: Walter de Gruyter, 1980, 461p.), lists materials focused on the explication, historical background or development, and so forth, of specific terms and concepts found in Patristic writings. The first half of the volume covers Greek, the second half Latin terms. Separate indexes are provided for the authors of works cited and for Patristic or ancient authors to whom they refer.

338. **Catalogo di manoscritti filosofici nelle biblioteche italiane.** 11 vols. Vols. 1–8: Florence: Leo S. Olschki, 1980–1996. Vols. 9–11: Florence: Sismel—Edizioni del Galluzo, 1999–2003. (Subsidia al Corpus philosophorum Medii Aevi, Unione Accademica Nazionale).

A union catalog of medieval and early modern philosophical manuscripts held by Italian libraries. Primary arrangement is by localities, within that by individual libraries; but it should be noted that some localities, notably Florence and Siena, are spread among several nonsequential volumes. Each library's holdings are generally arranged by manuscript author. The catalog includes manuscripts by major figures, for example, Albertus Magnus, Thomas Aquinas, as well as many minor ones. Information provided includes detailed bibliographic and physical descriptions, and sometimes secondary references. Each volume has several indexes: of manuscripts by location and holding library, of incipits (opening phrases), and of author and subject names together with titles of anonymous works. Volume 11 is a cumulated index.

339.   Kohl, Benjamin G. **Renaissance Humanism, 1300–1550: A Bibliography of Materials in English.** New York: Garland, 1985. 354p. (Garland Reference Library of the Humanities, vol. 570).

More than a philosophical movement, Renaissance humanism is characterized by Kohl as "a literary culture, an understanding and appreciation of literature, history, philosophy and aesthetics," communicated through particular rhetorical forms and based in the revival and careful study of Greek and Roman literature and culture (pp. xv, xvii). Despite the absence of any philosophical giant on the order of a Plato, Aquinas, or Kant, it did have a strong philosophical strain running through it, marked by the revival of Platonism, the fusion of Christian and Stoic ethics, the search for a *philosophia perennia,* and frequent embrace of philosophical syncretism. In the absence of any full-scale bibliography devoted to Renaissance philosophy, Kohl provides valuable coverage of this aspect of Renaissance humanism among others, including such philosophical or borderline-philosophical thinkers as Pico della Mirandola, Erasmus, and Thomas More. Both primary texts and secondary studies are included. An exception to the English-language-only limitation of scope is the inclusion of bibliographies in foreign languages. Kohl claims near-exhaustiveness for articles and books published through 1982 and includes a few items from 1983 (p. xii). He does not provide annotations.

340.   Lohr, Charles H. **Commentateurs d'Aristote au moyen-âge latin: Bibliographie de la literature secondaire récente / Medieval Latin Aristotle Commentators: A Bibliography of Recent Secondary Literature.** Fribourg, Switz.: Éditions Universitaires; Paris: Éditions du Cerf, 1988. 255p. (Vestigia, 2).

This bibliography of secondary studies complements an inventory of medieval Latin commentaries on Aristotle compiled by Lohr and published in the annual *Traditio,* volumes 23–30, from 1967 to 1974. Biographical, bibliographical, and other studies on authors of this important medieval genre are arranged under the names, in Latin form, of their subjects. Precise dates of coverage are not identified, but publication dates of the literature listed appear to fall primarily in the period 1964–1987. There is no index. Preface in French in English.

341.   Schönberger, Rolf, and Brigitte Kible. **Repertorium edierter Texte des Mittel-alters aus dem Bereich der Philosophie und angrenzender Gebiete.** Berlin: Adademie, 1994. 888p.

Documents editions of original philosophical texts and philosophically relevant texts from adjacent areas such as theology, mysticism, and Medieval science. Covers the period from Alcuin to Nicolas of Cusa, roughly 800–1450. Encompasses both independent publications and editions published in collections, periodicals, *Festschriften,* and so forth. Includes numerous minor authors. Some restrictions are imposed for voluminously published authors such as Aquinas and Raymond Lull (see preface, p. x), who nonetheless have hundreds of entries each. Spurious works are listed under the name of the erroneously ascribed author followed by "Pseudo." Names are entered by their Latin forms, but are cross-referenced in the name index by their common equivalents in various European languages. There are also indexes for editors and for the titles of works that are the subjects of commentaries.

342.   Schulthess, Peter, and Ruedi Imbach. **Die Philosophie im lateinischen Mittelalter: Ein Handbuch mit einem bio-bibliographischen Repertorium.** Vol. 2: **Von Alcuin bis Nicolaus Cusanus: Bio-bibliographisches Repertorium der Philosophie im lateinischen Mittelalter,** comp. by Ruedi Imbach and Doris Nienhaus. 605p.

See entry 350.

343.   Steenberghen, Fernand van. **La bibliothèque du philosophe médiéviste.** Louvain: Publicationes Universitaires; Paris: Béatrice-Nauwelaerts, 1974. 540p.

Strictly speaking, this is a collection of descriptive and critical reviews of books relating to medieval philosophy published previously in the *Revue neoscholastique de philosophie* (1928–1945), the *Revue philosophique de Louvain* (1946–1973), or elsewhere. Works reviewed include monographic studies, bibliographies and other "scholarly instruments," textual editions and translations. Because Van Steenberghen, a distinguished historian of Medieval philosophy, seemingly reviewed most of the important books in the field that emerged over the course of his long career, this is, in effect, an extensive and extensively annotated bibliography of candidates for "the library of the philosopher/medievalist" published from 1925 to 1973.

344.   Vasoli, Cesare. **Il pensiero medievale: Orientamenti bibliografici.** Bari: Laterza, 1971. 302p. (Picola biblioteca filosofica Laterze).

A handy, pocket-sized bibliography on medieval thought from "the barbaric age" through Wycliff and Huss, concentrating on philosophy but also encompassing theology, spirituality, and science. Primary arrangement is by major periods, with subsections for specific individuals. One chapter is devoted to *filosofie orientale,* meaning Byzantian, Arabic, and Jewish philosophies. Materials cited are in many languages, including English, French, German, Latin, and Spanish, but Italian works are most heavily represented. No indexes are provided (the one thing so labeled is really a table of contents).

DICTIONARIES, ENCYCLOPEDIAS, AND HANDBOOKS

345.   Evans, G. R. **Fifty Key Medieval Thinkers.** London: Routledge, 2002. 183p. (Routledge Key Guides).

Offers introductory sketches, particularly appropriate for undergraduate students, on key medieval thinkers from Augustine (353–430) to Gabriel Biel (d. 1495). Not all would be considered philosophers, even using the fluid categories appropriate for this period when philosophy was not sharply demarcated from theology—Francis of Assisi, for example, is seldom if ever classed as a philosopher—and some, such as Jerome and Dante, have their reputations mainly in other intellectual domains. But at least 20 would be counted as "regulars" in the cast of medieval philosophy—appearing, for example, also in Hackett's *Medieval Philosophers* (entry 347)—while many others, such as Hildegard of Bingen, Joachim of Fiore, Ramon Llull, and John Wyclif, play contributory roles that may be overlooked in more narrowly focused works. Articles include brief bibliographies and suggestions for further reading.

346.   Gracia, Jorge and Timothy Noone, eds. **A Companion to Philosophy in the Middle Ages.** Malden, Mass.: Blackwell, 2003. 739p. (Blackwell Companions to Philosophy, 24).

Following a brief introductory overview by editor Gracia are seven concise essays on some salient features in the historical development of medieval philosophy. These include, for example, the ancient and Patristic background, the important place of the School of Chartres, the role of religious orders, and the meaning and significance of "scholasticism." The bulk of this volume, however, comprises an alphabetically arranged biographical dictionary of medieval philosophers, 137 men and one woman (Hildergard of Bingen), spanning in time from Augustine (354–430) to Gabriel Biel (d. 1495). As one might surmise from this large total number—nearly a hundred more than are included in Hackett's *Medieval Philosophers* (entry 347)—it encompasses many comparatively minor figures, about some of whom relatively little has been written. The vast majority, expectedly, are Christian philosophers, but at least 15 Islamic and Jewish philosophers are included as well, again not just the well-known, like Averroes and Maimonides, but also some lesser-known figures, for example, Albumasar and Gersonides. Articles range in length from less than 2 pages for the most obscure to 17 or 18 for the most famous, such as Ockham and Aquinas.

The editors "made a special effort to be cosmopolitan and inclusive insofar as the contributors are concerned" (preface), with impressive success. The 85 contributors are affiliated with universities throughout the Americas and Europe and work in diverse languages and scholarly traditions.

347.   Hackett, Jeremiah, ed. **Medieval Philosophers.** Detroit: Gale Research, 1992. 465p. (Dictionary of Literary Biography, vol. 115).

This attractive reference volume was the first in the mammoth and ongoing *Dictionary of Literary Biography (DLB)* publication project to be devoted entirely to philosophers. It shares the general characteristics of the *DLB* series: targeted at a student audience while offering utility to scholars as well, presenting essay-length treatments, often illustrated, of a specific category of writers—medieval philosophers in this case—with more than usual attention to biographical matters and to cultural and historical backgrounds. Its one questionable feature is a cumulative index for all volumes of the *DLB* to date (vols. 1–115), which occupies the last 75 of the volume's 465 pages. This feature recurs, rather wastefully it could be argued, in every *DLB* volume. Articles in this and other *DLB* volumes are also available online (text only) in the *Gale Literary Databases* collection from Thomson-Gale, accessible only through subscribing libraries.

The 41 philosophers selected by Hackett for this volume span the period from 345 (Augustine) to 1464 (Nicholas of Cusa) and include representatives of Islamic thought (e.g., Averröes, al-Fārābi, Ibn Bājja) and Jewish thought (e.g., Hasdai Crescas, Gersonides, Maimonides) as well as Christian philosophers both famous (Abelard, Aquinas, Boethius, Meister Eckhart) and lesser-known (Thomas Bradwardine, Giles of Rome, Richard Swineshead). Articles were contributed by a dozen or so leading specialists on medieval philosophy. Each article begins with a list of the philosopher's works and editions thereof in the original language and in English, and ends with a brief biography and a list of references to secondary sources.

348.   Malone, Edward A., ed. **British Rhetoricians and Logicians, 1500–1660. First Series.** Detroit: Gale, 2001. 432p. (Dictionary of Literary Biography, vol. 236). **Second Series.** Detroit: Gale, 2003. 473p. (Dictionary of Literary Biography, vol. 281).

Profiles, between the two volumes, around 50 late-Renaissance British writers on logic and rhetoric, two closely connected disciplines during this period. Few have high name recognition in the history of philosophy; a signal exception is Francis Bacon. The First Series volume appends a 36 page essay on Continental European Rhetoricians, 1400–1600, and their influence in Renaissance England, plus a glossary of terms and some definitions of logic and rhetoric from the time.

349.   Riedl, John Orth, et. al. **A Catalogue of Renaissance Philosophers (1350–1650).** Milwaukee: Marquette University Press, 1940. Reprint, Hildesheim, Germany: Georg Olms, 1973. 179p.

"Catalogue" is an apt term for this work which categorizes Renaissance thinkers into 102 different schools and movements, arranged in rough chronological sequence from early Italian Humanists to Occasionalists. "Philosopher" is interpreted liberally, so that "many scientists, ascetics, theologians and rhetoricians have been included . . . partly because some of their writings either were philosophical or had an influence on philosophy, and partly because their inclusion aids materially in the reconstruction of the comprehensive body of knowledge which the first philosophers of modern times received as their inheritance . . . " (foreword). Each entry consists of basic biographical data followed by a list of writings (with minimal bibliographic apparatus). "The biographical details selected were usually those that designated the education, teachers, university connections and pupils of a thinker, and such other details as might help to place him in some one or two of the maelstrom of conflicting tendencies in his lifetime." At the back are a table of universities, bibliography of basic secondary sources, and index of names.

350.   Schulthess, Peter, and Ruedi Imbach. **Die Philosophie im lateinischen Mittelalter: Ein Handbuch mit einem bio-bibliographischen Repertorium.** Zürich: Artemis & Winkler, 1996. 2 vols. Vol. 2: **Von Alcuin bis Nicolaus Cusanus: Bio-bibliographisches Repertorium der Philosophie im lateinischen Mittelalter,** comp. by Ruedi Imbach and Doris Nienhaus. 605p.

The first volume *(Teil I)* of this *Handbuch* constitutes a thematic historical survey of Latin Medieval philosophy from Alcuin to Nicolas of Cusa (ca. 800 to 1450), focusing particularly on the reception of classical texts and emphasizing many minor authors not typically mentioned in histories of Medieval philosophy. (Although the restriction to "Latin" serves principally to demarcate off the Islamic Arabic tradition, the latter's role in transmitting classical texts and learning receives considerable attention.) *Teil II* contains a complementary bio-bibliographical directory listing alphabetically virtually all known philosophical authors from the period covered, including some not mentioned in volume 1, with basic biographical details (birth and death dates; academic, religious, or professional affiliations; and brief characterization of his or her philosophical work) plus a bibliography. The latter, necessarily (and often highly) selective for all but very minor figures, includes both the principal primary texts, often sorted by categories such as commentaries and *questiones,* and secondary literature including references to a number of standard reference works consulted for this *Handbuch. Teil II* also serves as an index to *Teil I,* citing when applicable the relevant pages in the latter.

351.   Sheikh, M. Saeed. **Dictionary of Muslim Philosophy.** Lahore, Pakistan: Institute of Islamic Culture, 1970. 146p.

See entry 259 in chapter 9. This dictionary is devoted to *medieval* Muslim philosophers.

SOURCES ON INDIVIDUAL PHILOSOPHERS

ANSELM OF CANTERBURY, SAINT (1033–1109)

352.   Evans, G. R. **A Concordance to the Works of St. Anselm.** Millwood, N.Y.: Kraus International, 1984. 4 vols.

All significant words in the Latin text of Anselm's collected works are displayed in their context, usually 8 to 10 words of surrounding text. Each entry is referenced to work, chapter or section, page, and line. Frequent words such as *ab, ad,* and so forth, are listed in a separate index without context. A finding list enables the user to locate all the forms of a word (e.g., *accedo, accedendo, accessi,* etc.), while a "reverse vocabulary" index allows words with the same ending (e.g., *-enda, -alia*) to be identified for grammatical or stylistic analysis. The concordance is based on the *S. Anselmi Opera Omnia* edited by F. S. Schmitt (1938–61) and on the text of the *Philosophical Fragments* in *Memorials of St. Anselm* (1969), edited by F. W. Southern and F. S. Schmitt.

AUGUSTINE, SAINT (354–430)

353.   Andresen, Carl. **Bibliografia Augustiniana.** 2nd rev. ed. Darmstadt: Wissenschaftliche Buchgesellschaft, 1973. 317p.

Includes works by Augustine and about him, the latter mainly from the middle third of this century. Uses a classified arrangement (see classification table on pages 1–5) and is thoroughly indexed by authors, subjects, personal names (as subjects or in titles), and references to specific Augustinian works, Biblical texts, and classical authors. Also has a chronological list of Augustine's writings. The preface is in Latin and German.

354.   **Augustinus-Sekundärliteraturdatenbank—Augustine Secondary Literature Data Bank.** Zentrum für Augustinusforschung in Würzburg. http://www.augustinus. de/literaturdatenbank.asp (accessed October 24, 2005).

This electronic bibliography originated as a project designed to provide a foundation for the *Augustinus-Lexikon* (see entry 361), but enjoys a life and identity of its own. It includes some 27,500 entries, growing by hundreds per year, for secondary studies on Augustine. Access options offered include alphabetical listings sorted either by author or by title as well as author, title, or subject keyword searching with options for Boolean combinations and date limiting. Assigned subject keywords are based on the entry terms in the *Augustinus-Lexikon.* Candidates for addition to the bibliography can be submitted online via a link on the search screen. Updating occurs on a nearly daily basis.

Closed editions of the bibliography are also available on CD-ROM in conjunction with the first and second editions of the *Corpus Augustinianum Gissense* (entry 362).

355. Bavel, Tarsicius J. van, with F. Van der Zande. **Répertoire Bibliographique de Saint Augustin, 1950–1960.** The Hague: Martinus Nijhoff, 1963. 991p. (Instrumenta Patristica, 3).

Though covering a mere decade of Augustinian scholarship, this has an astonishing 5,502 entries, of which perhaps a third are cross-references. It offers the advantage, for those who read French, of substantial annotations, and uses a system of asterisks (one to three) to rate items according to level of readership and importance. A classified arrangement is used, supplemented by a subject index.

356. Donnelly, Dorothy F., and Mark A. Sherman. **Augustine's *De Civitate Dei: An Annotated Bibliography of Modern Criticism, 1960–1990.*** New York: Peter Lang, 1992. 109p.

Lists 64 studies on Augustine's most famous text, *De Civitate Dei* [The City of God], published in the United States and Canada over the three decades indicated in its title, as well as, in separate sections, 18 selected English-language studies published abroad and 13 of the most important pre-1960 publications. To describe the entries as annotated is to understate, given the often detailed summaries that average nearly a page in length. A list of Augustine's writings and a selected general bibliography, both unannotated, complete the volume.

357. Eckermann, Willigis, and Achim Krümmel. **Repertorium annotatum operum et tranlationum S. Augustini: lateinische Editionen und deutsche Übersetzungen (1750–1920).** Würzburg: Augustinus-Verlag, 1992. 552 pp. (Cassiciacum, Band 43/1).

Documents one aspect of the modern flowering of Augustinian scholarship: the proliferation of Latin editions and German translations of Augustine's works in the period reaching from 1750 to 1920, especially the first half of the nineteenth century. Entries are annotated with biographical information about editors, translators, and other contributors; brief characterizations of the nature, immediate purpose, publication circumstances, or content of the edition or translation; and identification of a holding library where the compilers personally examined a copy. Part 3 presents statistical data. There are indexes for names and for Augustine's letters and sermons.

358. Institut des Études Augustiniennes. Paris. **Fichier augustinien / Augustine Bibliography.** Boston: G. K. Hall, 1972. 4 vols. Microfilm ed.: 8 reels. **Premier supplement / First Supplement.** Boston: G. K. Hall, 1981. 516p.

Base volumes reproduce some 63,000 typewritten cards compiled by the Institut, established in 1943 as a center for Augustinian studies and bibliography. Access is by author (vols. 1–2) and by subject (vols. 3–4), the latter via a classified arrangement. Works by as well as about Augustine are listed. Some 13,000 additional cards, covering works published between 1971 and 1978 inclusively, are represented in the supplement.

The microfilm version of the base set is on 35mm film at 15X reduction.

359. Miethe, Terry L. **Augustinian Bibliography, 1970–1980, with Essays on the Fundamentals of Augustinian Scholarship.** Westport, Conn.: Greenwood Press, 1982. 218p.

Intended to supplement several older bibliographies, notably Andresen's (entry 353) and the *Fichier augustinien* (entry 358), Miethe's work takes in pre-1970 items if they were omitted from the earlier works. Included, for instance, are some 140 dissertations from the 1890s to 1970. Arrangement is by broad subjects, including sections for items relating to specific works by Augustine. Entries are unannotated. The four essays appended to the bibliography are misleadingly titled and add negligible value.

360. Fitzgerald, Allan D., general ed. **Augustine Through the Ages: An Encyclopedia.** Grand Rapids, Mich.: William B. Eerdmans, 1999. 902p.

Authoritative and broadly useful, this encyclopedia embraces the biographical, historical, and theological as well as philosophical dimensions of Augustine. Entries address numerous topics addressed in his writings, from abortion to worship; each of his more significant works; events, places, and people in his life; influences on his thought (e.g., Plato, Manicheism) and his own influences on later individuals (e.g., Gregory the Great, Aquinas, Calvin, Kierkegaard) and movements (Scholasticism, Renaissance, Reformation). Brief but scholarly bibliographies accompany every article. Other features include tables listing all of Augustine's works with their principal collective Latin editions and English translations, dates, and explanatory notes. Separate tables list known letters (under *epistulae*) and sermons. Contributors, 141 strong, represent three continents, though a majority are American.

361. Mayer, Cornelius, ed. **Augustinus-Lexikon.** Basel: Schwabe, 1986–. Vols. 1– (in progress).

"The *Augustinus-Lexikon* endeavors to give a comprehensive account of Augustine the individual, his milieu, and his thought. This undertaking may rightly claim its own special place alongside of other works of reference whose scope does not allow them to do justice to Augustine's surpassing influence" (preface to vol. 1). This self-congratulatory ascription, though written before the appearance of Fitzgerald's excellent and comprehensive English-language encyclopedia, *Augustine Through the Ages* (entry 360), would not necessarily retreat before Fitzgerald's work, because the *Augustinus-Lexikon* is more expansive still and another step up in scholarship. Launched with the formation of an editorial board as long ago as 1976, it remains far from complete as of late 2005. Only volume 1 (A-Con) and volume 2 (Cor-Fides) were completed, the latter still existing in the form of eight fascicles, a publication pattern expected to continue with future volumes. Fascicles 1 and 2 (Fig-Hier) of volume 3 were published in a combined issue in February 2005. The completed set is projected to have five volumes with a collective total of about 1,200 entries, plus an index volume.

While it covers much the same ground as the Fitzgerald encyclopedia—offering articles on events, persons, places, and objects important in Augustine's life and thought;

on his voluminous writings; and on significant concepts and topics in his thought—the *Lexikon* in contrast eschews any systematic treatment of "the history of his importance for posterity" (preface). Its multilingual character—with articles variously in English, German, or French, entry titles all in Latin—also makes it less accessible than Fitzgerald to most nonspecialists (whatever their own language), and the depth and breadth of its scholarship are more likely to exceed the needs, if not the comprehension, of nonspecialists. Somewhat forbidding, too, is its extensive use of abbreviations.

The bibliographic references accompanying each *Lexikon* article are compiled and made available separately on the Web site of the Zentrum für Augustinusforschung in Würzburg at *http://www.augustinus.de* (accessed October 24, 2005). Comprising some 4,800 items as of late 2005, this *Bibliographie des Augustinus-Lexikons* should continue to grow with the parent publication. It is not limited to materials on Augustine per se, because cited literature often relates to his background and context.

362. **Corpus Augustinianum Gissense 2 (CAG 2).** CD-ROM. Ed. Cornelius Mayer. Zentrum für Augustinus-Forschung in Würzburg. Basel: Schwabe, 2004. 1 disk accompanied by printed manual.

This CD-ROM contains in the first place Augustine's collected Latin works in what the editor and colleagues considered the best critical editions. The conventional reference value electronic texts afford by virtue of their amenability to computerized searching is significantly augmented here by incorporation of, in effect, a virtual lemmatized concordance to the more than 5 million words in the Augustinian corpus. This permits, for example, querying the database for all words built on the root "pagan-" to obtain a list of all the applicable words, which can be edited down if desired before eliciting a list of all occurrences in the complete text or within a specific work. References cite book and paragraph number. Also presented are frequencies of occurrence—meaning, however, the number of paragraphs in which the word occurs one or more times, not the absolute number of occurrences of the word. The database and index were originally produced at the Universität Giessen in close association with the Zentrum für Augustinus-Forschung in Würzburg and the ongoing project of the *Augustinus-Lexikon* (entry 361; see its preface, vol. 1, p. xiv). The first CD-ROM edition *(CAG 1)* was published in 1996 (Basel: Schwabe, 1996). The second edition claims numerous corrections to the text and an improved search interface offering four language options: German, English, French, and Spanish.

Importantly, both editions of the CD-ROM also contain the *Augustinus-Sekundär-literaturdatenbank* (see entry 354) as it stood at the time of publication. For the second edition, this entails a database of some 27,500 entries.

BOETHIUS, ANUCIUS MANLIUS SEVERINUS (CA. 480–CA. 526)

363. Kaylor, Noel Harold, Jr. **The Medieval *Consolation of Philosophy:* An Annotated Bibliography.** Hamden, Conn.: Garland, 1992. 262p. (Garland Medieval Bibliographies, vol. 7; Garland Reference Library of the Humanities, vol. 1215).

Kaylor's bibliography focuses on the role played in the vernacular (non-Latin) intellectual and educational life of medieval Europe by Boethius's *De Consolatione Philosophiae*.

Widely read in vernacular languages by nonscholars and used as a primary school text, its numerous translators included figures as notable as King Alfred, Chaucer, and Queen Elizabeth. Kaylor offers a brief survey of trends in scholarship and an annotated bibliography of scholarly studies (from the nineteenth century to 1992) in each of four chapters treating the Old English, Medieval German, Medieval French, and Middle English traditions. The annotations are brief and rather basic. A consolidated bibliography at the end of the volume includes some items not listed in the individual chapters, and vice versa.

DUNS SCOTUS, JOHN (CA. 1266–1308)

364. Schäfer, Odulfus. **Bibliografia de Viata, Operibus, et Doctrina Iohannis Duns Scoti.** Rome: Orbis Catholicus-Herder, 1955. 223p.

Nineteenth- and twentieth-century writings on Duns Scotus up to 1952 are arranged by author. There are separate indexes for subjects and for names of coauthors, editors, and other contributors, as well as cross-references for problematic Latin, French, and Spanish author names. The introduction is in Latin.

ERASMUS, DESIDERIUS (1466–1536)

365. **Catalogue of the Erasmus Collection in the City Library of Rotterdam.** Westport, Conn.: Greenwood Press, 1990. 678p. (Bibliographies and Indexes in Philosophy, 2).

Reproduced here are cards from the catalog of the municipal library of Erasmus's native city, Rotterdam, which houses the world's largest collection of books and articles by and about the Dutch humanist. As of 1989 (when this work was done) it comprised around 2,500 works by Erasmus, 500 edited by him, and 2,500 about him. Only a fraction of this is philosophical in nature, as the collection reflects the full range of Erasmus's interests and activities relating to classical scholarship and translation, theology, philosophy, pedagogy, pacifism, church reform, and more. Subject and author listings are separate.

PAUL OF VENICE (PAOLO NICOLETTI VENETO) (D. 1429)

366. Perreiah, Alan R. **Paul of Venice: A Bibliographical Guide.** Bowling Green, Ohio: Philosophy Documentation Center, Bowling Green State University, 1986. 175p. (Bibliographies of Famous Philosophers).

This volume stretches the title of the series in which it appears—a philosopher who rarely gets his own entry in philosophical dictionaries and encyclopedias hardly rates as famous—but it performs valuable service in documenting a figure of considerable intellectual stature who, around the turn of the fourteenth to fifteenth centuries, influenced both late medieval Scholasticism and early Renaissance Humanism. It provides for the first time a comprehensive bibliography of 279 extant manuscripts by Paul or ascribed to him, accompanied by a 45-page, heavily-documented discussion of the disputed *Logica Magna* which concludes that this work is not in fact by Paul but is inconclusive about the actual author. A 20-page biography introduces the volume.

THOMAS AQUINAS, SAINT (CA. 1224–1274)

367. Bourke, Vernon J. **Thomistic Bibliography, 1920–1940.** St. Louis: The Modern Schoolman, 1945. (Supplement to vol. 21). 312p.

Has 6,667 numbered and unannotated entries, arranged in an analytical subject scheme adapted with minor modifications from Mandonnet and Destrez, whose work (entry 369) is carried forward here. Like its predecessor, and also like its successor for the subsequent period (entry 370), this work functions to some extent, but not fully, as a bibliography for Thomism as a school of thought, as well as for St. Thomas as an individual (in any case a tenuous distinction, because Thomistic philosophy typically makes constant reference to St. Thomas and his writings). An index of proper names includes both authors and persons mentioned in titles.

368. Ingardia, Richard. **Thomas Aquinas: International Bibliography, 1977–1990.** Bowling Green, Ohio: Philosophy Documentation Center, Bowling Green State University, 1993. 492p. (Bibliographies of Famous Philosophers).

This latest Thomistic bibliography picks up chronologically where Miethe and Burke (entry 370) left off, with some overlap at the boundaries. Its 4,200 items representing less than a decade-and-a-half of scholarly activity testify to the continuing and widespread interest toward the end of the twentieth century in Aquinas and his philosophical thought (isolated here insofar as possible from theological matters) despite Thomism's declining stature in Catholic institutions. Separate sections, each arranged by language, cover primary and secondary sources, including significant book reviews; and there is a section on congresses, special collections, unpublished papers, and American dissertations. Authors' abstracts have been provided when available. There are seven indexes.

369. Mandonnet, P., and J. Destrez. **Bibliographie thomiste.** Le Saulchoir, Kain, Belgium: Revue des sciences philosophiques et theologiques, 1921. (Bibliotheque thomiste, no. 1). 2nd ed. Paris: Librairie Philosophique J. Vrin, 1960. 121p.

A list of 2,219 items, published up to 1920, classified under five major categories: (1) life and personality of St. Thomas; (2) works of St. Thomas; (3) philosophical doctrines; (4) theological doctrines; and (5) doctrinal and historical relations.

The second edition is basically a reprinting, with a new introduction.

370. Miethe, Terry L., and Vernon J. Bourke. **Thomistic Bibliography, 1940–1978.** Westport, Conn: Greenwood Press, 1980. 318p.

Continuing the efforts of Bourke (1945, entry 367) and Mandonnet and Destrez (1921, entry 369), this bibliography is arranged much like its predecessors. It has 4,097 unannotated entries. The introduction includes some discussion of new research tools and recent developments in Thomistic scholarship.

371. Deferrari, Roy Joseph. **A Latin-English Dictionary of St. Thomas Aquinas, Based on the "Summa Theologica" and Selected Passages of His Other Works.** Boston: St. Paul Editions, 1960. 1115p.

This is an abridgement of the *Lexicon of St. Thomas Aquinas* (entry 372). "It contains all the words and meanings given in the *Lexicon* and most of the research value, but the omission of examples more easily allows a choice of wrong meanings from among the many definitions given" (McLean, *Philosophy in the 20th Century: Catholic and Christian,* vol. 1, p. 5).

372.   Deferrari, Roy Joseph, Sister M. Inviolata Barry, and Ignatius McGuiness. **A Lexicon of St. Thomas Aquinas Based on the "Summa Theologica" and Selected Passages of His Other Works.** Washington, D.C.: Catholic University of America Press, 1948–53. 5 fascicles in 2 vols.

Designed to facilitate understanding of Aquinas's language generally "and not its philosophical and theological aspects exclusively," this lexicon "includes all the words in the *Summa Theologica* and such other words from the remaining works as seem in the judgment of the authors to be of great importance" (foreword). For each word, one or several differing English meanings are given, followed by illustrations of its use in each meaning. If a definition of a term is supplied by Aquinas himself, this precedes any other examples. The text used is that of the Leonine edition (Rome, 1888–1906) for the *Summa,* that of Vives (Paris, 1871–80) for other works.

373.   Schütz, Ludwig. **Thomas-Lexikon: Sammlung, Übersetzung und Erklärung der in sämtlichen Werken des h. Thomas von Aquin vorkommenden Künstausdrucke und wissenschaftlichen Aussprüche.** 2nd greatly enlarged ed. Paderborn: Ferdinand Schöningh, 1895. 889p. Variously reprinted, including New York: F. Ungar, 1957.

An older but much reprinted German dictionary keyed to Aquinas's Latin text, focusing, as its long title explains, on technical terms and specialized philosophical or theological vocabulary. For each term, it gives the direct German equivalent(s) with occasional explanatory comments, followed by illustrative quotations, often numerous though usually not exhaustive of Aquinas's use of the term.

374.   Stockhammer, Morris. **Thomas Aquinas Dictionary.** New York: Philosophical Library, 1965. 219p.

See entry 508 for a general comment on the series. This is strictly a compilation of quotes, the vast majority of them very short: usually a single sentence. Some entries, rather than presenting anything substantive, seem to serve an indexing function; such as, "horse and donkey," which offers this quote: "Horse and donkey are different beings, but both are animals." No entries are included that do not correspond to a word or words used in the quotations, thus none for "Cosmological Proof," "the Five Ways," "ontology," *"via negativa,"* or other such terms likely to come up in discussions of Aquinas's philosophy. Most quotes are from the *Summa Theologica,* a few from the *Summa Contra Gentiles.* Citations refer to the standard divisions of these works, including the numbered questions and answers characteristic of Aquinas's philosophical style.

375.   Deferrari, Roy Joseph, and Sister M. Inviolata Barry. **A Complete Index to the "Summa Theologica" of St. Thomas Aquinas.** Washington, D.C.: Catholic University of America Press, 1956. 386p.

This index is based on the Leonine edition of the *Summa* (Rome, 1888–1908) and certain passages from the Vives edition (Paris, 1871–1880) that are not included in the former. "Since this Index has been prepared for those interested in the content of St.Thomas' thinking rather than in his literary style, no attempt has been made to separate individual words into their inflectional forms as is the usual procedure in making an *index verborum.* . . . Likewise, words of no philosophical significance, such as *et, cum,* and *qui,* are omitted" (foreword). References are to standard divisions of the text, mainly numbered parts, questions, and articles.

376.   Index Thomisticus: Sancti Thomae Aquinatis Operum Omnium Indices et Concordantiae. Roberto Busa, S. J., editor-in-chief. [n.p.]: Frommann-Holzboog, 1974–1980. 3 vols. in 49 physical vols.

"This is a reference tool of such grandiose proportions that it cannot be ignored" (Miethe & Bourke, *Thomistic Bibliography 1940–1978,* p. xiii). Indeed, the *Index Thomisticus* takes the prize for the most voluminous print reference work (excluding continuations) to be recorded in this guide. It comprises three sections plus a supplement. Section 1, *Indices,* in 10 volumes, contains indexes of distribution, summaries of the dictionary, and indices of frequency. Sections 2 and 3 comprise the *Concordantiae:* complete concordances for, respectively, all of Aquinas's works, in 31 volumes, and for additions by other authors that are included in older editions of the *Opera Omnia,* in 8 volumes. Miethe and Bourke question the wisdom of including the latter, "since they represent neither the thought nor the language of Saint Thomas" (*op. cit.,* p. xiv). A small guide in Latin and English, *Clavis Indicis Thomistici* (Frommann-Holzboog, 1979, 47p.), was issued when the set was still incomplete; a larger introductory volume to the entire *Index* reportedly was to be published last, but has apparently not materialized.

The *Index Thomisticus* has been hailed as "of incomparable importance to Thomistic research" (*New Scholasticism* 50 [1976]:237–49). Miethe and Bourke, on the other hand, express reservations, fearing the potential for error in the computerized compilation (they cite an example) and suggesting that while "without doubt [it] has some utility for students of medieval Latin usage . . . the very size of the *Index* renders it cumbersome for the investigation of Saint Thomas' thought" (*op. cit.*, p. xiv).

Supplementing the *Index* are seven volumes containing Aquinas's complete Latin works, *S. Thomae Aquinatis Opera Omnia.* The full text was subsequently issued in digital format as *Thomae Aquinatis Opera Omnia cum Hypertextibus in CD-ROM* (Milan: Editoria Elettronica Editel, 1992; 2nd ed., 1996). This has substantial reference value of its own, not merely for its free-text searching capabilities but the added value of "hypertext" that summarizes all of the more than 10 million words into around 147,000 lemmatized forms. It does not, however, contain the indices and concordances of the printed *Index.*

377.   Thomae Aquinatis Opera Omnia cum Hypertextibus in CD-ROM. Roberto Busa, ed. 2nd ed. Milan: Editoria Elettronica Editel, 1996.

See entry 376.

VIVES, JUAN LUIS (1492–1540)

378.   Noreña, Carlos G. A Vives Bibliography. Lewiston, N.Y.: Edwin Mellen Press, 1990. 59p. (Studies in Renaissance Literature, vol. 5).

Though slim and avowedly not exhaustive, Noreña's work on Vives provides good and useful bibliographic coverage of the Spanish Renaissance philosopher and humanist. It is divided into seven sections: editions of Vives's *Opera Omnia,* critical editions of his works, translations by language, Vives and the Renaissance, biographical literature, secondary studies of Vives's thought, and bibliographical sources. Entries are not annotated.

13
Western Philosophy: Modern through Nineteenth Century

BIBLIOGRAPHIES

379. Emel'ianov, B. V., and V. V. **Kulikov. Russkie mysliteli vtoroi poloviny XIX –nachala XX veka: opyt kratkogo biobibliograficheskogo slovaria.** Ekaterinburg: Izd-vo Ural'skogo Universiteta, 1996. 383p.

See entry 398.

380. Ersch, Johann Samuel, and Christian Anton Geissler. **Handbuch der philosophischen Literatur der Deutschen, von der Mitte des 18. Jahrhunderts bis zum Jahre 1850.** Düsseldorf: Stern-Verlag Janssen, 1965. 218p. (Instrumenta Philsophica. Series Indices librorum, 1).

See entry 61.

381. Jessop, T. E. **A Bibliography of David Hume and of Scottish Philosophy from Francis Hutcheson to Lord Balfour.** London: A. Brown, 1938. Reissued, New York: Russell & Russell, 1966. Reprinted, New York: Garland, 1983. 201p.

See entry 439 regarding the Hume bibliography in part 1. The bibliography on Scottish philosophy is segregated as part 2 (pp. 75–190). "Scottish" is more than simply a geographical qualifier here; it designates a distinctive philosophical outlook that dominated philosophy in Scotland from Hutcheson (ca. 1725–) to the late nineteenth century. Indicative of this is the deliberate omission of Scottish thinkers during this period (particularly toward the end) who stood outside the tradition, which Jessop characterizes in these terms: "a liberal empiricism with an introspective bias in ethics and aesthetics, widening . . . into a philosophical attitude which, with growing objectivity, has given the major prerogatives to the intimations of experience rather than to the decrees of abstract thinking" (preface). It encompasses the Common Sense school most notably represented by Thomas Reid. This bibliography covers 79 writers individually and also includes contemporary reviews of their books. While Hume deeply influenced many of these philosophers, they were mostly critical of him.

382. Marti, Hanspeter, with Karin Marti. **Philosophische Dissertationen deutscher Universitäten, 1660–1750: eine Auswahlbibliographie.** Munich: K. G. Saur, 1982.

See entry 64.

383. Myerson, Joel, ed. **The Transcendentalists: A Review of Research and Criticism.** New York: Modern Language Association of America, 1984. 534p.

A broad intellectual and cultural movement not confined to one field, New England Transcendentalism is described by Myerson (pp. 1–2) as "essentially a religious orientation," closely associated with Unitarianism, but having its "most lasting impact on literature," especially via Emerson and Thoreau. However, it drew on, and had significant implications for, philosophy, particularly the areas of epistemology, philosophy of nature, and social philosophy. Myerson and 29 fellow scholars survey the movement in a series of 44 bibliographic essays. Twenty-eight of these deal with individual Transcendentalist thinkers from Bronson Alcott to Charles Stearns Wheeler, another 11, under the rubric "The Contemporary Reaction," with thinkers who were not allied with the movement but reacted to it or interacted with it (e.g., Orestes Browning, Hawthorne, Melville). Content and structure of the essays vary, but typically they include sections on bibliographies, manuscripts, editions, biographical studies, and criticism, and close with a paragraph of suggestions for further research. Pages 385–503 have an alphabetically arranged (by author) bibliography of works referred to in the essays, with full bibliographic details.

384.   Slater, John G., comp. **Bibliography of Modern American Philosophers.** Bristol, U.K.: Thoemmes Continuum, 2005, 3 vols.

     See entry 524.

385.   Slater, John G., comp. **Bibliography of Modern British Philosophers.** Bristol, U.K.: Thoemmes Continuum, 2004, 2 vols.

     See entry 525.

DICTIONARIES, ENCYCLOPEDIAS, AND HANDBOOKS

386.   Alekseev, Petr Vasil'evich. **Filosofy Rossii XIX–XX stoletii: biografii, idei, trudy.** 4th ed. Moscow: Akademicheskii Proekt, 2002.

     See entry 286.

387.   **Blackwell Companion to the Enlightenment.** John W. Yolton, et. al., eds. Oxford: Basil Blackwell, 1991. 581p.

     The Enlightenment was much more than a philosophical phenomenon, having wide repercussions in literature and the arts, religion, science, politics, and society. In the absence, however, of a reference work devoted exclusively to the philosophical thought of this important period, several general Enlightenment encyclopedias merit mention and recommendation in this chapter (see also entries 389, 399, and 403). Tellingly, perhaps, the Library of Congress (LC) classifies most of these under philosophy, presumably in recognition of the centrality to the Enlightenment period of its philosophical impulses.

     This *Blackwell Companion,* the oldest among these general reference works on the Enlightenment (and classified by LC under history rather than philosophy), still deserves inclusion for its strong coverage of the philosophical aspects. It offers entries on major philosophers such as Leibniz, Hume, and Kant; well-known French *philosophes* such as Diderot, Montesquieu, Rousseau, and Voltaire; but more importantly perhaps a host of less familiar figures such as François Hemsterhuys and William Molyneux. It also has articles on many of the philosophical and partly-philosophical topics that dominate the thought of this period: aesthetics, cosmology, democracy, equality, natural religion, necessity, progress, to name a few. Most articles, apart from brief biographical ones, include bibliographies.

388. Buhr, Manfred, ed. **Enzyklopädie zur bürgerlichen Philosophie im 19. und 20. Jahrhundert.** Cologne: Pahl-Rugenstein, 1988. 597p.

See entry 517.

389. Delon, Michel, ed. **Encyclopedia of the Enlightenment.** London: Fitzroy Dearborn, 2001. 2 vols.

See general comment under entry 387. This is an English translation of the *Dictionnaire européen des Lumières* (Paris: Presses universitaires de France, 1997, 1128p.). As such, it has a strong European flavor, including a marked focus on the Continent, in contrast to two other recent identically titled works (entries 399 and 403). Delon, himself a distinguished cultural historian at the Sorbonne, was assisted on this encyclopedia by some 200 international but mainly French contributors. Not surprisingly, the bibliographic references at the ends of most articles emphasize European-language sources. Among the more philosophically significant entries are, for example, authority, government, and power; civilization and civility; doubt, skepticism, and Pyrrhonism; God; history, philosophy of idea; materialism; natural law and the rights of man; reason; and utopia. There are no biographical entries, so this is not the place to look for surveys on the major Enlightenment thinkers.

390. Dematteis, Philip Breed and Leemon B. McHenry, eds. **American Philosophers Before 1950.** Detroit: Gale, 2003. 407p. (Dictionary of Literary Biography, vol. 270).

See entry 295.

391. Dematteis, Philip Breed and Peter S. Fosl, eds. **British Philosophers, 1500–1799.** Detroit: Gale, 2002. 456p. (Dictionary of Literary Biography, vol. 252).

Shares the qualities and features common to the *Dictionary of Literary Biography* series; see entry 347 for a general comment. The period covered by this volume encompasses several of the greatest British philosophers, who are also among the most important philosophers of all time: Bacon, Hobbes, Locke, Hume, and Berkeley. These are certainly given their due here. But many other figures are treated at often comparable and sometimes even greater length. These include, for instance, Jeremy Bentham, Edmund Burke, Joseph Butler, Samuel Clarke, David Hartley, Francis Hutcheson, Henry More, William Paley, and Thomas Reid. Worthy of special mention are six women philosophers—Mary Astell, Margaret Cavendish, Anne Conway, Damaris Cudworth, Catharine Trotter, and Mary Wollstonecraft—and several thinkers better known for their achievements in other arenas than as philosophers: Isaac Newton, Joseph Priestley, and Adam Smith.

392. Dematteis, Philip Breed, Peter S. Fosl and Leemon B. McHenry, eds. **British Philosophers, 1800–2000.** Detroit: Gale, 2002. 420p. (Dictionary of Literary Biography, vol. 262).

See entry 294.

393.   Dictionary of Eighteenth-Century British Philosophers. John W. Yolton, John Valdimir Price, and John Stephens, general eds. Bristol: Thoemmes Press, 1999. 2 vols.

This is the earliest published of three biographical encyclopedias covering British philosophers of the Modern period (see also entries 395 and 397) and sets the general pattern. (A similar volume, entry 530, covers the twentieth century.) It aims "to give readers a glimpse of an author's life, ideas and contribution to the history of thought and philosophy" (introduction). Its approximately 600 subjects include many "quasi-philosophers" in fields such as theology and the sciences. Particular effort has been made to recover awareness of obscure figures, and even some anonymous writers are represented in a 10-page section at the end on their works. In the case of major philosophers such as Berkeley, Butler, and Hume, there is a strong emphasis on representing their now lesser known as well as their most regularly discussed writings. Articles are contributed by approximately 100 scholars, many of them leading writers on Modern British philosophy. Each article includes a bibliography of the author's works and often of secondary sources, typically quite selective but likely to be more inclusive the less known the philosopher in question. Name index only.

394.   Dictionary of Modern American Philosophers. John R. Shook, general ed. Bristol, U.K.: Thoemmes Press, 2005. 4 vols.

See entry 529.

395.   Dictionary of Nineteenth-Century British Philosophers. W. J. Mander and A. P. F. Sell, senior eds. Bristol: Thoemmes Press, 2002. 2 vols.

Follows the general pattern set by the *Dictionary of Eighteenth-Century British Philosophers* (entry 393). Like that predecessor, it strives particularly to give "lesser, even quite obscure, authors their due" because they indicate the intellectual environment in which the better-known philosophers worked and often stimulated, propagated, and critiqued the latter's work (introduction). Around 600 philosophers are treated by 160 contributors. They include many subjects whose primary identification was not as philosophers, including some famous ones such as Coleridge and T. H. Huxley. There is some acknowledged overlap with the eighteenth-century volume and a subsequent twentieth-century volume in the case of individuals who published significantly in either of those centuries as well as the nineteenth.

396.   Dictionary of Seventeenth and Eighteenth-Century Dutch Philosophers. Wiep van Bunge, et. al., general eds. Bristol: Thoemmes Press, 2003. 2 vols.

While modeled on several works from the same publisher on British philosophers of the Modern period (entries 393, 395, and 397), this dictionary differs somewhat in including not just biographical entries—though there are some 365 of those—but also entries on Dutch universities, academies, publishing houses, and journals. It represents the philosophical and more broadly intellectual aspects of Holland's Golden Age and their significance for European thought and culture. Included are a number of foreign philosophers who lived or worked in Holland or exercised a major influence on its intellectual life, for example, Descartes, Pierre Bayle, and John Locke. Besides these and a few well-known native philosophers such as Spinoza and Grotius (Hugo de Groot), there are lesser figures familiar to specialists on the period (e.g., Boerhaave, Nieuwentijt) as well as many minor and neglected writers. Articles are contributed by more than 100 scholars, mostly Dutch.

397.   Dictionary of Seventeenth-Century British Philosophers. Andrew Pyle, general ed. Bristol: Thoemmes Press, 2000. 2 vols.

Observes the general pattern and central objectives set by the *Dictionary of Eighteenth-Century British Philosophers* (entry 393), with which it overlaps by duplicating coverage of individuals active in parts of both centuries. It includes some 400 philosophers, a designation interpreted generously to embrace not only many minor figures but a number of thinkers primarily identified with other domains such as poetry, science, mathematics, politics, and theology, for example, Dryden, Newton, Harvey, Raleigh. The designation "British," too, is applied somewhat broadly, sufficiently to include a number of Scots academics and English Catholics who lived and worked in France or the Low Countries, and a couple of foreigners treated as "honorary Britons" because of their special connections with British intellectual circles (introduction). More than 70 scholars contributed the articles.

398.   Emel'ianov, B. V., and V. V. Kulikov. Russkie mysliteli vtoroi poloviny XIX –nachala XX veka: opyt kratkogo biobibliograficheskogo slovaria. Ekaterinburg: Izd-vo Ural'skogo Universiteta, 1996. 383p.

This reference work on Russian thought from the mid-nineteenth century to the beginning of the twentieth century features entries exclusively on individual philosophers. Several thousand are represented here by, in most instances, the briefest of biographical details (often no more than dates of birth and death, and sometimes not even those), and a bibliography of writings that may range from a single article to a substantial list of publications plus references to secondary literature.

399.   Encyclopedia of the Enlightenment. Peter Hanns Reill, consulting ed.; Ellen Judy Wilson, principal author. New York: Facts on File, 1996. 485p.

See general comment under entry 387. Among several recent identically titled works (see entries 389 and 403), this is written particularly at the level of undergraduate and high school students as well as general readers. Its introduction endeavors to provide a brief general characterization of the Enlightenment and its key features while combating stereotypes. A number of the encyclopedia's more specifically philosophically oriented articles are handily identified by an entry for philosophy that exists exclusively of cross-references, including, for example, empiricism, Epicurean philosophy, moral philosophy, natural philosophy, political theory, rationalism, reason, science, and a few major biographical entries: Descartes (pre-Enlightenment but influential in the period), Kant, Leibniz, Newton, and Spinoza. These are hardly exhaustive, however, of the philosophical content: there are also entries for other major philosophers, for instance Rousseau, Locke, and Hume; for lesser known philosophers like Moses Mendelssohn; for quasi-philosophers such as the French *philosophes* Diderot and Voltaire; and for major philosophical texts such as Rousseau's *Social Contract* and Hume's *Treatise of Human Nature.*

400.   Garrett, Don, and Edward Barbanell, eds. Encyclopedia of Empiricism. Westport, Conn.: Greenwood Press, 1997. 455p.

See entry 638.

401.   Glendinning, Simon, ed. The Edinburgh Encyclopedia of Continental Philosophy. Edinburgh: Edinburgh University Press; Chicago: Fitzroy Dearborn, 1999. 685p.

See entry 564. Though oriented chiefly on twentieth-century Continental philosophy, this provides substantial coverage of nineteenth-century antecedents including Kantian Idealism, Hegelianism, British Idealism, Schleiermacher, Marx, Kierkegaard, Nietzsche, and others.

402.   Gordon, Haim. **Dictionary of Existentialism.** Westport, Conn.: Greenwood Press; London: Fitzroy Dearborn, 1999. 539p.

See entry 565. Includes coverage of the nineteenth-century wellsprings of Existentialism, notably Kierkegaard and Nietzsche.

403.   Kors, Alan Charles, ed. in chief. **Encyclopedia of the Enlightenment.** Oxford: Oxford University Press, 2003. 4 vols.

See general comment under entry 387. This is the most comprehensive of several recent reference works with identical titles (see entries 389 and 399). Readers interested in the Enlightenment's philosophical aspects could do well to begin with the four-page survey article under philosophy and the major related articles cross-referenced at its conclusion, which include, for example, aesthetics, economic thought, empiricism, human nature, materialism, moral philosophy, natural religion, political philosophy. Many additional philosophical or philosophically relevant entries can be identified in the topical outline of articles at the front of volume 1 under "Enlightenment Thought and 18th Century Culture," notably such subcategories as philosophy, human nature, natural religion, political philosophy, and so forth; the subcategory "tradition" which lists major schools and movements of thought such as empiricism, Epicureanism, rationalism, skepticism, utilitarianism; and under "biographies" the names of many major and minor philosophers. This encyclopedia even offers articles on the perspectives on the Enlightenment of, or its influence on, much later philosophers such as Foucault and Habermas or schools of thought such as the Frankfurt School.

404.   Mott, Wesley T., ed. **Biographical Dictionary of Transcendentalism.** Westport, Conn.: Greenwood Press, 1996. 315p.

See entry 383 for a general note on Transcendentalism. This biographical dictionary complements Mott's *Encyclopedia of Transcendentalism* (entry 405), even to the extent of including cross-references, indicated with double asterisks (**), to that companion work. Alphabetically arranged entries represent 204 individuals, not al of them allied with the Transcendentalist movement but related to it in diverse and sometimes complicated ways. Some were important contemporary or near-contemporary sources for, or influences on, Transcendentalism (e.g., Carlyle, Fourier, Hegel, Schelling; individuals in this category no longer alive by 1830 are treated in the companion *Encyclopedia*). Others were contemporary or later critics (e.g., Charles Hodge, John Dewey), were positively influenced by it (William James, John Muir), or had a complex and ambivalent relationship (Hawthorne). And there's at least one instance of someone described as "remarkably untouched" by it despite significant contacts with leading Transcendentalists: the poet Longfellow. Naturally, the key exponents and practitioners of Transcendentalism, such as Bronson Alcott, Orestes Brownson, William Ellery Channing, Ralph Waldo Emerson, Sarah Margaret Fuller, and Henry

David Thoreau, as well as many of its lesser lights are amply covered. Signed articles were contributed by some 90 scholars.

405. Mott, Wesley T., ed. **Encyclopedia of Transcendentalism.** Westport, Conn.: Greenwood Press, 1996. 280p.

See entry 383 for a general note on Transcendentalism. This encyclopedia complements Mott's *Biographical Dictionary of Transcendentalism* (entry 404), and includes many cross-references to the latter, indicated with double asterisks (**). Encyclopedia entries range over key Transcendentalist concepts and themes (e.g., idealism, nature, nonresistance), publication organs and literary venues (*The Harbinger,* journals), places and institutions that figured importantly in the movement's history (Concord, Mass.; Walden Pond; the Boston Athaneum), significant ventures and events (Brook Farm, Fruitlands, the Miracles Controversy), and elements in its environmental or historical context that shed light on one or another aspect of the movement (Compromise of 1850, Jacksonian Democracy, Perfectionism, Shakers). In addition, in a slightly surprising division of labor with the *Biographical Dictionary,* its has a good number of biographical entries for figures, especially philosophers from Plato and Epictetus to Kant and Herder, who particularly influenced its thought, provided they were deceased by 1830. Those alive by or after 1830 are treated in the companion work. The signed articles were contributed by 70 scholars from a variety of fields and backgrounds.

406. Nadler, Steven, ed. **A Companion to Early Modern Philosophy.** Malden, Mass.: Blackwell, 2002. 661p. (Blackwell Companions to Philosophy, 23).

Taking a chronological-thematic rather than an alphabetical approach to its period, this Blackwell Companion is perhaps more a conventional historical survey than a reference work, and at any rate may be considered a boundary case. It offers the benefit, however, of contributions by nearly 40 specialists covering not only the familiar landmarks and promontories of seventeenth- and eighteenth-century philosophy in Western Europe and Britain but also some of its less well-publicized nooks and crannies. Besides essays on each of the period's major figures—Descartes, Spinoza, Leibniz, Hobbes, Locke, Berkeley, Hume, Rousseau—it has individual essays on second-rank philosophers such as Pascal, Gassendi, Malebranche, Shaftesbury, Reid, Vico, and Moses Mendelssohn; on thinkers better known for contributions to science or other domains than as philosophers, such as Bacon, Boyle, Newton, Mandeville, Adam Smith, and Voltaire; and even some relatively unknowns, for example, Johannes Clauberg and Robert Desgabets. Other essays treat groups of thinkers or schools of thought: Occasionalism, Dutch Cartesian philosophy, Grotius and Pufendorf (philosophers of law), British philosophy before Locke, the Cambridge Platonists, the English Malebranchians, women philosophers in early Modern England, German philosophy after Leibniz, aesthetics before Kant, among others. While accepting the conventional demarcation of Western philosophy's "Modern" period as beginning with Descartes, the volume begins by tracing continuities with the Aristotelianism, Scholasticism, Platonism, and Humanism of preceding eras, and exploring the significance of the "new science" represented by Kepler, Galileo, and Mersenne. It stops short of Kant, whose philosophy, suggests Nadler, "does indeed represent so much of a break from what went before that it seems more of a new beginning than the culmination of a preceding tradition" (introduction).

SOURCES ON INDIVIDUAL PHILOSOPHERS

BERKELEY, GEORGE (1685–1753)

407. Jessop, Thomas Edmond. **A Bibliography of George Berkeley, with an Inventory of Berkeley's Manuscript Remains by A.A. Luce.** 2nd ed., revised and enlarged. The Hague: Martinus Nijhoff, 1973. 155p. (International Archives of the History of Ideas, 66).

Aims to list Berkeley's own writings "exhaustively," and writings on Berkeley adequately if somewhat less than exhaustively. For the former, editions and translations are listed, with detailed bibliographic descriptions and annotations (though not so full as those of Keynes; see entry 408). Writings on Berkeley are divided by subject areas, with those relating to his philosophy subdivided by countries (English-writing, French-writing, German-language, Italy, others). The inventory of manuscript remains and letters (part 3) is by their locations.

The first edition of this work was published by Oxford University Press in 1934.

408. Keynes, Geoffrey. **A Bibliography of George Berkeley, Bishop of Cloyne: His Works and His Critics in the Eighteenth Century.** Oxford: Clarendon Press; Pittsburgh: University of Pittsburgh Press, 1976. 285p. (The Soho Bibliographies, 18).

Compiled by a collector of Berkeleyana, this catalogue of early editions of Berkeley and his critics provides meticulous descriptions and annotations concerned with bibliographic and physical details and publishing history.

BRADLEY, FRANCIS HERBERT (1846–1924)

409. Ingardia, Richard. **Bradley: A Research Bibliography.** Bowling Green, Ohio: Philosophy Documentation Center, Bowling Green State University, 1991. 195p. (Bibliographies of Famous Philosophers).

Intended to reinvigorate Bradley's reputation and legacy, Ingardia's bibliography lists all of Bradley's own output and just over a thousand secondary sources, not counting book reviews which are listed with the entries for the books reviewed. It is a useful compilation, but the policy of providing only annotations reproduced from the *Philosopher's Index* or *Dissertation Abstracts* results in a scarcity of annotations (just 15 percent of entries) as well as imbalances with respect to their length or relevance, and undermines Ingardia's claim to surpass most other annotated bibliographies in providing information sufficient "for effective research needs" (introduction).

BURKE, EDMUND (1729–1797)

410. Gandy, Clara I., and Peter J. Stanlis. **Edmund Burke: A Bibliography of Secondary Studies.** New York: Garland, 1983. 357p.

Chapters especially relevant for study of the philosophical aspects of Burke's thought and activity are chapter 4 on his aesthetic theory, chapter 5 on his political thought, and chapter 6 on his ideas on economics, society, and religion. Each chapter is introduced by a brief overview. Many entries are annotated, sometimes at considerable length.

DESCARTES, RENÉ (1596–1650)

411. Chappell, Vere C. and Willis Doney. **Twenty-Five Years of Descartes Scholarship, 1960–1984: A Bibliography.** New York: Garland, 1987. 183p. (The Philosophy of Descartes).

Chappell and Doney pick up where Sebba's bibliography (entry 412) leaves off. They aim "to document the entire scholarly literature on Descartes, from 1960 through 1984, in most of the languages in which it has been produced and in all of the fields in which Descartes is currently a subject of interest" (introduction). However, they generally omit materials in languages other than Western European (e.g., Chinese, Japanese, Polish, Russian), lacking resources to verify them, but do refer to other sources where these may be pursued. They list 2,502 items alphabetically by author. An appendix covers editions and translations of Descartes's own writings. A meager subject index employs just 38 headings and subheadings, some with 200 to 300 entries referenced by number only.

412. Sebba, Gregor. **Bibliographia Cartesiana: A Critical Guide to the Descartes Literature, 1800–1960.** The Hague: Martinus Nijhoff, 1964. 510p. (International Archives of the History of Ideas, 5).

Lists about 3,000 books and articles in numerous languages. Features two parts: (1) "Introduction to Descartes Studies": 562 of the most significant works, including bibliographical, biographical, introductory, and general studies; and (2) an alphabetical bibliography, including items listed in part 1. Part 1 is fully and part 2 selectively annotated, with annotations often evaluative. Two subject indexes are provided: classified ("systematic") and alphabetical ("analytic").

413. Ariew, Roger, et. al. **Historical Dictionary of Descartes and Cartesian Philosophy.** Lanham, Md.: Scarecrow Press, 2003. 320p. (Historical Dictionaries of Religions, Philosophies, and Movements, 46).

Five well-published specialists on Descartes or the early Modern period in philosophy—Ariew, Dennis Des Chenne, Douglas Jesseph, Tad Schmaltz, and Theo Verbeek—collaborated to produce this exceptionally authoritative dictionary. It takes in all aspects of Descartes's life and thought, and a large swath of his influence in his lifetime and roughly the 75 years following. Entries encompass key concepts and ideas from his philosophy, elements of his scientific and mathematical work (as important in its time as his philosophical work), his major and many minor published writings, significant background to and influences on his thought, places and institutions that figured importantly in his life and career, and finally but not least, numerous individuals: "those who supported him, those who criticized him, those who corrected him, and those who together formed one of the major movements in philosophy: Cartesianism" (foreword). The work also includes a chronology, a 12-page introductory overview of Descartes's life and times, and a 42-page bibliography of (mainly English-language) primary and secondary sources.

414. Cottingham, John A. **A Descartes Dictionary.** Oxford: Basil Blackwell, 1993. 187p. (Blackwell Philosopher Dictionaries).

Aspiring "to appeal to the newcomer to Descartes, whether student or general reader, while also providing detailed critical comment and precise textual references for the more advanced reader," this dictionary succeeds on both counts. Cottingham presents an alphabetically arranged guide to key Cartesian concepts and topics, ranging over Descartes's ideas on cosmology, physics, physiology, psychology, theology, and ethics (including, for example, entries on atoms, circulation of blood, creation, morality, motion) as well as the epistemological and metaphysical core of his thought (with entries on, e.g., certainty, Cartesian circle, dreaming, method, mind and body, ontological argument). There is also an article on each of Descartes's significant writings (*Discourse on Method, Optics, Treatise on Man,* etc.). A six-page introduction conveys the essentials of Descartes's life and publishing history; individual entries often provide additional historical context for his ideas. Primary sources are cited throughout (referenced to standard editions both in the original French and Latin and in English), secondary sources only in the case of some contemporary or early commentators. A highly selective, four-page secondary bibliography is at the back.

415.   Morris, John, ed. and trans. **Descartes Dictionary.** New York: Philosophical Library, 1971. 274p.

One of a series of dictionaries on individual philosophers issued by the publisher; see entry 508 for a general comment. Better than some others in terms of scholarship, focus, and balance, this remains nonetheless merely a compilation of quotes. There are no systematic treatments of Descartes's terminology or views, nor do the quotes necessarily build a coherent picture. Expect no more than some salient or perhaps merely interesting statements on a given topic. Entries relating to Descartes's central concerns include demonstration, God, and mind, but others reflect his opinions on topics as varied as America, blushing, humility, and rats. Sources are identified with reference to the standard Adam-Tannery edition of Descartes's works.

416.   Cahné, Pierre-Alain. **Index du Discours de la Méthode de René Descartes.** Rome: Edizioni dell'Ateneo, 1977. 90p. (Lessico intellettuale europeo, XII; Corpus Cartesianum, 2).

The original French text of Descartes's little classic is subjected to an exhaustive analysis designed, seemingly, more for linguistic than for philosophical study. Besides a concordance of all significant words, there is a list of those not so significant (*mots outils*—mainly articles and prepositions) giving number of occurrences, plus a hierarchical index of words in order of frequency of occurrence. Page references are to the standard Adam-Tannery edition, using, somewhat confusingly, what looks like a four-digit number to represent separate page and line numbers (e.g., 2827 = page 28, line 27).

DIDEROT, DENIS (1713–1784)

417.   Spear, Frederick A. **Bibliographie de Diderot: Répertoire analytique international.** Geneva: Librairie Droz, 1980/88. 2 vols.

The first volume of Spear's secondary bibliography on the great Enlightenment *philosophe* and *Encyclopédie* editor covers studies published through 1975. Volume 2 supplements with coverage for 1976–1986. Entries are numbered continuously through the two volumes, the first listing 3,967 books, articles, and so forth, the second an additional 1,877 new items (entries 3968–5844) plus, in an appendix, new editions of works listed in volume 1. Materials in all European languages are included. A detailed, systematic subject arrangement reflects the immense range of Diderot's thought and activities, and includes separate sections for studies of each of his major writings. Each volume has a general index for names and subjects.

DILTHEY, WILHELM (1833–1911)

418. Herrmann, Ulrich. **Bibliographie Wilhelm Dilthey: Quellen und Literatur.** Weinheim: Julius Beltz, 1969. 237p.

Works by Dilthey are listed primarily in chronological sequence, with separate sections for collected works, translations, reviews, letters and diaries. Works about Dilthey—books, articles, dissertations, reviews—are arranged in 16 subject sections. An author index is provided.

EDWARDS, JONATHAN (1703–1758)

419. Johnson, Thomas Herbert. **The Printed Writings of Jonathan Edwards, 1703–1758.** Princeton: Princeton University Press, 1940. Reprinted, New York: Burt Franklin, 1970. 136p.

This standard bibliography of Edwards's works is arranged chronologically according to the first edition of each item, and includes detailed bibliographic descriptions for all the early editions. Entries include holding library codes. Index of titles includes numerous cross-references.

420. Lesser, M. X. **Jonathan Edwards: A Reference Guide.** Boston: G. K. Hall, 1981. 421p. (Reference Guides in Literature).

Primarily an annotated bibliography of writings about Edwards, arranged chronologically from 1729 through 1978. A chronology of works *by* Edwards (without bibliographic particulars) precedes the introduction, which is a 52-page bibliographic essay and overview of Edwards scholarship and interpretation. Index combines author, title, and subject entries, but subject entries are grouped together under Edwards's name.

421. Manspeaker, Nancy. **Jonathan Edwards: Bibliographical Synopses.** Lewiston, N.Y.: Edwin Mellen Press, 1981. 278p. (Studies in American Religion, vol. 3).

Includes a listing of Edwards's published works and a comprehensive though not exhaustive bibliography of books, chapters of books, articles, and dissertations about him, from his own time through 1980. "Most entries are annotated, though some are not and others are summarized so briefly as to make the comments of little value" (*Choice 19* [Dec. 1981]:490).

ENGELS, FRIEDRICH (1820–1895)

422. Eubanks, Cecil L. **Karl Marx and Friedrich Engels: An Analytical Bibliography.** 2nd ed. New York: Garland, 1984. 299p. (Garland Reference Library of Social Science, vol. 100).

Individual and collected works by Engels are listed on pages 16–23. Secondary studies that focus specifically on Engels can be identified through the indexes of books, articles, and dissertations. See also entry 471.

423. Rubel, Maximilien. **Bibliographie des oeuvres de Karl Marx. Avec en appendice un répertoire des oeuvres de Friedrich Engels.** Paris: Marcel Rivière, 1956. 273p.

See entry 472. The Engels appendix, on pages 239–58, lists 151 works by Engels in chronological sequence.

FICHTE, JOHANN GOTTLIEB (1762–1814)

424. Baumgartner, Hans Michael, and Wilhelm G. Jacobs. **J. G. Fichte-Bibliographie.** Stuttgart: Friedrich Frommann, 1968. 346p.

Lists works by Fichte, including editions and translations, and works about him, overwhelmingly in German but also in English and other languages. Coverage from 1791 through 1967. The arrangement is classified, with personal name index and title-keyword index.

425. Doyé, Sabine, et. al. **J. G. Fichte-Bibliographie (1968–1992/93).** Amsterdam and Atlanta, Ga.: Rodopi, 1993. 383p.

Supplements the 1968 Fichte bibliography by Baumgartner and Jacobs (entry 424). Lists new editions and translations (in 11 languages) of Fichte's work as well as secondary literature, a total of 2,187 items. Indexes of authors, subjects, personal names, and sources supplement the classified arrangement.

HEGEL, GEORG WILHELM FRIEDRICH (1770–1831)

426. Hasselberg, Erwin and Frank Radtke. **Hegels "Wissenschaft der Logik": Eine internationale Bibliographie ihrer Rezeption im 20. Jahrhundert.** Vienna: Passagen, 1993. 3 vols.

A comprehensive bibliography of writings on Hegel's *Wissenschaft der Logik* in all languages, arranged principally by country of publication. Most heavily represented is Germany (which shares volume 1 only with China), followed by Russia. U.S. and British publications are lumped together in one section, while "minor" countries (e.g., Belgium, Yemen, Puerto Rico) are grouped together at the end of volume 3 but still kept distinct. Annotations, some quite lengthy, are present for perhaps half of the entries—somewhat more for European-language publications, less for non-European, notably Chinese and Japanese.

427. Steinhauer, Kurt. **Hegel Bibliography: Background material on the International Reception of Hegel within the Context of the History of Philosophy / Hegel Bibliographie: Materialen zur Geschichte der internationalen Hegel-Rezeption und zur Philosophie-Geschichte. Teil 1: Bis 1975.** Munich: K. G. Saur, 1980. 894p. **Teil 2: 1976–1991, mit Nachträgen und Berichtigungen zu Teil I.** Munich: K. G. Saur, 1998. 2 vols.

Steinhauer's bibliography offers unusually comprehensive international coverage, including, for example, Japanese works. The initial volume and later supplement employ a similar internal arrangement comprising two principal sections: first a list of Hegel's works, including editions of complete and selected works, single editions, and correspondence; then a bibliography of secondary sources, arranged chronologically by decades, from 1802 to 1975 in Part 1 and from 1976 through 1990 (not 1991, as the title suggests) in Part 2. Addenda to Part 1 (previously omitted works) precede the post-1975 listings in both the primary and secondary sections of Part 2, while corrigenda are listed in separate sections occupying nearly 100 pages. Each volume has an index of authors, editors, and translators, and a subject index of German keywords. Pagination is continuous through the two parts, totaling 1,128 pages.

428. Burbidge, John W. **Historical Dictionary of Hegelian Philosophy.** Lanham, Md.: Scarecrow Press, 2001. 205p. (Historical Dictionaries of Religions, Philosophies, and Movements, 34).

This dictionary follows the general pattern set by the *Historical Dictionary of Nietzscheanism* in the same series (see entry 481). Its alphabetically arranged entries cover a similar range of topics: key concepts in Hegel's thought, his major writings, thinkers who influenced him and even more influenced *by* him throughout the nineteenth and into the twentieth century, adversaries and interpreters, and the significant events, institutions, and people in his life. More unusual is a 5-page glossary of German terms, perhaps more accurately a cross-reference guide to the corresponding English-language entries in the main body of the dictionary. The 30-page bibliography is dominated by divisions devoted to each of Hegel's major works, each subdivided into a primary bibliography of editions and translations and a secondary bibliography of selected sources (commentaries, interpretations, and, less often, polemical works) focused on that primary text.

429. Glockner, Hermann. **Hegel-Lexikon.** 2nd ed. Stuttgart: Frommann, 1957. 4 vols. in 2. (*Sämtliche Werke;* Jubiläumsausgabe, Bd. 23–26).

Issued in conjunction with Glockner's edition of Hegel's *Sämtliche Werke,* originally published 1927–1940 and variously reprinted, Glockner's *Lexikon* (modestly revised in this 1957 edition) constitutes in part an index to these collected works. It gives volume and page citations to significant passages involving the topics, expressions, individuals, or places listed as entry terms, often divided among various subtopics. But it goes beyond that, becoming a quotations dictionary that reproduces particularly momentous or memorable passages relating to selected subjects. Occasionally it also offers a clarifying comment, brief definition, or list of synonymous or related terms.

430. Inwood, Michael. **A Hegel Dictionary.** Oxford: Basil Blackwell, 1992. 347p. (Blackwell Philosopher Dictionaries).

For a series of philosopher dictionaries that aims to be "scholarly yet accessible" (cf. entry 490), Hegel presents more than a routine challenge. Observes a cover blurb on this work: "his innovative use of language, involving the influence of German etymology and his wide knowledge of the history of philosophy from its Greek origins, have helped to create his reputation for difficulty and obscurity." Inwood's efforts to present and clarify Hegel's key ideas within an alphabetical dictionary format do succeed in making Hegel more accessible to students at all levels, though that's not to say the going is generally easy. Novices, and even those beyond, may still suffer occasional bewilderment from Hegelian-style lines such as "The idea then reappears in the realm of nature, as the idea in its otherness, and in that of spirit, as the idea returning to itself out of otherness" (p. 125). But there is less of this than in most works on, let alone by, Hegel. Inwood sheds useful light on such Hegelian concepts as absolute, dialectic, idea, and spirit; on Hegel's views on, for example, art, beauty, and aesthetics, family and women, God, history, and the state; and on the context and content of each of Hegel's major writings. Most articles include discussion of the historical background—philosophical, linguistic, and so forth—of Hegel's terminology and ideas, but not, deliberately, of their subsequent development in post-Hegelian thought. There are two introductory essays, one titled "Hegel and His Language" and a second that provides a brief overview of Hegel's life and influence. A 13-page bibliography of primary and secondary sources (English-language only) is also included.

431. Jaeschke, Walter. **Hegel-Handbuch: Leben, Werk, Schule.** Stuttgart: J. B. Metzler, 2003. 583p. (Metzler Handbüchern).

See note on the series at entry 482. Provides an overview of Hegel's life, a detailed analysis of his works, and discussion of the early phase of his influence up to the emergence of "right" and "left" schools of Hegelianism.

HERDER, JOHANN GOTTFRIED (1744–1803)

432. Günther, Gottfried, Siegfried Seifert, and Albina A. Volgina. **Herder-Bibliographie.** Berlin: Aufbau, 1978. 644p.

Part 1 of this international bibliography lists primary literature, with special sections for collected works, letters, and translations (by language). Part 2 covers secondary literature, organized under a variety of thematic headings and subheadings. Some descriptive, though minimal, annotations are provided.

HOBBES, THOMAS (1588–1679)

433. Garcia, Alfred. **Thomas Hobbes: Bibliographie internationale de 1620 à 1986.** Caen: Centre de Philosophie politique et juridique, Université de Caen, 1986. 267p.

Garcia's bibliography, which is unannotated, begins with a chronological listing, followed by an alphabetical listing, of Hobbes's own works. A secondary bibliography (pages 18–215) lists books, articles, and essays on Hobbes in most European languages. The general index is poor: it lists mainly authors' names, seemingly redundant given that the secondary bibliography itself is arranged alphabetically by author, while incorporating just a very limited number of subject terms.

434. Hinnant, Charles H. **Thomas Hobbes: A Reference Guide.** Boston: G. K. Hall, 1980. 275p. (A Reference Guide in Literature).

Lists (in a single sequence) works about Hobbes as well as editions of works by Hobbes, from 1679 through 1976. Writings about Hobbes are annotated with brief descriptive annotations. A chronological list of Hobbes's writings is included in the introductory material. There is an index of names and subjects, with subject entries gathered under Hobbes's name.

435. Macdonald, Hugh, and Mary Hargreaves. **Thomas Hobbes: A Bibliography.** London: Bibliographical Society, 1952. 84p.

A descriptive bibliography of early editions of Hobbes, listing 109 items. Includes notes on circumstances of authorship and publishing history.

436. Sacksteder, William. **Hobbes Studies (1879–1979): A Bibliography.** Bowling Green, Ohio: Philosophy Documentation Center, Bowling Green State University, 1982. 194p. (Bibliographies of Famous Philosophers).

Dates of coverage indicated in the title represent the second and third centennials of Hobbes's death in 1679. Editions and translations of Hobbes's works, including some that saw their first publication after 1879, are listed in sections 1–3 and in section 7 (the latter a listing by editor and translator). Secondary literature is listed according to format (books, chapters of books, journal articles, etc.) in sections 4–6 and 8.

437. Martinich, A. P. **A Hobbes Dictionary.** Oxford: Basil Blackwell, 1995, 336p. (Blackwell Philosopher Dictionaries).

Following the general pattern of previous Blackwell Philosopher Dictionaries (see, e.g., entries 468 and 490), Martinich provides an introductory overview of Hobbes's life and historical context, a chronology of his life and work—adding in this case a separate chronology of pertinent English history, mainly seventeenth-century—an alphabetical dictionary of key terms and concepts in Hobbes's writings, and a bibliography. The 140 or so dictionary articles feature, of course, such quintessentially Hobbesian concepts as state of nature, right of nature, and sovereign, but also include Hobbes's ideas on, or their relation to, such diverse topics as absurdity, atheism, the Bible, geometry, kingdom of darkness, laughter, rhetoric, and soul. For most entries, says Martinich, he has "tried to answer three questions—How did Hobbes use the word? Where did he use it? and Why did he use it?—roughly in that order" (preface). The bibliography beginning on page 317 has three sections: works by Hobbes, annotated with particulars on publishing history and early editions; select seventeenth-century works relevant to Hobbes; and twentieth-century works, including some articles as well as books. There is a general index.

HUME, DAVID (1711–1776)

438. Hall, Roland. **Fifty Years of Hume Scholarship: A Bibliographical Guide.** Edinburgh: Edinburgh University Press, 1978. 150p.

Based partly on an earlier, privately published *Hume Bibliography, from 1930* (York: Roland Hall, 1971, 80p.), this carries forward the work by Jessop (entry 439). It covers the years 1925 to 1976, but also includes a separate list of the main writings on Hume from 1900 to 1924. Books, articles, and dissertations are listed by year of appearance. There are indexes for authors, for languages other than English, and a fairly detailed one for subjects. Worth noting is an introductory essay, "The Development of Hume Scholarship" (pp. 1–14).

439.   Jessop, Thomas Edmond. **A Bibliography of David Hume and of Scottish Philosophy.** London: Russell & Russell, 1938. Reissued, New York: Russell & Russell, 1966. Reprinted, New York: Garland, 1983. 201p.

See also entry 381. "Of Hume's works every edition that appeared in his lifetime has, I believe, been catalogued here, and probably almost all the subsequent editions whether in English or in translation. The list of writings about him is incomplete . . ., but it is full enough to give a proportioned view of the range, geographical as well as chronological, of the interest he excited" (preface).

JAMES, WILLIAM (1842–1910)

440.   Perry, Ralph Barton. **Annotated Bibliography of the Writings of William James.** New York: Longmans, Green, 1920. Reprinted, North Salem, N.H.: Verbeke, 1968. Reprinted, Folcroft, Pa.: Folcroft Library Editions, 1973. Reprinted, Dubuque, Iowa: William C. Brown, n.d. 69p.

"In view of the fact that much of James's most important thought appeared in the form of essays and reviews, often under a title which gave no clue to the contents, some such guide as this is indispensable . . ." (prefatory note). Perry provides a chronological list with brief summaries of subject matter or thesis for nearly every item cited, as well as tables of contents for books and collections of essays.

441.   Skrupskelis, Ignas K. **William James: A Reference Guide.** Boston: G. K. Hall, 1977. 250p. (Reference Guides in Literature).

Books and shorter writings about James in English are listed by year, from 1868 through 1974, and briefly summarized. Separate sections list selected writings in other languages, American dissertations, and some of James's "Spirit Writings" (works purported to have been transmitted after death through spiritualistic mediums). There is an integrated author, title, and subject index.

KANT, IMMANUEL (1724–1804)

442.   Adickes, Erich. **German Kantian Bibliography.** Boston: Ginn and Ginn, 1893–96. Reprinted, Würzburg: A. Liebing, 1966? Reprinted, New York: Burt Franklin, 1970. 623p.

This bibliography of writings both by and about Kant "which have appeared in Germany up to the end of 1887" (preface) is arranged chronologically in both parts; some exceptions and subtleties are explained in the preface. Adickes offers descriptive and critical comment for most items. A valuable resource on the first century of development of and reaction to Kantian philosophy. Name and subject indexes are provided.

443.   **Bibliographischer Informationsdienst, Kant-Forschungsstelle der Johannes Gutenberg-Universität Mainz.** http://www.kant.uni-mainz.de (accessed October 25, 2005).

See entry 450.

444.   Malter, Rudolf, and Margit Ruffing. **Kant-Bibliographie, 1945–1990.** Frankfurt am Main: Vittorio Klostermann, 1999. 976p. (Veröffentlichungen der Kant-Forschungsstelle am Philosophischen Seminar der Universität Mainz).

This bibliography was begun by Malter, who was editor of an annual Kant bibliography in the journal *Kant-Studien* for a number of years, and completed after his death by Ruffing. One or more companion volumes to cover the years 1749–1944 are reportedly planned (see, e.g., the Web site of the Kant-Forschungsstelle der Johannes Gutenbergsuniversität Mainz, entry 450). The present work attempts to present comprehensively all of the primary and secondary Kant literature of every kind and in any languages for its period, 1945–1990. While complete success seems unreachable, the more than 12,000 titles it records must put it very close to that goal. The international scope is exemplified by the presence particularly of many Chinese, Japanese, Russian, and Latin American publications. Titles in non-Western languages are generally translated into German rather than transliterated. Materials are listed by year of publication, grouped within each year into editions and translations of Kant's works, bibliographies and indexes, literature on Kant's life and work, and miscellaneous literature *(Verschiedenes)* dealing for example with Kantian scholarship, Kantianism, or the 250th anniversary of Kant's birth. The last-mentioned event even warrants special subdivisions in this category for 1974. There are indexes for works by Kant mentioned in the secondary literature (with their titles as translated into other languages grouped under the original German title) and for authors of secondary literature.

445.   Caygill, Howard. **A Kant Dictionary.** Oxford and Cambridge, Mass.: Blackwell, 1995. 453p. (Blackwell Philosopher Dictionaries).

Alphabetically arranged articles offer approaches to and paths through the complex body of Kant's thought that are alternative and complementary to the original writings and the many existing commentaries thereon, to the potential benefit both of specialists and of nonspecialists. The latter, however, will too often find Caygill's treatment of the more technical parts of Kant's philosophy little more accessible than the original works, despite the dictionary's stated intention to clarify Kant's ideas "for students and general readers alike" (cover blurb). The 250-plus entries include specifically Kantian concepts and terms such as antinomy of pure reason, categorical imperative, and thing-in-itself; many others in more general philosophical or even popular currency on which Kant had significant things to say (from absolute and abstraction to woman and world); and each of Kant's major writings, from the famous three *Critiques* to lesser-known works such as *Anthropology from a Pragmatic Point of View.* Many articles have valuable material on the historical background of Kant's terminology or his treatment of a particular topic, or the subsequent development of, or reaction to, his ideas. Two introductory essays offer, respectively, discussion of Kant's impact on philosophical language and information on his life and historical context.

446.   Eisler, Rudolf. **Kant-Lexikon: Nachschlagewerk zu Kants samtlichen Schriften, Briefen und handschriftlichem Nachlass.** Berlin: Mittler, 1930. Reprinted, Hildesheim, Germany: Georg Olms, 1961; pbk., 1964. Reprinted, New York: Burt Franklin, 1971. 642p.

Partly a dictionary and partly an index to Kant's works (though far from exhaustive), this reference work strives to let Kant "speak for himself" as much as possible while at the same time offering something more than a hodge-podge of quotations. Thus, Eisler has provided explanations of the (German) terms and such comment as he deemed necessary to show or clarify connections. There are numerous cross-references. Sources of quotations from Kant's works, including letters and manuscripts, are carefully identified.

447. Irrlitz, Gerd. **Kant-Handbuch: Leben und Werk.** Stuttgart: J. B. Metzler, 2002. 526p. (Metzler Handbüchern).

See note on the series at entry 482. Provides an overview of Kant's life and intellectual context, detailed analyses of his works, a brief chronology, and four-page bibliography.

448. Stockhammer, Morris. **Kant Dictionary.** New York: Philosophical Library, 1972. 241p.

One of a series of "dictionaries" on individual philosophers issued by the publisher; see entry 508 for a general comment. This exemplifies most of the worst faults of its genre. Some of its quotes do scant justice to the concepts they deal with, for example, those for categories and antinomy of pure reason; others, like that on the "manifold," are nearly meaningless without explanation or context. Of three quotes under categorical imperative, two are variant formulations of the principle so-named, but nothing explains what it *is,* or why it has variant formulations. Sources of quotes are identified by title only, making it well-nigh impossible to trace their context. This may frustrate even one's appreciation of some tantalizing quotes on nontechnical subjects: Bible, bigotry, "Kant's thirst," rape, tobacco, and so forth. Neither scholars, students in need of help, nor the merely curious end up well-served.

449. Hinske, Norbert, and Wilhelm Weischedel. **Kant-Seitenkonkordanz.** Darmstadt: Wissenschaftliche Buchgesellschaft, 1970. 299p.

Published as a supplementary volume to the Wissenschaftliche Buchgesellschaft edition of Kant's complete works, also known as the Weischedel edition. "It offers a thorough juxtaposition of all existing complete editions," including the original editions, Rosenkranz, Hartenstein 1 and 2, Kirchmann, the *Akademie*-edition (Preussische Akademie der Wissenschaften), Vorlander, Cassirer, and Weischedel. For each of Kant's works, it lists the volume or page numbers in each edition, followed by a detailed table matching page numbers in the original edition with those in the other editions. For the *Critique of Pure Reason,* it provides separate tables for what are known as the "A" and "B" editions. Foreword in German and English.

450. **Kant-Forschungsstelle der Johannes Gutenberg-Universität Mainz.** http://www.kant.uni-mainz.de/ (accessed October 25, 2005).

The most substantial resource to be accessed at this research center site is a running bibliography, dubbed *Bibliographischer Informationsdienst,* that provides notice of new publications in advance of the print bibliographies published annually in the journal *Kant-Studien.* This serves to fill a two-year delay in the latter bibliographies from bibliographic year to date of publication, necessitated by their aspirations to comprehensiveness. Other resources at this site include an index to proceedings of international Kant congresses since 1960, information about Kantiana collections held by the Kant-Forschungsstelle, a Kant portrait gallery, information pages for the Kant-Gesellschaft, and links to some related sites.

451. Martin, Gottfried, et. al. **Allgemeiner Kantindex zu Kants gesammelten Schriften.** Vols. 16/17, 20. Berlin: Walter de Gruyter, 1967–1969.

The *Allgemeiner Kantindex* aspired to be a comprehensive index to the Kantian corpus based on the so-called *Akademie*-edition of the *Gesammelte Schriften* (Berlin: 1902–1955). Its intended scope is explained in the *Vorwort* to volumes 16–17, the first to appear of what was to have been many volumes (no precise number was announced). However, publication was halted following the appearance of one additional volume (no. 20), due in part to the death in 1972 of the editor-in-chief, Professor Martin. Information from the publisher in early 1996 indicated that no further volumes of the *Allgemeiner Kantindex* were in preparation or planned. Of the three volumes issued, 16 and 17 contain an index of word frequencies in works published by Kant himself (as distinguished from those published posthumously), comprising the first nine volumes of the *Gesammelte Schriften (GS)*. Volume 20 is an index of personal names for volumes 1–23 of the *GS*, comprising published works, letters, and manuscripts. Unrealized volumes were to have provided location indexes to all significant words in the *GS*, word frequencies in writings not published by Kant himself, personal name and source indexes, and a subject index for the entire *GS*. As a provisional measure, a separate subject index for the *Critique of Pure Reason* only was issued (see entry 452), though this is not formally part of the *Allgemeiner Kantindex*. The more recently published *Kant-Konkordanz* (entry 452) picks up to some extent, but on a less ambitious scale, the unfinished work of the *Allgemeiner Kantindex*.

452. Martin, Gottfried, and Dieter-Jürgen Löwisch. **Sachindex zu Kants "Kritik der reinen Vernunft."** Berlin: Walter de Gruyter, 1967. 351p.

An alphabetical subject index to the German text of Kant's *Critique of Pure Reason* as published in the *Akademie*-edition of his *Gesammelte Schriften*. References give page numbers plus line numbers of relevant passages.

Though it bears a close relationship to the project of the *Allgemeiner Kantindex*, which was headed by Martin (see entry 451), this volume is not actually part of that unfinished series.

453. Roser, Andreas, and Thomas Mohrs, eds. **Kant-Konkordanz zu den Werken Immanuel Kants (Bände I–IX der Ausgabe der Preussischen Akademie der Wissenschaften).** Hildesheim: Olms-Weidman, 1992–1995. 10 vols. (Alpha-Omega, Reihe D, Deutsche Autoren, 1–10).

This concordance to the major writings comprised within the first nine volumes of the Preussischen Akademie der Wissenschaften edition of Kant's works (1902–1923) includes approximately half of all words occurring in Kant's text. It omits functional words such as *ab* and *und*, pronouns (with some exceptions, e.g. *ich*), as well as many nouns, adjectives, and verbs not deemed significant to the central philosophical, theoretical, and methodological aspects of Kant's writings. Words are displayed within a single line of context. Winfried Lenders, writing in the journal *Kant-Studien* (84, no. 1 (1993):103–08), subjects this work to harsh criticism. Lenders accuses the compilers of naivete or worse with respect to the principles and problems of concordance-building; criticizes the "subjective" character of their selectivity; points out significant shortcomings in the work (for instance, the failure to "gather" compound expressions such as *a priori* and compound verb forms such as *behält bei,* and numerous deficiencies in lemmatizing, i.e., the grouping together of inflected and variant forms of the same word, even the complete omission of significant variants such as *behauptete* and *behaupteten* for the verb *behaupten*); and questions the need for a printed concordance, especially one no better than this, at a time when availability of the full text in computer-readable form, together with increasingly sophisticated software programs for textual analysis, offer the scholar superior capabilities for the kind of textual research concordances have traditionally served. In light of these criticisms, Lenders belittles the work's pretensions, signaled in its introduction, to take up the unfinished task of Gottfried Martin's *Allgemeiner Kantindex* (entry 451).

KIERKEGAARD, SØREN AABYE (1813–1855)

454. Evans, Calvin D. **Søren Kierkegaard Bibliographies: Remnants, 1944–1980 and Multi-Media, 1925–1991.** Montreal: McGill University Libraries, 1993. 185p. (Fontanus Monograph Series, 2).

This uncommon bibliography on an uncommon philosopher takes as its specific purview items generally missed or omitted by other Kierkegaard bibliographies. In part 1, this restriction is applied rigorously: it includes only "remnants" of printed materials not picked up by other bibliographers, notably including a number of book reviews, books on broader subjects (e.g., Existentialism) that have substantive discussions on Kierkegaard, articles outside the fields of philosophy and theology (e.g., law, political science), unpublished manuscripts referred to in the literature, and dissertations from eight countries. Part 2, while not bound by the criterion of exclusivity, concentrates on a generally neglected category, "multi-media," meaning films, audio and video recordings, slides, radio and theater scripts, and music. The music category encompasses a remarkable number of compositions inspired by Kierkegaard or based on his work, from multiple versions of *Prayers of Kierkegaard* to *Kierkegaard: for four tubas.*

455. Himmelstrup, Jens, with Kjeld Birket-Smith. **Søren Kierkegaard: International Bibliography / International Bibliografi.** Copenhagen: Nyt Nordisk Forlag, Arnold Busck, 1962. 22p.

Covers the period from 1835 to about 1955 (the centennial of Kierkegaard's death), with more haphazard coverage to as late as 1960. Both of the main divisions—editions of Kierkegaard's works and literature about Kierkegaard—are arranged according to language. Arrangement within language sections is chronological in part 1, by author in part 2. Represented, in addition to the Scandinavian languages and the major languages of Western Europe, are Russian, other East European languages, Greek, Hebrew, and Japanese, though the preface warns that coverage for some of these is inevitably sketchy. Title page, preface, table of contents, and most headings are in Danish and English; subject index terms are in Danish only.

Himmelstrup's work was supplemented by Aage Jorgensen, *Søren Kierkegaard-litteratur 1961–1970: En Forelobig Bibliografi* (Maarslet, Denmark: Aage Jorgensen, 1971, 99p.).

456. Lapointe, Francois H. **Søren Kierkegaard and His Critics: An International Bibliography of Criticism.** Westport, Conn.: Greenwood Press, 1980. 430p.

Part 1, works by Kierkegaard, includes translations and groups materials by language. Part 2, works about Kierkegaard, employs a mixed arrangement by formats (books and reviews, dissertations) and subjects, including a chapter arranged by proper names. The bibliography encompasses publications through 1979, is selectively annotated, and includes an index of authors and editors.

457. Watkin, Julia. **Historical Dictionary of Kierkegaard's Philosophy.** Lanhan, Md.: Scarecrow Press, 2001. 411p. (Historical Dictionaries of Religions, Philosophies, and Movements, 33).

Shares the aims and general pattern set by the *Historical Dictionary of Nietzscheanism* in the same series (see entry 481). Differences include a considerably shorter introduction (10 pages) but considerably longer bibliography (just over 100 pages), and the inclusion of three appendices indicative of the peculiar challenges in understanding this often enigmatic thinker and writer. These appendices offer a quick overview of Kierkegaard's writings with some of the more intricate details of his authorship; a list of his pseudonyms and their meaning and usage; and "Some Historical Notes" including a list of monarchs relevant to Kierkegaard's life and times, key historical events, and places where he lived. Entries in the main body of the dictionary cover the usual range for this series: key concepts in Kierkegaard's thought, his major writings, persons who influenced or were influenced by him, adversaries and interpreters, and the significant events, institutions, and people in his life. There are some illustrations, including maps.

458. Hong, Nathaniel J., Kathryn Hong, and Regine Prenzel-Guthrie. **Cumulative Index to *Kierkegaard's Writings: The Works of Søren Kierkegaard.*** Princeton, N.J.: Princeton University Press, 2000. 560p. (Kierkegaard's Works, vol. 26).

Indexes the 25 volumes comprising the authoritative English-language edition of Kierkegaard's collected writings edited by Howard V. and Edna H. Hong (Princeton, 1978–2000). More than just a collocation of the indexes in the individual volumes, it merges them into a common format using revised and refined rubrics and imposing consistency in the entries. Besides a 360-page general index of topical, name, and place references, it provides separately six special rubrics entailing large numbers of entries and references: one for Kierkegaard's autobiographic references, pseudonyms, and references to his own works; another for Biblical references, both explicit and indirect; three covering the major themes of Christianity, God, and love; and a final one for analogies used by Kierkegaard. The volume also has a chronological table of Kierkegaard's published works and a collation of the present collected edition with the Danish and an older English edition.

459. McKinnon, Alastair. **The Kierkegaard Indices.** Leiden: E. J. Brill, 1970–1975. 4 vols.

Preparation of these *Indices,* sophisticated research tools "designed to encourage and assist serious scholarly study of Kierkegaard's published works" (introduction, volume 2), was accomplished by exploiting the power of computers even at what now seems a fairly crude stage of their development. The result might well intimidate anyone short of a true Kierkegaard specialist, but for the latter these may be indispensable time-savers. Titles and content of the four volumes are as follows:

1. **Kierkegaard in Translation / en traduction/ in Übersetzung** (1970, 133p.). Correlates the page numbers of both the third and second Danish editions of the Collected Works with those of "the best and most widely available English, French and German translations."

2. **Fundamental polyglot konkordanz til Kierkegaards Samlede Vaerker** (1971, 1137p.). This is a concordance of 586 of the most fundamental terms in Kierkegaard's writings, set in context, with reference to their occurrences in the Danish third and second editions and the corresponding pages and lines of the English, French, and German translations.

3. **Index verborum til Kierkegaards Samlede Vaerker** (1973, 1322p.). Indexes every word in Kierkegaard's writings except those included in volume 2 plus certain common articles and prepositions. Provides page and line locations in the Danish third edition only (but these may be correlated with other editions via the tables in volume 1).

4. **A Computational Analysis of Kierkegaard's Samlede Vaerker** (1975, 1088p.). Presents the various lexical properties of the Kierkegaard corpus with the use of rank and frequency lists and a number of summary tables and graphs.

LEIBNIZ, GOTTFRIED WILHELM (1646–1716)

460.   **Leibniz-Bibliographie.** [Band 1]: **Die Literatur über Leibniz bis 1980.** 2nd rev. ed. Based on work of Kurt Müller, ed. Albert Heinekamp. Frankfurt am Main: Vittorio Klostermann, 1984. 742p. Band 2: **Die Literatur über Leibniz 1981–1990.** Based on work of Kurt Müller, ed. Albert Heinekamp in collaboration with Marlen Mertens. Frankfurt am Main: Vittorio Klostermann, 1996. 267p. (Veröffentlichungen des Leibniz-Archivs, 10 and 12).

Lists writings on Leibniz's work, thought, and influence in classified subject arrangement. Coverage of the base volume extends from Leibniz's lifetime to 1980. Volume 2 supplements this with coverage through 1990, observing a largely parallel though somewhat expanded classification. Effort has been made to make bibliographic descriptions, particularly of the early literature, as complete as possible. Annotations are limited to bibliographic matters. Author and subject indexes are provided in both volumes.

461.   Ravier, Emile. **Bibliographie des oeuvres de Leibniz.** Paris: Libraire Félix Alcan, 1937. Reprinted, Hildesheim: Georg Olms, 1966. 704p.

Restricted to works *by* Leibniz, a vast body of writings with often complex publication histories. Sections cover, for example, books and articles published by Leibniz; anonymous reviews published by him; works written by him and published in his lifetime but by others; and works published posthumously (listed by century of publication). An appendix lists the contents of major collections of Leibniz writings, including his voluminous letters. Annotations, limited largely to bibliographic matters, are in French.

462.   Finster, Reinhard, et. al. **Leibniz Lexicon: A Dual Concordance to Leibniz's Philosophische Schriften.** Hildesheim: Olms-Weidman, 1988. [Vol. 1], 419p. [Vol. 2], 65 microfiche.

"The *Leibniz Lexicon* consists of two different concordances, a printed volume and a microfiche Key-Word-in-Context (KWIC) concordance. . . . Both are companions to the largest single collection of Leibniz's philosophical writings currently available, that is, the edition in seven volumes edited by C.I. Gerhardt between 1875 and 1890" (preface). The printed volume is devoted to the principal concepts of Leibniz's philosophical vocabulary, each represented by what the editors considered its most distinctive, significant, or representative occurrences, quoted in substantial context ranging from a brief phrase to an entire paragraph. Each quotation is in its original language, one of three in which Leibniz wrote: German, French, or Latin. The introduction explains how the editors handled dilemmas and complexities created by the trilingual source-text, for example, in regard to when and when not to group together similar or related terms in different languages. The microfiche concordance reproduces 13,449 pages of computer printout on 65 fiche, representing nearly exhaustively every word in Leibniz's entire vocabulary in all its occurrences in the Gerhardt edition, with a limited context for each occurrence. Exclusions (definite articles, relative pronouns, and so forth, as well as some minor special categories) are explained in the introduction to the printed volume, as are other matters pertaining to the content and use of the microfiche concordance. In both concordances, textual references are given uniformly as a sequence of three numbers representing volume, page, and line.

LOCKE, JOHN (1632–1704)

463.   Attig, John C. **The Works of John Locke: A Comprehensive Bibliography from the Seventeenth Century to the Present.** Westport, Conn.: Greenwood, 1985, 185p. (Bibliographies and Indexes in Philosophy, 1).

This primary bibliography, while it aims to be comprehensive, describes itself as an "interim checklist of editions" until a projected bibliography associated with the Clarendon edition of the *Works of John Locke,* in progress, is completed (p. xii). Locke's works are arranged chronologically by date of first publication, with the initial entry followed as applicable by: editions of the complete text in the original language; abridged versions and selections; translations of the full text, by language; abridgements and selections in translation. In many instances, these are followed by entries for early notices, attacks, and defenses of Locke's works by other authors, indicated by bracketed entry numbers. Along with a brief section listing early biographical sketches (inserted chronologically at the date of Locke's death, 1704), these take Attig's work into the realm of secondary bibliography, with the aim of setting the historical context for Locke's works in the controversies of his time. Extensive bibliographical annotations also contribute to this goal. An appendix lists incorrect or doubtful attributions. Name, title, and language indexes are provided.

464.   Christopherson, Halfdan Olans. **A Bibliographical Introduction to the Study of John Locke.** Oslo: Norske Videnskaps Akademi, 1930. Reprinted, New York: Burt Franklin, 1968. 134p.

This extended bibliographic essay treats Locke's writings in relation to their historical context and the development of Locke's thought, and discusses secondary works from 1704 to 1928 by thematic categories (e.g., writings relating to Locke's *Essay,* to his educational thought, to his political and economic writings). An author index is included.

465.   Hall, Roland, and Roger Woolhouse. **80 Years of Locke Scholarship: A Bibliographic Guide.** Edinburgh: Edinburgh University Press, 1983. 215p.

Materials on Locke from 1900 to 1980 are listed by year, and within each year by author. Indexes afford access by author, language, and subject. There are no annotations.

466.   Yolton, Jean S. **John Locke: A Descriptive Bibliography.** Bristol: Thoemmes Press, 1998. 514p. + 26 pp. of plates.

Seeks to fill a need intensified by the burgeoning of Locke scholarship and made urgent by work on the authoritative Clarendon Edition of Locke's collected writings. It covers all editions and translations of all of Locke's publications to 1801, including contributions to works by others, posthumous publications, collected editions, and published correspondence. Chapter 12 covers spurious works and doubtful attributions. Bibliographic descriptions include meticulously detailed physical descriptions and are often supplemented with extensive notes on publishing history. Also recorded are library or private collection locations of copies examined, and their previous owners when known. Chapter 13 makes a limited foray into secondary bibliography with a checklist of contemporary criticism of Locke through 1800. There are numerous indexes, including among others of editors and translators, illustrators, printers, and languages of texts.

467.   Yolton, Jean S., and John W. Yolton. **John Locke: A Reference Guide.** Boston: G. K. Hall, 1985. 294p. (A Reference Guide to Literature).

The Yoltons list and provide descriptive, generally noncritical annotations for more than 1,800 secondary works from 1689 to 1982, by year of publication. Indexes are provided for names (of authors and of persons mentioned in annotations) and for subjects, the latter tending to use overly broad categories.

468.   Yolton, John W. **A Locke Dictionary.** Oxford: Blackwell, 1993. 348p. (Blackwell Philosopher Dictionaries).

Yolton, a noted authority on Locke, presents the philosopher's use of key words from abstraction to zealots, including those linked to such central Lockean concerns as ideas and their various kinds (abstract or general ideas, complex ideas, simple ideas), property, qualities, revelation, and rights, among others. Often Yolton provides considerable historical background on traditional terms and concepts—very importantly, for instance, in his discussion of the specific targets of Locke's opposition to the concept of innateness. Locke's own words are frequently quoted (with specific citations to standard editions of his works), and special attention is paid to changes in his usage over time or in different writings. Bibliographies of Locke's works, of pre–nineteenth-century works referenced in the text, and of selected secondary sources are at the back.

469.   Harrison, John, and Peter Laslett. **The Library of John Locke.** 2nd ed. Oxford: Clarendon Press, 1971. 313p.

This aid to the study of intellectual influences on Locke, or of the intellectual climate and currents of his time, includes an essay by Laslett on "John Locke and His Books" and a catalogue of Locke's personal library (pp. 67–267). The work is illustrated.

MALEBRANCHE, NICHOLAS (1638–1715)

470.   Easton, Patricia, Thomas M. Lennon, and Gregor Sebba. **Bibliographia Malebranchiana: A Critical Guide to the Malebranche Literature into 1989.** Carbondale: Southern Illinois University Press, 1992. 189p.

Easton and Lennon update and extend in this work a privately printed 1959 bibliography by Sebba on Malebranche, a seventeenth-century philosopher-priest who extended the philosophy of Descartes and originated the extreme-dualist position known as Occasionalism. Part 1 lists works by Malebranche, while part 2 lists works about him in three sections: bibliography, biography, and studies. A majority of publications listed are in English or French, but materials in Dutch, German, Italian, Japanese, Latin, Polish, Russian, and Spanish are also included. Critical annotations in English accompany most entries. There is an index for subjects and names mentioned in citations or annotations.

MARX, KARL (1818–1883)

471.   Eubanks, Cecil L. **Karl Marx and Friedrich Engels: An Analytical Bibliography.** 2nd ed. New York: Garland, 1984. 299p. (Garland Reference Library of Social Science, vol. 100).

A 42-page introduction provides an overview of Marx's and Engels's most important writings, the Marx-Engels relationship, biographies, and the major interpreters. The bibliography itself, which is not annotated, lists individual and collected works by Marx and Engels, and, in separate sections, books, articles, and doctoral dissertations about them. Separate subject indexes also cover each of these types of material.

472.   Rubel, Maximilien. **Bibliographie des oeuvres de Karl Marx, avec en appendice un répertoire des oevres de Friedrich Engels.** Paris: Marcel Rivière, 1956. 273p. **Supplement,** 1960. 79p.

This catalog of Marx's extensive output (some 885 items, plus a handful of dubious works), arranged in approximate chronological sequence, includes references to collected editions, notably the *Marx-Engels Gesamtausgabe* (1927–1935). Annotations, in French, are concerned chiefly with bibliographic details and publication history, but occasionally comment on a work's content or significance.

473.   Stockhammer, Morris. **Karl Marx Dictionary.** New York: Philosophical Library, 1965. 273p.

See entry 508 for a general comment on the series of which this is a representative. Like its fellows, this "dictionary" presents quotes only, without context or explanation, which works somewhat better here than in most of the others, because Marx tends to be less than averagely technical or abstruse. Sources are cited by title only. A fairly good selection of quotes covers economic and political as well as philosophical topics. The *Communist Manifesto* and *Das Kapital,* predictably, are heavily mined, but 17 other works are drawn on as well. Translations, based on the *Gesamtausgabe* (Berlin and Moscow, 1927–35), are by Moore and Aveling.

MILL, JOHN STUART (1806–1873)

474. Laine, Michael. **Bibliography of Works on John Stuart Mill.** Toronto: University of Toronto Press, 1982. 173p.

This international bibliography, listing 1,971 items in many languages, is arranged by author, with a subject index (somewhat unsatisfactory in its use of broad subject terms with long series of reference numbers) and a separate index for names as subjects. Appendices list verse, cartoons, and portraits and other representations.

475. MacMinn, N., J. R. Hainds, and J. M. McCrimmon. **Bibliography of the Published Writings of John Stuart Mill.** Evanston, Ill.: Northwestern University Press, 1945. 101p. (Northwestern Studies in the Humanities, 12).

Edited from Mill's own manuscript, with corrections and notes. Reportedly "not quite complete" (*Encyclopedia of Philosophy,* vol. 5, p. 322).

MONTESQUIEU, BARON DE (1689–1755)

476. Cabeen, David Clark. **Montesquieu: A Bibliography.** New York: New York Public Library, 1947. 87p.

"Has 650-odd titles by and about M., most of them evaluated and located at New York Public Library, Columbia, or occasionally other important libraries. The *Bibliography* has 8-page index, including reasonably complete subject lists" (Cabeen, ed., *Critical Bibl. of French Literature* [1951], vol. 4, p. 157).

NIETZSCHE, FRIEDRICH (1844–1900)

477. Krummel, Richard Frank and Evelyn S. Krummel. **Nietzsche und der deutsche Geist.** 3 vols. Berlin: Walter de Gruyter, 1998. (Monographien und Texte zur Nietzsche-Forschung, Bände 3, 9, 40).

Described by reviewers as "monumental," this three-volume bibliography aspires to document well-nigh exhaustively the reception of Nietzsche's work in the German-speaking areas of Europe from 1867 until the end of World War II. Materials covered, in approximately chronological sequence, include not just scholarly books, journal articles, dissertations, and so forth, but every conceivable source including magazine and newspaper articles, biographies and autobiographies of individuals who interacted with Nietzsche, correspondence, even poetry. Entries are annotated, often extensively, with varying combinations of descriptive data, content notes, information on historical context, quotations from the cited work, and cross-references. Component volumes are as follows:

Band 1: **Ausbreitung und Wirkung des Nietzscheschen Werkes im deutschen Sprachraum bis zum Todesjahr: Ein Schrifttumsverzeichnis der Jahre 1867–1900.** 2nd rev. and enl. ed. 737p.

Band 2: **Ausbreitung und Wirkung des Nietzscheschen Werkes im deutschen Sprachraum vom Todesjahr bis zum Ende des Ersten Weltkrieges: Ein Schrifttumsverzeichnis der Jahre 1901–1918.** 2nd rev. and enl. ed. 861p.

Band 3: **Ausbreitung und Wirkung des Nietzscheschen Werkes im deutschen Sprachraum bis zum Ende des Zweiten Weltkrieges: Ein Schrifttumsverzeichnis der Jahre 1919–1945.** 931p.

The first editions of volumes 1 and 2 were published with minor title differences by Walter de Gruyter in 1974 and 1983, respectively. The revised and enlarged second editions were issued simultaneously with the first edition of volume 3.

478. Reichert, Herbert William, and Karl Schlechta. **International Nietzsche Bibliography.** Rev. and expanded edition. Chapel Hill: University of North Carolina Press, 1968. 162p. (University of North Carolina Studies in Comparative Literature, 45).

The first edition (1960) of this full though selective bibliography included 3,973 items in 24 languages, grouped by language. The revised edition adds 566 items that are grouped together rather than merged with the original entries. A subject index has been added. Some entries are briefly annotated.

479. Schaberg, William H. **The Nietzsche Canon: A Publication History and Bibliography.** Chicago: University of Chicago Press, 1995. 281p.

The bulk of this work constitutes what its author calls a "biobibliography" (p.189)—a meticulously detailed narrative history of Nietzsche's publications and their relationships to his life. It examines how, when, and why Nietzsche's works were written, when published and by whom, the number of copies printed, and the effect of sales (or lack thereof) on their author. Part 2 is a 35-page primary bibliography in roughly chronological sequence. Bibliographic descriptions include full renditions of title pages. Annotations incorporate physical descriptions (detailed paginations, bindings, size, etc.) and the most basic known facts of publication and sales history within Nietzsche's lifetime.

480. **Weimarer Nietzsche-Bibliographie (WNB).** Susanne Jung, et. al. Stuttgart: J. B. Metzler, 2000–2002. 5 vols. (Personalbibliographien zur neueren deutschen Literatur, Band 4/1–5).

Published under the auspices of the Stiftung Weimarer Klassik and its affiliated Herzogin Anna Amalia Bibliothek, whose combined extensive Nietzsche-related collections provide the basis for, but by no means exhaust, this superlatively comprehensive bibliography. Disclosure of the Anna Amalia Bibliothek's holdings serves to compensate for their relative inaccessibility during the period of communist-controlled East Germany (DDG), when it was named the Zentralbibliothek der deutschen Klassik. The five component volumes are as follows:

Band 1: **Primärliteratur 1867–1998.** 2000. 517p.

Lists editions of Nietzsche's output in six broad categories: collected editions, individual publications, musical works, letters, works on digital or audio media, and translations. The last-named section exemplifies the bibliography's exceptional comprehensiveness, including many translations in non-Western languages such as Arabic, Bengali, and Japanese, and Western minority languages such as Basque and Icelandic. Each section is divided into several subsections; within each of these the arrangement is chronological.

> Band 2: **Sekundärliteratur 1867–1998: Allgemeine Grundlagen und Hilfsmittel; Leben und Werk im Allgemeinen; biographische Einzelheiten.** 2002. 500p.
>
> Bard 3: **Sekundärliteratur 1867–1998: Nietzsches geistige und geschichtlich-kulturelle Lebensbeziehungen, sein Denken und Schaffen.** 2002. 1013p.
>
> Band 4: **Sekundärliteratur 1867–1998: Zu Nietzsches philosophisch-literarischem Werk insgesamt; zu einzelnen Werken.** 2002. 258p.
>
> Band 5: **Sekundärliteratur 1867–1998: Wirkungs- und Forschungsgeschichte. Register zu den Bänden 2–5.** 2002. 808p.

The four-volume secondary bibliography uses an elaborate systematic classification (displayed in full at the end of vol. 5) with numerous subheadings, sub-subheadings, and so forth, under the broad headings identified in each volume's subtitle. Arrangement within subsections is chronological, except that translations and reviews, regardless of their own dates, are listed immediately following the entry of the work translated or reviewed. Volume 5 has name and topical indexes covering the entire set.

481.   Diethe, Carol. **Historical Dictionary of Nietzscheanism.** Lanham, Md.: Scarecrow Press, 1999. 265p. (Historical Dictionaries of Religions, Philosophies, and Movements, 21).

The series editor's foreword aptly summarizes the aim and scope of this dictionary: "It informs us about Nietzsche the man as well as Nietzsche the philosopher. It describes his career and his thought," and "it also presents earlier thinkers who influenced Nietzsche's philosophy as well as his contemporaries, who agreed or disagreed with him, and others who perpetuated his memory and interpreted (or misinterpreted) his philosophical heritage for later generations." Besides alphabetically arranged entries covering the aforementioned range of topics, including entries on Nietzsche's major writings and key concepts in his thought, the dictionary also features a brief chronology of important dates in Nietzsche's life, a short glossary of terms, a substantial 40-page introductory essay emphasizing particularly the reception, dispersion, and influence of his thought, and a 32-page bibliography with its own 5-page introduction.

482.   Ottmann, Henning, ed. **Nietzsche-Handbuch: Leben, Werk, Wirkung.** Stuttgart: J. B. Metzler, 2000. 561p. (Metzler Handbüchern).

This is the first of several volumes on major philosophers issued in the series of *Metzler Handbüchern* on important German intellectual and cultural figures. Though promoted by the publisher and described by some reviewers as reference works *(Nachschlagewerke),* most must be considered borderline in that category. Like many other works on their subjects, they provide biographical information on the philosophers together with detailed summaries and analyses of their writings, and sometimes material on their influence. Their exceptional thoroughness and comprehensiveness, particularly in presenting individual writings, do contribute a considerable measure of reference value, as does their typically thorough indexing. Bibliographies provided are generally brief and, while authoritatively selective, otherwise unexceptional.

The volume on Nietzsche, while largely typical of the series, answers to the "reference work" label better than others, in that it includes a dictionary of Nietzschean concepts, theories, and metaphors from *Antisemitismus* to *Züchtung* (sect. 3). There are also sections on Nietzsche's sources and the influences on him, and on his impact on academic disciplines, genres, and countries. Some 70 Nietzsche authorities contributed to this *Handbuch.*

483.   Oehler, Richard. **Nietzsche-Register: Alphabetisch-systematische Übersicht über Friedrich Nietzsches Gedankenwelt.** Stuttgart: Alfred Kröner Verlag, 1965. 533p. (Kröners Taschenausgabe, vol. 170).

In his *Vorwort,* Oehler plausibly suggests that an aid to subject access is more essential for Nietzsche than for most other thinkers, due to the predominantly aphoristic form of his writings. This *Register* is an index to the main concepts and names in Nietzsche's works, keyed to the edition of the German text published as volumes 70 through 83 of Kröners Taschenausgabe. It references the most significant passages, not merely citing volume and page numbers but also quoting fragments of the text in which the terms are embedded.

PASCAL, BLAISE (1623–1662)

484.   Maire, Albert. **Bibliographie générale des oeuvres de Pascal.** Paris: L. Giraud-Badin, 1925–27. 5 vols.

Many secondary works are included in this bibliography along with exhaustive listings of editions, reprintings, and translations of Pascal's writings. Individual volumes are devoted to specific writings or groups of writings, for example, volume 4 deals with Pascal's most important philosophical work, the *Pensées.*

PEIRCE, CHARLES SANDERS (1839–1914)

485.   Ketner, Kenneth Laine, C. J. W. Kloesel, and Joseph M. Ransdell. **A Comprehensive Bibliography of the Published Works of Charles Sanders Peirce with a Bibliography of Secondary Sources.** Bowling Green, Ohio: Philosophy Documentation Center, Bowling Green State University, 1986. 337p. (Bibliographies of Famous Philosophers).

This is a minimally revised edition of Ketner, et. al., *A Comprehensive Bibliography and Index of the Published Works of Charles Sanders Peirce with a Bibliography of Secondary Studies* (Greenwich, Conn.: Johnson Associates, 1977). Part 1, besides being independently useful as a comprehensive bibliography, is also an index to the *Charles S. Peirce Microfiche Collection,* originally issued on 149 fiche by Johnson Associates in 1977 and since reissued, together with a 1986 supplement of 12 fiche, by the Philosophy Documentation Center. Like the collection itself, this bibliography/index is organized chronologically. Fiche numbers are indicated, and works by and about Peirce are distinguished by the letters "P" (Peirce) and "O" (others). Under an extremely broad definition of published works (indicated in the preface), Peirce's output is more enormous than usually thought, and far exceeds what's included in his *Collected Papers.* Part 2 is a supplementary bibliography of secondary works, arranged by author. It repeats the "O" items from part 1 but also includes many works not part of the microfiche collection. Regrettably, the opportunity to update this section for the revised edition was not seized (so that no works after 1977 are listed); instead, the preface refers to two nonmonographic supplements published elsewhere, which themselves provide coverage only through 1983.

486.   Robin, Richard S. **Annotated Catalogue of the Papers of Charles S. Peirce.** [n.l.]: University of Massachusetts Press, 1967. 268p.

This is a catalog of and guide to the Peirce papers in the Houghton Library at Harvard. Part 1 lists manuscripts, arranged by subject; part 2 lists correspondence.

PRICE, RICHARD (1723–1791)

487.   Thomas, D. O., John Stephens, and P.A.L. Jones. **A Bibliography of the Works of Richard Price.** Brookfield, Vt.: Scolar Press/Ashgate Publishing, 1993. 221p.

Not well-known now, Price (1723–1791) was influential in his time in British moral and political philosophy as well as several other fields: theology, economics, actuarial science, mathematics, and politics. Three brief secondary bibliographies included in this work (covering books and pamphlets, articles, and other works) show sparse scholarly activity relating to Price from about 1800 to 1970 but increasing attention and accelerating rates of publication in recent decades. Most of the volume is devoted to an exhaustive primary bibliography of Price's writings in all known editions and translations published in or shortly after his lifetime, with newer editions also recorded in notes. Antiquarian or rare book dealers and librarians will value the meticulous bibliographical descriptions, while scholars and students of philosophy and intellectual history will benefit from the narrative introductions that place each work in the context of Price's intellectual development.

ROUSSEAU, JEAN-JACQUES (1712–1778)

488.   Dufour, Théophile. **Recherches bibliographiques sur les oeuvres imprimées de J.-J. Rousseau.** Paris: L. Giroud-Badin, 1925. 2 vols. Reprinted, New York: Burt Franklin, 1971. 2 vols. in 1.

"Indispensable research tool. In addition to descriptions of printed editions of R.'s works, this work is particularly important because it lists R. manuscripts at Library of Neuchatel. Also lists books belonging to R." (Cabeen, ed., *Critical Bibliography of French Literature* [1951], vol. 4, p. 209).

489.   Sénelier, Jean. **Bibliographie générale des oeuvres de J.-J. Rousseau.** Paris: Encyclopedie Francaise, 1949. Reprinted, New York: Burt Franklin, [n.d.]. 282p.

"Elaborate and indispensable bibliography. Corrects and complements Dufour [entry 488] and extends research to date of publication. Chronological presentation. . . . Description and location of MSS. Dissemination of R.'s writings by countries" (Cabeen, ed., *Critical Bibliography of French Literature* [1951], vol. 4, p. 251).

490.   Dent, N. J. H. **A Rousseau Dictionary.** Oxford: Basil Blackwell, 1992. 279p. (Blackwell Philosopher Dictionaries).

Dent's work on Rousseau made a promising start for Blackwell's series of dictionaries on individual philosophers, a previously rare genre if we set aside the mainly-quotations "dictionaries" published by Philosophical Library from 1951 to 1972 (see entry 508). It established a successful model for the stated aim of the Blackwell series to be "scholarly yet accessible" (cover blurb), serving students and general readers as well as "those already familiar with the material who require a convenient reference source" (ibid.). Following an introductory essay, which handles biographical matters, plus a chronology, it has about 100 alphabetically arranged articles, all substantial (i.e., there are no short definitions), covering key ideas, concepts, and themes in Rousseau's thought or summarizing his major writings and placing them in historical context. Dent's interpretations of controverted areas of Rousseau's thought are responsible and not idiosyncratic, though perhaps overly defensive in Rousseau's behalf. Primary sources are cited extensively throughout. Secondary literature is not cited directly, but references for further reading accompany every entry and are keyed to a secondary bibliography of 349 books and articles.

SCHELLING, FRIEDRICH WILHELM JOSEPH VON (1775–1854)

491.   Schneeberger, Guido. **Friedrich Wilhelm von Schelling: Eine Bibliographie.** Bern: Francke, 1954. 190p.

Primary bibliography lists Schelling's published works, including books in numerous editions, journal articles and contributions to magazines and newspapers, as well as works for which he supplied introductions or notes, letters to and from him, and some works dedicated to him. Secondary bibliography lists 816 items in chronological arrangement from 1797 on. There are some annotations, mainly bibliographical and contents notes.

SCHILLER, JOHANN CHRISTOPH FRIEDRICH VON (1759–1805)

492.   Bärwinkel, Roland, et. al. **Schiller Bibliographie, 1975–1985.** Berlin: Aufbau, 1989. 527p. (Bibliographien, Kataloge, und Bestandsverzeichnisse).

Supplements entries 494, 495, and 496. Organization remains comparable to that used in the antecedent bibliographies, but there is more rearrangement of categories and revision of headings (from those in base volume for 1893–1958) than is the case with previous supplements. Translations of Schiller's works in particular receive expanded coverage, notably those in Russian and other East European languages.

493.   **Schiller-Bibliographie: Unter Benutzung der Trömelschen Schiller-Bibliothek (1865).** Ed. Herbert Marcuse. Hildesheim: H. A. Gerstenberg, 1971. 137p.

This 1971 publication is a photomechanical reprinting of a 1925 work published in Berlin by S. M. Fraenkel, which incorporated the work of Paul F. Trömel in his

Schiller-Bibliothek (Leipzig: Brockhaus, 1865). It is a primary bibliography of Schiller's works in three sections: (1) collected editions from 1802 to 1840; (2) individual works published from 1776 through 1805; (3) the most significant editions first published after Schiller's death in 1805, through 1923.

494.   Vulpius, Wolfgang. **Schiller Bibliographie, 1893–1958.** Weimar: Arion, 1959. 569p. (Bibliographien, Kataloge, und Bestandsverzeichnisse herausgegeben von den Nationalen Forschungs- und Gedenkstätten der klassichen deutschen Literatur in Weimar).

A primary and secondary bibliography encompassing the range of Schiller's work as philosopher, poet, and dramatist. The primary section is organized by genre categories, for example, poetry collections, philosophical-aesthetic writings, journalistic writings and reviews, letters, and so on. The secondary bibliography is divided into a variety of categories including, for example, Schiller's life, his style, his political-ideological worldview, and under "Schiller und die Nachwelt" aspects of his legacy such as publication history, Schiller societies, exhibitions, and so forth. There is a name index.

For continuing coverage, see entries 492, 495, and 496.

495.   Vulpius, Wolfgang. **Schiller Bibliographie, 1959–1963.** Berlin: Aufbau, 1967. 204p. (Bibliographien, Kataloge, und Bestandsverzeichnisse).

Continues entry 494, using a largely parallel scheme of organization.

496.   Wersig, Peter, and Wolfgang Vulpius. **Schiller Bibliographie, 1964–1974.** Berlin: Aufbau, 1977. 254p. (Bibliographien, Kataloge, und Bestandsverzeichnisse).

Supplements entries 494 and 495. The table-of-contents outline is nearly identical to that in the 1959–63 volume.

SCHOPENHAUER, ARTHUR (1788–1860)

497.   Hübscher, Arthur. **Schopenhauer-Bibliographie.** Stuttgart: Frommann-Holzboog, 1981. 331p.

Lists works by Schopenhauer, including translations, and works about him. Of 2,395 items, the vast majority are in German, some in other European languages, relatively few in English. An index of names is provided.

498.   Cartwright, David E. **Historical Dictionary of Schopenhauer's Philosophy.** Lanham, Md.: Scarecrow Press, 2005. 239p. (Historical Dictionaries of Religions, Philosophies, and Movements, 55).

Like other philosopher-oriented dictionaries in the same series, beginning with Diethe's work on Nietzsche (entry 481), this combines a focus on its subject's thought with generous attention to biographical matters. The latter include, in Schopenhauer's case, an uncommon share of colorful elements that are duly treated here—among others his famous poodles, his troubles with women and related misogyny, his personal antagonism toward Hegel, his collaboration with Goethe on color research and their subsequent falling-out. Entries on Schopenhauer's thought include principal themes such as his well-known philosophical pessimism, death, Will, Will to Life, art, representation, principle of sufficient reason. Entry terms or phrases in this category are usually accompanied by their German originals. Other entries relate to intellectual influences, not only many contemporaries (e.g., Fichte, Schelling) and predecessors in Western thought (Plato, Calderón de la Barca, Spinoza, Kant) but also Schopenhauer's strong interest in Eastern thought (Buddhism, Hinduism) and his appropriation from it of specific elements such as the "veil of *māyā*." Among entries discussing his influences on others are those on Hartmann, Nietzsche, Wagner, and Wittgenstein.

Cartwright provides a 45-page introductory overview of Schopenhauer's life and ideas, a chronology, and a 38-page bibliography including the primary sources in both German and English editions and secondary sources organized by broad themes.

499.   Spierling, Volker. **Schopenhauer-ABC.** Leipzig: Reclam, 2003. 256p.

A dictionary of 360 terms, phrases, and references of particular significance in Schopenhauer's philosophy. For some entries the exposition consists entirely of one or more quotes from Schopenhauer's own writings. Others offer (usually alongside quotes) explanatory comments, biographical or contextual information, and so forth, occasionally including material from other secondary sources. Most end with cross references to related entries. A blurb in front notes the inclusion of a number of amusing anecdotes about Schopenhauer.

500.   Wagner, Gustav Friedrich and Arthur Hübscher. **Schopenhauer-Register.** 2nd ed. Stuttgart-Bad Canstatt: Fr. Frommann, 1960. 530p. Reprint ed.: Stuttgart: Frommann-Holzboog, 1982. 530p.

A keyword index to Schopenhauer's works, keyed to the seven-volume compilation of his *Sämtliche Werke* edited by Hübscher (2nd ed., Wiesbaden: E. Brockhaus, 1946–51). It represents a revision and adaptation by Hübscher of Wagner's *Encyklopädisches Register zu Schopenhauer's Werken* (Karlsruhe: G. Braunsche, 1909). By Hübscher's own account, the latter remains of value for the way it gathered related terms under a common entry, whereas the present index provides an individual entry for every significant term and name. There is a separate index (pp. 505 ff.) for proverbs, maxims, expressions, precepts, and so forth, including also directly quoted passages from other authors, in German and in other languages.

SPENCER, HERBERT (1820–1903)

501.   Perrin, Robert G. **Herbert Spencer: A Primary and Secondary Bibliography.** Hamden, Conn.: Garland, 1992. 1005p. (Garland Reference Library of the Humanities, vol. 1061).

Perrin records, as exhaustively as seems humanly possible, all writings by and about Spencer in English dated from 1839 through 1992, some 2,082 items. Of these, 322 represent Spencer's own prolific output, ranging from letters to the 10-volume *System of Synthetic Philosophy.* The secondary bibliography reflects the intense interest in Spencer's ideas, particularly his evolutionary theory of progress and social Darwinism, during the latter half of the nineteenth century, as well as the precipitous decline of interest early in this century and its partial resuscitation in recent years. The arrangement of secondary literature into 13 broad subject chapters, such as biographical and general studies, ethics, biology, psychology, sociology, and social thought, compensates somewhat for the lack of a detailed subject index. There is a name index. The bibliography is prefaced by a 98-page survey of Spencer's life, career, and thought.

SPINOZA, BENEDICT (BARUCH) DE (1632–1677)

502.   Bamberger, Fritz. **Spinoza and Anti-Spinoza Literature: The Printed Literature of Spinozism, 1665–1832.** Ed. Laurel S. Wolfson and David J. Gilner. Cincinnati, Ohio: Hebrew Union College Press, 2003. 296p. (Bibliographica Judaica, 15).

Bamberger's bibliography represents the catalogue of his personal library of early Spinoza literature, subsequently acquired by Hebrew Union College-Jewish Institute of Religion and now housed at the latter's Jerusalem Campus in the Abramov Library. Each bibliographic entry is accompanied by an annotation by Bamberger containing, variously, information on the work's author, a summary of content or thesis, clarification of bibliographic matters, and references to related entries. A total of 664 items of secondary literature are listed chronologically, along with a handful of manuscripts and autograph letters and several dozen early editions of Spinoza's own works. An essay titled "Early Editions of Spinoza's *Tractatus Theologico-Politicus:* A Bibliohistorical Reexamination" precedes the bibliography.

503.   Boucher, Wayne I. **Spinoza in English: A Bibliography from the Seventeenth Century to the Present.** Leiden: E. J. Brill, 1991. 226p. (Brill's Studies in Intellectual History, 28).

Boucher's aim was to "to bring together, for the first time, citations to all of the books, book chapters or sections, dissertations, and scholarly papers on Spinoza in the English language, as well as citations to all translations of his works into English . . . from the late 17th century to the present" (preface). Acknowledging debts to earlier bibliographies, especially Oko's (entry 504), he not only updates these but also corrects and amplifies them by citing hitherto overlooked items, restoring useful information suppressed by older bibliographic conventions, and presenting full citations in a uniform style. At the same time, he omits extremely marginal works (containing just one or two references to Spinoza) that encumber Oko's work. Works by Spinoza are listed in chronological sequence, those about him (nearly 2,000 entries) alphabetically by author.

504.   Oko, Adolph S. **The Spinoza Bibliography.** Boston: G. K. Hall, 1964. 700p.

This work, published under the auspices of the Columbia University Libraries, reproduces catalog cards for about 7,000 items, accumulated by Oko over many years and in many cases bearing his annotations. Coverage is to 1942, with few entries dated later than 1940. Arrangement is according to a subject classification outlined in the front; inconveniently, headings are shown only at the beginning of each section and not repeated on each page. For each item, one location (only) is indicated, with preference given to Columbia, home of the Oko-Gebhardt collection of Spinoziana, and after that to Hebrew Union College, where Oko built up an extensive Spinoza library.

505. Préposiet, Jean. **Bibliographie Spinoziste.** Paris: Belles Lettres, [1973]. 454p. (Travaux du Centre de Documentation et de Bibliographie philosophiques de Besançon, 1. Annales littéraires de l'Université dé Besançon, 154).

Préposiet's extensive, multilingual primary and secondary bibliography includes both an alphabetical listing by authors *(répertoire alphabetique)* and a systematic subject listing *(registre systematique)*. The latter has chapters on Spinoza's life; his intellectual milieu; his own writings, with editions and translations listed by language; studies of individual works; the sources, diffusion, development, and influence of Spinoza's thought; and specific Spinozistic topics or themes, such as religion, politics, morality, freedom, art, and epistemology. Appendices reproduce several brief texts relating to Spinoza and give an inventory of his own library.

506. Wetlesen, Jon. **A Spinoza Bibliography, 1940–1970.** 2nd rev. ed. Oslo: Universitetsforlaget, 1971. 47p.

The title page states this second edition is "arranged as a supplementary volume to A. S. Oko's *Spinoza Bibliography*" (see entry 50). An earlier version (*A Spinoza Bibliography, Particularly on the Period 1940–1967;* Oslo: Universitetsforlaget, 1968, 88p.) also included selectively material covered by Oko, but in this edition Wetlesen has "omitted almost every reference to works published before 1940" (preface).

507. Giancotti Boscherini, Emilia. **Lexicon Spinozanum.** The Hague: Martinus Nijhoff, 1970. 2 vols. (International Archives of the History of Ideas, 28).

To serve the Spinoza-scholar who "asks from a lexicon not only rapid and easy orientation in the field of Spinozistic concepts, but also the means for terminological and conceptual analysis which is necessarily tied to the original language," this lexicon "sets for itself the following goals: the clarification of the meaning of terms and of concepts, the determination of their reciprocal connections and implications, the bringing out of the semantic ambiguity of some terms, on the one hand, and of the synonymity of other terms, on the other hand, and also the recognition of those elements which are needed for an historical reconstruction of the cultural and environmental milieu of Spinoza" (introduction). The lexicon encompasses all of Spinoza's works, the main part covering the terminology of his Latin texts, an appendix his Dutch-language writings. There is also a Latin-Dutch glossary. Preface and introduction are in both English and Italian.

508. Runes, Dagobert D. **Spinoza Dictionary.** New York: Philosophical Library, 1951. Reprinted, Westport, Conn.: Greenwood Press, 1976. 309p.

This is the first of a number of similar "dictionaries" issued over several decades by Philosophical Library. Though never formally designated a series, they are similar enough to warrant a general comment here. Each is confined strictly to quotations from the philosopher or (in one case) group of philosophers constituting its subject. The quotations relate to specific terms or concepts, and are accordingly arranged alphabetically, but they are not necessarily definitional or even explanatory. Often, they merely exemplify some of a philosopher's views or pronouncements on a topic.

The "dictionary" label for a compilation of quotations is neither unprecedented nor entirely inappropriate, but can easily mislead, evoking expectations of definitions or systematic explanations. Such expectations are often unjustifiably encouraged by this series through exaggerated claims in prefaces or cover blurbs. Furthermore, many of the volumes perform poorly even as quotation dictionaries—neglecting topics that are significant, even central, in a philosopher's thought (while sometimes including peripheral topics); making poor or inadequate selections of quotes; or failing to identify sources of quotes with any useful precision. Where the latter deficiency exists, one possible use of a quotations dictionary, namely, to locate specific passages and perhaps trace their context, is effectively frustrated.

Runes's *Spinoza Dictionary* is not only the first but one of the better efforts in the series. It offers a selection of quotes on matters most likely to be of interest to, and within the grasp of, the nonspecialist wishing to dip into Spinoza's thought, while dodging most of the terminological and stylistic difficulties which tend to make that thought so notoriously forbidding. The majority are drawn from the *Ethics,* but other works and Spinoza's voluminous correspondence are tapped as well. The average length of the quotes significantly exceeds that for the series as a whole, which generally counts as a virtue. Translations are mainly those of R. H. M. Elwes in *The Chief Works of Benedict de Spinoza,* 3rd ed. (1889). Sources of quotes are identified with a moderate degree of precision.

VICO, GIAMBATTISTA (1668–1744)

509. Gianturco, Elio. **A Selective Bibliography of Vico Scholarship (1948–1968).** Florence: Grafica Toscana, 1968. 104p.

Published as supplement to *Forum Italicum,* this is intended to continue and update Benedetto Croce and Fausto Nicolini's *Bibliografia Vichiana* (Naples: Ricciardi, 1947–48, 2 vols.). It lists selectively, for the period indicated, reprints of Vico's major works and secondary studies in many languages, predictably including numerous books and articles in Italian. The secondary section employs a thematic arrangement with subarrangement by author.

510. Verene, Molly Black. **Vico: A Bibliography of Works in English from 1884 to 1994.** Bowling Green, Ohio: Philosophy Documentation Center, Bowling Green State University, 1994. 183p.

Though not identified as a second edition, this work absorbs and updates the publisher's 1986 publication, *A Bibliography of Vico in English, 1884–1984,* compiled by Giorgio Tagliacozzo, Donald Phillip Verene, and Vanessa Rumble, which in turn displaced a slim 1978 bibliography by Robert Crease, *Vico in English: A Bibliography of Writings by and about Giambattista Vico (1668–1744)* (Atlantic Highlands, N.J.: Published for the Institute for Vico Studies by Humanities Press, 1978, 48p.). None of these three works carry annotations.

Among the 2,300 items cited are, in part 1, books, articles, dissertations and theses, reviews in English of works on Vico in non-English languages, and (by the twentieth century) materials from the popular press; in part 2, English translations of Vico's works and English-language reviews of his works in other languages; and in part 3, works in which Vico is briefly mentioned, cited, or discussed, even including some fiction in which he appears. There is, unfortunately, no subject index.

VOLTAIRE, FRANÇOIS-MARIE AROUET DE (1694–1778)

511.   Bengesco, Georges. **Voltaire: Bibliographie de ses oeuvres.** Paris: Emile Perrin, 1882–85. Reprinted, Nendeln, Liechtenstein: Kraus Reprint, 1967. 4 vols.

This catalog of Voltaire's prodigious output and numerous editions thereof includes a list of more than 10,000 letters in the Moland edition of Voltaire's collected works (Paris, 1877–1885) plus some others. Because Bengesco spreads his materials over a wide variety of rubrics, making it difficult to locate specific titles, an index, *Table de la bibliographie de Voltaire par Bengesco,* compiled by Jean Malcolm, was published, though much later (Geneva: Institut et Musée Voltaire, 1953, 127p.).

14

Western Philosophy: Twentieth and Twenty-first Centuries

GENERAL AND MISCELLANEOUS SOURCES

See sections below for sources specific to the Anglo-American and Continental traditions.

BIBLIOGRAPHIES

512.   Shook, John R., et. al. **Pragmatism: An Annotated Bibliography 1898–1940.** Amsterdam: Rodopi, 1998. 615p. (Value Inquiry Book Series, vol. 66).

Contains 2,794 main entries, most of them annotated, and an additional 2,200 references to reviews, summaries, and so forth, representing publications by Pragmatists and commentators on Pragmatism written internationally from 1898 to 1940. There are 12 major figures emphasized, among them several Italians: Peirce, James, Dewey, Mead, Vailati, F.C.S. Schiller, A. W. Moore, Boodin, Calderoni, Papini, Prezzolini, and C. I. Lewis. But dozens of minor Pragmatist writers are covered as well. The focus is on writings in English, French, German, and Italian, but there is a small number of writings in other languages. Arrangement is chronological, then alphabetical by author within each year. Annotations range from one line to over a half page. The introduction discusses sources and major studies on Pragmatism generally and on its key geographical centers or regions: Cambridge (Mass.), Chicago, Great Britain, Italy, France, Germany. Author and subject indexes.

DICTIONARIES, ENCYCLOPEDIAS, AND HANDBOOKS

513.   Alekseev, Petr Vasil'evich. **Filosofy Rossii XIX–XX stoletii: biografii, idei, trudy.** 4th ed. Moscow: Akademicheskii Proekt, 2002.

See entry 286.

514.   Bertens, Hans and Joseph Natoli. **Postmodernism: The Key Figures.** Oxford: Blackwell, 2002. 384p.

The remarkable diversity among the 57 individuals plus one collective (the Wooster theatre group) gathered here under the umbrella of "Postmodernism" is clarified considerably by the editors' introduction, which distinguishes three major and somewhat loosely related "fields of reference" for the concept of Postmodernism. First is a "set of literary and artistic practices" that emerged in the 1950s and flourished through much of the next three decades. Second is "a set of philosophical propositions that are centered around the rejection of Realist epistemology and of the Enlightenment project that builds upon that epistemology." Third is a set of theories and interpretations that "seek to describe a new sociocultural formation and/or economic dispensation that according to a number of theorists has at least in the Western world come to replace modernity" (pp. xii–xiii). It is the second, of course, and to a lesser extent the third, that accounts for the presence of a strong contingent of philosophers among artists, critics, and social theorists as diverse as John Cage, the Coen brothers, Antonio Gramsci, Frederic Jameson, Toni Morrison, Robert Venturi, and Kurt Vonnegut. Most of the philosophers are Continental, in fact French—Althusser, Baudrillard, Derrida, Foucault, Levinas, Lyotard, among others—but, exemplifying Postmodernism's trans-Atlantic reach even in philosophy, they also include two Americans, Thomas Kuhn and Richard Rorty.

Contributors are 47 academics from institutions mainly in the United States, United Kingdom, and Canada plus a few in other countries. While articles do not have their own bibliographies, they include references to a 32-page general bibliography at volume's end.

515. Brown, Stuart, Diané Collinson, and Robert Wilkinson, eds. **Biographical Dictionary of Twentieth Century Philosophers.** London: Routledge, 1996. 947p.

See entry 196.

516. Brown, Stuart, Diané Collinson, and Robert Wilkinson, eds. **One Hundred Twentieth-Century Philosophers.** London: Routledge, 1998. 241p.

See entry 197.

517. Buhr, Manfred, ed. **Enzyklopädie zur bürgerlichen Philosophie im 19. und 20. Jahrhundert.** Cologne: Pahl-Rugenstein, 1988. 597p.

This encyclopedia of *spätbürgerlichen,* or "late bourgeois," philosophy, a product of the German Democratic Republic shortly before German reunification, has become ironically enough a record of what turned out to be "late" Marxism—at least the official Marxism of a Marxist state in which Buhr was a leading thinker. It features a series of essays by various authors—arranged thematically, not alphabetically—describing, analyzing, and critiquing major topics, themes, and trends of nineteenth- and twentieth-century Western philosophy, particularly its Continental manifestations but also including the Anglo-American realm. Besides treatments of branches such as ethics, epistemology, logic, philosophy of history, and political philosophy, there are discussions of schools or trends such as idealism, hermeneutics, materialism, and psychoanalysis, and thematic essays on, for example, classical bourgeois versus "late bourgeois" philosophy, the struggle over "Philosophie und 'Nicht-Philosophie,'" signs of the anti-Enlightenment, and "rationality/history/philosophy."

518. Centro di Studi Filosofici di Gallarate. **Dizionario dei filosofi del Novecento.** Florence: Leo S. Olschki, 1985. 825p.

This Italian dictionary of twentieth-century philosophers features mainly biographical entries. The rare exceptions include articles on Soviet philosophy and on the Positivist *Encyclopedia of Unified Science.* Coverage ranges widely over Western philosophy and includes some quasi-philosophical writers such as Pirandello, Max Weber, and T. S. Eliot, plus a few interpreters of non-Western philosophy for Western audiences, such as Yu-lan Fung and Rabindanath Tagore. Coverage of Italian figures is particularly strong.

519. Emel'ianov, B. V., and V. V. Kulikov. **Russkie mysliteli vtoroi poloviny XIX–nachala XX veka: opyt kratkogo biobibliograficheskogo slovaria.** Ekaterinburg: Izd-vo Ural'skogo Universiteta, 1996. 383p.

See entry 398.

520. Lechte, John. **Fifty Key Contemporary Thinkers: From Structuralism to Postmodernity.** London and New York: Routledge, 1994. 251p.

Lechte's choice of fifty "key thinkers" falls heavily on European figures and embraces just two Americans, Chomsky and Peirce. "Contemporary" means roughly post-World War II, but some earlier thinkers qualify by dint of intellectual "contemporaneity" (preface). Articles plus bibliographies treat philosophers, linguists, social theorists, feminists, historians, and literati, grouped into nine categories such as structuralism, semiotics, second-generation feminism, post-Marxism, and postmodernity.

521. Sim, Stuart, ed. **Routledge Companion to Postmodernism.** New York: Routledge, 2001. 401p.

Originally published as the *Icon Critical Dictionary of Postmodern Thought* (Cambridge, U.K.: Icon Books, 1998) and subsequently as the *Routledge Critical Dictionary of Postmodern Thought* (New York: Routledge, 1999). Covers Postmodernism as a broad cultural and intellectual movement, characterized as "a rejection of many, if not most, of the cultural certainties on which life in the West has been structured over the last couple of centuries" (introduction). Thus it deals with postmodernism in, or its influences upon, architecture and art, literature, music, film and television, popular culture, science and technology, politics, and lifestyles. At the same time, it emphasizes philosophy's central role as "both a prime site for debate about postmodernism and a source of many of the theories of what constitutes postmodernism" and as "a form of scepticism" that underlies its various manifestations (p. 3). The work is divided into two sections. Part 1 offers thematic essays by various authors on postmodernism's role in the aforementioned domains as well as its relation to feminism and to the tradition of dissent, and concludes with a select bibliography. Part 2 is an alphabetically arranged dictionary of names and terms. The writing in both sections is exceptionally accessible for the most part. There is a general index.

522. Taylor, Victor E., and Charles Winquist. **Encyclopedia of Postmodernism.** London: Routledge, 2001. 466p.

Entries in this alphabetically organized encyclopedia present a mix of key terms, biographies, and disciplinary essays, the latter including a seven-page article on philosophy. Like the *Routledge Companion to Postmodernism* (entry 521) from the same publisher, it treats the broad complex of Postmodernism's intellectual and cultural manifestations and influences while emphasizing its philosophical core. The writing is not quite as accessible as that of the *Companion*, despite the professed aim to provide a volume "accessible to readers with general interest in postmodernism as well as those with specialized research agendas" (introduction). The editors even describe the volume itself as "postmodern, providing the reader with clarifications as well as contradictions in the field of postmodern studies" (ibid.). Nonetheless, the work provides a great deal of useful information and insight on this important movement. Signed articles are contributed by an international group of around 150 scholars. Most include bibliographies. General name and topical index.

ANGLO-AMERICAN PHILOSOPHY

BIBLIOGRAPHIES

523.   Shook, John R., et. al. **Pragmatism: An Annotated Bibliography 1898–1940.** Amsterdam: Rodopi, 1998. 615p. (Value Inquiry Book Series, vol. 66).

See entry 512.

524.   Slater, John G., comp. **Bibliography of Modern American Philosophers.** Bristol, U.K.: Thoemmes Continuum, 2005. 3 vols.

Slater's bibliography of American (including Canadian) philosophers complements his previously published *Bibliography of Modern British Philosophers* (see entry 525) and parallels it in every significant respect: the time period covered, criteria for inclusion, types of publications listed, alphabetical/chronological arrangement, even the conventions for identifying the presence of copies in the University of Toronto's Fisher Library collection built largely by Slater. While the bibliography lists philosophical books and other monographic publications issued as late as 2003, their authors—or, in the case of secondary studies, subjects—had to be born before 1935 to be included. Of the several most prominent names in late-nineteenth and twentieth-century American philosophy admitted by this criterion, three—Dewey, Peirce, and Santayana—are not in fact covered here; reference is made instead to existing comprehensive bibliographies (entries 538, 485, and 550, respectively). But others in this august company—James, Whitehead, arguably Quine and Rawls—are well covered, as are numerous important second-tier figures such as Morris Cohen, Herbert Feigl, W. E. Hocking, Susanne Langer, Ernest Nagel, Nicholas Rescher, and Richard Rorty. Also represented are a host of third-tier or downright obscure philosophical writers. The 1935 cut-off date, however, excludes some prominent contributors to philosophical debates of the last third of the twentieth century who were born too late, for example, Daniel Dennett, Saul Kripke, Thomas Nagel, Martha Nussbaum, Alvin Plantinga. As with his British bibliography, Slater does not specify a beginning date for this compilation. Few of the 800 thinkers he includes began publishing before 1850, but a handful have earlier publications listed, starting at least as early as 1836 (a sermon by Noah Porter, later professor of philosophy at Yale).

525.   Slater, John G., comp. **Bibliography of Modern British Philosophers.** Bristol, U.K.: Thoemmes Continuum, 2004. 2 vols.

Modern here does not designate, as conventional in the historiography of Western philosophy, the period encompassing the sixteenth through eighteenth centuries and, more debatably, part or all of the nineteenth. Neither is it equivalent to *contemporary.* The British—and a few Australian—philosophers covered by this bibliography were active in the latter part of the nineteenth through the initial years of the twenty-first century. None, however, were born after 1935, so that in nearly all cases they have completed their work. No precise starting date is identified. The vast majority of publications listed fall after 1850, but a few were published before that, as early at least as 1820. Around 800 thinkers are represented, ranging from giants such as Popper and Whitehead through important but second-tier figures (e.g., Anscombe, Broad, Joad) to relatively obscure writers. In the case of two giants, Russell and Wittgenstein, readers are referred to existing definitive bibliographies (entries 547 and 556). Included are thinkers known not primarily as philosophers but as, for example, theologians (John Baillie), historians (Herbert Butterfield), scientists (J. D. Bernal), or mathematicians (Charles Babbage). In such cases, bibliographic coverage is not restricted to their more philosophical works. Unaccountably omitted are T. H. Huxley and Herbert Spencer, whose philosophical credentials ostensibly exceed, and whose publication years match, those of others who are included.

The bibliography encompasses books and pamphlets but not articles unless issued or reprinted separately. Within these bounds, primary bibliographies are as complete as possible. Where applicable, there is also a secondary bibliography, sometimes including non-English works in major European languages. Entries in each section are ordered by publication date. Except for a minority marked by asterisks, works listed are represented by copies in the University of Toronto's Fisher Library, many of them collected and donated by the compiler of this work.

DICTIONARIES, ENCYCLOPEDIAS, AND HANDBOOKS

526.   Dematteis, Philip Breed and Leemon B. McHenry, eds. **American Philosophers Before 1950.** Detroit: Gale, 2003. 407p. (Dictionary of Literary Biography, vol. 270).

See entry 295.

527.   Dematteis, Philip Breed and Leemon B. McHenry, eds. **American Philosophers, 1950–2000.** Detroit: Gale, 2003. 432p. (Dictionary of Literary Biography, vol. 279).

Shares the qualities and features common to the *Dictionary of Literary Biography* series; see entry 347 for a general comment. This volume complements *American Philosophers Before 1950* by the same editors (entry 295). It profiles 28 significant philosophers from the second half of the twentieth century. For many of them, one will not readily find entries in other philosophical dictionaries, and certainly not extensive articles ranging from 6 to 20 pages. The majority of these thinkers share the broadly analytical orientation of American philosophy during this period, for example, Arthur Danto, Donald Davidson, Nelson Goodman, Carl Hempel, Saul Kripke, Ernest Nagel, Alvin Plantinga, Hillary Putnam, W.V.O. Quine, John Rawls, John Searle, Wilfrid Sellars. But a few work, or worked, largely or entirely outside the analytical tradition: Peter Bertocci, Brand Blanshard, Walter Kaufmann, Seyyed Nasr, Ayn Rand, Richard Rorty, and Paul Weiss, for example.

528.   Dematteis, Philip Breed, Peter S. Fosl and Leemon B. McHenry, eds. **British Philosophers, 1800–2000.** Detroit: Gale, 2002. 420p. (Dictionary of Literary Biography, vol. 262).

See entry 294.

529.   Dictionary of Modern American Philosophers. John R. Shook, general ed. Bristol, U.K.: Thoemmes Press, 2005. 4 vols.

This impressive dictionary is modeled after the series of dictionaries on British philosophers by century (entries 393, 395, 397, and 530) as well as those on Dutch and Irish philosophers (entries 396 and 282) published by Thoemmes. Coverage in this instance is not limited to one century, but neither is it comprehensive over all of

American philosophical history. Rather, it stretches from the post-Civil War era to the early twenty-first century, with the qualification that no philosophers born after 1941 are represented. Many of those born in the 1930s or early 1940s, however, were still active at the time of this dictionary's publication. Both "philosopher" and "American" are given broad and inclusive interpretations. Of the thousand or so thinkers included, as many as a quarter might be considered borderline philosophers more closely identified with domains such as theology (e.g., Charles Hodge, Langdon Gilkey), psychology (Rollo May, B. F. Skinner), economics (Milton Friedman, Kenneth Arrow), social and political activism (Jane Addams, Martin Luther King, Sojourner Truth), literature (Edward Bellamy, Ezra Pound), the arts (Charles Ives, Frank Lloyd Wright), or cultural criticism (Lewis Mumford, Susan Sontag). Foreign-born thinkers who spent parts of their intellectual careers in the United States or Canada are counted as American for this purpose, for example Theodor Adorno, Etienne Gilson, Alasdair MacIntyre, Herbert Marcuse, Jacques Maritain, Daisetz Suzuki, and Paul Tillich. While the titans of American philosophy (James, Peirce, Dewey, etc.) are not ignored, the particular strength of this dictionary is its coverage, often unique, of many second- and third-tier philosophers.

530.   Dictionary of Twentieth-Century British Philosophers. Stuart C. Brown and Hugh Bredin, eds. Bristol, U.K.: Thoemmes Continuum, 2005. 2 vols.

This is the fourth in a series of dictionaries of British philosophers and follows the pattern set by those for the seventeenth, eighteenth, and nineteenth centuries (entries 397, 393, and 395, respectively). It is the first, of course, to include some living philosophers. These are fewer in number than one might guess, however, because this dictionary is largely restricted to those born by or before 1935, for whom there's "a reasonable assumption that most will already have made their main contributions to the subject" (introduction). The choice of 1935 was also influenced by the intention to keep this dictionary to approximately the same size yet similar degree of comprehensiveness as its predecessors. Exceptions are made for some exceptionally important figures born after 1935 (e.g., Simon Blackburn, Roger Scruton) as well as those who have already died. Still, this leaves significant swaths of British philosophical activity in the last four decades of the twentieth century outside the scope of this work. At the other end of the chronological spectrum, minor philosophers active in both the nineteenth and twentieth centuries but already covered in the nineteenth-century dictionary are excluded here. Although this dictionary, like its predecessors, includes some borderline philosophers who would be classified first as scientists, art critics, sociologists, theologians, and so forth, comparatively fewer are not professional philosophers. A "supplementary list" at the back identifies individuals who "had some claim on inclusion in this Dictionary" but already had entries in one or several of four other dictionaries by the same publisher (entries 282, 395, 529, and the *Dictionary of British Classicists,* 2004, 3 vols.).

Altogether there are entries for around 500 philosophers ranging from the famous (Russell, Wittgenstein, Popper) to the obscure. For many of the latter, their article in this dictionary may represent the first and only secondary source. Length is not necessarily proportional to significance, as major figures may be given relatively brief treatment along with references to the existing secondary literature, while treatment of minor figures often varies depending on available sources of information and perhaps the energy or resourcefulness of contributors in ferreting it out. Some 200 contributors are identified at the front.

531.   Lott, Tommy L. and John P. Pittman, eds. **A Companion to African-American Philosophy.** Malden, Mass.: Blackwell, 2003. 465p. (Blackwell Companions to Philosophy).

See entry 815.

532.   Martinich, A. P. and David Sosa, eds. **A Companion to Analytic Philosophy.** Malden, Mass.: Blackwell, 2001. 497p. (Blackwell Companions to Philosophy).

Apart from a five-page introduction by editor Martinich, this volume presents the analytical tradition in twentieth-century philosophy through a series of biographical articles on 41 of its foremost practitioners. These are arranged in order of birth date, yielding a rough but by no means exact correspondence to the chronology of their respective subjects' major contributions to the tradition's development. Most of these figures were positioned squarely within the Anglo-American sphere with which the analytical tradition is strongly and sometimes exclusively associated. Several, however, did their initial work on the European continent, notably in the intellectual milieu of post-World War I Vienna, before emigrating to the United States, England, or Australia; and one of the movement's patriarchs, Gotlob Frege, spent his entire career in Germany. Also among the chosen 41 is one thinker who eventually became one of the movement's foremost critics, Richard Rorty. That Martinich can describe Rorty and fellow critics as "analytical philosophers in spite of themselves" in their attempts to make their positions clear and cogent (p. 4) probably exemplifies the extent to which analytical philosophy in its widest sense is more a philosophical style than a set of doctrines or a shared methodology.

In that wide sense, the 40 contributing authors are themselves eminent analytical philosophers.

SOURCES ON INDIVIDUAL PHILOSOPHERS

Collingwood, Robin George (1889–1943)

533.   Dreisbach, Christopher. **R. G. Collingwood: A Bibliographical Checklist.** Bowling Green, Ohio: Philosophy Documentation Center, Bowling Green State University, 1993. 139p. (Bibliographies of Famous Philosophers).

In addition to a full primary bibliography of Collingwood's writings, Dreisbach provides an extensive secondary bibliography, more comprehensive than that in the earlier bibliography by Taylor (entry 534), arranged by type of publication (books, articles, essays, reviews, etc.). Book entries include cross-references to reviews. The checklist is generally unannotated, but works having vague or nondescriptive titles are given brief notes to indicate their content or significance. Author and subject indexes are supplemented by a periodical source index for secondary works.

534.   Taylor, Donald S. **R. G. Collingwood: A Bibliography: The Complete Manuscripts and Publications, Selected Secondary Writings, with Selective Annotation.** New York: Garland, 1988. 279p. (Garland Bibliographies of Modern Critics and Critical Schools, vol. 11; Garland Reference Library of the Humanities, vol. 810).

Taylor provides a comprehensive primary bibliography of Collingwood's writings as a philosopher, historian, and archaeologist, including a large number of manuscripts and letters held by Oxford's Bodleian Library. The secondary bibliography, as the subtitle proclaims, is far more selective, being limited to just under 200 items concerned with two of Collingwood's central preoccupations: philosophy of history and aesthetics. A similar focus governs the selective provision of annotations in the primary bibliography.

Dewey, John (1859–1952)

535.　　Boydston, Jo Ann, ed. **Guide to the Works of John Dewey.** Carbondale: Southern Illinois University Press; London: Feffer & Simons, 1970. 396p.

Intended for use either as a complement to Dewey's *Collected Works* or as an independent resource, this guide comprises 12 essays by noted scholars surveying areas of Dewey's thought (psychology, ethics, theory of art, philosophy of religion, education and schooling, etc.). All but one (an essay titled "Dewey's Lectures and Influence in China") are followed by a checklist of his writings in that area, including unpublished writings, transcripts, and so forth, as well as published writings. A detailed subject and title index is provided.

536.　　Boydston, Jo Ann, and Kathleen Poulos. **Checklist of Writings about John Dewey, 1887–1977.** 2nd ed. Carbondale: Southern Illinois University Press; London: Feffer & Simons, 1978. 476p.

The contents of this bibliography are largely absorbed into *Works about John Dewey, 1886–1995,* entry 538. Exceptions are unpublished works—dissertations, theses, and papers presented at meeting—and some marginally substantive materials such as books with brief references to Dewey.

537.　　Boydston, Jo Ann, and Robert L. Andresen. **John Dewey: A Checklist of Translations, 1900–1967.** Carbondale: Southern Illinois University Press; London: Feffer & Simons, 1969. 123p.

The main section lists alphabetically 67 books and articles by Dewey, including collections of his writings, each followed by a list of translations by language. Separate sections list materials originally published in languages other than English: some (in French) subsequently translated into English, others (in Japanese and Chinese) not. A chronological list of translations is included in the introductory material.

538.　　Levine, Barbara. **Works about John Dewey, 1886–1995.** Carbondale: Southern Illinois University Press, 1996. 526p.

Incorporates most of the material listed in the *Checklist of Writings about John Dewey, 1887–1977,* 2nd ed. (entry 536). Along with some 2,000 items published from 1977 to 1995, it also included hundreds of pre-1977 items, and even two pre-1887 items, missed by its predecessor. Material is divided into books and articles, listed alphabetically by author, and reviews of Dewey's works, listed under the titles of the works reviewed (whose original publication data are also provided). Not included are dissertations and other unpublished works, ERIC documents, and articles in reference works. Author and title-keyword indexes.

539.　　Thomas, Milton Halsey. **John Dewey: A Centennial Bibliography.** Chicago: University of Chicago Press, 1962. 370p.

Dewey's books, articles, reviews, letters to editors, and so forth, published 1882 through 1960, are listed chronologically on pages 1–153, with reprintings and translations listed under the entry for the original edition. Entries for books include tables of contents. Writings about Dewey, including dissertations, are listed by author on pages 155–293. Reviews of books *about* Dewey are also listed here, but reviews of books *by* him are in the first part (in each case under the entry for the work reviewed). The second part is largely superseded by the Boydston and Poulos *Checklist* (entry 536), but Thomas's excellent, detailed subject index (integrated with author/title index) has no counterpart in the later work.

540. Winn, Ralph Bubrich, ed. **John Dewey: Dictionary of Education.** New York: Philosophical Library, 1959. 150p.

See entry 757.

541. Boydston, Jo Ann. **John Dewey's Personal and Professional Library: A Checklist.** Carbondale: Southern Illinois University Press, 1982. 119p.

"Compiled at the Center for Dewcy Studies, this bibliography is the most complete list of books in Dewey's personal library and in the libraries of his immediate family. All entries are annotated to include author inscriptions, notes and marginalia by Dewey, and other information necessary to trace the development of, and influence on, Dewey's thought" *(Harvard Educational Review* 53 [February 1983]:103).

Gilson, Etienne Henri (1884–1978)

542. McGrath, Margaret. **Etienne Gilson: A Bibliography / Une bibliographie.** Toronto: Pontifical Institute of Mediaeval Studies, 1982. 124p.

Lists 935 items by Gilson, an important Neo-Thomist philosopher in his own right as well as a major historian of philosophy. Includes works edited, prefaces, and book reviews. Also lists 260 items about Gilson, including five theses. Includes name and subject indexes.

Lovejoy, Arthur Oncken (1873–1962)

543. Wilson, Daniel J. **Arthur O. Lovejoy: An Annotated Bibliography.** New York: Garland, 1982. 211p. (Garland Bibliographies of Modern Critics and Critical Schools, vol. 2; Garland Reference Library of the Humanities, vol. 344).

Best known as a historian of ideas, Lovejoy also made contributions (though less influential) to important debates in American philosophy. Both aspects of his career, and other activities (e.g., his role in organizing the AAUP), are encompassed by this bibliography, which lists and amply annotates some 315 publications by Lovejoy and some 225 secondary sources.

Quine, Willard Van Orman (1908–2000)

544. Bruschi, Rita. **Willard van Orman Quine: A Bibliographic Guide.** Florence: La Nuova Italia Editrice, 1986. 199p.

Includes a primary bibliography of 281 publications by Quine (books, articles, reviews, introductions to books by others, etc.) from 1930 to 1984, followed by a secondary bibliography of 902 publications about Quine from 1939 through 1983. Both sections are organized chronologically. The secondary bibliography is selectively annotated. There are three indexes: subjects, "thinkers connected to Quine," and authors. Despite the work's European origin, the majority of entries represent English-language publications, as might be predicted from Quine's status as a leading Anglo-American philosopher.

Rawls, John (1921–2002)

545.   Wellbank, J. H., Dennis Snook, and David T. Mason. **John Rawls and His Critics: An Annotated Bibliography.** New York: Garland, 1982. 683p. (Garland Reference Library of the Humanities, vol. 303).

When this bibliography appeared, Rawls's own writings were modest in number (about two dozen, and among those only one book) but not in significance, as more than 2,500 secondary publications listed here attest. Most of these deal with Rawls' seminal work, *A Theory of Justice*. Annotations are often extensive. Arrangement is by author, with indexes for second authors, titles, reviews (including reviews of related works), and subjects or "concepts."

Rorty, Richard (1931–)

546.   Rumana, Richard. **Richard Rorty: An Annotated Bibliography of Secondary Literature.** Amsterdam: Rodopi, 2002. 135p. (Value Inquiry Book Series, 130; Studies in Pragmatism and Values).

Rumana records and selectively annotates citations to books, articles, and reviews dealing with Rorty, an American philosopher who began in the analytic tradition but turned into a critic of that tradition and has come to be regarded as a leading philosophical voice for Postmodernism, drawing on elements of American Pragmatism and Continental philosophy. Rumana's introduction observes that, of some 1,200 items cited, "only a small percentage are friendly to Rorty," and proceeds to explore why this might be so. It also explains Rumana's strategy in selecting entries for annotation: guided in part by where he felt comfortably knowledgeable, but in part also by a desire to annotate a representative sampling illustrating, for example, political critiques from both left and right, responses from admirers and defenders of specific philosophers whose ideas Rorty has adapted or critiqued, specific perspectives such as feminism, and interest in particular stages of Rorty's thought. Annotations are chiefly descriptive, and some include "see" references to other entries. The bibliography observes a single alphabetical arrangement by author, but there is a good subject index.

Russell, Bertrand Arthur William (1872–1970)

547.   Blackwell, Kenneth, Harry Ruja, et. al. **A Bibliography of Bertrand Russell.** London: Routledge, 1994. 3 vols. (The Collected Papers of Bertrand Russell).

From the uncommon quality and thoroughness of its scholarship to its elegant physical attributes (boxed set, heavy coated paper, gilt titles and top edge) to its hefty price, this work is marked for elite status: a Rolls Royce among bibliographical Fords and Chevies. A primary bibliography only (issued in connection with the McMaster edition of *The Collected Papers of Bertrand Russell*), it presents an authoritative and minutely detailed record of the public output of one of this century's most public philosophers, encompassing all sides of Russell's wide-ranging labors and interests, the popular as well as the scholarly and technical. Volume 1 catalogues separate publications through 1990—books, pamphlets, and leaflets—in every known edition, impression, and translation, each meticulously described to distinguish it from others, together with descriptions of the extant manuscript remains and listings of all full or partial reprintings (even anthologized extracts) the compilers were able to unearth and verify. Each entry notes locations in one or both of two major Russell library collections, at McMaster University and Toronto. Volume 2 covers serial publications—journal articles, newspaper columns, reviews, letters to editors, and so forth, again including reprintings—and also has a number of special sections: reports of speeches, interviews, multiple-signatory publications, original blurbs (endorsements of books published in advertisements or on book jackets), extracts published in booksellers' catalogues, audio recordings, films, and even a listing of spurious publications. Volume 3 provides comprehensive name, title, and subject indexes plus an index to the citations of manuscript files in the Russell Archives at McMaster.

548.   Martin, Werner. **Bertrand Russell: A Bibliography of His Writings, 1895–1976 / Eine Bibliographie seiner Schriften, 1895–1976.** Munich: K. G. Saur; Hamden, Conn.: Linnett Books, 1981. 332p.

A chronological bibliography of Russell's vast output, with commentaries in both English and German supplied for major works. An appendix includes a chronological index of main works, an index of translations by language, a very short (four-page) bibliography of secondary works, title index, and list of sources. Contains some spurious entries copied from previous bibliographies, according to Blackwell and Ruja (entry 547, vol. 1, p. xliii).

549.   Dennon, Lester, E., ed. **Bertrand Russell's Dictionary of Mind, Matter, and Morals.** New York: Philosophical Library, 1952. 290p.

Like a number of other "dictionaries" published by Philosophical Library (see entry 508 for a general comment), this is strictly a compilation of quotes. Besides being a source for Russell's views, asserts the preface, it can be used as a dictionary of terms related to the topics indicated in the title. While that's plausible for some entries, those on mind or justice, for example, or for the well-known definition of "number" from the *Introduction to Mathematical Philosophy,* the majority of entries provide no attempt at definition: see, for example, deduction, democracy, and freedom. Besides relatively pedestrian terms like the examples just cited, there are also intriguing, characteristically Russellian entries such as "America and tyranny of the herd," "beliefs, harmful," "democracy, future of," and "induction and sacred books." Sources of quotes are identified by title with page numbers.

This work is at least among the best of its breed. Because it's the only one whose subject enjoyed the opportunity to provide a preface (a characteristic statement of his approach to philosophy), it's worth noting that he apparently approved of the project.

Santayana, George (1863–1952)

550.   Saatkamp, Herman J., Jr., and John Jones. **George Santayana: A Bibliographical Checklist, 1880–1980.** Bowling Green, Ohio: Philosophy Documentation Center, Bowling Green State University, 1982. 286p. (Bibliographies of Famous Philosophers).

Primary sources, arranged chronologically, begin with Santayana's student efforts at the Boston Latin School and at Harvard—including even his drawings for the *Harvard Lampoon*—and also encompass reprintings, in full or in part, of his many books and articles. Entries for books include tables of contents. Manuscript collections are listed separately. Sections for works about Santayana cover books, articles, reviews (of books by and books about him), and dissertations. Author, title, and subject indexes are provided.

Whitehead, Alfred North (1861–1947)

551.   Woodbridge, Barry A. **Alfred North Whitehead: A Primary-Secondary Bibliography.** Bowling Green, Ohio: Philosophy Documentation Center, Bowling Green State University, 1977. 405p. (Bibliographies of Famous Philosophers).

Lists all of Whitehead's known writings and attempts to include all secondary materials through June 1976 "which might be of even negligible value to those studying Whitehead or the application of his thought . . . " (introduction). It is not actually quite as complete as this suggests, but it does have over 1,800 entries, not counting reviews (included selectively, and listed under the works with which they deal). Annotations, generally noncritical, are provided for works that lent themselves to brief summaries. There is a subject index.

Wittgenstein, Ludwig Josef Johan (1889–1951)

552.   Borgis, Ilona. **Index zu Wittgensteins "Tractatus logico-philosophicus" und Wittgenstein-Bibliographie.** Freiburg im Breisgau: Karl Alber, 1968. 113p.

The bibliography occupying roughly half of this book is international in scope and includes works (mainly notebooks, lectures, etc.) by Wittgenstein and works about him (books, dissertations, and articles). The book's other half contains a word index to the German text of Wittgenstein's *Tractatus,* a landmark of twentieth-century philosophy (see entry 560 for an index to the English translation). Reference is given to the numbered propositions that constitute the structure of the text, quoting those that are most significant while citing others by number only.

553.   Frongia, Guido and B. McGuinness. **Wittgenstein: A Bibliographical Guide.** Oxford: Basil Blackwell, 1990. 438p.

This is a translation, revision, and updating of a work published in Italian, *Guida all letteratura su Wittgenstein: storia e analisi della critica* (Urbino: Argalia, 1981), authored by Frongia alone. In addition to a list of Wittgenstein's published writings, it affords fairly exhaustive coverage of the early secondary literature (including even sources with minimal reference to him), becoming increasingly selective for the decades of the 1960s through 1980s, during which interest in Wittgenstein burgeoned. Coverage stops at mid-1987. English-language materials predominate, but early contributions and later works of international significance in major Western European languages are included. The 1,967-item secondary bibliography is arranged by year of publication, then by author. Indexes are provided for subject terms, subject names, and authors. A 38-page essay, "History of the Reception of Wittgenstein's Work," is at the front.

554.   Lapointe, Francois H. **Ludwig Wittgenstein: A Comprehensive Bibliography.** Westport, Conn.: Greenwood Press, 1980. 297p.

Covers works by and works about Wittgenstein, with the latter distributed among six chapters: (1) books, and reviews thereof (with lists of contents for anthologies); (2) dissertations; (3) studies of individual works by Wittgenstein; (4) general discussions; (5) studies relating Wittgenstein to other thinkers; and (6) studies listed under more than 200 subject descriptors. Many items are listed in more than one chapter. The book's coverage is international , through 1979.

555.   Philipp, Peter. **Bibliographie zur Wittgenstein-Literatur.** Revised, expanded, and edited by Frank Kannetzky and Richard Raatzsch. Bergen: Wittgensteinarkivet ved Universitetet i Bergen, 1996 (Skriftserie fra Wittgensteinarkivet ved Universitetet i Bergen, nr. 13; Working Papers from the Wittgenstein Archives at the University of Bergen, no. 13).

Lists books, articles, and dissertations about Wittgenstein, and even some literature that influenced his writings, from 1899 through 1995 with a few titles from 1996. Some 8,500 entries are listed alphabetically by author's last name (with first names represented by initials only) save for seven anonymous entries at the end. While this bibliography is comprehensive, its utility is limited by lack of a subject index or alternative subject access. It seems most useful for identifying new publications from about 1986–87, the terminal dates for the bibliographies by Shanker (entry 556) and Frongia and McGuinness (entry 553). This is facilitated by a chronological index, which lists pertinent authors' names under each year. Although this bibliography has been reported to be available online, that does not appear to be true as of late 2005.

556.   Shanker, V. A., and Stuart G. Shanker. **A Wittgenstein Bibliography.** London: Croom Helm, 1987. 352p. (Ludwig Wittgenstein: Critical Assessments, vol. 5).

Among the most comprehensive Wittgenstein bibliographies, this was issued separately as a fifth volume supplementing a four-volume anthology of essays and articles, *Ludwig Wittgenstein: Critical Assessments,* edited by Stuart G. Shanker (London: Croom Helm, 1986). The primary bibliography begins with G. von Wright's meticulous and foundational record of Wittgenstein's *Nachlass,* and proceeds to the most complete list possible of books, articles, lectures, conversation notes, letters, anthologies, collections, and derivative primary sources of Wittgenstein's thought published anywhere up to the time of compilation. The secondary bibliography, worldwide in scope, cites over 5,400 writings about Wittgenstein.

557. Glock, Hans-Johann. **A Wittgenstein Dictionary.** Oxford: Blackwell, 1996. 405p. (Blackwell Philosopher Dictionaries).

This alphabetically arranged dictionary "presents technical terms that Wittgenstein introduced into philosophical debate or transformed substantially, and also topics to which he made a substantial contribution. . . .Glock places Wittgenstein's ideas in their historical context, and indicates their impact on his contemporaries as well as their relevance to current debates. The entries delineate Wittgenstein's lines of argument on particular issues, assessing their strengths and weaknesses, and shed light on fundamental exegetical controversies" (cover blurb). The author aspires to address "three kinds of readers": academics both inside and outside philosophy needing to relate Wittgenstein's work to their own; Wittgenstein scholars, whom he suggests should find "a state-of-the-art discussion, as well as some new ideas"; and finally general readers (p. 1). Acknowledging the considerable challenges Wittgenstein's thought are apt to pose for the latter, Glock advises readers without background in analytic philosophy to read first the "Sketch of an Intellectual Biography" which precedes the alphabetical entries (p. 1). The work concludes with a substantial bibliography of secondary sources and a general index.

558. Richter, Duncan. **Historical Dictionary of Wittgenstein's Philosophy.** Lanham, Md.: Scarecrow, 2004. 242p. (Historical Dictionaries of Religions, Philosophies, and Movements, 54).

Richter's dictionary on Wittgenstein follows the general pattern for philosopher-oriented volumes in Scarecrow's "Historical Dictionaries" series set by Diethe's dictionary of Nietzscheanism (entry 481) and emulated subsequently by dictionaries on Kierkegaard (entry 457) and on Descartes and Cartesianism (entry 413). While focusing on Wittgenstein's philosophy, it also gives ample coverage to biographical matters, including his family background, Vienna and Cambridge phases, intellectual and personal associations, visits to Russia and the United States, his debated homosexuality, even his wartime service work at a London hospital. Treatment of Wittgenstein's thought includes succinct expositions of distinctive concepts and themes such as family resemblance, form of life, language-games, nonsense, the picture theory of language, the private-language argument, and propositions, as well as discussions of his views on general topics such as certainty, free will, induction, soul, and truth. Richter is candid about controversies in Wittgenstein interpretation, as on the question of whether he was a behaviorist or in what sense he was an "ordinary language" philosopher. Roughly a quarter of the entries are biographical, identifying and characterizing philosophers and others who influenced Wittgenstein, individuals who studied with or were influenced by him, and some intellectual rivals such as Heidegger and Popper. Finally, there are entries for each of his published works. Preceding the dictionary proper are a chronology and a 17-page introduction, and it is followed by a 40-page topically organized bibliography.

559. Kaal, Hans, and Alastair McKinnon. **Concordance to Wittgenstein's** *Philosophische Untersuchungen.* Leiden: E. J. Brill, 1975. 596p.

This is a word index to all significant words in the German text of Wittgenstein's *Philosophical Investigations* (third edition), which even in the British and American editions is printed side by side with the English translation. Short, often fragmentary quotations show the context for each occurrence of a word; locations are identified by both page and line numbers. A brief *Vorwort,* by the publisher, is in German, but there is an introduction in English.

560. Plochmann, George Kimball, and Jack B. Lawson. **Terms in Their Propositional Context in Wittgenstein's "Tractatus": An Index.** Carbondale: Southern Illinois University Press, 1962. 229p.

In contrast to the *Tractatus* index by Borgis (entry 552), this is an index to the English translation, not the German original. Unlike Borgis, too, it provides a contextual quote for each reference, not just the most significant occurrences. Also includes a German-English word list, a list of logical symbols, and a selective bibliography covering materials dealing with the *Tractatus* only.

CONTINENTAL PHILOSOPHY

BIBLIOGRAPHIES

561. Miller, Joan M. **French Structuralism: A Multidisciplinary Bibliography with a Checklist of Sources for Louis Althusser, Roland Barthes, Jaques Derrida, Michel Foucault, Lucien Goldmann, Jaques Lacan and an Update of Works on Claude Lévi-Strauss.** New York: Garland, 1981. 553p. (Garland Reference Library of the Humanities, vol. 160).

Focusing mainly on the period 1968–1978, Miller's multilingual bibliography extends and supplements Josué Harari's much slighter *Structuralists and Structuralisms: A Selected Bibliography of French Contemporary Thought (1960–1970)* (Ithaca, N.Y.: Diacritics, 1971, 82p.). Both treat Structuralism as a multidisciplinary movement while giving due to its pervasively philosophical character. Distinct parts cover (1) general and introductory works, (2) the seven leading figures named in the sub-title, (3) Structuralism as applied to various disciplines. The section on anthropologist Lévi-Strauss supplements C. and F. Lapointe's *Claude Lévi-Strauss and His Critics* (New York: Garland, 1977).

DICTIONARIES, ENCYCLOPEDIAS, AND HANDBOOKS

562. Critchley, Simon, and William R. Schroeder, eds. **A Companion to Continental Philosophy.** Malden, Mass.: Blackwell, 1998. 680p. (Blackwell Companions to Philosophy).

Aims to provide "an introductory but authoritative account" of the Continental tradition in philosophy "for the analytically trained philosopher, the interested academic in the humanities and social sciences, the postgraduate and undergraduate student in philosophy and related areas, and the lay reader" (p. 1). Though "Continental philosophy" often connotes twentieth-century developments, here it takes in the nineteenth century and its principal Continental figures—Fichte, Hegel, Marx, Kierkegaard, Nietzsche, and others. In part this is due to their significance as precursors to the twentieth-century Continental movements and thinkers—including the likes of Husserl, Heidegger, Sartre, De Beauvoir, Derrida, Foucault, Kristeva—treated in the later two-thirds of the volume. In part it is also because they already instantiate the "parting of the ways" between Continental and Anglophone philosophical streams whose twentieth-century manifestation includes what editor Critchley calls "the *de facto* distinction between analytic and Continental philosophy" (p. 3). The grounds and shortcomings of that distinction are discussed by Critchley in his introductory essay.

The volume's 56 chapters are devoted, with only a few exceptions, to individual thinkers, beginning (by way of background) with Kant and ending with the contemporary

French feminist philosopher Michèle Le Doeuff. They are grouped into nine parts focused sometimes on a distinct school of thought or philosophical method (e.g., "The PhenomenologicalBreakthrough," "CriticalTheory," "Hermeneutics"),sometimesonabroad theme (e.g., "Religion Without the Limits of Reason," "Continental Political Philosophy"), all the while following an approximately chronological line of development. There is a detailed name and subject index.

563. Embree, Lester, et. al, eds. **Encyclopedia of Phenomenology.** Dordrecht: Kluwer Academic, 1997. 764p. (Contributions to Phenomenology, vol. 18).

The preface to this work categorizes its 166 entries with unusual exactness as "about matters of seven sorts: (1) the four broad tendencies and periods within the phenomenological movement; (2) twenty-three national traditions of phenomenology; (3) twenty-two philosophical sub-disciplines . . . ; (4) phenomenological tendencies within twenty-one non-philosophical disciplines; (5) forty major phenomenological topics; (6) twenty-eight leading phenomenological figures; and (7) twenty-seven non-phenomenological figures and movements of interesting similarities and differences with phenomenology" (p. xiii). The single entry left unaccounted for is presumably that for phenomenology itself, which makes no attempt to provide an overview of the movement as a whole—a task delegated to the introduction—but consists entirely of cross-references. The encyclopedia aims to be accessible to advanced undergraduates as well as "professional colleagues of other orientations" (preface), but readers without some prior initiation in the language and methodology of phenomenology are likely to find much of it difficult going. Specialists and graduate or very advanced undergraduate students, however, will appreciate and benefit from the international cast of leading scholars of the movement who contributed the signed articles. General index.

564. Glendinning, Simon, ed. **The Edinburgh Encyclopedia of Continental Philosophy.** Edinburgh: Edinburgh University Press; Chicago: Fitzroy Dearborn, 1999. 685p.

Aims to provide the philosophical context for broader currents of Continental European thought that are of "increasingly intense interest" in English-speaking universities "by offering a comprehensive and in-depth overview of the central movements, authors, and themes that comprise what has become known as the Continental tradition of philosophy" (preface). While oriented chiefly on the twentieth century, this encyclopedia also reaches back to cover important nineteenth-century antecedents: Kantian Idealism, Hegelianism, Schleiermacher, Marx, Kierkegaard, and Nietzsche, among others. Eight sections, each comprising an introduction plus six or seven essays by diverse contributors, treat either a major school or movement, from nineteenth-century classical Idealism through Phenomenology, the Frankfurt School, and Structuralism to Post-Structuralism, or else a broad theme such as philosophy of existence or philosophies of life and understanding, which may subsume additional movements such as Existentialism as well as generalized surveys of such areas as philosophy of science and political philosophy. The constituent essays include bibliographies. Editor Glendinning provides a 17-page introductory over-view that demonstrates a degree of accessibility, even to the uninitiated, regrettably not maintained throughout (e.g., the introduction to the section on Post-Structuralism).

It's worth noting that this work represents, in some sense, an outside perspective on Continental philosophy, however sympathetic and knowledgeable the authors. Of 56 contributors, only 2 are academics working on the Continent. The rest, all but 3, are divided nearly evenly into U.S. and British scholars.

565.   Gordon, Haim. **Dictionary of Existentialism.** Westport, Conn.: Greenwood Press; London: Fitzroy Dearborn, 1999. 539p.

This dictionary encompasses Existentialism from the mid-nineteenth century—long before the term was coined—through its heyday in the 1950s and 1960s. Its introduction characterizes the movement in terms of three foci: the person as a whole being as he or she exists in the world; rebellion against the rationalism of philosophy's modern period; and freedom as central to human existence. Typical articles run from two to eight pages; few are less than a page. Biographical articles represent not only the Titans of the movement (Kierkegaard, Nietzsche, Heidegger, Sartre, et. al.) but also less well-known thinkers (e.g., Rosenzweig, Shestov), literary contributors (Dostoyevsky, Kafka), and some who influenced or were influenced by Existentialism though not considered party to it (Husserl, Bonhoeffer). Other entries cover terms and concepts specifically associated with Existentialism (e.g., authenticity, bad faith, *Dasein,* leap [of faith, etc.]) as well as more generic philosophical topics (ethics, freedom, God, knowledge, time, etc.). Articles in the latter category typically canvas the ideas of two to four major Existentialist thinkers. The 65 contributors hail from half a dozen countries including the United States, Britain, and Israel, though none from Existentialism's historical strongholds, France and Germany. Articles are signed.

566.   Murray, Christopher John, ed. **Encyclopedia of Modern French Thought.** London: Fitzroy Dearborn, 2004. 713p.

Modern French thought is not, of course, confined to philosophy, and the 234 articles in this alphabetically organized encyclopedia range over such fields as sociology, linguistics, anthropology, literary theory and criticism, political and social thought, psychoanalysis, and theology, as well as philosophy. But not only is philosophy a major player in French thought throughout the twentieth century and entering the twenty-first, it has been intertwined with the other areas aforementioned in ways that may be unparalleled outside France. That suggests this is a resource not to be overlooked by anyone interested in French philosophy of the past hundred years, particularly where it involves interdisciplinary topics such as art criticism and aesthetics, colonialism and postcolonialism, educational theory, feminism, humanism/antihumanism, or sexuality. Aside from the interdisciplinary value there is in any case an ample selection of entries one would expect in any encyclopedia on modern French philosophy, including its significant figures (De Beauvoir, Foucault, Kristeva, Levinas, Sartre, etc.) and movements (Deconstruction, Existentialism, Marxism, Phenomenology, Post-Structuralism) as well as approaches to standard topics such as knowledge and truth and philosophy of science.

567.   Stewart, David and Algis Mickunas. **Exploring Phenomenology: A Guide to the Field and Its Literature.** 2nd ed. Athens, Ohio: Ohio University Press, 1990. 181p.

The second edition of this guide differs from the first (Chicago: American Library Association, 1974, 165p.) only by the addition of a supplement beginning on p. 159. Written "for the non-specialist and... generally educated reader" (preface), it surveys the field in seven succinct chapters addressing general themes, the foundational work of Husserl, its later development, Existential Phenomenology, treatment of traditional problems (e.g., free will, perception, values), application to other disciplines (e.g., psychology, religion), and "ongoing tasks." Complementing each chapter is a selective yet substantial bibliography. Collectively these total 426 items, most with brief descriptive annotations. Books and articles in English are emphasized, but some foreign-language works are also listed. Bibliographies on individuals other than Husserl (e.g., Heidegger, Sartre) are relegated to an appendix. The 1990 supplement offers a brief survey of Phenomenology's evolution since 1974, emphasizing the upsurge of Hermeneutics and concern with the relation between philosophy and social sciences, and a 55-item bibliographical supplement. Bibliographies here complement Leonard Orr's *Existentialism and Phenomenology: A Guide for Research* (Troy, N.Y.: Whitston, 1978, 179p.) for the period 1950–1976.

SOURCES ON INDIVIDUAL PHILOSOPHERS

Beauvoir, Simone de (1908–1986)

568.   Bennett, Joy, and Gabrielle Hochmann. **Simone de Beauvoir: An Annotated Bibliography.** New York: Garland, 1988. 474p. (Garland Reference Library of the Humanities, vol. 774).

This secondary bibliography lists and annotates works on de Beauvoir and her writings in the major European languages from 1940 to 1986. Entries are organized into sections for general criticism, interviews, theses, reviews of books by de Beauvoir, reviews of books about de Beauvoir, and obituaries. Entry numbers have prefixes identifying their section or subsection, for example, "IN" for interviews, "SS" for reviews of *The Second Sex*. Because the index of authors and named persons refers to these prefixed numbers, it can be cumbersome to locate specific entries because the sections (and thus their prefixes) are not in alphabetical sequence and must often be located via the table of contents. A chronology of de Beauvoir's life precedes the bibliography proper.

Bergson, Henri-Louis (1859–1941)

569.   Gunter, P.A.Y. **Henri Bergson: A Bibliography.** Rev. 2nd ed. Bowling Green, Ohio: Philosophy Documentation Center, Bowling Green State University, 1986. 557p. (Bibliographies of Famous Philosophers).

This revised edition of the original 1974 bibliography lists, in separate chronologically arranged sections, 470 works by Bergson and 5,926 works about him, including dissertations. Annotations are provided for nearly all of the works *by* and many of the works *about*. Separate subject indexes, both very broad, cover the two sections. In the case of works *about*, the subject index is combined with an inadequate, selective author index, limited apparently to authors of major works.

Buber, Martin (1878–1965)

570.   Cohn, Margot, and Rafael Buber. **Martin Buber: Eine Bibliographie seiner Schriften, 1897–1978 / Martin Buber: A Bibliography of His Writings, 1897–1978.** Jerusalem: Magnes Press, Hebrew University; Munich: K. G. Saur, 1980. 160p.

The title is also in Hebrew, as is the foreword. A chronological listing of Buber's voluminous writings, including editions and translations—a total of about 1,500 items. Notes and comments are in English, "except where Hebrew items are concerned" (foreword). Indexes are provided for titles, titles in Hebrew, themes, and languages.

Supersedes Moshe Catanne's *Bibliography of Martin Buber's Works (1897–1957)* (Jerusalem: Bialik Institute, 1958).

571.   Moonan, Willard. **Martin Buber and His Critics: An Annotated Bibliography of Writings in English through 1978.** New York: Garland, 1981. 240p. (Garland Reference Library of the Humanities, vol. 161).

Writings by and about Buber are listed in separate sections, each arranged chronologically. Excellent descriptive annotations are provided for most "writings about." The latter are also indexed by author and subject, while "writings by" are indexed by title and translator. A commendable feature is a list of bibliographic sources consulted.

Camus, Albert (1913–1960)

572.   Fitch, Brian T., and Peter C. Hoy. **Albert Camus: Essai de bibliographie des études en langue française consacrées à Albert Camus (1937–1970).** 3rd ed. Paris: Minard, 1972. Unpaged. (Calepins de bibliographie, no. 1).

Includes writings on Camus in French, arranged chronologically. Indexed by author and, in the case of reviews of Camus's books, by title of the publication in which the review appeared.

573.   Hoy, Peter C. **Camus in English: An Annotated Bibliography of Albert Camus's Contributions to English and American Periodicals and Newspapers (1945–1968).** 2nd ed., revised and enlarged. Paris: Minard, 1971. Unpaged.

Materials listed in this slim bibliography are primarily literary and political statements, and include articles, excerpts from books, and interviews. First edition was a finely printed and illustrated limited edition of 250 numbered copies (Wymondham, England: Brewhouse Press, 1968, 29p.).

574.   Roeming, Robert F. **Camus: A Bibliography.** Madison: University of Wisconsin Press, 1968. 298p.

Has 3,432 unannotated entries, listing editions and translations of Camus's writings and works about Camus in all languages, arranged by author. Much of the material is literary or political. Has index of authors by language, a chronological index, and index of journals in which articles are published, but lacks any subject approach. Computer printout is clear but somewhat hard to scan.

Cassirer, Ernst (1874–1945)

575.   Eggers, Walter, and Sigrid Mayer. **Ernst Cassirer: An Annotated Bibliography.** New York: Garland, 1988. 483p. (Garland Bibliographies of Modern Critics and Critical Schools, vol. 13; Garland Reference Library of the Humanities, vol. 475).

Despite its avowed literary bias as part of a series devoted to critics and critical schools, this bibliography covers all aspects of the thought and writings of Cassirer, a German neo-Kantian philosopher and historian of ideas who culminated his career in the United States as a refugee from Nazism. The bibliography of his writings runs to 167 items, including 38 books, not counting translations, listed here with the entry for the original language. The secondary bibliography comprises over a thousand items, including 461 book reviews and 48 dissertations. Excellent, often lengthy annotations provided for all entries represent a Herculean labor that unfortunately left the compilers too spent (one surmises) to meet the need for subject indexing beyond a register of names.

Croce, Benedetto (1866–1952)

576.   Borsari, Silvano. **L'opera di Benedetto Croce.** Naples: Istituto italiano per gli studi storici, 1964. 619p.

Croce's works, listed here by year of publication from 1882 through 1962, number 4,530 items, including reviews, prefaces, edited books, and so forth. Translations are listed separately (items 4531–4659). Annotations are limited to bibliographic matters. Name and title index are combined.

577.   Cione, Edmondo. **Bibliografia Crociana.** [Rome]: Fratelli Bocca, 1965. 481p. (Biblioteca di scienze moderne, 155).

Parts 1–4, which list works by Croce, are largely superseded by Borsari (entry 576). Part 5 lists, chronologically, about 1,250 writings on Croce through 1954, and includes brief annotations. While the majority of items are in Italian, there are also many in English, French, German, and other languages.

Derrida, Jacques (1930–2004)

578.   Schultz, William R., and Lewis L. B. Fried. **Jacques Derrida: An Annotated Primary and Secondary Bibliography.** Hamden, Conn.: Garland, 1992. 882p. (Garland Bibliographies of Modern Critics and Critical Schools, vol. 18; Garland Reference Library of the Humanities, vol. 1319).

Writings by Derrida, the leading figure in the French Deconstructionist movement, are covered exhaustively in the primary section of this bibliography. Books (including translations), parts of books, articles, published interviews, reviews, and so forth, up to the time of compilation are all included, divided among French and English subsections. A secondary bibliography, occupying about four-fifths of the volume, lists and annotates 3,618 works about Derrida, some of which make only slight reference to him. There is an author and a name index. An introductory essay surveys questions and controversies raised by Derrida's work.

579.   Lucy, Niall. **A Derrida Dictionary.** Oxford: Blackwell, 2004. 183p.

"Derrida's terminology is notoriously difficult for readers to understand, and indeed defining Derridean terms runs counter (in a sense) to the spirit of his intellectual project" (cover blurb). In a similar vein, philosopher John D. Caputo's commendation of this dictionary (also on the cover) observes that it "spares us the tediousness of trying to formalize ideas whose very idea is that they cannot be formalized." This should provide ample notice to users not to set their expectations for clarity too high. But quite possibly many readers will conclude there is little or no gain in clarity at all over Derrida's own writings (try the entries for deconstruction, *differance,* or hymen, for example; perhaps the entries for postal metaphor and phonocentrism could be cited as contrary instances). Even so, the dictionary undoubtedly has utility in that, as the first-quoted blurb goes on to suggest, it "can offer points of entry into Derrida's complex and extensive works." In that light, Lucy was probably wise to limit his selection of entries to 40 key terms or phrases and six thinkers who figure significantly in Derrida's thought, each allotted anywhere from 1 full page (e.g., *aporia,* mark, Plato) to 13 pages (speech-writing opposition). Lucy's aim "to provide a series of outlines and interpretations of some of Derrida's key ideas and arguments" is implemented in part with many examples drawn from popular culture—not necessarily found in Derrida's own writings—as well as from personal experiences.

Foucault, Michel (1926–1984)

580.   Clark, Michael. **Michel Foucault: An Annotated Bibliography: Tool Kit for a New Age.** New York: Garland, 1983. 608p. (Garland Bibliographies of Modern Critics and Critical Schools, vol. 4; Garland Reference Library of the Humanities, vol. 350).

Attempts to be "totally comprehensive for works by and about Foucault in French and English" (preface). Extensively annotated, it provides lengthy summaries for the major books of this leading French Structuralist, and short summaries even (in many cases) for brief reviews. A section on background works selectively includes books and essays that are not primarily about Foucault but do mention him. Indexes for authors, book titles, article titles, and topics are included.

Gadamer, Hans-Georg (1900–2002)

581.   Makita, Etsuro. **Gadamer-Bibliographie (1922–1994).** Frankfurt am Main: Peter Lang, 1995. 349p.

A primary bibliography listing Gadamer's writings in five categories: (1) books, dissertations and *Habilitationsschriften;* (2) articles; (3) reviews; (4) short articles, letters, interviews, and so forth; (5) edited works, including collections edited by others. Except in the final section, arrangement is chronological within categories, or in some cases subcategories. Indexes of titles, reviews, and subjects.

Heidegger, Martin (1889–1976)

582.   Sass, Hans-Martin. **Martin Heidegger: Bibliography and Glossary.** Bowling Green, Ohio: Philosophy Documentation Center, Bowling Green State University, 1982. 513p. (Bibliographies of Famous Philosophers).

Works by Heidegger are listed by year of first publication, with later editions and translations following the original edition. This is followed by a listing of translations by language. Works about Heidegger (about 5,300 items) are listed by author, except for a separate chapter listing papers and addresses presented at Heidegger conferences. There is a subject index, but it is in German only, and is less discriminating than it might be, resulting sometimes in long lists of reference numbers. Other indexes include names (as subjects), editors and translators, titles of Heidegger's works, and reviews of his works. This compilation by Sass largely supersedes his earlier *Heidegger-Bibliographie* (Meisenheim am Glan: Anton Hain, 1968) and a supplement, *Materialen zur Heidegger-Bibliographie, 1917–1972* (idem, 1975). However, differences in arrangement—for example, a chronological ordering of the literature about Heidegger—may occasionally warrant reference to the earlier volumes.

The glossary, which occupies 64 pages, "presents the English, Chinese, French, Italian, Japanese and Spanish translations of just 100 words, fundamental to Heidegger's thinking" (p. 450). It is preceded by an appropriately Heideggerian rumination on questions about language.

583.   Denker, Alfred. **Historical Dictionary of Heidegger's Philosophy.** Lanham, Md.: Scarecrow Press, 2000. 378p. (Historical Dictionaries of Religions, Philosophies, and Movements, no. 30).

Follows in many respects the pattern set by the *Historical Dictionary of Nietzscheanism* (entry 481), though in this case the focus remains on the individual and does not take in those he influenced or any movement he inspired. But unlike the *Heidegger Dictionary* by Inwood (entry 585), focused almost exclusively on terminology, Denker's dictionary deals substantially with the biographical dimensions of its subject and with his historical context. This entails among other things some attention to the controversial issue of Heidegger's relation to Nazism. Entries range over events, institutions, and persons in Heidegger's life; thinkers who influenced him; individual writings, including some not yet translated into English; and, in generous measure, his specialized terminology as well as the general topics on which he wrote. Supplementing the alphabetical dictionary are an introduction to Heidegger's "life and path of thinking"; a chronology of events; a separate chronology of writings, lectures, courses, and seminars; German-English and Greek-English glossaries; and a 90-page bibliography that includes a complete inventory of the Heidegger *Gesamtausgabe* to date (Klostermann, 1976–) along with individually published works in German and English plus a selective but substantial secondary bibliography, arranged thematically.

584.   Dreyfus, Hubert L., and Mark A. Wrathall, eds. **A Companion to Heidegger.** Malden, Mass.: Blackwell, 2005. 540p. (Blackwell Companions to Philosophy).

This is the first and so far (late 2005) only Blackwell Companion to be devoted to a single philosopher. It surveys Heidegger's thought and career in partly chronological, partly thematic fashion. Following an introduction by the editors are 30 essays grouped into three parts. Part 1, dealing with the early Heidegger, addresses various themes and streams of influence (German Idealism, Nietzsche, Phenomenology, etc.) and also his notorious involvement with Nazism. Part 2 has nine essays dealing with *Being and Time,* Heidegger's *magnum opus.* Part 3 considers his later thought and contains critical responses including consideration of his relations to pragmatism, religion, and ecology. Bibliographies accompanying the articles usually include both references and suggestions for further reading. The 30 contributors, mostly North American scholars, include at least 2 who are significant philosophers in their own right, Richard Rorty and Charles Taylor.

585.   Inwood, Michael. **A Heidegger Dictionary.** Oxford: Blackwell, 1999. 283p. (Blackwell Philosopher Dictionaries).

Having previously tackled Hegel in a dictionary in the same series, Inwood here takes on a philosopher of equally notorious difficulty. The focus in this dictionary is on one locus of that difficulty, Heidegger's terminology and its associated complex web of concepts, explorations, and questions. Thus the usual introductory essay is devoted in this case to "Heidegger and His Language" and not, for instance, a biographical overview. Nearly all of the 100 entries represent either an important term (e.g., authenticity, *Dasein, Logos,* negation, thing), a pair or group of closely associated terms (God and theology; ground and abyss; nothing and negation; thinking and questioning; time, temporality, and timeliness), or a compound expression (abandonment of being; being-with, present-at-hand). Even the occasional exception, such as an entry for Nietzsche, represents a subject addressed by Heidegger in his published writings. Inwood seeks to clarify Heidegger's often innovative philosophical language by exploiting the full range of his work, including many as yet untranslated lectures, drawing on etymological explorations, frequent quotations, and contextual information, and making heavy use of cross-references. The result will undoubtedly be helpful to serious Heidegger scholars and others willing to bring some perseverance to the effort to understand this demanding thinker, but it will neither make the task easy nor, probably, rescue Heidegger entirely from his reputation for obscurity. The work has both a general index and an index of foreign words and expressions.

586.   Thöma, Dieter, ed. **Heidegger-Handbuch: Leben, Werk, Wirkung.** Stuttgart: J. B. Metzler, 2003. 574p. (Metzler Handbüchern).

See note on the series at entry 482. A biographical overview and detailed expositions of Heidegger's works, typical of the series, are joined in this instance by an extensive section on his "context and influence," occupying more than a third of the volume. This examines Heidegger's relationships to many individual philosophers, to various branches of philosophy or other disciplines, and to specific philosophical schools or movements. There is also a substantial chronology. Some 50 scholars contributed to this work.

587.   Feick, Hildegard. **Index zu Heideggers "Sein und Zeit."** 2nd rev. ed. Tübingen: Max Niemeyer, 1968. 132p.

An index to key terms in the German original of *Being and Time,* giving not merely locations but in most cases quotations showing the context of their use, and also citing occurrences in *other* works of Heidegger. The second edition updates the first (published in 1961) by incorporating references to works of Heidegger's later years. A *Seiten-Konkordanz,* in back, cross-references works which have been published in several different editions.

588.   Landolt, Eduard. **Systematischer Index zu Werken Heideggers:** *Was ist das—Philosophie?; Identität und Differenz; Gelassenheit.* Heidelberg: Carl Winter Universitätsverlag, 1992. 319p.

This volume contains separate indexes to three works by Heidegger, identified in the subtitle. For each work, occurrences of the most significant terms are listed with quotations of their surrounding context (sometimes several sentences), while somewhat less significant terms are usually indexed via cross-references to the aforementioned quotations for major terms. A separate section is provided in each case for Greek terms used by Heidegger. Landolt's *Vorwort* provides an orientation to the indexes and elaborate coaching for their effective use.

Husserl, Edmund (1859–1938)

589. Lapointe, Francois. **Edmund Husserl and His Critics: An International Bibliography (1894–1979), Preceded by a Bibliography of Husserl's Writings.** Bowling Green, Ohio: Philosophy Documentation Center, Bowling Green State University, 1980. 351p. (Bibliographies of Famous Philosophers).

Part 1, devoted to Husserl's writings, includes sections on the Husserl Archives and the *Husserliana,* published conversations, correspondence, and editorial work. Part 2, devoted to works about Husserl, employs some divisions by subject (general discussions, studies and reviews of individual works, proper names, and subject descriptors) combined with some divisions by format (books and reviews, dissertations); there is some cross-listing, but no apparent consistency. An appendix lists 266 addenda.

590. Spileers, Steven. **Edmund Husserl Bibliography.** Dordrecht: Kluwer Academic, 1999. 450p.

Lists primary and secondary literature from 1887 to 1997 restricted to the following languages: German, English, French, Italian, Spanish, Portuguese, and Dutch. This restriction admits translations into any of these languages of sources originally written in excluded languages, for example, Polish or Japanese. Secondary literature includes books, articles, and dissertations if not also published as books. Additional details and subtleties of inclusion criteria are spelled out at some length in the introduction. Within both the primary and secondary sections, entries are grouped by language in the order aforementioned. Within each language group, they are ordered chronologically in the case of Husserl's works (using for translations their own publication dates, not those of the original), and alphabetically by author in the case of secondary works. Subject access to the secondary sources is afforded by indexes of names, of keywords, and of the titles of Husserl's works they discuss. There are also indexes of translators, editors, and authors.
Several categories of materials are listed in special sections: bibliographies; editions of Husserl's writings and collected letters in the *Husserliana* series; edited collections with articles or selections by or about Husserl; and texts by other authors in the Husserl-edited *Jahrbuch für Philosophie und Phänomenologische Forschung.*

591. Cairns, Dorion. **Guide for Translating Husserl.** The Hague: Martinus Nijhoff, 1973. 145p. (Phaenomenologica, 55).

For translators aiming at publication, this is an essential tool; but any English-speaker endeavoring to read Husserl in the original German may find it equally useful. Essentially a glossary of key terms and expressions, Cairns's guide gives translations in standard English editions of Husserl's works, cites general German-English dictionaries, and indicates preferred translations where options exist. In numerous instances, French renderings are also cited as an additional aid.

Jaspers, Karl (1883–1969)

592. Rabanus, Christian. **Primärbibliographie der Schriften Karl Jaspers'.** Tübingen: A. Francke, 2000. 399p. (Basler Studien zur Philosophie, 11).

Places Jaspers's works in chronological sequence by initial publication year, with subsequent reprintings, editions, and translations, regardless of date, immediately following the entry for the original publication. Coverage extends from Jaspers's 1909 dissertation to 1997 and includes many writings first published posthumously. Before 1969, the year of Jaspers's death, the compiler seeks to represent republications and translations exhaustively; after that date, the criteria for inclusion are narrowed somewhat to admit only the more significant (see explanation, p. 7). Supplementary sections list publications for which Jaspers served as editor, recordings of lectures and addresses, and microfilm publications. A title index is subdivided by languages. There is also a name index.

Issued under the auspices of the Karl Jaspers Stiftung in Basel, this bibliography builds on the privately printed *Karl Jaspers: Eine Bibliographie,* Band 1: *Die Primärbibliographie* by Gisela Gefken and Karl Kunert (Oldenburg, 1978).

Kristeva, Julia (1941–)

593.   O'Grady, Kathleen. **Julia Kristeva: A Bibliography of Primary and Secondary Sources in French and English, 1966–1996.** Bowling Green, Ohio: Philosophy Documentation Center, Bowling Green State University, 1997. 110p.

Claiming creation of this bibliography as "an important feminist act . . . by marking a place for women in the history of the production of knowledge" (pp. v–vi), O'Grady catalogs as exhaustively as possible French and English-language materials by and about Kristeva, whose work ranges widely across philosophy, linguistics, semiotics, psychoanalysis, and literary theory, and who has drawn both positive and negative response within feminist thought. Primary sources, including works of fiction, are listed chronologically, with translations immediately following the entry for the original publication in, usually, French, sometimes English. Secondary sources are divided into books, scholarly articles (essays and reviews), dissertations, newspaper and magazine articles, and bibliographies. Placed between the primary and secondary sections is the borderline category of interviews, some 51 of which are listed. The volume also includes an overview of Kristeva's work and critical reaction thereto, a *curriculum vitae* supplied by Kristeva, name index, and a subject index for secondary sources only. No annotations.

594.   Volat, Hélène. **Julia Kristeva: œuvres et critique, 1966–1994.** Paris: Lettres Modernes, 1996. ca. 200p. (unpaged). (Les carnets bibliographiques de la Revue des lettres modernes; La revue des lettres modernes, no. 1317–1325).

Though published in France with French-language introduction, chapter headings, and so forth, this bibliography was compiled in the United States. The introduction acknowledges some limitations resulting from reliance on American library resources, for example in identifying certain French dissertations, book reviews, or newspaper articles. While in principle all languages are included, materials in French and English predominate, with English notably well represented—due, says Volat, to Kristeva's immense audience in Anglophone countries. Arrangement in both the primary *(œuvres)* and secondary *(critique)* sections is principally by date of publication. Reprints and translations are listed under the year of their own publication but cross-referenced under the original. Multiple indexes include author and several discrete title indexes but no subject index.

As of late 2005, updates to this printed bibliography, along with much of its original content somewhat differently arranged, could be found on a Web site maintained

by Volat at the State University of New York at Stony Brook, http://ms.cc.sunysb.edu/
~hvolat/kristeva/kristeva.htm (accessed October 26, 2005).

Lukács, Georg (Gyorgy) (1885–1971)

595.   Lapointe, Francois H. **Georg Lukács and his Critics: An International
Bibliography with Annotations (1910–1982).** Westport, Conn.: Greenwood Press,
1983. 403p.

Lists only materials *about* Lukács, a Hungarian Marxist philosopher and literary
critic with a considerable reputation even outside East European Marxist circles. Divisions
cover (1) books and reviews; (2) dissertations and theses; (3) essays and articles; (4) items
arranged by proper names (relating Lukács to other thinkers). Parts 1 and 3 are divided
according to language. Many of the 2,100 entries are annotated, often at length, with some
of the annotations lifted from other sources such as *Dissertation Abstracts International.*

Marcel, Gabriel (1889–1973)

596.   Lapointe, Francois H., and Claire C. Lapointe. **Gabriel Marcel and His Critics:
An International Bibliography (1928–1976).** New York: Garland, 1977. 287p. (Garland
Reference Library of the Humanities, vol. 57).

Lists, without annotations, 3,001 items through early 1976, including works
by and about Marcel. Covers Marcel's activity as dramatist and literary critic as well
as his more strictly philosophical work. Combines certain divisions by format (books,
dissertations, articles) with divisions arranged by proper names and subjects. There is an
index of authors and editors.

Maritain, Jacques (1882–1973) and Raïssa (1883–1960)

597.   Gallagher, Donald A., and Idella Gallagher. **The Achievement of Jacques and
Raïssa Maritain: A Bibliography, 1906–1961.** Garden City, N.Y.: Doubleday, 1962. 256p.

An extremely comprehensive if not exhaustive international bibliography of
books, booklets, parts of books, articles, prefaces, forewords, introductions, and translations.
Lists hundreds of items by and about Jacques Maritain, the leading Thomist philosopher of
this century, and scores of items by and about his wife, Raïssa, less famous but also a well-
published author of philosophical, theological, and literary works. A 30-page introduction and
a chronology of the Maritains' lives precede the bibliography. A subject index is included.

Merleau-Ponty, Maurice (1907–1961)

598.   Lapointe, Francois, and Claire C. Lapointe. **Maurice Merleau-Ponty and His
Critics: An International Bibliography (1942–1976); Preceded by a Bibliography of
Merleau-Ponty's Writings.** New York: Garland, 1976. 169p. (Garland Reference Library
of the Humanities, vol. 51).

Works by Merleau-Ponty are arranged in five sections: monographs and reviews
thereof; dissertations; studies of individual works of Merleau-Ponty; studies relating him
to others thinkers; and items arranged by subject. Cross-references make this otherwise

cumbersome division workable, though they are not always adequate. As to coverage, the closing date should more accurately be given as 1975; even at that, there are some significant gaps in coverage of articles and dissertations from 1973 to 1975.

Ortega y Gasset, José (1883–1955)

599. Donoso, Antón and Harold Raley. **José Ortega y Gasset: A Bibliography of Secondary Sources.** Bowling Green, Ohio: Philosophy Documentation Center, 1986. 449p.

The 4,125 items recorded in this comprehensive secondary bibliography includes materials "made public" (as the introduction puts) in all formats: not only the usual published materials—books, articles, essays, even encyclopedia entries and substantial discussions in more general works—but also theses, some letters, radio transcripts, and audiovisual media. They represent many countries of origin and many languages, though materials in Spanish and English predominate. Entries are not annotated. There is a fairly good subject index, although its references to entry numbers only can make for some cumbersomeness in use, especially for broad subjects with many references.

600. Rukser, Udo. **Bibliografía de Ortega.** Madrid: Revista de Occidente, 1971. 417p. (Estudios Orteguianos, 3).

Identifies 1,957 books and articles by and about Ortega y Gasset, arranged by country of origin from South Africa to Yugoslavia. Has an author index.

Ricœur, Paul (1913–)

601. Vansina, Frans D. **Paul Ricœur: Bibliographie primaire et secondaire—Primary and Secondary Bibliography,1935–2000.** Leuven: University Press: Uitgeverij Peeters, 2000. 544p. (Bibliotheca ephemeridum theologicarum Lovaniensium, 148).

Updates *Paul Ricœur: Bibliographie systématique de ses écrits et des publications consacrées à sa pensée (1935–1984)—A Primary and Secondary Systematic Bibliography (1935–1984)* (Leuven: Peeters, 1985) by the same compiler. Ricœur's own writings and translations thereof are categorized into books, articles, and minor texts (very brief communications, etc.). Works about Ricœur are categorized into books, dissertations, articles, and book reviews. In both sections, arrangement within each genre category is first by language, then by year of publication. There are separate indexes for primary and secondary sections, in each instance including a name index and subject indexes in both French and English.

Sartre, Jean-Paul (1905–1980)

602. Belkind, Allen. **Jean-Paul Sartre: Sartre and Existentialism in English: A Bibliographical Guide.** Kent, Ohio: Kent State University Press, 1970. 234p. (The Serif Series: Bibliographies and Checklists, no. 10).

Part 1 lists English translations of Sartre's works, including philosophical and literary works, film scripts, magazine articles, prefaces and introductions to books by others, and interviews. Parts 2 through 4 list writings in English about Sartre, including books, pamphlets, and dissertations (annotated), periodical articles (minimally annotated), and reviews. Appendix gives list of sources. There is an index of authors, editors, and translators.

603.   Contat, Michel, and Michel Rybalka. **Les Écrits de Sartre: Chronologie, bibliographie commentée.** Paris: Gallimard, 1970. 788p. English edition (revised): **The Writings of Jean-Paul Sartre.** Volume 1, **A Bibliographical Life.** Trans. by Richard C. McCleary. Evanston, Ill.: Northwestern University Press, 1974. 654p. (Northwestern University Studies in Phenomenology and Existential Philosophy).

Includes a detailed chronology of Sartre's writing and publishing activities, plus a profusely annotated bibliography of his published works, also in chronological sequence. An appendix lists films scripted by Sartre or based on his writings. A second appendix, in the French edition only, reproduces some "rediscovered texts." Indexes of titles, names/ subjects, and (in the French edition only) periodicals in which Sartre published.

The English edition includes revisions and updating to spring 1973, and integrates "a concise bibliography of Sartre's translations into English" (p. xix).

604.   Lapointe, Francois H., and Claire Lapointe. **Jean-Paul Sartre and His Critics: An International Bibliography (1938–1980).** 2nd ed., revised and annotated. Bowling Green, Ohio: Philosophy Documentation Center, Bowling Green State University, 1981. 697p. (Bibliographies of Famous Philosophers).

Contains 10,908 numbered entries, grouped partly according to format (books and reviews thereof; dissertations), partly according to subject (studies of individual works; names; topics). Arrangement within each group is by language: English, French, others. Annotations, added since the first edition (same publisher, 1975), are frequent for books and general essays or articles, sporadic for other categories (none are supplied for dissertations).

605.   Rybalka, Michel, Michel Contat, et. al. **Sartre: Bibliography 1980–1992.** Paris, CNRS, 1993; Bowling Green, Ohio: Philosophy Documentation Center, Bowling Green State University, 1993. 247p. (Bibliographies of Famous Philosophers).

Issued simultaneously in France with the title *Sartre: Bibliographie, 1980–1992* and minus the English introduction. Picking up where Francois and Claire Lapointe (entry 604) left off, this bibliography records the addition of another 3,400 publications and 200 dissertations to the literature by and on Sartre over the dozen or so years it encompasses. Main entries are presented in chronological order—for each year, new writings or editions of Sartre first, then works about him—and there is a full name index as well as a subject index for Sartre's own works only. All headings are in French; the English edition merely adds some introductory pages. Works included are in English, French, German, Italian, and Spanish.

606.   Wilcocks, Robert. **Jean-Paul Sartre: A Bibliography of International Criticism.** Edmonton: University of Alberta Press, 1975. 767p.

Wilcocks ascribes to his work a dual nature as "a compilation of the essential scholarly and critical texts" that also attempts "to offer commentary on, and to quote from, press articles and reviews which may not be readily available" (introduction). By press articles he means "material in the daily, weekly, or sometimes monthly, press of an ephemeral nature, normally news items or journalists' comments on Sartre's activities"—some so ephemeral that Wilcocks sees fit to designate them with the code letters "N.W.C.," that is, "Not Worth Consulting" (but he also suggests "the reader may ignore this piece of advice"). This popular or less scholarly material remains the special strength of Wilcocks's bibliography, together with its arrangement according to various of Sartre's activities: fiction, drama and cinema, literary criticism, philosophy, politics, and some general categories.

Schweitzer, Albert (1875–1965)

607. Griffith, Nancy Snell, and Laura Person. **Albert Schweitzer: an International Bibliography.** Boston: G. K. Hall, 1981. 600p.

Covers the many facets of Schweitzer's life and thought, and includes writings in many languages as well as some nonprint materials. Works by Schweitzer are annotated, works about him infrequently. Chapter 6 deals specifically with Schweitzer's philosophical work, including his concept of "reverence for life," but some material of philosophical interest may also be found in the sections "Theology and Religion" and "Albert Schweitzer and World Peace."

Teilhard de Chardin, Pierre (1881–1955)

608. McCarthy, Joseph M. **Pierre Teilhard de Chardin: A Comprehensive Bibliography.** New York: Garland, 1981. 438p. (Garland Reference Library of the Humanities, vol. 158).

Lists, without annotations, 621 works by Teilhard de Chardin, and 4,317 works about him. The former are arranged chronologically, except for collaborative works (collected at the end, by name of first coauthor). "Works about," arranged by author, include principally items in French, German, and English, and some in other languages, with English translations of non-English titles supplied where not obvious. A subject index is included.

609. Cowell, Siôn. **The Teilhard Lexicon: Understanding the Language, Terminology, and Vision of the Writings of Pierre Teilhard de Chardin: The First English-Language Dictionary of His Writings.** Portland, Ore.: Sussex Academic Press, 2001. 232p.

The *Teilhard Lexicon* aims "to enable researchers and students to better understand the specialized language of Teilhard's transdisciplinary approach, which he found himself compelled to develop as a means of expressing that extraordinary vision of a universe in process of convergence towards a cosmic center of unity he identifies with the Cosmic Christ" (cover blurb). Some entries represent standard terms and concepts to which Teilhard gave particular meanings or interpretations (e.g., activation, evolution, obligation, the One), others are Teilhardian neologisms (e.g., agaposphere, God-ahead, Omegalization).

Cowell's work builds upon Claude Cuénot's *Nouveau lexique Teilhard de Chardin* (Paris: Editions de Seuil, 1968, 224p.).

Tillich, Paul (1886–1965)

610. Crossman, Richard C. **Paul Tillich: A Comprehensive Bibliography and Keyword Index of Primary and Secondary Writings in English.** Metuchen, N.J.: American Theological Library Association and Scarecrow Press, 1983. 181p. (ATLA Bibliography Series, no. 9).

Though considered primarily a theologian, Tillich was arguably the most philosophical of modern theologians, and unquestionably one who has drawn an unusual amount of attention from philosophical quarters. Though much of his mature career was spent in the United States, his philosophical roots were Continental. Crossman's bibliography covers English-language books, articles, dissertations, and (more selectively) book reviews through roughly 1981, concerned with any aspect of Tillich's thought and in a few cases with his personal life. Separate keyword indexes are provided for subject-terms and personal names; the former suffers somewhat from a lack of discrimination common with this mode of indexing.

Unamuno y Yugo, Miguel de (1865–1936)

611. Valdés, Mario J., and Maria Elena de Valdés. **An Unamuno Source Book: A Catalogue of Readings and Acquisitions with an Introductory Essay on Unamuno's Dialectical Enquiry.** Toronto and Buffalo, N.Y.: University of Toronto Press, 1973. 305p.

This specialized work is designed to aid the scholar interested in influences on the thought of the important Hispanic thinker Miguel de Unamuno y Jugo. "The bulk of the work consists of a complete register of the 5,700 volumes at Salamanca, Unamuno's home, including titles discovered in Unamuno's personal catalog (1900–1917) but now missing from the collection. Systematic perusal of the *Obras completas* (Vergara ed.) provided further references to books, newspapers, and journals that Unamuno read or to which he contributed material and that are not in the Salamanca collection. These are listed in two appendices, with references to the *Obras completas*. Bibliographic entries are complete, and most are annotated with symbols indicating significant aspects of each title" (*American Reference Books Annual,* 1974, entry 1195).

Part III
BRANCHES
OF PHILOSOPHY

15
Aesthetics, Philosophy of Art and of Art Criticism

BIBLIOGRAPHIES

612.   Albert, Ethel M. and Clyde Kluckhohn. **A Selected Bibliography on Values, Ethics and Esthetics in the Behavioral Sciences and Philosophy, 1920–1958.** Glencoe, Ill: Free Press, 1959. 342p.

See entry 644. Works on aesthetics are not segregated but are interspersed among works on ethics or on value judgments in general, in chapters demarcated along disciplinary lines. Most aesthetics-related entries can be identified, however, via the "Guide to the Bibliography" at the front, effectively a classified topical index. See especially outline rubrics V.6 and VIII.

613.   Baxandall, Lee. **Marxism and Aesthetics: A Selective Annotated Bibliography: Books and Articles in the English Language.** New York: Humanities Press, 1968, 1973. 261p.

Baxandall's aim is to "afford a guide to the chief Marxist theoretical contributions, practical studies and controversies" represented in English-language works (including translations) up to early 1967. A vast miscellany of sources, beginning with the foundational works of Marx, Engels, Plekhanov, Mehring, Lenin, and Lukács, are cited and annotated, with "descriptive rather than judgmental" annotations. "Decisions as to whether some writings 'really' were Marxist had no place. . . .When in doubt the compiler opted to include rather than exclude" (introduction).

A reviewer of this work in *American Reference Books Annual* (vol. 2, 1970, p. 42) complained that the compiler "is not familiar with the basic principles of bibliographical organization, nor is he accurate and there are many errors." The first criticism perhaps applies to the unusual arrangement by authors' nationality or language-grouping; even if justifiable in this instance, this approach should have been supplemented with adequate subject access. There are indeed topic indexes for each of the 36 geographical and linguistic divisions, but only a very limited general topic index.

614.   Draper, John William. **Eighteenth Century English Aesthetics: A Bibliography.** Heidelberg: Carl Winters Universitätsbuchhandlung, 1931. (Anglistische Forschungen, Heft 71.) Reprinted, New York: Octagon Books, 1968. 140p.

Covering one of the liveliest periods of thinking about aesthetics, this bibliography lists contributions by artists and critics as well as philosophers. Works relating to specific art forms (parts 2 through 5) far outnumber the general works on aesthetics in part 1. An appendix titled "Some Recent Comments on Eighteenth Century Aesthetics" lists selected secondary materials.

615.   Gayley, Charles Mills and Fred Newton Scott. **A Guide to the Literature of Aesthetics.** Berkeley: Supplement to the Report of the Secretary of the Board of Regents, University of California, 1890. Reprinted, New York: Burt Franklin, 1974. 116p.

Lists primarily nineteenth-century works, mainly books, but also some periodical literature (grouped under the titles of the periodicals). Materials in English, French, and German are included. Many appear also in later bibliographies, but a good number are not readily identifiable otherwise. The only annotations are those that indicate the specific sections of general and collective works that deal with aesthetic issues. Arrangement is by subject.

616. Hammond, William A. **A Bibliography of Aesthetics and of the Philosophy of the Fine Arts from 1900 to 1932.** Rev. ed. New York: Longmans, Green, 1934. Reprinted, New York: Russell & Russell, 1967. 205p.

This selective, largely unannotated, and dated bibliography remains valuable for the period it covers. Included are books, articles, and some doctoral dissertations and book reviews. Chapters 1–3 list general treatises and histories; 4–15 cover narrower topics, including individual art forms, problems concerning style and symbolism, and the relation of art to psychology, morality, and religion.

617. Shields, Allan. **A Bibliography of Bibliographies in Aesthetics.** San Diego: San Diego State University Press, 1974. 79p.

Shields lists bibliographic sources published from 1900 through 1972 (with a scattering of slightly earlier items). Besides a very small number of book-length works, he includes bibliographies and bibliographic essays in journals and collections, and selected (but numerous) works which include some significant bibliographic material, even bibliographic footnotes. Chapters cover works in aesthetics and its history generally and works relating to specific arts, to aesthetic education, and to psychology and art.

DICTIONARIES, ENCYCLOPEDIAS, AND HANDBOOKS

618. **Ästhetische Grundbegriffe: historisches Wörterbuch in sieben Bänden.** Ed. Karlheinz Barck, et. al. Stuttgart: J. B. Metzler, 2000–. 7 vols. (projected).

As of October 2005, the seven volumes promised in the subtitle are complete through volume 6, covering *Tanz* through *Zeitalter/Epoche*. Volume 7 will be an index, due to appear shortly. The work aspires to serve scholars and students in all the aesthetic disciplines as well as the interested public, and to provide communications bridges between the various disciplines, between the scholarly and public domains, and between aesthetic theory and practice *(Vorwort)*. Taking seriously the notion of *Grundbegriffe* proclaimed in its title, it doesn't offer short articles on matters of detail but sticks to lengthy treatments of 170 broad concepts, or groups of related concepts, deemed foundational or found to be most pervasive from historical as well as interdisciplinary perspectives. Examples include *appolonisch-dionysisch, Ausdruck, Chaos-Ordnung, Mimesis/Nachahmung, Négritude/ Black Aesthetics/créolité, Pathos/pathetisch, Postmoderne.* Bibliographic references, typically encompassing materials in the major European languages including English, are confined to footnotes, for the most part, especially those citing historical sources. However, a *Siglenverzeichnis* at the front of each volume lists major reference works and collected editions of philosophers and other writers on aesthetic subjects, while selective bibliographies at the ends of articles identify the most essential works and representative contemporary literature.

619.   Childers, Joseph, and Gary Hentzi, eds. **The Columbia Dictionary of Modern Literary and Cultural Criticism.** New York: Columbia University Press, 1995. 362p.

Standing in the intersection of literary theory and criticism with the broader realm of cultural and social theory and criticism, this dictionary draws its terms from many disciplines that contribute to this contemporary hybrid field, including among others psychoanalysis, semiotics, political philosophy, media studies, and feminist studies, and occasionally aesthetics or philosophy of art in their traditional guises. Entries include, for example, absurdism, decentering, decode, deconstruction, forces of production, form, patriarchy, schizoanalysis, and sex/gender system. The authors' foremost concern, they say, was "the needs of the nonacademic reader or beginning student who encounters an unfamiliar term and requires a summary of its most important meanings, usages, and associations," while they anticipate "nevertheless, that readers with some background in the field of theory and criticism will find the book useful as a reference tool" (preface). Articles typically run from a few sentences to a page or two, and most include one or several bibliographic references. There is also a 27-page general bibliography at the end. Name index only.

620.   Cooper, David E. **A Companion to Aesthetics.** Oxford.: Basil Blackwell, 1992. 466p. (Blackwell Companions to Philosophy).

Cooper's *Companion* takes "aesthetics" as equivalent to "philosophy of art," and "art" itself broadly so as to include literature as well as visual and performing arts. There are 130 articles ranging from 1,200 to 4,000 words in length dealing with key concepts of the field (beauty, expression, humour, ineffability, popular art, taste, etc.); with major aesthetic theories and schools or broad domains of theory (e.g., Chinese and Japanese aesthetics, feminist criticism, Marxism and art, Medieval and Renaissance aesthetics, modernism and postmodernism, religion and art); and with prominent theorizers, ancient to contemporary (e.g., Plato, Kant, Ruskin, T. S. Eliot, Gadamer, Sartre, Ernst Gombrich, Julia Kristeva). A longer article titled "Theories of Art" can be recommended as a good starting point and overview for readers new to the field.

Cooper draws no narrow lines between philosophy of art and adjacent regions— criticism, psychology or sociology of art, and so forth—yet keeps clearly philosophical issues central. While primarily Anglo-American in perspective, his work reflects the increased receptivity to Continental philosophy of recent years and, to a lesser degree, increased interest in Eastern thought.

621.   **Encyclopedia of Aesthetics.** Michael Kelly, ed. in chief. New York: Oxford University Press, 1998. 4 vols.

Authoritative and comprehensive, this encyclopedia has some 600 articles by 450 contributors seeking to offer "a combination of historical reference material and critical discussions of contemporary aesthetics intended for general readers and experts alike" (preface). Alphabetically arranged entries include terms and concepts (e.g., avant-garde, fashion, representation, sublime), traditions and schools of thought (Black Aesthetic, Chinese aesthetics, Formalism, Marxism), artistic movements (Baroque, Expressionism,

Suprematism), specific art forms and genres (architecture, dance, literature, photography), historical periods (Roman, Medieval), and many individual thinkers, not only philosophers but also major artists and critics whose reflections on the nature and significance of the arts have been influential. Contributors comprise an international contingent of scholars representing a wide spectrum of university departments (philosophy, art, architecture, classics, literature, music, theatre, etc.) as well as museums or other arts institutions, and also some independent scholars and artists. Among them are many of the leading writers in the field, including such prominent names as Rudolf Arnheim and Arthur Danto. Index.

622.   **Kratkii slovar' po èstetike.** Ed. Mikhail Fedotovich Ovsiannikov and V.A. Razumnii. Moscow: Izdvesto Politicheskoi Literatury, 1963. 542p. 2nd ed., Moscow: Prosveshchenie, 1983. 223p.

"Covers about 250 terms and concepts of Marxist-Leninist aesthetics" (DeGeorge, *The Philosopher's Guide,* p. 90, referring to first edition). Ovsiannikov was a major Soviet theoretician in this field, with numerous other publications on aesthetics to his credit.

623.   Macey, David. **The Penguin Dictionary of Critical Theory.** London: Penguin Books, 2000. 490p.

See entry 795.

624.   Saisselin, Remy G. **The Rule of Reason and the Ruses of the Heart: A Philosophical Dictionary of Classical French Criticism, Critics, and Aesthetic Issues.** Cleveland: Case Western Reserve University Press, 1970. 308p.

Saisselin's work has two parts. The first is arranged alphabetically by key terms in aesthetics and criticism from the period of French classicism, roughly the 1630s to the late 1700s. An expository and interpretive essay is provided for each term. The second part deals with specific writers, for example, Corneille, Diderot, Montesquieu, Rousseau, Voltaire. Numerous cross-references connect the various articles. "On the whole, . . . a worthwhile effort to show both the theoretical background and the practice of French classicists" (*Modern Language Journal* 52 [April 1972]:651).

625.   Souriau, Étienne. **Vocabulaire d'esthétique.** Paris: Presses Universitaires de France, 1990. 1415p.

Souriau's is not exclusively or even primarily a dictionary of philosophical aesthetics; many entries address terms and concepts of art history, art techniques, typology, and so forth. For French-language readers, however, it is a rich and scholarly resource with substantial philosophical material as well as information on many other terms and concepts important to understand in thinking philosophically about the arts and aesthetics. Of some 37 contributors, 5 are identified as "professeur de philosophie." Among the more philosophically oriented or relevant entries are *acculturation, action, existence, expression/exprimer, formaliste/formalisme, harmonie, Idéalisme, imitation, Kantienne (esthétique), Marxiste (esthétique), plaisir esthétique, Structuralisme, sublime.*

626.   Wolfreys, Julian, et. al., eds. **The Continuum Encyclopedia of Modern Criticism and Theory.** New York: Continuum, 2002. 882p.

Aims to offer "the student of literary and cultural studies a comprehensive, single-volume guide to the history and development of criticism in the humanities as the twenty-first century opens." It "takes the reader through introductions to historically influential philosophers, literary critics, schools of thought and movements from Spinoza and Descartes to phenomenology and Heidegger, from Coleridge and Arnold to contemporary debates in the areas of cultural studies and post-marxism. . . ." (foreword). Not an alphabetically organized encyclopedia, it divides its attention geographically first of all, its three major parts each comprising a series of articles by different contributors that trace a more or less chronological line of development within a particular region: (1) "Critical Discourse in Europe"; (2) "Theories and Practice of Criticism in North America"; (3) "Criticism, Literary and Cultural Studies in England, Ireland, Scotland and Wales." While the orientation is broadly interdisciplinary throughout, the centrality of philosophy is clear from many articles devoted to individual philosophers as diverse as Kant, Nietzsche, Pierce, Lukács, De Beauvoir, Derrida, Wittgenstein, and J. L. Austin, and others dealing with recognized philosophical schools such as Phenomenology, the Frankfurt School, Structuralism, and Post-Structuralism. Supplementing the thematic material is a 40-page glossary. An index covers both the essays and the glossary.

Contributors, more than 80 strong, represent mainly universities throughout the United States, the United Kingdom, and Australia.

OTHER REFERENCE SOURCES

627.   Aesthetics On-line. American Society for Aesthetics. http://aesthetics-online. org (accessed October 26, 2005).

Along with information and business matters specifically for members of the American Society of Aesthetics, this site offers a number of generally useful and publicly accessible aesthetics-related resources. Among these are directories with links to online bibliographies, teaching resources, course syllabi and descriptions, calls for papers, other aesthetics organizations' home pages, aestheticians' personal Web pages, journals, centers and institutes, and miscellaneous Web sites. Also available are a calendar of events, guides to graduate study in aesthetics in North America and the United Kingdom, and a list of aestheticians' email addresses.

16
Epistemology, Metaphysics, and Philosophy of Mind

BIBLIOGRAPHIES

628. **Contemporary Philosophy of Mind: An Annotated Bibliography.** Compiled by David Chalmers. http://www.u.arizona.edu/~chalmers/biblio.html (accessed October 26, 2005).

Among the most substantial philosophical bibliographies to be found on the Web, this is eminently worthy of inclusion in this guide, particularly as there is no current print bibliography with comprehensive coverage of the very active area of philosophy of mind. Its compiler, David Chalmers, is a leading American philosopher in this field. Although the question of persistence arises especially for Web resources tied to a particular individual, the substantial scope, quality of scholarship, and already impressive longevity of this online bibliography suggest the likelihood that it will endure in some form. At this writing it was last updated October 13, 2005, and lists 8,142 books and articles. These are placed in a classified arrangement featuring six major headings: consciousness and qualia; mental content; metaphysics of mind; philosophy of artificial intelligence; philosophy of psychology; consciousness in the sciences. Beneath these is a two-level hierarchy of subheadings and sub-subheadings. Under the third heading, for example, can be found subsection 3.2, "Reduction," and under that several sub-subsections such as 3.2a, "Reduction and Multiple Realizability" and 3.2b, "Nonreductive Materialism." Within each level, entries are listed alphabetically by author. Some but not all include one- to two-sentence descriptive annotations. A valuable recent addition is the inclusion of numerous links to online texts via Google Scholar, including links to other sources that cite the work in question.

629. Emmett, Kathleen, and Peter Machamer. **Perception: An Annotated Bibliography.** New York: Garland, 1976. 177p. (Garland Reference Library of the Humanities, vol. 39).

Concentrates on the philosophical literature on perception from the period 1935–1974. Some works from other areas of philosophy and from other disciplines, particularly psychology of perception, are included when, in the compilers' judgment, they "have been or should be important to philosophers interested in perception" (preface). The bibliography is arranged by author. A subject index gives access both by concepts and divisions of the field (e.g., awareness, cognitive theories, illusion, intentionality, neurophysiology, realism, primary qualities, sense datum, touch) and by the names of significant figures whose theories are discussed (D. M. Armstrong, J. L. Austin, Ayer, Berkeley, Chisholm, Hume, Locke, Merleau-Ponty, G.E. Moore, H. H. Price, Russell, Ryle, Wittgenstein, and others). Name entries sometimes reference works by the individual in question, sometimes not.

Annotations, largely descriptive, are provided for most of the nearly 1,500 items listed.

630. Harlow, Victor E. **A Bibliography and Genetic Study of American Realism.** [n.l.]: Harlow Publishing Co., 1931. Reprinted, New York: Kraus, 1970. 132p.

Harlow defines Realism as "the philosophic assertion of the most general assumption of all naive experience, to-wit, that the world we experience is real, and independent of our experiencing or knowledge of it" (p. 2). Its origins as an "explicit doctrine" in America are traced to William James. Other major figures include Ralph Barton Perry, Roy Wood Sellars, Arthur Lovejoy, and (under the rubric Critical Realism) George Santayana. Materials are organized by five periods of development, each treated with a short narrative followed by a lengthy bibliography. Writings and writers critical of Realism in its various forms, for example, Josiah Royce, are also included.

DICTIONARIES, ENCYCLOPEDIAS, AND HANDBOOKS

631. Bechtel, William and George Graham, eds. **A Companion to Cognitive Science.** Malden, Mass.: Blackwell, 1998. 791p. (Blackwell Companions to Philosophy, 13).

Provides an authoritative and, despite the confines of a single volume, fairly expansive overview of the current state of the multidisciplinary field of cognitive science (cf. entries 635, 636, and 641). This includes specific attention to its philosophical dimensions, though material of interest to philosophers, particularly philosophers of mind, is surely not limited to specifically philosophical essays such as Owen Flanagan's discussion of consciousness. Not an alphabetically organized dictionary, this Companion features 60 essays, almost all around 10 pages in length, gathered under 5 broad headings: areas of study in cognitive science, methodologies, "stances" (i.e., doctrinal positions, more or less), controversies, and, finally, "cognitive science in the real world" (areas where important applications or implications are seen or foreseen, including education, ethics, legal reasoning, and science). These are preceded by an extremely perspicuous 100-page historical introduction, "The Life of Cognitive Science," excellent for getting a sense of the field's development and the various streams that flowed into it, including some that have largely dried up. A welcome reference feature is an alphabetical dictionary of "selective biographies of major contributors to cognitive science," around 150 of them, on pages 750–776. This includes a number of philosophers, for example, Brentano, Patricia and Paul Churchland, Daniel Dennett, Jerry Fodor, John Searle, Wittgenstein. Indexes of subjects and of authors mentioned or cited.

632. Burkhardt, Hans and Barry Smith, eds. **Handbook of Metaphysics and Ontology.** Munich: Philosophia, 1991. 2 vols.

Embodying the conviction that the history of metaphysical thinking and current work in metaphysics can be mutually illuminating, this handbook includes articles reflecting recent scholarship on historical figures (e.g., Aristotle, Bruno, Hegel, Ockham, Parmenides), schools (Arabic school, Encyclopaedists, Port-Royal, Würzburg school), periods (Greek metaphysics, Renaissance philosophy), and concepts (hylomorphism, logos, plenitude), as well as articles on numerous topics and issues that occupy contemporary metaphysicians (abstraction, chaos theory, emergence, essentialism, intentionality, possible worlds, quantum physics, supervenience) and on some leading contemporary practitioners (Chisholm, Hidebrand,

Fodor, Gurwitsch, Kripke, Segelberg). Also among the 470 or so total articles are many on the logical and mathematical tools of metaphysics and on the application of metaphysical ideas within linguistics, psychology, cognitive science, and mathematics.

To a significant extent, this work straddles the Continental/Anglo-American divide, particularly in its treatment of historical topics. Attention to recent and contemporary Continental thought focuses on schools sympathetic to and active in metaphysical thinking, such as the schools of Brentano and Husserl and Neo-Thomism. The roster of more than 250 contributors is impressively international, including large numbers from the United States, Britain, and Western Europe and smaller numbers from Canada, Australia, Latin America, Poland, Israel, and scattered other locations.

633.   Dancy, Jonathan and Ernest Sosa. **A Companion to Epistemology.** Oxford: Blackwell, 1992. 541p. (Blackwell Companions to Philosophy).

Dancy and Sosa enlisted the aid of an impressive group of Anglo-American scholars to produce this companion to epistemology, or theory of knowledge. Articles, which are signed, range from 250 to 3,500 words in length and vary in their level of technicality depending on the subject matter and sometimes the predilections of contributors. Beginning students and general readers will find many articles helpful, others too advanced (e.g., convention). Entries include important thinkers on epistemology (e.g., A. J. Ayer, Descartes, Richard Rorty, Bertrand Russell) as well as terms and concepts (epoche, evidence, knower paradox, necessary/contingent, etc.) and more general topics such as feminist epistemology, Pragmatism, self-knowledge and self-identity, and so forth. Despite a strong Anglo-American emphasis, there is attention to Continental epistemology with a survey article on that topic and individual articles on, for example, Derrida, Foucault, hermeneutics, and phenomenology, among others.

634.   **Dictionary of Philosophy of Mind.** Edited by Chris Eliasmith. http://philosophy. uwaterloo.ca/MindDict/ (accessed October 26, 2005).

This online dictionary has proven itself among the most durable and oft-linked philosophical dictionaries on the Web. Its front-line definitions tend toward the ultrasuccinct, but in many (not all) instances they are accompanied by links to more expansive discussions or bibliographic references. The discussions vary considerably in length but can run to the equivalent of several printed pages (e.g., quantum theories of consciousness). Though uneven both in its coverage and in scholarly authority, this can be a useful, tolerably reliable tool for undergraduate students and even graduate students or professional philosophers who lack close familiarity with philosophy of mind. According to its home page, "The dictionary has a policy of blind peer review for all submissions. . . . Advisory, editorial, and review boards have been established." Articles are signed.

635.   Dunlop, Charles E. M., and James H. Fetzer. **Glossary of Cognitive Science.** New York: Paragon House, 1993. 146p. (Paragon House Glossary for Research, Reading, and Writing).

Within a very compact format, this glossary offers a helpful, wide-ranging compilation of definitions and brief explanations of terminology, names, and other references prevalent in the interdisciplinary field of cognitive science. It is aimed at students and teachers, not specialists. Abundant cross-references help the user to fill in any gaps left by a given explanation and with a little persistence to construct succinct overviews of significant areas from linked entries. Cognitive science, as its name suggests, investigates the nature of cognition: in humans, in animals, and, at least conditionally, in machines, inclining as it does (controversially) toward treating cognition as a set of processes that can at least in theory be carried out by a computer. It straddles the disciplines of computer science, psychology, linguistics, philosophy, and neuroscience; contributions from all of these except neuroscience are encompassed here. Rapid developments in this field have somewhat dated this dictionary but not rendered it obsolete.

636. **Encyclopedia of Cognitive Science.** Lynn Nadel, ed. in chief. New York: Nature Publishing Group, 2003. 4 vols.

This encyclopedia, says its preface, "captures current thinking about the workings of the mind and brain, focusing on problems that are as old as recorded history, but reflecting new approaches and techniques that have emerged since the 1980s" (p. xi). Its interdisciplinary concerns overlay large areas of psychology, philosophy, linguistics, computer science, and neuroscience, and also draw on anthropology, biology, economics, education, and others. For scholars and students in philosophy of mind who believe they have something to learn from the other disciplines, this is a valuable resource. And though specifically philosophical articles constitute a minority, they are substantial both in number and content. Several are found under entry headings of the form "X, philosophical issues about," with the X's ranging over such topics as action, computation, consciousness, innateness, pain, representation, self, and split brains. Entries of the form "philosophy of X" make up another significant group; here the X's include language, linguistics, mind, neuroscience, and science. But less transparently philosophical entries abound as well: anomalous monism, Chinese Room Argument, eliminativism, epiphenomenalism, mind-body problem, supervenience, and Turing Test, to cite some leading examples. One area slighted, arguably, is biographical articles on prominent philosophers of mind to match those on prominent psychologists, artificial intelligence researchers, and so forth. David Chalmers, a leading contemporary philosopher of mind, served as Section Editor for philosophy.

An unusual feature of this work is the grading of articles according to levels of readership: introductory, intermediate, and in-depth.

637. Fetzer, James H., and Robert F. Almeder. **Glossary of Epistemology / Philosophy of Science.** New York: Paragon House, 1993. 149p. (Paragon House Glossary for Research, Reading, and Writing).

The two disciplines covered by this compact work share a concern with the nature of knowledge: "ordinary knowledge" in the first case, "scientific knowledge" in the second. Like other Paragon glossaries (see, e.g., entry 635), this one aims to help students and teachers by providing very brief explanations of concepts commonly encountered in the literature of the field (or in this case two related fields) as well as concise identification of its leading thinkers and their core ideas. The intention to stay "down to earth" (preface) for the benefit of the nonspecialist is largely successful, although occasionally the demand for brevity gets in the way of clarity, for example, in the entries for strong knowledge and possible-world semantics.

638. Garrett, Don, and Edward Barbanell, eds. **Encyclopedia of Empiricism.** Westport, Conn.: Greenwood Press, 1997. 455p.

This concise encyclopedia embraces empiricism in the broad sense of a philosophical emphasis on experience as a source of knowledge. At the same time, it places Empiricism, a specific philosophical movement of the seventeenth and eighteenth centuries centered in Great Britain, at center stage. David Hume claims the longest article, and other leading Empiricists are prominently featured as well, as are preoccupations of the Empiricist movement such as causation, ideas, induction, and our knowledge of space. But concern with the historical antecedents of Empiricism, its wider intellectual context, and especially the subsequent development of its themes, as well as with empiricism as a broader tendency of thought, yields extensive coverage of topics beyond the usual Empiricist focus. Thus there are substantial articles on Aristotle, on Bertrand Russell, and on Isaac Newton's complex relationship to empiricist convictions. Less prominent philosophical lights, such as Pierre Gassendi, Thomas Reid, and Ernst Mach receive proportionately more attention here than in general philosophical histories or reference works. Also treated are related movements or schools of thought, including Skepticism, Behaviorism, Logical Positivism, Operationism, and Pragmatism. The signed articles, by around 75 contributors, include bibliographies. There is an index.

639. Guttenplan, Samuel, ed. **A Companion to the Philosophy of Mind.** Oxford: Blackwell, 1994. 642p. (Blackwell Companions to Philosophy).

Guttenplan opens, in part 1, with an extended "Essay on Mind," just over a hundred pages long, and follows that with an alphabetical, encyclopedic-dictionary format in part 2. The essay, intended especially for readers unfamiliar with the field, offers an alternative and supplementary way of navigating through its subject matter and provides frequent cross-references to the articles in part 2.

A remarkable feature of this work is the first-person articles contributed by prominent contemporary philosophers of mind on their own ideas and viewpoints. Such "self-profiles" are provided by, among others, Noam Chomsky, Donald Davidson, Daniel Dennett, Fred Dretske, Jerry Fodor, Hilary Putnam, and John Searle. In addition to these, the list of contributors includes a number of other names well-known in contemporary Anglo-American philosophy—the domain represented almost exclusively in this *Companion.* Total entries number around a hundred, and many of the articles run from half a dozen to a dozen pages in length, for example, those on artificial intelligence, epiphenomenalism, psychoanalytic explanation, Ludwig Wittgenstein. Only a few are less than a page, for example, anomalous monism, eliminativism, type/token. Almost all end with bibliographies, some quite lengthy. A detailed subject/name index begins on page 623.

640. Hetherington, Norriss S., ed. **Encyclopedia of Cosmology: Historical, Philosophical, and Scientific Foundations of Modern Cosmology.** New York: Garland, 1993. 686p. (Garland Reference Library of the Humanities, vol. 1250).

Cosmology—the study of the universe as an orderly system, its fundamental structure, and its evolution—is a subject permeated with philosophical ramifications. This is certainly true historically, as many prescientific cosmologies sprang from philosophical (as well as, of course, religious) motives, speculations, and arguments. Hence the entries in this encyclopedia for individual philosophers such as Artistotle, Avicenna, Buridan, Descartes, Kant, and Plato, and for predominantly philosophical cosmologies such as Atomist, Chinese, Early Greek, and Romantic cosmologies. But modern scientific cosmology, too, remains more self-consciously than most scientific disciplines embedded in a web of philosophical assumptions, implications, questions, and debates. Hetherington's preface notes that "a strong philosophical component is evident in working scientists' reflective account of their work in modern cosmology" and calls attention to several articles in which philosophical aspects of modern cosmology are explicitly addressed, namely, those on the anthropic principle, creation in cosmology, multiple universes, philosophical aspects of the origins of modern cosmology, and plurality of worlds.

641. Houdé, Olivier, ed., with Daniel Kayser, et. al. **Dictionary of Cognitive Science: Neuroscience, Psychology, Artificial Intelligence, Linguistics, and Philosophy.** New York: Psychology Press, 2004. 428p.

The subtitle of this dictionary signals the main disciplines that contribute to, and sometimes critique (especially in the case of philosophy), the interdisciplinary enterprise that forms its subject. A translation of a French work, *Vocabulaire de sciences cognitives* (Paris: Presses Universitaires de France, 1998), it assembles contributions from 60 international scholars to explain and explore 120 of the field's significant terms and concepts. Among the more philosophical or philosophically pregnant entries are, for instance, abduction, emergence, epistemology, identity, intentionality, naturalization, propositional attitude, qualia, rationality, and reductionism. The introduction includes a section specifically addressing the contribution of philosophy to cognitive science, and articles often have distinct sections on the philosophical dimensions of their topic alongside sections on other disciplinary perspectives. Bibliographies appended to the articles list English-language sources, a fair number of them of later vintage than the 1998 French edition of this work.

642. Kim, Jaegwon, and Ernest Sosa, eds. **A Companion to Metaphysics.** Oxford: Blackwell, 1995. 540p. (Blackwell Companions to Philosophy).

With the help of nearly 160 contributors, among them many leading writers on metaphysical topics in contemporary Anglo-American philosophy, Kim and Sosa provide a reference guide to metaphysics focused chiefly on the Western tradition and, in the twentieth century, the analytic tradition. Some attention is given to non-Western metaphysics, primarily in the form of concise survey articles (two to five pages) on metaphysics in, respectively, Africa, China, and India (there is a similar article for Latin America, where philosophy stands largely within the Western tradition). Likewise, there is some minimal coverage of metaphysics in Continental European philosophy, for example, the entries for Heidegger, Husserl, and Structuralism. Certain areas of metaphysics covered by other Blackwell Companions, such as those on ethics and philosophy of mind, are treated more briefly here than they might otherwise be. The alphabetical arrangement of entries is complemented by a thorough name/subject index.

643. **The MIT Encyclopedia of the Cognitive Sciences.** Robert A. Wilson and Frank C. Keil, eds. Cambridge, Mass.: MIT Press, 1999. 964p.

Like most reference works on cognitive science (e.g., entries 636 and 641), this takes full account of the field's interdisciplinary character, encompassing philosophy along with psychology, neuroscience, computational intelligence (the term preferred here to "artificial intelligence"), linguistics, and several other areas of research whose relevance bears especially on the broad rubric of "culture, cognition, and evolution." The latter and each of the aforementioned disciplines are treated to introductory essays preceding the alphabetically organized main part of the encyclopedia. Thus readers interested in philosophical material will benefit from editor Wilson's overview (pp. xv–xxxvii) of philosophical issues, debates, and positions, which references many if not all of the entries relevant to philosophy. These include such standard topics in philosophy of mind as the Chinese Room Argument, consciousness, dualism, emergentism, epiphenomenalism, mental causation, physicalism, qualia, and reductionism, among many others, as well as biographical entries for some historical (but generally not contemporary) contributors to the philosophical debates such as Descartes, Kant, and James. A number of entries explore philosophical issues surrounding topics in other domains, for example, "Connectionism, philosophical issues" and "Linguistics, philosophical issues." Occasionally, however, this encyclopedia disappoints by failing to indicate or explore the philosophical ramifications of data from other fields, for example those concerning the binding problem, blindsight, and "split brain" phenomena.

17
Ethics

BIBLIOGRAPHIES AND INDEXES

644. Albert, Ethel M. and Clyde Kluckhohn. **A Selected Bibliography on Values, Ethics and Esthetics in the Behavioral Sciences and Philosophy, 1920–1958.** Glencoe, Ill: Free Press, 1959. 342p.

Prepared under the auspices of Harvard's Laboratory of Social Relations and Stanford's Center for Advanced Study in the Behavioral Sciences, this bibliography covers literature on values from many perspectives. Only pages 225–299 are devoted to philosophy per se, but sections devoted to other disciplines—anthropology, psychology, sociology, political science, economics, and others—also offer grist for philosophical mills. While arrangement is by disciplines, a "Guide to the Bibliography" at the front gives topical access across disciplinary boundaries or perspectives. An author index is also provided. Many entries include a brief, usually single-sentence summary of content or thesis

645. **Bibliography of Bioethics.** Detroit: Gale Research, 1975–1980. Vols. 1–6. New York: Free Press; London: Collier Macmillan, 1981–1983. Vols. 7–9. Washington, D.C.: Kennedy Institute of Ethics, Georgetown University, 1984–. Vol. 10–.

This annual bibliography has been edited from its inception by LeRoy Walters, joined as of volume 10 (1984) by one or more co-editors. It encompasses three broad dimensions of bioethics identified in the introduction, printed with minor variations in all volumes: (1) "the ethics of the professional-patient relationship": the "duties of health professionals" and "the rights of patients"; (2) "research ethics, the study of value problems in biomedical and behavioral research"; and (3) "the quest to develop reasonable public policy guidelines for both the delivery of health care and the allocation of health care resources, as well as for the conduct of biomedical and behavioral research" (vol. 31, page 3). This represents a somewhat more circumscribed scope than that of the *Encyclopedia of Bioethics,* for example (entry 691), as it excludes topics such as the environment or animal rights except as they impinge directly on human health or health care. Within this defined scope, the bibliography aims at comprehensive coverage of English-language periodical articles and monographs, listed in separate sections. Besides books, "monographs" encompasses reports, pamphlets, and audiovisual materials, generally in small numbers. As of 2005, the staff of the Kennedy Institute of Ethics, which compiles the bibliography, was directly monitoring some 200 journals and newspapers and regularly searching 31 indexes, bibliographic databases, and review journals for additional pertinent citations (vol. 31, pp. 4–7).

The core of the bibliography is constituted by two subject indexes, one for periodical articles and essays, a separate one for monographs. These have varied over time in format and content, but in the 2005 volume (the latest at this writing) they include numerical subject codes, usually more than one per entry, keyed to a classification scheme printed on the back flyleaf. In the subject index for articles and essays, entries also include "subject captions" that characterize items using a six-fold typology: analytical, case study, empirical, legal, popular, or review. Abstracts accompany only a minority of entries, but when provided they tend to be substantial, typically 100 to 400 words. Other indexes include an author index for articles and essays, a title index for monographs. The author index includes full bibliographic data for each indexed article, a practice that began with volume 18 (1992). In recent volumes, referral from the author index to main entries in the subject section, for example to check for an abstract, is cumbersome and potentially frustrating: it requires coordinating subject classification numbers referenced in the author index with the alphabetically arranged headings in the subject section via the classification table on the flyleaf. For monographs, by contrast, the subject section itself is organized by the numbered classification scheme.

Virtually all listed documents are in the collections of the National Reference Center for Bioethics Literature (NRCBL) at the Kennedy Institute of Ethics (see entry 718). Entries for monographs include their NRCBL library call numbers.

Much of the content of this bibliography is now available online in two databases maintained by the Kennedy Institute: *ETHX on the Web* and *Genetics and Ethics* (entries 653 and 654). As of October 2005, article citations were represented in these databases from 1988 forward, monographs from 1975 forward. The contents of volumes 1–27 (1975–2001) were formerly available online and on CD-ROM under the title *BIOETHICSLINE,* discontinued as a separate entity in 2001. *BIOETHICSLINE*'s records were absorbed into two larger National Library of Medicine databases: *PubMed/ MEDLINE* for periodical articles, *LOCATORPlus* for books and related documents. Current records are also added to these databases. For 1974 through 1995, the cumulated contents of the bibliography were included on the CD-ROM version of the revised (second) edition of the *Encyclopedia of Bioethics* (entry 692).

646.   Bibliography of Society, Ethics and the Life Sciences. Hastings-on-Hudson, N.Y.: Institute of Society, Ethics and the Life Sciences; The Hastings Center. 1973–1979/80.

During the years it appeared, this publication offered excellent selective coverage for the wide range of ethical issues relating to medicine, health care, and biological science. From 1975 on, however, it duplicated to a large extent the *Bibliography of Bioethics* (entry 645), although it did offer, as an advantage over the latter, annotations for selected items. Arrangement is topical, with broad problem areas (behavior control; genetics, fertilization, and birth; health care delivery; etc.) subdivided for more specific issues. The successive volumes incorporate selectively the more important items listed in earlier volumes.

While discontinued under the above title, this bibliography was supplemented for 1980–83 by the *Hastings Center's Bibliography of Ethics, Biomedicine, and Professional Responsibility* (entry 657).

647.   Bick, Patricia Ann. Business Ethics and Responsibility: An Information Sourcebook. Phoenix, Ariz.: Oryx, 1988. 204p. (Oryx Series in Business and Management, 11).

Bick's bibliographic guide, covering a wide range of ethical issues associated with business activity, cites and in most cases annotates with succinct descriptions 1,018 items published between 1980 and 1986 and in the United States alone. It overlaps significantly with the business ethics bibliography by Donald Jones and Patricia Bennett for 1981–1985 (entry 662). Bick divides her compilation into chapters dealing with general sources and general issues, including the teaching of business ethics and its incorporation into an organization; corporate social responsibility, including issues of shareholder activism and collective versus individual responsibility; self-regulation through professionalism and codes of conduct; international business, including multination/host relationships and international codes; internal corporate affairs, including employee rights, whistleblowing, discrimination, comparable worth, and harassment; external corporate affairs, including issues of advertising, marketing, product safety, and environmental protection; and the role of organized religion in business. A surprise, perhaps, is an entire chapter on South Africa, which raised highly publicized ethical issues for U.S. and multinational business during the period covered. There are also chapters listing reference sources and research centers and organizations.

648.   Bioethics Literature Review. Frederick, Md.: University Publishing Group, 1986–. Vols. 1–.

A monthly serial publication, the *Bioethics Literature Review* provides comprehensive bibliographic and abstracting coverage over a broad range of topics in bioethics, including medical ethics and policy issues, human experimentation, genetic engineering, mental health, and animal rights. It regularly reviews a large number of journals specific to the field, and also, on a selective basis, journals in broader or related fields, including most major law journals, and even some general publications such as the *New York Times* and *Washington Post.* Among the most philosophically oriented journals it covers are *Ethics,* the *Journal of Medicine and Philosophy, Philosophy and Public Affairs,* and the *Review of Metaphysics.*

649.   Bol, Jan Willem, et. al. Marketing Ethics: A Selected, Annotated Bibliography of Articles. Chicago: American Marketing Association, 1993. 75p. (Bibliography Series, American Marketing Association).

A useful and authoritative, if by now somewhat dated, bibliography on a specialized area of business ethics, covering the period 1980–1992. Topics addressed include advertising, international marketing, sales practices, retailing, and public relations, among others. Cited articles are drawn from 43 selected scholarly marketing or business journals, including the *Journal of Business Ethics* and *Business and Professional Ethics Journal.* Helpful descriptive annotations accompany each entry. Author index.

650.   Carman, John, Mark Juergensmeyer, et. al. A Bibliographic Guide to the Comparative Study of Ethics. Cambridge: Cambridge University Press, 1991. 811p.

Produced under the sponsorship of the Berkeley-Harvard Program in Comparative Religion, this guide focuses heavily on religiously-based ethics, as witness chapter titles such as "Hindu Ethics," "Ethics in the Japanese Religious Tradition," Ancient Greek Religious Ethics," "Jewish Ethics," as well as four chronological chapters on Christian ethics. But as there is often no clear demarcation between religious and philosophical ethics—especially, though not only, in non-Western traditions such as Buddhism and Taoism—there is ample material here either centrally or tangentially relevant for the philosophical study of ethics. The latter is also addressed squarely in chapter 15, "Modern Western Philosophical Ethics," which lists and annotates major twentieth-century English-language source materials. Every bibliographic entry includes an annotation plus a number of letter-codes that categorize the work in question in relation to a set of cross-cultural topics and genres developed for the entire volume. Preceding each chapter's bibliographies are a narrative survey of the tradition under scrutiny and a "tradition outline" that serves as a key to the organization of the bibliographic material. An index allows comparison of the treatment of 24 topics (e.g., equality, evil, moral accomplishment, wealth) across traditions.

651. Elliston, Frederick A., and Jane van Schaik. **Legal Ethics: An Annotated Bibliography and Resource Guide.** Littleton, Colo.: Fred B. Rothman, 1984. 199p.

"This monograph is intended as a reference guide for teachers of professional responsibility and legal ethics, legal scholars and philosophers conducting research on the practice of law" (preface). The field of legal ethics, the authors go on to note, "has come to attract the attention of other academics, notably philosophers working in the emerging discipline of professional ethics," whose interests typically extend beyond formal codes or rules. "Accordingly, the bibliography is much broader in scope than the issues raised by the Model Rules" of the American Bar Association. Part 3, "Related Materials," lists and annotates general books and some articles on ethical theory, philosophical approaches to professional ethics, and philosophy of law.

652. **Ethics Index.** CD-ROM. Evanston, Ill: American Theological Library Association, 1994–1996.

The CD-ROM *Ethics Index* was issued thrice a year for just a few years in the mid-1990s. The final cumulated edition, released in June 1996, was reported to contain nearly 50,000 records in every field of ethics, including 25,000 essays from more than 2,000 book titles and more than 15,000 articles from nearly 200 ethics journals, both general and specialized, starting from 1990. Though updating ceased in 1996, the existing discs remain available (as of mid-2004) in at least a few dozen U.S. libraries, according to OCLC's *WorldCat*, and certainly retain some value for the period they cover. While issued by a theologically oriented association, the *Ethics Index* incorporated philosophical and legal as well as theological perspectives in many areas of ethics. Indexed journals were mostly English-language, but included a few foreign-language journals, too. The index did not provide abstracts, but a fairly liberal use of assigned subject headings compensated somewhat for this lack. A thesaurus of subject terms and other documentation accompanied the discs.

653. **ETHX on the Web: A Bibliographic Database on Bioethics and Professional Ethics.** http://www.georgetown.edu/research/nrcbl/databases/ (accessed October 27, 2005).

A bibliographic and index database prepared by the Library and Information Services Group of the Kennedy Institute of Ethics at Georgetown University (see entry 718). Its content overlaps substantially but not fully with the printed annual volumes of the *Bibliography of Bioethics* (entry 645); the latter is described as containing a selected subset of the database content, and some of its early volumes have been subsumed into the database only in part. Database records for books and other monographs also coincide substantially with those published in *New Titles in Bioethics* (entry 671). Because the database is updated monthly, its coverage is usually more current than that of the two print publications. As of late 2005, *ETHX on the Web* reportedly covers monographs from 1975 forward, periodical articles primarily from 1988 forward. It contains over 210,000 total records. The database is publicly accessible and free of charge at this time. Search options include basic, advanced, and Boolean searches.

A subset of *ETHX on the Web* is made available separately as the *Genetics and Ethics* database (entry 654).

654.   Genetics and Ethics. http://www.georgetown.edu/research/nrcbl/databases/ (accessed October 27, 2005).

The *Genetics and Ethics* database is a subset of the *ETHX on the Web* database maintained by the Kennedy Institute of Ethics (entry 653) and is accessed from the same page on the Institute's Web site. Because items that have something to do with genetics have been preselected, they can be searched without the need to include the term "genetics" or its variations. As of late 2005, it is reported to contain some 27,000-plus records drawn from the 210,000 or more included in *ETHX on the Web.*

655.   Goldstein, Doris Mueller. Bioethics: A Guide to Information Sources. Detroit: Gale Research, 1982. 366p. (Gale Information Guide Library; Health Affairs Information Guide Series, vol. 8).

Goldstein identifies and annotates organizations, programs, and special library collections concerned with bioethics in part 1, as well as printed information sources distributed between parts 2 ("General Sources . . . ") and 3 ("Topical Sections"). The latter includes brief bibliographies of background works on ethical theory and general works on bioethics, as well as sections on specific areas of concern within the field of bioethics: abortion, genetic intervention, behavior control, human subjects research, death and dying, among others. Most publications listed date from 1973 through 1981, though special effort was made to identify the most significant pre-1973 writings.

656.   Gothie, Daniel L. A Selected Bibliography of Applied Ethics in the Professions, 1950–1970: A Working Sourcebook with Annotations and Indexes. Charlottesville: University Press of Virginia, 1973. 176p.

Includes chapters on ethical issues in the areas of business and management, engineering, government and politics, health sciences, law, science, and social sciences. Most of the books and articles listed are not rigorously "philosophical," but do address issues of philosophical import. The majority of journal articles cited come from professional journals in the fields to which they relate. Annotations are usually too brief and perfunctory to be of any real use.

In the area of business and management only, Gothie's work is supplemented by three bibliographies by Donald G. Jones (entries 660, 661, and 662).

657.   The Hastings Center's Bibliography of Ethics, Biomedicine, and Professional Responsibility. Compiled by the staff of the Hastings Center. Frederick, Md.: University Publications of America, 1984. 109p.

This is "both a continuation of and a departure from the previous bibliographies [see entry 646] prepared by The Hastings Center" (preface). Many classic books and articles listed in the earlier volumes are repeated here, but the emphasis is on publications from 1978 through 1982, with a few from 1983. A section titled "Applied and Professional

Ethics" has been added. Entries are selectively annotated. There is no subject index, but a detailed subject classification is reflected in the table of contents.

658. Herring, Mark Youngblood. **Ethics and the Professor: An Annotated Bibliography, 1970–1985.** New York: Garland, 1988. 605p. (Garland Reference Library of the Humanities, vol. 742).

Documents and annotates 1,905 books and articles relating to ethical issues that confront professors and others in higher education, often extending also to education at lower levels. The issues involve matters as varied as tenure, governance, collective bargaining, academic freedom, copyright, merit pay, student rights, sex education, moral and religious education, plagiarism, alcohol and drug abuse, athletes, testing, admissions policies, and grading. Items listed include discussions in professional development and news publications, such as the *Chronicle of Higher Education,* as well as scholarly studies. Annotations, largely descriptive, are supplied for all entries. Author, title, and subject indexes.

659. **International Society of Environmental Ethics Bibliography.** http://www.cep.unt.edu/bib/index.htm.

See entry 714.

660. Jones, Donald G. **A Bibliography of Business Ethics, 1971–1975.** Charlottesville: University Press of Virginia, 1977. 207p.

Published under the aegis of the Center for the Study of Applied Ethics at the Colgate Graduate School of Business Administration, University of Virginia, this work updates Gothic's *Selected Bibliography of Applied Ethics in the Professions* (entry 656), but has narrowed the focus to business ethics. Few of the roughly 2,000 books and articles listed take a distinctly philosophical approach (many present background information or discussion), but they do relate to issues of ethics and values that have philosophical presuppositions and implications. Annotations are sporadic and generally so brief as to be barely useful.

The bulk of the bibliography divides into two sections characterized by the editors as comprising microethics and macroethics (introduction), the former dealing with specific issues in such areas as accounting, advertising, employee relations, and so forth, the latter with broad issues regarding business aims and practices in relation to the environment, minorities, multinational enterprise, safety and health, and so forth. Flanking these major divisions are a shorter section for general works and two highly selective sections titled "Theoretical and Applied Ethics" and "Religion and Business Ethics."

661. Jones, Donald G. and Helen Troy. **A Bibliography of Business Ethics, 1976–1980.** Charlottesville: University Press of Virginia, 1982. 220p.

Supplementing Jones's bibliography for 1971–75 (entry 660), this work retains basically the same arrangement, though a few topical sections have been relabeled or somewhat reorganized, and some new ones added (e.g., insurance, bribery and unusual foreign payments, whistle blowing, women in business). Sections titled "Codes of Conduct and Self-Regulation" and "Teaching and Training in Business Ethics" have been added near the end.

662. Jones, Donald G., and Patricia Bennett. **A Bibliography of Business Ethics, 1981–1985.** Charlottesville: Center for the Study of Applied Ethics, University of Virginia, 1986. 309p. (Mellen Studies in Business, vol. 2).

This is the fourth of a series of bibliographies from the University of Virginia's Center for the Study of Applied Ethics, and the third edited or co-edited by Jones (see entries 660, 661, and 662). Content and arrangement remain largely the same as in the volume for 1976–1980. There is substantial overlap in coverage and content with Patricia Ann Bick's *Business Ethics and Responsibility* (entry 647), but there are differences in organization as well as citations unique to each work even for the overlapping years.

663. Jones, Donald G. and Elaine L. Daly. **Sports Ethics in America: A Bibliography, 1970–1990.** New York: Greewood Press, 1992. 291p. (Bibliographies and Indexes in American History, no. 21).

Lists 2,863 articles and books on, or relevant to, the multifaceted and widely discussed subject of sports ethics, primarily in relation to the American scene. They are distributed among five categories: (1) general works and philosophy; (2) the team, the players, and the coaches; (3) the game, competition, and contestants; (4) sports and society; and (5) reference works. Numerous narrower topics provide further subdivisions, such as recruiting, gambling and point shaving, violence, academics and athletes, minorities and sport, sport and religion, women and sport. Articles are drawn widely from popular magazines and professional news and opinion publications as well as scholarly research journals. Few come from philosophy journals. Entries are unannotated but include subject descriptors, usually several of them, which are picked up in the subject index. These include descriptors for specific sports. There is also an author index.

664. Kistler, John M. **Animal Rights: A Subject Guide, Bibliography, and Internet Companion.** Westport, Conn.: Greenwood Press, 2000. 228p.

Kistler lists and annotates some 900 books, and references some 1,200 online sources, on animal rights and related issues. These are organized into six chapters: (1) general works, (2) animal natures, (3) fatal uses of animals, (4) nonfatal uses of animals, (5) animal populations, and (6) animal speculations—the latter concerned with sources that explore animal rights issues from religious or "paranormal" perspectives. Each chapter has a short introduction that outlines the major questions and controversies and describes some of their historical, social, or political context. Kistler's aim is not to be exhaustive for specialists but to provide helpful guidance for a wide range of readership.

Web sites are not generally accorded their own entries here. Rather, they are incorporated in the annotations for books and usually represent a site where one may find the entire book, an article by the same author, a review, or more information on the same topic. Rightly noting the instability of internet sites and addresses, Kistler provides helpful suggestions in his introduction for locating material that may have moved or finding alternate sources.

665. Leming, James S. **Foundations of Moral Education: An Annotated Bibliography.** Westport, Conn.: Greenwood Press, 1983. 325p.

This bibliography focuses on the philosophical and psychological bases for "any examined approach to moral education" (introduction). It covers primarily but not exclusively literature published from the mid-sixties through 1981—some 1,500 books, articles, dissertations, and ERIC documents. The philosophical dimension of its subject takes in questions regarding, for example, the aims of moral education, indoctrination and neutrality, and the relationship of religion to morality generally as well as moral development specifically. It also opens, however, onto the entire domain of moral philosophy. The selectivity mandated here is adeptly handled; in fact, Leming's 21 pages on ethical theory make an excellent selective, concise, annotated bibliography on twentieth-century philosophical ethics through 1981. An author index and (somewhat weak) subject index are included.

666. Magel, Charles R. **A Bibliography on Animal Rights and Related Matters.** Washington, D.C.: University Press of America, 1981. 602p.

While interest in animal rights as a serious philosophical subject has mushroomed in the last half century (see the evidence up to 1980 in the section "1951–80: Animals and Ethics"), that it is not a new topic is clear from the abundance of historical material included in this bibliography, even restricted as it is to Western thought and English-language materials.

If the ethics of human treatment of animals is the focus, an impressive array of related matters accounts for a majority of entries. These include: philosophical and religious views on the nature of animals; expressions of attitudes toward animals, including literary and artistic; scientific and historical studies of a wide range of uses and treatment of animals alleged by some to violate their rights (meat consumption, animal experimentation, hunting, etc.); animal protection and welfare movements, organizations, and laws; suggested alternatives in human treatment of animals. Bibliographic entries number 2,771, and include some general or obliquely related works, citing specific relevant sections. Arrangement is somewhat complex: by subject, sometimes subdivided chronologically, with separate sections for special formats (government documents, films, periodicals) and nonbibliographic entries (e.g., organizations). Annotations are the exception, not the rule.

Magel's own bias as a fairly radical proponent of animal liberation is undisguised, but materials contrary to his position are by no means slighted. For complementary and updated coverage of this topic, see entries 667 and 668.

667. Magel, Charles R. **Keyguide to Information Sources in Animal Rights.** London: Mansell; Jefferson, N.C.: McFarland, 1989. 267p.

In this guide, Magel provides a series of concise bibliographic essays surveying the literature on animal rights and related issues from Pythogoras (sixth century B.C.) to its burgeoning in recent times, and follows these with a chronologically arranged annotated bibliography. The present work partly updates but does not fully supplant Magel's 1981 bibliography (entry 666), which cast a wider net over related and tangential topics. Part 3 provides a list of 181 selected animal rights and animal welfare organizations worldwide. Seven appendices list audiovisual materials, musical recordings, and periodicals, reproduce the texts of two major animal rights declarations, and provide information on sources of products which have not been tested on animals and on animal ingredients in products.

668. Manzo, Bettina. **The Animal Rights Movement in the United States, 1975–1990: An Annotated Bibliography.** Metuchen, N.J.: Scarecrow Press, 1994. 296p.

Manzo's bibliography on the animal rights movement documents its organizational aspects and political and educational activities as well as its philosophical arguments and debates. The starting date of its coverage coincides roughly with the publication of Peter Singer's influential *Animal Liberation: A New Ethic for Our Treatment of Animals.* It is a selective bibliography of around 1,300 citations to books, journal and magazine articles, government publications, and reports. Focusing, as its title indicates, on the movement in the United States, it nonetheless includes some English-language citations from other countries. Philosophical material is mainly collected in the two chapters headed "Philosophy" and "Ethics." Seven other chapters deal with religions, law, and specific categories of animal rights issues such as circuses, fur, vegetarianism, and experimentation.

669.   Matczak, Sebastian A. **Philosophy: A Select, Classified Bibliography of Ethics, Economics, Law, Politics, and Sociology.** Louvain: Editions Nauwelaerts; Paris: Beatrice-Nauwelaerts, 1970. 308p. (Philosophical Questions Series, no. 3).

See entry 778.

670.   Miller, Albert Jay, and Michael James Acri. **Death: A Bibliographical Guide.** Metuchen, N.J.: Scarecrow, 1977. 420p.

See entry 811.

671.   **New Titles in Bioethics,** 1975–. Washington, D.C.: National Reference Center for Bioethics Literature, The Joseph and Rose Kennedy Institute of Ethics, Georgetown University. Quarterly, annual cumulation.

A quarterly bibliography based on recent additions to the monograph collections of the National Reference Center for Bioethics Literature (NRCBL; see entry 718). An annual cumulation is published separately. Format and organization are similar to those of the annual *Bibliography of Bioethics* (entry 645), but the latter lists journal articles whereas *New Titles in Bioethics* is confined to books and some other monographic publications such as audiovisual materials. At this writing in October 2005, issues from July–Sept. 2003 through January–March 2005 could be viewed online at the NRCBL Web site (http://www.georgetown.edu/research/nrcbl/publications/newtitles/index.htm). The content of this publication is incorporated also in the Kennedy Institute of Ethics *ETHX on the Web* database (entry 653).

672.   Roth, John K., et. al. **Ethics: An Annotated Bibliography.** Pasadena, Calif.: Salem Press, 1991. 169p. (Magill Bibliographies).

This selective guide to books in the field of ethics is intended not for scholars but for undergraduate students, advanced high school students, and general readers. Its annotations are often evaluative as well as descriptive. It begins, appropriately, with a section titled "Beginning Ethics," which lists and describes introductory texts and anthologies. Part 2, "Thinking About Ethics," includes a chronological survey of the major primary sources from the classical period to the twentieth century; a section on histories of ethical theory, whether comprehensive or focused on a specific period, school, or movement; and finally a section on systematic treatments of theoretical problems in ethics, which moves to a generally more difficult level. Part 3, "Applying Ethics," fills more than half the volume and reflects the burgeoning of applied studies in the 1980s and 1990s. It lists sources under the following specific domains of application: economics and business; the environment; the media; public policy; international relations; gender and sexuality; race and ethnicity; medicine and health, life and death; genocide and the Holocaust. There is an author index only.

673. Triche, Charles W. III and Diane Samson Triche. **The Euthanasia Controversy, 1812–1974: A Bibliography with Select Annotations.** Troy, N.Y.: Whitston, 1975. 242p.

For anyone interested in the history of euthanasia debates, this bibliography covering the better part of the last two centuries is a valuable resource. Though selective, it aims to be "near complete" (preface) and documents a vast amount of material in newspapers and popular magazines as well as scholarly writings. Some foreign-language materials are included. There are two principal sections. One lists and annotates books and essays, including, in the case of major works or collections, the individual essays or chapters. The other lists periodical literature under 19 subject categories including, for example, cases of mercy killings, decisions and medical ethics, extraordinary means, general writings for and against euthanasia, the law and euthanasia, the morality of euthanasia, statistics, suicide, and terminal patient care. This section is very selectively annotated. General author index.

DICTIONARIES, ENCYCLOPEDIAS, AND HANDBOOKS

674. Barber, Nigel. **Encyclopedia of Ethics in Science and Technology.** New York: Facts on File, 2002. 386p.

The author identifies his primary target audience as "users of high school, public, and college libraries," which appears appropriate assuming the envisioned college audience is mainly lower-level or junior college students. When he goes on to suggest other uses or users ranging from organizations concerned with science and technology or with ethics to college level teachers and even graduate-level courses in professional ethics (introduction), he drifts into puffery. As the sole author responsible for all 400 entries, Barber cannot muster the scholarship and specialist expertise exemplified in several other reference works that either focus on or encompass the same domain (see, e.g., entries 682 and 690). He does present much useful and solid information on a host of standard topics—mainly areas of scientific practice, application, or "fall-out" that raise ethical issues, together with illustrative cases, but also ethical theories, general concepts, and key thinkers. However, articles as well as bibliographies generally stay at an introductory level, at times to the point of superficiality (though following cross-references sometimes leads to more in-depth treatment of a topic and is therefore recommended). In places the work loses its focus. Lengthy articles on the histories of science and technology that make little or no connection with ethics may have a justification as useful background. But that rationale hardly extends to other articles, for example, those on Copernicus, Euclid, Vesalius, or topics in philosophy of mind, whose relevance to ethical issues is neither stated nor likely to be transparent to the work's primary audience.

675. Becker, Lawrence C. and Charlotte B. Becker, eds. **Encyclopedia of Ethics.** 2nd ed. New York: Routledge, 2001. 3 vols.

This encyclopedia belongs on any list of core reference titles in philosophy. Its team of over 325 contributors and consulting editors includes many prominent thinkers on philosophical ethics writing in English (e.g., Sissela Bok, R. M. Hare, Alasdair McIntyre, Martha Nussbaum), but those of lesser prominence, too, have usually made substantial contributions to the subjects on which they write here. Some 600 articles, typically 2 to 5 pages in length, cover a wide diversity of topics, from more-or-less predictable schools, theories, concepts, and key thinkers to significant areas of moral decision-making and controversy. Among the less predictable in the latter categories are articles on academic freedom, forgiveness, land ethics, moral luck, racism and related issues, and several on the professional ethics of specific fields. Unusual also is an article on women moral philosophers and a sequence of 12 essays under "History of Western Ethics" surveying the major historical periods. Among entries new to the second edition, which significantly expands the two-volume first edition (Garland, 1992), are genetic engineering, Aldo Leopold, multiculturalism, political correctness, public and private morality, and self-esteem. There is some attention to non-Western philosophical thought about ethics, with articles on, for example, China, Confucian ethics, India, Japan, and also to religious ethics, with at least one entry for each of the world's major religions. The focus, however, is philosophical, not religious ethics, and chiefly Western.

All articles include bibliographies, generally excellent and often extensive. Along with a subject index, there is a citation index which references all cited authors, corporate authors, journals cited *in toto,* and legal cases.

676.   Bekoff, Marc, and Carron A. Meaney, eds. **Encyclopedia of Animal Rights and Animal Welfare.** Westport, Conn.: Greenwood Press, 1998. 446p.

Philosophical aspects of animal rights and welfare find an important place in this dictionary alongside the sociology of human treatment of and relationships to animals, political and legal measures on behalf of animals, religious perspectives on animals and their welfare, and the history and present state of animal rights and protection movements. Among articles with a specifically philosophical focus, several deal with the application of general ethical theories and principles to animals; see, for example, the entries for animal rights, moral agency and animals, utilitarianism, and virtue ethics. Others address metaphysical questions, often intertwined with empirical issues, regarding the nature and capacities of animals and what implications these have for their morally appropriate treatment; examples here include the entries on animal cognition, anthropocentrism, behaviorism, marginal cases, moral standing of animals, pain, and species essentialism. There are also entries on philosophers whose ideas have been influential in this area, such as Descartes, Kant, Nietzsche, and Schopenhauer. Of the dictionary's roughly 130 contributors, 28 are identified as philosophy professors.

Bibliographies accompany most articles, and there is a general bibliography at the end. A directory of organizations that provide information or educational materials relating to animal welfare is appended.

677.   **Bioethics for Students: How Do We Know What's Right? Issues in Medicine, Animal Rights, and the Environment.** Stephen G. Post, general ed. New York: Macmillan Reference U.S.A., 1999. 4 vols.

Consistent with its title, this work aims to introduce issues in bioethics to "young people" (introduction)—presumably meaning high school and perhaps early college-age students, though the reading level is not further specified. Its articles are based "to a large extent" on those in the second (1995) edition of the authoritative *Encyclopedia of Bioethics* (cf. entry 691), and it even lists and acknowledges the editors of that work and the authors of the original articles. Alphabetically arranged sections address broad topics such as animals, death and dying, genetics, population, religious perspectives, sex and gender, and transplants and other technical devices. Subtopics within sections vary in their organization. A "general topics" section at the end collects entries that do not fit under one of the major rubrics, for example, advertising, circumcision, quality of life. The format of the work is designed to appeal to its intended audience, with many photographs, sidebar definitions, quotations, and bold section headings. It also includes suggestions for related readings; appendices with selected legal cases, medical codes and oaths, and general bibliography; and a comprehensive index.

678.   Bowman, James S. and Frederick A. Elliston. **Ethics, Government, and Public Policy: A Reference Guide.** New York: Greenwood, 1988. 341p.

Despite its subtitle, this must be considered a borderline reference work. It offers 12 essays, framed by an introduction and concluding analysis, on significant aspects of ethics in government and public policy, but these probably do not come close to a comprehensive overview. Reference value is enhanced, however, by a common structure shared by most of the essays, which includes an introduction to the subject matter, a "background and literature review" section, and at the end a substantial bibliography. Topics addressed include, for example, individual ethics and organizational morality, controversies in risk analysis, negotiating rules, equal opportunity and affirmative action in employment decisions, fraud and waste in government, and morality in foreign policy. Most discussions mix considerations of principle with practical issues concerning the "management" of ethics in government and public policy arenas.

679.   Burley, Justine, and John Harris, eds. **A Companion to Genethics.** Oxford: Blackwell, 2002. 489p. (Blackwell Companions to Philosophy).

A number of the Blackwell Companions to Philosophy fall on the borderline of the category "reference works," but this one especially. A thematically organized survey of its subject, it lacks even the reference features of some other thematically organized Companions, such as a glossary or extensive bibliography. Nonetheless, it offers a valuable and convenient overview and stocktaking of the multifaceted ethical debates surrounding the science of genetics and its actual or potential applications. There are 34 essays by 36 authors or co-authors grouped under 5 headings: (1)" Genetics: Setting the Scene"; (2) "Genetic Research"; (3) "Gene Manipulation and Gene Selection"; (4) "Genotype, Phenotype, and Justice"; (5) "Ethics, Law, and Policy." Noted genetics researcher Sir David Weatherall provides an afterword. Name/subject index.

680.   Canto-Sperber, Monique, ed. **Dictionnaire d'éthique et de philosophie morale.** 4th ed., rev. & augm. Paris: Presses universitaires de France, 2004. 2,199p.

The first edition of this well-received French dictionary appeared in 1996 and was followed in short order by three successively revised and expanded editions in 1997, 2001, and 2004. One U.S. scholar has characterized it as "an indispensable philosophical tool" (Laurence Thomas in *Ethics* 113 [2003]:685). It is particularly valuable for its continental

European perspective. However, the roughly 275 contributing authors include British and North American as well as French and other continental scholars. Besides ethical theories, schools of thought, and general ethics concepts, the 300 or so articles treat a wide range of applied ethics, from areas of application such as *éthique pénale* and nanotechnologies to specific ethical (or unethical) practices or principles such as *consentement et consentement informé, crime contre l'humanité, développement durable,* and *le principe du double effet.*

681. Chadwick, Ruth, ed. **The Concise Encyclopedia of Ethics in Politics and the Media.** San Diego: Academic Press, 2001. 335p.

This is in large part a derivative work: all but two of its 33 articles are drawn from the *Encyclopedia of Applied Ethics* (entry 690), though over half of these with some updating of content or bibliography. The new entries deal with campaign journalism and with ethics and media quality. The two spheres selected for attention here, politics and the media, interact extensively in contemporary society and share many analogous, overlapping, or mutually interacting ethical concerns, identified by editor Chadwick as centering around five key themes: professional ethics, democratic participation, minority issues, privacy, and freedom and responsibility (preface). In some articles, the connection between the two domains is very strong, for example, those on campaign journalism, censorship, confidentiality of sources, freedom of the press, pornography, and privacy versus the public's right to know. Others are more exclusive either to the realm of politics, such as those on civil disobedience, gun control, political obligation, and warfare strategies and tactics, or to the media domain, notably those on broadcast journalism, media depiction of ethnic minorities, objectivity in reporting, and tabloid journalism. Entries are arranged in a single alphabetical sequence.

682. Chadwick, Ruth, ed. **The Concise Encyclopedia of the Ethics of New Technologies.** San Diego: Academic Press, 2001. 404p.

Like entry 681, this is in large part a derivative work drawn from the *Encyclopedia of Applied Ethics* (entry 690). Of its 37 entries, 23 are taken verbatim or with minor updates from the parent work, 9 have more substantial updating (particularly those relating to genetics), and 5 are new articles. The "new technologies" in view here are predominantly biotechnologies, including especially reproductive, genetic, and health-care technologies, but there are also articles on, for example, computer and information ethics, hazardous and toxic substances, and nuclear power. Helping to frame issues specific to these various technology domains is a selection of more general articles, for instance those on consequentialism and deontology, feminist ethics, human nature, "playing God," and slippery slope arguments. The five entries new to this volume are cloning, geneticization, health technology assessment, intrinsic and instrumental value, and novel foods.

683. Childress, James F. and John Macquarrie, eds. **The Westminster Dictionary of Christian Ethics.** Philadelphia: Westminster, 1986. 678p.

Though theological ethics is its foremost concern, this dictionary (a revision of Macquarrie's *Dictionary of Christian Ethics* published by Westminster in 1967) also affords substantial coverage of philosophical perspectives, concepts, issues, and thinkers. Illustrative of philosophically oriented entries are catagorical imperative, choice, Confucian ethics, emotivism, Kantian ethics, natural law, right and wrong, and virtue. Such entries are often authored by contributors with well-established reputations in philosophy, such as A. C. Ewing and R. M. Hare. Whereas Macquarrie's original edition had articles on individual thinkers, including philosophers such as Aristotle, Bradley, and Mill, these have now been replaced by or absorbed into articles on the major traditions, movements, or themes these thinkers initiated or shaped: Aristotelian ethics, Idealist ethics, Utilitarianism, and so forth. The revised dictionary also reflects the dramatic growth in the realm of applied ethics since the 1967 original, with many more articles on topics in biomedical, environmental, political, and professional ethics. Contributors in this domain include leading scholars such as Childress himself, Lisa Sowle Cahill, Warren Reich, and LeRoy Walters.

Given the attention to both philosophical and theological concerns, there is sometimes less effort to bridge these two domains than one would hope, but the new edition has improved on the original in this respect. Theologically, the dictionary has a liberal-Protestant bent, yet is quite ecumenical, counting among its contributors a number of prominent Catholic, Evangelical, Orthodox, and Jewish scholars.

684.   Clarke, Paul Barry, and Andrew Linzey. **Dictionary of Ethics, Theology, and Society.** London: Routledge, 1996. 926p.

See entry 785.

685.   Cohen, Eliott D. and Deni Eliott. **Journalism Ethics: A Reference Handbook.** Santa Barbara, Calif.: ABC-Clio, 1997. 196p. (Contemporary Ethical Issues).

A useful, well-rounded reference resource for students and teachers of journalism, professional journalists, general readers, and philosophers or philosophy students interested in the application of ethics in particular professions. Setting a pattern for other volumes in its series (cf. entries 686, 688, and 704), it provides an introduction to its subject, including methods of analysis in journalism ethics and its relationship to law; a chronology of salient events in the field's development; biographical sketches of key contributors to the field, several of them also contributors to this volume; concise articles on 22 central topics such as journalistic objectivity, images and stereotypes, privacy, conflict of interest, and deception of sources; summaries of significant court cases; a compilation of codes of journalism ethics; a 20-page bibliography of both print and nonprint resources; a directory of organizations; and a glossary of terms.

686.   Dienhart, John William and Jordan Curnutt. **Business Ethics: A Reference Handbook.** Santa Barbara, Calif.: ABC-Clio, 1998. 444p. (Contemporary Ethical Issues).

The lengthiest of several volumes in the Contemporary Ethical Issues Series, this follows the general pattern for the series (cf. entries 685, 688, and 704) with minor variations. The authors' own description is largely apt: "As a reference work, this book is uniquely helpful. Beyond a bibliography of print and nonprint resources (including Web sites), we have also included information about ethical codes, professional and business organizations devoted to business ethics, short biographies of the leading figures in business ethics, and a list of important courts decisions, laws, and regulatory agencies" (preface). Add to that inventory, however, an introduction, which gives a general characterization of business ethics and discusses its "tools," and nearly 300 pages of articles on specific ethical issues and problem areas, organized thematically into four broad categories: the consumer, the corporation, the employee, and the environment. There is also a brief glossary. Both authors are philosophy professors.

687. Duncan, A. S., G. R. Dunstan and R. B. Welbourn, eds. **Dictionary of Medical Ethics.** New rev. ed. London: Darton, Longman & Todd; New York: Crossroad, 1981. 459p.

Though dated in a field where development has been rapid in the last few decades, this remains the only concise dictionary on medical ethics apart from Hedges's *Bioethics, Health Care, and the Law* (entry 699), which has a more strongly legal focus. Contributors are mainly British, and the majority are physicians, giving a somewhat different orientation from most American writings in this realm. Most articles still have some value for basic exposition of ethical issues in health care or related background information, and even their bibliographies of pre-1981 literature. For a more reliable picture of the current state of discussion or practice, however, users should consult more recent sources, notably Hedges's work and the third edition of the *Encyclopedia of Bioethics* (entry 691).

688. Elfstrom, Gerard. **International Ethics: A Reference Handbook.** Santa Barbara, Calif.: ABC-Clio, 1998. 240p. (Contemporary Ethical Issues).

Designed to meet a diverse panoply of reference needs concerning its topic at the level of students and general readers, this handbook on international ethics provides an introduction to the field, including its history, basic concepts, and methodology; a chronology; biographical sketches of key "issue makers and ethicists"; concise articles on 22 central topics such as free trade agreements, human rights, international systems of law, national sovereignty, refugees, war, and women's status; a compilation of significant documents; 40 pages of bibliography of both print and nonprint resources; a directory of organizations; and a glossary of terms.

689. **Encyclopaedia of Religion and Ethics.** Ed. James Hastings with the assistance of John A. Selbie . . . and other scholars. New York: Scribner's; Edinburgh: T. & T. Clark, 1908–22. 12 vols. plus index.

See entry 765.

690. **Encylopedia of Applied Ethics.** Ruth Chadwick, ed.-in-chief. San Diego: Academic Press, 1997. 4 vols.

This multidisciplinary work offers 282 articles concentrating on "areas . . . regarded as central in contemporary society such as issues concerning the environment, law, politics, the media, science and engineering, education, economics, the family and personal relationships, mental health and social work, policing and punishment, minority rights" (preface, vol. 1). Entries predominantly designate broad domains of application such as those aforementioned or more specific ethical problem areas such as animal research, birth control, internet protocol, media ownership, nuclear deterrence, plagiarism and forgery, property laws, safety laws, whistle-blowing, and zoos and zookeeping, among a multitude of others. But there are also articles dealing with specific ethical theories (e.g., consequentialism and deontology, Epicureanism, virtue ethics), moral traditions (Greek ethics, Islam, Thomism), or general concepts deployed in ethical discourse (autonomy, collective guilt, paternalism). Articles observe a standard format that begins with an outline, glossary, and defining statement, provides a discussion of typically 5,000 to 6,000 words, and concludes with cross-references and bibliography. There is a detailed subject index.

691.   Encyclopedia of Bioethics. 3rd ed. Stephen G. Post, editor in chief. New York: Macmillan Reference USA: Thomson/Gale, 2004. 5 vols.

For purposes of this encyclopedia, "bioethics" encompasses a vast range of ethical issues and value-related problems in the life sciences and health care. That its opening article happens to deal with probably the most prominent of these, abortion, seems fitting. But succeeding articles deal with issues as diverse as advertising of health care, behavior modification therapy, environmental ethics, genetic discrimination, informed consent in human research, population ethics and policies, sexual ethics, smoking, and warfare as it relates to medicine, public health, and use of biological and chemical weapons. Just as the second edition (New York: Macmillan; London: Simon & Schuster and Prentice Hall International, 1995, 5 vols.) introduced a number of topics new or newly prominent at that time—for example, AIDS, ecofeminism, hospice care—this third edition introduces new entries for topics that have emerged or gained urgency or increased attention over the past decade, for example, artificial nutrition and hydration, bioterrorism, cloning, dementia, and ethical and health issues of immigration. As the introduction notes, several broad topical areas "have been thoroughly redesigned, and are essentially new," for instance death and dying, law and bioethics, organ and tissue transplantation, and religion and ethics. It also reports that half of the content is "entirely new," while the remainder consists of "deeply revised and updated articles" excepting only a few articles deemed "classic" (p. xiii). The table of contents indicates which articles have been revised and by whom.

Not only articles on issues specific to bioethics but also articles providing essential background for intelligent discussion and assessment of those issues—on basic ethical concepts and principles, comprehensive ethical theories, religious traditions, historical perspectives, and surveys of disciplines bearing on bioethics—remain an important feature of this encyclopedia, and can often serve general uses beyond their application to bioethics. For instance, the survey under "ethics" (with five individually authored articles on the task of ethics, moral epistemology, normative ethical theories, social and political theories, and religion and morality) may profitably be used to supplement material in the *Encyclopedia of Ethics* (entry 675) or the general *Routledge Encyclopedia of Philosophy* (entry 150), or even substitute for these where they're not available. Equally valuable is the appendix containing the texts of major codes, oaths, and directives related to bioethics, which has grown from just over 200 pages in the second edition to nearly 300.

This is an interdisciplinary work, covering historical, theological, scientific, legal, and social scientific aspects as well as philosophical. The philosophical perspective is heavily represented, however, and many of the roughly 450 contributors are philosophers or teach in philosophy departments (though identification extends only to institutional affiliation). Besides disciplinary diversity, the contributors, whose ranks include virtually every major American writer in the field, represent broad diversity in ideological, political, and theological perspectives. Bioethics is enhanced, says the editor, "by dialogue between different traditions of thought, both secular and religious, reflecting the diversity of the public square" (p. xii). Even so, some perspectives, say those of the so-called Christian Right or of strictly official Catholicism, may not consider themselves as well represented as they could or should be. No one, however, can justly deny the encyclopedia's solid credentials or its foundational and even defining role for the field of bioethics.

692.   Encyclopedia of Bioethics. Rev. ed. CD-ROM. New York: Macmillan Library Reference/Simon & Schuster Macmillan, 1996.

This CD-ROM file contains the text of the second edition of the *Encyclopedia of Bioethics,* which has already been supplanted by a third edition (entry 691). The latter, however, has not been issued in this format. Also included on the disc is a cumulation of the annual *Bibliography of Bioethics* (see entry 645) from its inception in 1974 through the year 1995, a bonus not publicized on the disc label or the cover of the accompanying documentation. Both components can still perform some useful service if used with due regard for their limits and supplemented as appropriate by reference to their respective updates, which in the case of the bibliography includes the two online databases of the Kennedy Institute of Ethics cited in entries 653 and 654. An impressive array of retrieval and navigational aids facilitates consultation of both the encyclopedia and bibliography.

693.   Encyclopedia of Ethical, Legal, and Policy Issues in Biotechnology. Thomas H. Murray and Maxwell J. Mehlman, eds. New York: John Wiley, 2000. 2 vols. (Wiley Biotechnology Encyclopedias).

One of four encyclopedias in a series that otherwise deals with the scientific aspects and applications of biotechnology, this delves into the ethical issues raised by developments in this rapidly expanding field and the related issues posed for public policy and law. Though its concerns overlap to a considerable extent with those of the larger and wider ranging *Encyclopedia of Bioethics* (entry 691), it offers additional perspectives as well as more detail or more specific focus on topics within its narrower purview, which appears to be biological technologies operating at the cell or sub-cell (e.g., gene) level. It has, for instance, no less than seven articles dealing with different aspects of, or perspectives on, gene therapy, and an equal number on "human enhancement uses of biotechnology." Other major topics include, for example, agricultural biotechnology, cloning, genetic information, human subjects research, patents and licensing, and reproduction ethics relating specifically to biotechnology matters such as prenatal testing and sex selection. The 112 entries are arranged alphabetically. Contributors include many experts affiliated with research or policy institutes or with government agencies involved in policy roles, as well as university professors. Most write at a level appropriate for other specialists though often accessible to an educated general audience as well. Articles include references keyed by number to entries in the (often extensive) accompanying bibliographies.

694.   Ethics and Values. Danbury, Conn: Grolier Educational, 1999. 8 vols.

This set of eight somewhat slim volumes is "intended to help students come to grips with important issues of morality that bear on all our lives" (introduction). The students in question are presumably those in intermediate through secondary grade levels. The encyclopedia presents around 200 2- to 3-page articles arranged A–Z, the majority of them on specific areas of ethical decision and debate such as abortion, censorship, harassment, medical ethics, sexual behavior, and violence. A few, such as those on bullying and peer pressure, seem particularly pertinent for a teenage audience. Other articles deal with general ethical concepts—for example, character, good, ideals, rules, virtue—or with important background concepts or issues, such as belief, class, consequences, dogmatism, emotions, human nature, ideology, religion. There are no entries for technical terms of ethical theory like utilitarianism or deontological ethics, nor are these used in presenting the various sides on debated issues. The work does have articles on major religious, philosophical, and political systems that often undergird moral beliefs, including, for example, atheism, Buddhism, Christianity, communism and socialism, Hinduism, Islam, Judaism, and Taoism. Articles generally avoid taking sides, though it's sometimes questionable whether each of several opposing sides is displayed to equal advantage.

695. Ferm, Virgilius Ture Anselm, ed. **Encyclopedia of Morals.** New York: Philosophical Library, 1956. Reprinted, New York: Greenwood Press, 1969. 682p.

Though dated, Ferm's encyclopedia offer several features that afford it some continuing utility and interest. While philosophical concerns dominate, it also gives considerable attention to religious views and perspectives and, what is more unusual, to empirical description of moral systems observed in practice. For the latter, Ferm selected, with the advice of a group of anthropologists including Melville Herskovits, "a fairly generous slice of interesting examples of social behavior among societies quite unfamiliar to most readers" (preface), including groups as diverse as the Rio Grande Pueblo Indians, Aztecs, Aboriginals of Yirkalla (Australia), and Riffians (Moroccan Berbers). These certainly do not exhaust the world's variety, but are representative and offer food for philosophical reflection as well as engrossing social science. This material complements the more standard articles on religious systems (e.g., Christian, Jewish, Hindu) or subsystems (Quaker, Puritan, Jesuit), individual thinkers (e.g., Aquinas, Sidgwick, Schlick), and specific ethical theories or schools (e.g., Utilitarianism). In lieu of short definitions of terms, numerous cross-references direct the reader to broader topics where such terms are treated "in context."

Contributors include distinguished scholars of the previous generation such as Lewis White Beck, William Frankena, Walter Kaufmann, and Frederick Sontag.

696. Frederick, Robert E., ed. **A Companion to Business Ethics.** Oxford: Blackwell, 1999. 464p. (Blackwell Companions to Philosophy).

Provides a comprehensive thematically organized overview of the field of business ethics under four broad rubrics. Part 1 examines business ethics from the perspectives of diverse normative and meta-ethical theories including Utilitarianism, Kantianism, virtue ethics, Pragmatism, ethical relativism, feminist theory, and Postmodernism. Part 2 considers ethics in specific business "disciplines" such as management, finance, accounting, and marketing as well as its relationship to economics and other social science disciplines applied to business. Part 3 deals with a selection of specific yet broadly relevant issues pertaining to international business, corporate moral agency, employee rights, work, environmental responsibility, social responsibility, and business ethics and religion. Part 4 reviews the historical origins of business ethics and examines facets of its contemporary practice such as regulatory efforts, codes of conduct, investigation of ethical breaches and due process, and corporate leadership. Special reference features include a 13-page bibliography and 2 appendices containing directories of Web resources and U.S. and international business ethics organizations.

697. Frey, R. G. and Christopher Hea Wellman, eds. **A Companion to Applied Ethics.** Malden, Mass.: Blackwell, 2003. 698p. (Blackwell Companions to Philosophy, 26).

"Applied ethics," observe the editors, "is the largest growth area of philosophy today, and we here feature a variety of original pieces designed to capture the breadth and depth of the writing in the general field today. Our aim has been to select the best philosophers we could on some of the topics we thought likely to be of interest to a broad public of specialists and non-specialists alike . . . " (preface). The 50 essays are not explicitly divided into any categories. And while loose thematic groupings are discernible—roughly, political and social ethics, bioethics, professional ethics, and environmental ethics, with some miscellaneous topics interspersed—the chapters, as the editors state, "may be read in any order." Had they been arranged alphabetically, as they easily might have been (with most existing chapter titles serving unchanged as entry terms), this would be deemed an encyclopedic dictionary, no questions asked. As it is, its status as a "reference work" will appear less certain. Doubts on that score might focus more appropriately on the fact that contributors often go beyond describing issues to arguing a particular viewpoint. Nonetheless, that there is a good deal of reference value in this work need not be questioned. The essays generally provide excellent entrees into significant topics in applied ethics ranging from broad subdivisions of the field, such as bioethics and business ethics, to specific issues like racism, sexism, genetic engineering, surrogate motherhood, experimentation on human subjects, corporate responsibility, whistle-blowing, computer ethics, and values in nature. A few topics the editors judged worthy of inclusion were nonetheless omitted because they felt unable to find excellent philosophers to take them on (preface).

A number of the areas treated succinctly in this work are covered more expansively in separate Blackwell Companions devoted to bioethics (entry 702), genetics (entry 679), and business ethics (entry 696).

698.   Grenz, Stanley J. and Jay T. Smith. **Pocket Dictionary of Ethics.** Downers Grove, Ill.: InterVarsity Press, 2003. 128p.

Provides brief, very basic and nontechnical explanations of around 300 terms common in writings and debates about ethics. Entries include concepts from both philosophical and theological ethics as well as topics in areas of application such as bioethics, sexual ethics, and the ethics of warfare. Biographical entries are limited to a few classical thinkers. This aptly titled pocket guide evinces the broadly evangelical Protestant perspective associated with its publisher, but it stays mainly descriptive rather than prescriptive even when summarizing Christian views on issues.

699.   Hedges, Richard. **Bioethics, Health Care, and the Law: A Dictionary.** Santa Barbara, Calif.: ABC-Clio, 1999. 234p. (Contemporary Legal Issues).

This dictionary focuses on ethics issues specific to the field of human health care, though it occasionally intrudes into issues of the wider domain of bioethics, for example animal experimentation. It also has a particular concern with the law—meaning U.S. law—as a codification of society's decisions on many of these issues. Written for "readers at many educational levels" both inside and outside the health care professions (preface), it mainly provides succinct explanations of terms and concepts (e.g., deontological theory, informed consent, nonmaleficence) together with succinct overviews of key issues surrounding specific medical practices or procedures (e.g., autopsy, in vitro fertilization, nutrition and hydration), conditions or situations (AIDS, coma, conjoined twins), and economic, legal, and social provisions that affect the availability, distribution, cost, and quality of health care or its specific applications (e.g., advanced directives, ethics committees, health insurance, managed care). There are also a small number of entries for key individuals, organizations, famous cases, and the most important legal cases or statutes. The dictionary provides clear and useful introductions to these topics, though health care professionals, patients, or patients' relatives confronting concrete ethical questions or dilemmas will probably want and need greater depth such as afforded by the *Encyclopedia of Bioethics* (entry 691). There is a short general bibliography, but individual articles include no bibliographic references.

700.   Hester, Joseph P. **Encyclopedia of Values and Ethics.** Santa Barbara, Calif.: ABC-Clio, 1996. 376p.

Hester's introduction to this encyclopedia, of which he is the sole author, strongly suggests a primarily descriptive intent: to describe the values and ethics of contemporary America and the historical, religious, philosophical, ideological, and (cross-)cultural influences that have shaped them, as distinct from a focus on issues of validity, foundational principles, coherence, clarification, and sound application that are the stuff of philosophical ethics. The expectation thus raised by the introduction is borne out to a large extent in the body of the encyclopedia, yet there is rather more evaluative comment on and analysis of positions and arguments than one might infer from it. Hester's personal views and assessments play a substantial role in that regard. For beginning students and general readers primarily, the roughly 400 entries for terms, issues, movements, events, controversies, organizations, thinkers, and leaders offer much useful and interesting information and food for thought. However, the selection of topics or their treatment is sometimes idiosyncratic. For instance, there's a substantial article on alternative medicine, with little overt connection to ethics and values, but no entries for violence or war. Bibliographies suggest useful additional sources but reflect the scope of one man's reading and knowledge rather than the carefully weighed selections of specialists. All in all, this work will best serve as a supplementary but not a core resource on ethics and values, even for a general audience.

701.   Höffe, Otfried, et. al., eds. **Lexikon der Ethik.** 6th rev. ed. Munich: C. H. Beck, 2002. 317p.

Packing a great deal of material into a compact format, this German dictionary defines and explains key concepts of ethics (e.g., *kategorischer Imperativ, MetaEthik, Sittlichkeit*), canvasses views on significant ethical issues and problem areas (*Diskriminierung, Medizinische Ethik, Selbstmord, Sexualität*), and surveys major schools and periods of ethical theory (*Chinesische u. japanische Ethik, Marxistische Ethik, Utilitarismus*). There are no biographical entries, however. Höffe's *Lexikon* is particularly useful for Continental perspectives, references to Continental literature in its bibliographies, and concise information on Continental schools of thought, such as the *Konstruktive Ethik* of the Erlanger School, that are rarely represented in English-language reference works (even, for example, Becker and Becker's *Encyclopedia of Ethics,* entry 675). (The foregoing annotation is based on the 1992 fourth edition.)

A French translation of an earlier edition of this work, with some adaptation, was published as *Petit dictionnaire d'éthique* (Fribourg, Switz.: Ed. Universitaires; Paris: Ed. du Cerf, 1993, 371p.).

702.   Kuhse, Helga, and Peter Singer, eds. **A Companion to Bioethics.** Oxford: Blackwell, 1998. 512p. (Blackwell Companions to Philosophy).

While it provides a useful wide-ranging overview of the field of bioethics, its thematic organization and lack of special reference features (such as a glossary or extensive bibliography) place this in the "borderline reference work" category. There are 46 essays grouped into 14 sections covering broad themes such as issues involving embryos and fetuses, the "new" genetics, life and death issues, AIDS, experimentation with animals, ethical issues in the practice of health care, and the teaching and practice of bioethics. There is also a brief introduction and a general index.

703. **Lexikon der Bioethik.** Wilhelm Korff, et. al., eds. Gütersloh: Gütersloher Verlagshaus, 1998. 3 vols.

This German encyclopedia treats bioethical issues within an avowedly Christian and more specifically, though not so avowedly, Catholic orientation. This does not imply that a single perspective is presented on all issues. For example, the general topic *Ethik* is covered by three articles representing philosophical, Catholic, and Protestant perspectives. Bioethics is defined broadly to encompass the categories of medical ethics, human-ecological ethics, and environmental ethics. A detailed review of this work by Michael Werner, which notes both strengths and weaknesses but may be less than sympathetic to its religious orientation, concludes that "although in many areas there is useful and current information . . . the [*Lexikon der Bioethik*] is only a somewhat helpful tool for orientation in bioethical controversies because of its conceptual weakness, the fluctuating academic quality of the entries and the limited validity, in terms of worldview, of some ethical judgments. A work equal to the *Encyclopedia of Bioethics* [see entry 691] in the German language is still, therefore, not in sight" (http://micha.h.werner.bei.t-online.de/Werner-1998e.htm, accessed May 23, 2004).

704. Palmer, Clare. **Environmental Ethics: A Reference Handbook.** Santa Barbara, Calif.: ABC-Clio, 1997. 192p. (Contemporary Ethical Issues).

Aimed particularly, one gathers, at students and general readers, this handbook both provides an entree to environmental ethics and meets a variety of potential reference needs relating to this field. It includes an introductory overview; a chronology; biographical sketches of historically important figures and current contributors to the field; concise articles on 19 central topics such as biodiversity, climate change, Gaia, hunting and fishing, population, tourism, and waste; a section on U.S. laws, regulations, and court cases; codes of practice; a directory of organizations; a 28-page bibliography of both print and nonprint resources; and a glossary of terms.

705. Roth, John K., ed. **Ethics.** Rev. ed. Pasadena, Calif.: Salem Press, 2005. 3 vols.

Though it's not apparent from its title, this is an alphabetically organized encyclopedic dictionary. The first edition (Salem Press, 1994, 3 vols.) carried the series title "Ready Reference" and also appeared (with miniscule revisions) in a single-volume British edition with the more revealing title *International Encyclopedia of Ethics* (London: Fitzroy Dearborn, 1995, 988p.). "Ethics" is interpreted broadly by this encyclopedia to encompass issues of social and political as well as personal ethics, and the examination of these issues from a wide range of perspectives: religious, legal, sociological, and psychological as well as philosophical. Traditional philosophical ethics is well represented by many and substantial entries both topical (e.g., consequentialism, hedonism, is/ought distinction, metaethics, supererogation, universalizability) and biographical or historical (Confucian ethics, Epicurus, Existentialism, Kant, Post-Enlightenment ethics, Spinoza, etc.). But the special strength of this work is its wide-ranging coverage of applied ethics, including the areas of animal rights, bioethics, environmental ethics, political and judicial ethics, the ethics of science and computing, civil and human rights, military ethics, the ethics of sex and gender, and the ethics of the arts and censorship. As compared with the standard *Encyclopedia of Ethics* by L. and C. Becker (entry 675) and Chadwick's *Encyclopedia of Applied Ethics* (entry 690), Roth's work is aimed more at students and general readers, less at scholars, but the coverage he offers is broad, detailed, and respectably authoritative. Many articles from the first edition have been revised for the second, and there are now over a thousand entries, up from 817 in the first edition. New entries include both emerging areas of ethical concern (e.g., computer misuse, corporate compensation, lotteries, outsourcing, even cell phone etiquette) as well as entries reflective of events currently or recently in the news (Iraq, Jihad, Napster, Roman Catholic priests scandal, Rwanda genocide). There is a substantial list of contributing authors, though fewer prominent names will be found among these than are presented by the Beckers and by Chadwick.

The second edition achieves enhanced visual appeal over the first, as well as increased utility for the intended audience, with many illustrations, charts, graphs, maps, and sidebars. Bibliographies, generally short but nonetheless helpful, are provided with articles exceeding 500 words. Special features include timelines for the history of ethics and selected topics (e.g., apartheid); ready-reference listings of basic information at the head of each article (e.g., dates, "type of ethics," definition, significance, etc., as applicable), a general bibliography; a glossary; a list of Nobel Peace Prize winners; and indexes by categories, persons, and subjects.

706.   Singer, Peter, ed. **A Companion to Ethics.** Oxford: Blackwell, 1991. 565p. (Blackwell Companions to Philosophy).

Departing from the pattern of most Blackwell Companions to Philosophy that preceded it, Singer's work avoids the alphabetical dictionary/encyclopedia format, ostensibly to avoid treating ethics "as something remote, to be studied only by scholars locked away in universities" (introduction). Instead, it offers a more systematic "journey" through philosophical ethics via 47 essays, by an equal number of authorities, on major topics in the field: its history (e.g., the origin of ethics, ancient ethics, the great ethical traditions), its most fundamental questions and the principal answers thereto (e.g., natural law, the social contract tradition, egoism, virtue theory, all in a section titled "How Ought I to Live?"; and intuitionism, naturalism, subjectivism, and relativism, all under "The Nature of Ethics"); some important areas of application (e.g., world poverty, environmental ethics, euthanasia, sex, animals, business ethics, crime and punishment); and, finally, five significant sources of challenge and critique for the entire enterprise of ethics, discussed under the titles "The Idea of a Female Ethic," "The Significance of Evolution," "Marx Against Morality," "How Could Ethics Depend on Religion?" and "The Implications of Determinism." As much an introduction and survey text as a reference work, this Companion nonetheless distinguishes itself for reference functions by at least three features: an outline of contents that includes an abstract for each essay; an exceptionally detailed index; and an uncommonly authoritative group of contributors, including a number of prominent contemporary names in the field (e.g., Kurt Baier, R. M. Hare, Mary Midgley, Robert Solomon).

Singer, an Australian philosopher who has since moved to Princeton and earned some notoriety for his personal views, acknowledges the slant of his work toward the Western tradition (p. xxii), though he is not so explicit about its Anglo-American slant when it comes to recent and contemporary thought. He has included, however, essays on Indian,

Buddhist, Classical Chinese, and Islamic ethical traditions (paralleling essays on Jewish and Christian ethics), and there are occasional references to non-Western ethics in other essays.

707.   Slovar' po ētike. Ed. I. S. Kona. 5th ed. Moscow: Izd-vo Politicheskoi Literatury, 1983. 445p.

For anyone who can read Russian, or has access to a translator, this dictionary of ethics can be an excellent source on Marxist-Leninist ethics and formerly officially sanctioned Soviet perspectives on morality. It covers the history of ethical thought as well as specific topics in moral and social philosophy. First published in 1965 under the title *Kratkii slovar' po ētike,* it saw a rapid succession of later editions under the present title in 1970, 1975, and 1981.

708.   Terkel, Susan Neiburg and R. Shannon Duvall, eds. Encyclopedia of Ethics. New York: Facts on File, 1999. 302p.

Titled identically with the three-volume work by Becker and Becker (entry 675), this *Encyclopedia of Ethics* also shares a similar range of topics but is pitched at high school and early undergraduate students and general readers. Articles tend to be brief, ranging from around 75 words to around 1,500. The majority fall into four major categories that are helpfully defined in the introduction: descriptive ethics, metaethics, normative ethics, and applied ethics. In the latter category particularly, the editors strive to maintain a contemporary focus, selecting "the most pressing and significant problems" likely to interest students (introduction). Biographical entries are included fairly selectively and seek to "offer a balance . . . between those who have made erudite contributions and those who have contributed little academic discourse but much to the intense public debate about ethics" (preface). The editors acknowledge including some women "who may appear to be somewhat obscure and unknown" but whose contributions they regard as seminal even so. Individual articles do not have bibliographies. A five-page general bibliography, while useful, could have been more so if divided into at least a few broad categories.

709.   Wells, Donald A., ed. An Encyclopedia of War and Ethics. Westport, Conn.: Greenwood, 1996. 539p.

This encyclopedia focuses on principles and practices on both sides of a traditional distinction relating to the ethics of warfare: the ethical justification, or absence thereof, for engaging in warfare *(jus ad bellum)* and the moral restraints, if any, governing the conduct of warfare *(jus in bello)*. With regard to the former, it gives attention, for example, to both the extreme negative position, absolute pacifism, and to the important "just war" tradition, which also encompasses numerous issues in the second category. Entries include important concepts and terms (e.g., aggression, the combatant–noncombatant distinction, intentionality and double-effect); key documents and cases (the Geneva conventions of 1949, Red Cross Draft Rules for Civilian Protection, Nuremberg Trials); major thinkers on war and morality (Jane Addams, Carl von Clausewitz, Meng-tzu), major religious, philosophical, and ideological traditions (Christianity, Hinduism, Maoism); specific techniques, methods, and instruments of war that raise special issues (fragmentation bombs, guerila warfare, incendiaries, nuclear war); notorious breaches or alleged breaches of moral conduct in war (the Holocaust, the My Lai incident, war crimes in the former Yugoslavia); and collateral phenomena of warfare (collateral damage, conscription, environmental effects, prisoners of war). Among some regrettable omissions are articles on revolution, civil war, or occupation and the special ethical issues these might raise.

One additional but somewhat disappointing category of entries is that of specific wars or quasi-wars, such as the Arab-Israeli Wars of 1948–72 or the invasion of Grenada, confined to post-World War II events and usually involving the United States. Though presumably intended to relate theory to practice, these articles too often lack an explicit focus on the ethical issues at stake, as is the case for those on the Korean War, the Bay of Pigs incident, and Haiti.

Despite its several defects, this encyclopedia is solid and helpful on the whole, and benefits from the work of nearly four dozen well-credentialed contributors.

710. Werhane, Patricia H., and R. Edward Freeman, eds. **Blackwell Encyclopedic Dictionary of Business Ethics.** Malden, Mass.: Blackwell, 1998. 712p. (The Blackwell Encyclopedia of Management).

This dictionary, aimed broadly at academics, students, and business practitioners, was initially published in 1997 as volume 11 of the 12-volume *Blackwell Encyclopedia of Management,* then issued separately. Its 300 or so articles include entries on specific areas of business (e.g., advertising, finance, human resources, real estate sales), treating the key ethical issues and standards of each; on specific ethically challenging or ethically problem-atic practices (e.g., affirmative action, alcohol and tobacco advertising, insider trading); on business ethics in various countries or regions (including Africa, Canada, Europe, Israel, Japan, Russia, South Africa, and the United States); on general ethical theories and concepts (e.g., altruism and benevolence, compensatory justice, impartial spectator theories); and on key figures in the history of business ethics and its multidisciplinary tributaries (e.g., Aristo-tle, Drucker, Nozick, Rawls, Adam Smith). Most articles include bibliographies, sometimes listing a dozen or more sources. Contributors are predominantly U.S. university professors, either in business administration and related areas (accounting, economics, public adminis-tration, etc.) or in philosophy.

OTHER REFERENCE SOURCES

711. **Applied Ethics on WWW.** Administered by Chris MacDonald. URL: http://www.ethicsweb.ca/resources.

See entry 716.

712. **Center for Study of Ethics in the Professions (CSEP), Illinois Institute of Technology.** http://ethics.iit.edu/ (accessed October 28, 2005).

The CSEP Web site is particularly useful for its extensive Codes of Ethics Online. Contents range from codes for wide-ranging professions with many members, such as those of the American Medical Association and National Society of Profes-sional Engineers, to codes for narrow specialties like those of the Weimaraner Club of America or the American Rock Art Research Association. Other useful features of this site include links to other ethics centers and resources and access to the catalog for the Center's extensive library on professional ethics, which can serve as a virtual bibliography of the field.

713. **Codes of Professional Responsibility: Ethics Standards in Business, Health, and Law.** 4th ed. Rena A. Gorlin, ed. Washington, D.C.: Bureau of National Affairs, 2000. 1149p.

Codes of ethics or professional conduct adopted and sometimes enforced (to varying degrees) by professional associations rarely engage in overt philosophical justification or analysis of the standards they promulgate. Yet they are often products of philosophical reflection, among other contributories, and in any case they provide material for further philosophical reflection on the specific matters they cover or on general principles. Thus this compilation can be a valuable resource for philosophers and students thinking about applied or even theoretical ethics. Represented are some 60 codes or similar documents ("statements of principles," "ethical guidelines," etc.) within the three domains listed in the subtitle, which are broader than might appear—including, for instance, architecture, computing, engineering, and journalism under "business," and mental health and social work under "health." Bonuses provided by this volume are a directory of organizations and programs concerned with professional responsibility, both U.S.-based and worldwide (pp. 815–879), and an extensive guide to information resources including periodicals, reference works, and Web sites (pp. 881–969). Indexes of issues, professions, and organizations.

714.   Environmental Ethics. Center for Environmental Philosophy, University of North Texas. http://www.cep.unt.edu (October 29, 2005).

Besides providing information about the Center for Environmental Philosophy and its activities, this Web site hosts the *International Society of Environmental Ethics Bibliography,* which at last available count (2003) had over 13,000 entries. It also offers a good selection of links to other environmental ethics sites as well as a number of more general ethics or philosophy Web sites.

715.   Ethics Updates. Edited by Lawrence M. Hinman. Values Institute, University of San Diego. http://ethics.sandiego.edu (accessed October 29, 2005).

The *Ethics Updates* site describes itself as "designed primarily to be used by ethics instructors and their students" and "intended to provide updates on current literature, both popular and professional, that relates to ethics." Offerings at this Web site are divided into three major categories: ethical theory, applied ethics, and a general "resources" category. Each of the first two is subdivided into 14 specific topics (e.g., under the first, ethical relativism, rights theories, utilitarianism; under the second, environmental ethics, euthanasia, poverty and welfare, etc.), with varying menus of resources offered. Typically they include bibliographies and literature surveys as well as links to online texts, papers, and the Web sites of related organizations, sometimes including advocacy groups. They may also include, more sporadically, links to video resources at a companion *Ethics Videos* Web site, powerpoint presentations (many by the site's founder and editor, Lawrence Hinman), online discussions and lectures, or links to legal document or decisions. Subcategories under the general "resources" heading include a collection of case studies accompanied by online discussion folders, a guide to writing ethics papers, an ethics glossary, a calendar of events (conferences, seminars, etc.), and curricular resources for both K–12 and higher education.

716.   Ethicsweb.ca. Administered by Chris MacDonald. http://www.ethicsweb.ca (accessed October 29, 2005).

This Canadian Web site fronts a dozen or more distinct Web sites concerned with applied ethics including, among others, *BusinessEthics.ca, EthicsCommittee.ca* (devoted to resources for ethics committees in health care), *FeministEthics.ca, MedicalEthics.ca, NonProfit Ethics.com, ProfessionalEthics.ca,* and *StemCells.ca.* Most of these include internal divisions for Canadian resources and international resources, with the latter well represented. Of particular value within the *Ethicsweb.ca* site itself is a section titled *Applied Ethics on WWW.* This provides a well-organized general directory and gateway (with no apparent Canadian bias) to Web resources categorized by the major areas of applied ethics: business, health care, research, science and technology, animal welfare, environmental, computer, professional, media, public sector and government, and international. Standard subcategories are applied to each area as applicable, for example, organizations, topics and issues, codes of ethics, publications.

717.   International Directory of Bioethics Organizations. Ed. Anita L. Nolen and Mary Carrington Coutts. Washington, D.C.: National Reference Center for Bioethics Literature, Kennedy Institute of Ethics, Georgetown University, 1993. 371p. (Bioethics Resource Series, vol. 1).

This directory, now seriously dated, provided information on 278 organizations in 41 countries involved with issues of medical ethics: institutions offering academic degrees in the field, associations, research centers, and groups offering ethics consulting services. An updated print edition is not foreseen (information as of May 2004), but a current, online version of the directory is maintained by the National Reference Center for Bioethics Literature on its Web site at http://www.georgetown.edu/research/nrcbl/linksorgs.htm (cf. entry 718).

718.   National Reference Center for Bioethics Literature, Kennedy Institute of Ethics. http://www.georgetown.edu/research/nrcbl/nrc/index.htm (accessed October 29, 2005).

This important Web site for bioethics provides access to the Kennedy Institute's own databases, *ETHX on the Web* (entry 653) and *Genetics and Ethics* (entry 654), as well as links to the databases of the National Library of Medicine. Also offered are "Quickbibs" bibliographies on over a dozen prominent bioethics topics such as assisted suicide and stem cell research, and an online form for requesting a custom bibliographic search. Another valuable resource here is an international directory, by countries, of bioethics organizations, with links to their Web sites. Additional features of the site include information about the collections, services, programs, and publications of the NRCBL, and links to information about the wider activities, programs, and partnerships of the Kennedy Institute of Ethics.

719.   Professional Codes of Conduct in the United K.5ingdom: A Directory. 2nd ed. New York: Mansell/Cassell, 1996. 438p.

Serves a function similar to that of entry 713, which compiles chiefly U.S. codes, but includes an even larger number of codes in full—around 200—and provides brief descriptions of around 300 additional codes of U.K. professional organizations. Entries are arranged alphabetically by the name of the organization. Includes a 20-page introduction and comprehensive subject index.

720. **Source Book in Bioethics: A Documentary History.** Albert R. Jonsen, Robert M. Veatch, and LeRoy Walters, eds. Washington, D.C.: Georgetown University Press, 1998. 520p.

Gathers key documents from the last half century "that have both defined the fundamental issues in the field of bioethics and established ways of managing them in our society" (cover blurb). "Bioethics" for this purpose is construed somewhat narrowly as confined to human-related issues, especially medical ethics. There are 46 documents grouped into 5 parts, dealing with ethical issues concerning human subjects research, death and dying, human genetics, human reproductive technologies and arrangements, and the changing health care system. Examples include the "Nuremberg Code," the "Tuskegee Syphilis Study" final report, the New Jersey Supreme Court decision "In the Matter of Karen Quinlan," the President's Commission report on "Screening and Counseling for Genetic Conditions," the "Instruction on Respect for Human Life" of the Catholic Congregation for the Doctrine of the Faith, and the "Uniform Anatomic Gift Act." Brief introductions to each document are provided by the editors, all eminent scholars in the field of bioethics.

18
Logic and the Philosophies of Mathematics, Science, and Social Sciences

BIBLIOGRAPHIES

721. Ashworth, E. J. **The Tradition of Medieval Logic and Speculative Grammar from Anselm to the End of the Seventeenth Century: A Bibliography from 1836 Onwards.** Toronto: Pontifical Institute of Medieval Studies, 1978. 111p.

Records secondary works (books, articles, some lengthy book reviews, and a few dissertations) and modern editions of texts concerned with formal logic from the period indicated in the main title. Its scope is conceived "as including such topics as consequences, syllogistic, supposition theory, and speculative grammar, but as excluding such topics as the categories, the struggle between nominalism and realism, and pure grammar" (pref.). Lists 879 items in two parts covering respectively the period up to and after Paul of Venice. Four indexes cover names, texts, translations, and subjects.

722. Blackwell, Richard J. **Bibliography of the Philosophy of Science, 1945–81.** Westport, Conn.: Greenwood Press, 1983. 585p.

Offers comprehensive coverage of the vast literature on the philosophy of science from the years designated in its title. In this period, Blackwell notes, the field emerged as "not only a separate and distinctive branch of philosophy but more significantly as a role model which has had considerable impact on the more traditional parts of philosophy," and often beyond philosophy, as in "one preeminent case, Kuhn's notion of cognitive paradigms" (introduction). The bibliography comprehends both issues concerning the methodology, epistemology, and conceptual framework of science, and issues raised by specific scientific concepts, doctrines and theories, such as quantum mechanics and relativity theory in the physical sciences, biological species and evolution in the biological sciences. Excluded are cognate areas such as philosophy of logic and mathematics, philosophy of technology, philosophy of social sciences, and value issues raised by the natural sciences.

Items cited include books, articles in journals and collections, and book reviews, but not dissertations. Arrangement is topical, and there is an author index. Appendices list volumes in three major series in the philosophy of science, which are also frequently referenced in the bibliography.

723. Cassel, Jeris F., and Robert J. Congleton. **Critical Thinking: An Annotated Bibliography.** Metuchen, N.J.: Scarecrow, 1993. 403p.

See entry 748.

724. Risse, Wilhelm. **Bibliographia Logica.** Hildesheim: Georg Olms, 1965–1979. 4 vols.

No other branch of philosophy presently possesses a bibliography quite so extensive and comprehensive as this one for logic, which is a by-product, as the *Vorwort* explains, of Risse's systematic history of the development of logic, *Die Logik der Neuzeit* (1964–).

Volume 1 (1965, 293p.) lists in chronological arrangement monographs published from 1472 to 1800. Volume 2 (1973, 494p.) does the same for the period 1801–1969. Both volumes cite holding libraries (mainly European but also some American) for most of the works listed. Volume 3 (1979, 412p.) lists articles published both in periodicals and in anthologies, arranged according to a detailed classification system outlined in the front. Volume 4 (1979, 390p.) is a catalogue of 3,006 manuscripts, arranged by author if known and by title if anonymous, with separate sections for medieval and more recent manuscripts. Holding libraries or archives are indicated.

All volumes are thoroughly indexed.

725. Robert, Jean-Dominique. **Philosophie et science: Eléments de bibliographie / Philosophy and Science: Elements of Bibliography.** Paris: Beauchesne, 1968. 384p. (Bibliothèque des archives de philosophie, nouvelle série, 8).

Prior to Blackwell's 1983 work (entry 722), Robert's was the closest thing to a full-scale general bibliography of the philosophy of science. Its focus, however, is the relations between philosophy and science—or as the introduction puts it, "the problems set up both by the distinction between philosophy and sciences and also their necessary connection"—rather than philosophy of science as such. Many works by scientists which bear on these issues are included, among them a number of popular writings addressed to a wide public. Writings in French are probably most numerous, but English runs a very respectable second, with other European languages also well represented.

The majority of entries are grouped under *Travaux catalogues par nom d'auteurs* (works listed by authors' name). They are *coded* to indicate subject matter: for example, "B" for works relating to biology, "PY" for physics. Sections 3 and 4 are supplements to the main body of the bibliography, covering the years 1965–1966 and 1966–1967.

DICTIONARIES, ENCYCLOPEDIAS, AND HANDBOOKS

726. Baggini, Julian and Peter S. Fosl. **The Philosopher's Toolkit: A Compendium of Philosophical Concepts and Methods.** Malden, Mass.: Blackwell, 2003. 221p.

If logic in its broadest sense is concerned with how conclusions can be supported, then this can be characterized as a compendium of logical tools available to, and used by, philosophers—or anyone else. In any case, logic in the narrower (but still broad) sense embodied in many first-year logic texts accounts for a good share of the tools systematically catalogued and concisely described in this guide, particularly its first two chapters on "basic" and "further" tools for argument. Later chapters range increasingly beyond standard logic topics. "Tools for Assessment" addresses such matters as category mistakes, the is/ought gap, Leibniz's law of identity, and Ockham's razor. "Tools for Conceptual Distincitions" addresses, for example, the analytic/synthetic, necessary/sufficient, and type/token distinctions. "Tools for Radical Critique" discusses lines of critique as varied as class critique, empiricist critique of metaphysics, feminist critique, pragmatist critique, and Sartrean critique of "bad faith." Finally, "Tools at the Limit" takes on several controverted topics including basic beliefs, Gödel and incompleteness, possibility and impossibility, self-evident truths, and underdetermination of theory.

727. Bynum, William F., E. J. Browne, and Roy Porter, eds. **Dictionary of the History of Science.** Princeton: Princeton University Press, 1981. 494p.

Topics in the philosophy of science are a minority, but a substantial minority, among those covered by this excellent reference work. It usefully supplements existing dictionaries devoted specifically to philosophy of science (notably entries 730 and 742), and its combination of philosophical and historical material can offer some special benefits. An analytical table of contents in the front helpfully identifies 130 entries relating specifically to philosophy of science. Thirty-three of these are indicated to have bibliographies. Topics are as diverse as causality in quantum physics, Mill's canons, paradox of the ravens, and theory-laden terms. Other philosophical (or philosophically infused) topics are listed under the heading "Human Sciences" and include chain of being, man–machine, mind–body relation, and Social Darwinism.

There are no biographical entries as such, but a biographical index at the back gives basic biographical data as well as references to pertinent articles. It includes numerous philosophers, both classical (Bacon, Descartes, Leibniz, Mach, Spencer) and recent or contemporary (Carnap, Nagel, Popper).

728. Detlefsen, Michael, David Charles McCarty, and John B. Bacon. **Logic from A to Z.** London: Routledge, 1999. 116p.

This is in considerable part a derivative work: a cover blurb proclaims that it was "first published in the most ambitious international philosophy project for a generation: the *Routledge Encyclopedia of Philosophy.*" Yet despite this frank and unqualified acknowledgement, this is *not* simply a reprinting or reformatting of the article "Logical and mathematical terms, glossary of" in the print version of the *REP* (entry 150), although that constitutes its core. For example, *Logic from A to Z* has 36 entries (not counting cross-references) under "A," while the *REP* article has just 9. And under "M," the entry count is 15 versus 8. In addition, some duplicated entries have had minor revisions, for example, those for "analytic/synthetic" and "normal form (conjunctive)." Thus even individuals and libraries that have the print *REP* may find this a worthwhile supplementary resource for the technical vocabulary of formal logic and philosophy of mathematics. Those with access to the online *REP* (entry 152) will find the additions and revisions incorporated there.

Another useful feature here is a table of logical symbols. Occasionally, the work falls short. For instance, it lacks entries for "modal logic" or "modality" though these occur in the definitions of other terms such as "*de re / de dicto*" and "syllogism, modal." (In the full *REP,* this omission from the glossary is remedied by several independent articles on modal logic.)

A companion volume for informal logic is entry 745.

729. **Dictionary of Logic as Applied in the Study of Language: Concepts/Methods/ Theories.** Ed. Witold Marciszewski. The Hague: Martinus Nijhoff, 1981. 436p. (Nijhoff International Philosophy Series, vol. 9).

While the main theme of this dictionary is the application of logic in the study of language, many of its articles should be of more general interest to logicians, philosophers of science and mathematics, information scientists, and others. It does presuppose an advanced level of knowledge of the general field of logic. The 72 articles (there are no short definitions) treat topics as diverse as analyticity, the method of counterexample, decidability, definition, Gödel's theorem, many-valued logic, Polish notation, quantifiers, questions, logical syntax, trees, truth, and the theory of types. Each article includes bibliographic references, and there is a general bibliography at the back (dominated by English-language writings, perhaps surprising in view of the fact that the editor and 13 of 15 contributors are Polish scholars). Also at the back are an index of symbols and a subject index and glossary, the latter serving mainly to correlate synonymous terms and expressions.

730.   Durbin, Paul T. **Dictionary of Concepts in the Philosophy of Science.** Westport, Conn.: Greenwood Press, 1988. 362p. (Reference Sources for the Social Sciences and Humanities, no. 6).

Durban describes his work as presenting a "summary of approximately 100 basic controversies (or would-be controversies) covering all the subfields of contemporary philosophy of science. . . . The most likely users of the book are upper level undergraduate students taking a philosophy of science course or thinking about doing so, graduate students similarly situated, or educated general readers. . . . " (introduction). Entries represent concepts around which controversies have grown up, including substantive scientific concepts (e.g., causality, evolution, forces and fields, quantum mechanics), methodological concepts (e.g., confirmation, falsification, hypothetico–deductive method), and domains of scientific thought or inquiry (e.g., astronomy, sociobiology). Articles include bibliographies. Index.

731.   Erickson, Glenn W., and John A. Fossa. **Dictionary of Paradox.** Lanham, Md.: University Press of America, 1998. 220p.

Not all paradoxes examined in this alphabetically arranged dictionary are philosophical, for example the paradox of acting and the productivity paradox. A good majority, however, are philosophical in nature or have philosophical import. Notable in the former category are various logical paradoxes, such as the famous liar's paradox and paradoxes of material implication, and paradoxes of self-reference such as those of cognitive relativism and the verification principle. There are also paradoxes relevant to philosophical domains such as ethics (e.g., the paradox of loyalty and the victim's paradox), political philosophy (e.g., the paradox of libertarianism and the paradoxes of voting), and philosophy of religion (e.g., the Eden paradox and the goodness problem). Paradoxes from other fields that have philosophical import include, for instance, Einstein's clock paradox and the Einstein-Podolsky-Rosen paradox from physics, and a variety of paradoxes from mathematics and set theory. Many entries follow a common pattern: formulation, explanation, and resolution (the latter usually presenting suggested or debated rather than definitive resolutions). Most also have references to related readings. A few articles discuss categories of paradox such as literary, logical, and mathematical.

732.   Fetzer, James H., and Robert F. Almeder. **Glossary of Epistemology/Philosophy of Science.** New York: Paragon House, 1993. 149p. (Paragon House Glossary for Research, Reading, and Writing).

See entry 637.

733.   Feys, Robert, and Frederic B. Fitch. **Dictionary of Symbols of Mathematical Logic.** Amsterdam: North Holland, 1969. 171p. (Studies in Logic and the Foundations of Mathematics).

That the label "dictionary" may not entirely fit this work is suggested both in the preface by Feys, the original editor, and the foreword by Fitch, who completed the project. Its purpose is "to enable the reader to find with some ease the meaning and interpretation of symbols currently used in mathematical logic," particularly in a handful of classic and standard texts (identified in the front) and in the *Journal of Symbolic Logic.* It is "intended for readers not having previous knowledge of mathematical logic as well as for logicians who want an explanation of a notation outside their usual fields" (preface), but would be difficult for a beginning student to use. The order of presentation is *systematic,* partly because "the language of mathematical logic is ... the language of a *formalized* theory," the exact meanings of whose symbols may not be grasped intuitively or given direct verbal translations, but must be understood in the context of the corresponding formalized system with its axioms, rules, and definitions.

Apart from preliminaries, there are nine chapters covering the following areas of logic: propositional calculus; first-order functional calculus; functional calculus of higher orders, and the theory of types; combinatory logic; calculus of classes; calculus of relations; arithmetic formalized as an independent discipline; numbers as defined within systems of logic; and metamathematics. Indexes of names, subjects, and symbols follow.

734.   Grattan-Guinness, Ivor. **Companion Encyclopedia of the History and Philosophy of the Mathematical Sciences.** London: Routledge, 1993. 2 vols.

The 176 articles in this *Companion Encyclopedia* are arranged into several sections ranging from Ancient and non-Western traditions through the influence and role of mathematics in contemporary culture. Philosophical issues associated with mathematics, while they do not play the major role throughout, receive attention at numerous points and most concentratedly in section 2.12 ("The philosophical context of medieval and Renaissance mathematics"), most of part 5 ("Logics, set theories, and the foundations of mathematics," including section 5.9, "Some current positions in the philosophy of mathematics"), section 6.9 ("The philosophy of algebra"), section 7.8 ("The philosophy of geometry to 1900"), and section 10.17 ("Philosophies of probability").

735.   Greenstein, Carol Horn. **Dictionary of Logical Terms and Symbols.** New York: Van Nostrand Reinhold, 1978. 188p.

"The primary objective ... is to present compactly, concisely, and side by side a variety of notational systems currently used by logicians, computer scientists, and engineers" (preface). That objective, and the considerable success with which it is achieved, should be appreciated by anyone who has ever contended with the differences among notational systems. Familiar, and less familiar, logical expressions, from simple connectives to basic argument forms, are shown not only in such notational systems as Boolean, Polish, Peano-Russell, Hilbert, and set-theory, but even in such modes of representation as logic gates, truth tables, Euler and Venn diagrams, and squares of opposition. In addition to coverage of the more conventional areas of logic—sentential, quantificational, syllogistic, and modal—there are separate sections for notation in epistemic, doxastic, deontic, and tense logics. Greenstein has also gone beyond her stated primary objective by providing two additional and highly useful features: a list of abbreviations and acronyms prevalent in logical and computer literature, and a 77-page glossary of logical terms.

736.   **Handbook of Philosophical Logic.** 2nd ed. Ed. D. M. Gabbay and F. Guenthner. Dordrecht, Netherlands: Kluwer Academic, 2001–. Vols. 1–.

A systematic survey of the key topics of philosophical logic rather than, say, an alphabetically arranged encyclopedia, this can be considered borderline as a reference work. However, in its comprehensiveness, and as the product of a collaborative effort by an international team of authorities, it does perform an encyclopedic function, or something close to it. As such it should prove useful, as the editors aver of the 4-volume first edition (Dordrecht: D. Reidel, 1983–89), not just to logicians or philosophers in general but also to linguists, mathematicians, and "consumers of logic in many applied areas" including computer science and artificial intelligence (vol. 1, preface). Perhaps regrettably, the editors have found that since the first edition "the subject has evolved and its areas have become interrelated to such an extent that it no longer makes sense to dedicate volumes to [specific] topics," though the volumes do, as they say, "follow some natural groupings of chapters" (ibid.). The second edition is projected to reach around 18 volumes. The latest at this writing is Volume 11, published in March 2004.

737.   Jacquette, Dale, ed. **A Companion to Philosophical Logic.** Malden, Mass.: Blackwell, 2002. 576p. (Blackwell Companions to Philosophy, 22).

Like some other Blackwell Philosophy Companions, this is borderline as a reference work—organized thematically rather than alphabetically and lacking special reference features apart from a short "Resources for Further Study" section (pp. 771–75) that includes some internet sites and a list of organizations—but it pulls together an unusually comprehensive and authoritative overview of its expansive field within the compass of a single volume. Around 50 authorities representing universities throughout the world, many of them leaders in the field, contributed the previously unpublished articles. All, says the editor, "are intended for an introductory audience, and can be read with good understanding by beginning students who have completed a first course in symbolic logic"—possibly a slightly optimistic assessment for some instances. All articles include bibliographic references, many also suggestions for further reading. No grand organizing scheme is transparent—the preface describes some "invisible divisions"—but the 46 articles are clustered into 14 of "the most important topic areas in philosophical logic from the standpoint of students as well as professionals in the field" (preface). Examples include "Historical Development of Logic"; "Symbolic Logic and Ordinary Language"; "Modal Logics and Semantics"; "Inductive, Fuzzy, and Quantum Probability Logics"; "Logic, Machine Theory, and Cognitive Science."

738.   Kondakov, Nikolai Ivanovich. **Logicheskii slovar'-spravochnik.** 2nd ed. Moscow: Nauka, 1975. 720p. German translation, **Wörterbuch der Logik.** Ed. Erhard Albrecht and Gunter Asser. Leipzig: Bibliografisches Institut, 1978. 554p.

This Russian work—note the German version—is probably the most comprehensive encyclopedic dictionary of logic built on an alphabetical arrangement and also centrally concerned with definitions. An earlier Russian edition was published in 1971 under the title *Logicheskii slovar'*.

739. Lecourt, Dominique, ed. **Dictionnarie d'histoire et de philosophie des sciences.** Paris: Presses universitaires de France, 1999. 1,032p.

Similar in concept to the 1981 *Dictionary of the History of Science* (entry 727), this more recent French dictionary integrates treatment of the philosophy of science with extensive coverage of the history of science that so often informs it. Historically oriented articles deal with the many branches of science from geology to astrophysics; with key theories, scientific breakthroughs, and inventions; with notable figures and institutions; and with substantive concepts of science that have raised philosophical issues, such as *anti-matière, force, infini,* and *"masse (de Newton à Einstein)."* Entries closely identified with philosophy of science explore aspects and issues of scientific method, for example, *adduction, induction, modèle;* the broad interpretation of science's results, for example, *formalisme, réalisme;* and wider philosophical problems raised in particularly pointed ways in the context of science, for example, *causalité, necessité, rationalité.* In contrast to its English-language counterpart, Lecourt's dictionary includes biographical articles both on history's leading scientists and on philosophers who have thought and written about the nature of science. There are separate indexes of names and subjects.

An international contingent of more than 150 scholars collaborated on this project.

740. Malone, Edward A., ed. **British Rhetoricians and Logicians, 1500–1660. First Series.** Detroit: Gale, 2001. 432p. (Dictionary of Literary Biography, vol. 236). **Second Series.** Detroit: Gale, 2003. 473p. (Dictionary of Literary Biography, vol. 281).

See entry 348.

741. Mittelstrass, Jürgen, et. al. **Enzyklopädie Philosophie und Wissenschaftstheorie.** Vols. 1 and 2: Mannheim: Bibliographisches Institut-Wissenschaftsverlag, 1980, 1984. Vols. 3–4: Stuttgart: J. B. Metzler, 1995–1996.

See entry 175.

742. Newton-Smith, W. H., ed. **A Companion to the Philosophy of Science.** Malden, Mass.: Blackwell, 2000. 576p. (Blackwell Companions to Philosophy, 18).

Provides encyclopedic, alphabetically organized treatment of philosophy of science in both its contemporary guise and, to some degree, its historical development. Articles range from 3 to 20 pages in length. Their topics range over comprehensive philosophies of science (descriptive/normative accounts of the nature and aims of science, for example, logical positivism, logical empiricism, realism and instrumentalism); philosophical problems surrounding specific aspects of scientific methodology or practice (e.g., explanation, induction, inference to the best explanation, observation and theory); philosophical issues raised by particular scientific disciplines or subject areas (e.g., biology, computing, quantum mechanics, social science); and philosophically problematic concepts used in substantive scientific discourse (e.g., causation, laws of nature, reduction, and space, time, and relativity). There are also biographical articles on 20 leading thinkers who shaped the modern Western conception of science, whether philosophers (e.g., Locke, Hume, Mill), practicing scientists (Galileo, Darwin, Einstein), or both (Descartes, Leibniz, Mach, and, arguably, Newton), or who count among the handful of most influential figures in twentieth-century philosophy of science (e.g., Feyerabend, Kuhn, Popper, Quine). Includes an index.

A new two-volume English-language work to be titled *The Philosophy of Science: An Encyclopedia* has been announced by Routledge. Edited by Sahotra Sarkar and Jessica Pfeifer, this shows promise of being even more comprehensive and detailed than the Blackwell *Companion* described previously. It will feature both topical and biographical entries. Some early notices indicated publication in spring 2004, but at this writing in November 2005 the work has not yet appeared and no revised projection is available.

743. Seiffert, Helmut and Gerard Radnitzky, eds. **Handlexikon zur Wissenschaftstheorie.** Munich: Ehrenwirth, 1989. 502p.

About 100 articles, from *Abstraktion* to *Wissenssoziologie,* cover the philosophy or theory of *Wissenschaft*—a concept lacking an exact equivalent in English and somewhat variable according to context, but often used, as here, to encompass both the natural sciences, or *Naturwissenschaften,* and so-called *Geisteswissenschaften,* "human sciences" or "human studies," including, for example, history, sociology, economics, and linguistics. Articles address broad issues concerning the nature and methods of knowledge in these domains (e.g., *Erkenntnistheorie, Methode, Sozialwissenschaften, Wissenschaftsgeschichte*); the nature and methodology of specific disciplines (e.g., *Geschichtstheorie, Handlungstheorie, Mathematik, Semiotik*); schools of thought (e.g.. *Marxismus, Positivismus, Pragmatismus*); and major concepts, methodologies, controversies, and so forth (e.g., *Dialektik, Induktion, Modalität, Szientismus, Teleologie*). Both the bibliographies accompanying each article and selected bibliography of core literature at the front emphasize German-language sources almost but not quite exclusively. Contributors include a number of scholars prominent in (though not necessarily outside) Germany but also a few names familiar in Anglo-American philosophical circles: for example, Karl Popper (on *Falsifizierbarkeit*), Paul Feyerabend (on *anarchische Erkenntnistheorie, Rationalismus,* and *Relativismus*), and John Eccles (on *Geist-Leib-Problem*).

744. Turner, Bryan S., ed. **The Blackwell Companion to Social Theory.** 2nd ed. Malden, Mass.: Blackwell, 2000. 570p. (Blackwell Companions to Sociology).

This *Companion* is concerned not so much with the content of social theories as with metalevel philosophical theories about the nature and aims of social science and analysis of social phenomena. William Outhwaite addresses this concern in broad terms in chapter 2, "Philosophy of Social Science." Other chapters explore specific viewpoints or positions, some of which are largely internal to sociology or the social sciences generally (e.g., Rational Choice Theory, Systems Theory, Symbolic Interactionism), while others are associated with wider philosophic or intellectual movements such as Phenomenology, Structuralism, Feminism, Postmodernism. Though not squarely in the category of "reference work," this *Companion* provides a useful thematic survey, with extensive bibliographies, of twentieth-century and particularly recent developments in this field.

745. Warburton, Nigel. **Thinking from A to Z.** 2nd ed. London: Routledge, 2000. 150p.

This handy work covers informal logic in the widest sense of the term, and casts its net even wider to encompass other dimensions of critical thinking. Warburton's introduction identifies four principal types of entry: (1) "those which deal with common moves in arguments such as the *companions in guilt move*"; (2) "those which focus on seductive reasoning errors such as the *correlation = cause confusion* and the *Van Gogh fallacy*"; (3) "entries on techniques of persuasion and avoidance, such as the *no hypotheticals move* and the *politician's answer*"; and (4) "those which examine psychological factors which can be obstacles to clear thought such as *wishful thinking*" (p. ix). Given the largely negative cast of this typology, it is worth adding that topics covered include not only bad forms of reasoning or arguing but also sound moves and argument forms, such as counterexample and Ockham's razor. Entries typically provide a short explanation followed by examples. Entry terms show a preference for "the most memorable names" (p. x), and traditional Latin designations are usually cross-referenced to their nearest English equivalents: *modus ponens,* for instance, to "affirming the antecedent."

The second edition has 16 entries that were not in the first (Routledge, 1996).

19
Philosophy of Education

BIBLIOGRAPHIES

746.   Baatz, Charles Albert. **The Philosophy of Education: A Guide to Information Sources.** Detroit: Gale Research, 1980. 344p. (Gale Information Guide Library; Education Information Guide Series, vol. 6).

Building on an earlier bibliography by Broudy (entry 747) and employing a modification of its organizational scheme (explained in the first chapter), Baatz concentrates on the literature published since Broudy's work, that is, from 1967 to 1978, although a scattering of older works is also included. The number of books and articles listed, and in most cases briefly annotated, is estimated in the neighborhood of 2,000. Chapter 12 is a very selective bibliography for general philosophical background. Indexes by author, subject, and (for books only) title are included.

747.   Broudy, Harry S. et. al. **Philosophy of Education: An Organization of Topics and Selected Sources.** Urbana: University of Illinois Press, 1967. 287p. **Supplement.** 1969. 139p.

A prominent dimension of this work, signaled in the subtitle, is its endeavor to develop a structure for philosophy of education and, derivatively, its bibliography. The resulting scheme is diagrammed in the form of a grid, each cell of which represents the intersection of one of four broad problem areas (nature and aims of education; curriculum design and validation; organization and policy; teaching and learning) with one of eight areas of philosophical inquiry (epistemology; metaphysics; ethics and value theory; aesthetics; logic, semantics, language; philosophy of science; man and society; philosophy of religion). Each division of the bibliography corresponds to a cell in the grid, except for a substantial philosophical background section and two others outside the scheme: one titled "Educational Research and 'the Science' of Education," the other on the nature and status of philosophy of education. A vast number of books and articles, mostly published during the middle third of this century, are listed and briefly described.

The *Supplement* lists an additional 526 items.

748.   Cassel, Jeris F., and Robert J. Congleton. **Critical Thinking: An Annotated Bibliography.** Metuchen, N.J.: Scarecrow, 1993. 403p.

"Critical thinking" became something of a buzzword as well as the label for an identifiable movement in U.S. education at all levels during the late seventies to early nineties. Selectively yet in depth, Cassel and Congleton document slightly more than a decade's worth (1980–1991) of literature from and about that movement, examining or advocating critical thinking from a wide range of theoretical, empirical, and applied perspectives. Some 930 items are cited and annotated. Chapters cover, for instance, definitions and concepts; research; professional development and teacher training; testing and evaluation; and teaching in specific subject areas. Neither the exclusive property of nor merely a branch of philosophy, "critical thinking" does draw importantly on philosophical resources, and it raises philosophical issues—one reason, no doubt, why it is not characterized by unanimity about its concepts, goals, and methods. In that regard, it is helpful that Cassel and Congleton's chapters on debated theoretical matters include cross-references so that one can trace who is responding to whom. The book includes author and subject indexes.

749.   Leming, James S. **Foundations of Moral Education: An Annotated Bibliography.** Westport, Conn.: Greenwood Press, 1983. 325p.

> See entry 665.

750.   Miller, Albert Jay. **A Selective Bibliography of Existentialism in Education and Related Topics.** New York: Exposition Press, 1969. 39p.

> Except for a few older items included to give some historical perspective, this bibliography lists literature published from 1953 to 1968. Books and articles are separated, but there is no attempt to differentiate or structure the rather surprising miscellany of topics, the relation of some of which to Existentialism is far from clear.

751.   Powell, John P. **Philosophy of Education: A Select Bibliography.** 2nd ed. Manchester: Manchester University Press, 1970. 51p.

> Powell lists, without annotations, 707 items, divided among 26 sections. The 4 opening sections include books; the remainder, devoted to specific topics such as knowledge, moral education, curriculum, and punishment, focus on journal articles published from 1950 to 1970.

DICTIONARIES, ENCYCLOPEDIAS, AND HANDBOOKS

752.   Chambliss, J. J., ed. **Philosophy of Education: An Encyclopedia.** Hamden, Conn.: Garland, 1996. 720p.

> The first and arguably still the most comprehensive encyclopedic work devoted to philosophy of education, this excellent resource offers 228 articles by 184 contributors representing both the philosophy and education fields as well as, in smaller numbers, a variety of other disciplines. The introduction states the work is "addressed to general readers, university students, and scholars" (p. vii), but presumably means to include practicing educators as well, because it also avers that, the work's theoretical emphasis notwithstanding, "many articles show the significance of theory for practice" (ibid.) The encyclopedia's wide-ranging content includes strong coverage of the history of philosophical thought about education, from the Greeks to the present, with many entries on influential thinkers (e.g., Isocrates, Plato, Rousseau, Dewey) and schools of thought (Cynics, Epicureanism, Romanticism, Pragmatism). Many entries represent topics specific to or closely associated with education, such as academic freedom, civic education, discipline, intelligence, *Paidea,* physical education, teaching and learning, and explore the philosophical issues surrounding these concepts or practices. Others

represent topics central to philosophy, such as empiricism, equality, epistemology, freedom and determinism, rationalism, and rights, and explore the ramifications of these for education. Finally, there are many articles that address from a philosophical perspective education's relationships to its wider social context, such as those on gender and sexism, home and family, minorities, multiculturalism, race and racism, and sociology. Bibliographies, sometimes extensive, accompany all articles.

753.   Curren, Randall, ed. **A Companion to the Philosophy of Education.** Malden, Mass.: Blackwell, 2003 (Blackwell Companions to Philosophy).

Surveys philosophy of education from classical theories to contemporary issues. Its 45 articles are organized thematically, not alphabetically, in four principal parts. Part 1 describes no less than 14 historical and contemporary movements from the Socratic movement to postmodernism. Part 2 examines specific issues relating to teaching and learning, from the broadly general ("the nature and purpose of education") to specific educational practices (motivation and classroom management, the measurement of learning) to specific educational subjects (teaching science and arithmetic, aesthetics and art education, moral education, teaching literature). Part 3 concerns the politics and ethics of schooling, dealing with themes such as educational choice, children's rights, educational equality, multicultural education, inclusion and justice in special education, and sex education. Part 4 is devoted to issues specific to higher education, including its aims, academic freedom, research ethics, affirmative action, the professor-student relationship, and the regulation of student life.

Contributors, about 50 of them, represent an impressive diversity of academic specializations, mainly in departments of education and philosophy but some others as well—for example, ancient thought, English, law, management, politics, psychology—and an equally impressive array of affiliations with academic institutions in the United States, Britain, and elsewhere.

754.   Palmer, Joy A. et. al., eds. **Fifty Major Thinkers on Education: From Confucius to the Present.** London: Routledge, 2001. 254p. (Routledge Key Guides).

Not all important thought about education counts as philosophy, but a large proportion of the ideas of thinkers included in this dictionary falls readily into that category. Indeed, at least half of the 50 figures, though not necessarily their educational ideas, appear also in any reasonably comprehensive philosophical dictionary—say the *Oxford Companion to Philosophy* (entry 131). That includes such philosophical stalwarts as Plato, Aristotle, Augustine, Locke, Rousseau, Kant, Hegel, Mill, Nietzsche, Whitehead, and Russell, as well as individuals with lower philosophical profiles but perhaps greater renown in other domains, such as al-Ghazali, Erasmus, Comenius, Mary Wollstonecraft, Gandhi, and Rabindanath Tagore. Others thinkers profiled in this dictionary are as diverse as Jesus, John Wesley, Pestalozzi, Darwin, Matthew Arnold, Louisa May Alcott, Durkheim, W.E.B. Du Bois, and Montessori. Each article provides biographical data, an outline of the subject's principal activities and achievements, and an assessment of his or her influence, and is accompanied by a bibliography of major writings and suggested secondary readings.

See entry 755 for a companion volume on later thinkers.

755.   Palmer, Joy A. et. al., eds. **Fifty Modern Thinkers on Education: From Piaget to the Present Day.** London: Routledge, 2001. 290p. (Routledge Key Guides).

Complements entry 754. Fewer high-profile philosophers appear in this volume than in the companion volume, in part no doubt because of the ascendancy of empirical approaches to the study of education and the emergence of educational theory and policy as specialties in several disciplines and even an independent field. Among the prominent philosophical names here are Wittgenstein, Heidegger, Simone Weil, Lyotard, Foucault, and Habermas. Less well-known philosophers include Michael Oakeshott, Israel Scheffler, and Jane Martin. But many figures included here who are not known principally as philosophers have significant philosophical strands woven through their thought or have had their ideas subjected to philosophical scrutiny and challenge. Examples include Piaget, B. F. Skinner, Paolo Freire, Ivan Illich, Lawrence Kohlberg, Neil Postman, and Howard Gardner.

756. Winch, Christopher and John Gingell. **Key Concepts in the Philosophy of Education.** London: Routledge, 1999. 282p. (Key Concepts Series).

Elucidates over 150 key terms and concepts prevalent in philosophical discussion of education, presented alphabetically. These include schools of thought such as behaviourism, existentialism, instrumentalism, progressivism; areas of education such as physical education, religious education; educational activities and practices such as assessment, co-education, discipline, pedagogy, reading; proffered educational outcomes such as autonomy, competence, democracy, literacy; and many pertaining to education's social context or the scientific, philosophical, or political assumptions that inform it, for instance equality, homosexuality, human nature, justice, metaphysics, pluralism, postmodernism, relativism, rights, truth. Articles tend to range from half a page to half a dozen pages. Bibliographic references, used sparingly, are keyed to 23-page general bibliography at the back. Name and subject indexes.

757. Winn, Ralph Bubrich, ed. **John Dewey: Dictionary of Education.** New York: Philosophical Library, 1959. 150p.

Like some other dictionaries issued by its publisher (see entry 507 for a general comment), this is entirely a compilation of quotations from a major philosopher. The difference in this case is a more limited subject matter. It covers Dewey's thought on education (mostly of a philosophical cast) and also some of the larger philosophical context for that thought. Entries for educational topics such as discipline, methods of instruction, reading, and teaching are joined by quotes on broader but related Deweyan themes such as art, democracy, experience, happiness, and value. Sources of quotes are identified by title only.

OTHER REFERENCE SOURCES

758. **Philosophy of Education Society.** http://cuip.net/pes/ (accessed October 29, 2005).

The PES Web site serves principally to provide information about the society, its activities, publications, and membership. It includes a directory of members. Under the rubric "Resources," it also provides links to Web sites for affiliated societies, online syllabi and other teaching and research resources, and job listings.

20
Philosophy of Religion

BIBLIOGRAPHIES

759. McLean, George F. **A Bibliography of Christian Philosophy and Contemporary Issues.** New York: Ungar, 1967. 312p. (Philosophy in the 20th Century: Catholic and Christian, vol. 2).

> See entry 824.

760. Wainwright, William J. **Philosophy of Religion: An Annotated Bibliography of Twentieth-Century Writings in English.** New York: Garland, 1978. 776p.

> Wainwright characterizes his work as "addressed to professional philosophers and graduate students who work in the analytic tradition" and whose focus is philosophical problems rather than "the systems of individual philosophers or the history of philosophical movements" (introduction). The majority of items listed (books, portions of books, and articles) represent the Analytic tradition, but works of "Process philosophers, Neo-Scholastics, Idealists, theologians, historians of religion, psychologists, and so on" are cited when the compiler thought they would (or should) interest Analytic philosophers.
>
> Annotations, provided for all 1,135 entries, are typically critical as well as descriptive and sometimes run a full page or more. The eight chapters cover the following broad areas: the divine attributes, argument for the existence of God, the problem of evil, mysticism and religious experience, miracles, faith and revelation, religious language, and the justification of religious belief. An index of authors, editors, and reviewers is provided.
>
> Wainwright's bibliography is supplemented by Robert G. Wolf's *Analytic Philosophy of Religion: A Bibliography 1940–1995* (entry 762).

761. Whitney, Barry L. **Theodicy: An Annotated Bibliography on the Problem of Evil, 1960–1990.** New York: Garland, 1993. 650p. (Garland Reference Library of the Humanities, vol. 1111).

> Whitney's bibliography on a central topic of philosophical theology—theodicy, or "the attempt to reconcile belief in God with the world's suffering"—comes probably as close to comprehensiveness for the three decades he covers as reasonable aspiration allows, given, as he puts it, "an immensely complex issue and one which has virtually endless peripheral sub-themes" (preface). The main body of his work is divided into seven chapters focusing on major contemporary options: free will theodicy, "best possible world" theodicy, natural evil theodicy, John Hick's Irenaean theodicy, process theodicy, and miscellaneous other philosophical theodicies. Each chapter comprises two to five subdivisions within which both books and articles are listed in a single sequence by author. In several chapters (not all), entries representing central writings, all annotated with brief summaries, are segregated from (apparently less central) entries for "related publications," all unannotated. Four appendices, filling nearly 40 percent of the volume, take on some of the more

significant "peripheral sub-themes": Biblical theodicy, historical theodicy (discussions of major positions on theodicy from the past, notably those of Augustine, Aquinas, Leibniz, Hume, and Kant), "suffering of God" theodicy, and, under the heading "miscellaneous," such special topics as pain and theodicy, theodicy in literature, Jewish and Holocaust theodicy, Satan and theodicy, and women and theodicy. All of these topics, while acknowledged as "important in their own right," are judged by Whitney to be "not as central to the current philosophical and analytical theological debates" represented in his chapters (p. 6). A final appendix (E) is devoted to dissertations. Entries in all the appendices are, with a few exceptions, unannotated. Separate author indexes cover the chapters and the appendices.

In addition to a general introduction, Whitney provides useful introductions to each of his chapters and appendices, with overviews of the topics covered.

762. Wolf, Robert G. **Analytic Philosophy of Religion: A Bibliography, 1940–1996.** Bowling Green, Ohio: Philosophy Documentation Center, 1998. 722p.

Wolf documents the flourishing of philosophy of religion in the analytic domain in the twentieth century, especially its last four decades, listing over 5,000 books and articles. His compilation supplements as well as partly overlaps William J. Wainwright's *Philosophy of Religion: An Annotated Bibliography of Twentieth-Century Writings in English* (entry 760), but lacks the latter's annotations and is more narrowly focused on analytic philosophy. Items are often cross-listed under several headings. Books, for example, are first listed separately in chapter 1 (divided into monographs, collections of original papers, and anthologies of republished material), then again in subject-oriented sections where applicable, intermingled with journal articles and essays in collections. Chapter and subchapter topics include the logical background crucial to much contemporary analytic philosophy of religion (chapter 2), specific issues debated within the field (e.g., religion and science, theistic arguments, the problem of evil, the nature of God, miracles, morality and divine command ethics) (chapters 3–10), and analytically oriented studies of major thinkers from Plato to the present who have engaged religion philosophically (chapters 11–16). Coverage of journal literature extends beyond that accessible through the *Philosopher's Index* (entries 47 and 48), encompassing many articles published in theological, interdisciplinary, or, at times, obscure journals. Author index.

DICTIONARIES, ENCYCLOPEDIAS, AND HANDBOOKS

763. Chapman, Colin. **An Eerdmans Handbook: The Case for Christianity.** Grand Rapids, Mich.: William B. Eerdmans, 1981. 313p.

See entry 819.

764. Clark, Kelly James, Richard Lints, and James K. A. Smith. **101 Key Terms in Philosophy and Their Importance for Theology.** Louisville, Ky.: Westminster John Knox Press, 2004. 116p.

This compact dictionary indeed counts exactly 101 entries. A few, however, are actually pairs or other combinations of related terms, such as analytic/continental philosophy, dualism/monism, or immutability and impassibility, while 19 are names of important philosophers. The authors "attempted to determine the philosophical terms, concepts, and names that the theology student is likely to encounter," addressing "classical philosophical and theological questions as well as contemporary concerns" (intro.). Except for a handful of terms at home in specialized regions of philosophical theology—for example, omniscience and foreknowledge, ontotheology—most entries could be found in any reasonably comprehensive philosophical dictionary. But explanations here focus on aspects most relevant for theological study. Trying "to assume little philosophical knowledge" and aiming at "maximizing accessibility," the authors largely succeed in achieving their aims. A brief bibliography accompanies each article, and there is a cross-reference index.

765.   **Encyclopaedia of Religion and Ethics.** Ed. James Hastings with the assistance of John A. Selbie . . . and other scholars. New York: Scribner's; Edinburgh: T. & T. Clark, 1908–22. Variously reprinted. 12 vols. plus index.

For two-thirds of a century this was the most comprehensive English-language encyclopedia on religion, and it remains unique in its extensive coverage of philosophical matters. (See entry 766, however, for a recent comprehensive encyclopedia of religion that pays substantial attention to philosophy.) Philosophical content in Hastings includes especially topics in Eastern philosophy, philosophy of religion, and religious apologetics (e.g., arguments for the existence of God, theodicy, the relation between faith and reason); metaphysical issues of significance for religious thinking (immortality, the mind–body problem, naturalism, libertarianism and necessitarianism); and topics in philosophical ethics (ethical idealism, natural law, Utilitarianism). Though severely dated by 80-plus years of newer developments, this can be an exceptionally valuable guide to the thought and literature of the late nineteenth and early twentieth centuries. Because topics are often under headings not obvious or familiar to contemporary students, consultation of the very thorough index volume is strongly advised.

766.   **Encyclopedia of Religion.** 2nd ed. Lindsay Jones, editor in chief. Detroit: Macmillan Reference USA, 2005. 15 vols.

The second edition of this leading reference work on religion pays substantially more focused attention to philosophy than did the first edition edited by Mircea Eliade (New York: Macmillan, 1986, 16 vols.). Philosophy-related content, while just a small fraction of the total, adds up to a substantial resource that should not be overlooked for philosophical topics directly concerned with religion or treated with a particular eye to their import for religion. In addition to overview articles on philosophy and philosophy of religion, the encyclopedia offers articles on broad traditions such as Chinese, Indian, and Islamic philosophies; specific schools or movements such as Analytic philosophy, Empiricism, Structuralism, Confucianism, Cārvāka, Nyāya; subdisciplines such as epistemology and metaphysics; issues such as free will/determinism, intelligent design, and theistic arguments; and most of the leading Western and non-Western philosophers. Much of the extensive coverage of non-Western religions, where the boundary with philosophy is often not clearly drawn, will be relevant for study of non-Western philosophy. Noteworthy also is an article specifically concerned with philosophy's relation to religion.

767.   Evans, C. Stephen. **Pocket Dictionary of Apologetics & Philosophy of Religion.** Downers Grove, Ill.: InterVarsity Press, 2002. 125p.

Billed on its cover as aimed at beginning students of either apologetics—the rational defense, broadly conceived, of Christian faith—or philosophy of religion, this could be a handy resource also for pastors, religious educators, youth ministers and other church workers. Evans, who has a distinguished record of publications in both domains addressed variously to scholarly specialists, interdisciplinary audiences, and general readers, here draws on his wide expertise to offer succinct definitions for some 300 entries. They include technical terms such as *a posteriori,* foundationalism, and middle knowledge; biographical entries for leading apologists and philosophers of religion; movements and positions in philosophy and theology, for example, antirealism, exclusivism, postmodernism; and apologetic arguments from the cosmological to the teleological and the Pascalian wager. The definitions, while elementary, are never superficial; and while often imbued with Evans's own perspective as a Christian philosopher, they are never tendentious or disrespectful of other viewpoints.

768. **Handbook of Contemporary Philosophy of Religion.** Dordrecht: Kluwer Academic, 2000–02. Vols. 1–3. Forthcoming volumes to be published New York: Springer.

The current publisher's Web site promotes this as "a reference series that focuses on the primary issues and approaches to contemporary philosophy of religion" (http://www.springer.com/sgw/cda/frontpage/0,,5–40385–69–33114272–0,00.html, accessed October 29, 2005). It may be regarded as straddling the borderline of the "reference work" category, having in many ways the character of a conventional monographic series, whose individual volumes in this case provide thematic or chronological surveys of various aspects of philosophy of religion in the twentieth and into the twenty-first century. It does show promise of ultimately providing the kind of thorough coverage of its defined subject area that one might look for in a substantial and comprehensive subject encyclopedia, which as yet does not exist for this field. As of late 2005, the three volumes listed as follows had been published by Kluwer. Volumes 4 and 5, to be published by Springer, are projected to deal respectively with the comparative approach to philosophy of religion and with Process philosophy of religion. Plans for the series do not appear to foresee a settled number of volumes or list of topics.

769. Volume 1: Eugene Thomas Long. **Twentieth-Century Western Philosophy of Religion, 1900–2000.** 2000. 538p.

Divides into four roughly chronological divisions, surveying the major approaches, schools of thought, or "strands" within philosophy of religion that emerged or gained particular prominence in each era, including several covered thoroughly in other published or projected volumes.

770. Volume 2: Brian J. Shanley. **The Thomist Tradition.** 2002. 238p.

Begins with an overview of Thomism in the twentieth century, then surveys Thomist treatments of specific issues such as the status of religious truth claims, suffering and evil, theology and science, morality, human nature and destiny, and religious pluralism.

771. Volume 3: James Franklin Harris. **Analytic Philosophy of Religion.** 2002. 432p.

Discusses the development and nature of analytic philosophy, then examines the major issues that have occupied the analytic approach to philosophy of religion as it developed over the last half of the twentieth century and continues actively at the start of the twenty-first. Among these are religious language, the nature of God, arguments for God's existence, religious experience, religion and science, the problem of evil, religion and ethics, and religious pluralism.

772.   Quinn, Philip L., and Charles Taliaferro, eds. **A Companion to the Philosophy of Religion.** Oxford: Blackwell, 1997. 639p. (Blackwell Companions to Philosophy).

"This *Companion* is a guide to philosophy of religion for nonspecialists, but it will also engage specialists. It aims to provide the reader with a fairly detailed map of the territory covered by philosophical thought about religion in the English-speaking world" (introduction). Contributing to this map are many of the most influential figures who have shaped the field over the last several decades of the twentieth century: Stephen Davis, Antony Flew, John Hick, Basil Mitchell, Kai Nielsen, Alvin Plantinga, Ninian Smart, Eleanore Stump, Nicholas Wolterstorff, Keith Yandell, to name but a few. There are 77 contributors in all. Organization is thematic, not alphabetical, with essays grouped under 11 broad themes. They begin with discussions of philosophical issues in the world's major religions; move through historical overviews of the Western tradition and some twentieth-century currents; then take up specific topics and problems centered around the themes of religious language, attributes commonly assigned to God (omnipotence, omnipresence, goodness, foreknowledge, etc.), justification of religious belief and challenges to such belief, theism and modern science, theism and ethics, and philosophical reflections on characteristically Christian as opposed to broadly theistic doctrines (e.g., trinity, incarnation, atonement, survival of death). The final section discusses new directions in the field impelled by feminism, religious pluralism, and comparative philosophy of religion. Includes index.

773.   Thistleton, Anthony C. **A Concise Encylopedia of the Philosophy of Religion.** Oxford: Oneworld, 2002. 344p.

While indeed relatively concise, Thistleton's encyclopedia is considerably more expansive than Evans's *Pocket Dictionary of Apologetics and Philosophy of Religion* (entry 767) and sticks closer to topics and debates central to academic philosophy of religion. On the other hand, it is written more at the level of undergraduate students and general inquirers than Quinn and Taliaferro's *Companion to the Philosophy of Religion* (entry 772). Thistleton, the sole author, writes from many years of experience teaching philosophy of religion as well contributing substantially to the discipline, notably in the area of philosophical hermeneutics. His alphabetically arranged entries range over significant concepts (e.g., fideism, foundationalism), arguments (cosmological argument, free-will defense), major topics and areas of debate (evil, language in religion, revelation), philosophical and religions traditions (Buddhist philosophy, Zoroastrianism), schools of thought (Empiricism, Postmodernism, Scholasticism), and the field's most important thinkers throughout history, from Plato to Plantinga. As several of the aforementioned examples demonstrate, coverage extends to non-Western philosophy, though it is decidedly weighted toward Western. Articles are mostly brief, usually less than a page, and do not include bibliographies or bibliographic citations. A chronology of major thinkers and events is at the end of the volume, along with an index.

21
Social, Political, and Legal Philosophy

See also the Ethics chapter (chap. 17) for sources relating to ethics in government, politics, law, and international relations.

BIBLIOGRAPHIES

774. Albert, Ethel M. and Clyde Kluckhohn. **A Selected Bibliography on Values, Ethics and Esthetics in the Behavioral Sciences and Philosophy, 1920–1958**. Glencoe, Ill: Free Press, 1959. 342p.

See entry 644.

775. Bastide, Georges. **Ethics and Political Philosophy.** New York: Cultural Center of the French Embassy, 1961. 96p. (French Bibliographical Digest, no. 34).

Also published in French as *Bibliographie Française: Morale et philosophie politique* (Paris: 1961), this lists 711 French books and journal articles from the period 1946–1958. Among authors included are Raymond Aron, Simone de Beauvoir, Julien Benda, Jaques Maritain, Pierre Teilhard de Chardin, and Simone Weil. Many entries, especially those for books, have brief annotations.

776. **Bibliographie der Sozialethik: Grundsatzfragen des öffentlichen Lebens / Bases for Social Living,** 1961/63–1977/79. Ed. Arthur F. Utz, et. al. Freiburg im Breslau: Herder, 1963–1980. Vols. 3–11.

Volumes 1 and 2 of this series, covering 1956 to 1961, were published with the eventual subtitle as the main title (given in French and Spanish as well as German and English) and an explanatory subtitle: *Grundsatzfragen des öffentlichen Lebens: Bibliographie (Darstellung und Kritic), Recht, Gesellschaft, Wirtschaft, Staat / Bases for Social Living: A Critical Bibliography Embracing Law, Society, Economics, and Politics* (Freiburg im Breslau: Herder, 1960–1962).

Books and articles in the four major European languages, and some in others, are listed according to a classification scheme outlined in the front of each issue. (Headings in the outline are in German, French, and English). The headings for the five major divisions are (1) "Principles of Social Doctrine," (2) "Philosophy of Law," (3) "The Social Order," (4) "The Economic Order," and (5) "The Political Order." A sampling of topics reflected in the subheadings may suggest the strongly philosophical bent of this regrettably short-lived bibliographic resource: social philosophy, social justice and social charity, nature and aim of the state, ethics of social economy, private property, the just price, history of political economy, civil rights and liberties.

There is only an author index, but this includes authors mentioned in the titles of works cited.

777. Goehlert, Robert, and Clair Herczeg. **Anarchism: A Bibliography.** Monticello, Ill: Vance Bibliographies, 1982. 122p. (Public Administration Series, Bibliography no. P-902).

Covers both the theory and practice of anarchism. Under "Philosophy of Anarchism" are sections on works relating anarchistic ideas to ideas on socialism, nonviolence, the state, education, economics, and art. Individual anarchist thinkers covered in separate sections include Bakunin, Godwin, Paul Goodman, Kropotkin, Proudhon, and Stirner.

778. Matczak, Sebastian A. **Philosophy: A Select, Classified Bibliography of Ethics, Economics, Law, Politics, and Sociology.** Louvain: Editions Nauwelaerts; Paris: Beatrice-Nauwelaerts, 1970. 308p. (Philosophical Questions Series, no. 3).

This bibliography is intended to present the more important works relating to philosophical ethics, ethical problems and value issues raised in or by the social science disciplines mentioned in the subtitle, and the philosophical underpinnings of those disciplines. Each area is covered in a separate chapter, which opens with a brief sketch of the most important philosophical problems followed by four to six sections devoted to general studies, studies of particular periods (chronological), materials on special questions, periodicals, and (in some chapters) introductory bibliographies and works relating to particular countries. Entries are not annotated.

This work remains valuable for interdisciplinary research and study, though in addition to being now dated, it is less reliable than it should be. Reviewers commented on the omission of important, even standard works, for example, some of Hannah Arendt's writings, or works of either Galbraith or Friedman on capitalist economics (cf. *American Reference Books Annual,* 1971, entry 1330; *Review of Metaphysics* 31 [September 1977]:121–22). Editions cited are not always standard, and English translations of foreign-language works may be overlooked or ignored.

779. Nettlau, Max. **Bibliographie de l'anarchie.** Paris: Bibliothéque des "Temps Nouveaux," no. 8, 1897. Reprinted, New York: Burt Franklin, 1968. 294p.

Compiled by an authority on philosophical anarchism, this "remains the basic bibliography of the early material on the various radical movements of the 19th century . . ." (DeGeorge, *The Philosopher's Guide,* p. 101). It includes chapters on the "classic" proponents and exponents of anarchism (Proudhon, Bakunin, and Kropotkin) but also on specific variants and movements (e.g*., l'anarchisme-individualiste, le mutuellisme*), including American versions associated with such authors as Josiah Warren, Lysander Spooner, and B. R. Tucker. Most chapters begin with background notes. Annotations, though sometimes extensive, are generally limited to bibliographic matters.

780. **Social Theory: A Bibliographic Series.** Compiled by Joan Nordquist. Santa Cruz, Calif.: Reference and Research Services, 1986–2003. Nos. 1–68.

This prolific but now terminated series features relatively short bibliographies—typically 60 pages with around 500 entries—of materials in English on social-philosophical theories or by and on individual theorists. For the most part, these are European or of European origin and, also for the most part, of a radical or leftist orientation. The "English-only" rule is broken in some cases to list books in the original languages by the philosophers concerned. Although physically the bibliographies have the appearance of desk-top publishing efforts, they serve reasonably well to provide quick access to English-language sources on thinkers and movements for which more substantial and comprehensive coverage often is not yet available, or to update older sources. Some subjects in the series have themselves been updated with second or even third issues. The bibliographies are not annotated, and the subject indexing provided, based on title keywords-in-context, is limited and in many cases spotty (e.g., only secondary sources may be indexed, and sometimes expected indexing terms are missing).

All issues were compiled by Joan Nordquist. Information supplied by the publisher in March 2004 confirms that the series has now ceased.

1. **Jurgen Habermas: A Bibliography.** 1986
2. **Jacques Derrida: A Bibliography.** 1986.
3. **Louis Althusser: A Bibliography.** 1986.
4. **Michel Foucault: A Bibliography.** 1986.
5. **Jacques Lacan: A Bibliography.** 1987.
6. **Claude Levi-Strauss: A Bibliography.** 1987.
7. **Antonio Gramsci: A Bibliography.** 1987.
8. **Talcott Parsons: A Bibliography.** 1987.
9. **Herbert Marcuse: A Bibliography.** 1988.
10. **Theodor Adorno: A Bibliography.** 1988.
11. **Georg Lukacs: A Bibliography.** 1988.
12. **Mikhail Bakhtin: A Bibliography.** 1988.
13. **Max Weber: A Bibliography.** 1989.
14. **Hannah Arendt: A Bibliography.** 1989.
15. **Walter Benjamin: A Bibliography.** 1989.
16. **Julia Kristeva: A Bibliography.** 1989.
17. **Martin Heidegger: A Bibliography.** 1990.
18. **Max Horkheimer: A Bibliography.** 1990.
19. **Ernst Bloch: A Bibliography.** 1990.
20. **French Feminist Theory: Luce Irigaray and Helene Cixous: A Bibliography.** 1990.
21. **Jean François Lyotard: A Bibliography.** 1991.
22. **Jurgen Habermas (II): A Bibliography.** 1991.
23. **Simone de Beauvoir: A Bibliography.** 1991.
24. **Jean Baudrillard: A Bibliography.** 1991.
25. **Felix Guattari and Gilles Deleuze: A Bibliography.** 1992.
26. **Deconstructionism: A Bibliography.** 1992.
27. **Michel Foucault (II): A Bibliography.** 1992.
28. **Feminist Theory: A Bibliography.** 1992.
29. **Jean-Paul Sartre: A Bibliography.** 1993.

30. **Radical Ecological Theory: A Bibliography.** 1993.

31. **French Feminist Theory (II): Michele le Doeff, Monique Wittig, Catherine Clement: A Bibliography.** 1993.

32. **Mikhail Bakhtin (II): A Bibliography.** 1993.

33. **Georges Bataille: A Bibliography.** 1994.

34. **Roland Barthes: A Bibliography.** 1994.

35. **Theodor Adorno (II): A Bibliography.** 1994.

36. **Ecofeminist Theory: A Bibliography.** 1994.

37. **Jacques Derrida (II): A Bibliography.** 1995.

38. **Simone Weil: A Bibliography.** 1995.

39. **Julia Kristeva (II): A Bibliography.** 1995.

40. **Feminist Theory: Women of Color: A Bibliography.** 1995

41. **Feminism and Postmodern Theory: A Bibliography.** 1996.

42. **Martin Heidegger (II) : A Bibliography.** 1996.

43. **Rosa Luxemburg and Emma Goldman: A Bibliography.** 1996.

44. **French Feminist Theory (III): Luce Irigaray and Helene Cixous: A Bibliography.** 1996.

45. **Emmanuel Levinas: A Bibliography.** 1997.

46. **Hannah Arendt (II) : A Bibliography.** 1997.

47. **Pierre Bourdieu: A Bibliography.** 1997.

48. **Queer Theory: A Bibliography.** 1997.

49. **Jurgen Habermas (III) : A Bibliography.** 1998.

50. **Postcolonial Theory: A Bibliography.** 1998.

51. **Hans-Georg Gadamer: A Bibliography.** 1998.

52. **Feminist Literary Theory: A Bibliography.** 1998.

53. **Paul Ricœur: A Bibliography.** 1999.

54. **Anarchism: Contemporary Theories: A Bibliography.** 1999.

55. **Postcolonial Theory (II): Literature and the Arts: A Bibliography.** 1999.

56. **Marxism and Ecology: A Bibliography.** 1999.

57. **Maurice Merleau-Ponty: A Bibliography.** 2000.

58. **Herbert Marcuse (II) : A Bibliography.** 2000.

59. **Agnes Heller and the Budapest School: A Bibliography.** 2000.

60. **Feminist Theory (II) : A Bibliography.** 2000.

61. **Henri Lefebvre and the Philosophies Group: A Bibliography.** 2001.

62. **C.L.R. James: A Bibliography.** 2001.

63. **Frederic Jameson: A Bibliography.** 2001.

64. **Feminism and Psychoanalysis: A Bibliography.** 2001.

65. **Frantz Fanon: A Bibliography.** 2002.

66. **W. E. B. Du Bois: A Bibliography.** 2002.

67. **John Rawls: A Bibliography.** 2003.

68. **Antonio Negri: A Bibliography.** 2003.

DICTIONARIES, ENCYCLOPEDIAS, AND HANDBOOKS

781. **Blackwell Dictionary of Twentieth-Century Social Thought.** William Outhwaite and Tom Bottomore, eds. Oxford: Basil Blackwell, 1993. 864p.

Ranging widely "from the social sciences to philosophy, political theories and doctrines, cultural ideas and movements, and to the influence of the natural sciences" (preface), this authoritative work can complement general philosophical dictionaries and encyclopedias with its coverage of twentieth-century social and political philosophy as well as, to a lesser extent, the philosophy of the social sciences. Examples of articles with significant philosophical content or import are those on base and superstructure (in Marxist thought), historicism, hermeneutics, justice, Maoism, Neo-Darwinism, Neo-Kantianism, pragmatism, positivism, social choice, sociobiology, utopia, and utilitarianism. There are no biographical entries. References for further reading accompany all articles.

782. **Blackwell Encyclopedia of Political Thought.** Ed. David Miller, et. al. Oxford: Basil Blackwell, 1987. 570p.

A superb resource for Western political philosophy and adjacent areas of political theory, this encyclopedia is the work of over 100 contributors, chiefly British and American, among them some prominent names in the field: Shlomo Avineri, Brian Barry, Maurice Cranston, Eugene Kamenka, and Robert Nisbet, for instance. Entries range from brief definitions of technical terms to substantial articles that analyze central concepts such as authority, freedom, justice, representation, and violence, or consider ideologies such as anarchism, feminism, libertarianism, nationalism, and social Darwinism in relation both to historical context and to contemporary politics. The ideas and influence of some 120 significant political thinkers, from Lord Acton to Mary Wollstonecraft, are described in biographical entries. Non-Western thought is represented in a minimal way by survey articles on Chinese, Hindu, and Islamic political thought, and by an occasional entry such as those for Gandhi and the Islamic philosopher Ibn Khaldoun.

783. Cashmore, Ellis, and Chris Rojek. **Dictionary of Cultural Theorists.** London: Arnold; New York: Oxford University Press, 1999. 497p.

The editors' introductory statement of purpose also characterizes nicely the often hard-to-penetrate nature of texts in cultural theory. "This book is a primer. In no sense is our intention to be exhaustive, nor even comprehensive, in our coverage of the field. It is a preparatory guide intended to lead students through what sometimes seems like the torments of the damned" (introduction). Further, they add, "we are attempting a practical solution to a practical problem: How can educators today help students to assimilate the complex traces, twists and turns of recent social and cultural theory in a quick and effective way, wasting the least possible time?" Suggesting that an approach "that concentrates on the ideas associated with flesh-and-blood theorists . . . gives a concreteness to the issues involved," they offer sketches of more than two hundred leading theorists of culture of the nineteenth and twentieth centuries. Though only a minority are ordinarily classed as philosophers, all or most approached culture or aspects of culture from within their diverse fields—sociology, psychology, anthropology, political science, history, and others—with a decidedly philosophical bent. Alphabetically, they run from Adorno to Žižek; chronologically, from Wollestonecraft to Judith Butler. Each article surveys its subject's main concepts and arguments, major works, and formative influences; provides links to related figures; and suggests sources for further reading. The predominantly left-of-center social-political tendency of the field of cultural theory is in evidence here, but a number of figures are included who do not share and may be critical of that orientation, for example, Allan Bloom and Robert Nisbet. Contributors are predominantly British academics.

784.   Childers, Joseph, and Gary Hentzi, eds. **The Columbia Dictionary of Modern Literary and Cultural Criticism.** New York: Columbia University Press, 1995. 362p.

See entry 619.

785.   Clarke, Paul Barry, and Andrew Linzey. **Dictionary of Ethics, Theology, and Society.** London: Routledge, 1996. 926p.

Focusing primarily on the interplay between theology and society, this reference work pays a good deal of attention to philosophical matters. It generally does a better job than the *Westminster Dictionary of Christian Ethics* (entry 683) in bringing together philosophical and theological (as well as, in this case, social-scientific) perspectives on and contributions to specific topics, though within the narrower scope of social and political ethics. Examples of the more philosophically oriented or philosophically interesting articles are those on deconstruction, evil, evolution, free will, government, individualism, justice, lying, Marxism, natural rights, political correctness, power, and violence. Each article typically defines its concept; describes the principal ideas behind it; analyzes the history, development, and contemporary relevance of those ideas; and concludes with a substantial bibliography. Among the dozens of contributors 10 or so are identified as affiliated with philosophy departments; none of these are as prominent as some among the theologians and theologically-oriented ethicists, for example, Lisa Sowle Cahill, Stanley Hauerwas, Martin Marty, Michael Novak, Rosemary Radford Reuther, and John Howard Yoder. Theologically, the work tends toward the center-to-left end of the spectrum of Christian theology, and atheist and agnostic positions are also represented.

786.   Cranston, Maurice W., and Sanford A. Lakoff, eds. **A Glossary of Political Ideas.** New York: Basic Books, 1968. 180p. British edition, **A Glossary of Political Terms,** ed. Maurice W. Cranston. London: Bodley Head, 1966. 110p. (A Background Book).

This dictionary, though somewhat dated, still offers an excellent introduction to many central concepts of political philosophy (and political theory more generally) that, while ubiquitous in political discourse, are problematic in that they carry evaluative meanings, or heavy loads of philosophical freight, or both. Definitions are provided where possible, ambiguities are exposed where not. Among the 51 terms included are: common good, communism, conservatism, democracy, equality, human rights, justice, liberalism, progress, reactionary, state, utopia/utopian. Each article includes a brief bibliography of mainly standard and classic sources.

The American edition has been somewhat altered from the British original so as to serve better an American audience.

787.   Edgar, Andrew, and Peter Sedgwick, eds. **Cultural Theory: The Key Thinkers.** New York: Routledge, 2002. 288p.

Complementing the editors' *Key Concepts in Cultural Theory* (entry 788), this volume focuses on the individual thinkers prominent in the field of "cultural theory" as it defines itself today plus those who represent its most influential historical antecedents, reaching back to Plato and Aristotle. Cover or jacket blurbs identify these as "the literary critics, sociologists, artists, philosophers and writers who have shaped contemporary culture and society, and the way in which we view them." A more complete characterization, however, would need to intimate the field's more specific methodological proclivities and social-political leanings to shed light on what connects the somewhat disparate group of thinkers included here, ranging from Matthew Arnold to Luce Irigaray, Max Weber to Jacques Derrida, and what might exclude others such as John Locke, Friedrich von Hayek, or Ayn Rand, whose influences on contemporary society and culture or the way some people understand them are no less consequential than those of, say, Emmanuel Levinas, Walter Benjamin, or Julia Kristeva. That understood, this is a useful resource on a significant realm of recent and contemporary thought, offering reasonably clear and self-contained articles though marred by occasional lapses into obscure terminology or dense exposition apt to baffle the uninitiated. Supplementing its biographical articles are a brief glossary of key concepts, a 38-page bibliography of primary and secondary sources, and an index.

788.   Edgar, Andrew and Peter Sedgwick, eds. **Key Concepts in Cultural Theory.** New York: Routledge, 1999. 506p. index. (Key Concepts Series).

Cultural theory "takes as its domain of enquiry all aspects of culture" and is distinguished by "its espousal of a multi-disciplinary approach" (introduction). Consonant with that description, this encyclopedic dictionary includes among its 280 or so entries a broad range of specific cultural phenomena—for example, architecture, cinema, comics, folk music, television, youth culture—and terms drawn from a variety of disciplines— for example, archetype, Baroque, behaviorism, hypothetico-deductive method, ideology, social contract. But cultural theory is defined not just by its subject matter and interdisciplinary methodologies but also by a loosely affiliated family of perspectives and doctrines which tend to challenge orthodoxies and assumptions in traditional disciplines, to interpret cultural phenomena in political or economic terms, and to share a left-of-center social-political orientation often focused on issues of race, class, and gender. These characteristics emerge, though not fully explicitly, in the editors' introduction, and they resonate in many entries more distinctive of the field, such as, culture industry, deconstruction, *écriture feminine,* false consciousness, grand narrative, patriarchy, post-colonialism, power, queer theory. They color much of the rest of the dictionary as well, though this is not to say its approach is wholly uncritical.

Most articles are reasonably clear, self-contained, and potentially helpful even to the uninitiated. Some, however, exemplify the field's tendencies toward obscurity and intentional subversions of conventional terminology, and "insider" references are regrettably frequent. Articles (the majority by the editors) are signed, though contributors are identified by name only.

See entry 787 for a companion work on cultural theorists.

789.   Goodin, Robert E., and Philip Pettit, eds. **A Companion to Contemporary Political Philosophy.** Oxford: Blackwell, 1993. 679p. (Blackwell Companions to Philosophy).

A three-fold division dominates the organization of this volume. Part 1 consists of seven essays on the contributions to contemporary political philosophy of six different disciplines: philosophy itself, with analytical and continental philosophy treated in separate essays, followed by history, sociology, economics, political science, and legal studies. Part 2 has essays on six major ideologies: anarchism, conservatism, feminism, liberalism, Marxism, and socialism. Part 3, roughly half the volume, offers 28 articles on "special topics." These include such staples of political argument as autonomy, contract and consent, democracy, distributive justice, equality, liberty, power, rights, the state, and welfare. Among others less predictable are essays on community, "dirty hands" (regarding the oft-alleged transcendence of politics over ordinary morality), discourse, efficiency, environmentalism, sociobiology, toleration and fundamentalism, and trust. Within each of the three parts, articles are arranged alphabetically by title—the only bow to the dictionary format followed by some other Blackwell Companions. The shortest article (virtue) runs 6 pages, the longest (economics) 34 pages. Each essay is by a different author. Several prominent names occur among the contributors, for example, Anthony Quinton, Gerald Dworkin, and John Passmore. While historical background frequently receives incidental attention, the contemporary focus proclaimed in the title prevails both in the essays and in the lists of bibliographic references and suggestions for further reading following each essay. There is a detailed name/subject index.

790.   Gray, Christopher Berry, ed. **The Philosophy of Law: An Encyclopedia.** New York: Garland, 1999. 2 vols. (Garland Reference Library of the Humanities, vol. 1743).

This authoritative work gathers contributions from more than three hundred scholars, including philosophers and legal scholars in about equal numbers plus a smattering from other disciplines, to cover "virtually all topics under discussion in the recent literature of philosophy of law" (introduction). It focuses particularly on issues relevant to contemporary North America, but also includes substantial international and historical perspectives. Contributors represent over 40 countries.

Entries are arranged alphabetically, but there is 10-page classified subject list at the front. This has four major rubrics. "Historical philosophy of law" comprises articles on philosophy of law in various eras of Western history and on twentieth-century legal cultures defined typologically (e.g., common law, socialist, aboriginal) or geopolitically (e.g.,Western European, Latin American, Chinese, Islamic). "Schools and methodologies of philosophy of law" encompasses the major theories and approaches in the field: natural law, legal positivism, chaos theory, the exegetical school, and existential, feminist, libertarian, Marxist, and postmodern philosophies of law, among many others. Under "Personages in philosophy of law" are listed, by historical periods, some 90 influential thinkers and one group of thinkers (Frankfurt School). "Jurisdictional philosophy of law" classifies entries specific to the jurisdictions of public law and private law and their many subcategories: constitutional, criminal, administrative, property, contract, and so forth. Finally, "Systematic philosophy of law" identifies entries on general concepts (e.g., powers and rights, prima facie obligation, civility, distributive justice, autonomy), on methods and the contributions of related disciplines (e.g., empirical evidence, legal ontology, political philosophy, religion and theology, psychiatry), and issues surrounding legal interpretation and argumentation (e.g., skepticism, analogy, objectivity, arbitration, legislative intent). Articles conclude with bibliographies and cross-references. Comprehensive index.

791.   Hansom, Paul, ed. **Twentieth-Century American Cultural Theorists.** Detroit: Gale, 2001. 490p. (Dictionary of Literary Biography, vol. 246).

This volume profiles 34 American cultural theorists and complements Hansom's two volumes on European cultural theorists in the same series (entry 792). Far fewer, proportionally, are individuals who routinely find their way into philosophical reference works than is the case for the European group. Just three, in fact, fall safely into that category: John Dewey, Richard Rorty, and George Santayana. Others embraced under the cultural theory label here comprise a diverse group of writers and thinkers that includes, for example, anthropologist Ruth Benedict, psychoanalyst Karen Horney, social critics Paul Goodman and Christopher Lasch, literary critics Northrop Fry and Granville Hicks, feminist theorists Betty Friedan and Gloria Steinem, race theorists W.E.B. Du Bois and Cornel West, historians Richard Hofstadter and Gary Wills, economist Thorstein Veblen, and linguist and political critic Noam Chomsky. Needless to say, philosophy and philosophically relevant material are not restricted to those identified formally as philosophers.

792.   Hansom, Paul, ed. **Twentieth-Century European Cultural Theorists. First Series.** Detroit: Gale, 2001. 447p. (Dictionary of Literary Biography, vol. 296). **Second Series.** Detroit: Gale, 2004. 450p. (Dictionary of Literary Biography, vol. 246).

See entries 787 and 788 for characterizations of cultural theory. Among the 53 European, including British, theorists profiled in these two volumes, at least half are routinely counted among the ranks of philosophers and make regular appearances in philosophical reference sources. Chronologically they range from Brentano (1838–1917) to Kristeva (still active). Philosophically they are as diverse as Hannah Arendt and Jacques Derrida, a range that also encompasses the lesser diversities of, for example, Adorno, Gadamer, Heidegger, Husserl, Lukács, Lévinas, and Sartre. Other writers and thinkers here represent areas as such sociology, anthropology, psychoanalysis, literary and media criticism, and linguistics, and include, for example, Terry Eagleton, Umberto Eco, Frantz Fanon, Freud, Jung, Frank Kermode, Claude Lévi-Strauss, Georg Simmel, and Max Weber.

These volumes share the qualities and features common to the *Dictionary of Literary Biography* series; see entry 347 for a general comment. See also entry 791 for a companion volume on American cultural theorists.

793.   Hollis, Daniel W. **The ABC-Clio World History Companion to Utopian Movements.** Santa Barbara, Calif.: ABC-Clio, 1998, 303p.

In the history of social-political philosophy, Utopian theory and speculation constitute a small but significant chapter. And in the overall history of Utopianism, the philosophical element plays just one part among religious, literary, and social science elements on the theoretical side and, on the applied side, the many attempts to implement Utopian schemes in the real world. Hollis's dictionary is concerned with all of these aspects, and philosophy is not its dominant theme. But there is a good representation of philosophically grounded Utopias and philosophically oriented proponents as well as critics of Utopian ideas. Entries of particularly philosophical interest include those on Anarchism, Concrete Utopia, Feminist Utopias, the Frankfurt School, Maoism, Marxism, Pansophism, Positivism, Transcendentalism, and Utopian Socialism. Although there are no biographical articles on Utopian theorists, cross-references abound from names of individuals to pertinent movements (e.g., Bloch to Concrete Utopia, Fourier to Utopian Socialism) or specific texts (e.g., Bacon to *New Atlantis,* Skinner to *Walden Two*). Some attention is given to Utopian strains in non-Western thought, for example, in Buddhism and Taoism. Surprisingly, there is no entry for, and only brief reference to, the prototype theoretical Utopia in Western philosophy, Plato's *Republic.* For that topic and other complementary coverage of Utopian thought, reference is recommended to the *Historical Dictionary of Utopianism* by James M. Morris and Andrea L. Koss (Lanham, Md.: Scarecrow Press, 2004) and Richard C. S. Trahair's *Utopias and Utopians: An Historical Dictionary* (Westport, Conn.: Greenwood Press, 1999, 480p.), whose British edition (London: Fitzroy Dearborn, 1999) carries the more descriptive subtitle "An Historical Dictionary of Attempts to Make the World a Better Place and Those Who Were Involved." Each of these dictionaries parallels Hollis's in many respects and in others supplement it (both provide biographical articles, for instance), but on the whole each offers less systematic treatment of explicitly philosophical material. In all three dictionaries, however, food for philosophical thought is on offer throughout, particularly regarding the tensions between freedom and social order that have provoked much Utopian thinking (and critiques thereof) and posed a central challenge for much Utopian experimentation.

794.　　Lipset, Seymour Martin, ed. **Political Philosophy: Theories, Thinkers, Concepts.** Washington, D.C.: Congressional Quarterly, 2001. 510p.

The three terms in the subtitle represent an actual three-part demarcation of the content of this resource for which the label "encyclopedia" would not be inappropriate. Section 1, "Political Philosophies," contains 40 entries on broad political theories, from authoritarianism to twentieth-century European theory and also including, for instance, capitalism, Confucianism, corporatism, fascism, Hinduism, Leninism, nationalism, and Postmodernism. Section 2, "Political Philosophers," has entries for 26 major thinkers from Althusius to Wollestonecraft and including, for example, Burke, Gandhi, M. L. King, Jr., Machiavelli, Nietzsche, Plato, Rousseau, de Toqueville, and Weber. Section 3, "Philosophical Concepts and Issues," treats 34 topics from anarchy to war and civil conflict and including, for example, autonomy, class, consent, democracy (with eight distinct entries on various aspects), human rights, justice, legitimacy, popular sovereignty, and representation. Arrangement of entries within each section is alphabetical. Articles average nearly five pages in length, and there are no short entries. Contributors are 46 scholars affiliated mostly with major American, British, and Canadian universities. Bibliographies accompany each article, and there is a comprehensive index.

795.　　Macey, David. **The Penguin Dictionary of Critical Theory.** London: Penguin Books, 2000. 490p.

Libraries classify this dictionary among works on literary criticism, which does figure prominently in its content, but its own entry for "critical theory" indicates something much broader: "The term can be used quite loosely, as in the present dictionary, to refer to a whole range of theories which take a critical view of society and the human sciences or which seek to explain the emergence of their objects of knowledge" (p. 74). The ambiguity about its range of concern is symptomatic, no doubt, of what the preface characterizes as "the rise of interdisciplinarity within the modern human sciences" that "can itself be seen as a product of the collapse, or calling into question, of the old disciplines." The entry on critical theory is also forthright about its left-leaning sociopolitical orientation. The work shares many entries with the *Columbia Dictionary of Modern Literary and Cultural*

Criticism (see entry 619 in chapter 15), and likewise many entries with *Key Concepts in Cultural Theory* in the present chapter (entry 788). Some indeed are at home chiefly in the realms of literary criticism or, more broadly, aesthetics and art criticism (e.g., irony, mimesis, New Criticism, surrealism), but many have far wider ramifications (e.g., civil society, foundationalism, lesbian feminism, patriarchy, seduction theory). There are also biographical entries for important contributors to critical theory, mainly representing recent Continental philosophy and allied domains (e.g., Derrida, Deleuze, Kristeva), as well as some critics of aspects of its enterprise (e.g., Alan Sokal).

796.   Patterson, Dennis. **A Companion to Philosophy of Law and Legal Theory.** Cambridge, Mass: Blackwell, 1996. 602p. (Blackwell Companions to Philosophy).

Unusually for the series, this Blackwell Companion to Philosophy addresses itself in the first instance to a very narrowly defined audience: first-year American law students. It was conceived, says the editor, in direct response to "the need of the beginning student to get a handle quickly on the vast and diverse theoretical landscape that is the first year's experience" (preface). That focus notwithstanding, it is evident that a wider readership is also in view, if secondarily. The editor explains that he asked each of his authors, whom he describes as "the best writers in contemporary jurisprudence," both to survey their assigned topics and to indicate their own views where appropriate so that the resulting entries "would be of interest both to beginning students and [to] other professionals" (preface). The work's 42 thematically organized essays deal with philosophical and theoretical issues surrounding law and legal systems under four rubrics. Part 1 deals with particular areas of law, for example, property law, criminal law, Constitutional law (divided into four specific aspects), comparative law. Part 2 surveys contemporary schools of legal philosophy and interpretation, for example, natural law theory, legal positivism, feminist jurisprudence, legal formalism, deconstruction. Part 3 considers relationships between law and disciplines such as anthropology, sociology, theology, and literature. Finally, part 4 takes up a variety of specific topics subjected to extensive philosophical analysis and debate, including legal enforcement of morality, punishment and responsibility, the welfare state, the authority of law, and analogical reasoning.

797.   Raynaud, Philippe and Stéphane Rials, eds. **Dictionnaire de philosophie politique.** 3rd ed. Paris: Presses universitaires de France, 2003. 892p.

The first edition of this French reference work on political philosophy was issued in 1996, the second, minimally revised, in 1998. An encyclopedic dictionary, it offers substantial articles on important political philosophers from the ancients to the present; on theories and schools of thought; on concepts such as *autorité, communauté,* and *tolérance;* and on philosophical debates surrounding political phenomena such as *état et société civile, factions et parties, guerre et paix.* The 140 articles are contributed by 92 international authors, including some American scholars, for example, the University of Chicago's well-known Allan Bloom.

798.   **Routledge Dictionary of Twentieth-Century Political Thinkers.** Robert Benewick and Philip Green, eds. London: Routledge, 1992. 244p.

Of 159 political thinkers represented here by short biographical/intellectual sketches and brief bibliographies, many are seldom or never counted as philosophers: Ben

Gurion, Castro, Hitler, the Ayatollah Khomeini, and Booker T. Washington, to name a few scattered widely across the political spectrum. The third or more regularly classed as philosophers are nearly as diverse in their own way: Theodor Adorno, Hannah Arendt, Michel Foucault, Antonio Gramsci, Julia Kristeva, Kropotkin, Jacques Maritain, Robert Nozick, Karl Popper, John Rawls, Leo Strauss, Michael Walzer, and Simone Weil, to name a representative sample. Quasi-philosophers and others inviting philosophical attention include Mary Daly, J. K. Galbraith, Gandhi, F. von Hayek, Martin Luther King, Pareto, Ayn Rand, and B. F. Skinner. Unusually well represented are African, Asian, and Latin American thinkers, for instance Leonardo Boff, Gustavo Gutiérez, "Che" Guevera, Li Dazhao, Ling Quichao, Jayaprakah Narayan, Julius Nyerere, and Ali Shari'ati.

799.   Sheldon, Garrett Ward. **Encyclopedia of Political Thought.** New York: Facts on File, 2001. 342p.

Aimed presumably at high school and early college students and at general readers, this encyclopedia "is intended to present, in clear and concise form, the many ideas, concepts, persons, and movements in the world's political history. It covers everything from abstract ideas (like *freedom* and *justice*) to major thinkers (Aristotle, St. Thomas Aquinas, Locke, Marx) and contemporary movements (feminism, environmentalism, pacifism) from around the world (Western, Indian, Islamic, Chinese)" (preface). One part of this self-description needs some qualification: while there is indeed coverage of non-Western political thought, the emphasis is overwhelmingly Western. There is also a strong emphasis on the twentieth century. As for the conception of "political thought" employed, this is not confined to political philosophy, especially in any rigorous sense. But standard topics of political philosophy such as authority, democracy, general will, natural law, property, and rights are well represented, along with political philosophers, not just "big names" like the examples aforementioned but also less familiar figures such as Hannah Arendt and Giovanni Gentile. Two of the encyclopedia's five contributing authors are identified as professors of philosophy.

OTHER REFERENCE RESOURCES

800.   Wilcox, Laird, and John George. **Be Reasonable: Selected Quotations for Inquiring Minds.** Buffalo, N.Y.: Prometheus Books, 1994. 361p.

This volume (from a publisher closely associated with liberal social philosophy and the American Humanist Association) collects quotations "meant to challenge tendencies toward censorship and suppression of ideas as well as the stifling effects of 'politically correct' behavior" (book jacket). The quotations are divided among chapters on such topics as civil liberties; fanatics and true believers; logic; propaganda and persuasion; reason, rationalism, and free thought; and utopianism, idealism, and reformist zeal. Sources include philosophers, political leaders, political scientists, Supreme Court justices, writers, and others. Most of these speak or write on the side of intellectual liberty and free expression, but a few voices from the opposition (e.g., Hitler and the Ayatollah Khomeini) are also included. Within chapters, the quotations are arranged in alphabetical order by name of author or source document, and there is an index of names.

22
Other Branches of Philosophy and Special Topics

ENVIRONMENTAL PHILOSOPHY

801.   Jamieson, Dale. **A Companion to Environmental Philosophy.** Malden, Mass.: Blackwell, 2001. 531p. (Blackwell Companions to Philosophy).

   If borderline as a reference work, this volume may well realize its editor's hope that it is "the best single volume collection on the subject that is currently available" (preface). It surveys and explores a wide range philosophical issues and perspectives related to the natural environment. Ethical questions—how humans *ought to* relate to the environment—figure pre-eminently among them, but also considered are metaphysical, theological, and even epistemological issues that influence and often undergird ethical claims and attitudes. There are 36 articles organized thematically under 4 rubrics. Part 1 surveys the heritages of 10 "cultural traditions" including the world's major religions, the classical Greek tradition, and modern and contemporary philosophy with respect to their views of nature and human responsibility for the environment and the resources or impediments (often both) they offer for constructing an environmental philosophy. Part 2 surveys contemporary environmental ethics with two general articles on meta-ethics and normative ethics and four on specific schools of thought: sentienism, land ethic, deep ecology, and ecofeminism. Part 3 considers the contributions of neighboring disciplines: literature, aesthetics, economics, history, ecology, and law. Part 4 explores 13 specific problem areas in environmental philosophy, among them the place and value of wilderness, population issues, the question of obligations to future generations, issues surrounding biodiversity, the moral status of animals, environmental justice, technology, consumption, issues raised by the environmental consequences of colonization (terrestrial or extraterrestrial), and the question of civil (or uncivil) disobedience on behalf of environmental convictions.

802.   Palmer, Clare. **Environmental Ethics: A Reference Handbook.** Santa Barbara, Calif.: ABC-Clio, 1997. 192p. (Contemporary Ethical Issues).

   See entry 704.

803.   **Environmental Ethics.** Center for Environmental Philosophy, University of North Texas. http://www.cep.unt.edu.

   See entry 714.

PHILOSOPHY OF HISTORY

804.   Hughes-Warrington, Marnie. **Fifty Key Thinkers on History.** London: Routledge, 2000. 363p. (Routledge Key Guides).

Of the 50 thinkers on history represented here—selected, explains the author, not "on the basis of impact or significance alone, but rather of challenge" (preface)— perhaps no more than 18 are commonly counted among the ranks of philosophers. These include figures who engaged in what is called "substantive" or "speculative" philosophy of history, offering philosophical interpretations of "history" as the course of world events, and those concerned with "critical" or "analytical" philosophy of history, which addresses philosophical issues surrounding "history" as a branch of knowledge. Leading thinkers in the former category include Kant, Hegel, Marx, Spengler, Toynbee, and, latterly, Francis Fukuyama. The second group includes, for example, Collingwood, Croce, Dilthey, Carl Hempel, Thomas Kuhn, Ricœur, Vico, and W. H. Walsh. A few among the philosophers fit less readily into this twofold categorization: Foucault, Heidegger, Ibn Kahldoun, Michael Oakeshott. Of the other thinkers profiled in this volume, the great majority were or are practicing historians, from Herodotus to feminist historian Sheila Rowbotham. But these, too, in many instances engaged in philosophical reflection on their discipline or its subject matter, and their ideas as well as their practice provide much that is of interest for philosophers of history.

Articles in this Routledge Key Guide are accompanied by more extensive bibliographies than is typical of the series.

PHILOSOPHY OF LANGUAGE AND SEMIOTICS

805.   Kellerwessel, Wulf. **A Bibliography on Reference and Some Related Topics in Analytical Philosophy.** Frankfurt am Main: Peter Lang, 1996. 239p.

" 'Reference,' " explains the compiler in his introduction, "means a function of language or the use of language which connects *parts of the language* . . . and singles out concrete *parts of the non-linguistic world* (i.e., persons, animals, individual things . . .)." This seemingly commonplace feature of language has been, as he notes, a central theme within Analytical philosophy, one that has generated an astonishingly large and diverse body of writings. Kellerwessel documents 2,114 English-language and German-language books and articles devoted to this topic, whose chief home is in philosophy of language but whose ramifications also reach into logic, metaphysics, and even philosophy of mind. Arrangement of entries is by author in a single alphabetical sequence. Each entry includes one or more "headwords," or descriptors, indicative of the work's content or central concerns. There is an index based on these headwords.

806.   Colapietro, Vincent M. **Glossary of Semiotics.** New York: Paragon House, 1993. 213p. (Paragon House Glossary for Research, Reading, and Writing).

Semiotics, the general theory of "signs" broadly conceived—from footprints to fossils to traffic signals to bodily gestures to literary texts to visual art works, and so forth, insofar as each conveys meaning or "stands for" for something beyond itself—is both a wide-ranging and a controversial domain of study whose influence is felt in many disciplines, including anthropology, literary theory and criticism, psychology, and sociology. Though it has scientific aspirations, its principal roots are in philosophy as well as linguistics, and it remains deeply imbedded in philosophical issues, as attested by this sampling of entries: behaviorist theory of meaning; Cartesian, Cartesianism; Cassirer, Ernst; deconstruction, deconstructionism; ideological superstructure; immediate knowledge; verifiability principle; Wittgenstein, Ludwig.

Many entries represent technical terms of the field and its near neighbors: abduction, decoder, deep structure, hermeneutics, illocution, reference, and zoosemiosis, for example. Because the glossary is "designed for people who have little or no acquaintance with the field of . . . semiotics" (introduction), definitions and articles are brief and minimally technical. They include no bibliographic references, but a selected bibliography of around 50 items, heavily dominated by philosophical names and titles, appears at the back of the volume.

807.   Dictionary of Logic as Applied in the Study of Language: Concepts/Methods/ Theories. Ed. Witold Marciszewski. The Hague: Martinus Nijhoff, 1981. 436p. (Nijhoff International Philosophy Series, vol. 9).

See entry 729.

808.   Hale, Bob, and Crispin Wright. **A Companion to the Philosophy of Language.** Oxford: Blackwell, 1997. 721p. (Blackwell Companions to Philosophy).

Like some other volumes in the Blackwell Companion series, this employs primarily a thematic rather than alphabetical organization. Its reference value is enhanced, however, by a 38 page alphabetical glossary. There are 25 essays of substantial length, written by active British and American contributors to the field, that comprise the main body of the work. These are divided into three sections: (1) "Meaning and Theories of Meaning"; (2) "Language, Truth, and Reality"; (3) "Reference, Identity, and Necessity." Apart from brief comments on the contours of the field in a two-page preface, there is no introductory overview. The editors' aim was for each essay to provide "a survey and analysis of recent trends in work on the topic in question, offering a bibliography of the more important literature and incorporating a substantial research component. Accordingly, these are essays for a philosophically experienced—advanced undergraduate, graduate, or professional—readership" (preface). A comprehensive index covers both the essays and the glossary.

809.   Lamarque, Peter V., ed. **Concise Encyclopedia of Philosophy of Language.** Kidlington, Oxford, U.K.: Pergamon, 1997. 599p.

This is substantially a derivative work, all but one of its articles having been drawn, with varying degrees of updating and revision, from the authoritative *Encyclopedia of Language and Linguistics,* edited by Ron E. Asher (Oxford: Pergamon Press, 1994, 10 vols.). At its core are some 80 articles commissioned by Lamarque as the *ELL*'s Subject Editor for philosophy. Supplementing these are additional articles selected for their relevance or interest for philosophers of language. These include, as Lamarque takes pains to acknowledge, "articles mostly, but not exclusively, of an empirical nature," for example on apes and language, pragmatics, and language acquisition in the child (foreword).

The encyclopedia's overall organization is thematic, but within each of eight theme sections (following a general introduction in section 1) entries are arranged alphabetically. The eight sections cover language, metaphysics, and ontology; language and mind; truth and meaning; reference; language and logic; formal semantics; pragmatics and speech act theory; and key figures (biographical entries plus some collective biographical articles, for example, medieval philosophy of language). Many articles are quite technical, particularly those in the intersection of language and logic. Others are more accessible, making this encyclopedia useful for diverse levels of readership. Name and subject indexes.

PHILOSOPHY OF TECHNOLOGY

810. Mitcham, Carl, and Robert Mackey. **Bibliography of the Philosophy of Technology.** Chicago: University of Chicago Press, 1973. 205p.

This excellent bibliography, comprehensive and international though not exhaustive, covers a varied literature on "philosophic problems revolving around technology and its meaning to man and society" published from 1925 to 1972. It is organized by five categories: (1) comprehensive philosophical works; (2) ethical and political critiques; (3) religious critiques; (4) metaphysical and epistemological studies, including those concerned with cybernetics and artificial intelligence; and (5), in an appendix, classical documents (mostly from the period prior to 1925) and background materials, including basic histories of technology. Sections 2 and 3 distinguish and segregate works deemed primary and secondary in terms of philosophic content or merit. Arrangement within sections is chronological. Lack of an author index may be a deficiency. Many items have descriptive annotations, and English translations are supplied for non-English titles.

SPECIAL TOPICS

DEATH

811. Miller, Albert Jay, and Michael James Acri. **Death: A Bibliographical Guide.** Metuchen, N.J.: Scarecrow, 1977. 420p.

Encompasses materials dealing with aspects of death from many perspectives: medical, legal, psychological, sociological, theological, and so forth, as well as philosophical. Coverage extends from ancient beginnings to roughly 1974. Most philosophical materials can be located via two subject index entries: "philosophy and death," which cross-references related entries including "attitudes toward death among philosophers," "existentialism and death," and various entries beginning with the word "immortality"; and "ethical problems," which cross-references "euthanasia" and "right to die."

Samuel Southard's *Death and Dying: A Bibliographical Survey* (New York: Greenwood Press, 1991, 513p.) updates and supplements as well as overlaps with Miller and Acri's work, but has a smaller proportion of specifically philosophical material.

812. Triche, Charles W. III and Diane Samson Triche. **The Euthanasia Controversy, 1812–1974: A Bibliography with Select Annotations.** Troy, N.Y.: Whitston, 1975. 242p.

See entry 673.

EVENTS

813. Casati, Roberto and Achille C. Varzi. **50 Years of Events: An Annotated Bibliography, 1947 to 1997.** Bowling Green, Ohio: Philosophy Documentation Center, Bowling Green State University, 1997. 402p.

This misleadingly, perhaps mischievously, titled bibliography is concerned with the philosophical understanding of events as a conceptual and ontological category. This subject, which also encompasses the analysis of specific types of events such as actions, mental events, performances, and processes, has generated a large amount of discussion across many philosophical subdisciplines, especially metaphysics, logic, and the philosophy of language, spilling over as well into allied disciplines such as linguistics and cognitive science. The compilers identify more than 1,800 items in this widely scattered literature, beginning with a seminal 1947 essay by Hans Reichenbach on the logical form of action sentences. They include books, journal articles, collective works and individual contributions thereto, and, more selectively, reviews, dissertations, and technical reports. Reprintings are extensively cited but with no pretense to completeness. Primary arrangement is by author. A detailed subject and name index (including names as subjects) serves well for tracing specific topics, connections, or strands in the debates. Most entries include annotations, varying considerably in length and detail.

TIME

814. Das, T. K. **The Time Dimension: An Interdisciplinary Guide.** New York: Praeger, 1990. 344p.

The phenomenon of time raises issues and avenues for investigation across many fields of study. Das, whose interest in this topic emerged, perhaps surprisingly, from the field of management and organizational studies, organizes his bibliography primarily according to disciplines, including, for example, biology, economics, history, literature, psychology, and sociology, though there are also chapters for general and miscellaneous works and one on calendars and clocks. Philosophy is combined in a chapter with physics, presumably because these often overlap in their respective interests in specific attributes, paradoxes, and puzzles of time. Additional philosophical or philosophically relevant material is scattered throughout other chapters, most especially the chapter on history, which lists a number of items on time's relationship to history, a significant topic within the philosophy of history. Books and journal articles are listed, but not dissertations or other categories of material. Entries are unannotated. Author index only.

Part IV
MISCELLANEA

23
Sundry Currents, Schools, and Movements

This chapter cover six diverse philosophical currents, schools, or movements: African American philosophy, Christian philosophy, feminist philosophy, Freethought, Jewish philosophy, and Marxist philosophy. What these have in common is simply that they do not fit tidily into the categories defined for previous chapters. They are all within the orbit of Western philosophy, or largely so, but most run through more than one of the major periods that conventionally demarcate the history of Western philosophy. The few that are predominantly twentieth- and twenty-first century movements resist ready categorization into the Anglo-American and Continental strains. Moreover, none is confined to any one branch of philosophy, or perhaps a couple of branches, even if in several instances their concerns concentrate on certain areas, such as social-political philosophy or philosophy of religion, more than others.

AFRICAN AMERICAN PHILOSOPHY

815. Lott, Tommy L. and John P. Pittman, eds. **A Companion to African-American Philosophy.** Malden, Mass.: Blackwell, 2003. 465p. (Blackwell Companions to Philosophy).

African American philosophy as conceptualized in this work is something more than philosophy done by African Americans over the span of African American history. It is, rather, a more specific field of thought and inquiry that emerged in the political and social situation of the 1960s. The editors describe it as "thoroughly interdisciplinary with a large, but not exclusive, focus on social, political, moral, and cultural issues"—a focus they also maintain in this volume, even as they acknowledge that "the full sweep of African-American philosophic thought" also encompasses other domains and topics that they "elected not to represent" (preface). An opening essay by Cornell West seeks to define contemporary African American philosophy in relation both to European and American mainstream philosophy and several historic strains in African American thought. Other essays, many by leading African American scholars, address a wide range of topics including the moral and political legacy of slavery, Africa and diaspora thought, black feminism, race classification, white supremacy, integration, affirmative action, aesthetics, black cinema, rap, and sports and African Americans.

While a valuable survey of its field, this volume fits less clearly in the "reference work" category than some other Blackwell Philosophy Companions and offers no special reference features such as a glossary of terms or extensive bibliography.

CHRISTIAN PHILOSOPHY, INCLUDING SCHOLASTICISM / THOMISM

Many philosophers throughout Western philosophical history, beginning a few centuries after Christ, have identified themselves with Christianity, though varying widely in their specific theological persuasions, in degrees of orthodoxy, and in the extent to which distinctly Christian ideas or motivations figure in their philosophies. Some Christian philosophers known particularly for the religious cast of their thought are Saint Augustine (see entries 353–362), Blaise Pascal (entry 484), George Berkeley (entries 407–408), Jonathan Edwards (entries 419–421), Søren Kierkegaard (entries 454–459), Gabriel Marcel (entry 596), Paul Tillich (entry 610), Pierre Teilhard de Chardin (entries 608–609), and a large group of philosophers gathered under the banner of Scholasticism or, somewhat more narrowly, Thomism, the more recent phases of which are often designated as Neo-Scholasticism and Neo-Thomism. For the medieval origins of Scholasticism, see chapter 12, including resources on individual philosophers, notably Saint Thomas Aquinas (entries 367–377), Saint Anselm of Canterbury (entry 352), and John Duns Scotus (entry 364). See also entries on twentieth-century Neo-Thomist philosophers Jacques Maritain (entry 597) and Etienne Gilson (entry 542) in chapter 14. Many Christian philosophers and philosophical discussions of Christian faith are represented in the sources on philosophy of religion listed in chapter 20.

816. McLean, George F. **An Annotated Bibliography of Philosophy in Catholic Thought, 1900–1964.** New York: Ungar, 1967. 371p. (Philosophy in the 20th Century: Catholic and Christian, vol. 1).

"This comprehensive and annotated bibliography . . . has been compiled as an aid to the professor, student, and general reader. . . . The term 'Catholic thought' is understood as extending to works in or about the tradition of St. Augustine, St. Thomas Aquinas and other Scholastics, as well as to works by or about Catholics of the more recent existential, personalist, or phenomenological orientations" (preface). Part 1 begins with chapters on "research instruments" and introductory works, followed by 11 chapters "corresponding to the accustomed subject divisions of philosophy courses" (logic, epistemology, cosmology, psychology, etc.). Ethics is covered by two chapters: one on general ethics, the other on special ethics with subsections for legal, medical, sociological, domestic, political, economic, industrial, Marxian, and international ethics . Part 2 consists of four chapters concerned with different schools of Catholic/Christian philosophy: Augustinian, Thomistic, Franciscan, and "Personalist-Existentialist-Phenomenological."

Each entry, in addition to a descriptive and sometimes critical annotation, includes a code letter or letters indicating level(s) of readership, from A ("readers without a formal introduction to the study of philosophy") to D ("scholars").

817. McLean, George F. **A Bibliography of Christian Philosophy and Contemporary Issues.** New York: Ungar, 1967. 312p. (Philosophy in the 20th Century: Catholic and Christian, vol. 2).

This is a selective, classified listing of books and articles from 1934 through 1964 concerned with the relationship between philosophy and religion and with issues common to philosophical and religious thought. "Christian" is interpreted in a broad sense for the purpose of this volume, and non-Christian writings that bear on the issues are included. Chapter headings are: (1) Christian Philosophy; (2) Contemporary Philosophies; (3) Philosophy and Technology; (4) Philosophy of Man and God; (5) The Problem of God in a Secular Culture; (6) Religious Knowledge and Language; (7) Moral Philosophy; (8) Teaching Philosophy. English-language materials are emphasized, but coverage is international, with non-English materials following English in any given section. An appendix lists philosophy dissertations presented in U.S. and Canadian Catholic universities.

Unlike its companion volume on Catholic philosophy (entry 816), this bibliography is not annotated and is accordingly less useful, because there is often no clue to the cited work's perspective on the issue it addresses, or even its relevance.

818. Redmond, Walter Bernard. **Bibliography of the Philosophy in the Iberian Colonies of America.** The Hague: Martinus Nijhoff, 1972. 174p. (International Archives of the History of Ideas, 51).

The title's reference to "the" philosophy presumably reflects, deliberately, the fact that philosophy in the Spanish and Portuguese colonies meant *Scholastic* philosophy. In fact, Redmond chose 1810 as the approximate closing date for his bibliography because "both the 'pure' and the 'modern' scholasticism"—two currents distinguished in his preface—"tend to be supplemented after 1810 by non-Scholastic philosophies." (A few important later Scholastic works do get registered, however). Primary materials listed (1,154 items) are mainly "the traditional philosophy (and theology) *cursus* (classroom treatises on logic, physics, psychology, metaphysics, ethics, and the various theology courses) and *conclusiones* (or *theses, asserta,* etc.; lists of opinions defended in scholastic functions), but some other material has also been included (articles in periodicals, 'study plans,' etc.)" (preface). Manuscripts as well as printed works are listed, and many entries indicate locations of manuscripts or printed copies. A separate and much shorter section lists and annotates secondary literature (275 items).

819. Blanc, Élie. **Dictionnaire de philosophie ancienne, moderne et contemporaine.** Paris: P. Lethielleux, 1906. Reprinted, New York: Burt Franklin, 1972. 1,248 columns. **Supplément (années 1906, 1907, 1908)** bound with main work. 154 columns (Burt Franklin Bibliography and Reference Series, 461; Philosophy & Religious History, 117).

See entry 162.

820. Brugger, Walter. **Philosophisches Wörterbuch.** 17th ed. Freiburg im Breisgau: Herder, 1985. 592p.

See entry 170.

821. Brugger, Walter and Kenneth Baker. **Philosophical Dictionary.** Spokane, Wash.: Gonzaga University Press, 1972. 460p.

See entry 119.

822. Chapman, Colin. **An Eerdmans Handbook: The Case for Christianity.** Grand Rapids, Mich.: William B. Eerdmans, 1981. 313p.

This handbook of Christian apologetics—the endeavor to make a reasonable case for Christianity and to defend it against philosophical and other objections—is designed for a popular, nonscholarly audience. While much of its material is theological or historical rather than philosophical, a number of philosophical topics are addressed: traditional theistic proofs, the problem of evil, verification in philosophy and in science, the meaning of life, the relation between reason and faith, and others. Particularly pertinent is the section on "Understanding and Testing the Alternatives," which offers sketches of 10 "key thinkers" (Aquinas, Descartes, Locke, Hume, Rousseau, Kant, Hegel, Kierkegaard, Marx,

Freud) and 10 "-isms" (Catholic Scholasticism, deism, rationalism, atheism, agnosticism, mysticism, pantheism, Marxism, existentialism, humanism). Though intentionally elementary and at times shallow, the work is well done on the whole, taking into consideration its undisguised bias and the intended audience. A special asset is the wealth of pithy quotes selected to illustrate or characterize specific arguments, positions, or trends of thought. As with other *Eerdmans Handbooks* (. . . *to the Bible, to the World's Religions, to the History of Christianity,* etc.), numerous illustrations and creative design add life as well as visual interest.

823.   Evans, C. Stephen. **Pocket Dictionary of Apologetics & Philosophy of Religion.** Downers Grove, Ill.: InterVarsity Press, 2002. 125p.

See entry 767.

824.   **Handbook of Contemporary Philosophy of Religion**. Vol. 2: Brian J. Shanley. **The Thomist Tradition.** 2002. 238p.

See entry 770.

825.   Kennedy, Leonard A., C.S.B. **A Catalogue of Thomists, 1270–1900.** Houston, Tex.: Center for Thomistic Studies, University of St. Thomas (distr. Notre Dame, Ind.: University of Notre Dame Press), 1987. 240p.

Kennedy lists as exhaustively as he could manage philosophers and theologians in the tradition of St. Thomas Aquinas—some 2,000 of them—from the lengthy period indicated in his title, and provides minimal information on each: name, dates, principal works, and sources for additional biographical and bibliographical information. The overall arrangement is chronological, by centuries, and within that by religious order and finally (for some orders) by country. While better sources are available for major Thomist writers, Kennedy's compilation is useful for research on lesser-known figures and, through the tabulations incorporated in his table of contents as well as the introduction, an overview of the interest in Thomistic thought at various times and among different religious groups. Criteria for inclusion are explained in the introduction; a name index is at the back.

826.   Mondin, Battista. **Dizionario Enciclopedicao di Filosofia, Teologia e Morale**. Milano: Masimo, 1989. 855p.

See entry 181.

827.   **New Catholic Encyclopedia.** 2nd ed. Detroit: Thomson/Gale; Washington, D.C.: Catholic University of America, 2003–2004. 15 vols.

Though not in the first place a philosophical encyclopedia, the second edition of the *New Catholic,* like its first-edition predecessor (New York: McGraw-Hill, 1967, 15 vols. plus supplements 16–19, 1974–1996), is simply too rich a philosophical resource to overlook. By no means confined to Catholic philosophy or philosophers, it has articles on a surprisingly high proportion of topics and figures likely to be treated in any comprehensive philosophical encyclopedia, including many in non-Western philosophy. As is to be expected, treatment is invariably from a Catholic perspective, more evident in some articles than in others but rarely if ever so heavy-handed as to render them nonuseful for non-Catholic readers. Many relevant entries are cross-listed under "Philosophy" and "Philosophy, history of" in the index (vol. 15), but these are far from exhaustive of the encyclopedia's philosophical content. Catholic philosophers, from the famous (e.g., Aquinas, Marcel) through the somewhat well-known (Gilson, Lonergan, Maritain) to the relatively obscure (De Rayemaeker, Mercier) come in for special attention, of course, as do topics of special interest for Catholic thought (e.g., natural law, Neo-Scholasticism and Neo-Thomism, soul–body relationship). But there are also, just to give a flavor, articles on Plato and Platonism filling a combined 11 pages, on Kant and Kantianism for a similar combined length, and 5 pages each on movements as diverse as Logical Positivism and Deconstructionism.

828. Wuellner, Bernard, S. J. **Dictionary of Scholastic Philosophy.** 2nd ed. Milwaukee: Bruce, 1966. 339p.

"This dictionary, covering most of the technical language used in all branches of scholastic philosophy, is meant chiefly for undergraduate students" (preface). Many others, nonetheless, should find it at least equally useful. Preference is given to terms found in or defined by Aristotle and Aquinas, the twin springs of Scholasticism, but ample heed is given also to the concepts of later thinkers such as Duns Scotus and Suarez and prominent Neo-Scholastics such as Gilson and Maritain. Particular attention is given to compound terms and phrases, which are usually placed under the entry for the principal term. For example, under the entry for cause are located such expressions as "cause of being *(causa in esse),*" "dependent (subordinate) cause," and "false cause, fallacy of." A weakness, perhaps unavoidable, is that many definitions are quite abstract and employ other Scholastic terms that may be as unfamiliar as the term being defined. Some backtracking will usually overcome the problem.

Twenty tables and diagrams bring together many of the most significant classifications and distinctions that are characteristic of Scholastic thought: categories of being, divisions of efficient causes, divisions of the good, types of law and their relations, figures of the syllogism, and others.

FEMINIST PHILOSOPHY

For sources on women philosophers (not all of them feminist philosophers) see entries 35, 36, 203, 274, 853, and 854. See also sources on two important twentieth-century feminist philosophers, Simone de Beauvoir (entry 568) and Julia Kristeva (entries 593 and 594).

829. Code, Lorraine, ed. **Encyclopedia of Feminist Theories.** London: Routledge, 2000. 530p.

Feminist theory is not coterminous with feminist philosophy. But the latter constitutes one important part of feminist theory among others that can be categorized within the domains of sociology, anthropology, psychology, political theory, jurisprudence, economics, literary theory, and others. At least equally significantly, feminist theory often represents the mutual interpenetration of philosophy and these various disciplines. An observation under this encyclopedia's entry for philosophy reflects at least one side of this dynamic: "In maintaining strong links with feminist theorizing in other areas, feminist philosophy is also bringing new dimensions of interdisciplinarity and political awareness to philosophy. . . ."

Besides the entry for philosophy, others in this work with a strong philosophical focus are those on deconstruction, epistemology, essentialism, ethics, metaphysics, methodology, and Post-Structuralism/Postmodernism. And among 60 biographical entries for important feminist theorists are a number for figures regularly classified as philosophers, such as Angela Davis, De Beauvoir, Irigaray, Kristeva, and Jane Martin. The encyclopedia concentrates on what is termed second-wave feminist theory as it has developed since the 1960s, and primarily on the English-speaking world, with a substantial exception for French feminist theory.

Some 260 contributors, along with 11 consulting editors, are drawn widely from the major English-speaking nations plus a few others. Their institutional (mainly major university) affiliations are identified, but regrettably not their departmental affiliations or fields of study.

Most articles are accompanied by brief bibliographies combining "references and further reading." There is a general index.

830. Humm, Maggie. **Dictionary of Feminist Theory.** 2nd ed. Columbus, Ohio: Ohio State University Press; Hemel Hempstead, U.K: Prentice Hall/Harvester Wheatsheaf, 1995. 354p.

See entry 829 for a comment on the relationship between feminist theory and feminist philosophy. Unlike the *Encyclopedia of Feminist Theories,* this dictionary, whose first edition appeared in 1989, is the work of a single author. Though comparable in the scope of its coverage and the number and types of entries, it is generally written at a somewhat more accessible level, one of its professed aims being to assist university students who struggle with forbidding terminology (preface). Another interesting difference is that its biographical entries include some male thinkers who contributed to or influenced feminist theory, for example, Barthes, Freud, Marcuse. Humm describes her selection of topics as "almost wholly shaped by French and Anglo-American theory. I have for the most part selected writing which is shaped by three concerns: first the redefining of the *content* of knowledge; second the development of an alternative epistemology; and, finally, the mapping of possible new configurations of knowledge" (preface). Articles do not have bibliographies but most incorporate one or several references to a general bibliography at the back of the volume. There is no index.

831. Jaggar, Allison M. and Iris Marion Young. **A Companion to Feminist Philosophy.** Malden, Mass.: Blackwell, 1998. 703p. (Blackwell Companions to Philosophy, 12).

Following a brief general introduction, this Blackwell Companion offers 58 assays on various dimensions of and issues within feminist philosophy, organized thematically under 10 headings. These are (1) the Western canonical tradition; (2) Africa, Asia, Latin America, and Eastern Europe; (3) language; (4) knowledge and nature; (5) religion; (6) subjectivity and embodiment; (7) art; (8) ethics; (9) society; and (10) politics. There is no glossary or similar reference aid as found in some other Blackwell Companions to Philosophy that share a thematic arrangement, but the work does feature an unusually extensive bibliography (pp. 591–675). There is a general index.

Among the volume's more than 60 writers, the typical contributor is a professor of philosophy or women's studies, or both, at a U.S. university or college. But a few are in other disciplines such as political studies, law, or theology, and there is significant representation from Canada, Britain, Australia, and several non-English-speaking countries.

832.   Switala, Kristin. **Feminist Theory Website.** http://www.cddc.vt.edu/feminism/ (accessed October 29, 2005).

This Web site features mainly bibliographies of feminist theory and biographical sketches of feminist theorists. Feminist philosophy is well represented along with other strains of feminist theory, particularly within two of the site's major categories: fields within feminism and individual feminists. (The third major category is national and ethnic feminisms.) "Fields within feminism" include, besides philosophy, several narrower categories as well as related fields with philosophical import, notably aesthetics, critical theory, epistemology, essentialism, ethics, liberal feminism, Marxism, and Postmodernism.

FREETHOUGHT

833.   Brown, Marshall G. and Gordon Stein. **Freethought in the United States: A Descriptive Bibliography.** Westport, Conn.: Greenwood, 1978. 146p.

"Freethought may be defined as thought which is free of dogmatic assumptions (usually those of religious dogma) and which seeks to answer all questions through rational inquiry. As such, it includes atheism, rationalism, and secular humanism" (preface). Philosophical thought is but one element in freethought thus broadly defined, and judging by this bibliographic guide, not necessarily the most important. Nonetheless, significant philosophical positions within and philosophical influences upon American freethought are among the matters covered here, and covered in a way not likely to be paralleled elsewhere.

834.   Stein, Gordon. **Freethought in the United Kingdom and the Commonwealth: A Descriptive Bibliography**. Westport, Conn.: Greenwood Press, 1981. 193p.

This work by Stein complements his earlier joint effort with Marshall Brown, *Freethought in the United States* (entry 833). Like the latter, it is not exclusively or even predominantly concerned with philosophic thought, but does present significant philosophical material in a particular context and from a perspective not readily duplicated elsewhere. Four narrative chapters describe the British literature from about 1624 to the present; an alphabetical list of works cited is at the end of each chapter. Appendices cover freethought in Commonwealth countries, library collections on freethought, theses and dissertations, and works in progress.

JEWISH PHILOSOPHY

For resources on some individuals prominent in the history of Jewish philosophy, see the entries for Philo of Alexandria (entries 315–317), Baruch Spinoza (entries 502–508), and Martin Buber (entries 570–571).

835.   Isaacs, Ronald H. **Every Person's Guide to Jewish Philosophy and Philosophers.** Northvale, N.J.: Jason Aronson, 1999. 283p.

For the most part, Isaacs's guide comprises a standard historical survey. Its reference value, however—particularly in the absence of any English-language dictionary or encyclopedia devoted to Jewish philosophy—is enhanced by inclusion of a 16-page "glossary of philosophic terms" that has entries not just for concepts but for important philosophers and texts. Some entries deal with persons or topics not covered elsewhere in the volume. The survey section, following an introductory chapter, moves more or less chronologically from the beginnings of Jewish philosophy and Philo Judaeus to the philosophies of four branches of contemporary Judaism: Orthodox, Reform, Conservative, and Reconstructionist. Intervening chapters are mostly devoted to 35 individual philosophers, including, for example, Moses Maimonides, Levi Ben Gershom, Spinoza, Moses Mendelssohn, Leo Baeck, Franz Rosenzweig, Martin Buber, Joshua Heschel, and Emil Fackheim. A few chapters treat wider realms such as medieval Jewish philosophy and theology after the Holocaust. The text tends to assume some familiarity with Judaism generally, and sometimes uses Hebrew terms without explanation.

836. Kilcher, Andreas B., Otfried Fraisse, and Yossef Schwartz, eds. **Metzler Lexikon jüdischer Philosophen: Philosophisches Denken des Judentums von der Antike bis zur Gegenwart**. Stuttgart: J. B. Metzler, 2003. 476p.

The editors devote a 12-page introductory discussion to the challenge of defining the concept "Jewish philosophy." For the purpose of this biographical dictionary, suffice it to say, the criterion for who is a "Jewish philosopher" is not adherence to Judaic religion in a traditional sense, or in any sense at all, but neither is it simply a matter of race or ethnicity. It encompasses ethnically Jewish philosophers in whose thought Judaism or their own Jewishness figures in some significant way, but excludes those in whose thought it plays no role or only a marginal one. This leaves out Husserl and Popper, for instance, while admitting Freud and Derrida. The example of Freud signals that "philosopher" is also interpreted broadly. Articles on 189 individuals are presented in chronological rather than alphabetical sequence, from Philo of Alexandria through French philosopher Sarah Kofman (born 1934). Treatments are scholarly and authoritative, contributed by 86 scholars from institutions in Europe, Israel, and the United States. Bibliographies at the end of every article, while weighted somewhat toward German-language sources, often cite works in English, French, Hebrew, and occasionally other languages.

MARXIST PHILOSOPHY

For some individual Marxist philosophers, see entries relating to Friedrich Engels (entries 422–423), Georg Lukács (entry 595), and Karl Marx (entries 471–473). Philosophers whose primary identification is not with Marxism but who incorporate Marxist elements in their thought and are sometimes classified as Neo-Marxists include Jacques Derrida (entries 578–579), Michel Foucault (entry 580), Julia Kristeva (entries 593–594), Maurice Merleau-Ponty (entry 598), and Jean-Paul Sartre (entries 602–606).

837. Baxandall, Lee. **Marxism and Aesthetics: A Selective Annotated Bibliography: Books and Articles in the English Language**. New York: Humanities Press, 1968, 1973. 261p.

See entry 613.

838. **Bibliographie Philosophie,** 1967–1987. Berlin: Akademie für Gesellschaftswissenschaften beim Z.K. der S.E.D., Institut für Marxistisch-leninistische Philosophie, Zentralstelle für philosophische Information und Dokumentation, 1967–1987. Vols. 1–21.

See entry 78.

839. Bochenski, Joseph M., et. al., eds. **Guide to Marxist Philosophy: An Introductory Bibliography.** Chicago: Swallow Press, 1972. 81p.

"This book is a guide to readings. . .written for English-speaking students. . . . [O]nly the minimum has been said about the [Marxist] doctrines, in order to indicate the nature of the books recommended" (introduction).

Following an initial chapter on the philosophical background of Marx (Hegel and Feuerbach) are chapters devoted to six basic varieties of Marxism: (1) the thought of Marx himself; (2) German Classical Marxism, originating with Engels; (3) Soviet Marxism-Leninism; (4) Neo-Marxism, including interaction and dialogue with Existentialism, Freudianism, and Christianity; (5) Chinese Marxism; and (6) "the New Left." (This last chapter, dominated by Marcuse, reflects the political atmosphere of the late sixties and early seventies.) Listing just over 150 sources, mostly books, this very selective guide has been judged rather biased by some reviewers; but the editors would likely defend their choices with reference to, among other criteria, their intent to avoid secondary literature by those (on any side) "whose desire is not to instruct but to gain partisans" (introduction).

840. Lachs, John. **Marxist Philosophy: A Bibliographical Guide.** Chapel Hill: University of North Carolina Press, 1967. 166p.

Lachs lists, without annotations, 1,557 items published through 1966: books, journal and encyclopedia articles, and discussions in general histories of philosophy, in English, French, and German, but emphasizing books and especially books in English. He includes some materials which are only obliquely philosophical but do throw light on the underlying philosophical theories—for example, on Soviet educational practice or on the genetics controversies centering around Lysenko. There are 38 chapters, beginning with an introductory comment and a chapter on the classics (works of Marx, Engels, Lenin, Stalin, and Mao). Others cover Marxist themes (Dialectical Materialism, the class struggle); Marxist treatments of specific areas and topics (freedom, ethics, aesthetics); Marxist philosophy in specific countries or regions (United States, Soviet Union); and special types of works (journals of special relevance, bibliographies and reference works). Within chapters, English works are listed first, then French, then German; within each language grouping, books precede articles. An author index is provided.

841. Bottomore, Tom, et. al. **Dictionary of Marxist Thought.** 2nd ed. Cambridge, Mass.: Blackwell, 1992. 647p.

Though by no means confined to Marxist *philosophy,* this dictionary does provide extensive coverage of philosophical concepts (e.g., alienation, dialectics, historical materialism, praxis, truth), Marxist treatments of specific areas of philosophy (aesthetics, ethics, theory of knowledge), the philosophical background of Marxism (Feuerbach, Hegel, "Young Hegelians"), philosophical schools and movements within Marxism (Frankfurt School, Legal Marxism, revisionism, Western Marxism), and individual Marxist philosophers (Althusser, Luxemburg, Marcuse, Plekhanov). In addition, a survey article on philosophy discusses the role of philosophy in Marxism and Marxism's status as philosophy. Entries added to the second edition (some but not all representing new developments) include analytical Marxism, Sergei Eisenstein, gender, market socialism, and William Morris. Postscripts are used to update some older articles, notably those on Marxism in Eastern Europe (reflecting the collapse of communist regimes which preceded this edition) and on Soviet Marxism (still predating the fall of communism and the break-up of the U.S.S.R.). Even in the face of earth-shaking changes in Marxism itself, this remains a valuable resource on Marxist thought and the best source that is at once in English, in dictionary format, and not itself a work of Marxist partisanship.

842.   Buhr, Manfred, ed. **Enzyklopädie zur bürgerlichen Philosophie im 19. und 20. Jahrhundert.** Cologne: Pahl-Rugenstein, 1988. 597p.

See entry 517.

843.   Buhr, Manfred, and Alfred Kosing. **Kleines Wörterbuch der marxistisch-leninistischen Philosophie.** 7th rev. ed. Berlin: Dietz, 1984. 334p.

This compact dictionary does not restrict itself to specifically Marxist-Leninist topics and thinkers; it takes in, as its foreword explains, any philosophical concepts and names important for study of the works of Marx, Engels, Lenin, and contemporary (at the time of its writing) Marxist-Leninist philosophers, and for understanding the "ideological class-struggle between socialism and imperialism." Consequently, it is close to, if not quite, a general philosophical dictionary with a Marxist perspective. Separate indexes are provided for "key words" (entries for concepts, philosophical schools and branches, etc.) and for personal names.

844.   **Filosofskaia entsiklopediia.** F. V. Konstantinov, general editor. Moscow: "Sovetskaia entsiklopediia," 1960–70. 5 vols.

See entry 183.

845.   **Filosofskii entsiklopedicheskii slovar'.** 2nd ed. Ed. S. S. Averintsev, et. al. Moscow: "Sovetskaia éntsiklopediia," 1989. 814 p.

See entry 185.

846.   Frolov, Ivan Timofeevich, ed. **Dictionary of Philosophy.** Translated from the Russian; ed. Murad Saifulin and Richard P. Dixon. Moscow: Progress Publishers; New York: International Publishing Co., 1985. 464p.

See entry 127.

847.   Gorman, Robert A., ed. **Biographical Dictionary of Marxism.** Westport, Conn.: Greenwood Press, 1986. 388p.

"This volume contains biographical essays for over 210 Marxian philosophers and activists from almost fifty nations on five continents" (preface). While the categories of "philosopher" and "activist" overlap—notably in the instances of Engels, Lenin, Mao, and Marx himself—many (probably a majority) of the figures profiled here would scarcely be classed as philosophers and are known rather as political leaders or as Marxist economists, historians, social critics, and so forth. Yet they are brought together in this volume on the basis of a philosophical criterion: their common adherence to materialist or "orthodox"

Marxism, elucidated by Gorman in his introduction. This separates them from the figures included in the companion volume on Neo-Marxism (entry 848). Articles range from a half page to three pages in length and provide biographical details, summaries of their subject's contributions to Marxist theory or practice, and bibliographies, mostly brief, of primary and secondary sources.

848.   Gorman, Robert A., ed. **Biographical Dictionary of Neo-Marxism.** Westport, Conn.: Greenwood Press, 1985. 463p.

A companion to Gorman's *Biographical Dictionary of Marxism* (entry 847), this volume, too, includes and excludes individuals on the basis of a philosophical criterion: those represented here, while they all owe intellectual debts and in many cases a strong sense of allegiance to Marx, have rejected or distanced themselves from the materialist foundation of orthodox Marxism. In addition to 205 biographical entries, there are 10 entries for important groups, movements, or journals. Individuals readily recognized as philosophers comprise a larger proportion in this work than is the case for the volume on materialist Marxists. Prominent among them are, for example, Adorno, Benjamin, Bloch, De Beauvoir, Derrida, Feyerabend, Foucault, Gramsci, Habermas, Kristeva, Lukács, Lyotard, Marcuse, Merleau-Ponty, and Sartre. Many intellectuals from other arenas also appear here, for example, W.E.B. Du Bois, Frantz Fanon, Erich Fromm, Anthony Giddens, Emma Goldman, Michael Harrington, Jean Jaurés, C. Wright Mills, Wilhelm Reich. Noteworthy, too, is the inclusion of numerous figures from Third-World and former Eastern Bloc countries who are little known to English-speaking readers.

849.   Klaus, Georg and Manfred Buhr. **Philosophisches Wörterbuch.** 8th corrected ed. Berlin: Das Europäische Buch, 1972. 2 vols.

See entry 173.

850.   **Kratkii slovar' po èstetike.** Ed. Mikhail Fedotovich Ovsiannikov and V.A. Razumnii. Moscow: Izdvesto Politicheskoi Literatury, 1963. 542p. 2nd ed., Moscow: Prosveshchenie, 1983. 223p.

See entry 622.

851.   **Slovar' po ētike.** Ed. I. S. Kona. 5th ed. Moscow: Izd-vo Politicheskoi Literatury, 1983. 445p.

See entry 707.

24
Directories and Miscellaneous Reference Sources

DIRECTORIES

For directories to philosophy-related internet sites, see chapter 6.

852. **Directory of American Philosophers, 2004–2005.** 22nd ed. Heather K. Michon, managing ed. Archie J. Bahm, founding ed. Charlottesville, Va.: Philosophy Documentation Center, 2004. 698p.

New editions of this directory have been published every two years since the first edition of 1962/63. Minor changes in organization and content have occurred over time, along with periodic changes in editorial direction. The largest section of this as of previous issues is a directory of U.S. university and college philosophy departments arranged first by states, then alphabetically by institutions. Information provided includes departmental addresses, phone and fax numbers, e-mail addresses, Web site URLs, department chairs, and faculty members listed with their ranks and philosophical specialties. Additional sections cover graduate assistantships, research centers and institutes, societies, journals, and publishers. A separate division of the *Directory* covers Canada in similar fashion. An alphabetical directory of philosophers, with addresses, consolidates coverage of the United States and Canada and includes some individuals with graduate philosophy degrees but not currently affiliated with any college or university department. Finally, there is a brief statistical section. Indexes are provided for institutions, centers and institutes, societies, journals, and publishers.

853. **Directory of Women in Philosophy, 1981–82.** Ed. Caroline Whitbeck with Deanna Barousse. Bowling Green, Ohio: Philosophy Documentation Center, Bowling Green State University, 1981. 38p.

Too dated to serve its original directory function, this alphabetical directory and two preceding editions dated 1976–1977 and 1979–1980 (issued under Whitbeck's name alone) may have some historical utility in providing a picture of women's participation in academic philosophy in the United States and Canada in the late 1970s and early 1980s. In addition to institutional address and telephone number, it gives information about degrees held, fields of specialization, position, dissertation, and publications (up to six). Indexed by state and country and by fields of specialization.

For a current directory of women philosophers, see entry 854.

854. **Directory of Women Philosophers.** American Philosophical Association, Committee on the Status of Women. http://dacnet.rice.edu/Services/DWP (accessed October 29, 2005).

An online directory of American women philosophers, searchable by name, by institutional affiliation, and by area of specialization. The directory lists both well-established figures and junior members of the profession, but it is far from a complete list of American women philosophers. Sample searches in October 2005 failed to turn up a number of individuals known to me, including several who are relatively prominent. Short records returned by searches include only basic data about affiliation and areas of specialization and competency, but have links to extended records that include mail and email addresses, source of Ph.D., limited information about publications, and occasionally a Web site link.

855.   Guide to Graduate Programs in Philosophy. 2000 ed. Newark, Del.: American Philosophical Association, University of Delaware, 2000. 353p.

      Provides information on more than 175 graduate philosophy programs in the United States and Canada. Includes information on available areas of specialization, program requirements, admissions, financial aid, interdisciplinary research opportunities, faculty and their areas of research, and contact information. No comparative rankings are made. See entry 866 for a Web site that provides rankings.

856.   International Directory of Bioethics Organizations. Ed. Anita L. Nolen and Mary Carrington Coutts. Washington, D.C.: National Reference Center for Bioethics Literature, Kennedy Institute of Ethics, Georgetown University, 1993. 371p. (Bioethics Resource Series, vol. 1).

      See entry 717.

857.   International Directory of Philosophy and Philosophers, 2003–2004. 13th ed. Ramona Cormier, ed. Heather K. Michon, managing ed. Paul Kurtz and Gilbert Varet, founding eds. Charlottesville, Va.: Philosophy Documentation Center, 2001. 764p.

      This directory encompassing more than 130 countries, but excluding the United States and Canada, complements the *Directory of American Philosophers* (entry 852) and alternates with it on a biennial publishing schedule of new editions. It is similar to the *DAP* in the categories of information it includes and also, now, in its arrangement—in contrast to earlier editions, in which all information on a given country was grouped together. The overarching scheme now consists of five sections covering respectively university and college philosophy departments, research centers and institutes, societies and associations, journals, publishers, and a sixth containing an alphabetical listing of some 13,000 university-affiliated philosophers. Each of the first five sections, but not the sixth, is subdivided by countries. Information supplied for departments or faculties of philosophy includes, as available, address, phone and fax numbers, e-mail address, Web site URL, names of faculty members with their rank and fields of specialization, enrollments, and highest degree granted. Consult the preface for other details of coverage and arrangement. Indexes are provided for each of the five categories mentioned previously.
      Content and editors of previous editions have varied. The first edition, published with the bilingual title *International Directory of Philosophy and Philosophers/ Repertoire internationale de la philosophie et de philosophes* and edited by Gilbert Varet and Paul Kurtz (New York: Humanities Press, 1965, 235p.), has some continuing value for its survey articles on philosophical activity and trends in individual countries, not repeated in later editions. Particularly good examples are the articles on South Africa and the U.S.S.R. Not every country covered in its directory was also represented by an article (there were, e.g., none for Australia, Austria, Bolivia, Indonesia, Turkey), but many were, even some

whose profile in the philosophical world has not been prominent (e.g., El Salvador, Finland, Portugal, Venezuela, and Yugoslavia). The articles were in English, French, or (less often) Spanish.

858.   The Philosopher's Phone and E-mail Directory, 1998–2001. Charlottesville, Va.: Philosophy Documentation Center, 1998–2000.

Formerly *The Philosopher's Phone Book* (1995–97), this directory of philosophers in the United States and Canada replicated in part the "Names and Addresses of Philosophers" section of the *Directory of American Philosophers* (entry 852), but added to each individual's entry his or her department or home phone number and e-mail address. Publication was suspended following the 2000–2001 edition, and the publisher confirms (November 1, 2005) that there are no plans to revive it.

859.   Spezialbibliotheken in Deutschland. Band 5: **Philosophie, Pädagogik, Religion.** Compiled by Petra Hauke. Bad Honeff: Bock & Herchen, 2002.

A directory of German libraries, listed alphabetically by location, whose collection emphases fall in the areas of philosophy, pedagogy, or religion. A majority of these turn out to be religious libraries, but there is a substantial representation of libraries specializing in philosophy or with particularly strong philosophy collections, including, for example, a number of general university libraries as well as university *Fachbibliotheken.* Data provided usually include, at minimum, street or mail addresses, phone and fax numbers, and specific collection emphases. They may additionally include, as applicable, email addresses, Web sites, hours, directors or supervisors, staffing, collection size, catalog availability, and participation in union lists and catalogs.

SELECTED ASSOCIATION WEB SITES

This section is limited to a few key Web sites for major philosophical associations, and only those whose sites offer substantial content beyond basic information about themselves. Directories with links to sites for numerous other organizations, including many specialized associations, societies, and research centers, can be found in the general internet guides listed in Chapter 6, and in several of the sites listed here. A few specialized organization Web sites that incorporate an exceptional amount of reference content are listed in the appropriate subject chapters.

860.   APA Online. American Philosophical Association. http://www.apa.udel.edu/apa/index.html (accessed October 29, 2005).

Member-oriented features at the American Philosophical Association's Web site include information about APA officers, governance, divisions, and meetings; policy statements; information on prizes and awards; and, in a "members only" section requiring log-in, the APA membership directory, a "Jobs for Philosophers" listing, and a grants and fellowships directory, among others. Publicly accessible resources that may be as useful for nonmembers as for members include a directory of Web pages for U.S. college and university philosophy departments, general information (including statistics) about the philosophical profession, a teaching resource center, and links to other philosophy-related Web sites. Regarding the latter, see also entry 103.

861.   L'Association canadienne philosophique / Canadian Philosophical Association.
http://www.acpcpa.ca/ (accessed October 29, 2005).

Like the APA Web site (entry 860), this provides both member-oriented features and generally useful resources. The former include information about the association's history and aims, officers, and structure; membership information and a list of members; and information about projects and publications, including full text to the association's *Bulletin*. Among the site's more broadly useful features are a publicly accessible page of Canadian job openings, and, under the heading "Resources," numerous links to related Web sites. The latter emphasize Canadian sites—philosophy departments, graduate programs, societies, institutes, journals, and grants—though some categories also have separate sections for selected foreign and international sites, and there is a category labeled "Various" with around 90 links to general resources such as online dictionaries, philosophy text sites, and so forth. Like the association, this site is "resolutely bilingual" throughout.

862.   SWIP: The Society for Women in Philosophy. http://www.uh.edu/~cfreelan/SWIP/ (accessed October 29, 2005).

Provides information about the society and its electronic discussion list SWIP-L, some statistics on women in philosophy, conference announcements, a directory of members' personal Web pages, and various categories (some better developed than others) of links to sites related to feminist philosophy or of special interest to women philosophers.

MISCELLANEOUS OTHER REFERENCE SOURCES

863.   Hoffman, Eric, ed. Guidebook for Publishing Philosophy. 1997 ed. Bowling Green, Ohio: Philosophy Documentation Center, Bowling Green State University, 1997. 255p.

A collaborative effort of the American Philosophical Association and the Philosophy Documentation Center, this guide provides helpful information for scholars wishing to publish in philosophy. Beginners especially will benefit, but experienced authors, too, may find useful reminders or ideas for new avenues of approach. Chapters by various authors discuss the perils of publishing, avoiding rejection by journals, book publishing, electronic publishing, presenting papers, resources for writing and publishing in the field, and even publishing in newspapers and general magazines. In addition, the volume includes directories of philosophy publishers and journals in the United States, the United Kingdom, and Canada, largely replicating material in by now superseded editions of the *Directory of American Philosophers* (entry 852) and *International Directory of Philosophy and Philosophers* (entry 857). Users of Hoffman's guide should, if possible, consult the most recent editions of those directories for updated information in this category.

The present work superseded two previous editions under the same title by Janice M. Moulton and by Marcia Yudkin and Janice Moulton (Newark, Del.: American Philosophical Association, 1977 and 1986, respectively). At this writing in October 2005, Hoffman's book, too, has gone out of print, but its text is freely accessible on the Philosophy Documentation Center's Web site at http://www.pdcnet.org/guide.html.

864.   Library of Congress Subject Headings in Philosophy: A Thesaurus. Barbara L. Berman, ed. Charlottesville, Va.: Philosophy Documentation Center, 2001. 262p.

Designed for use by librarians, information specialists, and researchers interested in the application of a standard set of subject descriptors to print and electronic or other nonprint resources in philosophy. Drawn from the comprehensive guide to subject headings published by the Library of Congress (LC), it lists headings authorized for use in the LC catalog and adopted by many other (particularly academic) libraries and union catalogs; cross-references to broader, narrower, and related terms; and extensive national, ethnic, and religious philosophies that can be used to formulate compound headings or subheadings. A special preface for philosophers by John Shook mainly explains the related LC classification scheme, alerting users, among other things, to areas outside the principal class numbers for philosophy (B), ethics (BJ), and aesthetics (BK) where philosophical materials may be classified.

865.   The Philosophical Calendar. Conference of Philosophical Societies (COPS). http://216.25.45.103/Philosophical_Calendar/ (accessed October 29, 2005).

"The on-line Philosophical Calendar is a free service of the Conference of Philosophical Societies (COPS). The Conference is the umbrella organization for philosophical societies in the United States and Canada. The Calendar welcomes notification of all conferences or other meetings that are of philosophical interest and that are open to philosophers. The Calendar also welcomes all calls for papers that are open to interested philosophers" (home page). Events are listed by year and month up to three years in advance, though it appears few are listed more than a year ahead. Calls for papers are listed separately.

866.   The Philosophical Gourmet Report: A Ranking of Graduate Programs in Philosophy in the English-Speaking World. Brian Leiter, ed. http://www.philosophical-gourmet.com/ (accessed October 29, 2005).

Leiter's site ranking philosophy graduate programs, though bound to engender some controversy, has become well-established and enjoys a remarkable degree of support. Its large advisory board, whose membership is listed on the site, counts representatives from many major graduate departments, a number of them very prominent philosophers. Rankings, based on mean scores in reputational surveys among several hundred philosophers throughout the English-speaking world, are provided separately for institutions in the United States, the United Kingdom, Canada, and Australia and New Zealand. There are also rankings (not geographically divided) by areas of specialization such as ethics, philosophy of science, and so forth, grouped into four or five ranges of mean scores plus an "also notable" category. Methods and criteria for the rankings are explained on the site in commendable detail. Ancillary resources include advice for applying to graduate schools, notices of faculty moves and retirements, and information about job placement and other factors that might affect a choice of graduate programs.

Appendix 1
Core Academic Titles

These titles are recommended as a core philosophy reference collection for institutions of higher education offering at least a bachelor's degree program and a full-orbed undergraduate philosophy curriculum. Online resources that are freely available on the Internet are excluded from this list, but not subscription-based online resources.

Sources are listed in order of entry numbers.

48. The Philosopher's Index, CD-ROM or online; or print version, entry 47, with **The Philosopher's Index: A Retrospective Index to U.S. Publications from 1940,** entry 49, and **The Philosopher's Index: A Retrospective Index to Non-U.S. English-Language Publications from 1940,** entry 50.

116. Audi, Robert, ed., **The Cambridge Dictionary of Philosophy,** 2nd ed.

131. Honderich, Ted, ed., **The Oxford Companion to Philosophy,** 2nd ed.

150. Routledge Encyclopedia of Philosophy (print), or online, entry 152.

196. Biographical Dictionary of Twentieth Century Philosophers, ed. Stuart Brown, Diané Collinson, and Robert Wilkinson.

201. Dictionary of the History of Ideas: Studies of Selected Pivotal Ideas, Philip P Wiener, editor in chief.

203. Kersey, Ethel M., with Calvin O. Schrag, consulting ed., **Women Philosophers: A Bio-Critical Source Book.**

207. New Dictionary of the History of Ideas. Maryanne Cline Horowitz, ed.

216. Carr, Brian, and Indira Mahalingam, eds., **Companion Encyclopedia of Asian Philosophy.**

238. Encyclopedia of Eastern Philosophy and Religion: Buddhism, Taoism, Zen, Hinduism, ed. Stephan Schuhmacher and Gert Woerner.

265. Wiredu, Kwasi, **A Companion to African Philosophy.**

277. Ayer, A. J. and Jane O'Grady, eds., **A Dictionary of Philosophical Quotations.**

563. Glendinning, Simon, ed., **The Edinburgh Encyclopedia of Continental Philosophy.**

619. Childers, Joseph, and Gary Hentzi, eds., **The Columbia Dictionary of Modern Literary and Cultural Criticism.**

621. Encyclopedia of Aesthetics, Michael Kelly, editor in chief.

633. Dancy, Jonathan and Ernest Sosa, **A Companion to Epistemology.**

642. Kim, Jaegwon, and Ernest Sosa, eds, **A Companion to Metaphysics.**

675. Becker, Lawrence C. and Charlotte B. Becker, eds., **Encyclopedia of Ethics,** 2nd ed..

690. Encyclopedia of Applied Ethics, Ruth Chadwick, editor in chief.

691. Encyclopedia of Bioethics, 3rd ed., Stephen G. Post, editor in chief.

742. Newton-Smith, W. H., ed., **A Companion to the Philosophy of Science.**

752. Chambliss, J. J., ed., **Philosophy of Education: An Encyclopedia.**

772. Quinn, Philip L., and Charles Taliaferro, eds., **A Companion to the Philosophy of Religion.**

783. Cashmore, Ellis, and Chris Rojek, **Dictionary of Cultural Theorists.**

794. Lipset, Seymour Martin, ed., **Political Philosophy: Theories, Thinkers, Concepts.**

829. Code, Lorraine, ed., **Encyclopedia of Feminist Theories.**

841. Bottomore, Tom, et. al., **Dictionary of Marxist Thought,** 2nd ed..

Appendix 2
Titles Especially Suited for Public and School Libraries

This appendix calls attention to titles that are particularly aimed at, or suited for, general readers or pre-college students and are therefore suggested for consideration by public and secondary school or occasionally lower school libraries. Titles published after 1995 are included only if they are still in print at the time this list is compiled in late 2005. This list does not represent a "recommended core philosophy reference collection" parallel to that for academic libraries in Appendix 1. Larger public libraries or those serving a highly educated population, and libraries serving secondary schools with a strong academic emphasis, should also consider acquiring at least some of the core academic titles in Appendix 1. Freely available online resources are not within the purview of this list.

Sources are listed in order of entry numbers.

115. Angeles, Peter A. **HarperCollins Dictionary of Philosophy,** 2nd ed..

128. Goring, Rosemary, ed.; Frank Whaling, consulting ed., **Larousse Dictionary of Beliefs and Religions.**

132. Hutchinson Dictionary of Ideas.

143. McLeish, Kenneth, ed., **Key Ideas in Human Thought.**

149. Rohmann, Chris, **A World of Ideas: A Dictionary of Important Theories, Concepts, Beliefs, and Thinkers.**

155. Sparkes, A. W., **Talking Philosophy: A Wordbook.**

197. Brown, Stuart, Diané Collinson, and Robert Wilkinson, **One Hundred Twentieth-Century Philosophers.**

199. Dehsen, Christian von, ed., **Philosophers and Religious Leaders.**

205. King, Peter J. **One Hundred Philosophers: The Life and Work of the World's Greatest Thinkers.**

214. Roth, John K., et. al., eds., **World Philosophers and Their Works.**

217. Collinson, Diané, Kathryn Plant, and Robert Wilkinson, **Fifty Eastern Thinkers.**

219. Leaman, Oliver, ed., **Encyclopedia of Asian Philosophy.**

221. McGreal, Ian P., ed., **Great Thinkers of the Eastern World: The Major Thinkers and the Philosophical and Religious Classics of China, India, Japan, Korea, and the World of Islam.**

249. Feuerstein, Georg, **Shambhala Encyclopedia of Yoga.**

268. Baggini, Julian and Jeremy Stangroom, eds. **Great Thinkers A–Z.**

269. Collinson, Diané, **Fifty Major Philosophers: A Reference Guide.**

272. McGreal, Ian P., **Great Thinkers of the Western World: The Major Ideas and Classic Works of More than 100 Outstanding Western Philosophers, Physical and Social Scientists, Psychologists, Religious Writers, and Theologians.**

276. Weate, Jeremy, **A Young Person's Guide to Philosophy: "I Think, Therefore I Am."**

674. Barber, Nigel, **Encyclopedia of Ethics in Science and Technology.**

677. Bioethics for Students: How Do We Know What's Right? Issues in Medicine, Animal Rights, and the Environment, Stephen G. Post, general ed.

694. Ethics and Values.

698. Grenz, Stanley J. and Jay T. Smith, **Pocket Dictionary of Ethics.**

699. Hedges, Richard, **Bioethics, Health Care, and the Law: A Dictionary.**

700. Hester, Joseph P., **Encyclopedia of Values and Ethics.**

705. Roth, John K., ed., **Ethics,** rev. ed.

708. Terkel, Susan Neiburg and R. Shannon Duvall, eds., **Encyclopedia of Ethics.**

745. Warburton, Nigel, **Thinking from A to Z,** 2nd ed.

767. Evans, C. Stephen, **Pocket Dictionary of Apologetics & Philosophy of Religion.**

787. Edgar, Andrew, and Peter Sedgwick, eds., **Cultural Theory: The Key Thinkers.**

798. Sheldon, Garrett Ward, **Encyclopedia of Political Thought.**

AUTHOR INDEX

Numbers in this index refer to entries, not pages. The letter "n" following an entry number indicates that the author is mentioned in the annotation. A bracketed number following an entry number—as in, for instance, "11[5]"—designates the specific volume of a multivolume set or the issue, volume, or part number of a series.

TITLE INDEX

Numbers in this index refer to entries, not pages. The letter "n" following an entry number indicates that the title is mentioned in the annotation. A bracketed number following an entry number—as in, for instance, "11[5]"—designates the specific volume of a multivolume set or the issue, volume, or part number of a series.

Ethics and Political Philosophy, 775
Ethics and the Professor: An Annotated Bibliography, 1970–1985, 658
Ethics and Values, 694
Ethics Index, 652
Ethics Updates, 715
Ethicsweb.ca, 716
ETHX on the Web: A Bibliographic Database on Bioethics and Professional Ethics, 653
Etienne Gilson: A Bibliography / Une bibliographie, 542
Europäische Enzyklopädie zu Philosophie und Wissenschaften, 177
Euthanasia Controversy, 1812–1974: A Bibliography with Select Annotations, 673
Every Person's Guide to Jewish Philosophy and Philosophers, 835
Everyman Dictionary of Religion and Philosophy, 139
Existentialism and Phenomenology: A Guide for Research, 567n
Exploring Phenomenology: A Guide to the Field and Its Literature, 567

Felix Guattari and Gilles Deleuze: A Bibliography, 780[25]
Feminism and Postmodern Theory: A Bibliography, 780[41]
Feminism and Psychoanalysis: A Bibliography, 780[64]
Feminist Literary Theory: A Bibliography, 780[52]
Feminist Theory: A Bibliography, 780[28]
Feminist Theory: Women of Color: A Bibliography, 780[40]
Feminist Theory (II): A Bibliography, 780[60]
Feminist Theory Website, 832
Fichier augustinien / Augustine Bibliography, 358
Fichte: Ein Verzeichnis westeuropäischer und nordamerikanischer Hochschulschriften, 1885–1980, 26[9]
Fifty Eastern Thinkers, 217
Fifty Key Contemporary Thinkers: From Structuralism to Postmodernity, 520
Fifty Key Medieval Thinkers, 345
Fifty Key Thinkers on History, 804
Fifty Key Words in Philosophy, 160
Fifty Major Philosophers: A Reference Guide, 269
Fifty Major Thinkers on Education: From Confucius to the Present, 754
Fifty Modern Thinkers on Education: From Piaget to the Present Day, 755
50 Years of Events: An Annotated Bibliography, 1947 to 1997, 813
Fifty Years of Hume Scholarship: A Bibliographical Guide, 438
Filone di Alessandria: Bibliografia generale 1937–1982, 315n
FILOS: Base de datos sobre filosofía en México, 90
Filosofisch Lexicon, 129n
Filosofskaia entsiklopediia, 183
Filosofskaia mysl' vostochnykh slavian: biobibliograficheskii slovar', 290
Filosofskii entsiklopedicheskii slovar', 184 (Gubskii), 185 (Averintsev)
Filosofskii slovar', 127n
Filosofy Rossii XIX–XX stoletii: biografii, idei, trudy, 286
FOLDOP, 126
Foundations of Moral Education: An Annotated Bibliography, 655
Francis bulletin signalétique 519: Philosophie/Philosophy, 41
Frantz Fanon: A Bibliography, 780[65]
Französische Existenzphilosophie, 11[9]
Frederic Jameson: A Bibliography, 780[63]
Free On-Line Dictionary of Philosophy (FOLDOP), 126
Freethought in the United Kingdom and the Commonwealth: A Descriptive Bibliography, 834
Freethought in the United States: A Descriptive Bibliography, 833
French Feminist Theory: Luce Irigaray and Helene Cixous: A Bibliography, 780[20]

Theodicy: An Annotated Bibliography on the Problem of Evil, 1960–1990, 761
Theodor Adorno: A Bibliography, 780[10]
Theodor Adorno (II): A Bibliography, 780[35]
Thinking from A to Z, 745
Thirty-Five Oriental Philosophers, 217n
Thomae Aquinatis Opera Omnia cum Hypertextibus in CD-ROM, 376n
Thomas Aquinas: International Bibliography, 1977–1990, 368
Thomas Aquinas Dictionary, 374
Thomas Hobbes: A Reference Guide, 435
Thomas Hobbes: Bibliographie internationale de 1620 à 1986, 433
Thomas von Aquin, 11[13/14]
Thomas-Lexikon: Sammlung, Übersetzung und Erklärung der in sämtlichen Werken des h. Thomas von Aquin vorkommenden Künstausdrucke und wissenschaftlichen Aussprüche, 373
Thomismus, 11[15/16]
Thomist Tradition, 770
Thomistic Bibliography, 1920–1940, 367
Thomistic Bibliography, 1940–1978, 370
Time Dimension: An Interdisciplinary Guide, 814
Tradition of Medieval Logic and Speculative Grammar from Anselm to the End of the Seventeenth Century: A Bibliography from 1836 Onwards, 336, 721
Transcendentalists: A Review of Research and Criticism, 383
Treasury of Philosophy, 215
Treasury of World Philosophy, 215
Twentieth-Century American Cultural Theorists, 791
Twentieth-Century European Cultural Theorists, 792
Twentieth-Century Western Philosophy of Religion, 1900–2000, 769
Twenty-Five Years of Descartes Scholarship, 1960–1984: A Bibliography, 411

Unamuno Source Book: A Catalogue of Readings and Acquisitions with an Introductory Essay on Unamuno's Dialectical Enquiry, 611
Univers philosophique, 164[1]
Utopias and Utopians: An Historical Dictionary, 793n

Vedanta Dictionary, 254
Vico: A Bibliography of Works in English from 1884 to 1994, 510
Vico in English: A Bibliography of Writings by and about Giambattista Vico (1668–1744), 510n
Viśistādvaita Works, Bibliography, 236
Vives Bibliography, 378
Vocabulaire d'esthétique, 625
Vocabulaire de sciences cognitives, 641n
Vocabulaire européen des philosophies: dictionnaire des intraduisibles, 189
Vocabulaire technique et critique de la philosophie, 169
Voces: Eine Bibliographie zu Wörtern und Begriffen aus der Patristik (1918–1978), 337n
Voltaire: Bibliographie de ses oeuvres, 511
Von Alcuin bis Nicolaus Cusanus: Bio-bibliographisches Repertorium der Philosophie im lateinischen Mittelalter, 350

Walter Benjamin: A Bibliography, 780[15]
W.E.B. Du Bois: A Bibliography, 780[66]
Weimarer Nietzsche-Bibliographie (WNB), 480
Westminster Dictionary of Christian Ethics, 683
Who's Who in the History of Philosophy, 204
Willard van Orman Quine: A Bibliographic Guide, 544

SUBJECT INDEX

Numbers in this index normally refer to entries, not pages. References to topics discussed in the introduction (chapter 1) are in italics and are preceded by the letters *p.* or *pp.* to indicate page numbers. The letter "n" following an entry number indicates that the item is mentioned in the annotation. A bracketed number following an entry number—as in, for instance, "11[5]"—designates the specific volume of a multivolume set or the issue, volume, or part number of a series.

Clement, Catherine
bibliography, 780[31]
Codes of ethics. *See* Professional ethics: codes, collections
Cognitive science. *See also* Mind, philosophy of
dictionaries, encyclopedias, and handbooks, 631, 635, 636, 641, 643
French, 641n
College and university philosophy departments
directories
U.S. and Canada, 852, 855, 860n, 861n
international, 857
graduate programs
directory, 855
rankings, 866
Web pages
directory, online, 103n
Collingwood, Robin George
bibliographies, 533, 534
Confucianism. *See also* Chinese philosophy
dictionary/encyclopedia, 256
Neo-Confucianism
biographical source, 251
glossary, 251
Contemporary philosophy. *See* Twentieth- and twenty-first-century philosophy
Continental philosophy, *pp. 3, 6–8. See also* Deconstruction; Existentialism; French philosophy; German philosophy; Italian philosophy; Phenomenology; Postmodernism; Post-Structuralism; Spanish philosophy; Structuralism
biographical source, 562
dictionaries, encyclopedias, and handbooks, 562–567
ethics
dictionaries, 701, 701n
Existentialism
dictionary, 565
Phenomenology
dictionaries, encyclopedias, and handbooks, 563, 567
sources on individual philosophers, 568–611
Cosmology
dictionary/encyclopedia, 640
Councils, institutes, and research centers, philosophical
directories, 852, 857
Web sites, 361n, 450, 712, 714, 715, 718
Critical theory. *See also* Cultural theory; Literary criticism and theory
dictionary, 795
Critical thinking
bibliography, 748
dictionary, 745

Croce, Benedetto
bibliographies, 576, 577
Cultural theory. *See also* Aesthetics; Literary criticism and theory; Social philosophy
biographical sources, 783, 787, 791, 792
American, 791
European, 792
dictionaries and encyclopedias, 619, 783, 787, 788, 795
Cynicism, Cynic philosophers
bibliography, 299

Databases. *See* CD-ROM resources; Internet resources
Death. *See also* Euthanasia
bibliographies, 811, 811n
Deconstruction, *p. 8. See also* Derrida, Jacques
bibliography, 780[26]
Deleuze, Gilles
bibliography, 780[25]
Derrida, Jacques, *pp. 7, 8*
bibliographies, 561, 578, 780[2, 37]
dictionary, 579
Descartes, René
bibliographies, 411, 412
dictionaries, 413–415
Discours de la methode
index, 416
Dewey, John
bibliographies, 535–539
translations, 537
dictionary, 757
education, views on
dictionary, 757
guide, 535
personal library, 541
Dictionaries and encyclopedias, general
Chinese, 122n
Dutch, 129n
English-language, 114–116
CD-ROM, 151
online, 126, 134–136, 144, 152, 156
French, 161–169
German, 119n, 130n, 170–178
online, 176
Italian, 179–182
Russian, 127n, 183–186
Spanish, 179n, 187
Diderot, Denis
bibliography, 417
Dilthey, Wilhelm
bibliography, 418

social philosophy and political philosophy
  bibliographies, 780
  dictionaries, encyclopedias, and handbooks, 781,
    789, 791, 792
  sources on individual philosophers, 533–560,
    568–611
world philosophy
  biographical sources, 196, 197

Unamuno, Miguel de
  personal library, 611
  sources of his thought, 611
United Kingdom. *See* British philosophy
United States. *See* American philosophy
University of Southern California, Hoose Library of
    Philosophy
  catalog, 14
University philosophy departments. *See* College and
    university philosophy departments
Utopianism
  dictionaries, 793, 793n

Values. *See also* Aesthetics; Ethics; Moral education,
    foundations of
  bibliography, 612
Vedānta. *See also* Hindu philosophy; Indian phi-
    losophy
  bibliographies
    Advaita Vedānta, 225[11]
    Bhedābheda, 225[3–5]
    Śudhādvaita Vedānta, 225[12]
    Viśistādvaita, 225[10]
  dictionaries/encyclopedias, 242, 254
    Advaita Vedānta, 242
Vico, Giambattista
  bibliographies, 509, 509n, 510, 510n
Viśistādvaita. *See* Vedānta
Vives, Juan Luis
  bibliography, 378
Voltaire, François-Marie Arouet de
  bibliography, 511
Vyākarana (Grammarian philosophy). *See also*
    Hindu philosophy; Indian philosophy
  bibliography, 225[9]
  dictionary/encyclopedia, 244

War and ethics
  dictionary/encyclopedia, 709
Web resources. *See* Internet resources
Weber, Max
  bibliography, 780[13]
Weil, Simone
  bibliography, 780[38]

Western philosophy, pp. 3–4, 6–11. See also indi-
    vidual countries or regions, e.g., British
    philosophy, French philosophy
  biographical sources, 268, 269, 271–275
  charts, chronological and thematic, 280
  history, general. *See also* Ancient philosophy;
    Medieval philosophy; Modern philosophy
    (through nineteenth century); Renaissance
    philosophy; Twentieth- and twenty-first-
    century philosophy
  bibliographies, 266, 267
  survey, juvenile readers, 276
  topical guide, 279
  quotations, 279
Whitehead, Alfred North
  bibliography, 551
Widener Library, Harvard University
  catalog, philosophy and psychology, 15
William of Ockham, *p. 11*
Wissenschaftstheorie. See also Science, philosophy
    of; Social sciences, philosophy of
  dictionaries, encyclopedias, and handbooks, 175,
    177, 743
Wittgenstein, Ludwig
  bibliographies, 26[12], 552–556
    dissertations and theses, 26[12]
  dictionaries, 557, 558
  Philosophische Untersuchungen
    concordance, 559
  Tractatus
    word indexes, 552, 560
Wittig, Monique
  bibliography, 780[31]
Women philosophers
  association
    Web site, 862
  bibliographies, 35–36
    online, 36n
  biographical sources, 203, 274
  directories, 853, 854
    online, 854
World philosophy. *See also* History of philosophy,
    comprehensive
  bibliographies, 13, 191, 192. *See also* Bibliogra-
    phies, general
  biographical sources, 196, 197
  country surveys, 198, 857
  dictionaries, encyclopedias, and handbooks, 164,
    196–198, 218
  directory, 857
  handbook, 198
  selections from philosophical texts, 215
World Wide Web sites. *See* Internet resources

About the Author

HANS E. BYNAGLE is Library Director and Professor of Philosophy at Whitworth College in Spokane, Washington. He earned a Ph.D. in philosophy from Columbia University, Master of Library Science from Kent State University, and his undergraduate degree in philosophy from Calvin College. In addition to two editions of a predecessor to this volume (*Philosophy: A Guide to the Reference Literature,* 1986 and 1997), he has authored more than a hundred reviews in philosophy, religion, and other areas. His current teaching and research focus is philosophy of mind.